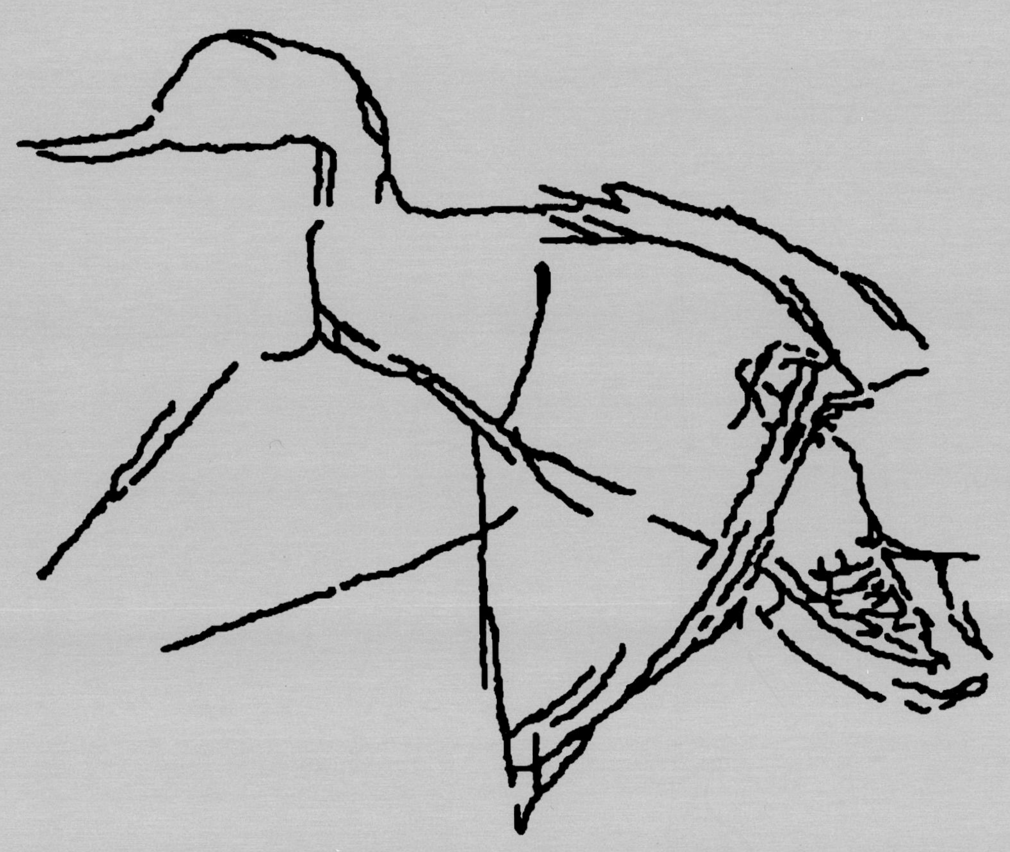

Hans Kleiber

(1887-1967)

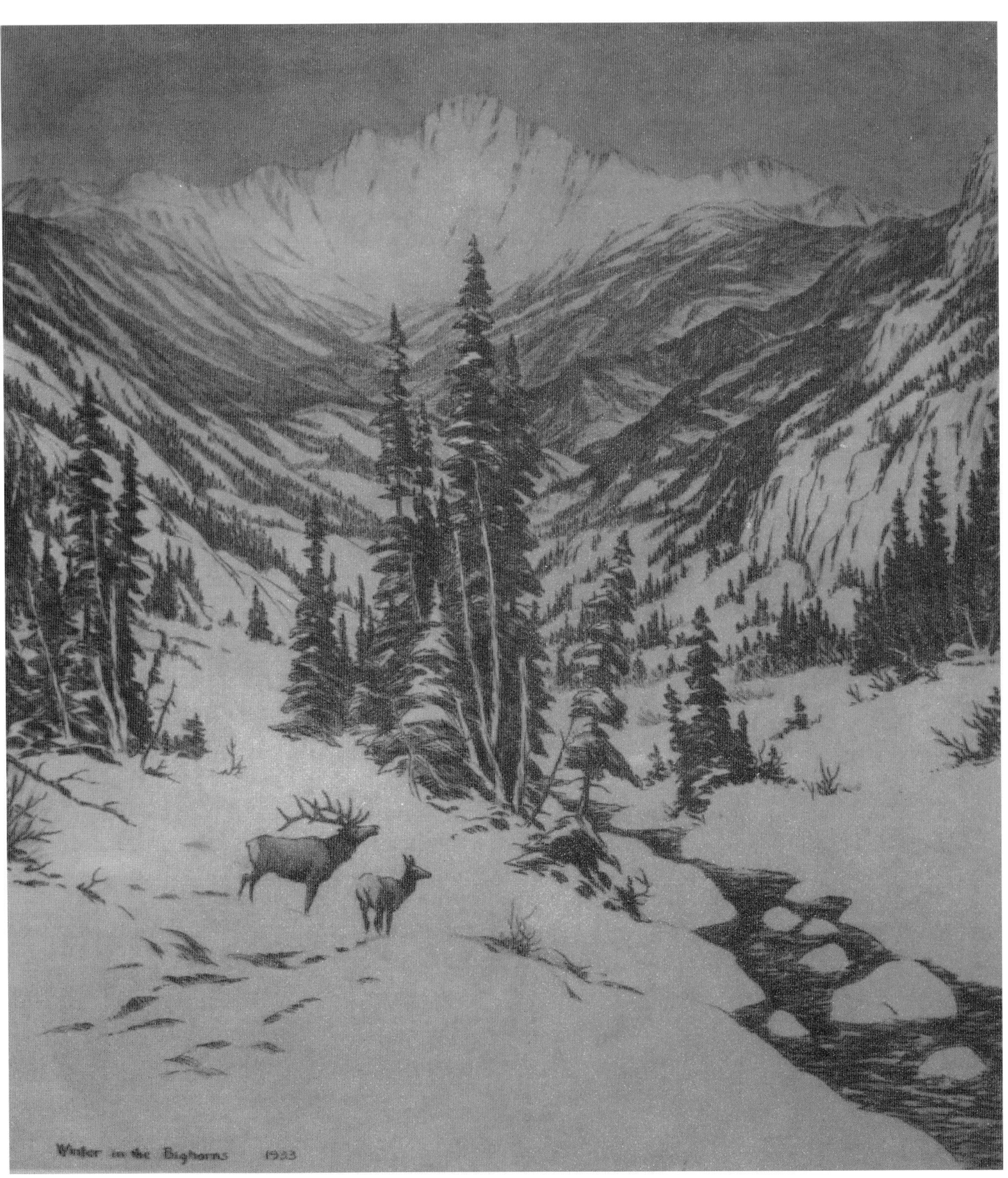
Winter in the Bighorns 1933

Hans Kleiber

(1887-1967)

Wyoming Printmaker
and
Artist

by

Marylee M. Moreland

and

Gary L. Temple

Marylee M. Moreland and Gary L. Temple
The Meadowlark Gallery, Inc.
118 North 29th Street
Billings, Montana 59101

The authors are pleased to present this First Edition of 2167 copies. A special limited edition of 167 copies are leather bound, numbered, and signed by the authors. This offering consists of 96 pencil signed impressions by Hans Kleiber, 15 pencil signed bathing impressions by Hans Kleiber, and 56 unsigned impressions by Hans Kleiber.

ISBN: 0-9643352-2-0

Printed in the good old United States of America

by
Advanced Litho Printing
226 9th Avenue South
Great Falls, Montana 59405
(406) 453-0393

For further information, assistance, and, or
authentication,
please feel free to contact:

Marylee M. Moreland and Gary L. Temple
The Meadowlark Gallery, Inc.
118 North 29th Street
Billings, Montana 59101
Telephone: (406)294-8575
www.meadowlarkgallery.com

---Table of Contents---

Hans Kleiber

"On any type of artwork one must verify everything and take nothing for granted."

The Authors

"No recent exhibitions or commissions except private ones. Being located on the highway to the Yellowstone, and fairly well known, many people stop at the studio. I sell all the work I can do. Watercolors, etchings, and colored etchings."

Hans Kleiber

Hans Kleiber

Dedication

Upon preparing this book for publication, we were often told about how we could go through a publishing company in China. The significant factors were fewer dollars and the fact that the publishing company in China could use non-environmental inks that are prohibited in the states. These inks supposedly result in brighter images. We have felt for many years and especially since September 11, and as well since events in the Middle East, that we needed to establish a relationship with a domestic United States company to publish this book. The result, we think, strongly indicates to us that the colors of red, white, and blue are much brighter.

This update of our two volume set of books on the printmaking career of Hans Kleiber is dedicated to my wife, Marylee M. Moreland. There are times when she says that the book is more mine than hers, but it would not be anything without our partnership. We are truly grateful for the endless discussions and theories that have evolved from our partnership. Her continued encouragement has made our Kleiber research and marriage stronger than ever.

We would like to thank the countless people who allowed us into their private worlds to "measure" their collections. For the most part, these collectors preferred and, or we preferred to have them remain anonymous. Nevertheless, we give our sincere thanks to them.

There are a few special individuals that we must formally thank and they are:

Hans Kleiber

Bill and Carole Ward of Saratoga, Wyoming

Carole Tucker formerly of the Golden Crown in Sheridan, Wyoming

Sue Near, Kirby Lambert, and Jennifer Bottomly-O'Looney of the Montana Historical Society in Helena, Montana

Sarah Boehme of the Buffalo Bill Historical Society in Cody, Wyoming

E. K. Kim, Susan Moldenhauer, and Sarah Gadd of the University of Wyoming Art Museum in Laramie, Wyoming

Alice Meister of the Sheridan County Parmly Library in Sheridan, Wyoming

Jennifer Alexander and Dominique Schultes of the Wyoming State Art Museum in Cheyenne, Wyoming

Dwight Layton and Ken Schuster of the Bradford Brinton Memorial in Bighorn, Wyoming

Thomas Olson of the Hangin' Tree Gallery in Sheridan, Wyoming

Richard Bodine and Charlene Bodine of Sheridan, Wyoming

Sam Scott and Mona Scott of Dayton, Wyoming

Special thanks to Jackie Inman of The Meadowlark Gallery.

Thank you to Hans Kleiber for showing us your "hand" several times.

Introduction

Early in 1991, we became interested in an artist by the name of Hans Kleiber. For several years prior to this we had observed his work in the market. At the C. M. Russell Art Auction Museum reception I commented about one work entitled, "Bucket of Blood Saloon." Our good friend Bill Ward said that he was not sure and would have to check his records to determine if it was an etching or a reduction. The term reduction was interesting, but more especially was the fact that no one had compiled the measurements of the various impressions done by Hans Kleiber.

Purely as a private resource for our own files, we began visiting galleries and asking them if we could measure any Hans Kleiber impressions that they might have on hand. One of the earliest visits to a gallery was that to the Hangin' Tree Gallery in Sheridan, Wyoming. The owner, Tom Olson, kind of shrugged his shoulders and said that it would not be a problem, but I am sure he wondered about these folks from Montana.

Another location was the Golden Crown in Sheridan, Wyoming, owned and operated by Carole Tucker. Carole and Vern Tucker, her former husband, had a long relationship with Hans Kleiber. Throughout the next many years of research, Carole became especially helpful. After many visits to private collectors and other galleries we discovered the complete "Tucker List" and realized that we had documented about sixty percent of it. At this point we decided that it was time to diligently work on documenting the impressions by the artist.

Hans Kleiber

Methods

Our research for this third book on the works of Hans Kleiber has been drawn from letters, the family history, public documents, museum collections, and private collections. We wanted to first record and identify various sizes of the impressions by Hans Kleiber. Second, we wanted to record the multiple titling done on the impressions by Hans Kleiber. Third, we wanted to determine the various forms of media that the artist used during his career, which included oil and watercolor. Fourth, we wanted to cover as thoroughly as possible the work of the artist with the Associated American Artists. Fifth, we wanted to examine some of his advertising ephemera. Sixth, we wanted to address the posthumous activities of the artwork of Hans Kleiber.

The focus of available information has influenced our narration of Kleiber's biography. The records of the artist were not available for any type of review after his death because the artist had requested that they be destroyed.[1]

---

[1] Carole Tucker had discussed with us that Hans Kleiber requested that all records of his art career be destroyed after his passing.

Hans Kleiber

Chapter One

Hans Kleiber (1887-1967)

"Hans Kleiber's imagination, at the age of eighteen, was so caught by Buffalo Bill, by Wister's "Virginian" and by Theodore Roosevelt's adventures in the "Big Horn" country that he went West to work in a lumber camp. The years that followed included U. S. forestry service throughout the Western states and gave Kleiber an unforgettable picture of the beauty and solemnity of the Western scene. Gradually he found himself drawn to a brush; later, he used his new-found talents at the etcher's plate. Perseverance and courage landed him in the top ranks; he has been called "Etcher Laureate of the Rockies." Self-taught, Kleiber has managed to capture in his etchings the calm and majesty of the West to which he feels close through his personal experiences. His work has been invited for exhibition by America's foremost art societies. Shortly after one of his first showings in the East the Society of American Etchers elected him to membership."[2]

Associated American Artists, 711 Fifth Avenue, New York 22, N. Y.

---

[2] Associated American Artists, 711 Fifth Avenue, New York 22, N. Y..

Hans Kleiber

Hans Kleiber was born in Cologne, Germany on August 24, 1887. "I was a boy of almost thirteen when we came to the United States, and of necessity I suppose, my people settled in a small manufacturing town in Massachusetts."[3] In 1905, he left home and never returned except for very short visits. A first choice or desire was to go into art, so he went to New York City for a few months. While there in New York City, a man advised him to go to the Forestry School then at Cornell University. Hans Kleiber found that he did not have the necessary qualifications, and also four years of additional schooling was not appealing. Deciding to go west, he became stricken with typhoid fever in Scranton, Pennsylvania and returned to his family in Massachusetts. In 1906 he came west to Denver, Colorado where he continued his pursuit of forestry. Employment agencies were the only conduit to being hired by the Forest Reserve at that time. He finally located two logging operations where they were sending men. The two locations were Flagstaff, Arizona and the other one was Ranchester, Wyoming. "I knew nothing about either and I felt like a mule between two bundles of hay. In my hotel room I finally paid my fee and decided to toss up for it and Ranchester turned up."[4]

Upon his arrival to the Big Horn country, he easily acclimated himself into the McShane Tie Camp at Woodrock. His first work for the Forest Service was a timber sale in the summer of 1906. In the

---

[3] "Reminiscences of Hans Kleiber, Early Day Forest Ranger, Big Horn National Forest" by Hans Kleiber, 1942; Sheridan County Historical Society.

[4] Ibid.

spring of 1908, he took his first Ranger Examination and found out that he did not qualify as he was not a United States citizen. His father had failed to fill out the necessary paperwork enabling his entire family to become United States citizens. On a trip back to Europe, Kleiber's father unexpectedly fell ill, and the time period for the completion of the papers lapsed. Nevertheless, citizenship was quickly formulated by Hans in 1911.

As with all of the Forest Service[5], fire prevention was a primary concern, especially during the summer months. Prior to his citizenship, the summer of 1910 indoctrinated Hans Kleiber well into the virtues of forest fires. In 1913, he built the telephone line to the Porcupine Ranger station and maintained several other telephone lines in the area. Kleiber's recollections of fire fighting became ever more intense during and after 1913. In the summer of 1914, he worked at the Tongue District.

The following winter he was sent to the south end of the Forest where he took over the Paintrock and Tensleep Districts. He crossed the divide between Tongue and Shell Creek with a pack outfit on

---

[5] We have heard many recollections of visits with Hans Kleiber about his duties in the Forest Service. In addition to monitoring timber sales, he would have to check the various logging camps. A further responsibility was keeping the soiled doves camps from getting too close to the logging camps. At one time an explanation was given for the five subjects of nudes that Kleiber produced; collectors were told that these images went back to his European memories when his mother would take the children swimming. We are prompted to accept the fact that some of his memories must have come from the soiled doves camps as well.

January 28, 1915. "I crossed just about where the highway is now and I doubt if I could have made it without help. The trip from Dayton to Hyattville took four days. It was pitch dark long before I got to Hyattville and as there were not lights and no roads in my direction, my only guide was the smell of burning cedar wood from some of the stoves in town. My overshoes were frozen into the stirrup, and Cavanaugh helped light me from the saddle at the livery barn."[6]

In June of 1915, he took over the Woodrock section of the Tongue District. At the end of the summer months in 1916, the fire season began, and it was not until a heavy snow cover came in October that the fire season was concluded. In the summer of 1916 or 1917, he was detailed to a Forest Planting Camp at Halsey, Nebraska. He was there about six weeks when an outbreak of small pox threatened to close down the entire camp. Kleiber and another Ranger left one night in what Kleiber referred to as leaving in somewhat of an unorthodox way.[7]

"The reason I bring up fires so often is that after all is said and done, they are the most destructive element in the Forest Service and the damage they leave in their wake takes nature generations to build up again in these Rocky Mountain Forest."[8]

In 1918, he was called upon to go to a major fire near Orofino, Idaho. He supervised about three

---

[6] "Reminiscences of Hans Kleiber, Early Day Forest Ranger, Big Horn National Forest" by Hans Kleiber, 1942; Sheridan County Historical Society.

[7] Ibid.

[8] Ibid.

hundred men in his camp. Kleiber commented extensively about the timber and the rainbow trout in the Weitas Creek which was a tributary of the Clearwater. He told the story of how he and another man went out one morning and caught enough trout by noon to feed more than one hundred men. The equipment used was quite elaborate, as it consisted of the use of a willow pole.

From 1919 to 1923, Kleiber was responsible for the Range Appraisal for the Washaki District, but more so, he was generally a Ranger-at-Large who by that time considered his work for the Forest Service as ended.

"I had gone into Forestry for the pure love of it. My years of work for the Service filled a niche in my life that nothing else could have filled with deeper satisfaction and enjoyment. The work itself and the money I got for it, while important enough in their way had always been of secondary consideration. To put it in its simplest form, it had been a way of life to me, and as such it was not easy for me at the time to turn my back to it, even though the urge under which I was doing it had probably stronger roots in me than I suspected."[9]

While traveling, Hans Kleiber began to write and comment about the places he so dearly loved. Several books have contained examples of his skill as an avid storyteller, writer and poet.

"Along about 1920 I began to think seriously of trying to put down some of the things that I had seen and felt about the landscapes and wildlife of the mountains but it wasn't for several years, until the

---

[9] Ibid.

summer of 1923 that I really made the break and then not all at once."[10] (Age: 36)

Much of the family history about Hans Kleiber has become simplified from various readings and research. The processes of being self taught does not simply evolve overnight. Kay Kleiber commented about the artist in 1923 had begun painting in oils and then began etching in 1927.[11] For example, one needs to refer to a letter by Hans Kleiber to Branson Stevenson in 1926.

"To begin with I used all zinc plates. Zinc hasn't the quality and the vitality like copper, but its cheaper and thought over the notations. Often when our idea is not quite clear in my mind I do it on zinc first and perhaps later on copper."[12]

"I went through about 35 plates in 6 weeks, experimenting day and night almost continually with lines and soft ground work."[13]

"I started in with using most any kind of paper, this is a poor policy its hard on your plates and it doesn't do justice to it in printing it."[14]

---

[10] Biographical Sketch by Hans Kleiber; Business Womens Club, Sheridan, Wyoming; May 22, 1936.

[11] Page 1, "Daydreams and Fantasies, Stories of the Secret Forest" by Hans Kleiber; published by Kay Kleiber, 1989. The process of etching did not simply occur overnight, see Appendix One.

[12] Letter to Branson Stevenson; January 18, 1926, See Appendix One.

[13] Ibid.

[14] Ibid.

"It wasn't until 1927 that people began to show some interest in what I was trying to do."[15] (Age: 40)

Over his career, Hans Kleiber sold his work at the various guest ranches around the Sheridan, Wyoming area. Many of the guests that came out to Wyoming were from the Boston, Massachusetts area.

"In 1928 Goodspeed's Book Shop in Boston gave me my first exhibition of etchings which proved a tremendous encouragement."[16] (Age: 41)

On one of his etchings, Hans Kleiber noted that it was a soft ground etching done in 1929. The bed size of his press was 8.875 inches by 6.875 inches. (Age: 42)

"In 1930 the(y), Goodspeed's Book Shop in Boston, gave another one-man show of my work and asked me to be present. I was scared to death but I went and felt it was the greatest ordeal I had ever been through. I suppose it is one of the necessary evils in an artist's career."[17] (Age: 43)

" Leaving the High Country", Silver Medal from The Print Makers Society of California, 1931. (Age: 44)

" Flight of Ducks, Lake Solitude," The Print Makers Society of California, 1933. (Age: 46) In

---

[15] Ibid.

[16] Ibid.

[17] Biographical Sketch by Hans Kleiber; Business Womens Club, Sheridan, Wyoming; May 22, 1936; See Appendix Two.

1933, this etching was used as a gift to the membership of the California Print Society. In their letter to their members they showed an edition size of 240. Later it was renamed by Kleiber as "Summer Guests."

The Associated American Artists began in 1934 and shortly after that " Deep in the Rockies" by Hans Kleiber was the first print marketed through them.

The Gordon Beer Art Galleries of Detroit, Michigan; April 1, 1937. (Age: 50)

In 1941, Hans Kleiber signed a contract with the American Artists Group, Inc., and sent to Mr. Golden a solicitation letter he had received from Brown and Bigelow. Mr. Golden dampened the effect of the letter in his reply to Kleiber on March 24, 1941. The Brown and Bigelow letter was apparently often sent to many artists. He referred to the fact of when Mr. Woiceske had turned them down that they had then recruited Mr. T. Jack Young and Mr. Richard Bishop. He stated that, "It is possible for you to earn as royalties on one picture a sum that would be equivalent to what they would pay for the use of six or seven of your etchings, so that I do not think you are losing a thing by turning them down."[18] (Age: 54)

He mentioned that during the month of December 1943, the National Gallery in Washington, D.C., had an exhibition of fifty of his etchings. Hans Kleiber did not attend, but did state that it was well attended, however, his financial return from it was just $22.65. He said, "That is a very fair sample."[19] (Age: 56)

---

[18]Associated American Artists, 711 Fifth Avenue, New York 22, N. Y.

[19] Ibid.

On February 2, 1944, Hans Kleiber protested the contract with Mr. Golden because he felt it was "difficult to subscribe to in that the protection it gives is extremely one sided. As it stands, you are given the exclusive right to reproduce any of my pictures, whether etchings or paintings, for a period of 3 years. This leaves me without any guarantees, financial or otherwise for that period unless it so happens that you do pretty well with my pictures."[20] (Age: 57)

He referred later in this letter to the fact that he received $50.00 in 1932 and $154.00 in 1931. "I look with envy sometimes at what some of the carpenters, ordinary mechanics, and coal miners in the local fields make here. But I have no choice except to stay with the game that I am in." He expressed several examples of losing various reproduction opportunities of his works because he had a contract with the American Artists Group (Associated American Artists).[21]

" Old Cottonwood Tree," " The Old Cottonwood," or " The Old Cottonwood Tree" was accepted into the Associated American Artists Show—First National Print Competition Exhibit held at the New York Galleries from June 15 to July 15, 1946. Prices were $5.00 each or six for $25.00. (Age: 59)

On June 1, 1947, he said in a letter to Mr. Golden that " Winter Residents" was in existence as an etching.[22] (Age: 60)

---

[20] Ibid.

[21] Ibid.

[22] Ibid.

On December 28, 1948, in a letter to Mr. Royden C. Berger of Connecticut Mutual Life Insurance Company of Hartford Connecticut, Kleiber makes reference to their representative in Sheridan, Wyoming, having an article in the local paper about the selection of a painting for their calendar. The local agent was C. V. Davis. A watercolor painting entitled "On the Range" was the work selected. Apparently the painting was of range horses that very well could be similar to the etching "Weathering a Storm."[23] (Age: 61)

Exhibition of watercolors at the Grand Central Galleries in New York during the March of 1950. (Age: 63)

In a letter dated March 10, 1951, he was referred to Hallmark Cards by Grand Central Galleries. He had to turn down their request as he had a contract with the American Artists Group.[24] (Age: 64)

[23] Ibid.

[24] Ibid.

August 11, 1952
In a letter to Mr. Golden, he referred to sending him a colored etching of " At the Hitchrack." He said that this, the colored etching, was something new in the way of coloring prints. (Age: 65)[25]

In a questionnaire, dated February 2, 1953, he described a piece that was being reproduced as a Christmas card.

"At the Hitchrack"—Etching painted with watercolor. Three cow ponies tied to a hitchrack on a snowy day outside of a cow camp at the foot of the Bighorn Mountains in Wyoming. Their riders are visiting or having a little game of poker near the stove in the cabin.

---

[25] Through our review of many water colored etchings and photogravures by Hans Kleiber, there have been some common variables that we have noted. For the most part, his water coloring of his impressions were usually done in "even" and loose styles with little concentrations of pigment on the overall work. We have noticed upon the inspection of some hand water colored impressions, the use of extremely heavy amounts of pigment. This causes us to speculate as to who actually colored the work. For example, we do know of one of the bathing scenes where the work is colored but to such an extent that the pigment shows a great deal of intense flesh tones and very high degrees of representational factors. Another work that we have inspected has again high concentrations of pigment. Most of Hans Kleiber's coloring, in our opinion, is very subtle and shows softness. We would suspect that those works with high pigmentation were done posthumously by other parties.

He mentions that he, "Began to color some of my etchings with watercolors a year or so ago and found quite a demand for them."[26] (Age: 66) 1951

In a letter to Sam Golden, February 26, 1957, Kleiber said that the making of a color plate for $400.00 was more than he could afford for producing a Christmas Card.[27] (Age: 70)

Hans Kleiber passed away on December 8, 1967. (Age: 80)

---

[26] Associated American Artists, 711 Fifth Avenue, New York 22, N. Y.

[27] Ibid.

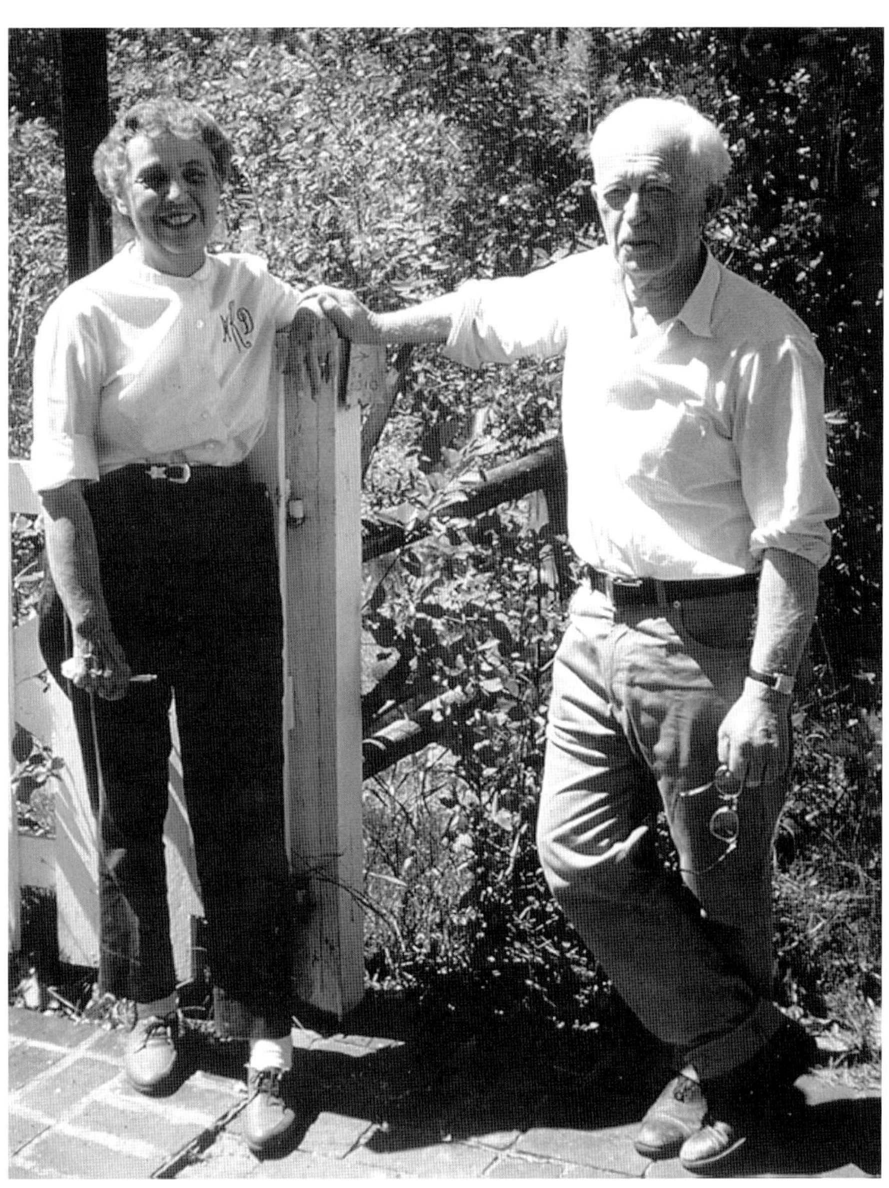

Missy and Hans Kleiber
April, 1965

Hans Kleiber

Chapter Two

Etching Versus Photogravure

A very common question after someone has walked through our gallery is, "Could you explain what is a photogravure?"

Do you remember when you were a young person in grade school and you stuck your fountain pen into a piece of paper to watch the ink spread out on it? A hand pulled etching is printed when the paper is usually wet so that the ink applies nicely to the paper. A photogravure impression is more of a stamping process upon the paper, as it does not necessarily have to be moist. Thus, the ink "lays" on top of the paper.

"What techniques would you recommend when attempting to determine the difference between a photogravure and a hand pulled etching?"

There have become many techniques that we have used over the years including magnification. If you are fortunate to have several impressions available, it becomes easier to point out the differences. Try standing back from several of them at an angle rather than looking straight at them. From this viewpoint you can see that some appear to be soft in the image while others may appear to "stand" on the paper. The softness of the image can indicate that it was printed with moist paper so we can draw the conclusion that it was most likely an etching. For example, we have determined that there were at least two types of photogravure processes. The first is very apparent as the ink does lay upon the paper, while the second is more sophisticated. With the second method, one must still go back to documentation having to do with the image sizes of the design of the impression.

In the book, "Hans Kleiber, Artist of the Bighorn Mountains" by Emmie Mygatt and Roberta Cheney,[28] typically the images that look the best are those that are photogravures. Photo, meaning photographic, allows the photogravure image to be printed better because it is stronger photographically. It is basically a mechanical stamping process. Remember that because it is a mechanical process, it is also done with a mechanical squeegee, making each photogravure impression exactly the same. I always remember with a grin, that when the photogravure term became accepted, one of our "colleagues" started telling their clients that these photogravures were actually drypoints.[29] In other words, the ill informed slight inference that photogravures are actually

---

[28] "Hans Kleiber, Artist of the Bighorn Mountains" by Emmie Mygatt and Roberta Cheney; The Caxton Printers, Ltd., Caldwell, Idaho; 1975.

[29] "How to Identify Prints" by Bamber Gascoigne, Thames and Hudson, 1991, Section 11:

'But in the late nineteenth century, as an extension of the Etching Revival, drypoint became a medium much used for its own sake without the partnership of etched lines. It had the immediate attraction of allowing the artist to create the plate himself, ready for printing, without even the use of acid. And in the somewhat precious fashion of the time for very limited editions, it seemed almost a virtue that drypoint will produce only a small number of good impressions, since the raised metal burr is extre mely vulnerable both to the wiping process and to the pressure during printing."

drypoints is like comparing apples to oranges. This supposed comment indicates that the sources have not even picked up and read reference books as to the processes of printmaking.

"Most discussions of photogravure today revolve around the technique as it is currently practiced in commercial industry. In this application the photographic image is exposed on a sensitized copper plate through a special gravure halftone screen."[30] The plate has the ink applied each time with a mechanical squeegee and the impression is printed with usually dry paper. All of the impressions have no variation in their total value of the ink printed.

In the process of photogravure there are no restrictions set to only one plate being produced, thus it is a fair assumption on our part that many plates were made resulting in a large production of impressions. This is not an attempt to ridicule or taint the career of Hans Kleiber but rather to properly document his marketing techniques. He was simply an artist attempting to make a living. Hans was able to present to a potential customer several options. The customer could purchase the actual hand pulled etching that was signed in graphite, or a usually smaller version that was signed in graphite, or another version where his cursive signature was reproduced as well.[31]

---

[30] "Printmaking, History and Process" by Donald Saff and Deli Sacilotto; Holt, Rinehart, and Winston, 1978; page 173.

[31] The artist was able to charge the highest fee for the hand pulled etching; then a medium figure for the smaller photogravure with his graphite signature, and the most economical price for the ones that reproduced his cursive signature.

Hans Kleiber

When we were getting ready to publish our first volume, "Hans Kleiber, A Reference Manual" in 1994, we had to go out on a limb with some basic assumptions of logic and analysis from others as well. One morning in the basement of the Montana Historical Society in Helena, Montana, Marylee made the observation that "Frontier Days" looked exactly like another impression we had examined in another collection. We decided at that point to expand our analysis by bringing in further magnification of the impressions and as well the paper used by the artist. We felt that we had reached some valid conclusions but did not have the proof; for after all we were just a couple of mere researchers from Montana. Sensing that we were taking a major step, we sent off packages to other researchers. Basically our same conclusions came back to us.

When our first volume went out on the market to the public, it initially appeared that we had possibly created chaos in the Kleiber market and nothing more. We were then asked by Audrey Olsen of the Great Falls Advertising Federation to conduct a seminar at the C. M. Russell Art Show and Auction. The seminar would be on our research of Hans Kleiber and the writing of our first volume.

In preparing for the seminar, we began to compile slides for the presentation. A photogravure is very easy to spot because after all it is photographic in its nature. Upon reviewing slides for our seminar, I noticed that one impression, "Camp at Elk Lake" appeared to be very flat when the slide was shown on a screen. I went to our database and totally by random selection called a collector in Sheridan, Wyoming who owned the work. I asked them if they would mind sending it up to us so that we could examine it again. When the impression arrived, we took it out of its matting and framing and were pleasantly greeted.

We finally received the final and absolute confirmation from the artist himself. There in the top margin of the impression of " Night Camp" was written by Hans Kleiber, the following: "Cost of printing by Anderson-Lamb Photogravure Corporation, 46-48 Fulton Street, Brooklyn, New York; Approximately $1.00 per print." On the back side of the impression the following was also written by Kleiber, "This is the original size of the plate. Its of the campground at the south end of Elk Lake on Piney Creek–Bighorns. Hans"

The artists had shown us his hand.

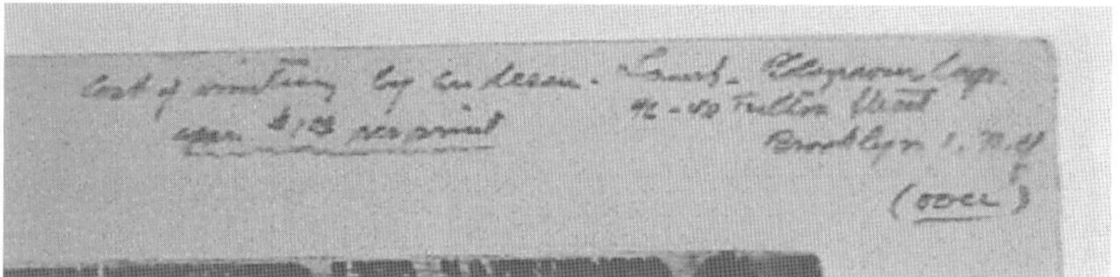

Hans Kleiber

Chapter Three

Economic Perspectives

When a customer comes into the gallery and comments that they own a Kleiber, we often ask them when they purchased it, where it was purchased, and if they remember the price. One Montana legislator could remember in the early 1970's of going down to the Snook Art Company in Billings, Montana and purchasing framed little Kleiber etchings for Christmas gifts for not over $50.00.

Probably our most favorite memory of the economic history of the Kleiber print market was when we asked a man who had stopped in the gallery the same question. He paused for a moment and said, "Eight brookies." It turns out that he often went fishing up above Kleiber's studio and on his way home, Kleiber would trade him an impression for a mess of fish.

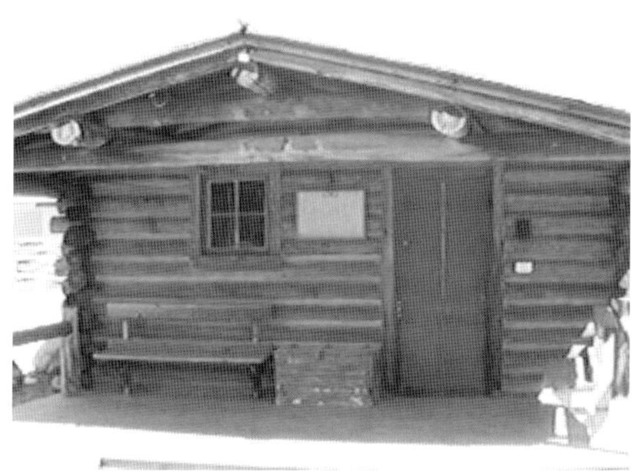

The Kleiber studio after it was moved to the Main Street of Dayton, Wyoming.

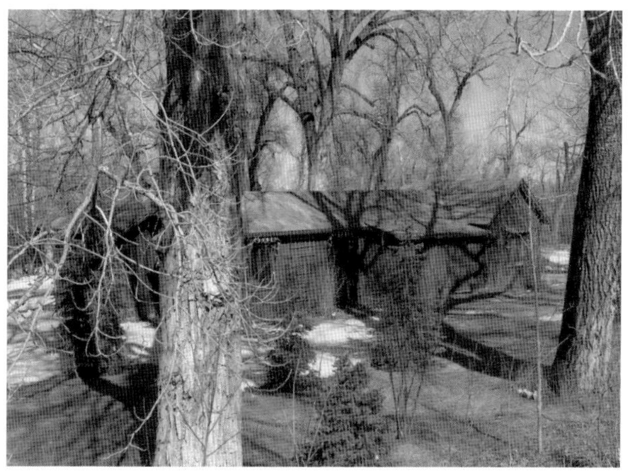

Present day photograph of the former Kleiber home in Dayton, Wyoming. The studio was located behind the house towards the creek.

Hans Kleiber

Chapter Four

"Brotherhood of Forgers, Fakers and Crooks"[32]

The World of Canceled Plates From A Different Perspective

We first listened to a seminar that Harold Davidson gave on the works of Edward Borein at the C. M. Russell Show. He was clicking well on all eight cylinders and then some. The seminar was very enjoyable. Surprisingly, no one from the Great Falls Advertising Federation felt that the tapes should be duplicated for the public. To this day, it is still an amazement, for over the past years they have brought in some excellent speakers. The seminars have had a range of speakers but are typically very poorly attended or appreciated. The primary interest of the seminars and the Great Falls Advertising Federation usually had to do with reproduction artists who were a stark contrast from the works of Charles M. Russell. One client of ours said, "Would Charlie Russell be as great today if he had done what Bev Doolittle did?"

History was always in the making when it came to Harold Davidson. We have heard from time to time about someone complaining about an opinion given by Harold, but then they usually get very quiet as they do not know how to substantiate their side. Harold Davidson was a true gentleman in the authenticity world. He was a definite pleasure from our first telephone conversation to the first day that we formally met him.

[32] "Edward Borein The Update" by Harold G. Davidson; Harold G. Davidson, Santa Barbara, California, 1991, page 205.

Hans Kleiber

Early on in our research of Hans Kleiber, we asked Harold if he would consider sharing with us the method or process he used to evaluate impressions. You will notice that we used the term impression, since it is becoming more and more common as the term etching is used too frequently in the market. After the telephone request, Harold immediately opened up and went into an in depth list of possible ways to consider an impression. He told us about taking the impression out into the strong sunlight and rolling the paper to study how the ink laid. Harold discussed the aspects of the paper and the meeting of the ink. The key thing about Harold Davidson was the fact that he was never over cautious about discussing the world of impressions and how to evaluate them.

We have often met folks who almost withdraw into themselves when asked questions on their area of expertise. They tend to feel that knowledge is power. We have practiced due diligence, which we feel eventually helps the market. In other words, tell them everything you know and everything you do not know. We have practiced this concept of due diligence in all of our research and additionally in our published books on Hans Kleiber.

During the course of our research, certain factors did not always become apparent until we stumbled on them many times. One of the classic myths of the art world is that after an artist dies, the value of his or her work goes up. Actually it goes down for about ten to twelve years after the death of the artist.[33] For example, if John Doe Artist were to die, then many who owned one of his works would bring it out onto the market thinking that it would go up in value. The determining factor is, as more works become available, the supply increases thus lessening the demand. "All was quiet on the Borein front until about 1960. The artist's work was selling at low prices, and the forgers were not tempted because of the poor returns on their artistic efforts."[34]

Forgeries are not the present problem in the Kleiber market today, but rather the sorting out of some of the posthumous activities since 1967. We have commented before about the reprinting of the Frontier Series by his son after his father's death.[35]

Recently, we have become aware of highly unusual canceled plates arising on the market. We can only speculate as to their origins, but it appears that posthumous activities were done after his death.

---

[33] Bernard Ewell graciously shared with us the "Myths of the Art Market." In less than two per cent of the art market do these myths actually apply. First, art has value. Second, art increases in value. Third, art is a good investment. Fourth, the bigger the name of an artist, the higher the value of his work. Fifth, when an artist dies, the value of their work goes up.

[34] "Edward Borein The Update" by Harold G. Davidson; Harold G. Davidson, Santa Barbara, California, 1991; page 205.

[35] See Appendix Three.

Hans Kleiber

There are legitimate canceled plates on the market that were used by Hans Kleiber. For the most part, Hans Kleiber did not cancel his own plates but preferred to use them until they "went blind."[36] After the Wyoming artist E. W. "Bill" Gollings death, the local Sheriff discovered Hans Kleiber in Gollings' studio canceling the plates by scratching a large "X" across each one. The Sheriff took the plates away from Kleiber, and many years later those same plates were purchased by a Gollings collector. Kleiber plates that were actually canceled by the artist are rare. We have examined canceled plates with a jewelers engraving as "Hans Kleiber 1887-1967" or "Cancelled Hans Kleiber 1887-1967." We can only suggest, that on a case by case basis, plates with a jewelers engraving should be held in suspicion until authenticated.[37]

The detail views to the left and above are examples of posthumous cancelations.

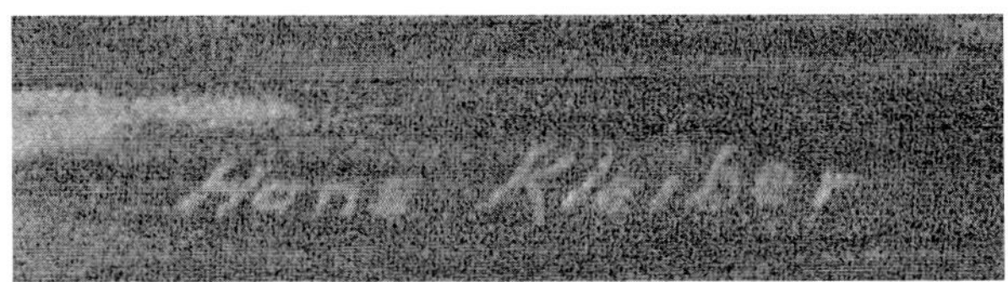

The above is a detailed view of the etched name of the artist within the plate of "Mallard Drake on Snow." This prevents any future printing of the plate as then the name would appear in reverse.

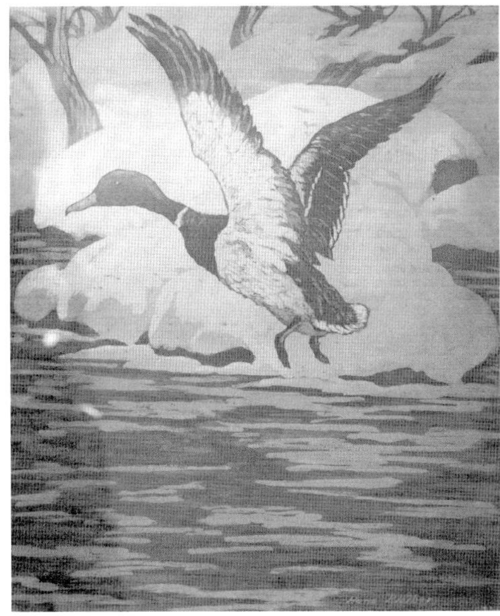

Canceled zinc plate of "Mallard Drake on Snow"
Plate Size: 10 inches high by 8 inches wide
Etched signature in lower right.

---

[36] Carole Tucker.

[37] For example, the plate used for the hand pulled etching of "At The Hitchrack" had in the top right corner the indication of bending of the plate possibly done by it being dropped on that one corner. The plate was then reworked, but impressions do still show that damaged area in the top left corner, see "At The Hitchrack."

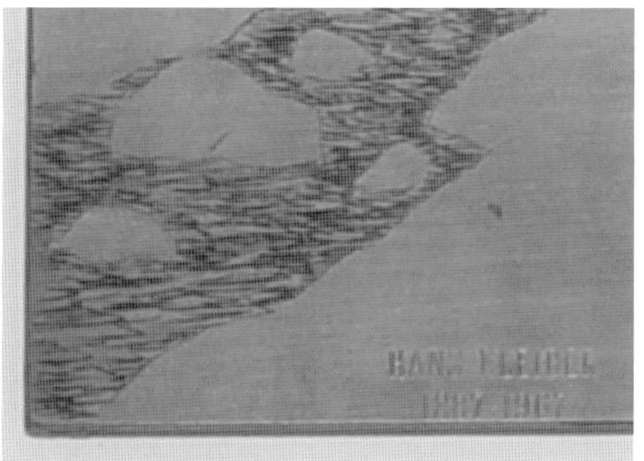

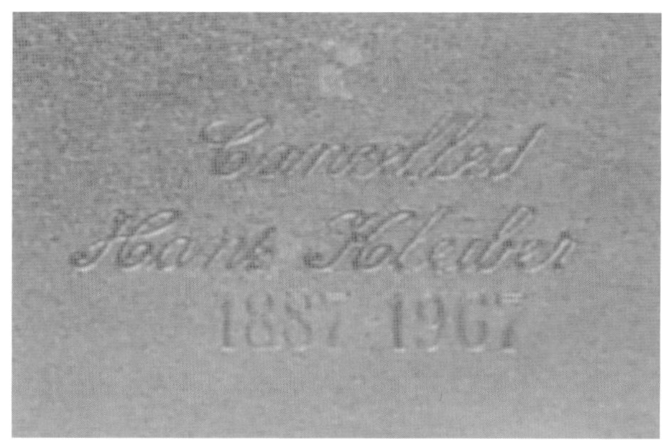

The following are detail views of the edge of plates that have not been canceled posthumously but were created and used by the artist. Many years ago, Robert F. Morgan visited with us about what and what not to look for regarding a supposed Charles M. Russell painting. We can always remember him telling us that the last thing you look at is the signature area.

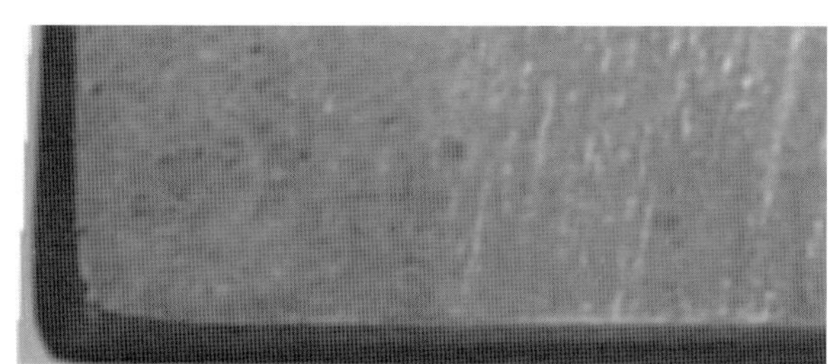

Left bottom corner of "Crows Flying South."

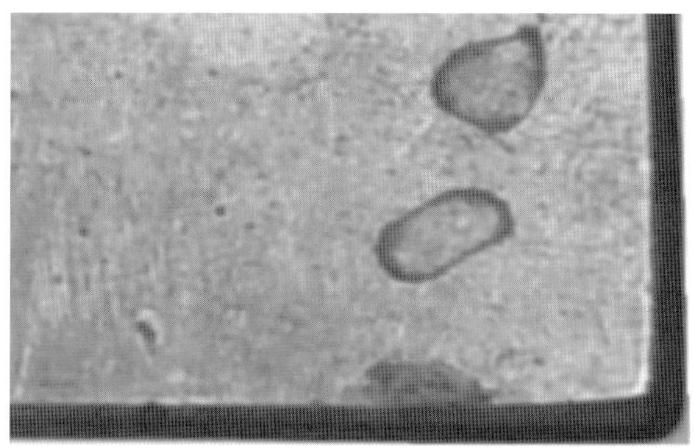

Right bottom corner of "Crows Flying South."

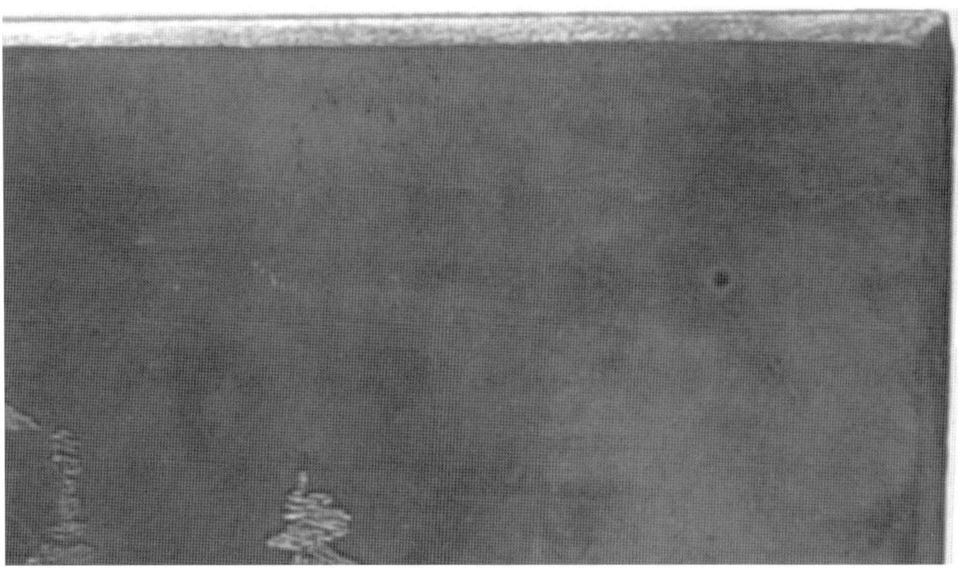

On the above detail view of a corner of a plate, please note the beveling process by the artist or printmaker.

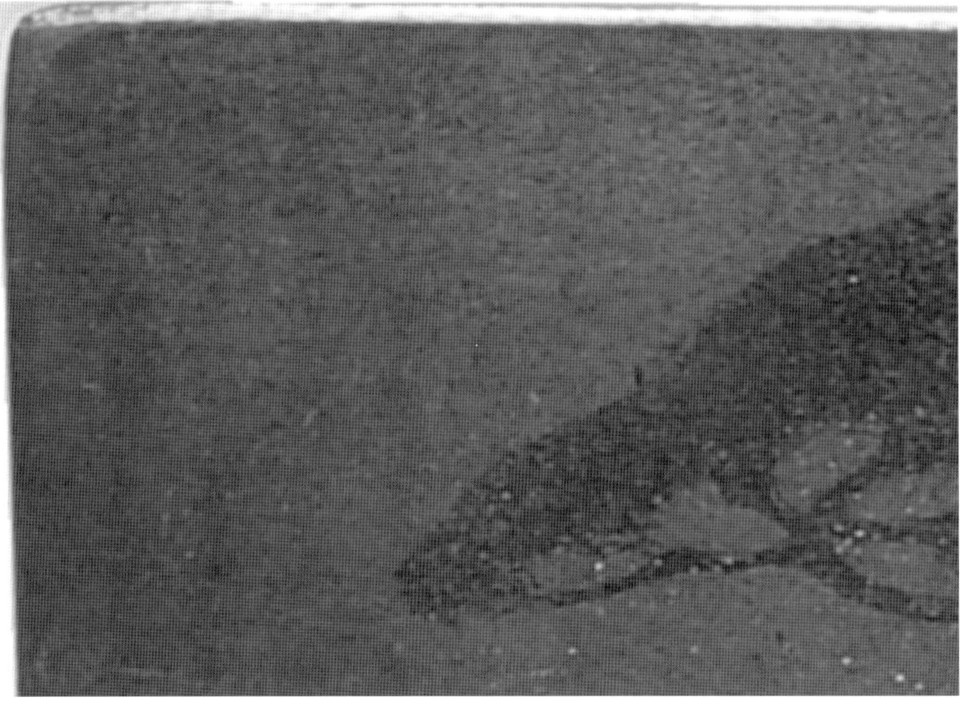

This is a detail view of the top corner of "Evening on the Range." Again, notice the beveling of the edge of the plate and the condition of the overall area.

First, we examined plates where we could readily see that they had been used in a printing process. Also, in our review of several plates that came from the family by descent, there was no indication of any plates being canceled with the jewelers engraving other than ones with certain factors. These factors included: the same type of beveling the edges of the plate, extreme lack of printing use, lack of wear to the front of the plate, and then usually plates of impressions that were printed as photogravures. Later in this book, the reader will see examples of some jeweler engraved plates that were also the same size as the hand pulled etchings.

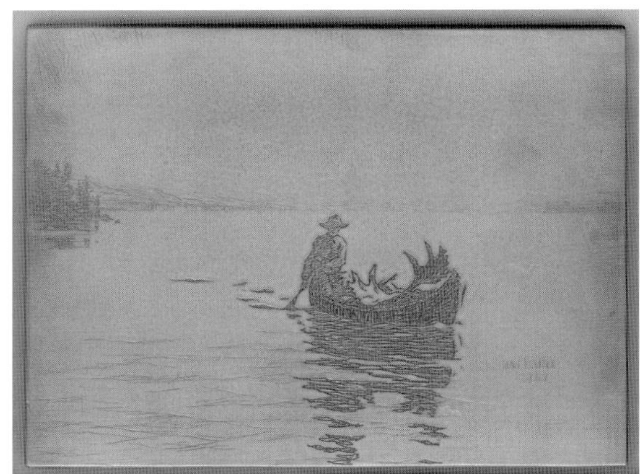

Recently we were offered the supposed canceled plate of the Second State of "Returning from the Hunt." The actual size of the subject plate was approximately 5.5 inches high by 7.5 inches wide and the type of metal was copper.[38]

---

[38] During the completion of our second volume of "Hans Kleiber, A Reference Manual" there was a conflicting discovery. Our source for the image of "Bound for the Hunt" a.k.a. "Starting on a Hunt" a.k.a. "Starting on the Hunt" came from the University of Wyoming. It was an unusual discovery for it showed that the hand pulled etching was smaller than the photogravure state, see page 83 and 84 of Volume II of "Hans Kleiber, A Reference Manual." Another impression was that of "Moose Swimming," where the photogravure state was larger than the hand pulled impression, see page 185 of Volume II of "Hans Kleiber, A Reference Manual." The authors fully admit that we made a mistake as well an assumption that with "Returning from the Hunt" was done in the same manner. Actually as this analysis will show, the hand pulled etching was the larger state and the photogravure was the smaller state.

Hans Kleiber

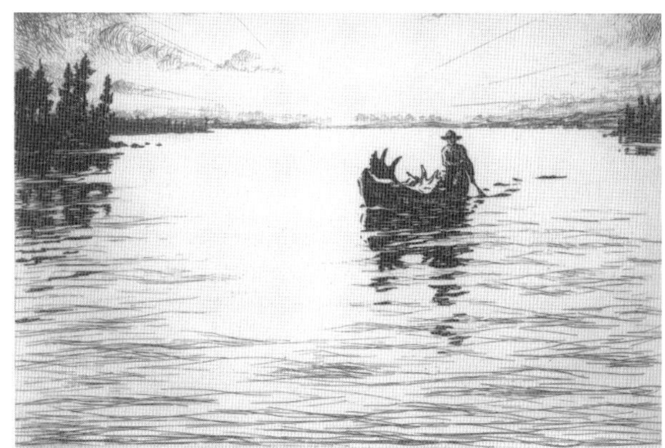

"Returning from the Hunt"
First State
Medium: Etching
Image: 7.75 inches high by 11.25 inches wide

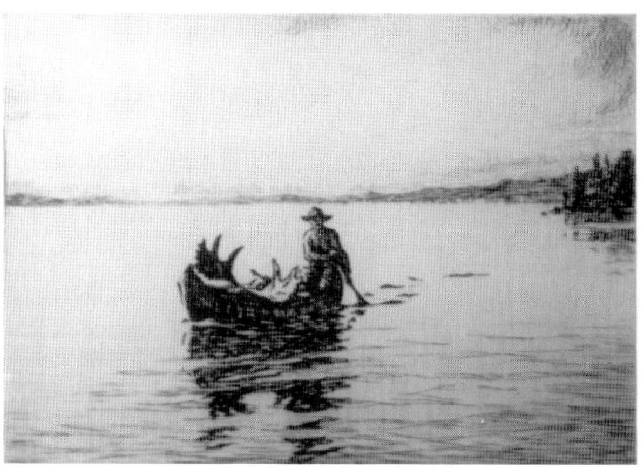

"Returning from the Hunt"
Second State
Medium: Photogravure
Image: 5.25 inches high by 7.375 inches wide
Title and signed by the artist in graphite.

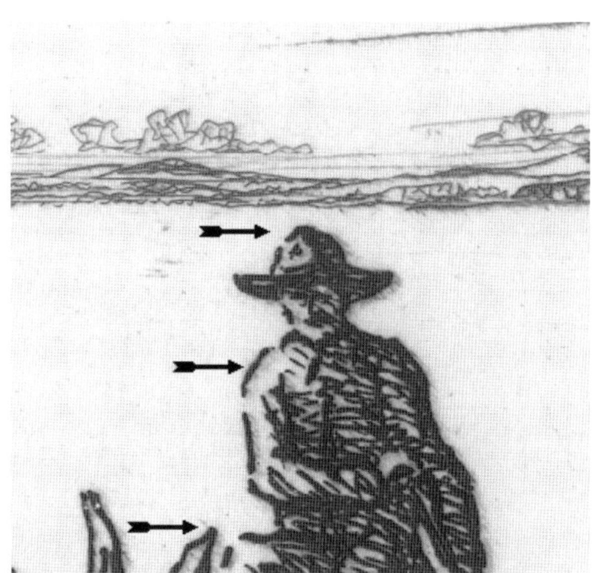

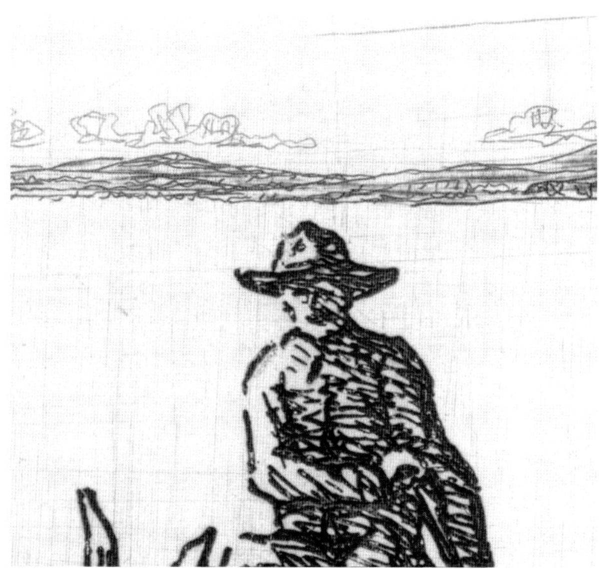

On the left is a detail view of the hand pulled etching of the First State of "Returning from the Hunt." Note the three identifying arrows where the ink has been absorbed into the paper. Also note the softness of the texture of the impression upon the paper. The reason for this is that the paper is moist when it is printed. On the right is a detail view of the photogravure of "Returning from the Hunt," Second State. The ink actually is laying upon the paper. One can actually feel the layers of ink upon the top of the paper of the photogravure with your finger tip.

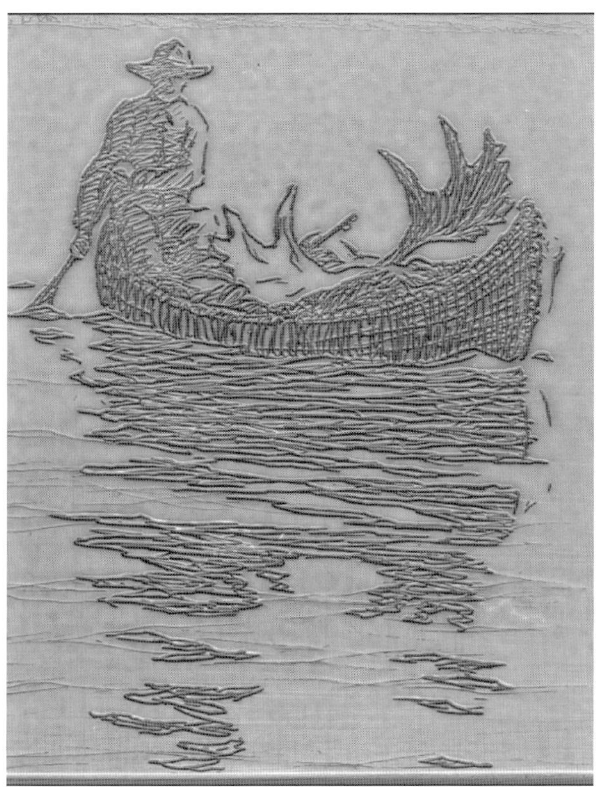

This page encompasses five detail views of which three are of the subject copper plate presented as the actual working plate for the photogravure of "Returning From The Hunt". The image to the left shows the overall flatness of the etched lines. The center left detail view is an enlarged view of the ripples in the water. Notice how the etched ripples are all even. Below is the detail view of the man. All of the etched lines are very even with no contrast, this is a clear indication of the design being produced photographically. Note at the bottom of this page, the two detail views of an actual etched copper plate by a contemporary artist.

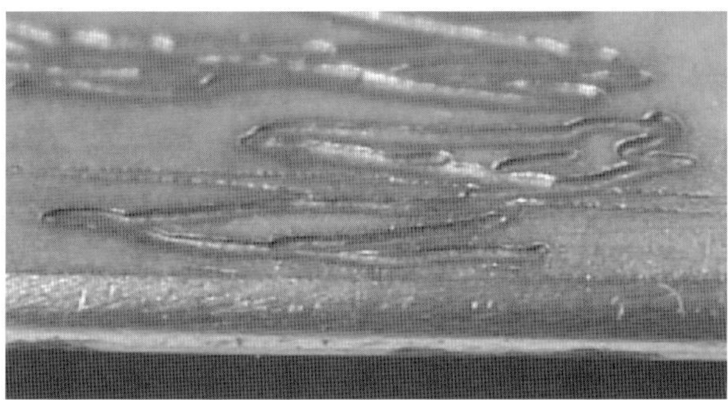

Detail view of the ripples in the water and the edge of the plate.

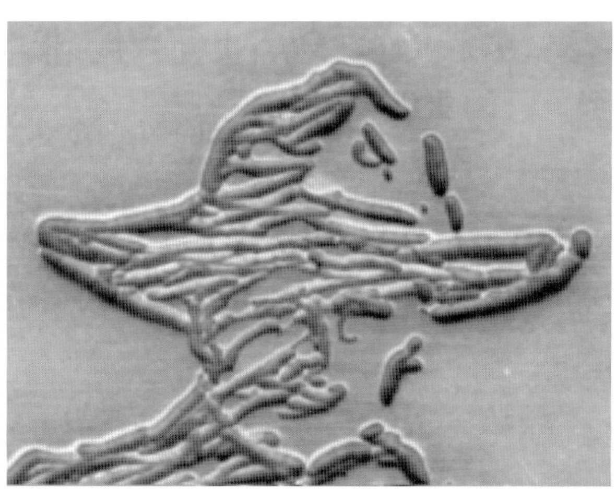

Detail view of the man's face and hat.

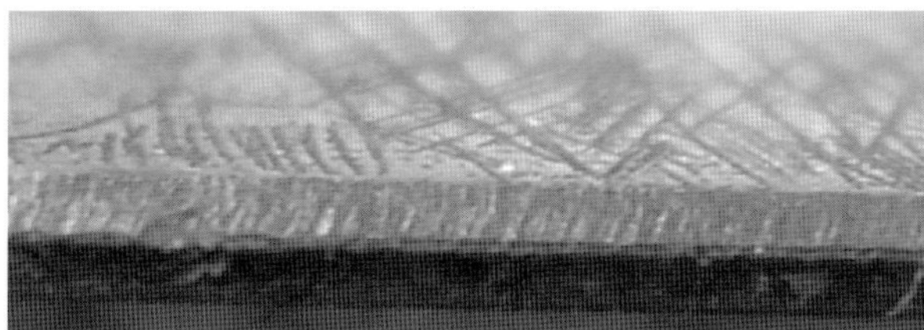

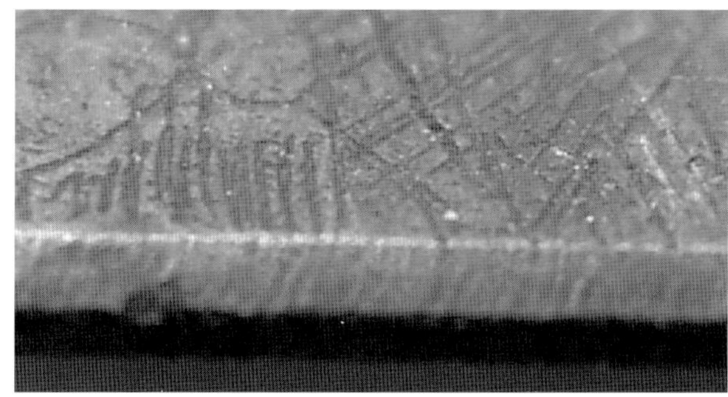

Detail views of an etched copper plate by a contemporary artist.

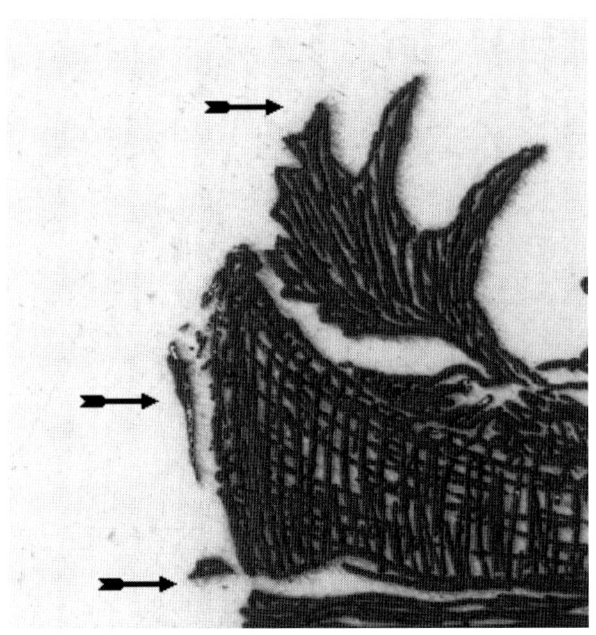

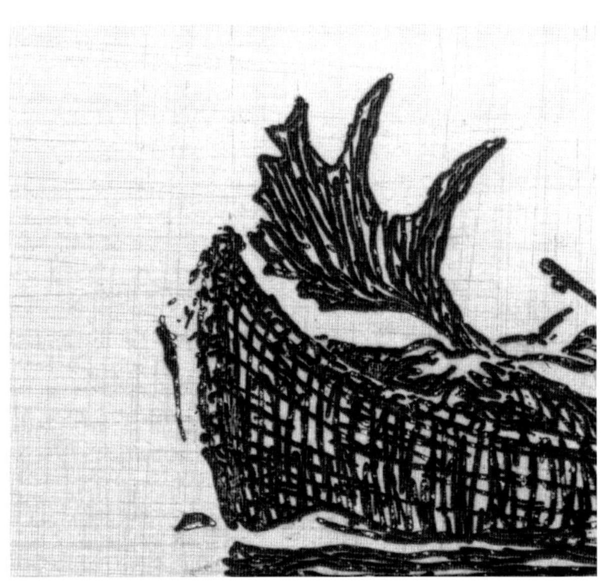

On the left is another detail view of the hand pulled etching, First State of "Returning From The Hunt." Note the areas identified with arrows as to the absorption of the ink during the printing. On the right is another detail view of the photogravure, Second State of "Returning From The Hunt."

Now that we have reviewed the impressions, the subject canceled plate must be reviewed as well. Notice the evenness of the edge of the plate and also the lack of any type of wear upon the face of the plate. This plate was not a working plate but rather a photo-engraving from a printed impression. Upon further review of detailed views of the edges of the plate, one can see an even rounding of the plate edge which was done more for decorative purposes than printing. Questions have been asked if we have ever examined a photogravure plate from an impression. The assumption here is that only one plate was used for a photogravure. Due to the process of printing photogravures, several plates were used, enabling the printing process to be done more efficiently.

Detail view of a corner of the jeweler canceled plate of the Second State of "Returning from the Hunt."

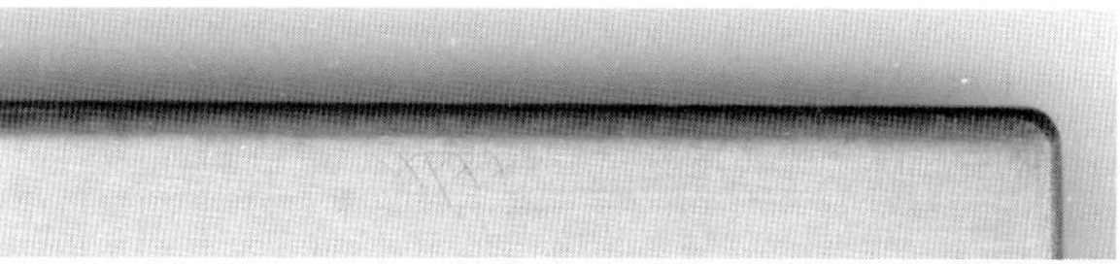

Another view of a corner of the jeweler canceled plate.

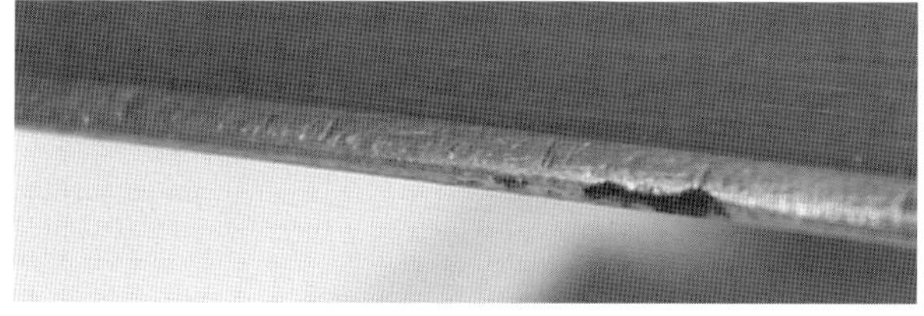

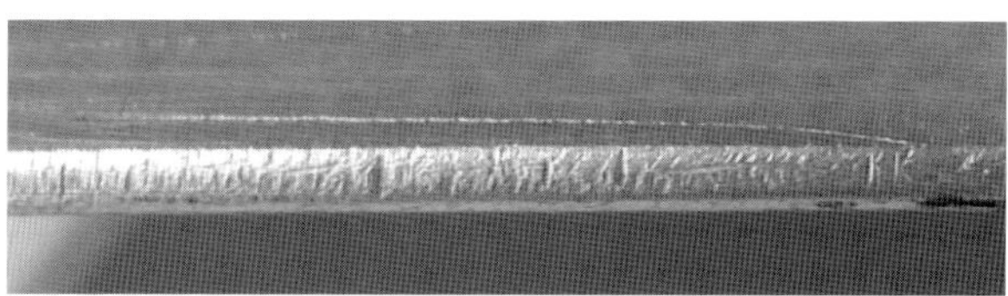

Magnified examples of the edge of the plate of the jeweler canceled plate of the Second State of "Returning from the Hunt."

Hans Kleiber

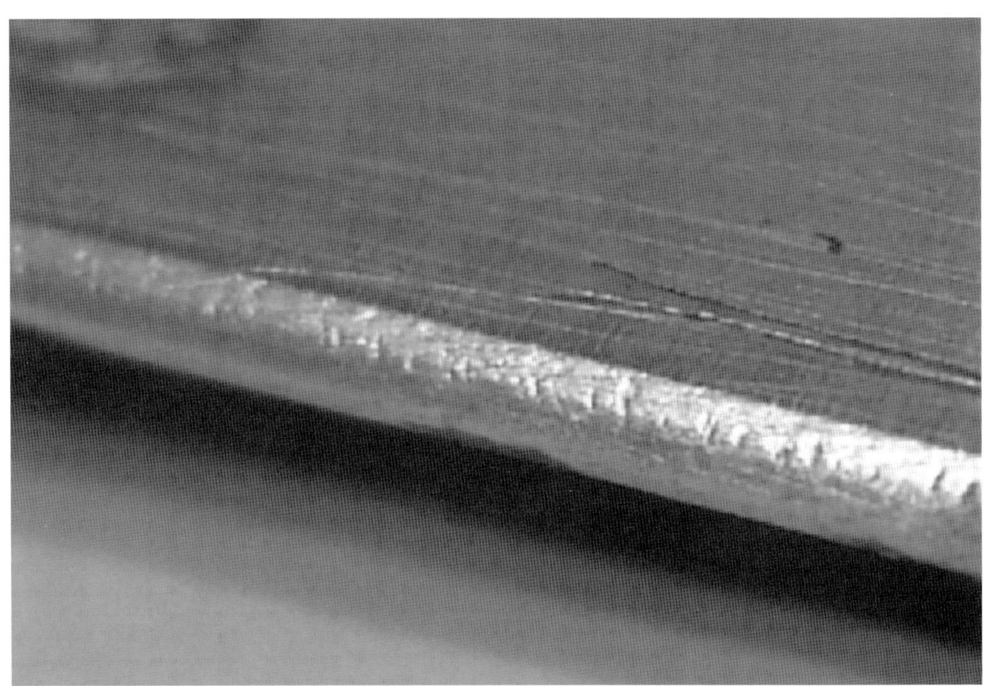

The following are examples of jeweler canceled plates. The original designed plates based upon the production that we have seen would show much more wear than is indicated by these photo-engravings.

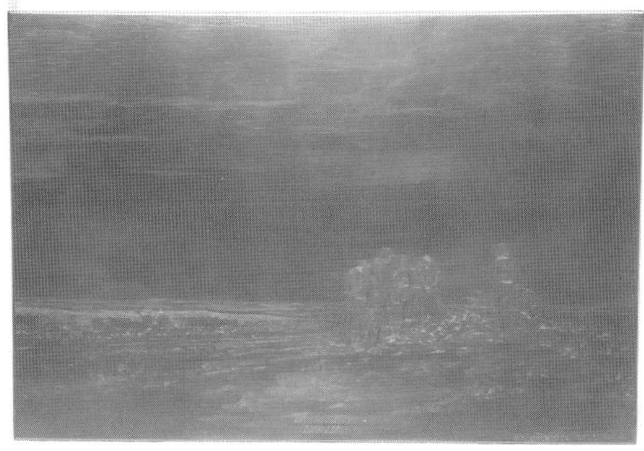

"A Burial on the Prairie"
Image: 7 inches high by 10 inches wide

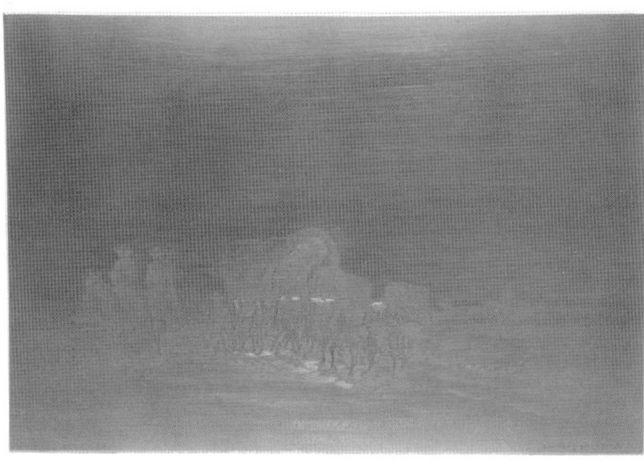

"Across the Prairies"
Image: 5.5 inches high by 7.75 inches wide

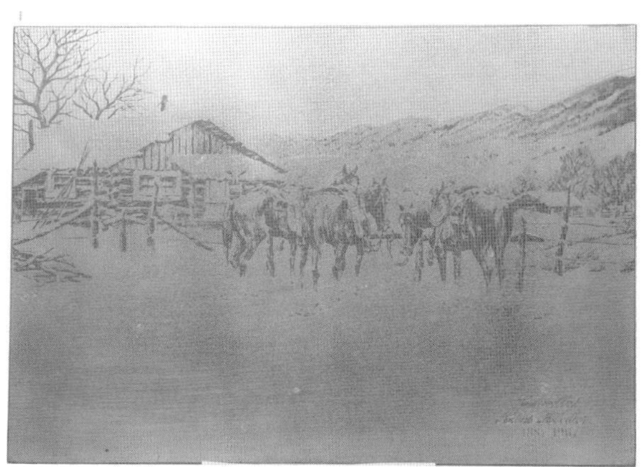

"At the Hitchrack"
Image: 5.75 inches high by 8 inches wide

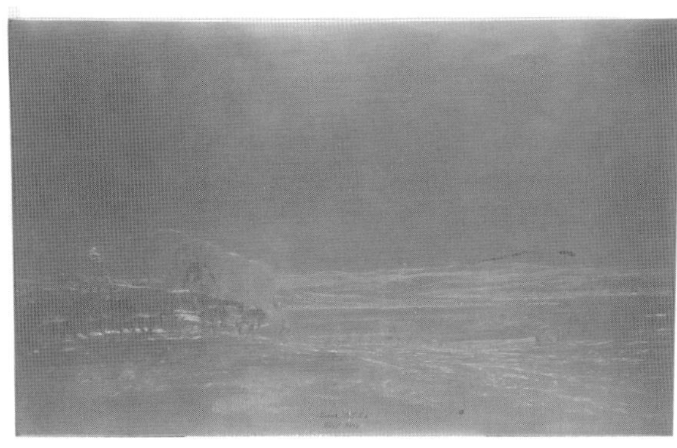

"Crossing the Platte"
Image: 7 inches high by 11 inches wide

For example, all of the plates displayed show remarkably good condition considering the number of impressions created from each design. Yes, plates can be cleaned, but also a suggestion was made that the plates were milled down so that the face was brought back to a clean condition. We would suggest that the milling would remove more of the plate than desired, including a good portion of the etching if they were the original designs. For example, the smallest milling would possibly be that of one thousandth of an inch, but it would still cause problems to the acid etched areas. The milling process would leave tool marks upon the copper. Another question had to do with the fact that they might have used a high grit sanding tool on the plate. This procedure would cause "fish hooking" upon the plate from an oscillating sander. Both the process of the milling and the sanding, no matter how fine, would leave clear evidence of the procedure used.

The creation of these photo engraved "plates" from printed impressions was an attempt to immediately bring in income. At the time of the death of Hans Kleiber, it was apparent to those immediate parties as to sources that the artist used to create photogravures. Keep in mind that we are talking about from after 1967 to the 1970's when the Kleiber dollar market was extremely different than present day. The creation of "plates" was then a very easy task. Canceled plates, or purported canceled plates of the artist, would bring a larger fee than the printed impressions left to the estate. The primary selling point would have been that the "canceled plate" was the only one and thus deserved a higher selling price.

Is that signature correct?

When we had built up our inventory to more than thirty five impressions, we still felt the concern to further analyze the signatures of Hans Kleiber. We asked a handwriting expert from a local county law enforcement agency to help us.

Hans

In writing his first name, Hans was usually completed in five up strokes, and sometimes he would close the s at the end.

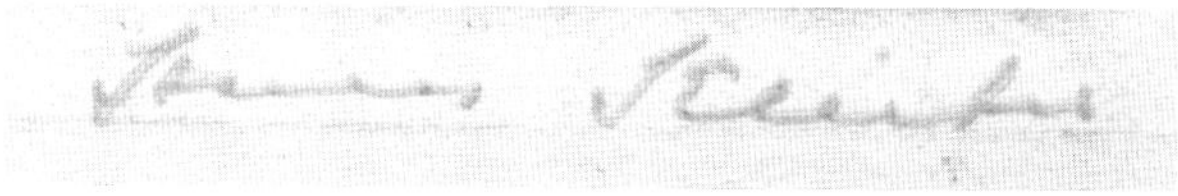

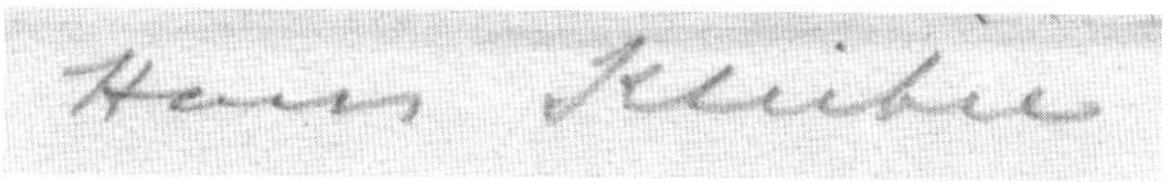

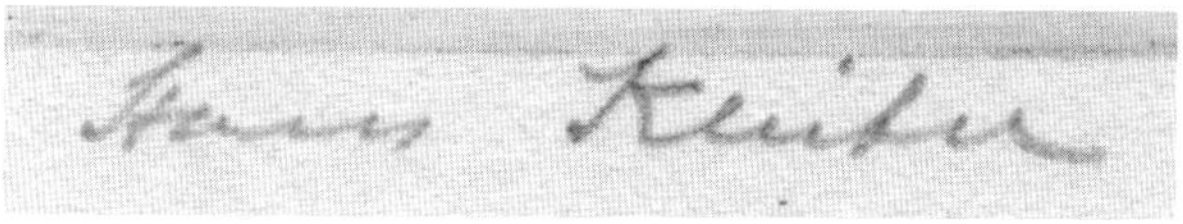

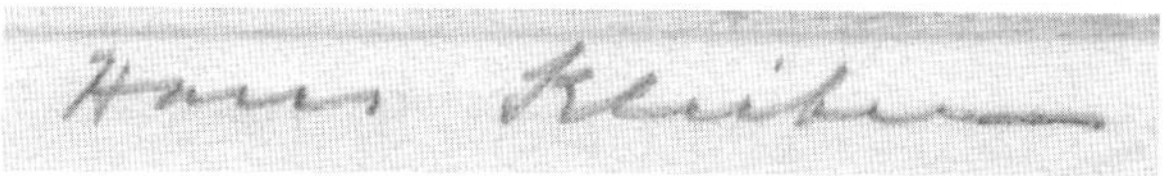

Kleiber

In writing his last name, Hans would at times break the name in his rhythm of writing between Klei and ber. As with all signatures, there is a certain rhythm to each individual signing.

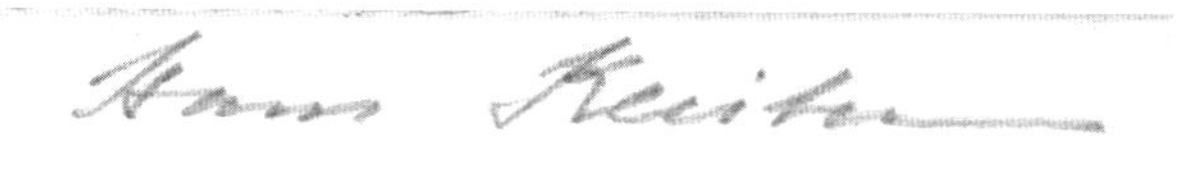

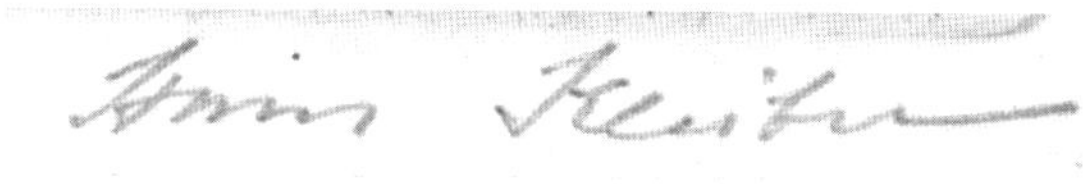

Hans Kleiber

The lower case g was not always closed in his titling.

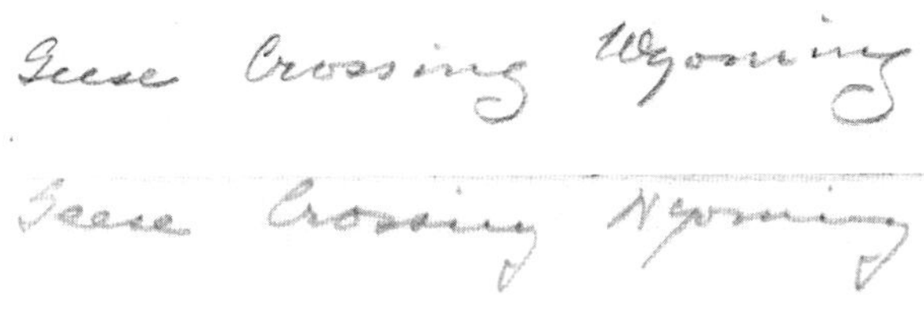

With a forgery or an incorrect signature, one tends to find definite inconsistencies and pen stoppages.

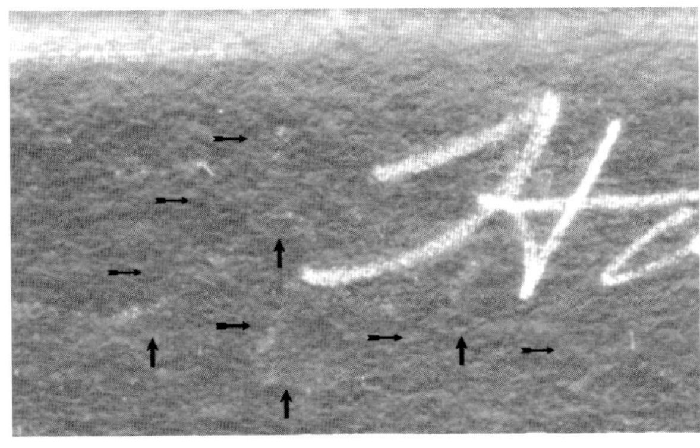

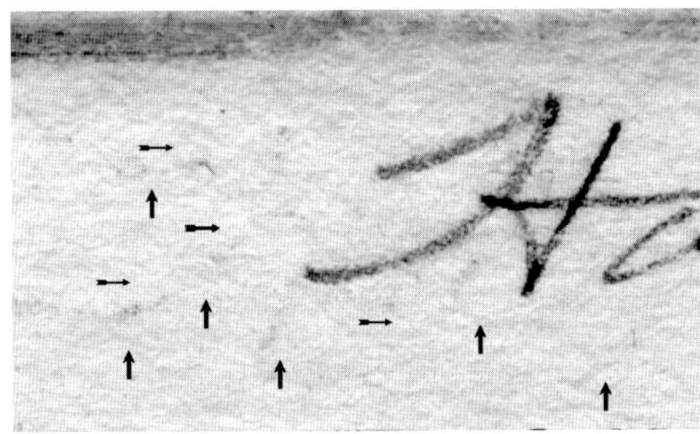

Under magnification, rolling the impression in the sun, the sly fellow comes through. Notice how they attempted to sign Hans, made a mistake and erased it.

The above two detail views and the overall view of the supposed signature is a good example of a forged signature attempt. This was a posthumously copied signature. Notice how the H and the K are heavier than the rest of the attempted signature. Note the angle of the signature. Arrows indicate areas where "someone" erased and restarted.

Actual correct signature of the artist.

Nobody writes the same way all of the time. For example, place ten checks in front of you and sign them right away. Compare each letter in the signing of the signature. A recent presented Kleiber impression clearly showed the title and signature area being printed rather than cursively signed, indicative of a posthumous activity.

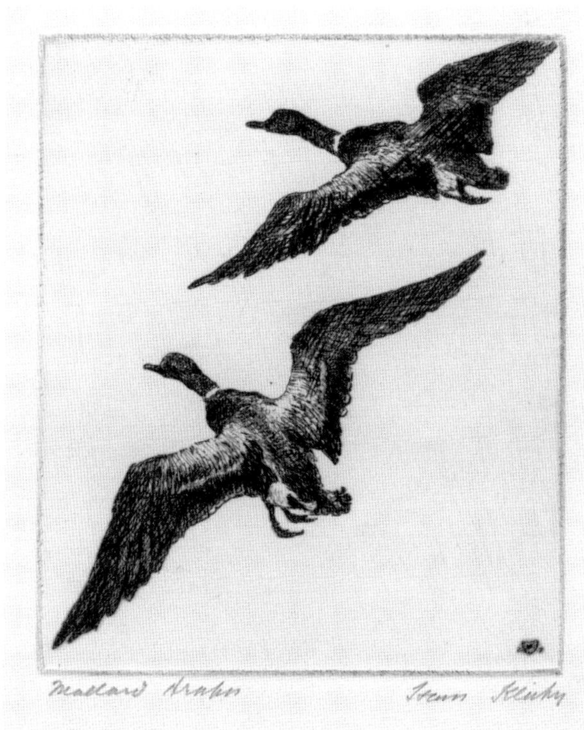

Actual titled and signed work by the artist.

Mallards in Flight Hans Kleiber

Posthumous printed title and name.

Mallards in Flight Hans Kleiber

Detail view of the posthumous printed title and name.

Printed by Stuart Kleiber (son) from the original plate by Hans Kleiber

The above is an example of the printed statement done on the restrikes posthumously.

Chapter Five

Gallery Ephemera

Goodspeed's Book Shop
of
Boston, Massachuesetts,
Fall, 1930

Gordon Beer Art Galleries of Detroit, Michigan, April 1, 1937

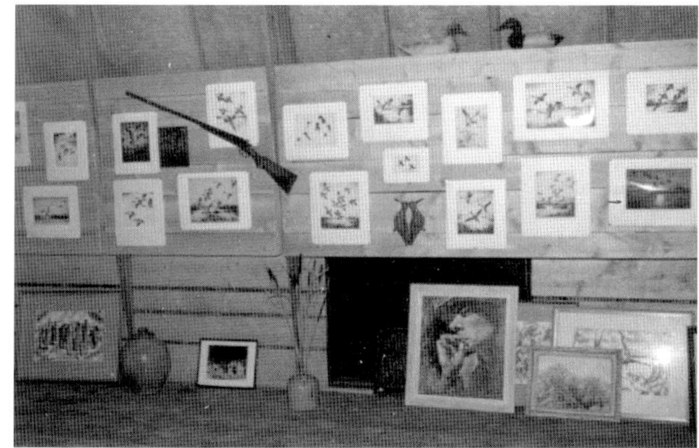

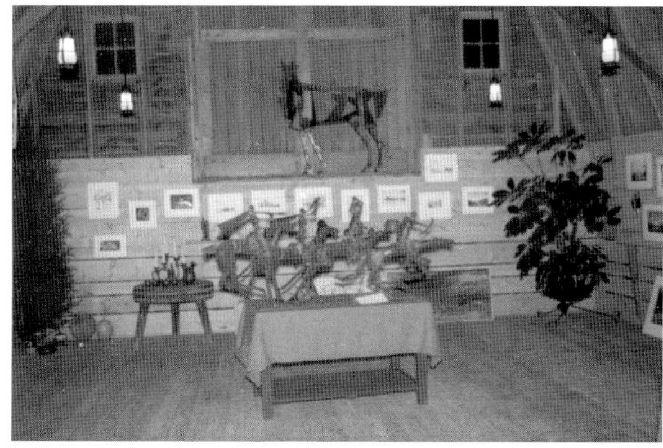

Early photographs of the Brown Barn Gallery in Billings, Montana as of December, 1964. As one can see, all of the impressions were basically sold unframed, since they were considered inexpensive works of art. Etchings or impressions were parlor items, usually kept in a drawer until they were ready to be admired.

Hans Kleiber

1930 | Nº 202 A

ETCHINGS
BLOCK-PRINTS
WATER-COLORS
by

Samuel Chamberlain
Decaris
Clark Fay
Sears Gallagher
Arthur Hall
Norma Hall
Hans Kleiber
Yngve E. Soderberg
George C. Wales
C. I. Wylde

PUBLISHED BY
GOODSPEED'S BOOK SHOP
7 ASHBURTON PLACE BOSTON

FALL 1930

Hans Kleiber

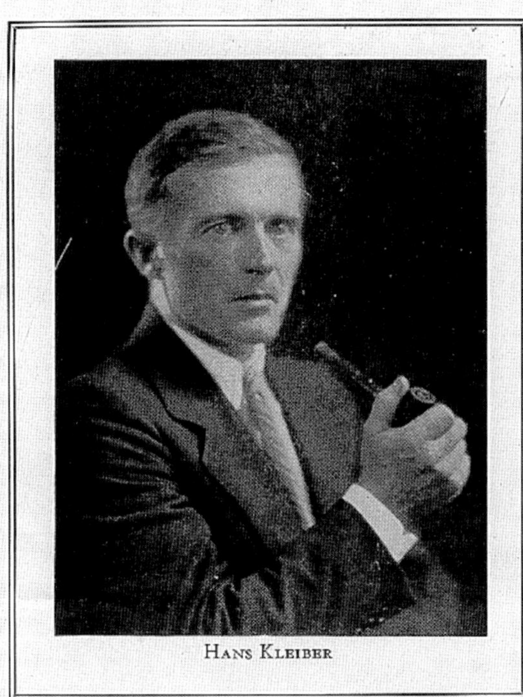

HANS KLEIBER

"WE ARE often urged to think of a picture as a window in our wall, from which we may snatch glimpses of the subjects and places that interest us most. This is a particularly apt way in which to consider the work of Hans Kleiber, a Wyoming etcher, whose subject is the out-of-doors in which he lives. Through the one-pane windows of his prints we look out across the wide country which is such a satisfactory antidote to the smoke of eastern cities. . . . This is the country that Mr. Kleiber knows best for he has been riding mountain trails for many years. Sometimes it has been as a forest ranger, more often as a guide, but he has been continuously storing up the impressions that he now sets down upon his copper plates. Until quite recently he has been able to work but spasmodically at his art, for a month of enthusiastic experimentation in the studio has had to be earned by several months of labor at a more lucrative occupation.

In this mountain group we find more rugged scenes. The interwoven planes of the Big Horns, eroded canyons, twisted and leaning evergreens, deer, and elk, and mountain sheep, — all these have caught his eye and he has portrayed them in the faithful and sympathetic drawing that has characterized his work from the first time he attempted to master the technique of etching."

Russell Kettell

Born in Germany in 1887.
Came to United States in 1900.
Studied drawing and painting in New Jersey for a short time.
Joined American Forestry Service in Wyoming, 1908.
Continued sketching and began etching only a few years ago.
Prints represented in many Public and Private Collections.
Now living in Dayton, Wyoming.

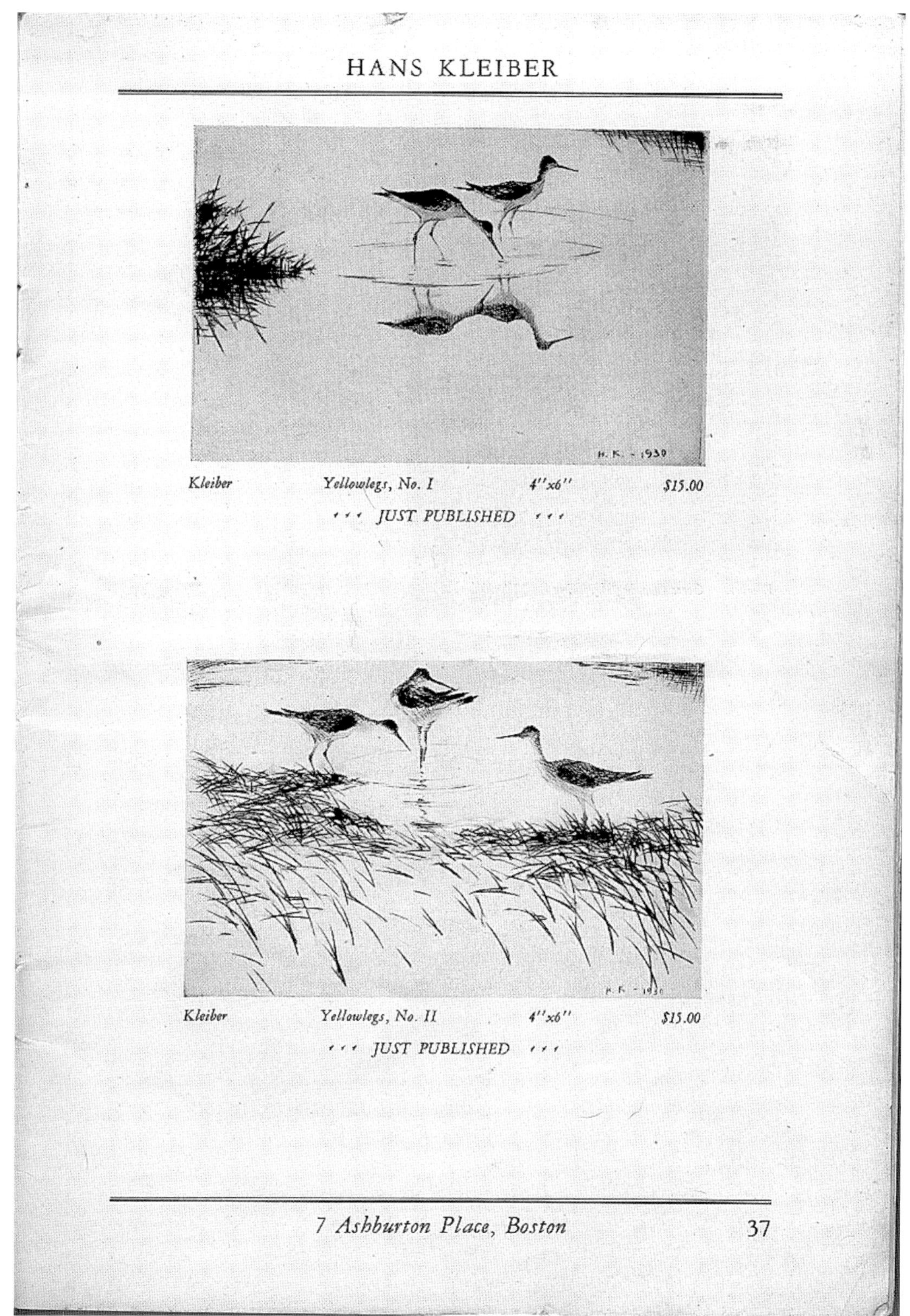

HANS KLEIBER

Kleiber *Yellowlegs, No. I* *4"x6"* *$15.00*

... JUST PUBLISHED ...

Kleiber *Yellowlegs, No. II* *4"x6"* *$15.00*

... JUST PUBLISHED ...

7 Ashburton Place, Boston 37

Hans Kleiber

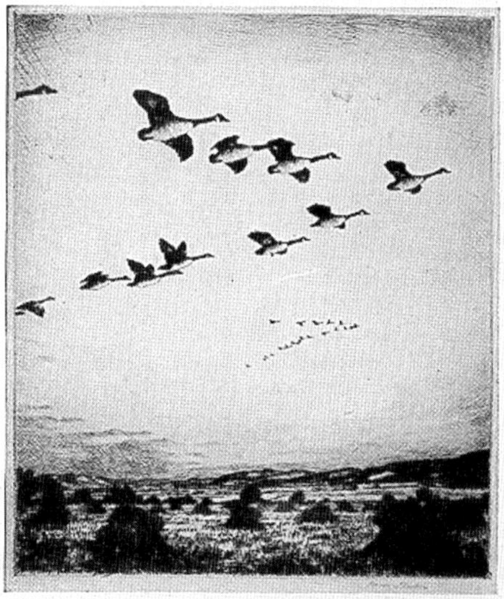

Kleiber Geese Crossing Wyoming 12″x10″ $30.00

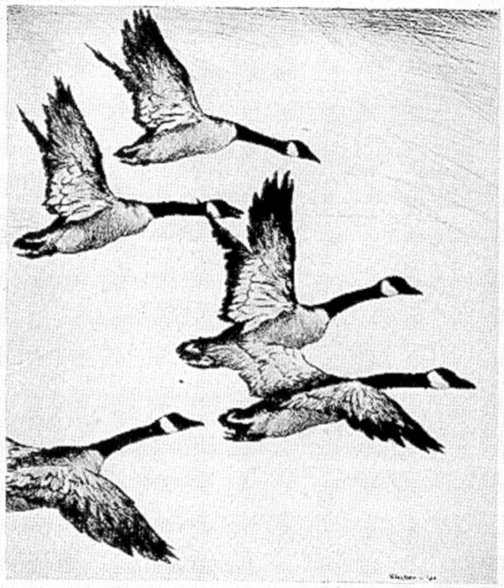

Kleiber In Full Flight 13″x11″ $25.00

HANS KLEIBER

Kleiber *A Rising Flock* *10"x7½"* *$25.00*

Kleiber *A Fisherman* *10"x7¾"* *$18.00*

7 Ashburton Place, Boston 39

Hans Kleiber

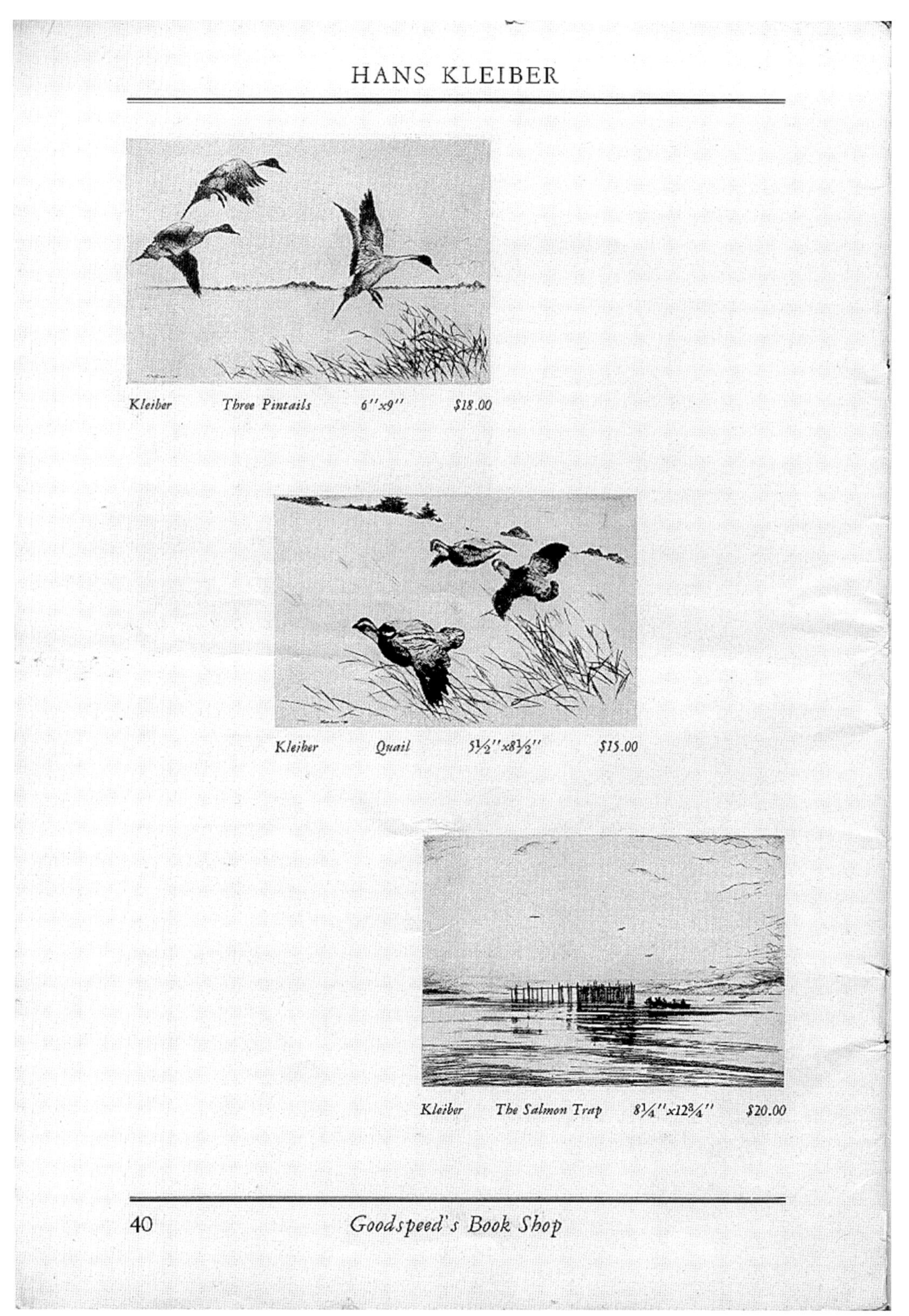

HANS KLEIBER

Kleiber *Three Pintails* *6"x9"* *$18.00*

Kleiber *Quail* *5½"x8½"* *$15.00*

Kleiber *The Salmon Trap* *8¼"x12¾"* *$20.00*

40 *Goodspeed's Book Shop*

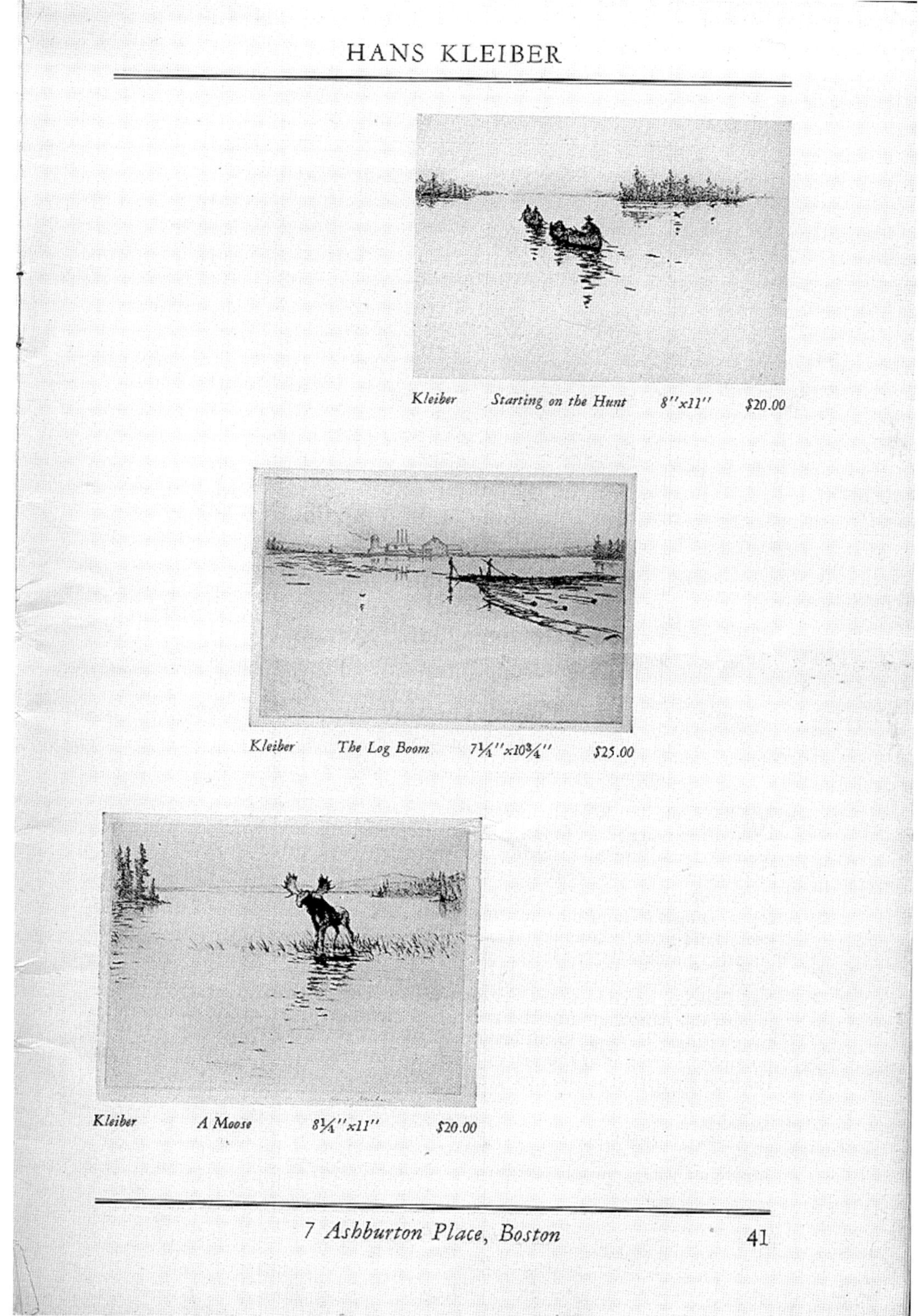

HANS KLEIBER

Kleiber Starting on the Hunt 8"x11" $20.00

Kleiber The Log Boom 7¼"x10¾" $25.00

Kleiber A Moose 8¼"x11" $20.00

7 Ashburton Place, Boston 41

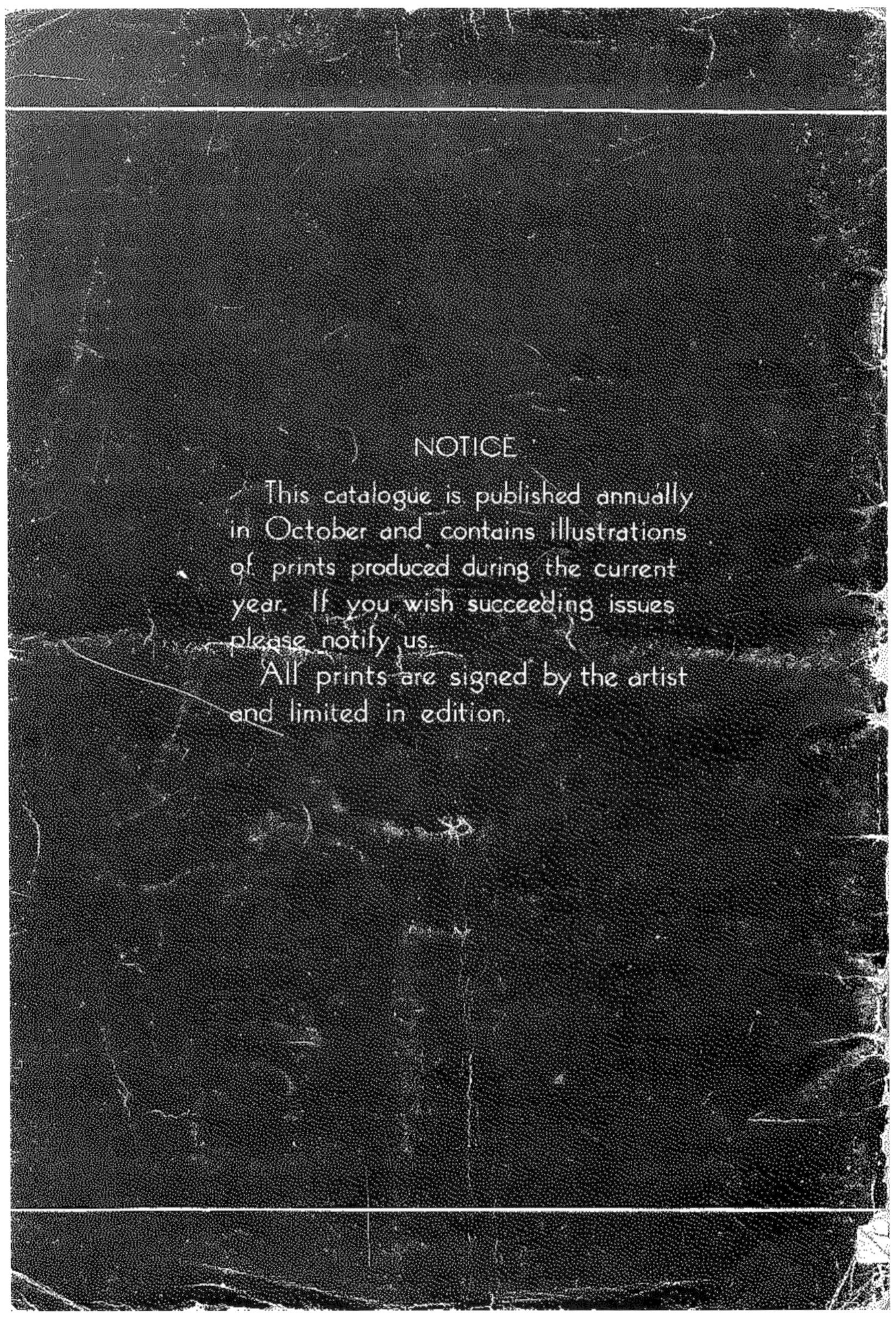
NOTICE

This catalogue is published annually in October and contains illustrations of prints produced during the current year. If you wish succeeding issues please notify us.

All prints are signed by the artist and limited in edition.

"Catalog of Ninety One Etchings by Hans Kleiber by The Gordon Beer Art Galleries of Detroit, Michigan

The following are the edition sizes of Hans Kleiber on April 1, 1937, according to the "Catalog Of Ninety One Etchings by Hans Kleiber" by The Gordon Beer Art Galleries of Detroit, Michigan:

Title	Size	Edition
A Flock Of Ducks	5x4	200
A Likely Stream	8x11	100
A Moose	8x11	150
A Quiet Stream	4x5.5	200
A Rising Flock	10x7	150
A Rough Stream	3.5x5	200
A Sheep Wagon	6x9	200
Around the Camp Fire	6x8	200
Big Horn Peaks	3.5x5.5	200
Big Horn, Wyoming	5x7	200
Blackbirds	6x4.5	200
Blackbirds	12x9	100
Bon Voyage, II	5x7	200
Burial on the Prairie	7x10	150
Canadian Goose	5x7	200
Chickadees	3.5x5	200
Crossing the Platte	7x11	150
Curlews	7x11	100
Dayton, Wyoming	5.5x8	150
Doe and Fawn	6x5	200
Duck Hunters	4.5x6.5	200
Elk, Winter	5x3.5	200
Evening	8.5x11	100
Evening, Ducks	3.5x5	200
Evening on the Yellowstone	5x4	200
Evening on Tongue River, Wyoming	4x6	200
Fishermen's Camp at Elk Lake	4.5x6	200

Hans Kleiber

Title	Size	Edition
Fishing on Jackson Lake, Wyoming	4.5x6	200
Fishing on Upper Piney Creek	5.5x4.5	200
Flying Geese	4x5.5	200
Frightened Finches	6x5	200
Geese Crossing Wyoming	12x11	100
Geese, Mating Time	7x11	150
Geese on the Pacific	8x13	100
Geese Overhead	5x8	200
Grouse Hunter	4.5x6	200
Honkers in Flight	9x9	100
Hunting Pheasants	7x12	100
In Full Flight	13x11	100
Kearney Lake	4.5x3.5	200
Lake Adelaide	5.5x7	200
Lake Geneva	4.5x3.5	200
Lake o' the Woods II	5x6.5	200
Lake Solitude, II	6x5	200
Landing One	4x6	200
Leaving the Frontier	7x10	150
Leaving the High Country	8x13	100
Little Goose, Wyoming	6x8	200
Looking for Pheasants	5x6.5	200
Magpies	9x7.5	100
Magpies	3.5x5.5	200
Mallard Drake	7x6	200
Mallards, a Pair	3.5x5	200
Mallards, Evening, II	6x8	150
Marsh Along Snake River	4x6.5	200
Northern Lights	12x10	100
On Lake La Croix	5.5x7.5	200
On the Canyon Rim	6x8	200
On the Oregon Trail	7x10	150
Oregon Trail I	3x5	200
Oregon Trail II	3.5x4.5	200
Out of the Clouds	6x8	200

Title	Size	Edition
Phalaropes	4.5x3.5	200
Pintails Coming In	11x13	100
Ptarmigan	5x6	200
Quail	5x7	200
Sheep Creek Ridge	5x6.5	100
Sheepherder	4x5.5	200
Sheep on the Range	4x5.5	200
Shooting from a Blind	5x6.5	200
Snow in the Rockies	9x12	100
Stormy Afternoon	3.5x5	200
Stormy Evening	5x4	200
The Log Boom	7.5x11	100
The Lone Fisherman	13x9	100
The Strike	6x8	150
The Tetons	5x4	200
Three Pintails	6x9	150
Through the Clouds	8x10	150
Trail Herd	5x7	200
Two Geese	5x4.5	200
Two Honkers	7x9	150
White Water	6x8	200
Winter Guests	11x14	100
Winter Guests	3.5x5.5	200
Winter in the Bighorns	13x11	100
Winter in Wyoming, I	7x9	150
Winter in Wyoming, II	7x9	150
Winter Trail	8x13	100
Yellowlegs, III	4x3.5	200

PRICE LIST OF ETCHINGS BY HANS KLEIBER

APRIL 1, 1937

No.	Title	Price
A- 1	Kearney Lake	$ 5.00
A- 2	Stormy Afternoon	5.00
A- 3	Mallards, A Pair	5.00
A- 4	A Rough Stream	5.00
A- 5	Lake Geneva	5.00
A- 6	Chicadees	5.00
A- 7	Oregon Trail	5.00
A- 8	Elk, Winter	5.00
A- 9	Blackbirds	5.00
A-10	Sheep on the Range	5.00
A-11	Oregon Trail, II	5.00
A-12	Bighorn Peaks	5.00
A-13	Yellowlegs III	5.00
A-14	Phalaropes	5.00
A-15	Evening, Ducks	5.00
A-16	Sheepherder	5.00
A-17	Magpies	5.00
A-18	Winter Guests	5.00
A-19	Two Geese	5.00
A-20	Evening on the Yellowstone	5.00
A-21	Fishing on Upper Piney Creek	6.00
A-22	A Quiet Stream	6.00
A-23	A Flock of Ducks	6.00
A-24	Evening on Tongue River	6.00
A-25	Flying Geese	6.00
A-26	Stormy Evening	6.00
A-27	Fisherman's Camp at Elk Lake	6.00
A-28	Landing One	6.00
A-29	The Tetons	6.00
A-30	Fishing on Jackson Lake	8.00
A-31	Marsh Along Snake River	8.00
A-32	Shooting From a Blind	8.00
A-33	Duck Hunters	8.00
A-34	Grouse Hunter	8.00
A-35	Sheep Creek Ridge	8.00
A-36	Looking for Pheasants	8.00
A-37	Canadian Goose	10.00
38	Bighorn, Wyoming	10.00
A-39	Quail	10.00
40	Bon Voyage, II	10.00
41	Little Goose, Wyōming	10.00
42	Ptarmigan	10.00
43	Frightened Finches	10.00
44	Lake Solitude	10.00
45	Lake Adelaide	10.00
46	Doe and Fawn	10.00
47	On Lake La Croix	10.00
48	Around the Camp Fire	10.00
A-49	A Couple of Mallards	15.00
50	The Sheep Wagon	15.00
51	Trail Herd	15.00
52	On the Canyon Rim	15.00
53	Lake o' the Woods	15.00
54	Mallard Drake	15.00
55	Out of the Clouds	15.00
56	White Water	15.00
57	Geese Overhead	15.00
58	Three Pintails	20.00
59	The Strike	20.00
60	Two Honkers	20.00
61	Mallards, Evening II	20.00
62	Winter in Wyoming II	20.00
63	Winter Wyoming, I	20.00
64	Geese, Mating Time	25.00
65	Dayton, Wyoming	25.00
66	Burial on the Prairie	25.00
67	Crossing the Platte	25.00
68	On the Oregon Trail	25.00
69	Leaving the Frontier	25.00
70	Through the Clouds	25.00
71	A Rising Flock	25.00
72	A Moose	25.00
73	The Log Boom	30.00
74	A Likely Stream	30.00
75	Magpies	30.00
76	Curlews	30.00
77	Geese on the Pacific	30.00
78	Hunting Pheasants	30.00
79	Winter Trail	30.00
80	Snow in the Rockies	30.00
81	Leaving the High Country	30.00
82	Honkers in Flight	30.00
83	Blackbirds	30.00
84	The Lone Fisherman	30.00
85	Evening	30.00
86	Winter in the Bighorns	40.00
87	In Full Flight	40.00
88	Winter Guests	45.00
89	Pintails Coming In	45.00
90	Northern Lights	45.00
91	Geese Crossing Wyoming	45.00

Publishers reserve right to advance prices, June 1, on any of these etchings, and to advance prices prior to that time on any etchings of which half the edition may be sold before June 1, 1937.

Chapter Six

DuPont Sporting Powders Advertisements

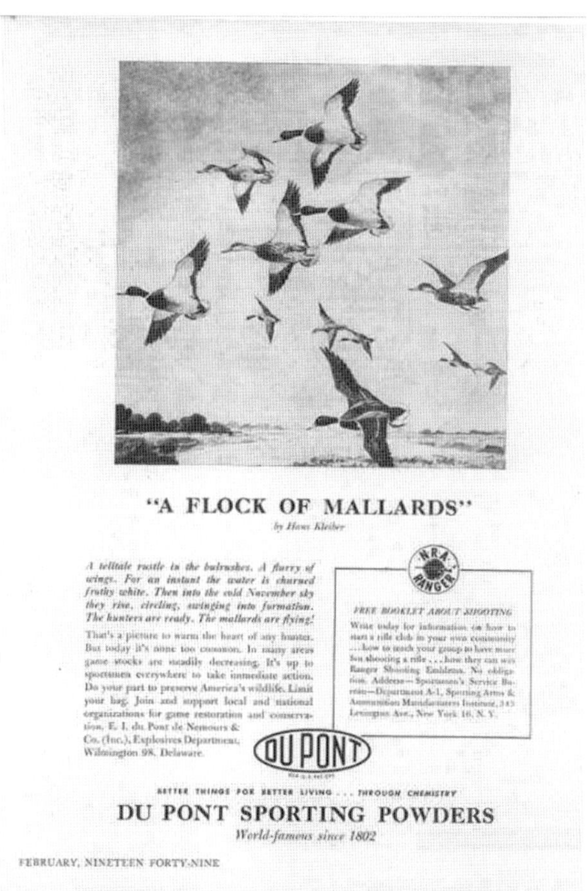

These are examples of some of the images that the DuPont Sporting Powders reproduced in their advertisements by Hans Kleiber. These examples are not all of them as we have also reviewed "Fall In The Rockies" and "Fighting Pheasants."

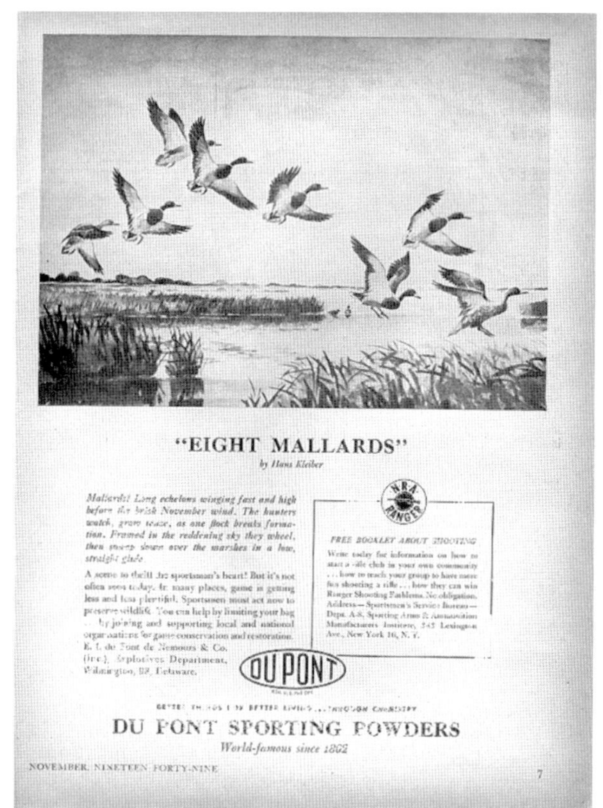

Hans Kleiber

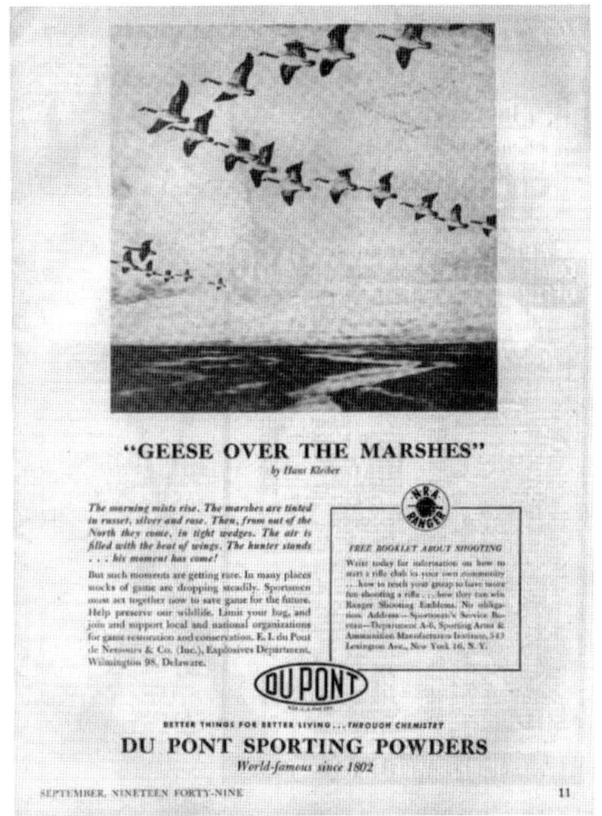

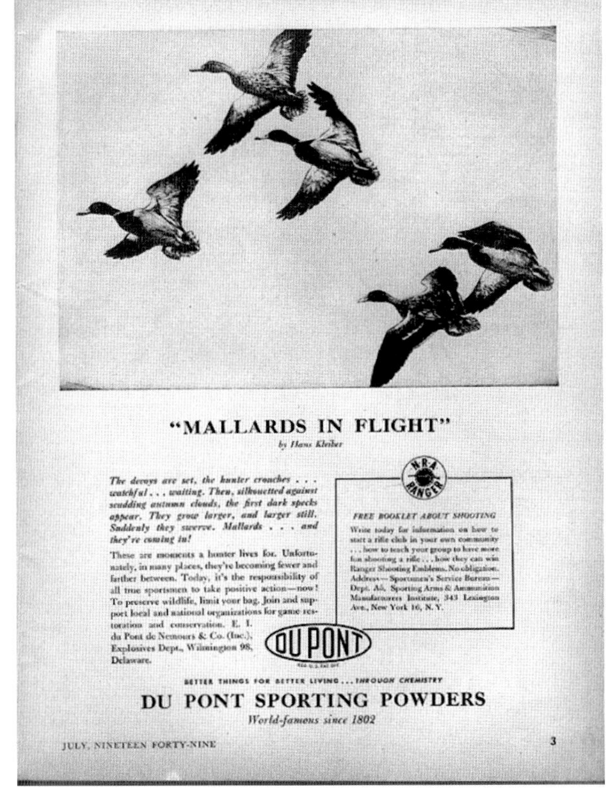

Chapter Seven

The "Tucker List"

Inventory Numbering System done by Carole A. Tucker and Missy Kleiber the summer before Hans Kleiber died.[39]

Stock Number	Description
1	Maligne Lake I
2	Disturbed or Lake Geneva
3	Range Horses
4	Ducks in the Mountains
5	Morning
6	Coming In (Aquatint)
6A	Coming In—Lake Geneva
7	Winter Guests I
8	Maligne Lake II
9	Pioneers I
10	Pioneers II
11	Bon Voyage
12	In the Absoraka or Across the Hills
13	Green River Lake

---

[39] This numbered list was received directly from Carole A. Tucker who owned the Golden Crown in Sheridan, Wyoming. Although the basic theory of this list was good, it still did not make note of the number of prints left in inventory or the image sizes for future reference. The inventory number was printed in pencil in the bottom right corner of the paper with a slash underneath it with the price of the print being written there. In cases where we could inspect an unframed print, we would try to note the number in the corner of the paper. In several cases, the inventory number and also the price were usually erased.

Hans Kleiber

14	Piney
15	In the Tetons
16	A Rough Stream
17	A Quiet Stream
18	Leaping Trout
19	Fishing on Paintrock
20	A Shaded Pool
21	Fishing on Piney
22	Maligne Lake
23	Fishing on the Big Horns or Lake Geneva
24	Snow in the Winter
25	Winter
26	The Old Homestead
27	The Spring Branch
28	The Big Horns
29	Solitude I (Mountains)
30	Timberline
31	The Skiers
32	In The Rockies
33	The Grand Tetons
34	Sheepherder I
35	On the Sheeprange
36	Winter on the Range (Sheep)
37	Range Horses
38	Mare and Colt
39	Cow and Calf
40	Winter Trail
41	Winter Feeding
42	The Wire Gate
43	Chickadees
44	Mountain Chickadees
45	Custer Battlefield
46	Cedar Waxwings
47	Jack Snipes
48	Frightened Geese
49	Ducks on Jackson Lake
49A	Ducks on Jackson Lake

50	Magpies
51	Leigh Lake (Tetons)
52	Stormy Afternoon
53	Stormy Evening
54	Winter Guests II
55	Evening
56	Two Geese
57	Blackbirds
58	A Pair of Pheasants
59	My Home Town—Dayton
60	Dayton, Wyoming
61	Christmas Eve, Dayton
62	Camp at Elk Lake
63	Winter in the Bighorns II
64	Hunting Pheasants
65	The Grouse Hunter
66	Duck Hunters
67	Shooting from a Blind or A Duck Blind
68	Grand Canyon
69	Mt. Moran
70	Mt. Shuksan—Olympics
71	The Bighorns—Teepee Creek
72	Big Horn Peaks—Sheep
73	Elk in the Big Horns I
74	Rapid Creek Ranch
75	Eatons Ranch—Canyon
76	Eatons Ranch—Buildings
77	Branding on the Range
78	Frontier Days
79	Along the Rockies
80	The Trailherd
81	Ride 'im Cowboy
82	At the Silver Dollar
83	At the Hitchrack
84	Waiting at the Gate
85	Winter Trail
86	Elk in the Big Horns
87	Leaving the Frontier

Hans Kleiber

88	Across the Prairies
89	Wrens
90	A Pair of Chickadees
91	Chickadees II
92	Titmice
93	Big Horn, Wyoming
94	Pheasants (In Flight)
95	Ptarmigan
96	Curlews
97	Solitude II (Birds)
98	Sheepherder II
99	Quail
100	On the Missouri
101	Plover
102	Mallard Drake
103	Pintails Loafing
104	Redheads Loafing
105	Disturbed Flock
106	In the Bighorns (Mountain Sheep)
107	Winter in the Bighorns
108	Little Goose Valley
109	The Lone Fisherman
110	In Full Flight
111	Pintails Coming In
112	Meade Creek Pond
113	Ducklings
114	Flying Wedges
115	Two Mallards or Pair of Couple
116	Coming In
117	Out of the Sky
118	Mallards—Evening II
119	A Swallowtail
120	The Strike
121	Lake Adelaide (Ducks)
122	Cloud Peak & Solitude
123	Around the Campfire
124	Jackson Lake & Tetons
125	Cooke City, Montana

126	Bucket of Blood Saloon I
127	At Yellowstone Lake
128	Killers
129	Sheep in the Big Horns
130	Three Pintails
131	Study of Magpies
132	Disturbed Pintails
133	Pintails Feeding
134	Snow Geese
135	Solitude (Moose)
136	Winter In Wyoming I (Sheep)
137	Winter In Wyoming II (Cattle)
138	Pheasants II
139	Rising Flock
140	Rising Flock (Colored)
141	Ducks in the Meadow
142	Virginia Deer
143	Virginia Deer (Tinted)
144	Drakes and Lillies
145	Drakes in Summer
146	Pintails and Mallards
147	Honkers in Flight
148	Pheasants III
149	Visitors
150	Leaving the Frontier
151	On the Oregon Trail
152	Across the Prairies
153	Evening on the Trail
154	Meneaska
155	A Burial on the Prairie
156	Fort Laramie 1846
157	Crossing the Platte
158	Knife River Post Office
159	Bucket of Blood Saloon
160	An Indian Scout (Jim Baker)
161	An Old Plainsman
162	Col. W. F. Cody
163	Chief Sitting Bull

Hans Kleiber

164	A Homesteader Plowing
165	Freemont Peak
165A	Freemont Peak
165B	Freemont Peak
166	Bayou Teche
	Old Paddle Wheeler
167	Disturbed Mallards
168	Drakes
169	Magpies
170	Mallard Drakes
171	Pintail Drakes
172	Morning on the Marshes
173	A Bull Moose
173A	Bull Moose
174	At Timberline
175	A Likely Stream
176	Winter Residents
177	Fall in the Rockies
178	Summer in the Rockies
179	Deep in the Rockies
180	Curlews
181	The Pond in the Hills
182	Coming In (Aquatint)
183	Evening
184	The Old Cottonwood
185	Morning in the Rockies
186	The Logboom
187	Weathering a Storm (Horses)
188	Winter Trail (Sheep)
189	At the Silver Dollar
190	Down from the Hills
191	Pinto Mare and Colt
192	Waiting at the Gate
193	Leaving the High Country
194	Weathering a Storm (Elk)
195	Returning from the Hunt
196	Cypress Swamp
196A	Cypress Swamp

197	Blackbirds II
198	Winter Guests I
199	Winter Guests II
200	The Lone Goose
201	Amber Water
201A	Amber Water
202	The Plume Hunter
203	Mallards in Flight
204	Canvasbacks in Flight
205	Black Ducks
205A	Black Ducks (Aquatint)
206	Bald Pates
206A	Bald Pates
207	Evening on the Marshes
208	Snow in the Rockies
208A	Snow in the Rockies
209	Winter in the Big Horns
210	Northern Lights
211	Geese Crossing Wyoming
212	The Grand Tetons
213	The Lone Fisherman
214	Geese over the Marshes
215	In Full Flight
216	Winter Guests
217	Pintails Coming In
218	Evening Star
218	Evening Star (Tinted)
219	Late Arrivals (Tinted)
220	Whistling Swans (Tinted)
221	The Sheep Wagon
222	Fishing in the Tetons or Fishing on Jackson Lake
223	Lake Geneva
223A	Lake Geneva
224	At the Hitchrack
225	Solitude
226	Milk Cows
227	In Full Flight

Hans Kleiber

228	Winter Guests
229	Mallards Coming In
229A	Mallards Coming In (Tinted)
230	A Pair of Shovellers
231	Winter (Farm)
232	Cliff Lake
233	Elk
234	Snow in the Rockies
235	Honkers Settling
236	Killdeer
237	A Pair of Pintails
238	A Pair of Mallards
239	Magpies
240	Lake Adelaide (Deer)
240A	Lake Adelaide
241	Evening on the Yellowstone
242	Mallards—Pair
243	On Tongue River or Ducks on the River
244	Landing One
245	Mallard Drakes
246	Mallards—Winter
247	Mallards or Mallards Rising
248	Plover
249	Phalaropes
250	Mount Rainier
251	Mount Rainier
252	Black Fox
253	On Little Goose (Cattle)
254	Antelope
255	Mallards Disturbed
256	Crowheart Butte
257	Disturbed Honkers
258	Doe and Fawn
259	Elk Fighting or Fighting It Out
260	Ducks in the Meadow

261	Evening on the Range
262	Mallards—Evening
263	Fishing on Piney
264	Trout and Lillies
265	Mallard Drakes
266	Evening
267	Elk in the Rockies
268	Sand Pipers
269	Sand Pipers II
270	Coming In—Evening
271	Fishing in the Big Horns
272	Sheep Wagon I
273	In the Forest
274	Evening at Lake Solitude
275	Dawn on the Range
276	Horse Creek, Wyoming
277	Disturbed
278	Geese Taking Wing
279	Geese Settling
280	Brant
281	Down the Missourie
282	Cock Pheasants
283	Fighting Pheasants
284	Flying Honkers
285	Avocet
286	Evening on the Marshes
287	Canadian Geese
288	Grand Teton
289	Mount Baker
290	Two Honkers
291	Mather Peak, Wyoming
292	Geese—Mating Time
293	Rainbow Water
294	Geese Rising
295	Spoonbills (Colored)
296	Mallard Drake on Snow (Aquatint)
297	Geese over the Pacific
298	Salmon Trap

Hans Kleiber

299	Flying Geese
300	Canadian Goose
301	Ducks Rising
302	At Jackson Lake
303	Buffalo Days
400	Hunting Pheasants
401	Lake LaCroix-Minnesota (Moose)
401A	Lake LaCroix
402	Square Top or Table Mountain (Green River)
403	A Flock of Honkers
404	A Mixed Flock
405	Grand Chenier
406	The Tetons, Wyoming
407	Mount Moran, Wyoming
408	Through the Clouds
409	Barataria
410	(Same As 128)
411	Flying Against the Wind
412	The Campfire
413	The Bathers (5 Prints)
414	Pike's Peak
415	Uncle Ben
416	Longs Peak
416A	Longs Peak
417	Hitting the Water
418	Egrets
418A	Egrets
419	Frightened Finches
420	Crows in the Fall
421	Summer Guests
422	(Same As 174)
423	Geese Overhead
424	Starting on the Hunt
425	Snake River Marshes
426	Midway
427	Deadwood Coach

428	Watering Sheep
429	On Yellowstone Lake (Ducks)
430	An Evening Flight
431	Late Afternoon
432	Two Geese
433	Mallards Mating Time
434	Sheep Creek Ridge
434A	Sheep Creek Ridge
435	Elk or Elk—Big Horns
436	A Bronc Buster
437	The Poachers
438	Campfire
439	Elk at Night
440	Evening on the Yellowstone
441	Casting from a Boat
442	Fighting Blue Jays
443	Honkers in Flight
444	Lake LaCroix—Ducks
445	White Water
446	Solitude (Elk)
447	Lake O' The Woods
447A	Lake O' The Woods
448	Yellow Legs I
449	Yellow Legs II
450	Shooting Pheasants
451	Deadwood Coach on Bozeman Trail
452	Rainbow Water
453	The Fisherman
454	**No Etching Assigned**
455	Little Goose
456	A Bit of Forrest
457	Howland Island in the South Pacific
458	Cow Moose and Calf
458A	Cow Moose and Calf
459	On The Canyon Rim
460	Old Pines on Sheep Creek

Hans Kleiber

461	Swallowtails
462	Mountain Chickadees
463	Poplars I
464	Poplars II
465	Teal
466	Mallards Dropping In
467	Lake DeSmet, Wyoming
468	Loon Lake, Minnesota
469	Fishing—Evening
470	A Glimpse of St. Marys Lake Glacier Park
471	Stormy Sunset
472	Moose Swimming
473	Mallards Flying
474	On Top of the Big Horns
475	Fargo Medicine Lake—1930
476	On the Trail
477	**No Etching Assigned**
478	Geese (Aquatint)

Chapter Eight

Frontier or Pioneer Series[2]

"A Burial on the Prairie"

"A Homesteader Plowing"

"Across the Prairies"

"An Indian Scout"

"An Old Plainsman"

"Bucket of Blood Saloon"

"Chief Sitting Bull"

"Col.W. F. Cody 1846-1917"

"Crossing the Platte"

"Evening on the Trail"

"Fort Laramie 1846"

---

[40] There has been some confusion as to where the Pioneer or Frontier theme originated. Some individuals have reported to us that they believe it was simply a marketing theme by some of Kleiber's galleries. This could very well be the case as it has been made reference to from early on. One of the other comments that has been made refers to the unusual theme inconsistencies of the various impressions.

Hans Kleiber

"Knife River Post Office"

"Leaving the Frontier"

"Meneasky"

"On the Oregon Trail"

Chapter Nine

Unpublished Impressions

It has been our pleasure to review many plate designs by Hans Kleiber. Many of these plates might have been printed by the artist but based upon his market at the time were possibly not that popular so he stopped. Are they more collectible than others, not necessarily? We simply are providing you with these additional designs for your reference. The plates did have notations as to suspect titles, but we could not verify that they came direct from the artist. We have indicated those that have been dated and, or titled in the plate.

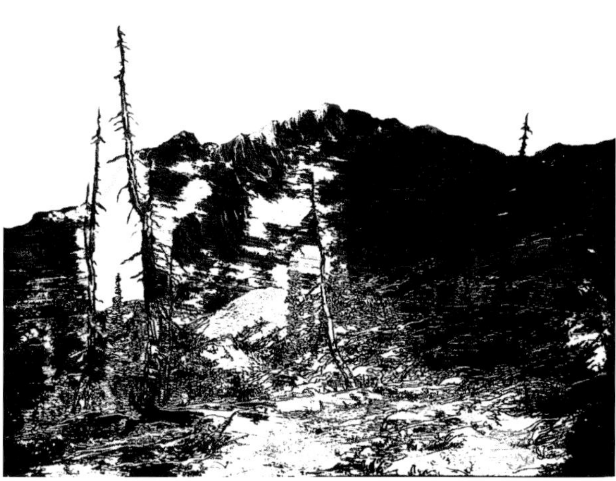

"Untitled--Black Tooth Mountain"
Plate Size: 6.25 inches high by 8 inches wide
Dated in plate 1926.

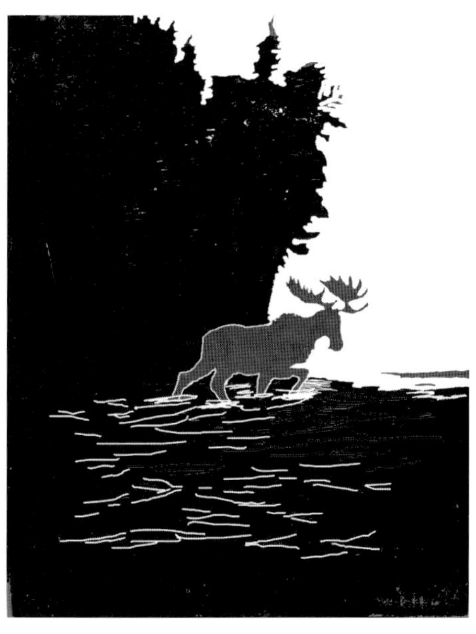

"Untitled--Bull Moose on the Run"
Plate Size: 10.5 inches high by 8 inches wide

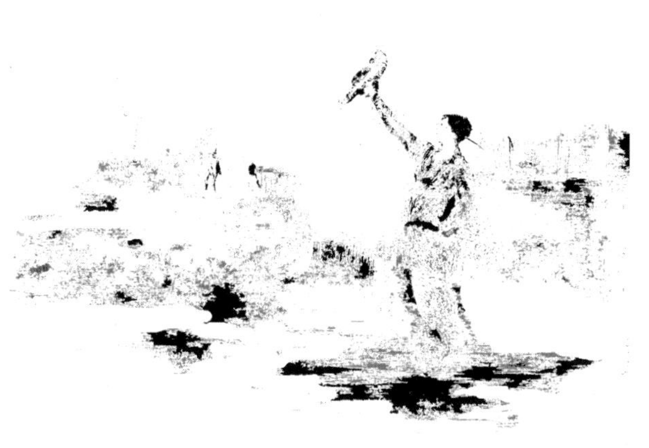

"Bronco Buster, No. 2"
Plate Size: 8.5 inches high by 11 inches wide
Please also refer to "Bronco Buster."

Hans Kleiber

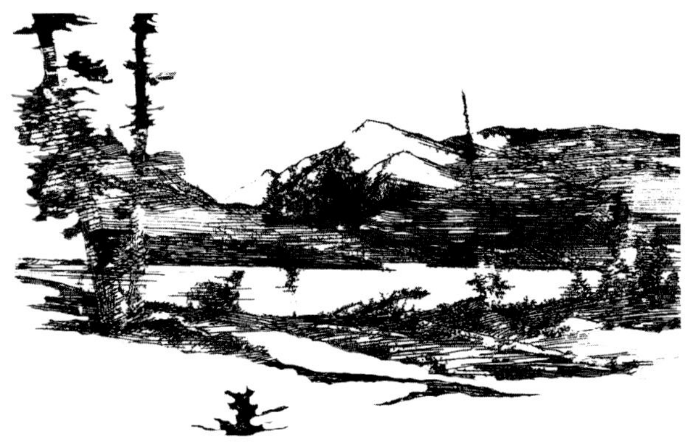

"Untitled--Cloud Peak"
Plate Size: 5.75 inches high by 8.25 inches wide
Dated in plate 1927.

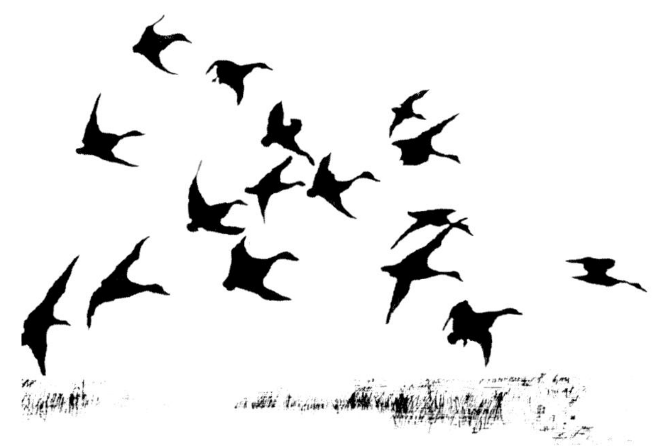

"Untitled--Drifting In"
Plate Size: 7.5 inches high by 10 inches wide

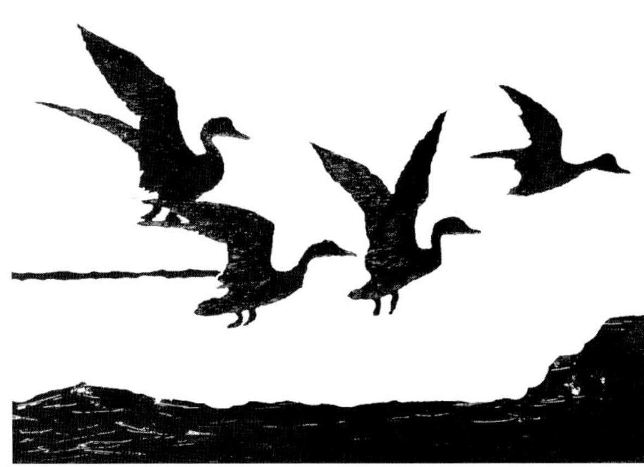

"Untitled--Ducks Taking Wing"
Plate Size: 5.25 inches high by 7 inches wide

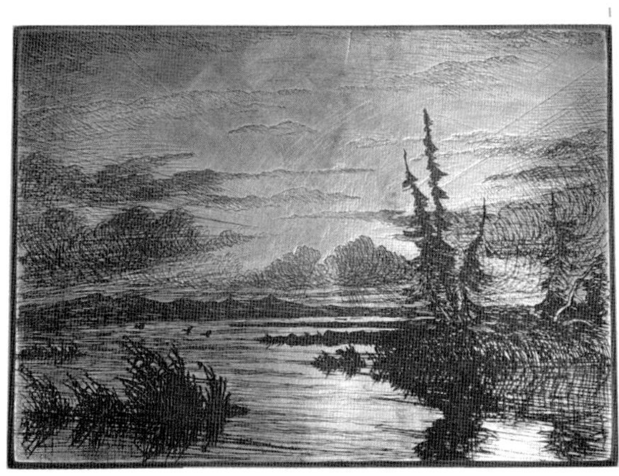

"Untitled--Elk Lake"
Plate Size: 5 inches high by 6.5 inches wide

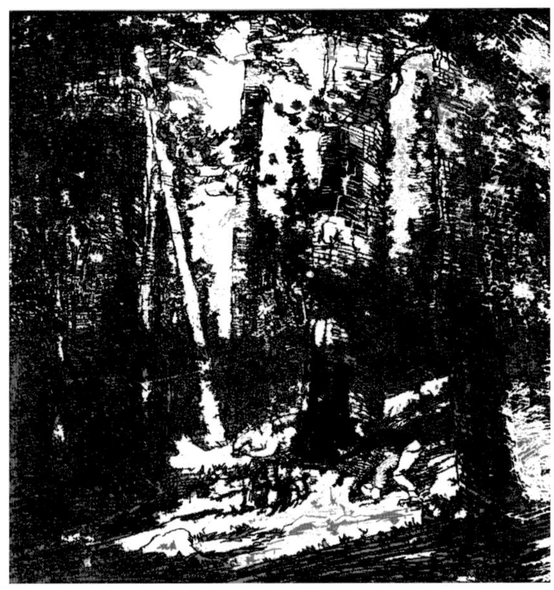

"Untitled--Falling Timber"
Plate Size: 7 inches high by 6 inches wide
In the bottom one third of the design there are two men using a saw to cut down a tree.

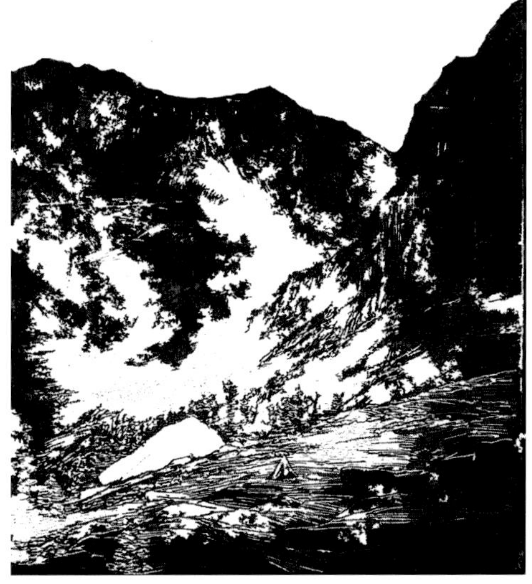

"Untitled--Fremont Peak"
Plate Size: 6.5 inches high by 5.25 inches wide
Dated in plate 1927.
In the bottom center of the image one can see a mountain pole tent where a party is camping.

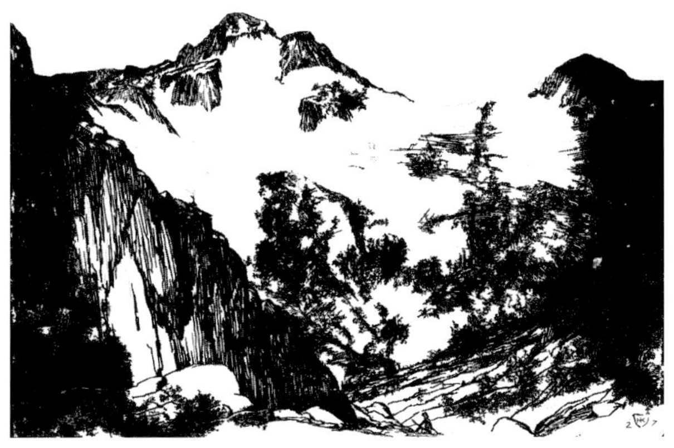

"Untitled--High Mountain Scene"
Plate Size: 7 inches high by 9 inches wide
Dated in plate 1927.

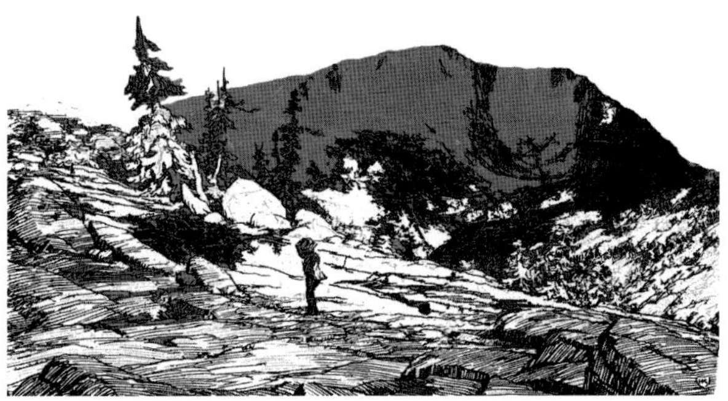

"Untitled--In the Wind River"
Plate Size: 5.25 inches high by 7.5 inches wide

Hans Kleiber

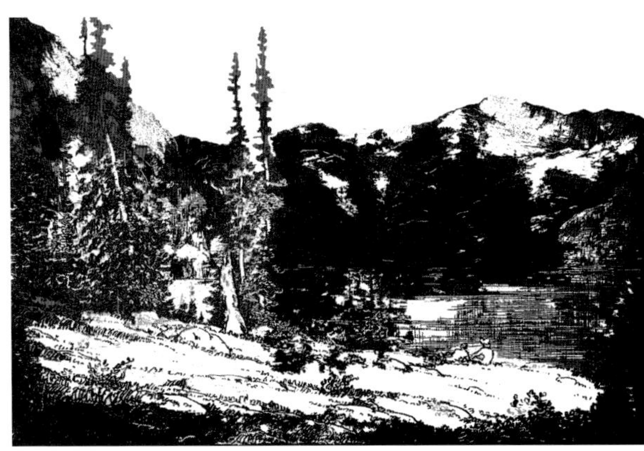

"Untitled--Lake Solitude"
Plate Size: 5.125 inches high by 7.5 inches wide
In the bottom center of the image one can see a couple sitting on the shore of the lake.

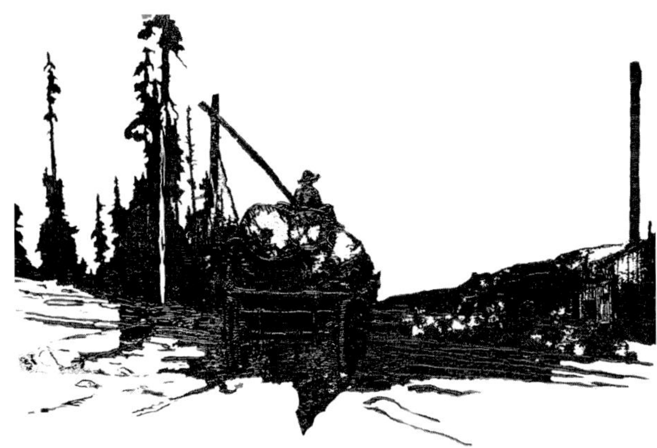

"Untitled--Logging Wagon"
Plate Size: 5 inches high by 7 inches wide
The viewer is looking at the back end of a wagon with a driver on it and several logs. Off to the right there is a type of cabin or logging shack.

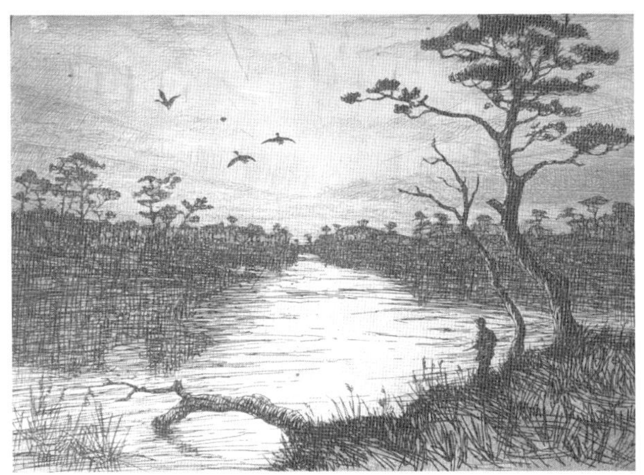

"Untitled--Loon Lake"
Plate Size: 6.5 inches high by 8.5 inches wide

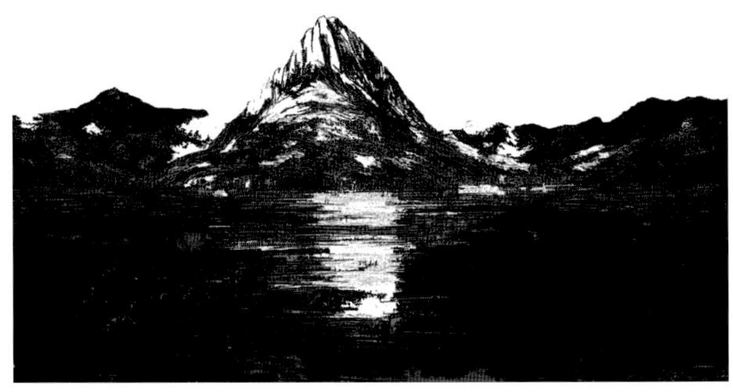

"Untitled--Mountain Lake"
Plate Size: 7 inches high by 12 inches wide

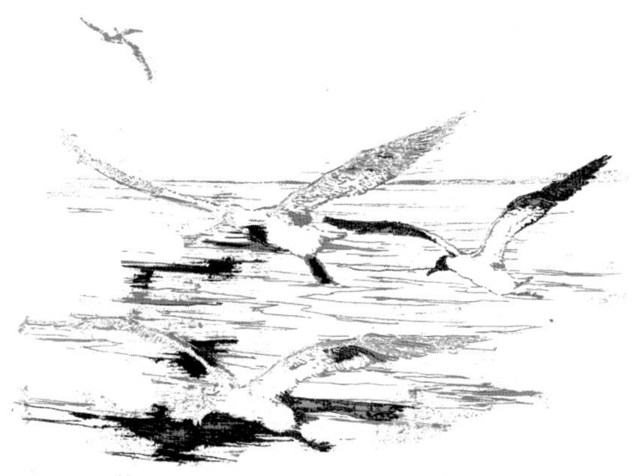

"Untitled--Seagulls"
Plate Size: 5 inches high by 6 inches wide
Dated in plate 1927.

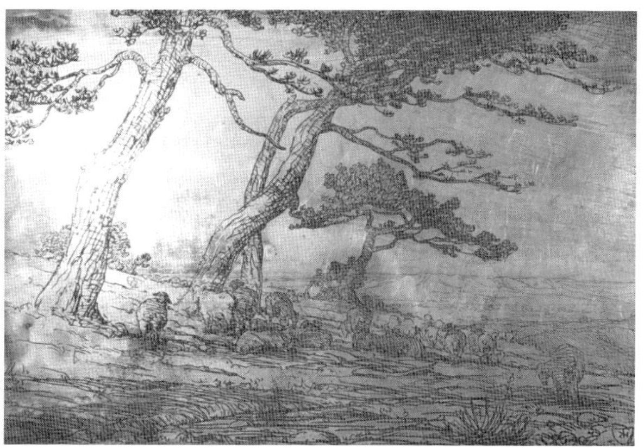

"Untitled--Sheep in the Hills"
Plate Size: 5 inches high by 7 inches wide
Dated in plate 1927.

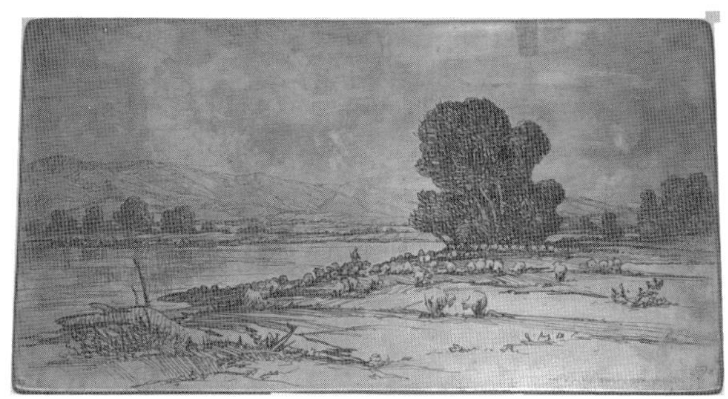

"Untitled--Sheep on the River"
Plate Size: 5 inches high by 8.5 inches wide
Dated in plate 1927.

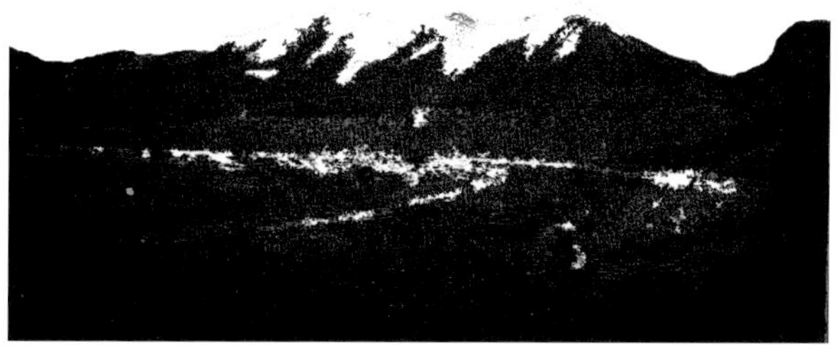

"Untitled--Tetons"
Plate Size: 4.25 inches high by 7 inches wide

Hans Kleiber

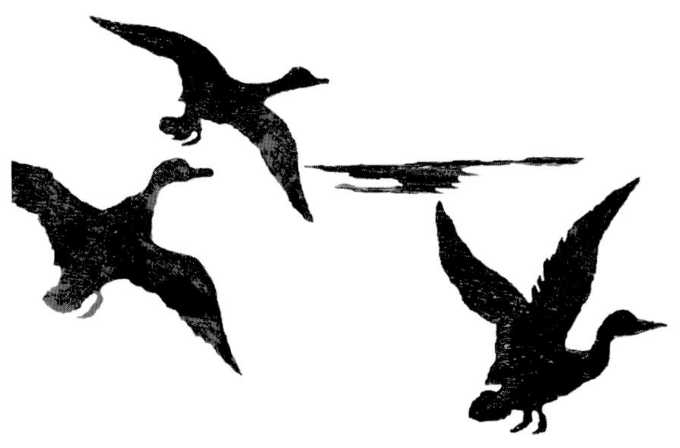

"Untitled--Three Ducks"
Plate Size: 6 inches high by 8 inches wide

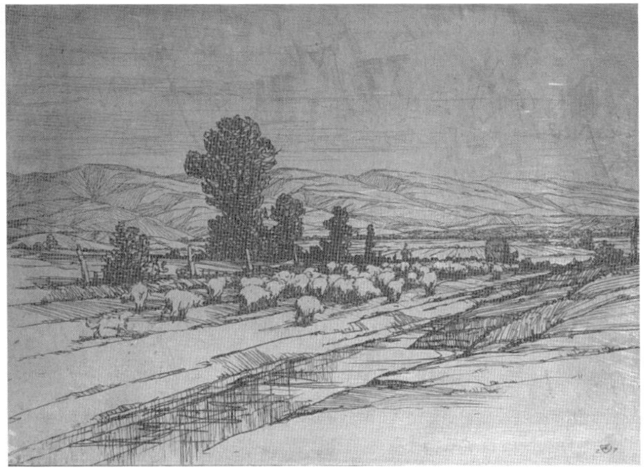

"Untitled--Trailing Sheep"
Plate Size: 6.25 inches high by 8 inches wide

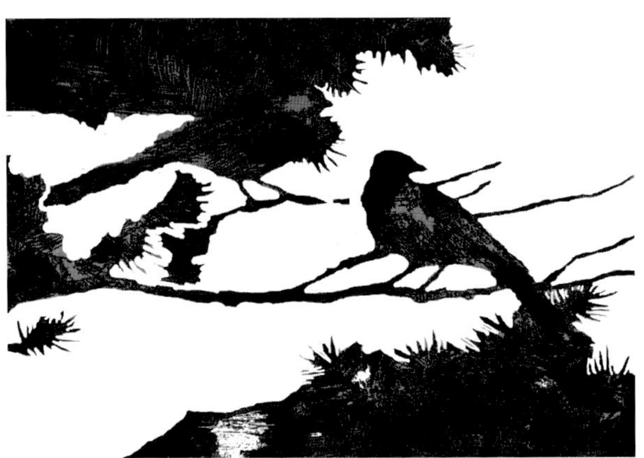

"Whiskey Jacks 1931"
Plate Size: 5 inches high by 7 inches wide
"Whiskey Jacks" is titled in the plate.

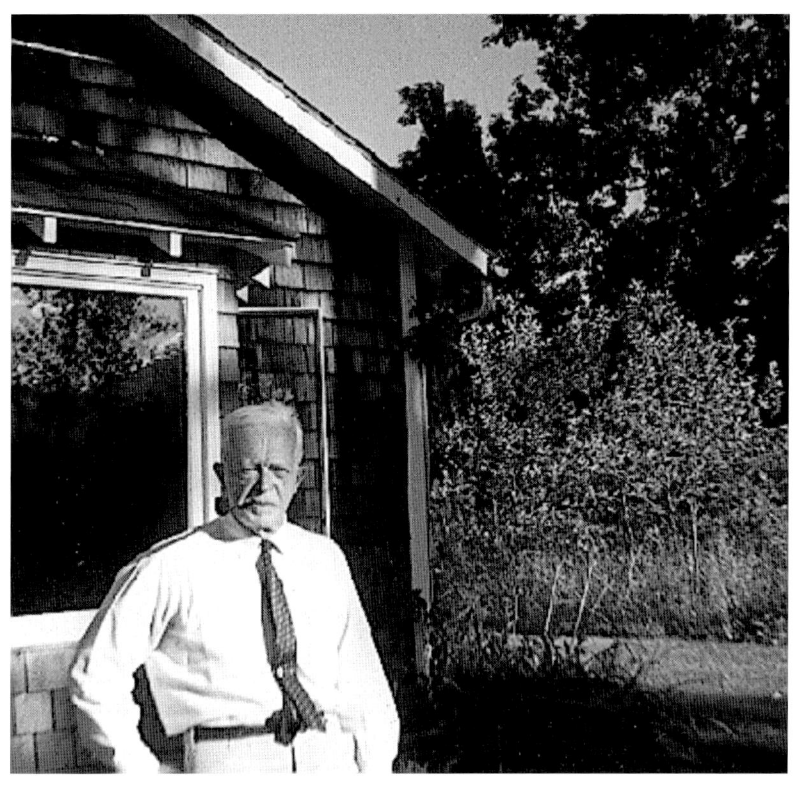

Chapter Ten

Impressions

Hans Kleiber

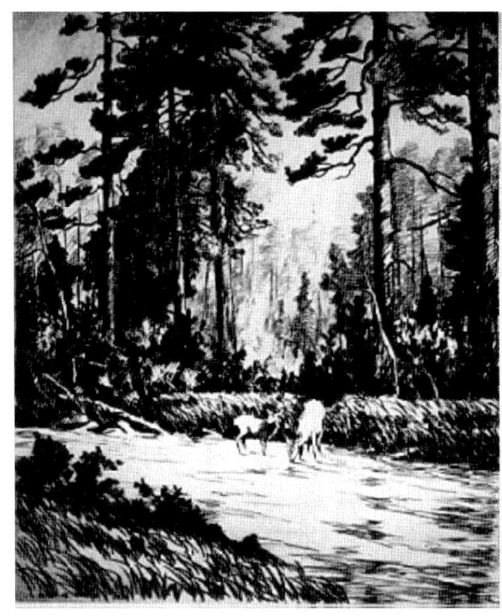

"A Bit of Forest"
First State
Medium: Etching
Image: 10.75 inches high by 8.625 inches wide

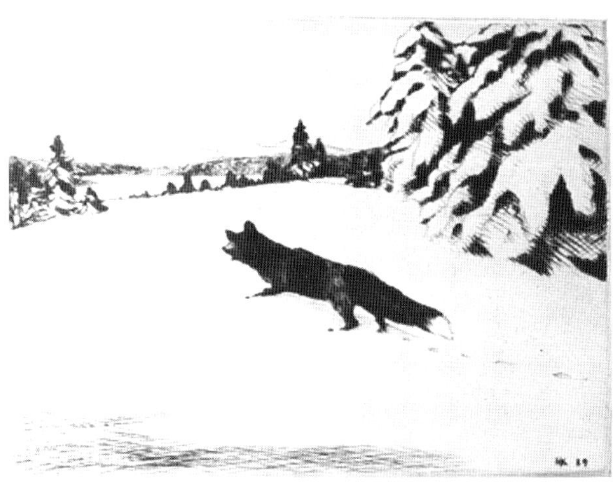

"A Black Fox"
"A Bush Fox"
"Black Fox"
Medium: Etching
Image: 4.125 inches high by 5.4375 inches wide

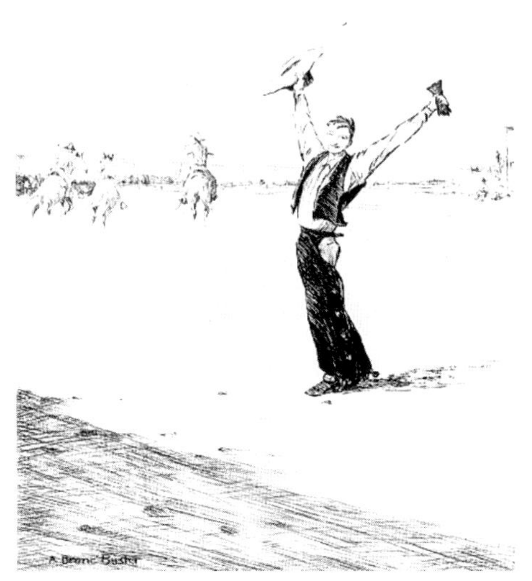

"A Bronc Buster"
Medium: Etching
Image: 6.3125 inches high by 4.875 inches wide

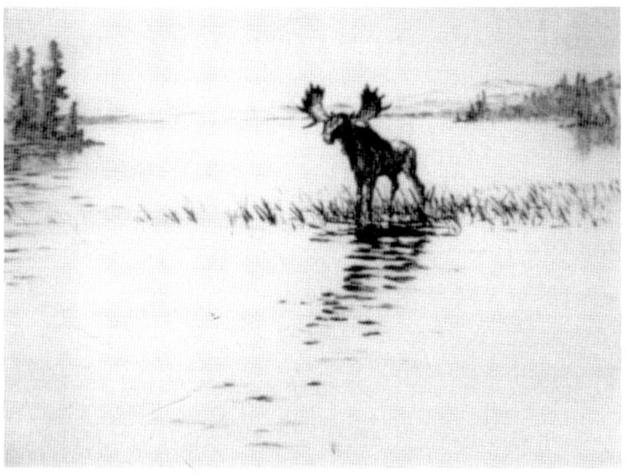

"A Bull Moose"
"A Moose"
"Moose"
Medium: Etching
Image: 8.25 inches high by 10.75 inches wide

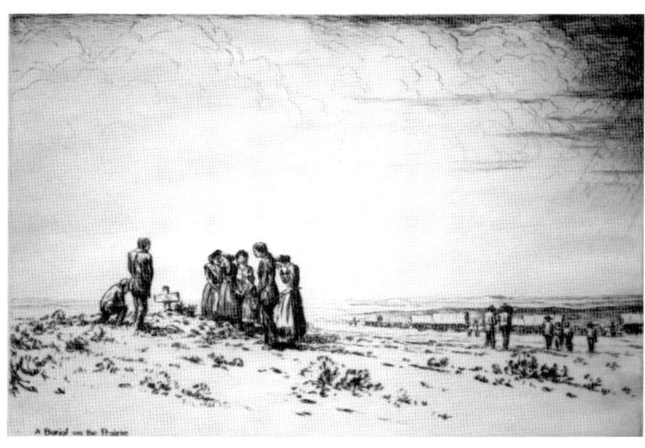

"A Burial On The Prairie"
Medium: Etching
Image: 6.75 inches high by 9.75 inches wide

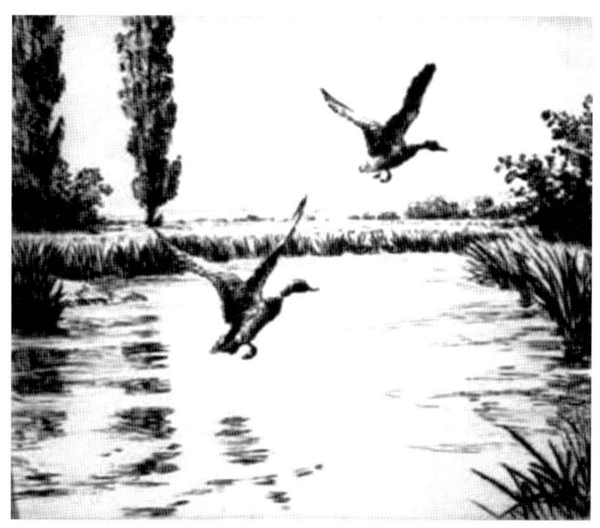

"A Couple of Mallards"
Second State of "Poplars I"
Medium: Etching
Image: 5.25 inches high by 6.75 inches wide

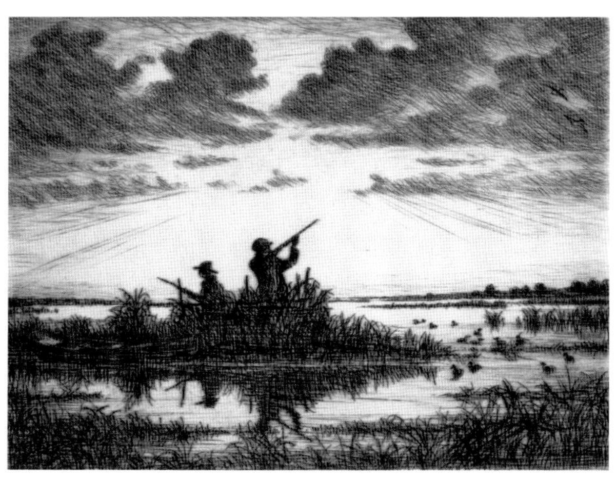

"A Duck Blind"
"Shooting From a Blind"
Medium: Etching
Image: 4.75 inches high by 6.25 inches wide

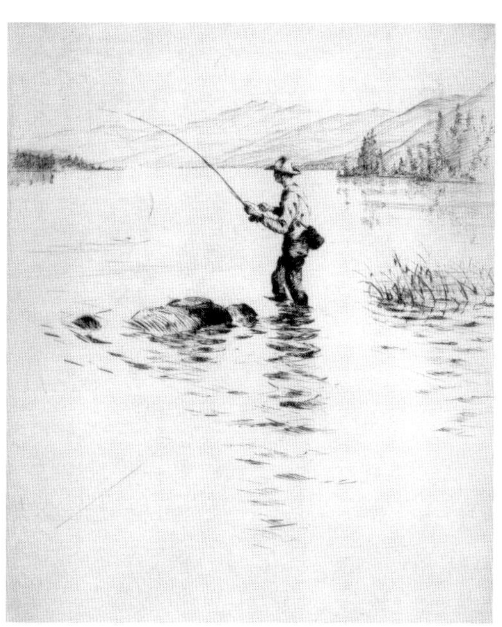

"A Fisherman"
Medium: Etching
Image: 9.8125 inches high by 7.8125 inches wide

Hans Kleiber

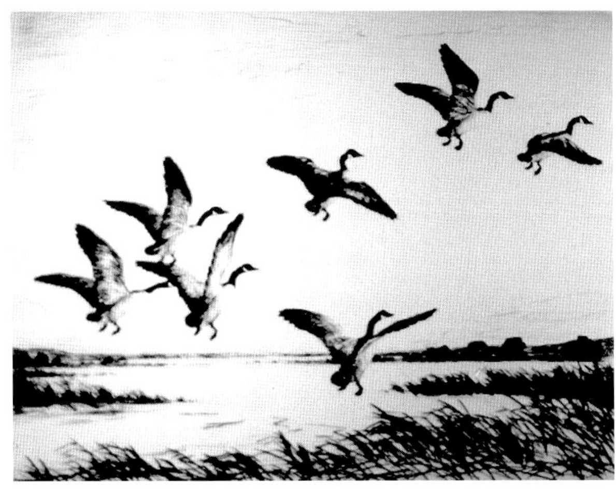

"A Flock of Honkers"
First State
Medium: Etching
Image: 7.75 inches high by 9.75 inches wide

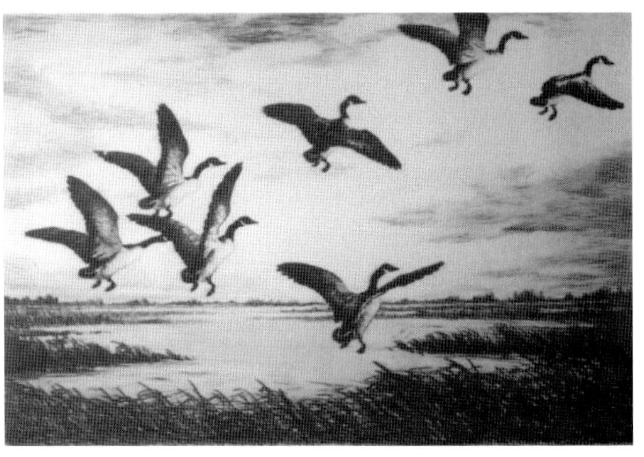

"A Flock of Honkers"
"Flock of Honkers"
Second State of "A Flock of Honkers"
Medium: Etching
Image: 6.75 inches high by 9.625 inches wide

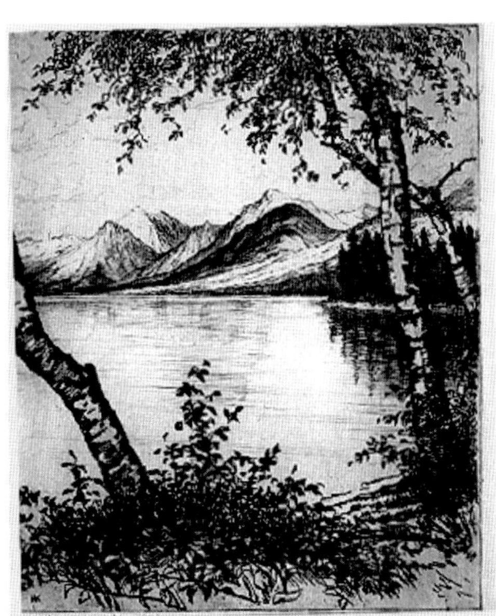

"A Glimpse of St. Mary's Lake, Glacier Park"
"St. Mary's Lake - Glacier Park"
Medium: Photogravure
Image: 11.75 inches high by 9.75 inches wide

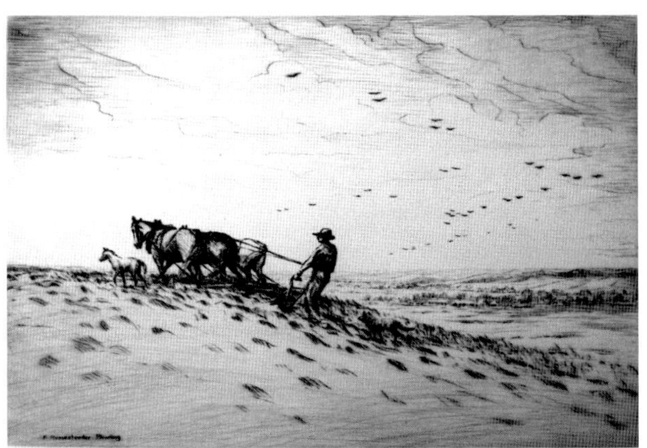

"A Homesteader Plowing"
Medium: Etching
Image: 6.875 inches high by 9.875 inches wide

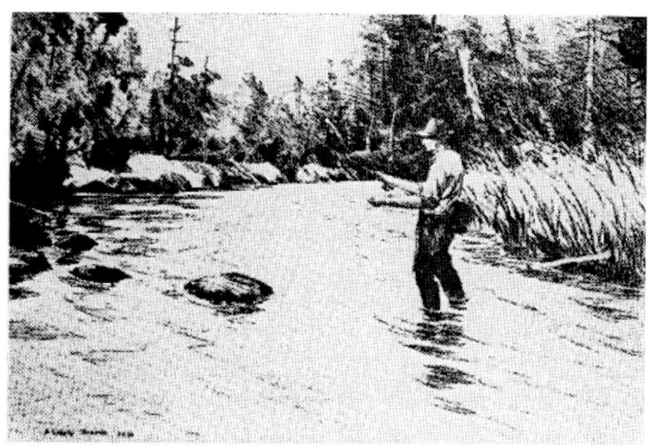

"A Likely Stream"
Medium: Etching
Image: 7.75 inches high by 11.25 inches wide

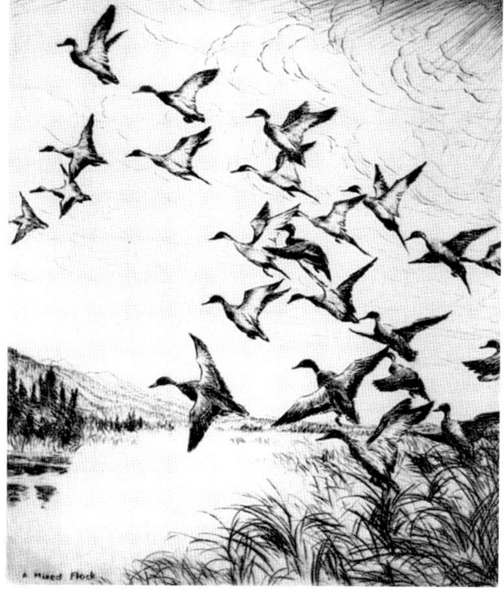

"A Mixed Flock"
Medium: Etching
Image: 8.3125 inches high by 6.875 inches wide

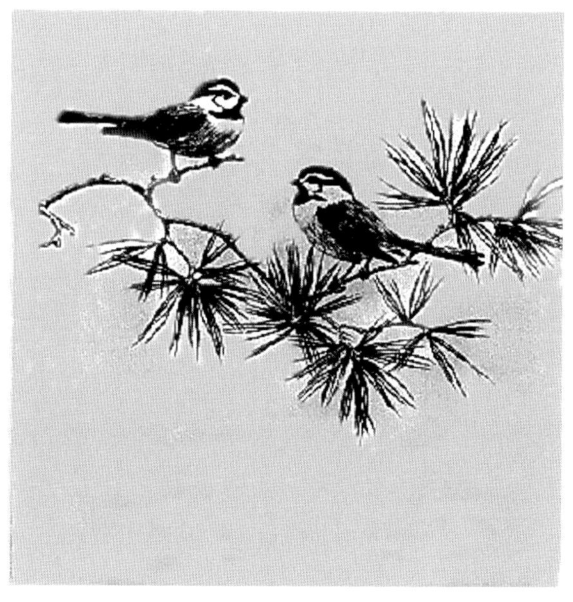

"A Pair of Chicadees"
"A Pair of Mountain Chicadees"
"Pair of Chicadees"
Second State of "Mountain Chicadees"
Medium: Photogravure
Image: 6.75 inches high by 5.75 inches wide

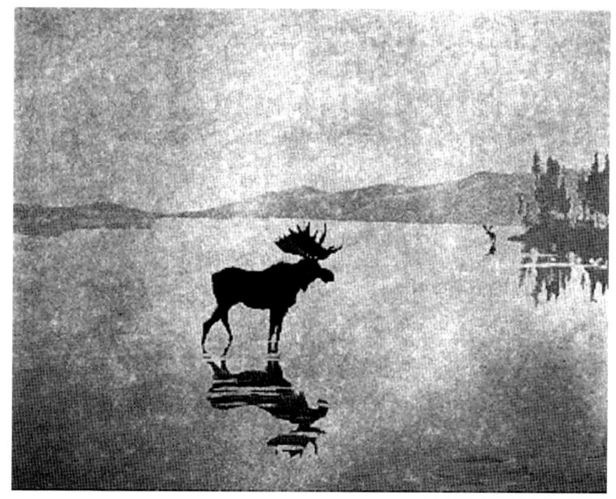

"A Moose"
"Moose - Night"
Medium: Etching
Image: 9.75 inches high by 11.75 inches wide

Hans Kleiber

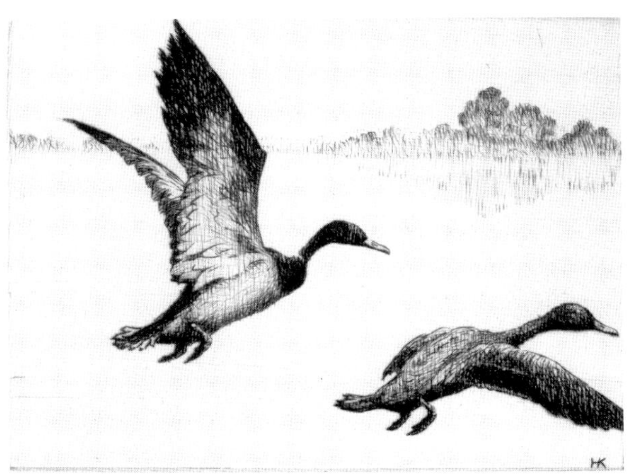

"A Pair of Mallards"
"Mallards, A Pair"
Medium: Etching
Image: 3.5 inches high by 4.875 inches wide

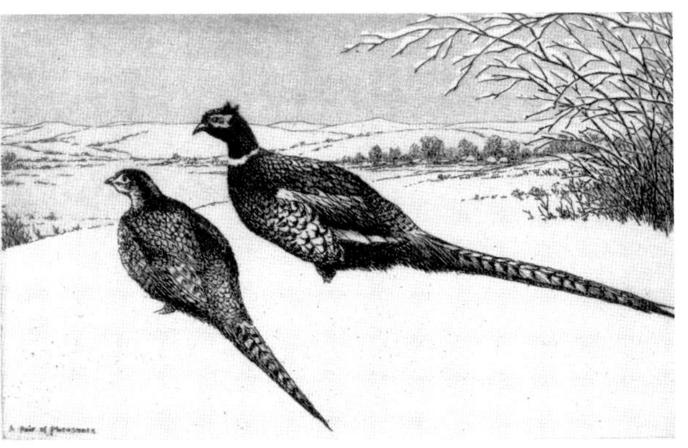

"A Pair of Pheasants"
Medium: Photogravure
Image: 3.75 inches high by 5.75 inches wide

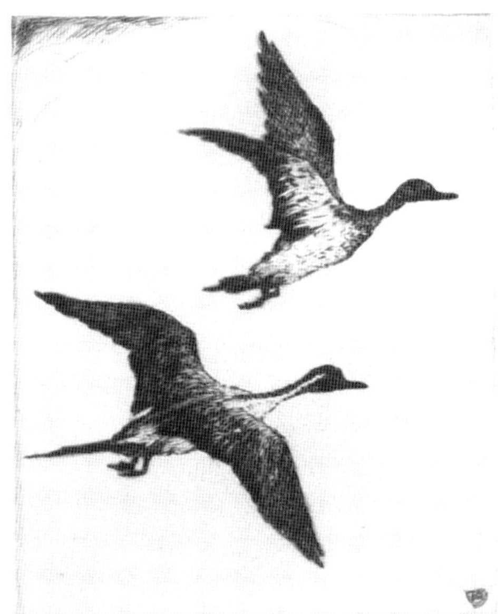

" Pair of Pintails"
Medium: Etching
Image: 4.875 inches high by 3.875 inches wide

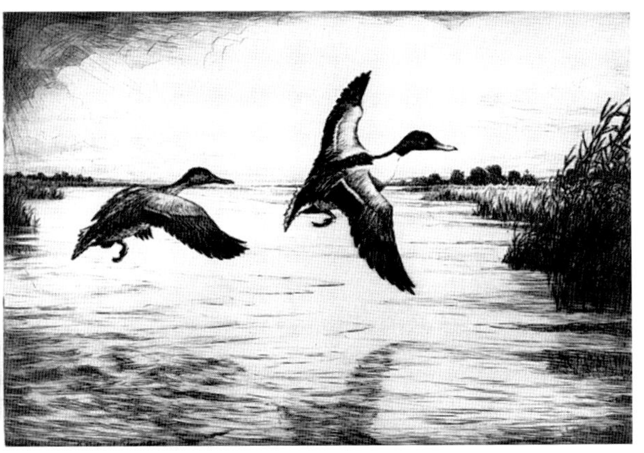

"A Pair of Shovellers"
Medium: Etching
Image: 6.75 inches high by 9.75 inches wide

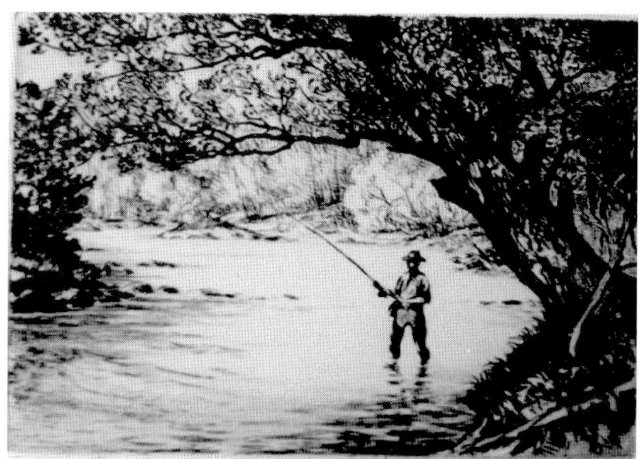

"A Quiet Stream"
Medium: Etching
Image: 3.8125 inches high by 5.3125 inches wide

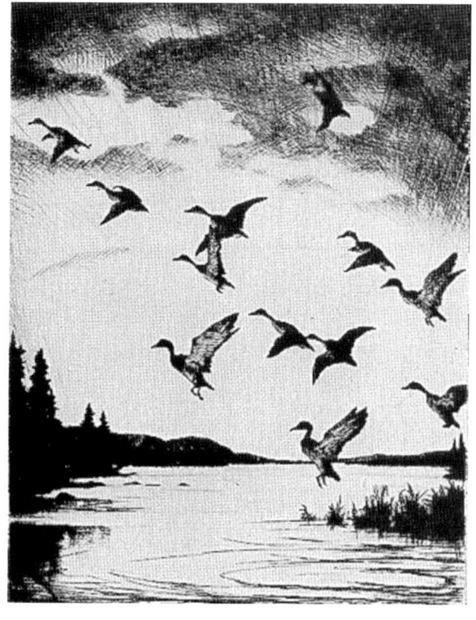

"A Rising Flock"
Medium: Etching
Image: 9.75 inches high by 7.25 inches wide

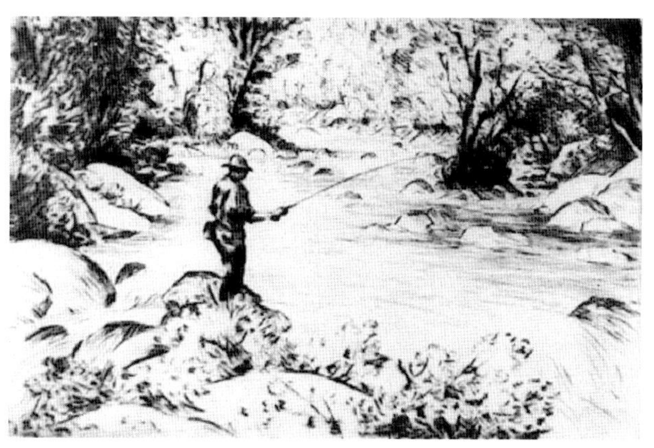

"A Rough Stream"
Medium: Etching
Image: 3.25 inches high by 4.75 inches wide

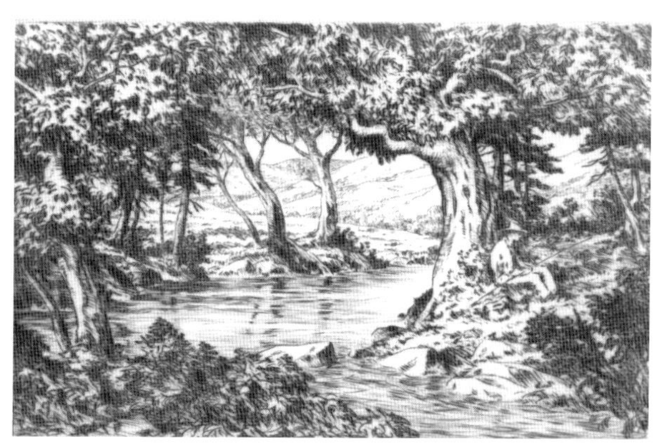

"A Shaded Pool"
Medium: Etching
Image: 3.75 inches high by 5.875 inches wide

Hans Kleiber

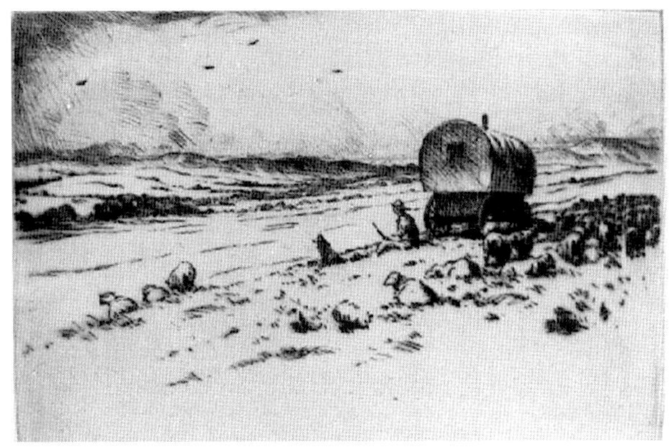

"A Sheep Wagon"
"Sheep Wagon II"
"The Sheep Wagon"
Medium: Etching
Image: 6.3125 inches high by 9.1875 inches wide

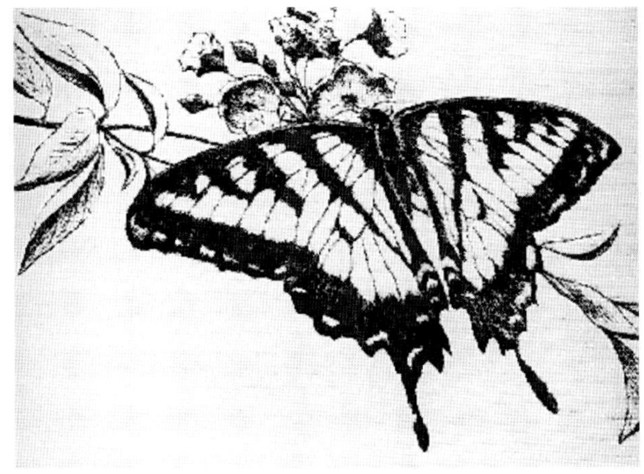

"A Swallow Tail"
Medium: Etching
Image: 5.875 inches high by 7.75 inches wide

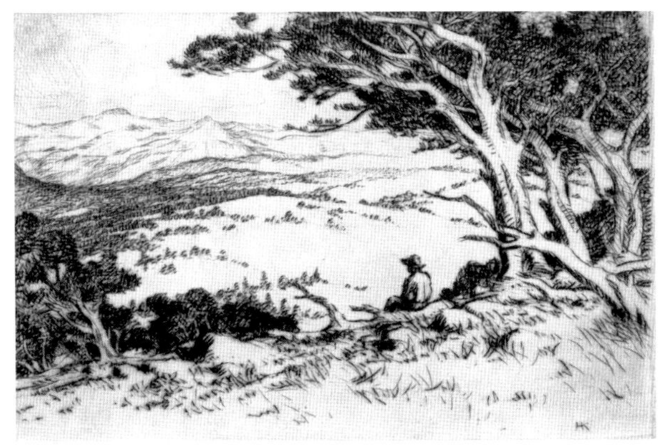

"Across the Hills"
"The Absoraka"
"The Absorakas"
Medium: Etching
Image: 4.375 inches high by 5.75 inches wide

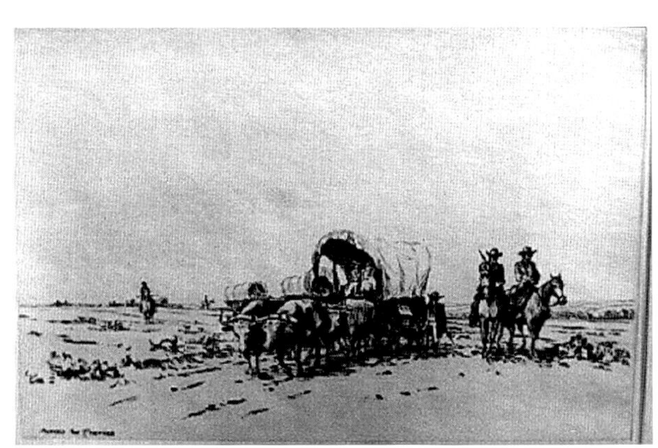

"Across the Prairies"
Medium: Etching
Image: 6.75 inches high by 9.75 inches wide
Medium: Photogravure
Image: 5.25 inches high by 7.5 inches wide

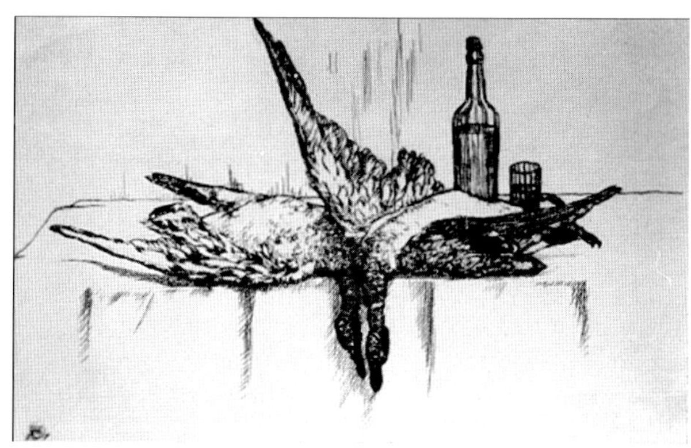

"After the Hunt"
Medium: Etching
Image: 4.875 inches high by 7.3125 inches wide

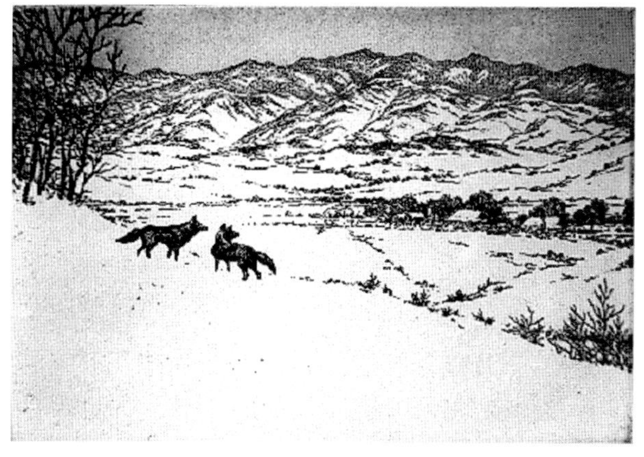

"Along the Bighorns"
"Along the Rockies"
Medium: Photogravure
Image: 4.75 inches high by 6.75 inches wide

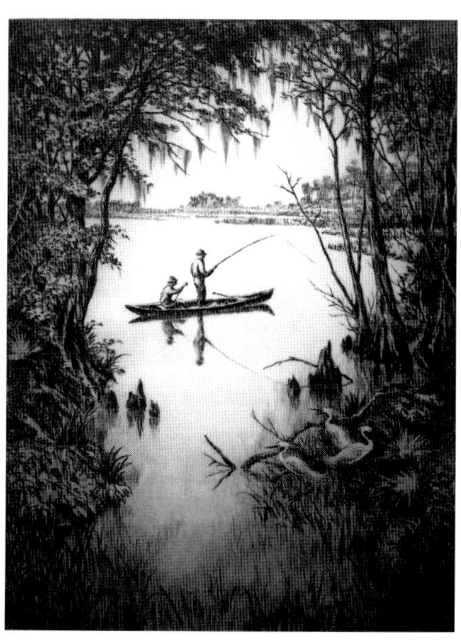

"Amber Water"
Medium: Etching
Image: 10.75 inches high by 7.75 inches wide

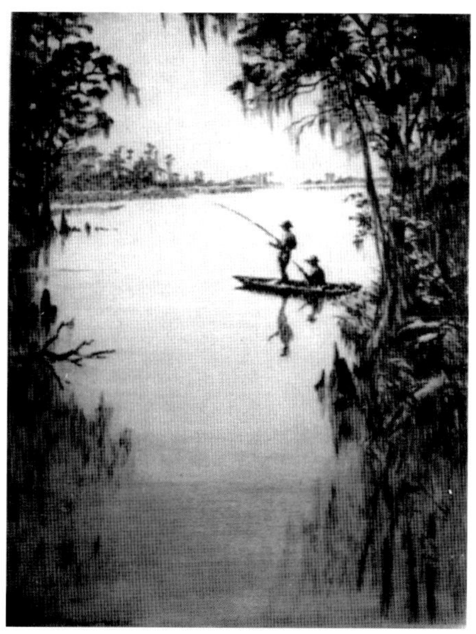

"Amber Water"
Medium: Etching
Image: 11.875 inches high by 8.875 inches wide

Hans Kleiber

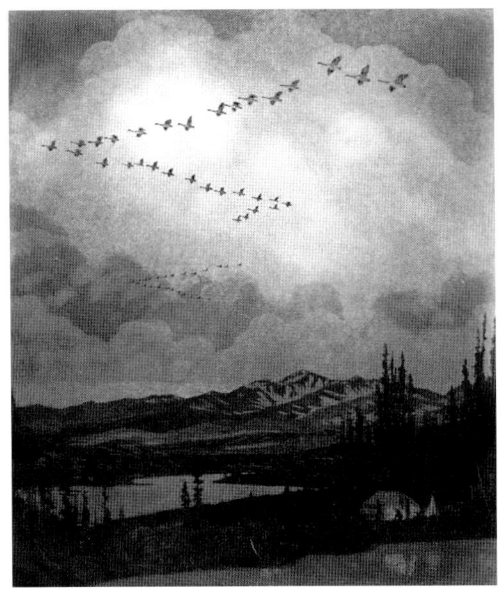

"An Evening Flight"
"An Evening Flock"
"Evening Flight"
Medium: Etching
Image: 11.875 inches high by 9.875 inches wide

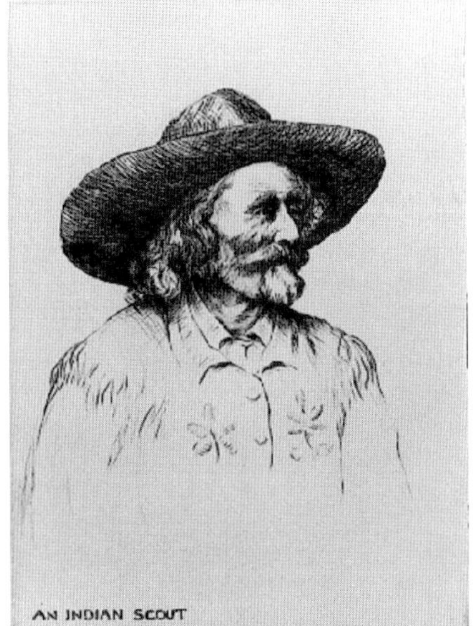

"An Indian Scout"
"An Indian Scout - Jim Baker"
Medium: Etching
Image: 6.875 inches high by 4.625 inches wide

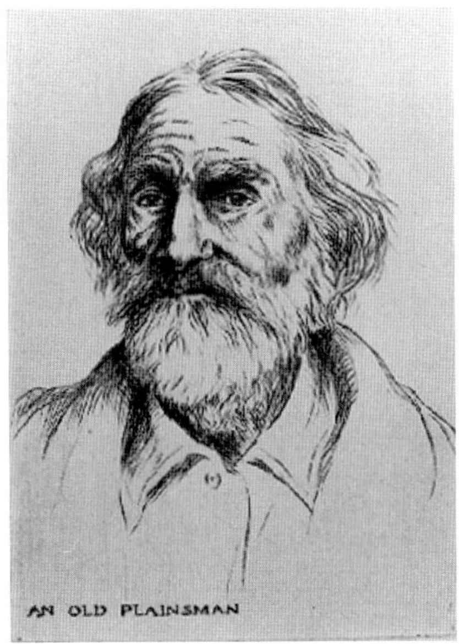

"An Old Plainsman"
Medium: Etching
Image: 6.75 inches high by 4.75 inches wide

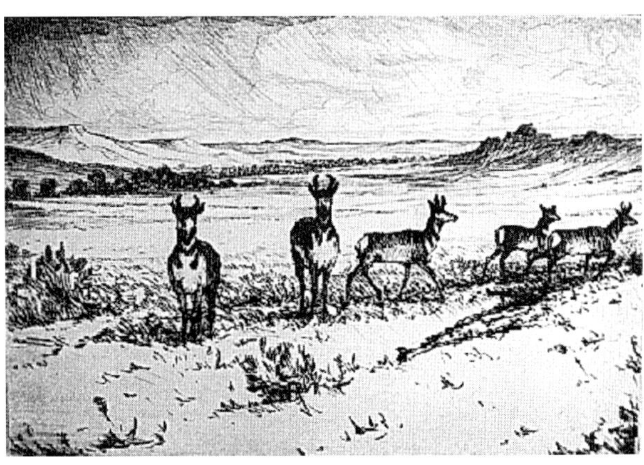

"Antelope"
"Antelope on Head of Black Thunder"
Medium: Etching
Image: 4.875 inches high by 6.75 inches wide

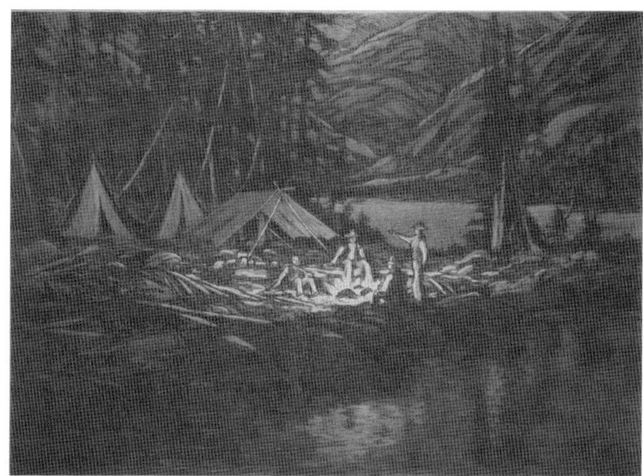

"Around the Campfire"
Second State of "Campfire"
a.k.a. "Campfire II"
Medium: Etching
Image: 5.75 inches high by 7.75 inches wide

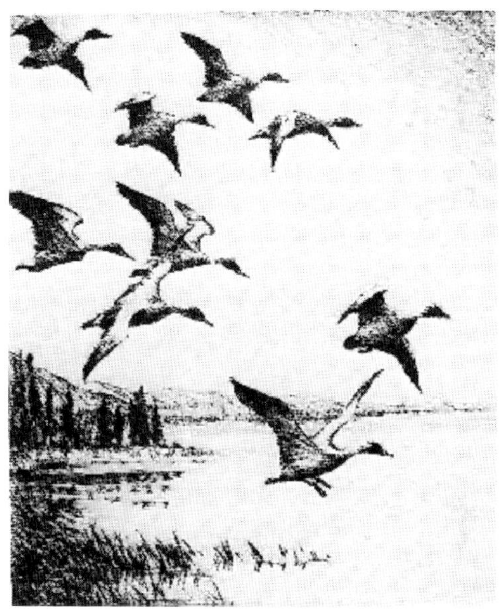

"At Jackson Lake"
Medium: Etching
Image: 5.3125 inches high by 4.375 inches wide

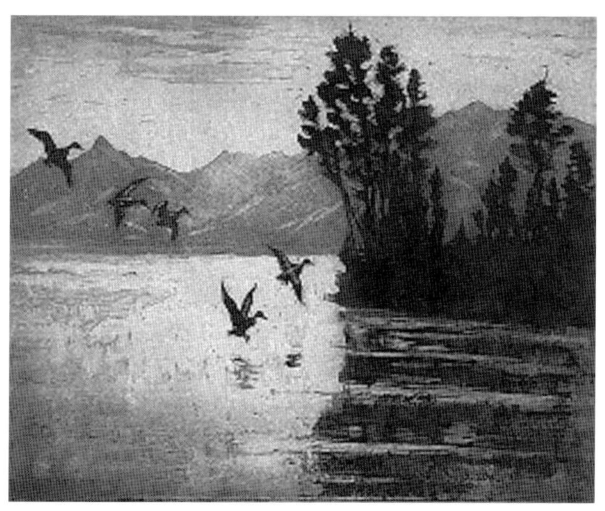

"At Jackson Lake"
Medium: Etching
Image: 8.75 inches high by 11.75 inches wide

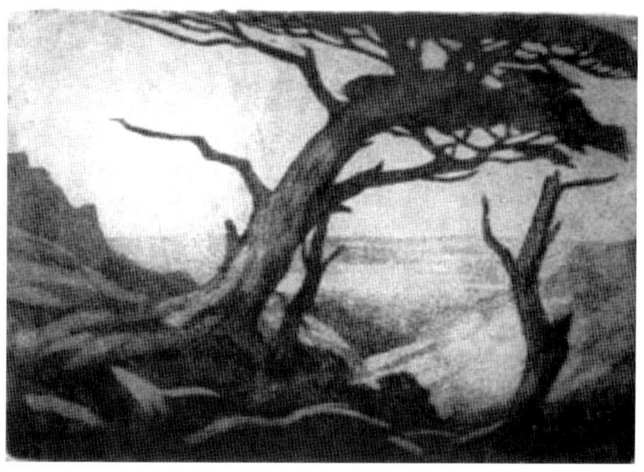

"At the Canyon Pine"
"On the Canyon Rim"
First State
Medium: Etching
Image: 6 inches high by 8.5 inches wide

Hans Kleiber

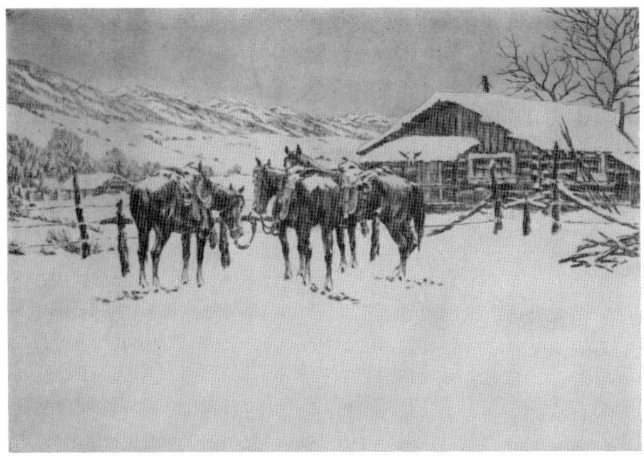

"At the Hitchrack"
Medium: Etching
Image: 9.5 inches high by 13.75 inches wide
Medium: Photogravure
Image: 5.5 inches high by 8 inches wide

The hand pulled etching by Hans Kleiber actually has two states due to artist error. In the top left corner of this impression one can see some slight wrinkles, see example. After examining the canceled plate, one can see where at one time it was damaged and repaired.

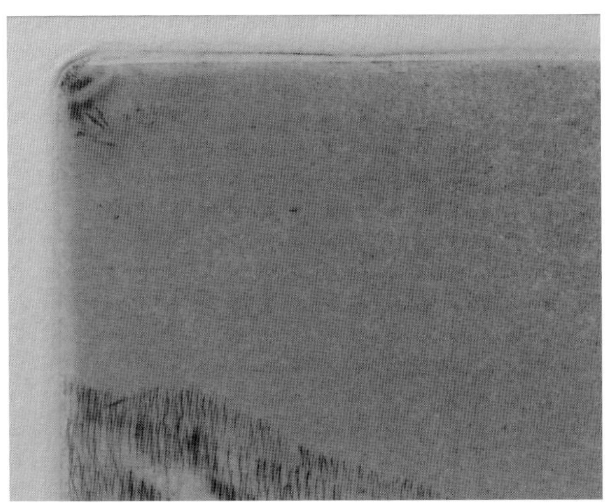

The above is a detail view of the upper left corner of the impression of the Second State of "At The Hitchrack."

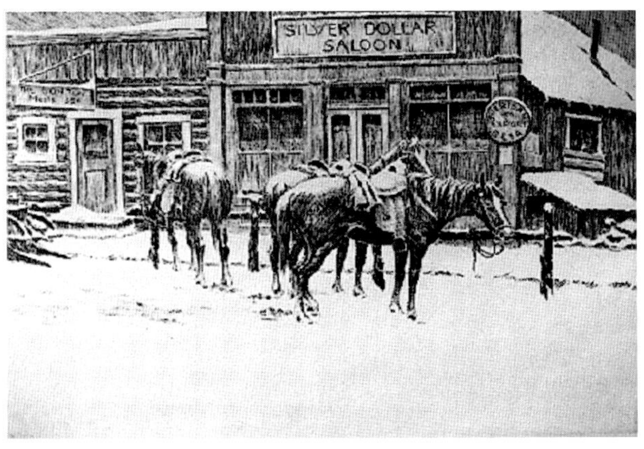

"At the Silver Dollar"
Medium: Etching
Image: 8.25 inches high by 11.75 inches wide
Medium: Photogravure
Image: 5.75 inches high by 8.25 inches wide

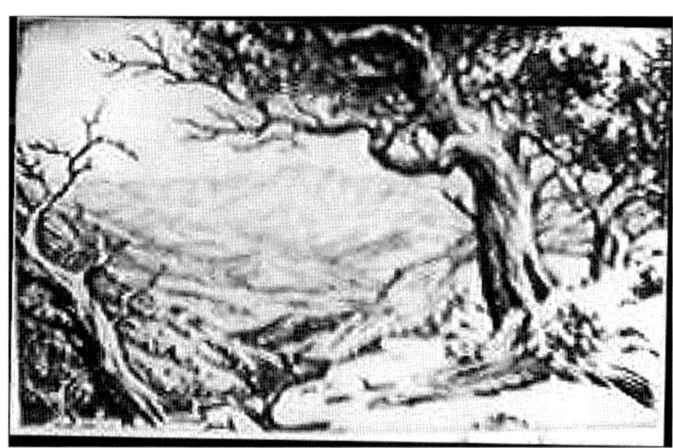

"At Timberline"
"Timberline"
Medium: Etching, Photogravure
Image: 3.875 inches high by 5.75 inches wide

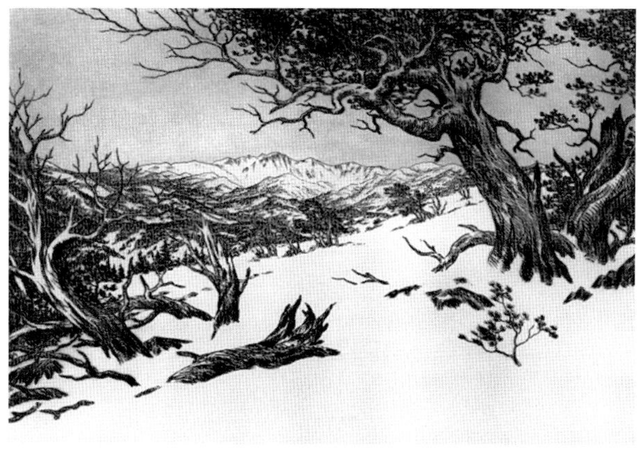

"At Timber Line"
"At Timberline"
Medium: Etching
Image: 7.75 inches high by 10.75 inches wide

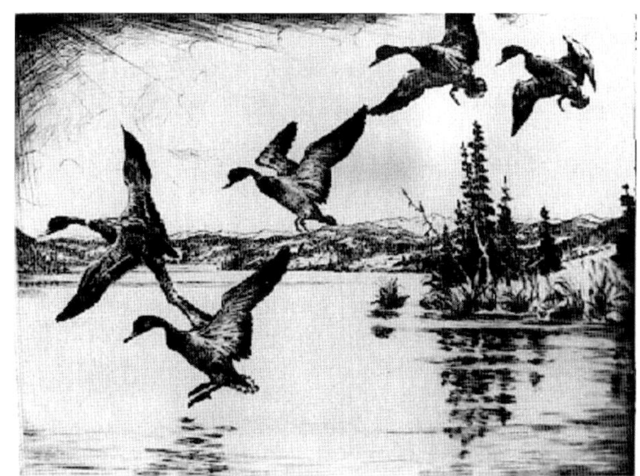

"At Yellowstone Lake"
"On Yellowstone Lake"
Medium: Etching
Associated American Artists
Image: 5.875 inches high by 7.75 inches wide

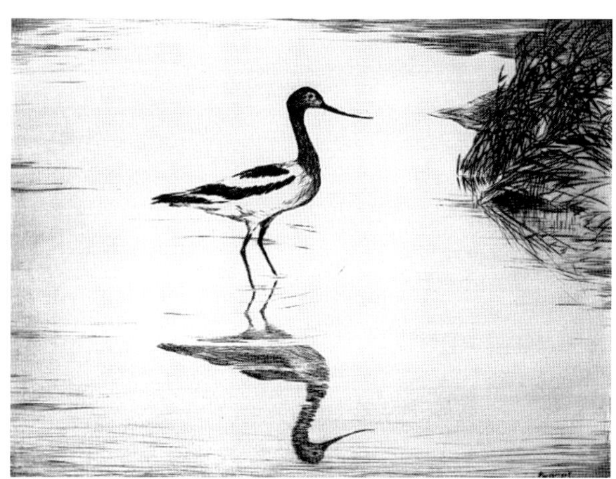

"Avocet"
Medium: Etching
Image: 6.875 inches high by 8.875 inches wide

Hans Kleiber

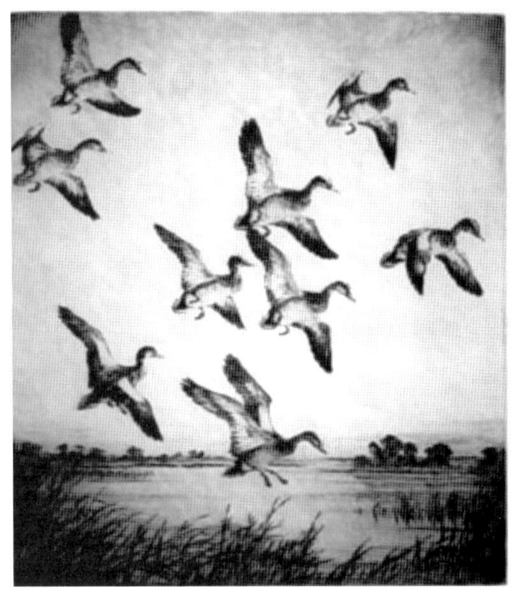

"Bald Pates"
Medium: Etching
Image: 10.75 inches high by 9 inches wide

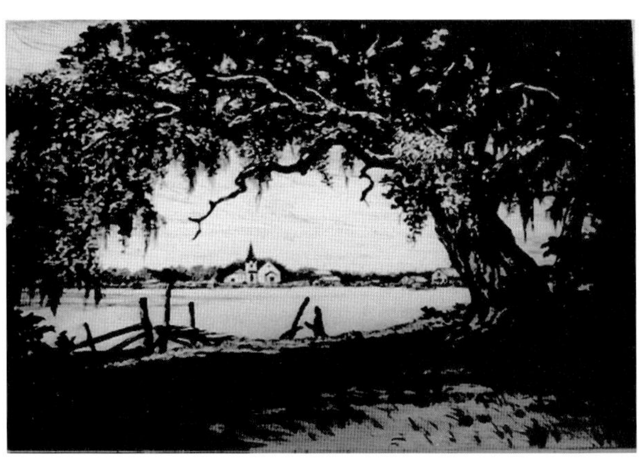

"Barataria, La."
Medium: Etching
Image: 6.8125 inches high by 9.875 inches wide

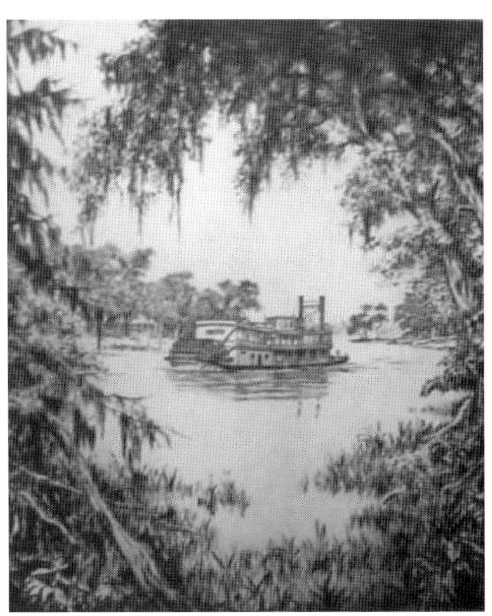

"Bayou Teche"
"Bayou Trip"
Medium: Etching
Image: 9.75 inches high by 7.75 inches wide

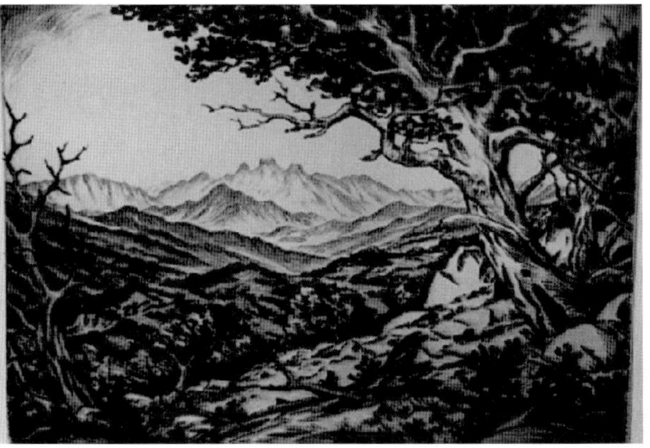

"Big Horn Peaks"
"The Big Horns"
Medium: Etching
Image: 4.875 inches high by 6.8125 inches wide

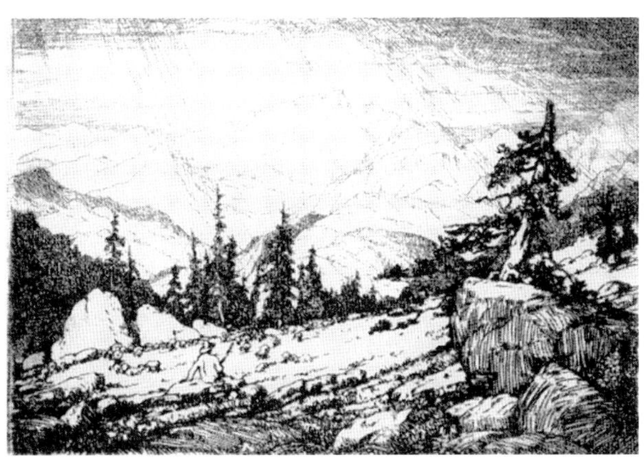

"Bighorn Peaks"
Medium: Etching
Image: 4.875 inches high by 6.875 inches wide

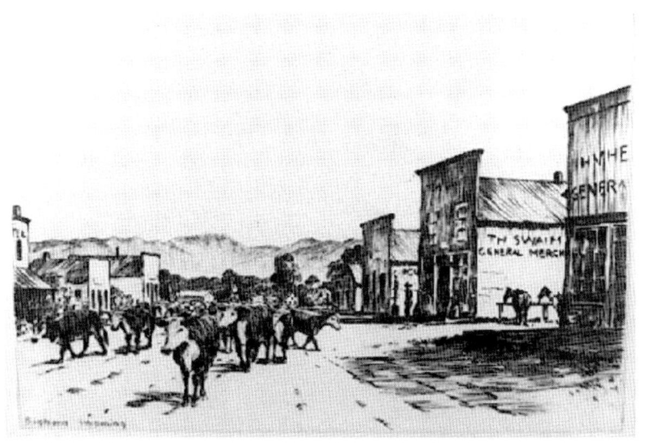

"Big Horn, Wyoming"
""Bighorn, Wyoming"
Medium: Etching
Image: 4.75 inches high by 6.75 inches wide

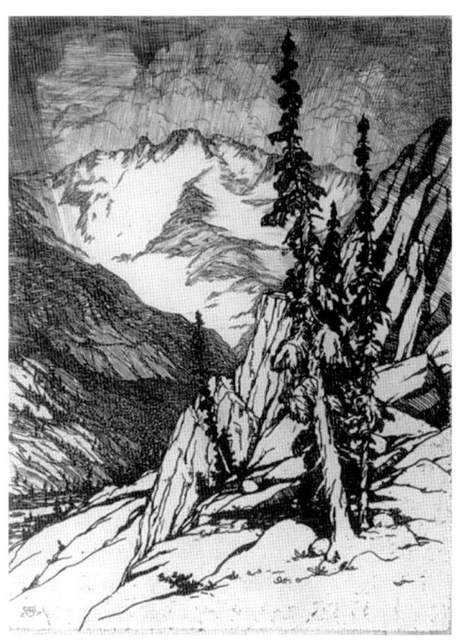

"Black Tooth, Wyoming"
Medium: Etching
Image: 8.5 inches high by 6.125 inches wide

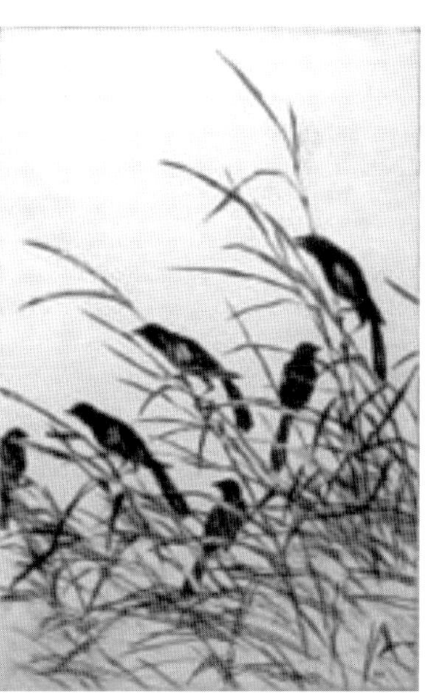

"Blackbirds"
Medium: Etching
Image: 5.75 inches high by 3.625 inches wide

Hans Kleiber

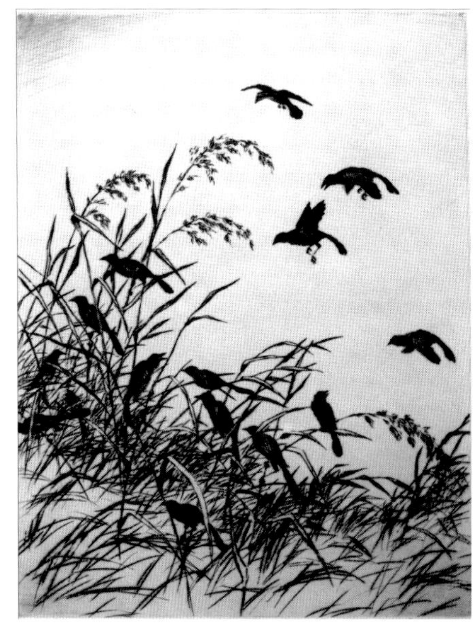

"Blackbirds"
"Blackbirds I"
"Blackbirds II"
Medium: Etching
Image: 11.75 inches high by 8.75 inches wide

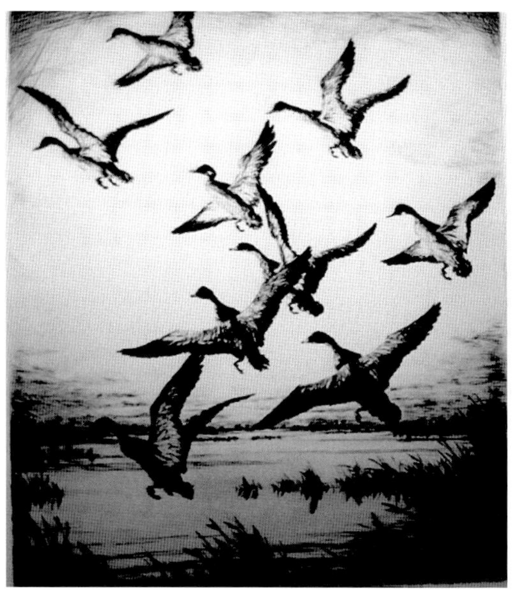

"Black Ducks"
"Marsh Ducks"
Medium: Etching
Associated American Artists
Image: 11.75 inches high by 9.75 inches wide

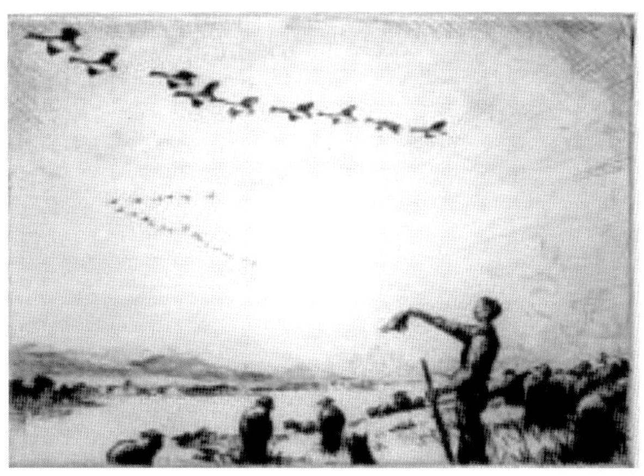

"Bon Voyage"
Medium: Etching
Image: 3.875 inches high by 5.375 inches wide

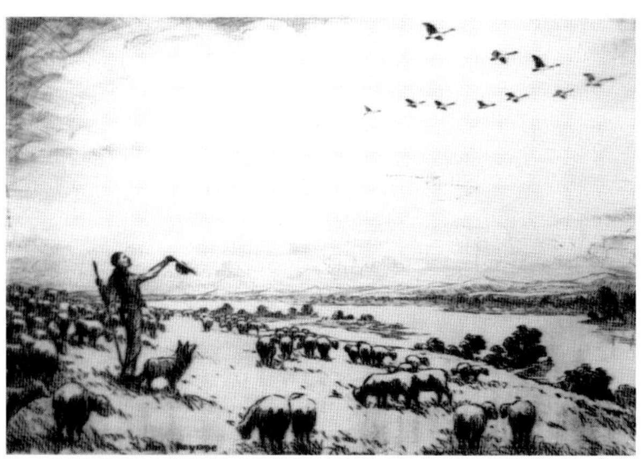

"Bon Voyage"
"Bon Voyage II"
Medium: Etching
Image: 4.75 inches high by 6.75 inches wide

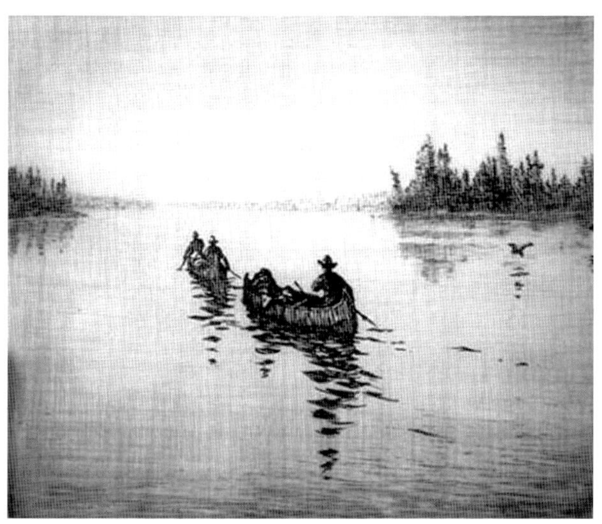

"Bound for the Hunt"
First State
Medium: Etching
Image: 6.125 inches high by 7.75 inches wide

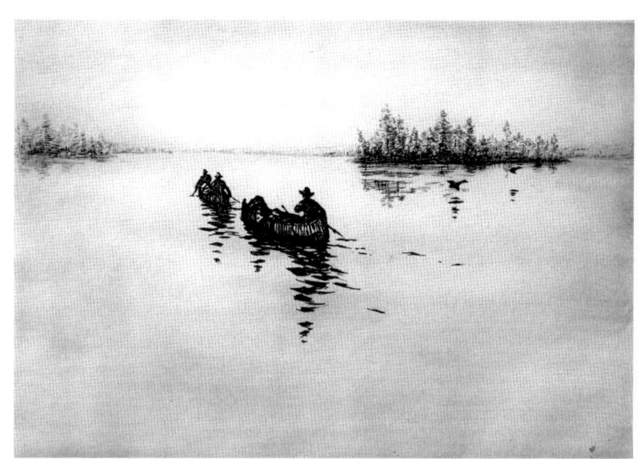

"Starting on a Hunt"
"Starting on the Hunt"
Second State of "Bound for the Hunt"
Medium: Photogravure
Image: 7.75 inches high by 10.75 inches wide

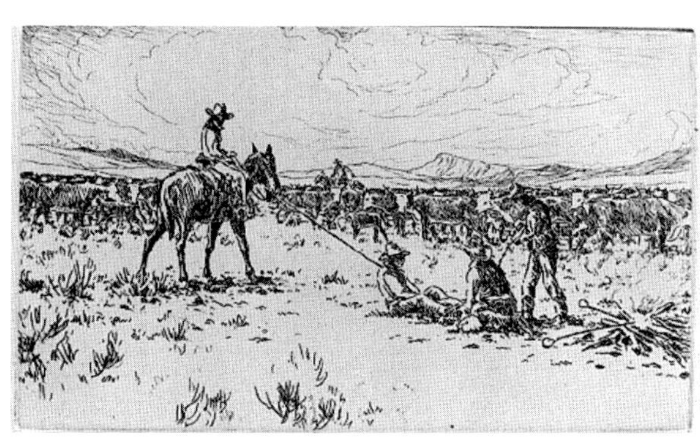

"Branding on the Range"
Medium: Photogravure
Image: 3.75 inches high by 6.25 inches wide

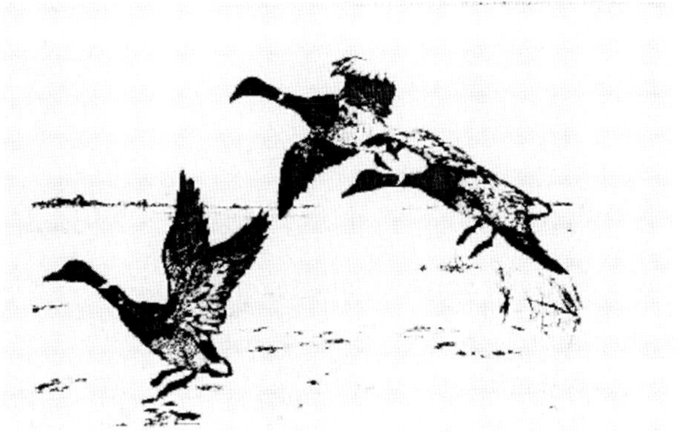

"Brant"
"Brant Settling"
Medium: Etching
Image: 6.375 inches high by 9.3125 inches wide

Hans Kleiber

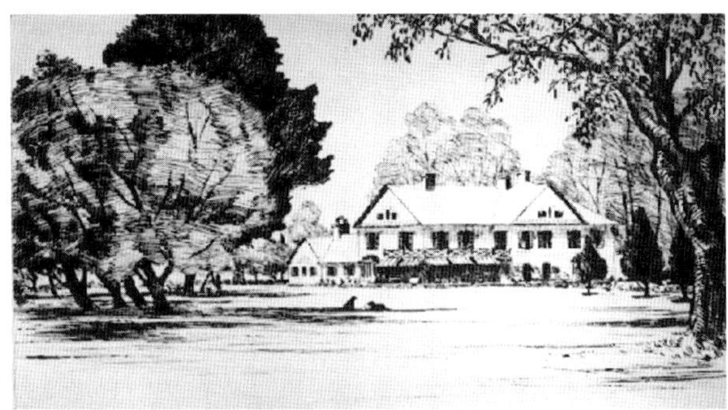

"Brinton Ranch, Bighorn, Wyoming 1930"
"Bradford Brinton House"
Medium: Etching
Image: 6.875 inches high by 11.875 inches wide

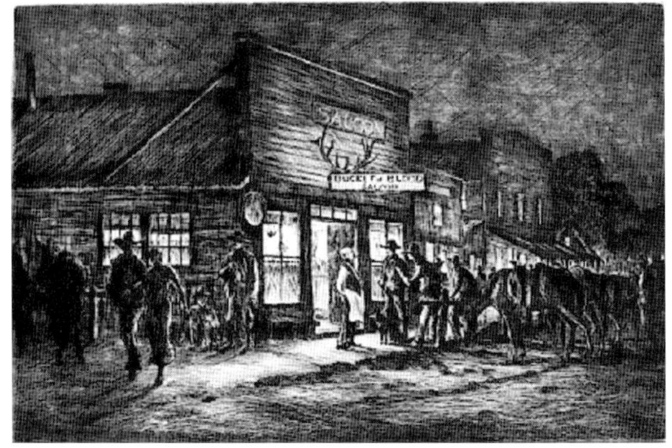

"Bucket of Blood Saloon"
"The Bucket of Blood Saloon"
Medium: Etching
Image: 6.75 inches high by 9.75 inches wide
Medium: Photogravure
Image: 5.25 inches high by 7.625 inches wide

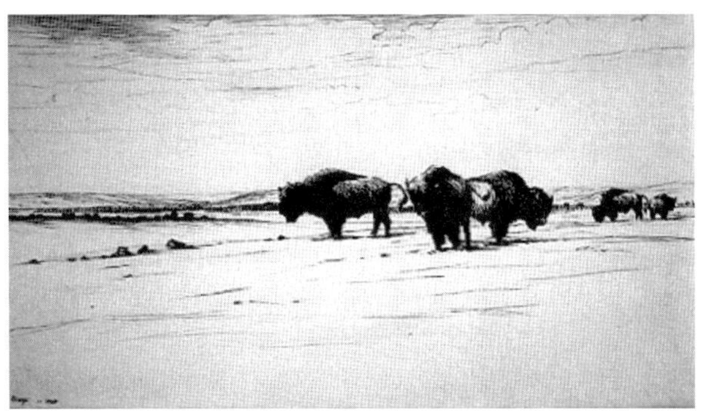

"Buffalo Days"
Medium: Etching
Image: 6.75 inches high by 12.75 inches wide

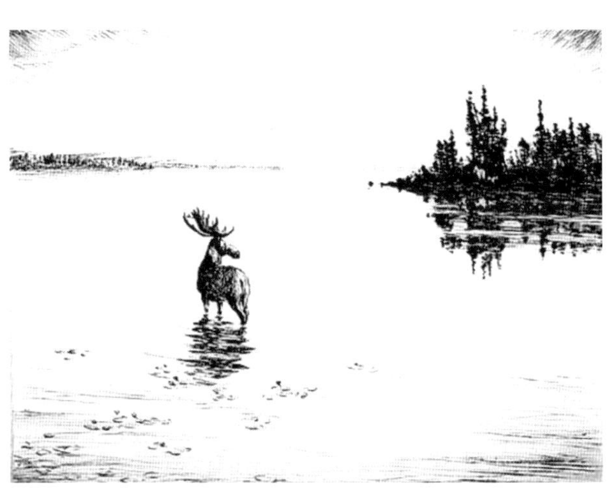

"Bull Moose"
Medium: Etching
Image: 8.25 inches high by 11.75 inches wide

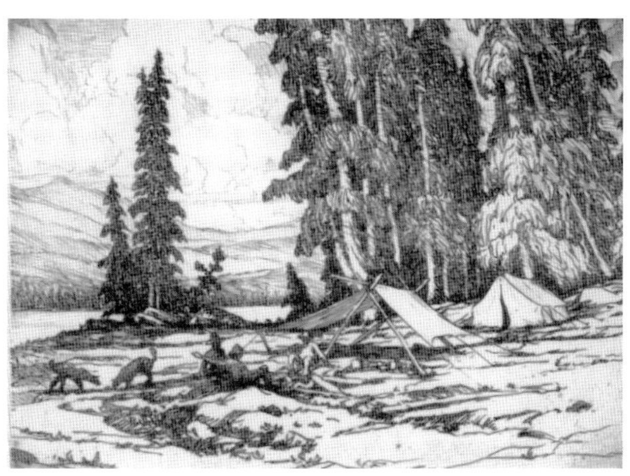

"Camp at Elk Lake"
"Camp at Elk Lake, Bighorns"
"Fisherman's Camp at Elk Lake"
"In Camp"
"In Camp at Elk Lake"
"Night Camp"
"The Camp at Elk Lake"
Second State of
"Camping at Elk Lake, Wyoming"
Medium: Photogravure
Image: 4.25 inches high by 5.875 inche wide

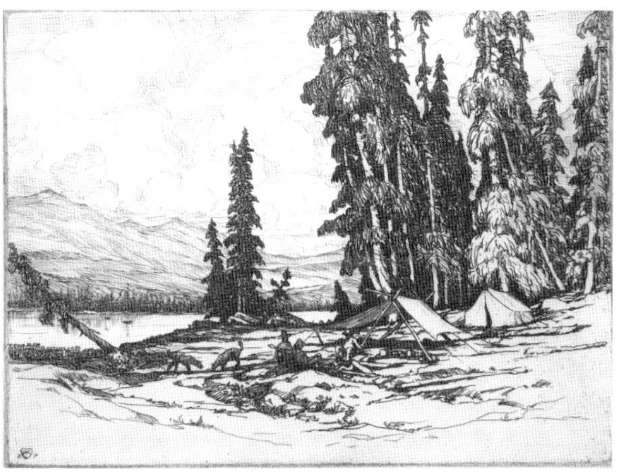

"Camping at Elk Lake, Wyoming"
First State
Medium: Etching
Image: 6 inches high by 8 inches wide

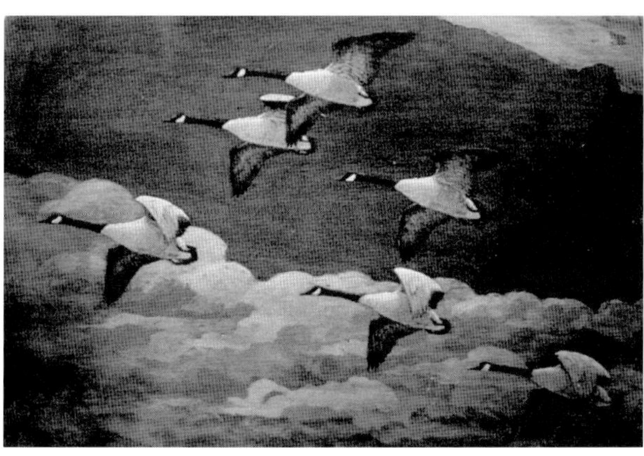

"Canada Geese"
"Honkers Flying"
"Honkers Flying - Night"
First State
Medium: Etching
Image: 8.875 inches high by 12.875 inches wide

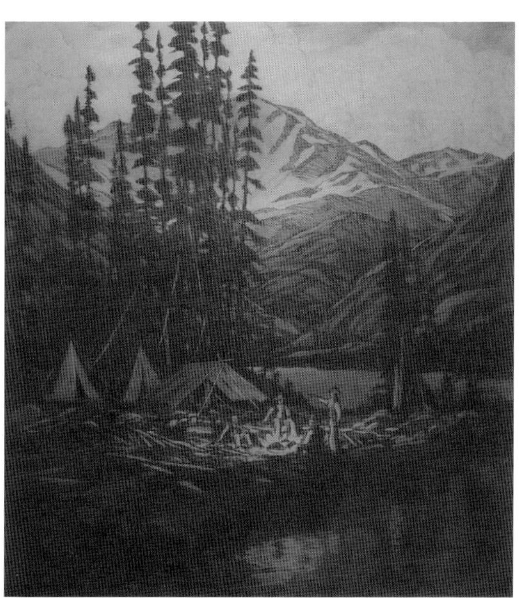

"Campfire"
"Campfire II"
"The Campfire"
Medium: Etching
Image: 8.875 inches high by 7.875 inches wide

Hans Kleiber

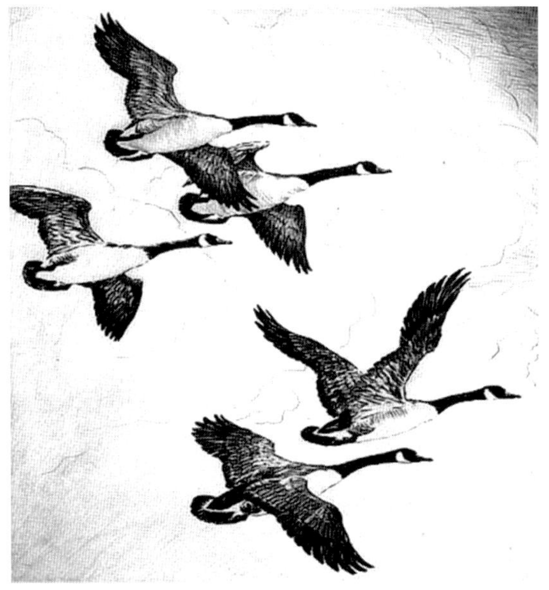

"Canadian Geese"
Medium: Etching
Image: 10.75 inches high by 8.625 inches wide

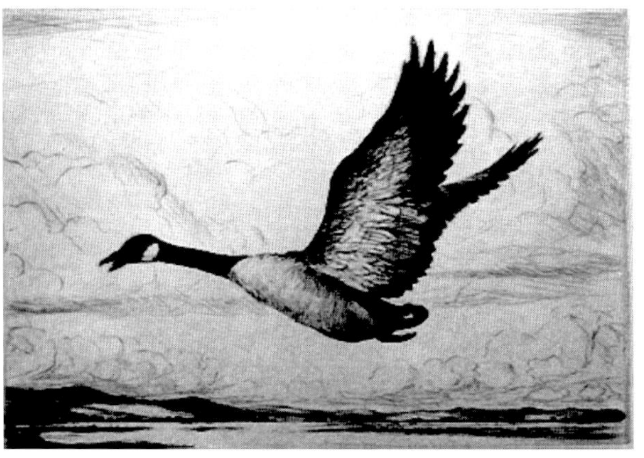

"Canadian Goose"
Second State of "Two Geese"
Medium: Etching
Image: 4.875 inches high by 6.75 inches wide

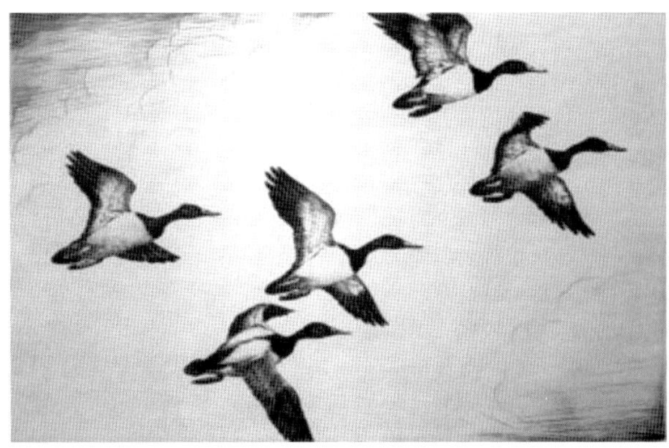

"Canvas Back in Flight"
Medium: Etching
Associated American Artists
Image: 7.625 inches high by 11.75 inches wide

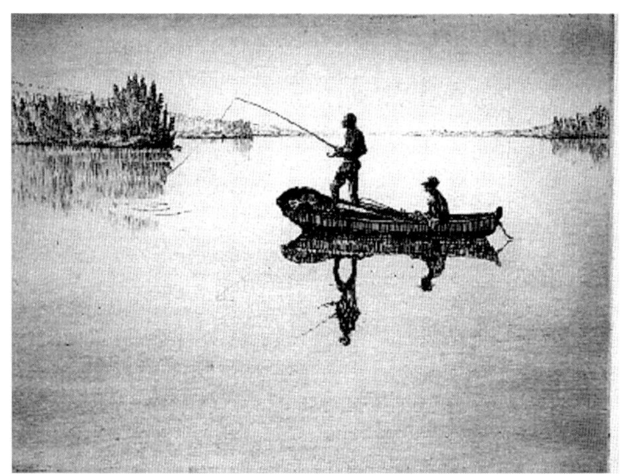

"Casting from a Boat"
Medium: Photogravure
Image: 6.875 inches high by 8.875 inches wide

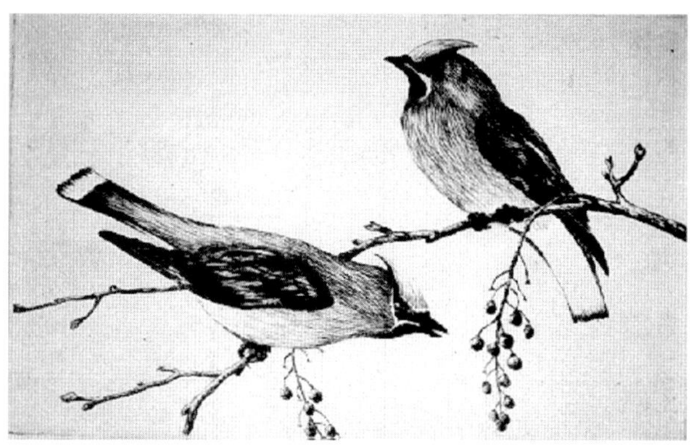

"Cedar Waxwings"
Medium: Etching
Image: 3.875 inches high by 5.875 inches wide

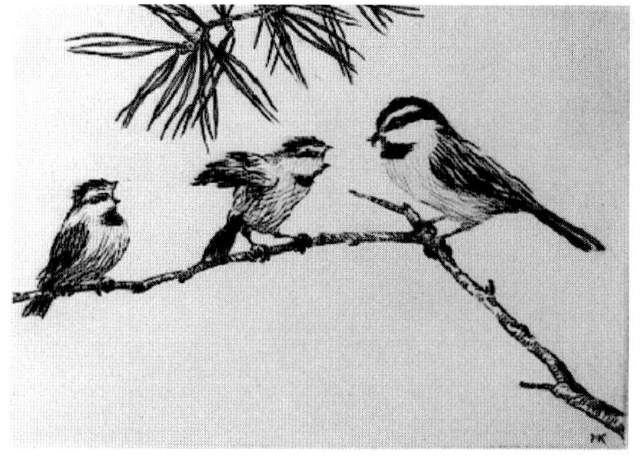

"Chicadees"
"Chicadees I"
Medium: Etching
Image: 3.5 inches high by 4.8125 inches wide

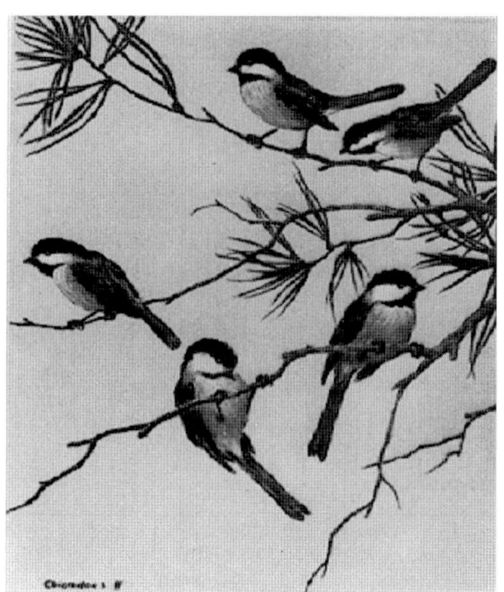

"Chicadees II"
"Medium: Etching
Image: 5.75 inches high by 4.75 inches wide

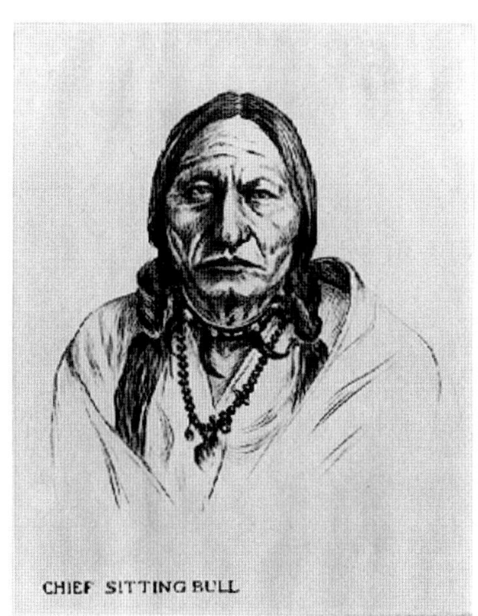

"Chief Sitting Bull"
Medium: Etching
Image: 9.25 inches high by 7.25 inches wide

Hans Kleiber

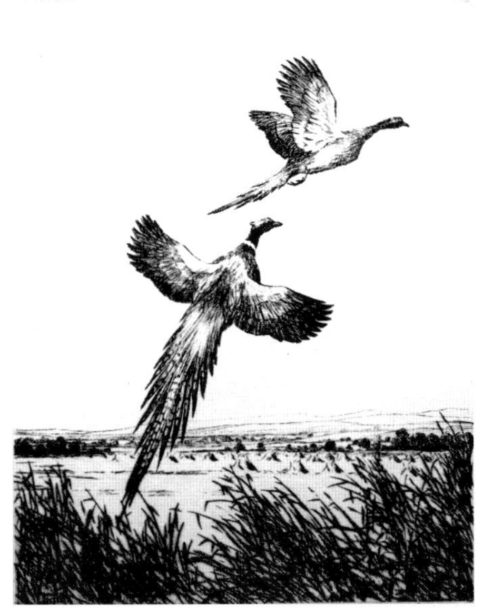

"Chinese Pheasants"
"Pheasants"
Medium: Etching
Image: 6.25 inches high by 4.875 inches wide

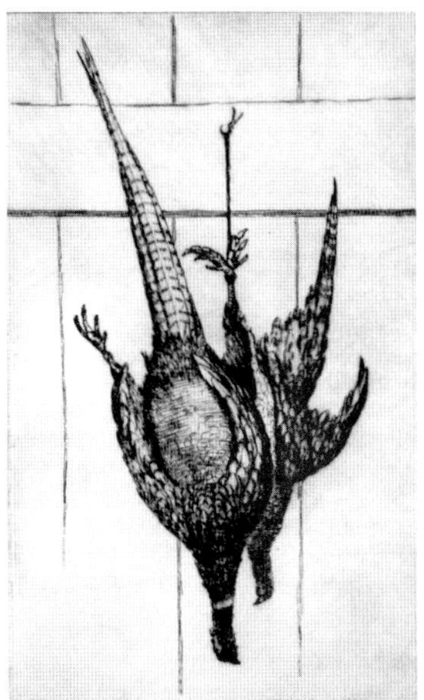

"Chinese Pheasants"
Medium: Etching
Image: 8.25 inches high by 4.75 inches wide

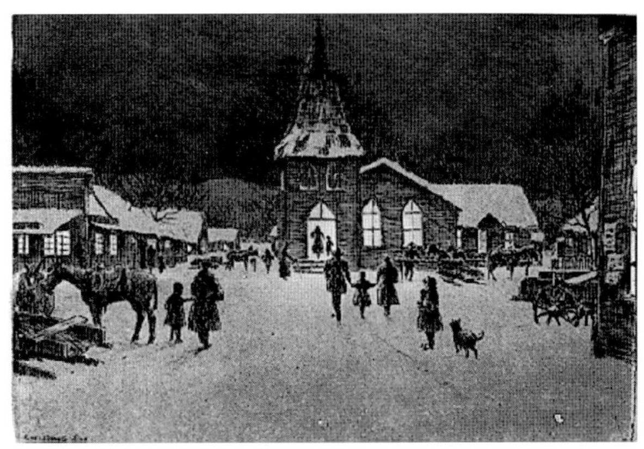

"Christmas Eve"
Medium: Photogravure
Image: 4.25 inches high by 6 inches wide

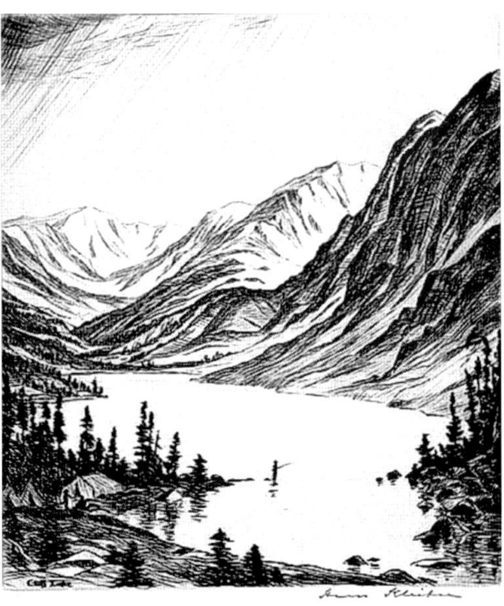

"Cliff Lake"
Medium: Etching
Image: 6.375 inches high by 4.875 inches wide

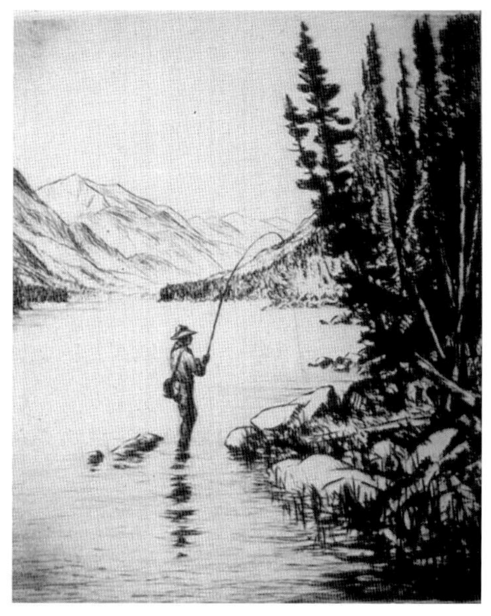

"Cliff Lake"
Medium: Etching
Image: 5.5 inches high by 4.5 inches wide

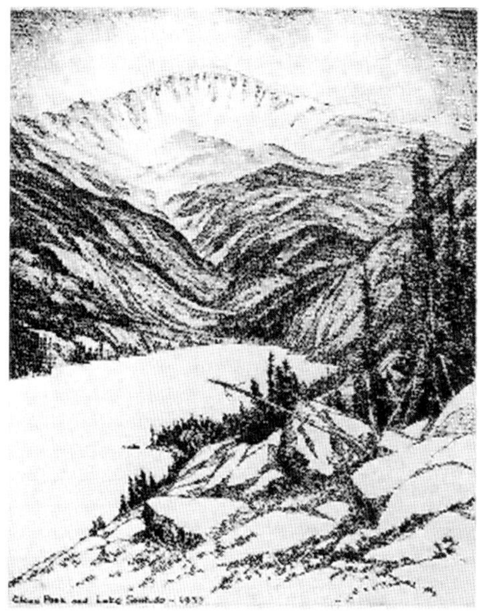

"Cloud Peak and Lake Solitude"
Medium: Etching
Image: 6.75 inches high by 5.25 inches wide

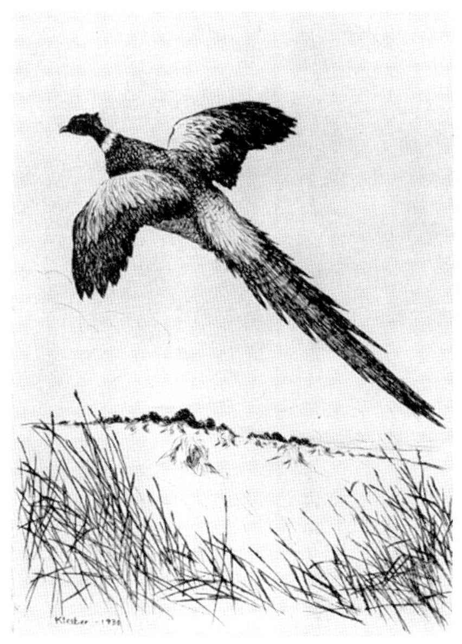

"Cock Pheasant"
Medium: Etching
Image: 8.875 inches high by 6.0625 inches wide

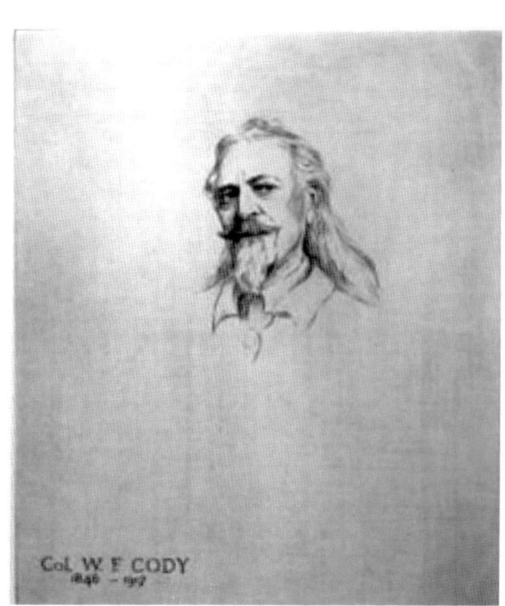

"Col. W. F. Cody 1846-1917"
Medium: Etching
Image: 8.25 inches high by 6.875 inches wide

Hans Kleiber

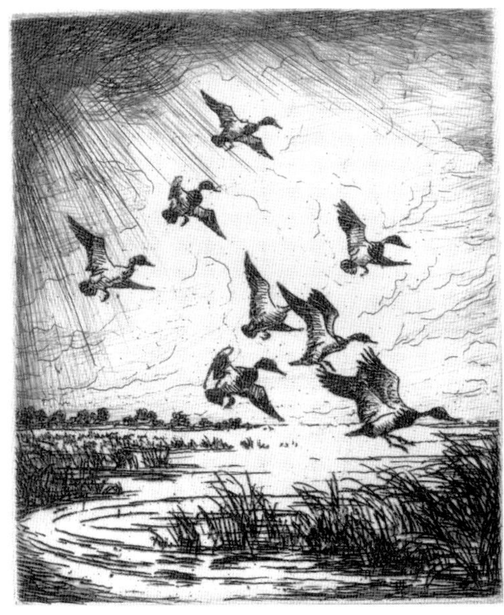

"Coming In"
Medium: Etching
Associated American Artists
Image: 3.25 inches high by 2.5625 inches wide

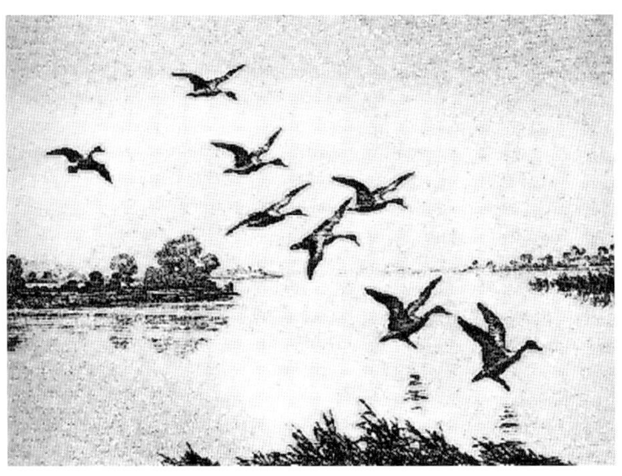

"Coming In"
"Coming In I"
Medium: Etching
Image: 5.75 inches high by 7.875 inches wide

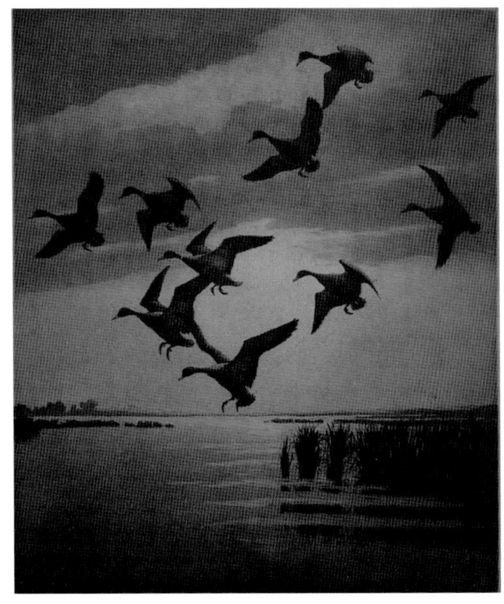

"Coming In"
"Coming In - Evening"
"Coming In #2"
"Flock Settling"
Medium: Etching
Image: 10.875 inches high by 8.875 inches wide

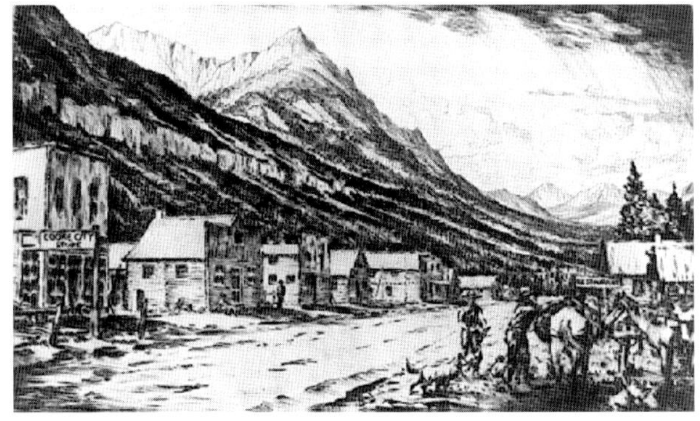

"Cooke City, Montana"
Medium: Etching
Image: 5.375 inches high by 8.625 inches wide

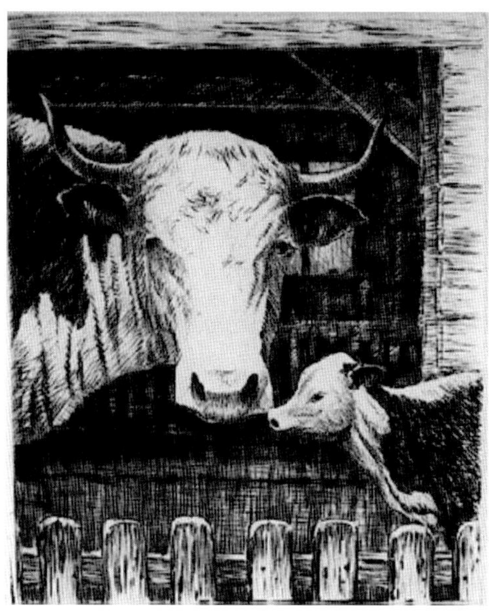

"Cow and Calf"
(Hereford)
Medium: Etching
Image: 4.875 inches high by 3.75 inches wide

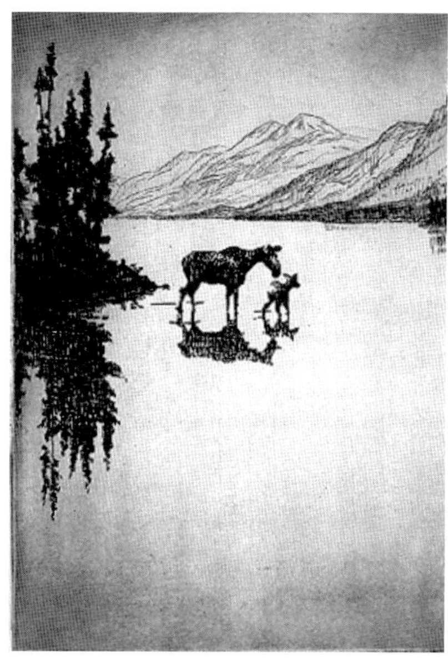

"Cow Moose and Calf"
"Moose Mother and Infant"
Medium: Photogravure
Image: 9.875 inches high by 6.75 inches wide

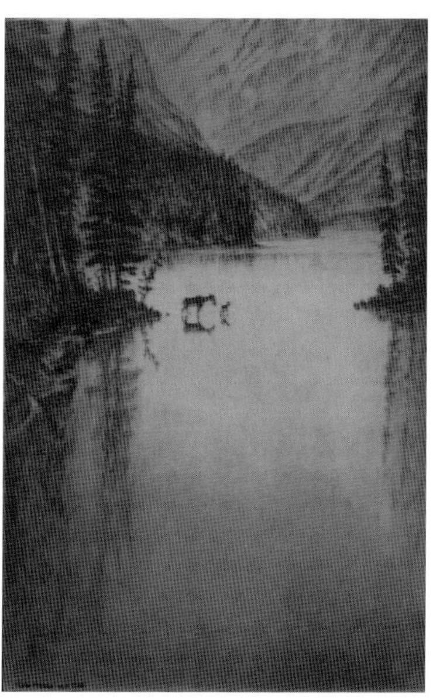

"Cow Moose and Calf"
"Solitude"
First State
Medium: Etching
Image: 11.625 inches high by 7.25 inches wide

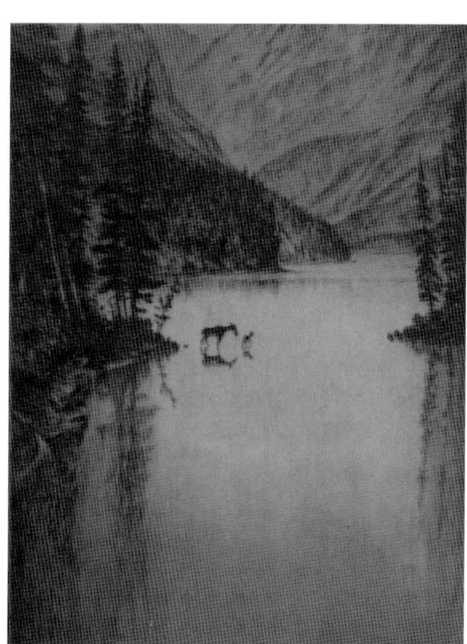

"Cow Moose and Calf"
"Solitude"
Second State of "Cow Moose and Calf"
Medium: Etching
Image: 9.625 inches high by 7.25 inches wide

Hans Kleiber

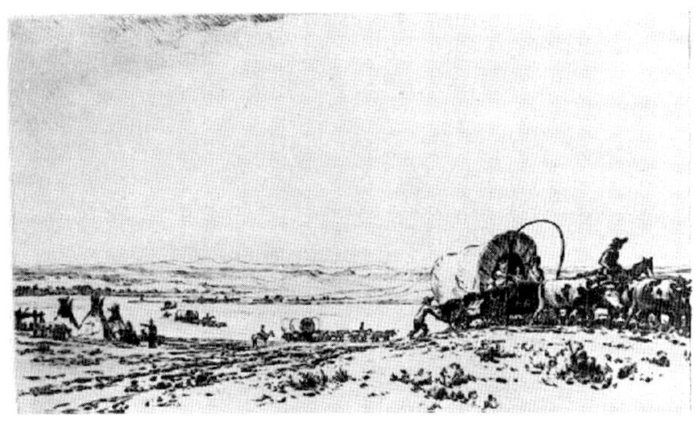

"Crossing the Platte"
Medium: Etching
Image: 6.75 inches high by 10.75 inches wide

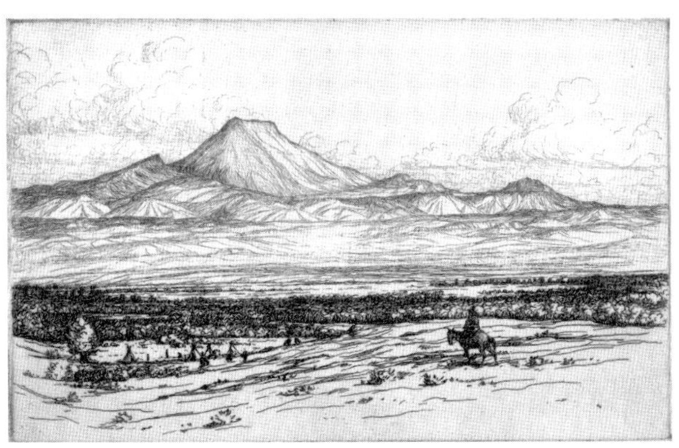

"Crowheart Butte"
"Crow Heart Butte - Wind River"
Medium: Photogravure
Image: 5.375 inches high by 8.25 inches wide

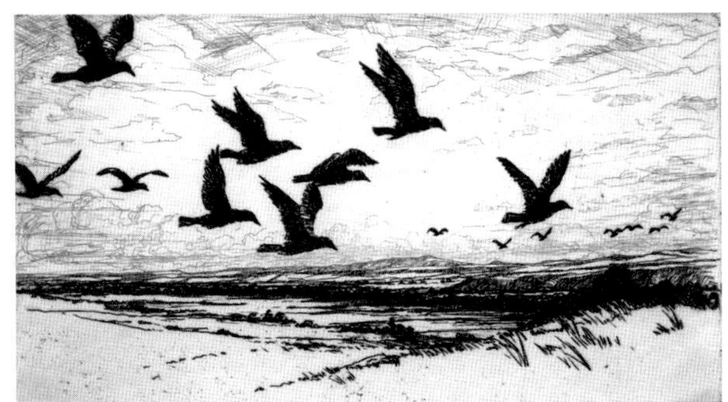

"Crows Flying South"
"Crows in the Fall"
Medium: Photogravure
Image: 5.25 inches high by 9.75 inches wide

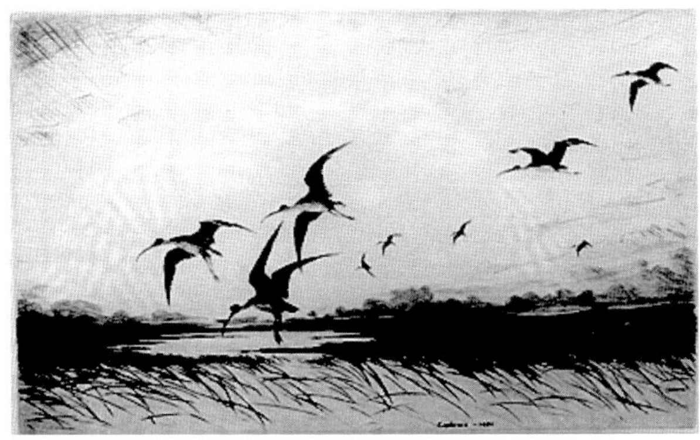

"Curlews"
First State
Medium: Etching
Image: 6.75 inches high by 10.75 inches wide

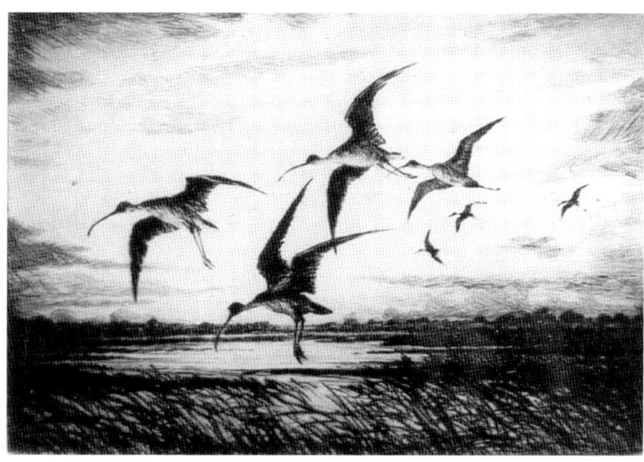

"Curlews"
Second State of "Curlews"
Medium: Etching
Image: 4.875 inches high by 6.8125 inches wide

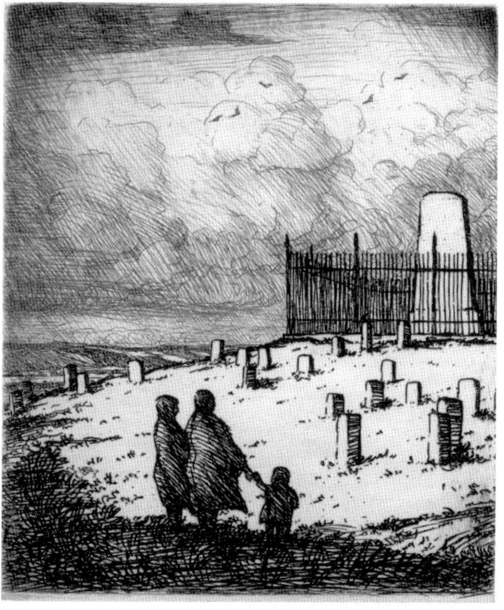

"Custer Battlefield"
Second State of "Custer Battlefied Monument, Montana"
Medium: Photogravure
Image: 4.875 inches high by 3.9375 inches wide

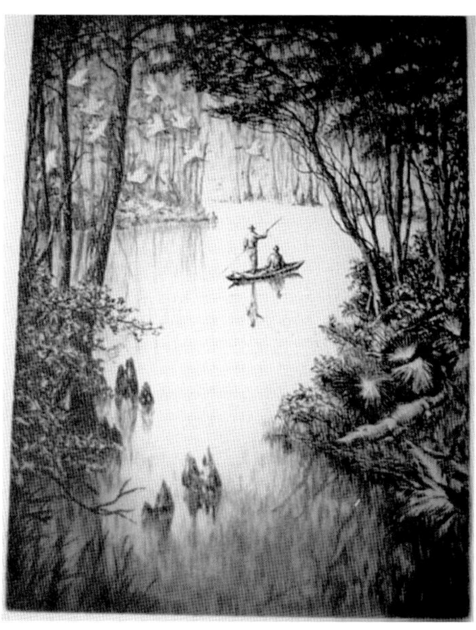

"Cypress Swamp"
Medium: Etching
Image: 10.875 inches high by 7.875 inches wide

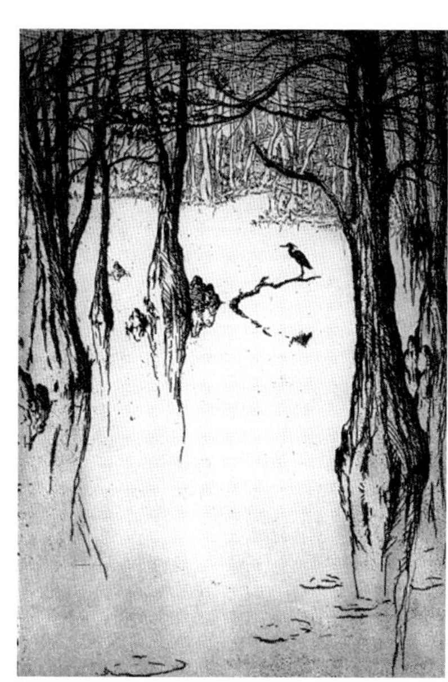

"Cypress Swamp"
Medium: Photogravure
Image: 11.75 inches high by 7.75 inches wide

Hans Kleiber

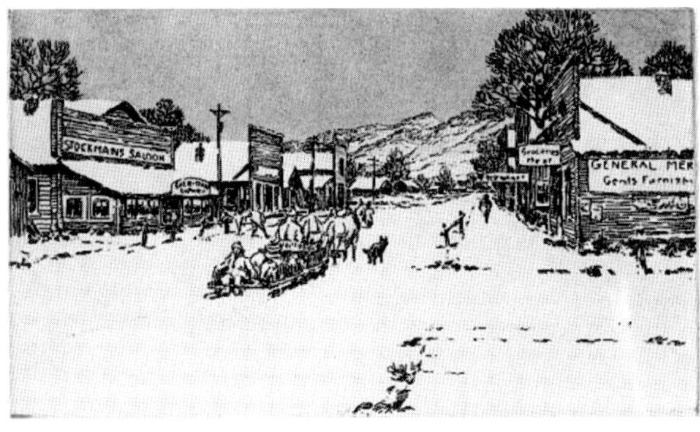

"Dayton, Wyoming"
Medium: Etching, Photogravure
Image: 3.75 inches high by 6.25 inches wide

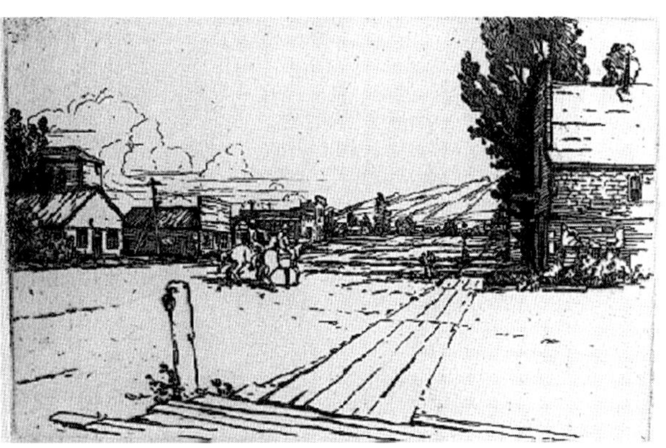

"Dayton, Wyoming"
Medium: Etching, Photogravure
Image: 5.25 inches high by 7.75 inches wide

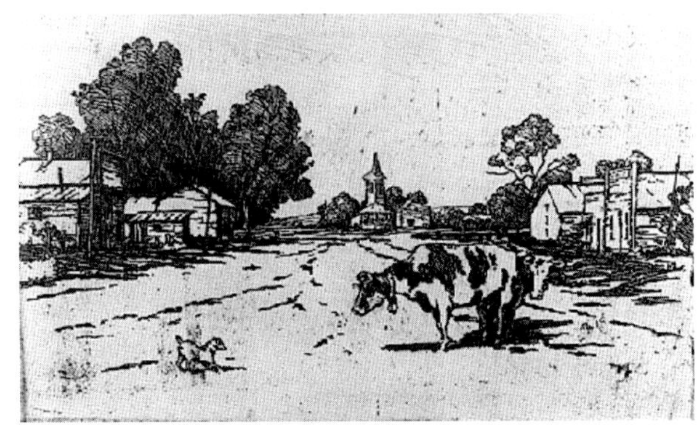

"Dayton, Wyoming"
"Dayton, Wyoming I"
Medium: Etching, Photogravure
Image: 4.875 inches high by 7.875 inches wide

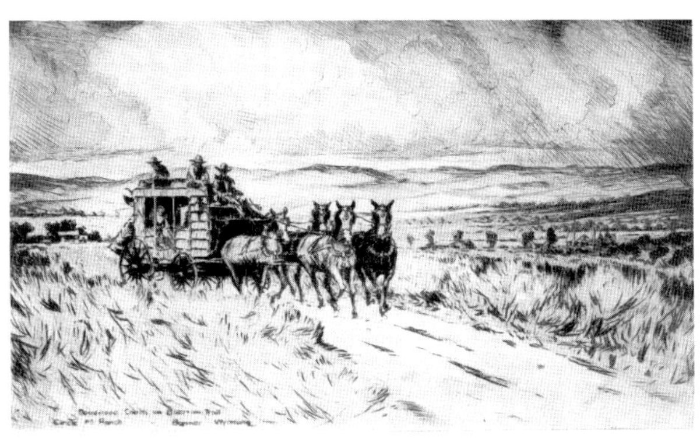

"Deadwood Coach on Bozeman Trail"
"Deadwood Coach on Bozeman Trail Circle M Ranch
Banner, Wyoming"
Medium: Etching
Image: 6.875 inches high by 10.75 inches wide
Medium: Photogravure
Image: 3.625 inches high by 5.875 inches wide

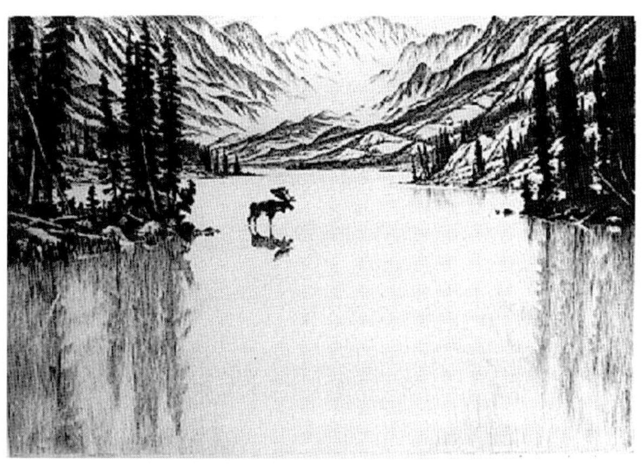

"Deep in the Rockies"
"Deep in the Rockies - Moose"
Medium: Etching
Associated American Artists
Image: 7.75 inches high by 10.75 inches wide

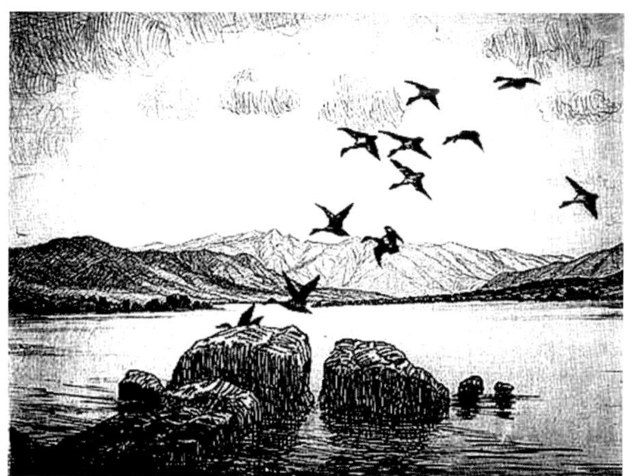

"Dinwoodie Lake"
"Dinwoodie Lake - Wyoming"
Medium: Etching, Photogravure
Image: 4.75 inches high by 6.75 inches wide

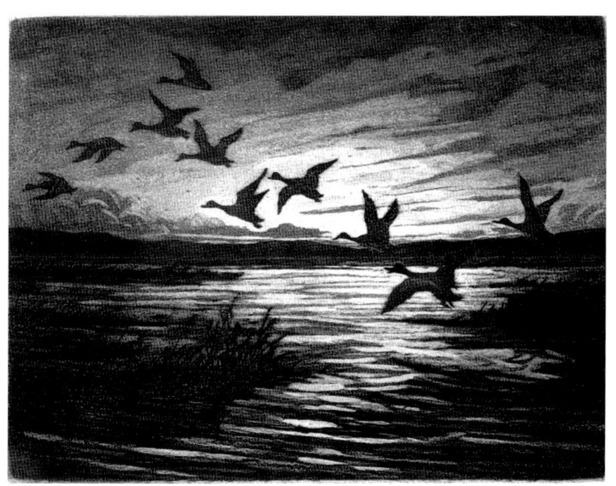

"Disturbed"
First State
Medium: Etching
Image: 6.375 inches high by 7.75 inches wide

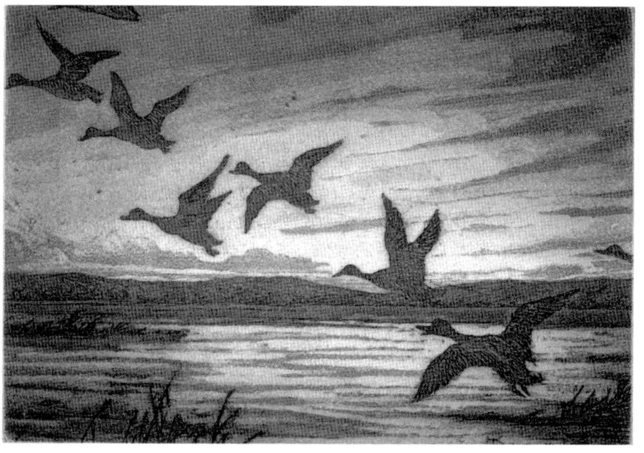

"Evening, Ducks"
"Morning"
Second State of "Disturbed"
Medium: Etching
Image: 3.5 inches high by 5 inches wide

Hans Kleiber

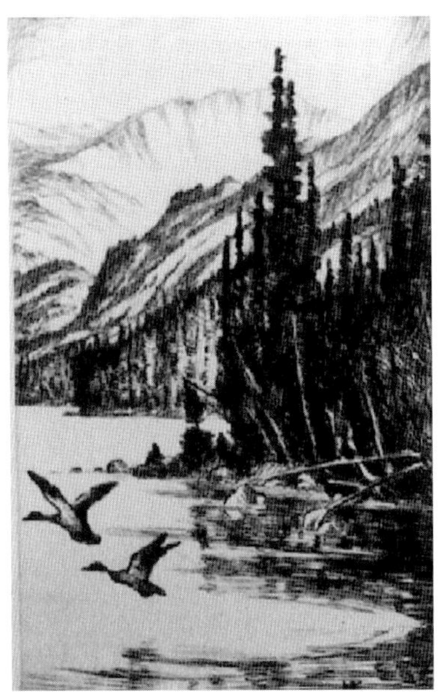

"Disturbed"
"Lake Geneva"
Medium: Etching
Image: 4.5 inches high by 2.75 inches wide

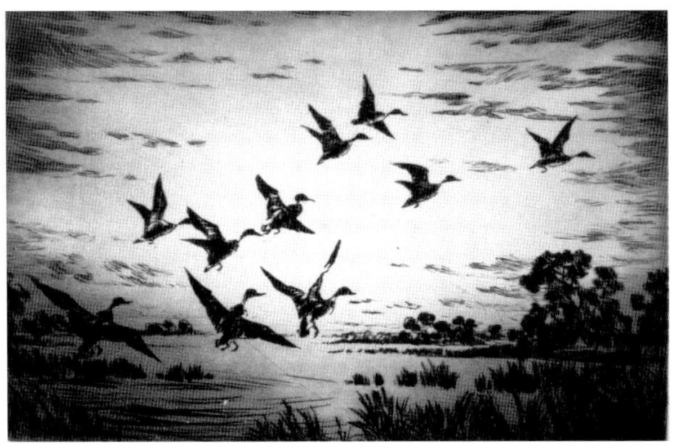

"A Disturbed Flock"
"Disturbed Flock"
Medium: Etching
Image: 4.75 inches high by 6.75 inches wide

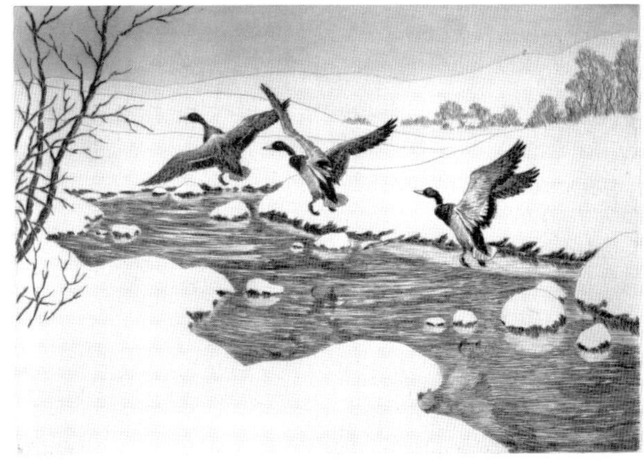

"Disturbed Mallards"
Medium: Etching
Associated American Artists
Image: 7.75 inches high by 10.75 inches wide

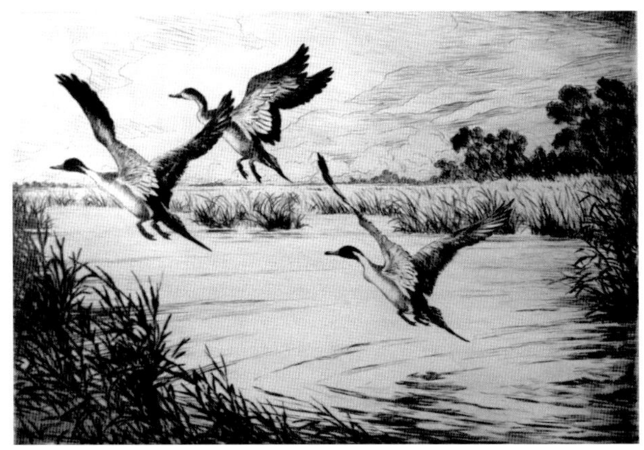

"Disturbed Pintails"
Medium: Etching
Associated American Artists
Image: 6.25 inches high by 8.75 inches wide

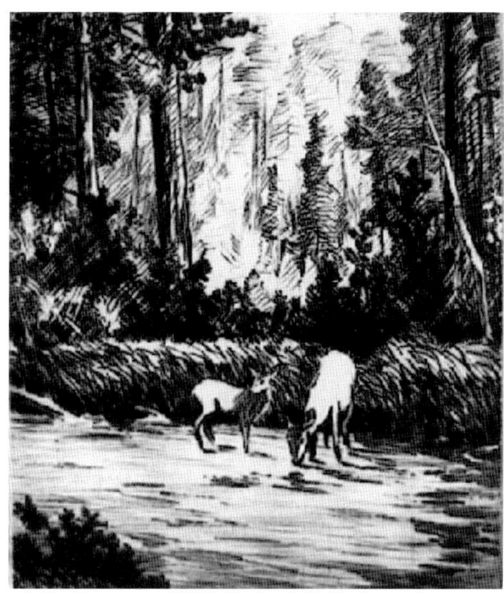

"Doe and Fawn"
Second State of "A Bit of Forest"
Medium: Etching
Image: 5.875 inches high by 4.75 inches wide

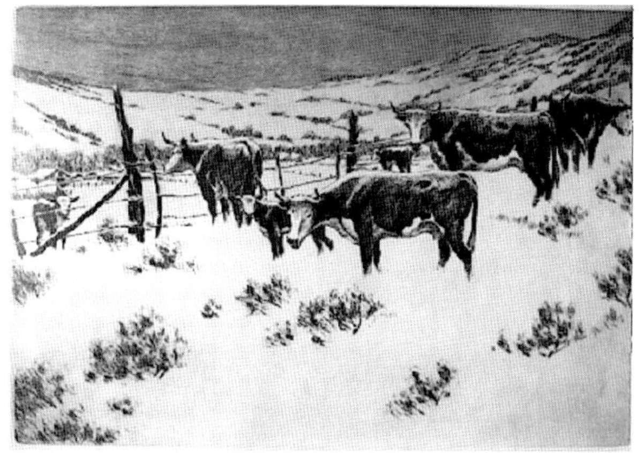

"Down from the Hills"
Medium: Etching
Image: 8 inches high by 11.75 inches wide

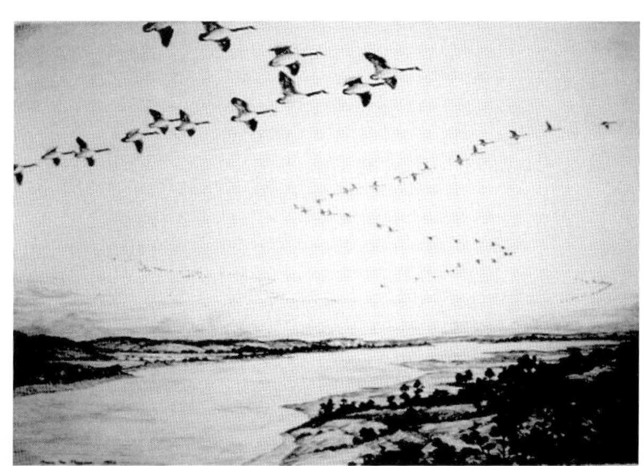

"Down the Missouri"
First State
Medium: Etching
Image: 10.75 inches high by 14.875 inches wide

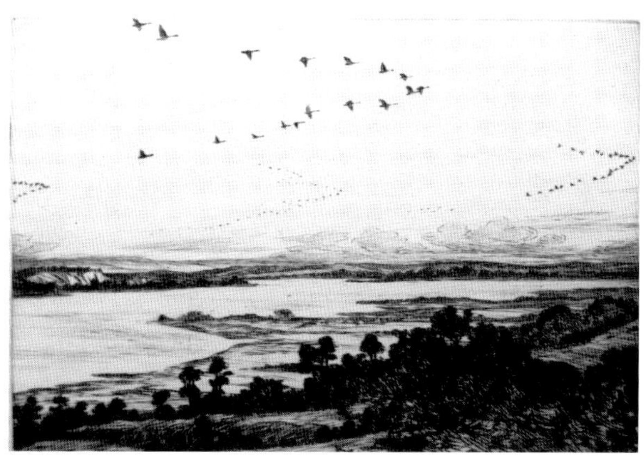

"Down the Missourie"
"On the Missouri"
Second State of "Down the Missouri"
Medium: Etching
Image: 4.75 inches high by 6.75 inches wide

Hans Kleiber

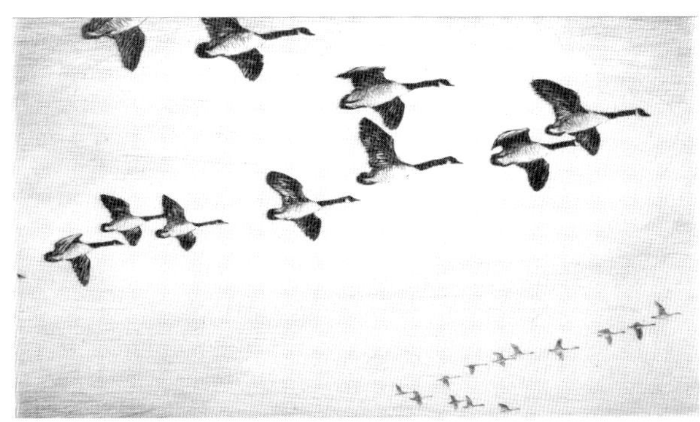

"Flying Wedges"
Third State of "Down the Missouri"
Medium: Etching
Image: 5 inches high by 7.875 inches wide

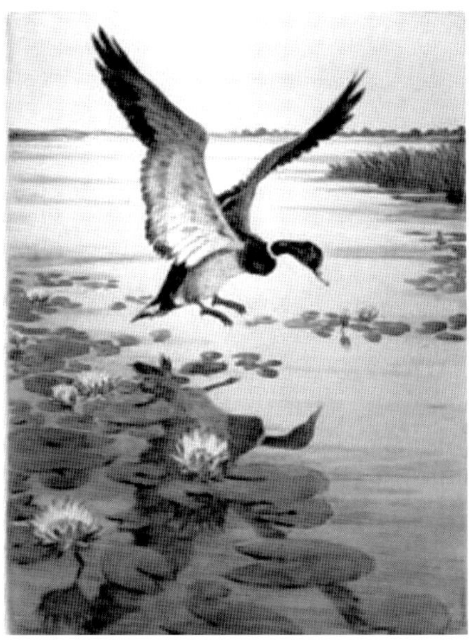

"Drake and Lilies"
"Drake and Lilies I"
Medium: Etching
Image: 8.75 inches high by 6.25 inches wide

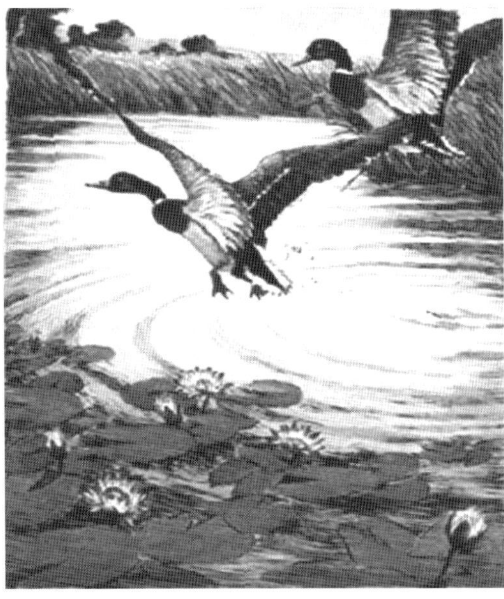

"Drakes and Lilies II"
"Drakes in Lilies II"
"Drakes In Summer"
Medium: Etching
Image: 8.75 inches high by 6.75 inches wide

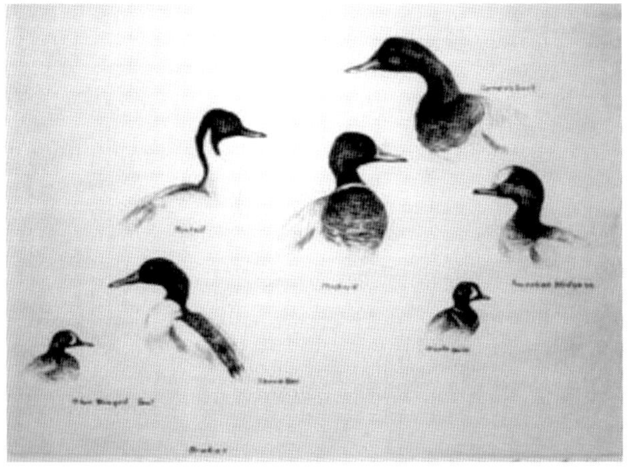

"Drakes"
Medium: Etching
Image: 7.5 inches high by 9.75 inches wide

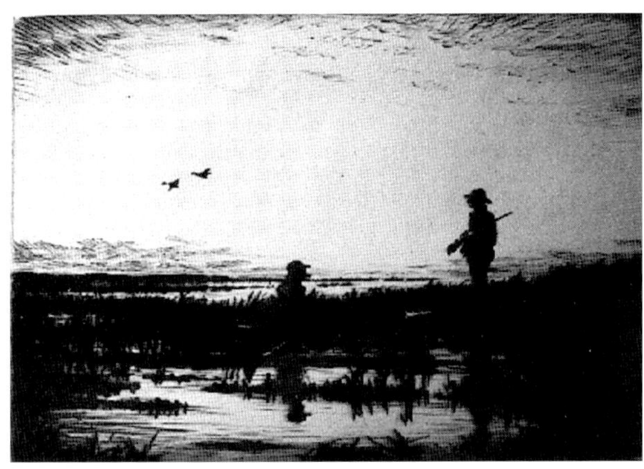

"Duck Hunters"
"Marsh Hunters"
"The Duck Hunters"
Medium: Etching
Image: 4.5 inches high by 6.25 inches wide

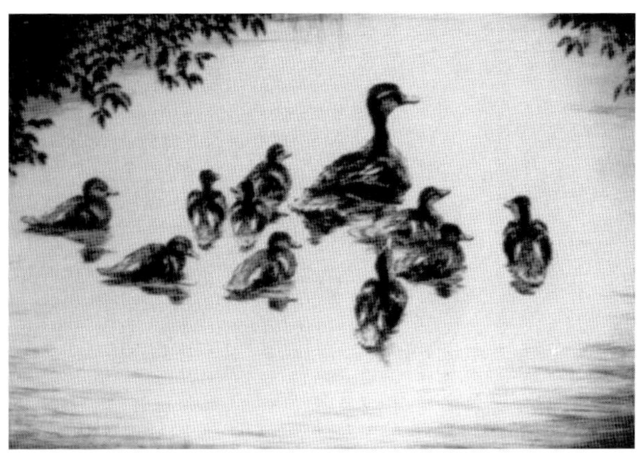

"Ducklings"
Medium: Etching
Image: 4.75 inches high by 6.75 inches wide

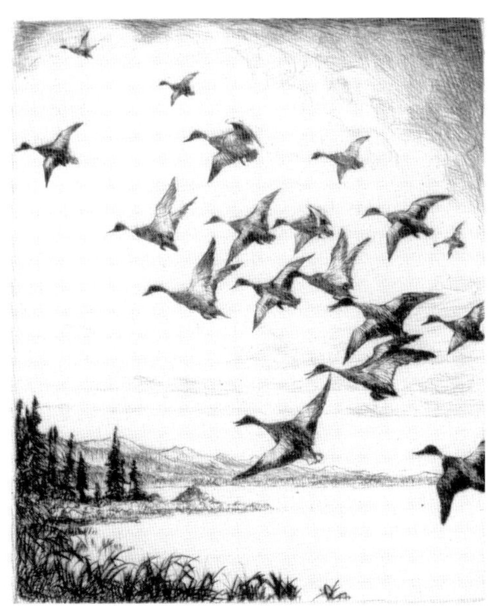

"Ducks Going South"
"Ducks on Jackson Lake"
Medium: Etching
Image: 4.875 inches high by 3.875 inches wide

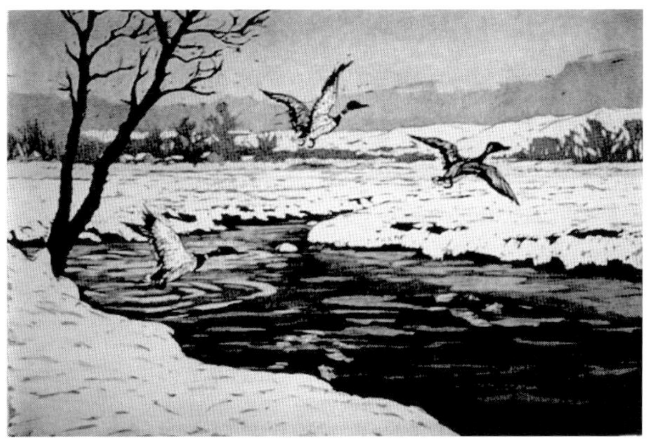

"Ducks in the Meadow"
Medium: Etching
Image: 6.6875 inches high by 9.75 inches wide

Hans Kleiber

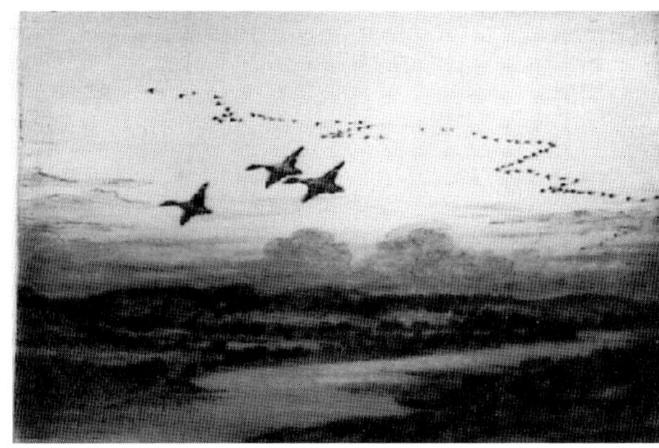

"Ducks in Wyoming"
"Ducks on the River"
"On the Tongue River"
Medium: Etching
Image: 4.0625 inches high by 5.8125 inches wide

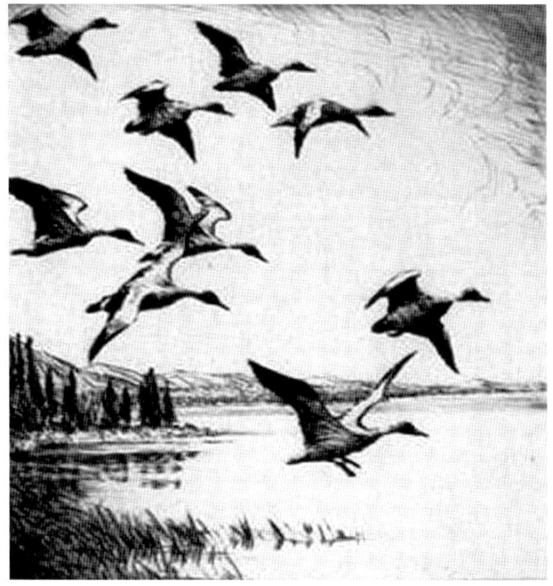

"Ducks on Jackson Lake"
Medium: Etching
Image: 5.375 inches high by 4.375 inches wide

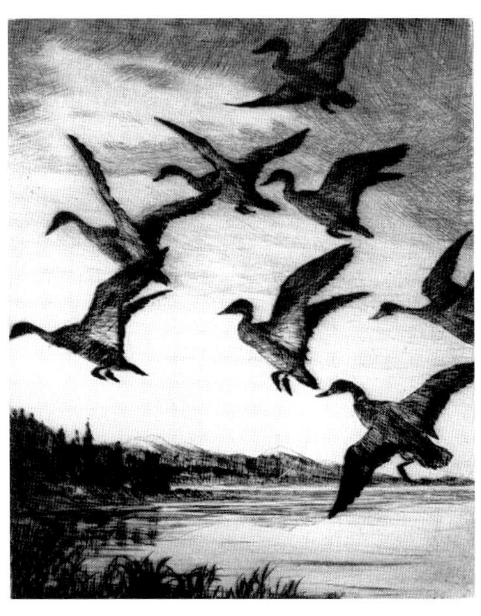

"Ducks Rising"
Medium: Etching
Image: 4.875 inches high by 3.875 inches wide

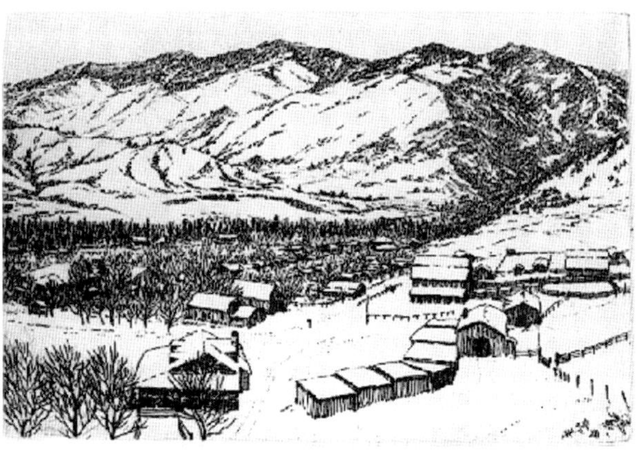

"Eaton's Ranch"
Medium: Photogravure
Image: 4.75 inches high by 6.75 inches wide

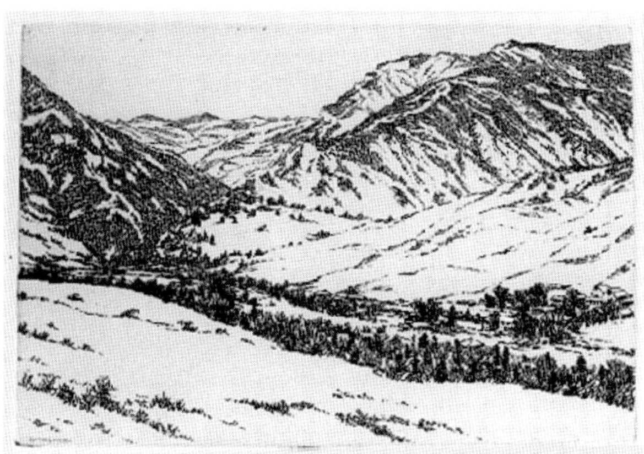

"Eaton's Ranch"
Medium: Photogravure
Image: 4.75 inches high by 6.75 inches wide

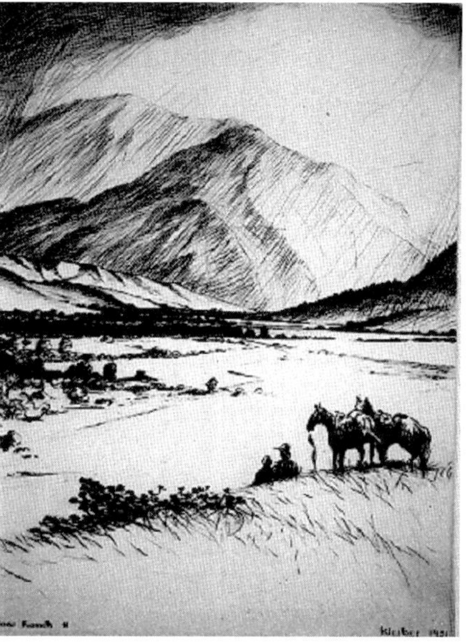

"Eaton's Ranch II"
Medium: Etching
Image: 7.875 inches high by 5.875 inches wide

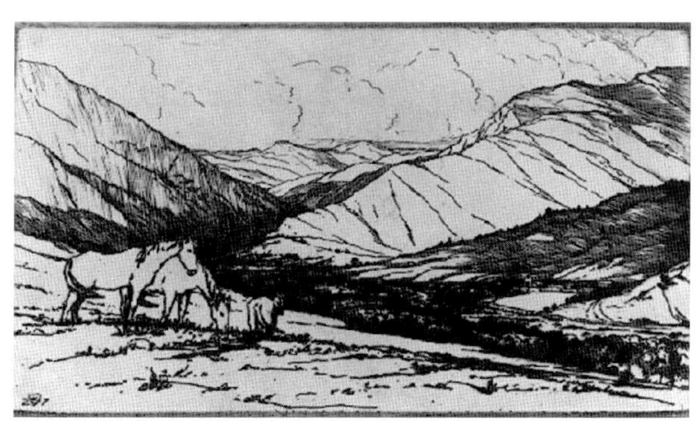

"Eaton's Ranch Wolf, Wyoming"
Medium: Etching
Image: 5.8125 inches high by 9.75 inches wide

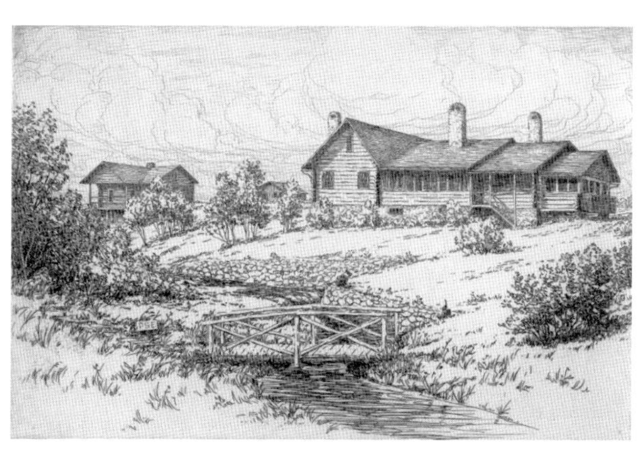

"Eddie Moore's House" (Banner)
Medium: Photogravure
Image: 7.875 inches high by 11.875 inches wide

Hans Kleiber

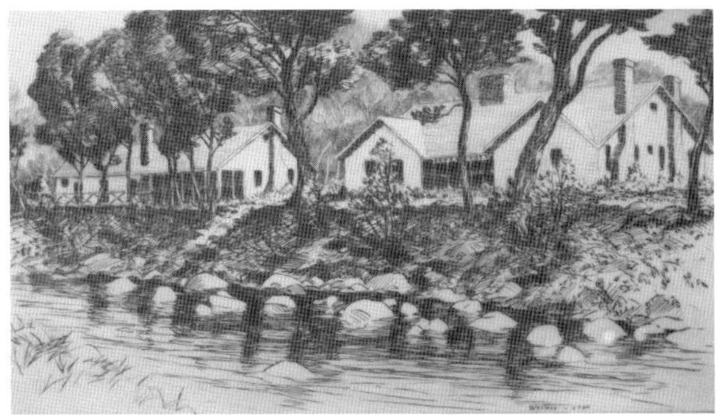

"Eddie Moore, Sr. House"
(Little Goose Dayton, Wyoming)
Medium: Etching
Image: 6.8125 inches high by 11.8125 inches wide

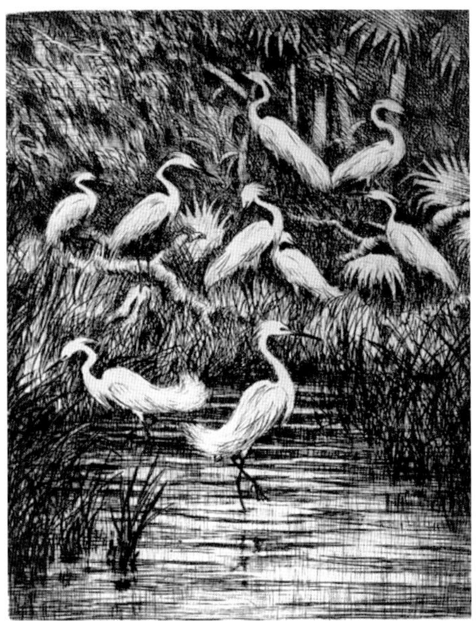

"Egrets"
Medium: Etching
Image: 7.875 inches high by 5.875 inches wide

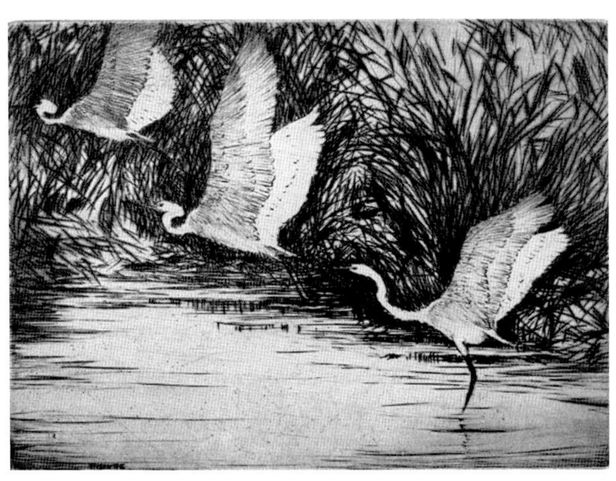

"Egrets"
Medium: Etching
Image: 5.125 inches high by 6.875 inches wide

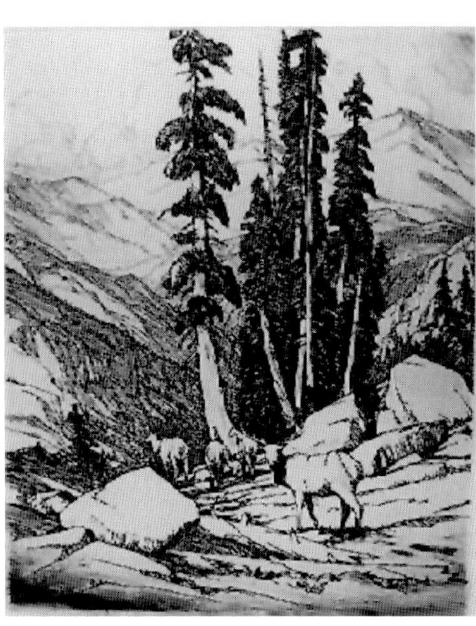

"Elk - Big Horns"
"Elk - Bighorns"
"Elk in Bighorns I"
Medium: Etching
Image: 6.75 inches high by 5.125 inches wide

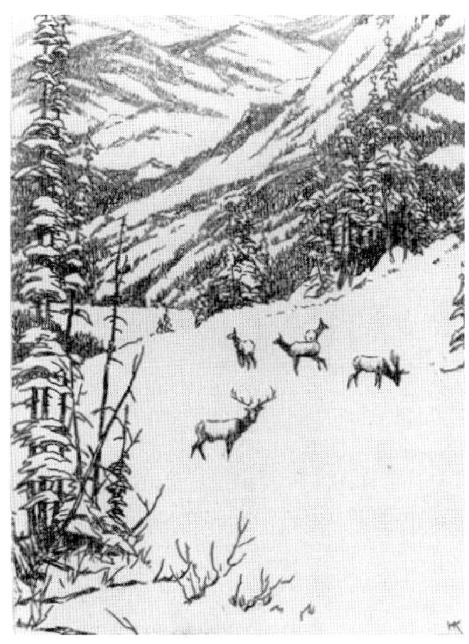

"Elk"
"Elk, Winter"
Medium: Photogravure
Image: 4.875 inches high by 3.5 inches high

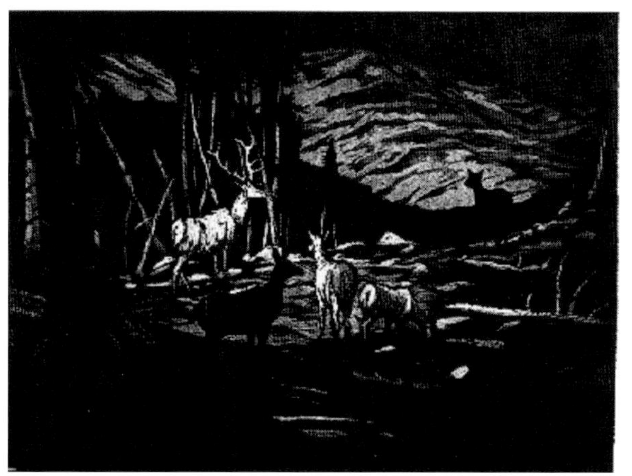

"Elk at Night"
Medium: Etching
Image: 7.75 inches high by 9.75 inches wide

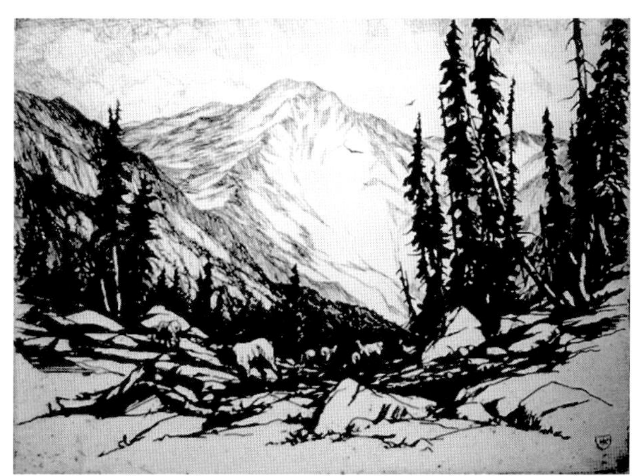

"Elk Bugling"
Medium: Etching, Photogravure
Image: 6.25 inches high by 8.25 inches wide

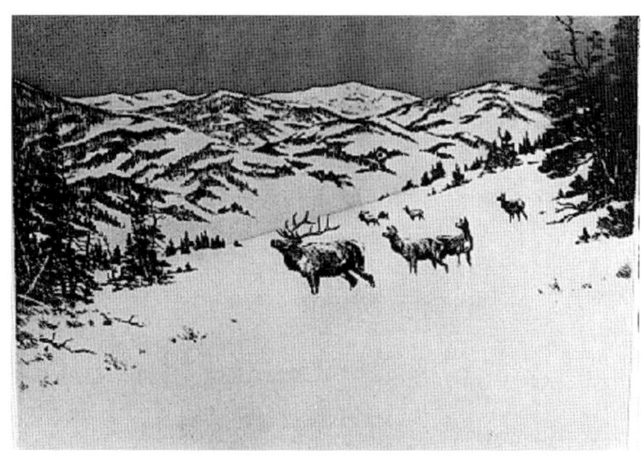

"Elk in the Bighorns"
"Elk in the Rockies"
Medium: Etching
Image: 9.75 inches high by 13.75 inches wide
Medium: Photogravure
Image: 5.75 inches high by 7.7875 inches wide

Hans Kleiber

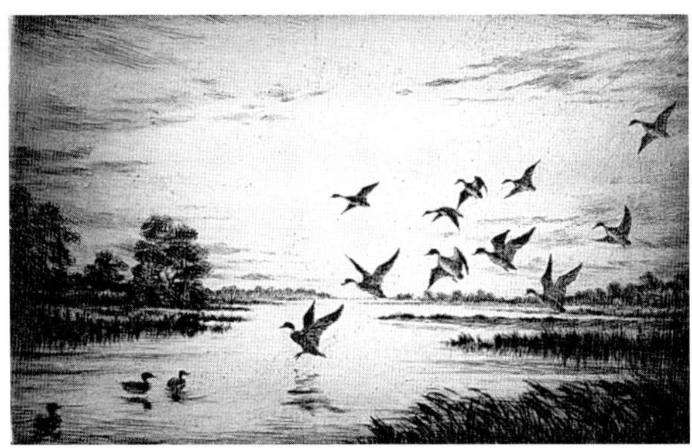

"Evening"
Medium: Etching
Image: 4.125 inches high by 6.375 inches wide

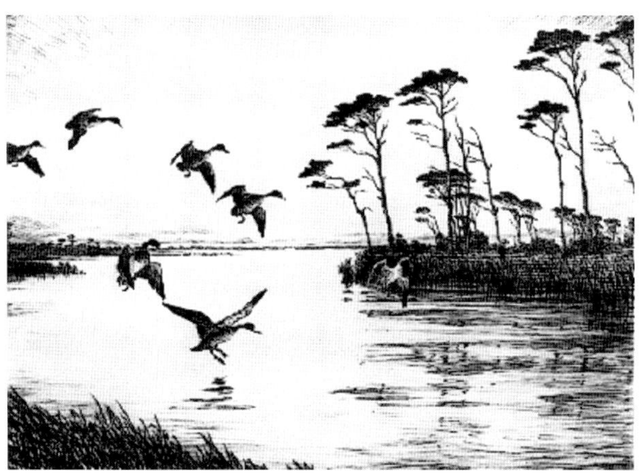

"Evening"
Medium: Etching
Associated American Artists
Image: 8.25 inches high by 10.75 inches wide

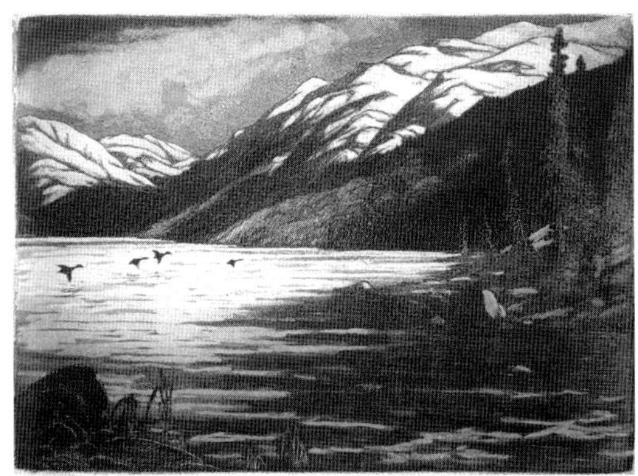

"Evening at Lake Solitude, Wyoming"
"Lake Solitude - Big Horns"
"Solitude"
Medium: Etching
Image: 5.75 inches high by 7.8125 inches wide

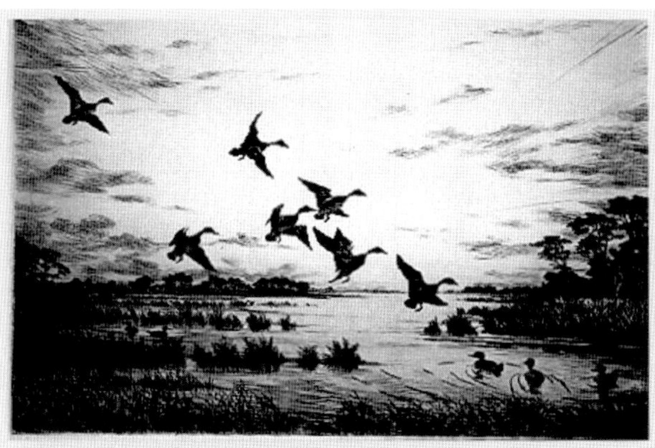

"Evening on the Marshes"
Medium: Etching
Image: 8.125 inches high by 11.75 inches wide

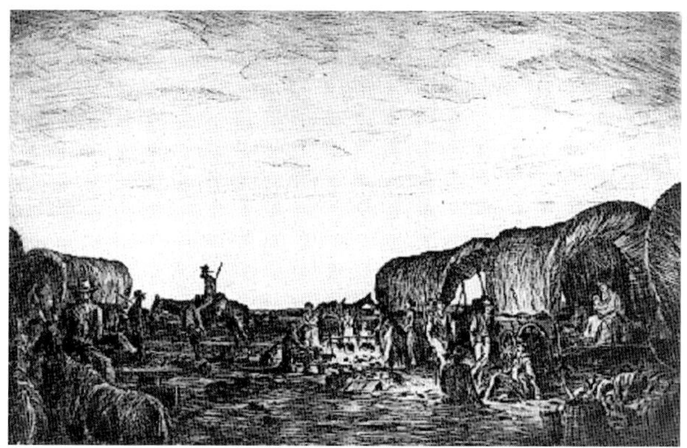

"Evening on the Trail"
Medium: Etching
Image: 6.75 inches high by 9.75 inches wide

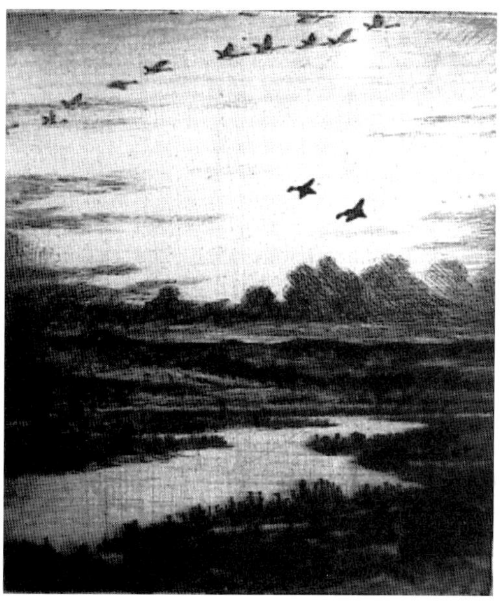

"Evening on the Yellowstone"
"On the Yellowstone"
Second State of
"Evening on the Yellowstone"
a.k.a. "On the Yellowstone"
Medium: Etching
Image: 4.875 inches high by 4.125 inches wide

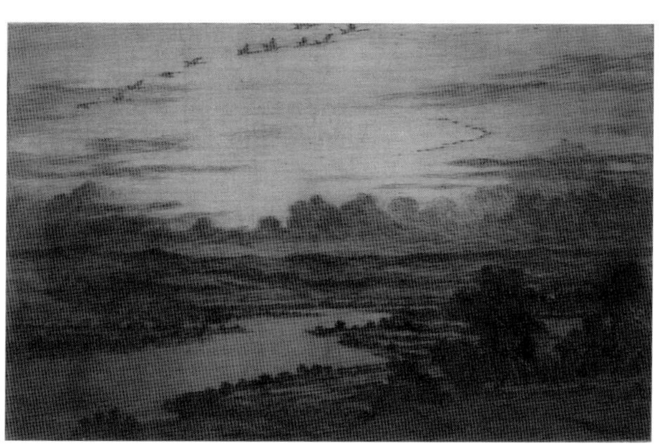

"Evening on the Yellowstone"
"On the Yellowstone"
Medium: Etching
Image: 4.9375 inches high by 7.4375 inches wide

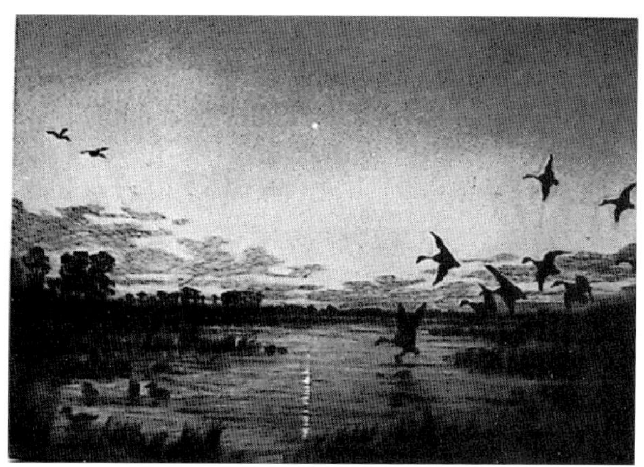

"Evening Star"
Medium: Etching
Image: 8.25 inches high by 11.75 inches wide
Medium: Photogravure
Image: 5.125 inches high by 7.125 inches wide

Hans Kleiber

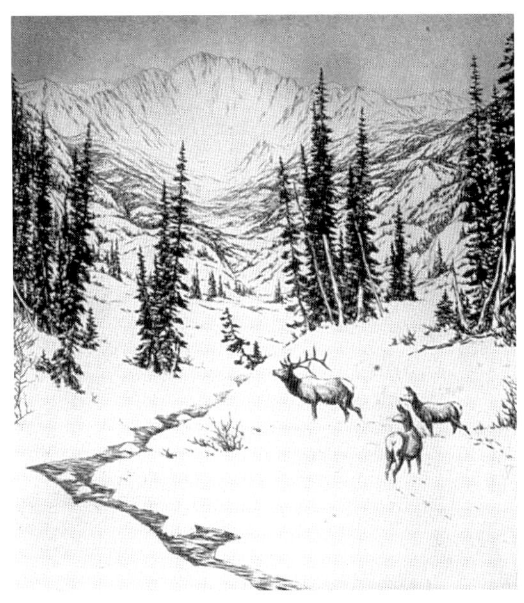

"Fall in the Rockies"
Medium: Etching
Associated American Artists
Image: 10.75 inches high by 9.25 inches wide

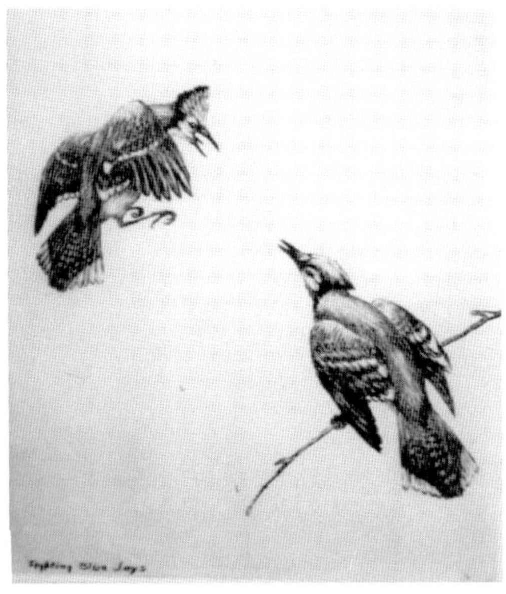

"Fighting Blue Jays"
Medium: Etching
Image: 5.75 inches high by 4.75 inches wide

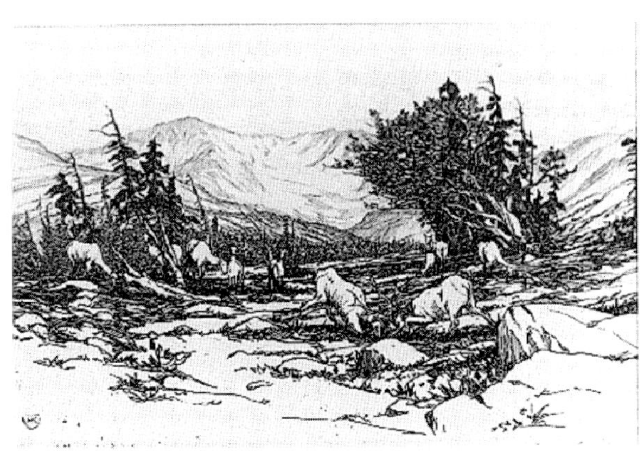

"Fighting It Out"
Medium: Photogravure
Image: 5.75 inches high by 9.75 inches wide

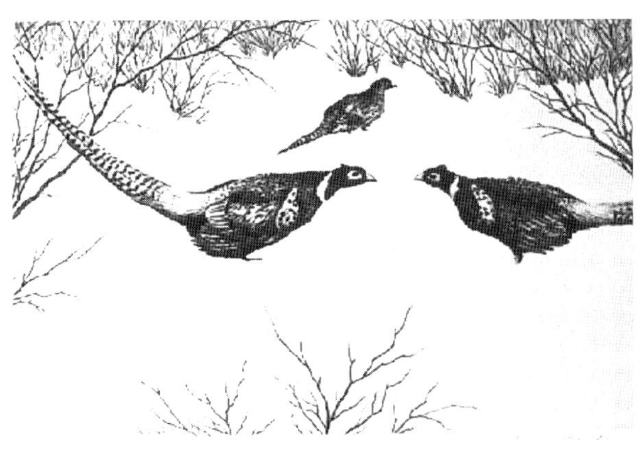

"Fighting Pheasants"
Medium: Etching
Associated American Artists
Image: 8.25 inches high by 11.75 inches wide

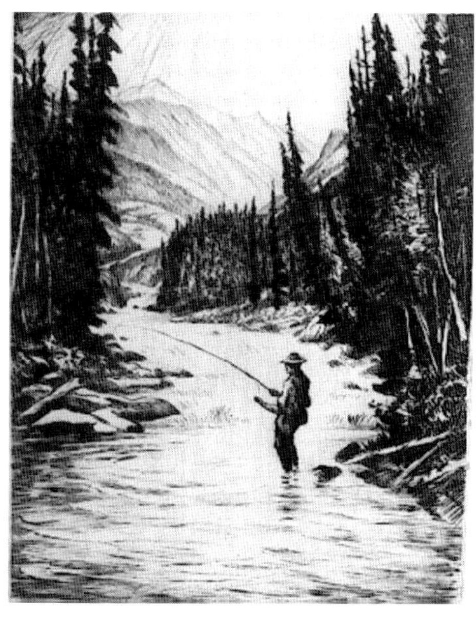

"Fishing in Piney"
"Fishing on Piney"
"Fishing on Piney, Bighorn"
"Fishing on Upper Piney Creek"
Medium: Etching
Image: 5.375 inches high by 3.875 inches wide

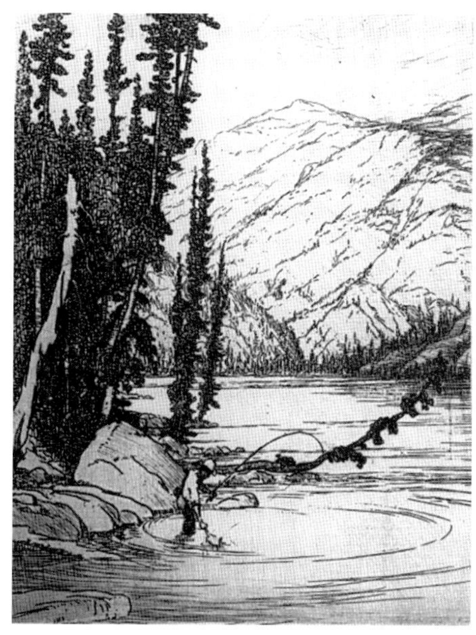

"Fishing in the Bighorns"
Medium: Photogravure
Image: 5.875 inches high by 4.375 inches wide

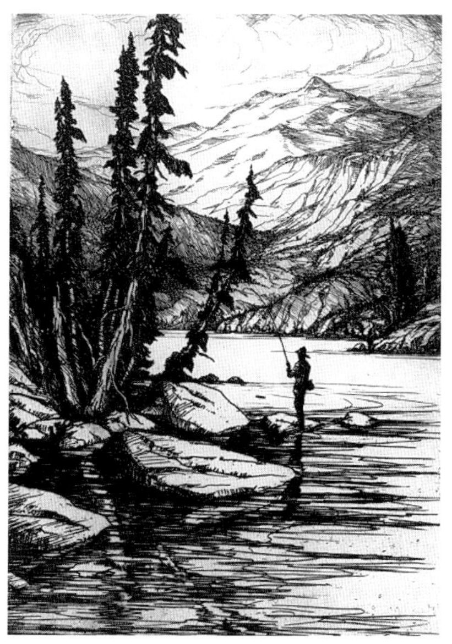

"Fishing in the Big Horns, Wyo."
Medium: Etching
Image: 9.1875 inches high by 6.25 inches wide

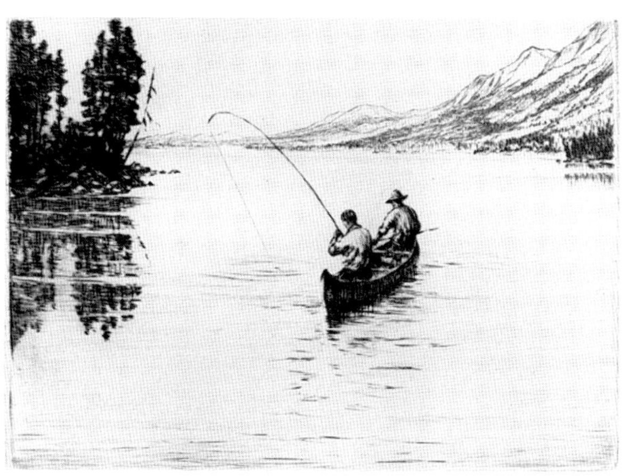

"Fishing on Jackson Lake"
Medium: Etching, Photogravure
Image: 4.375 inches high by 5.8125 inches wide

Hans Kleiber

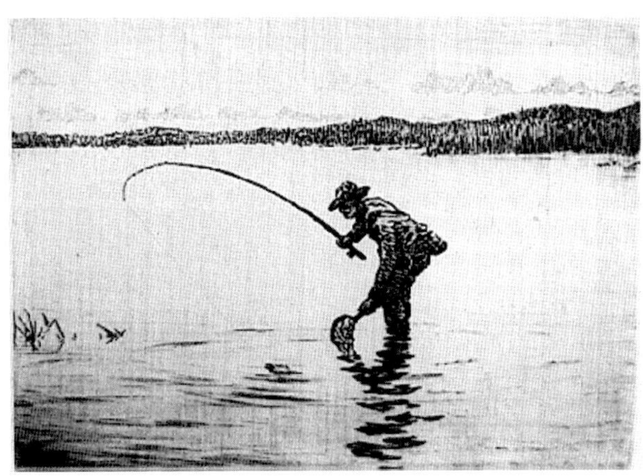

"Fishing on Jackson Lake, Wyoming"
"Landing One"
Medium: Etching, Photogravure
Image: 4.75 inches high by 5.875 inches wide

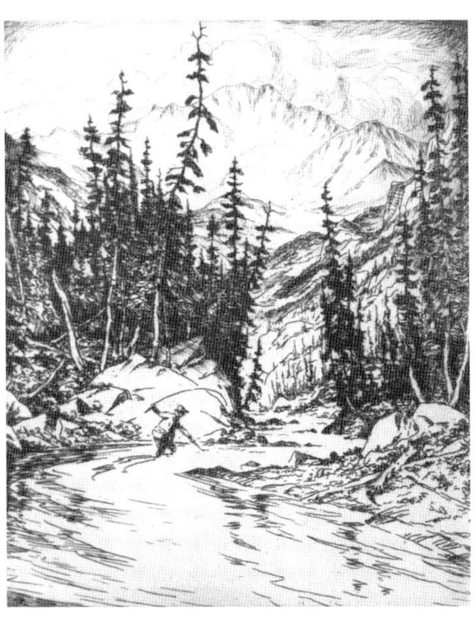

"Fishing on Paint Rock"
Medium: Photogravure
Image: 4.875 inches high by 3.75 inches wide

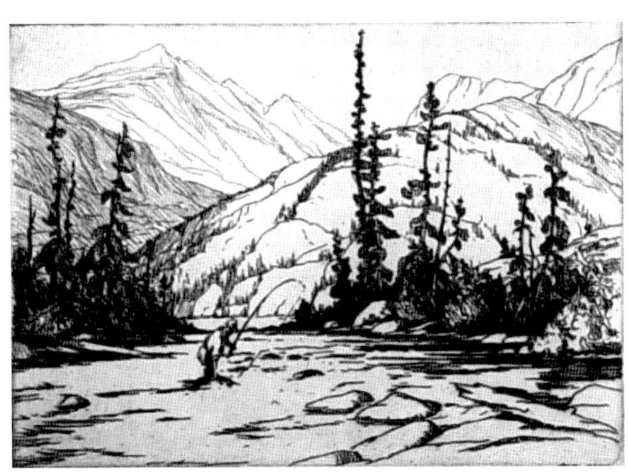

"Fishing on Piney"
"Fishing on Piney, Wyoming"
Medium: Photogravure
Image: 5.25 inches high by 7.25 inches wide

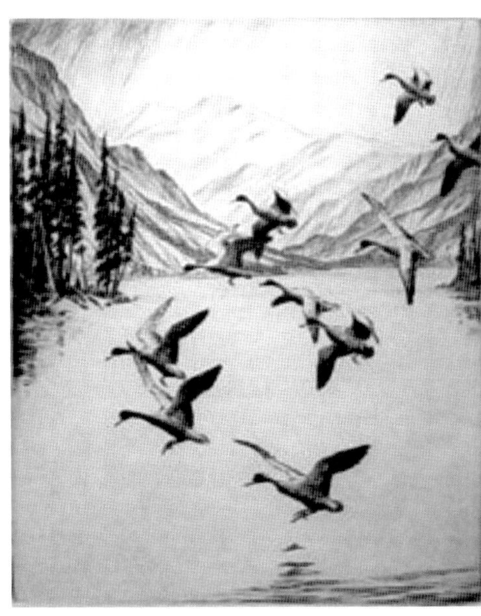

"Flight of Ducks, Lake Solitude"
"Summer Guests"
Medium: Etching
Image: 8.25 inches high by 6.5 inches wide

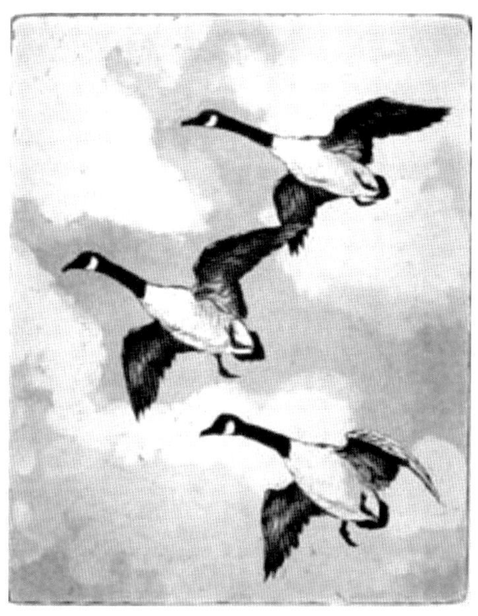

"Flying Against the Wind"
Medium: Etching
Image: 8.875 inches high by 6.8125 inches wide

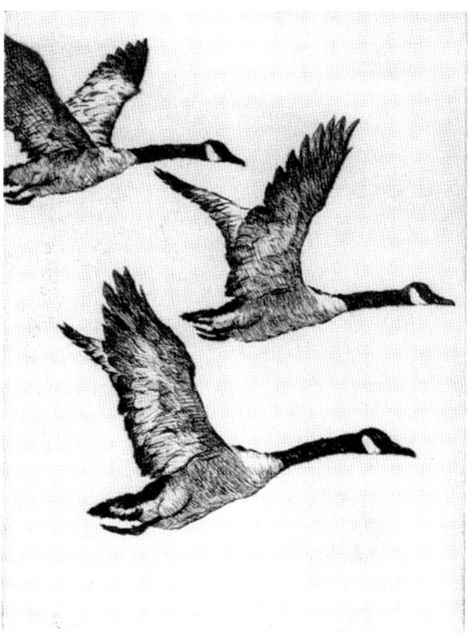

"Flying Geese"
Medium: Etching
Image: 9.3125 inches high by 6.75 inches wide

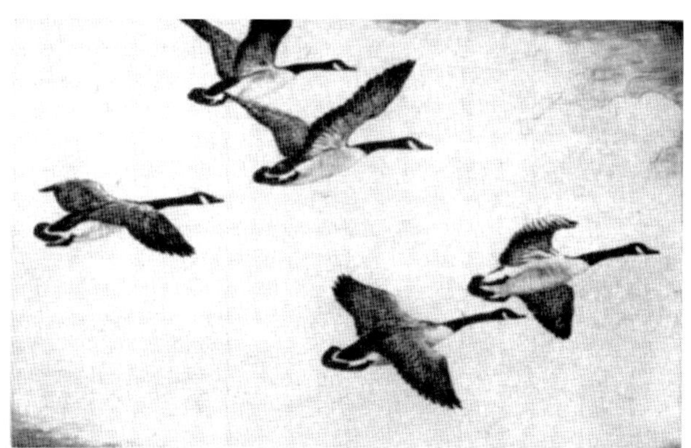

"Flying Honkers"
Medium: Etching
Image: 7.75 inches high by 11.75 inches wide

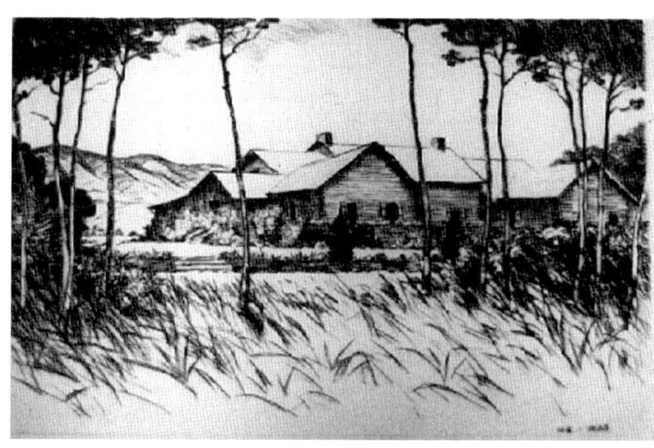

"Folly Ranch, Bighorn, Wyo."
(Main lodge at the Hidden Valley Ranch or the lower Folley Ranch lodges)
Medium: Etching
Image: 3.875 inches high by 5.875 inches wide

Hans Kleiber

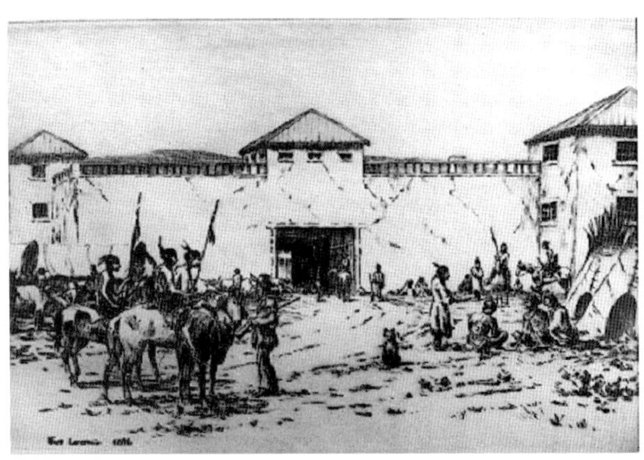

"Fort Laramie 1846"
Medium: Etching
Image: 6.75 inches high by 10.25 inches wide

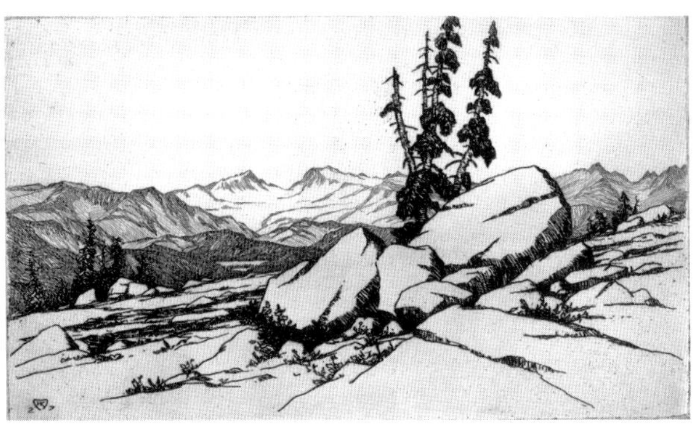

"Freemont Peak"
First State
Medium: Etching, Photogravure
Image: 5.25 inches high by 8.75 inches wide

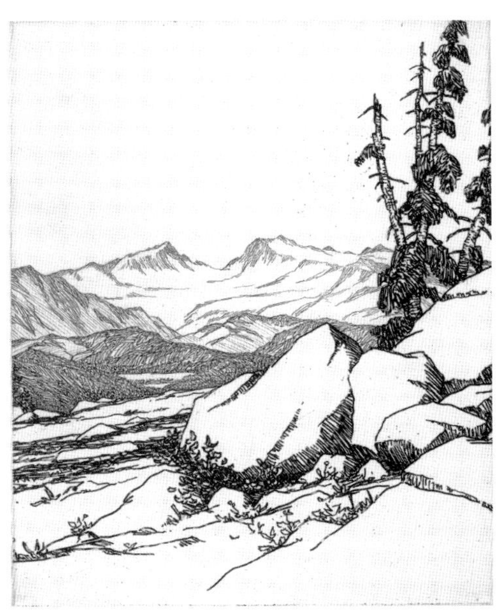

"Freemont Peak"
Second State of "Freemont Peak"
Medium: Photogravure
Image: 5.375 inches high by 4.375 inches wide

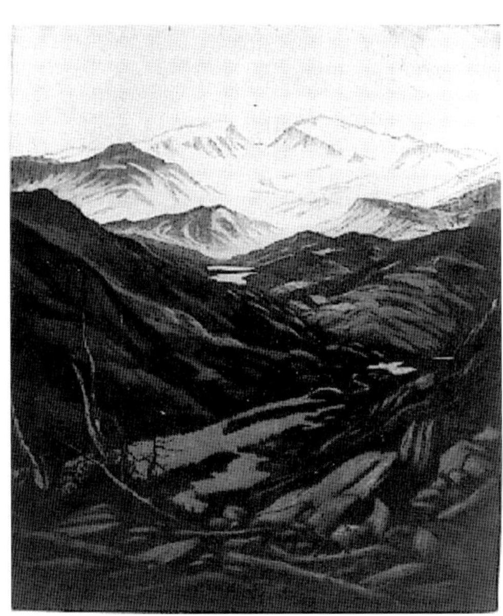

"Freemont Peak - Wind River"
Medium: Etching
Image: 9.625 inches high by 7.875 inches wide

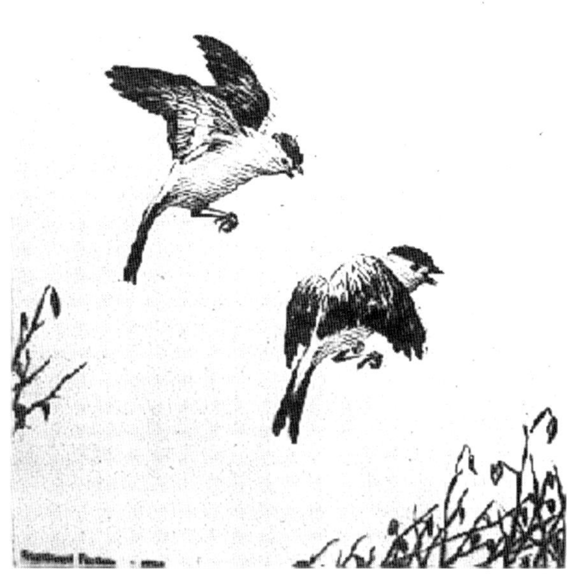

"Frightened Finches"
Medium: Etching
Image: 5.75 inches high by 5 inches wide

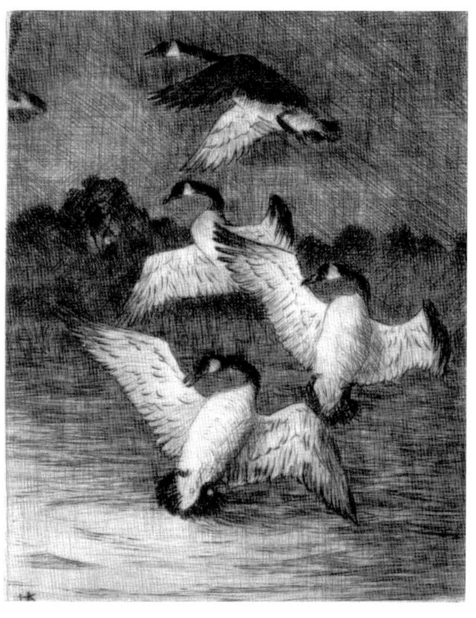

"Frightened Geese"
Medium: Etching
Image: 4.5 inches high by 3.5 inches wide

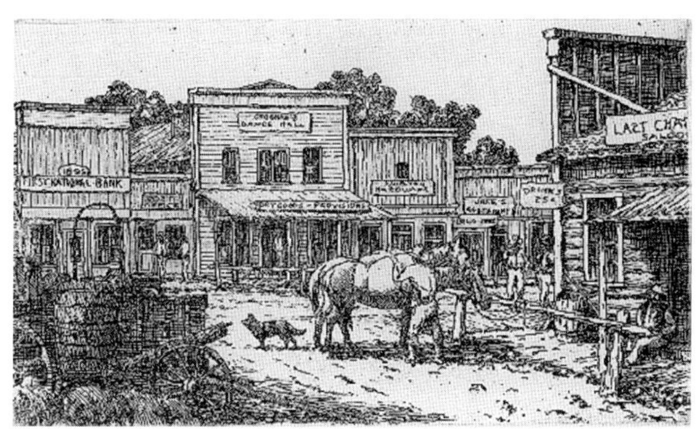

"Frontier Days"
Medium: Photogravure
Image: 3.75 inches high by 6.25 inches wide

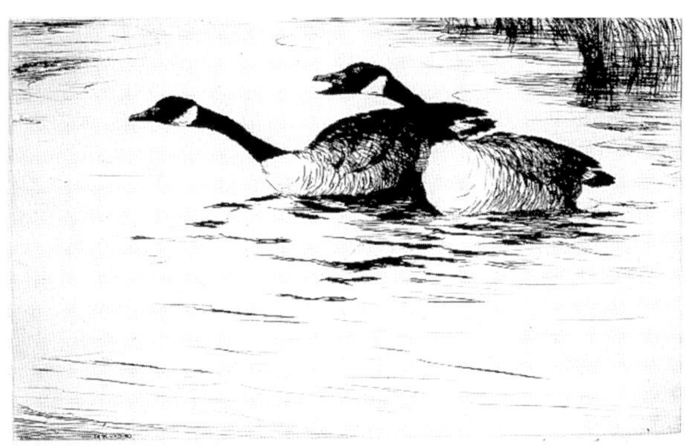

"Geese - Mating Time"
Medium: Etching
Image: 6.875 inches high by 10.875 inches wide

Hans Kleiber

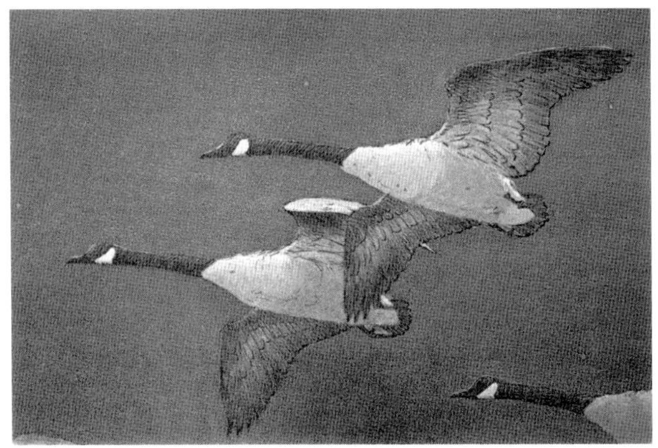

"Flying Geese"
"Geese - Night"
"Two Geese"
"Two Geese - Night"
Second State of
"Honkers Flying - Night"
Medium: Etching
Image: 3.875 inches high by 5.5 inches wide

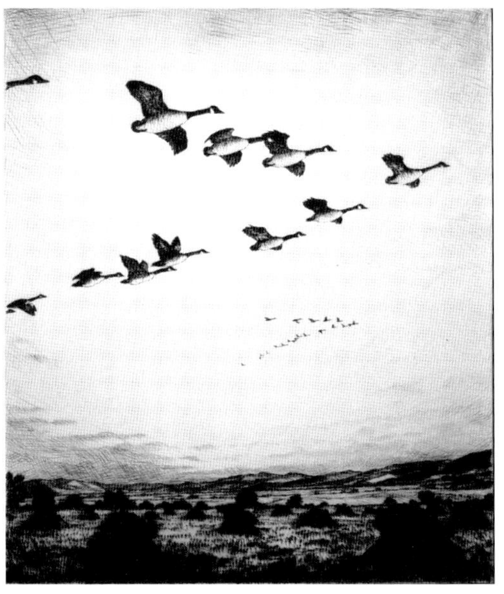

"Geese Crossing Wyoming"
Medium: Etching
Image: 11.75 inches high by 9.75 inches wide

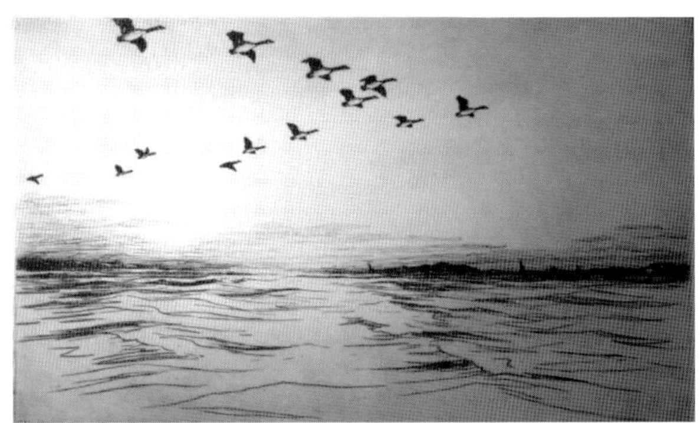

"Geese on the Pacific"
Medium: Photogravure
Image: 7.8125 inches high by 12.75 inches wide

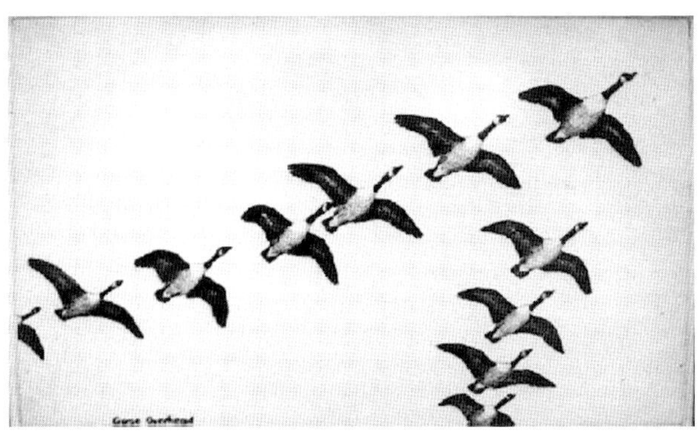

"Geese Overhead"
Medium: Etching
Image: 4.875 inches high by 7.875 inches wide

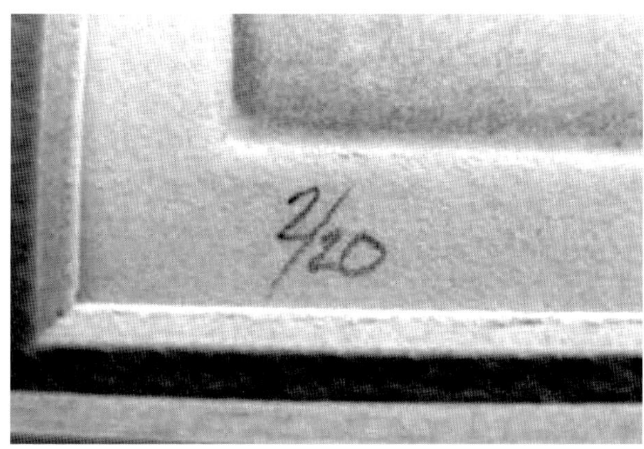

This is an example of a “dealer’ numbering the image
“Geese Overhead” by Hans Kleiber

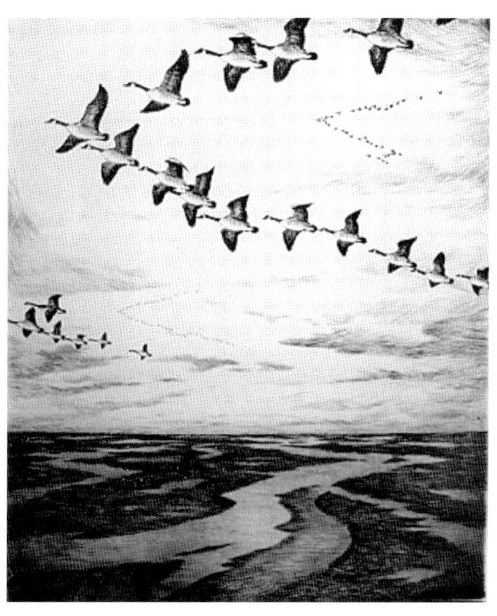

“Geese Over the Marshes”
Medium: Etching
Associated American Artists
Image: 11.75 inches high by 9.5 inches wide

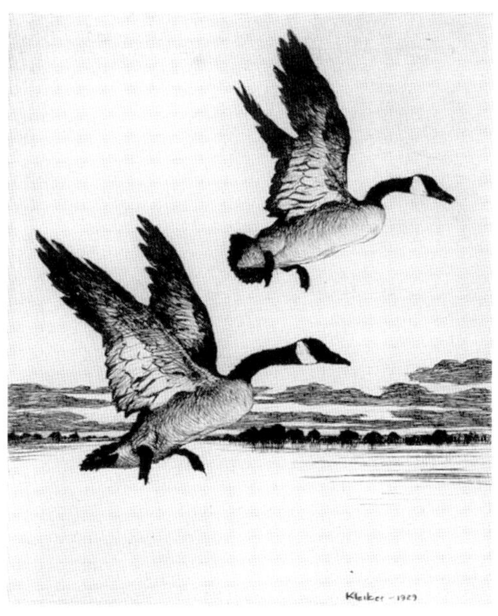

“Geese Rising”
Medium: Etching
Image: 9.8125 inches high by 7.875 inches wide

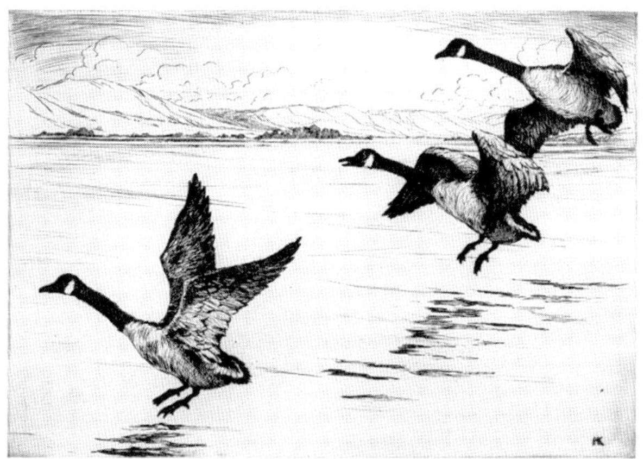

“Geese Settling”
Medium: Etching
Image: 8.8125 inches high by 12.3125 inches wide

Hans Kleiber

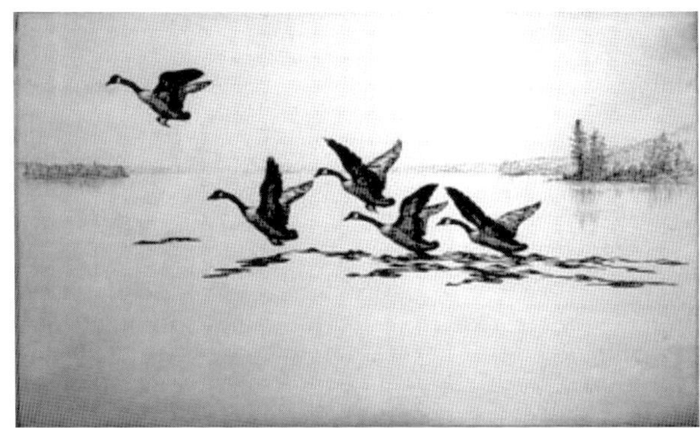

"Geese Taking the Air"
"Geese Taking Wing"
Medium: Photogravure
Image: 7.25 inches high by 11.875 inches wide

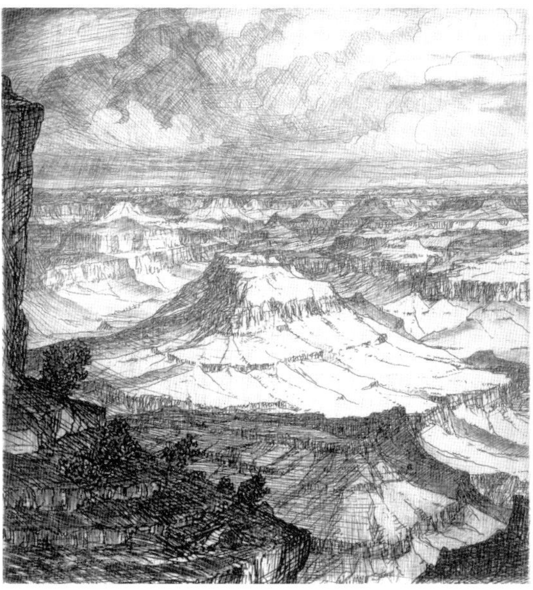

"Grand Canyon"
"The Grand Canyon"
Medium: Photogravure
Image: 5.375 inches high by 4.75 inches wide

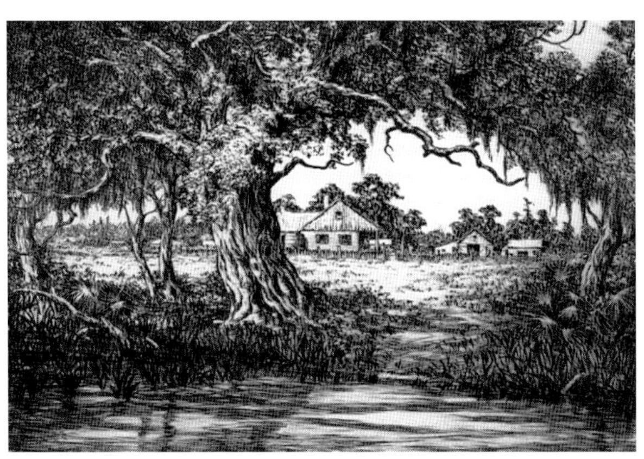

"Grand Chenier, La."
Medium: Etching
Image: 6.875 inches high by 9.875 inches wide

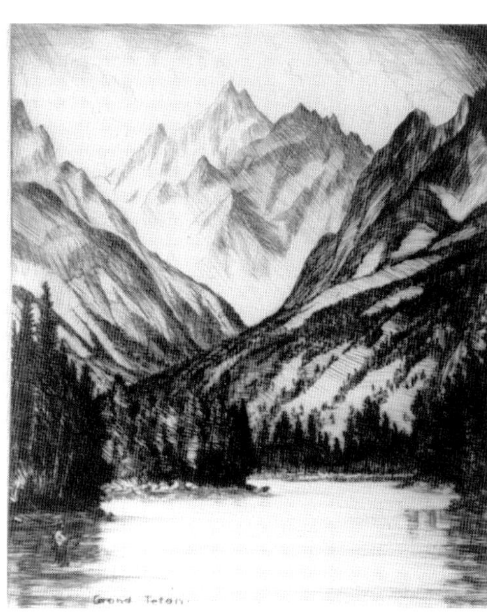

"Grand Teton"
Second State of "The Grand Teton"
Medium: Etching
Image: 5.125 inches high by 4.125 inches wide

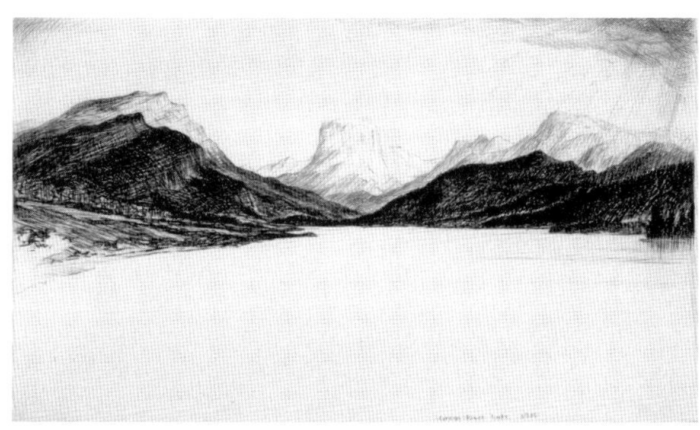

"Green River Lake"
Medium: Etching
Image: 5.875 inches high by 9.875 inches wide

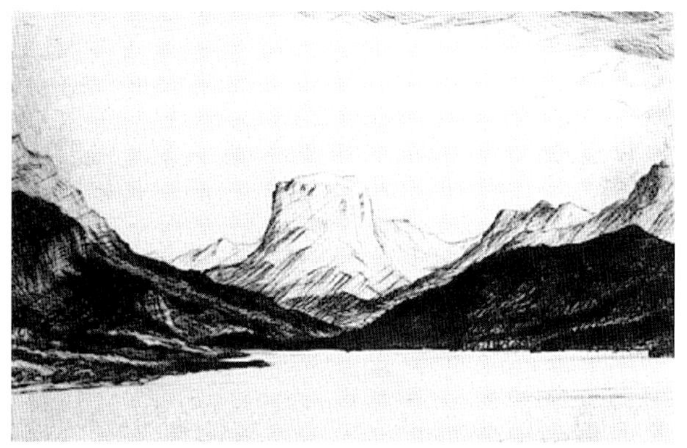

"Green River Lake"
Second State of "Green River Lake"
Medium: Etching
Image: 3.75 inches high by 5.75 inches wide

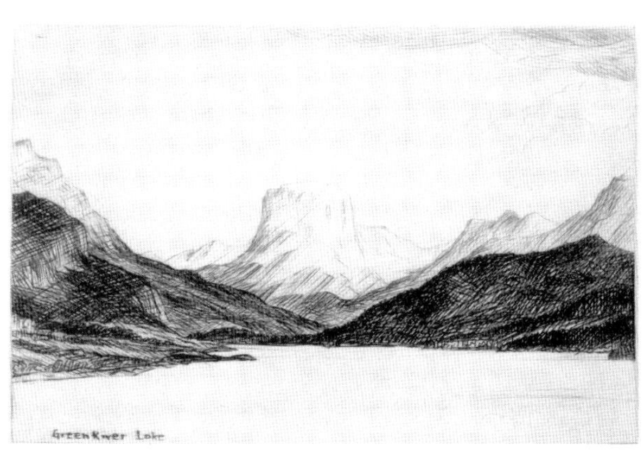

"Green River Lake"
Third State of "Green River Lake"
Medium: Etching
Image: 3.875 inches high by 5.875 inches wide

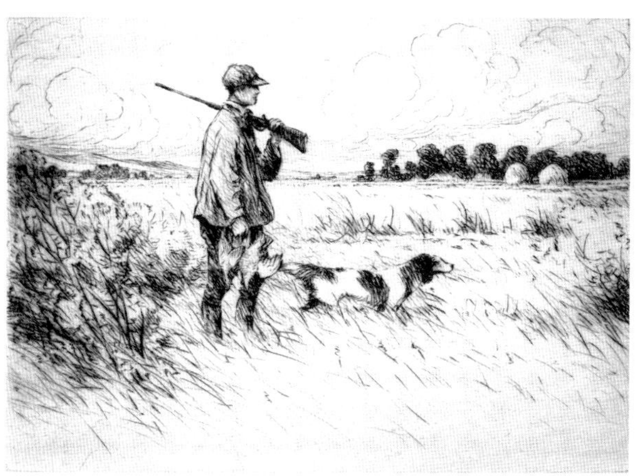

"Grouse Hunter"
"The Grouse Hunter"
Medium: Etching
Image: 4.5 inches high by 6.25 inches wide

Hans Kleiber

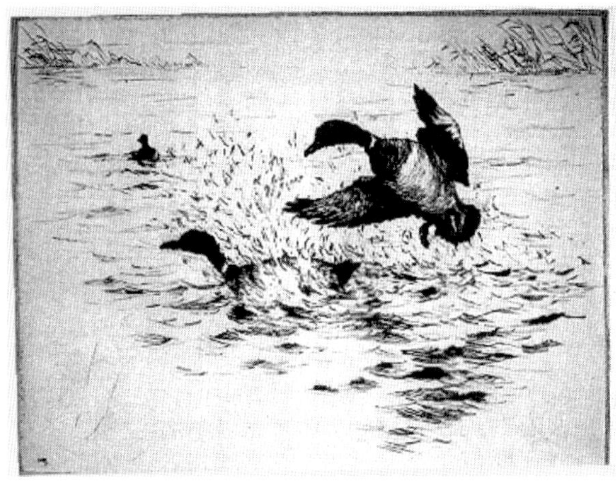

"Hitting the Water"
Medium: Etching
Image: 5.375 inches high by 6.875 inches wide

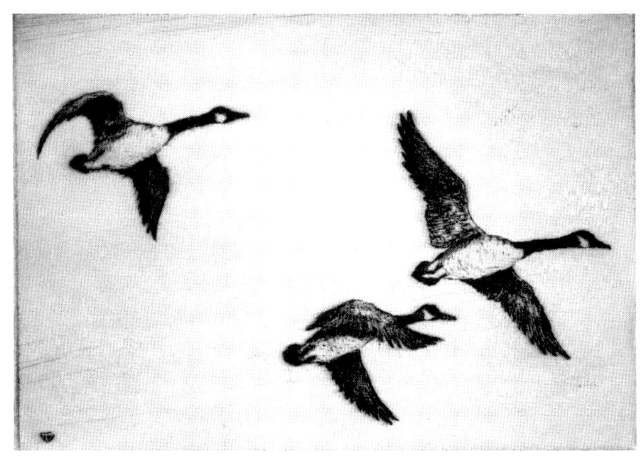

"Honkers in Flight"
Medium: Etching
Image: 4.875 inches high by 6.875 inches wide

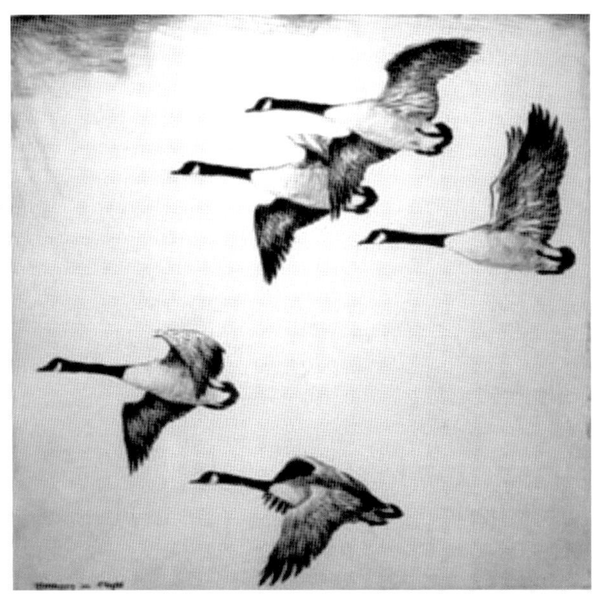

"Honkers in Flight"
Medium: Etching
Image: 8.625 inches high by 8.75 inches wide

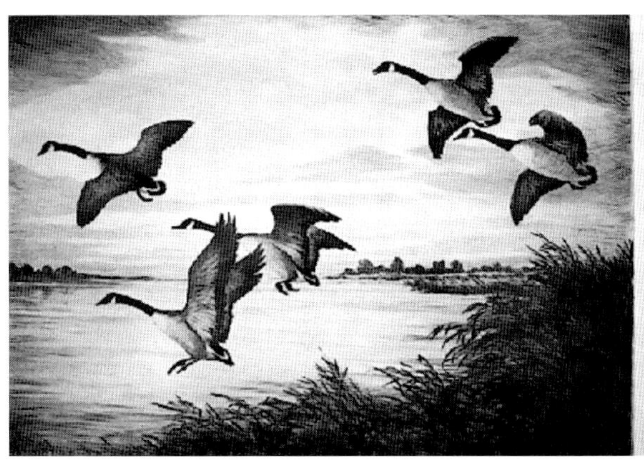

"Honkers Settling"
Medium: Etching
Image: 9.75 inches high by 13.75 inches wide

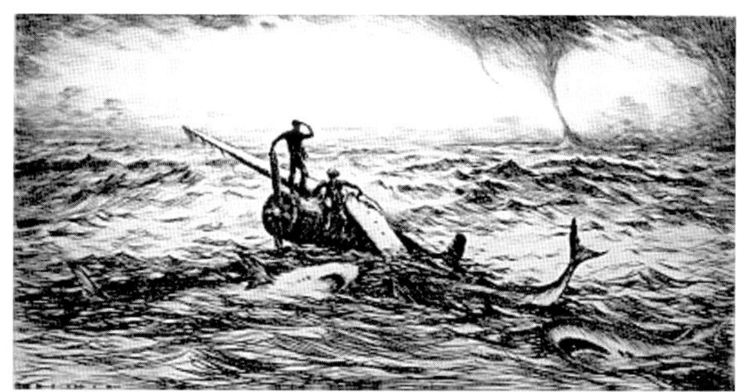

"Howland Island"
"Near Howland Island 1937"
First State
Medium: Etching
Image: 6.75 inches high by 12.75 inches wide

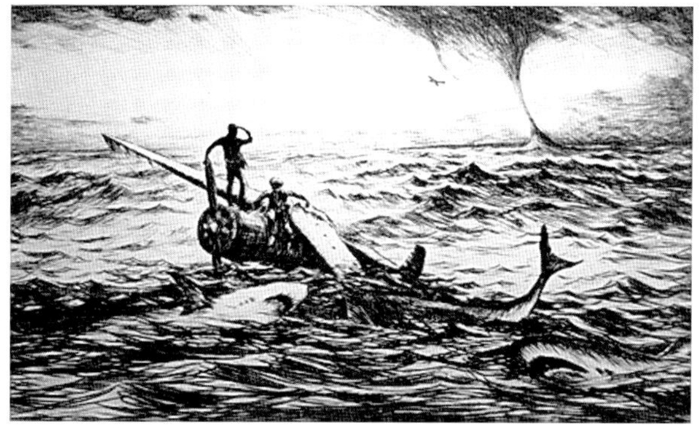

"In the South Pacific"
Second State of
"Near Howland Island 1937"
Medium: Etching
Image: 6.75 inches high by 11.75 inches wide

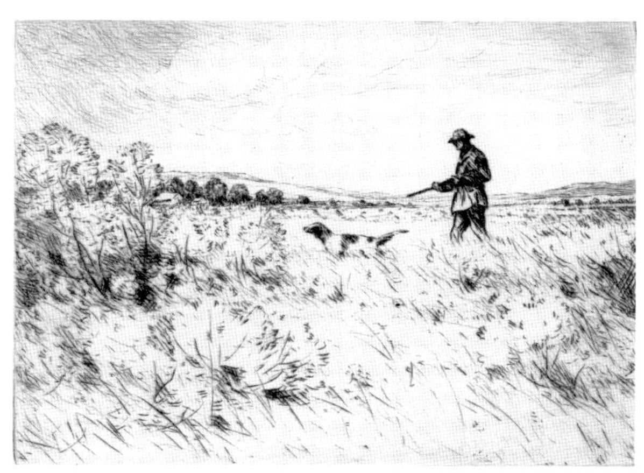

"Hunting Pheasants"
"Looking for Pheasants"
Medium: Etching
Image: 4.75 inches high by 6.5 inches wide

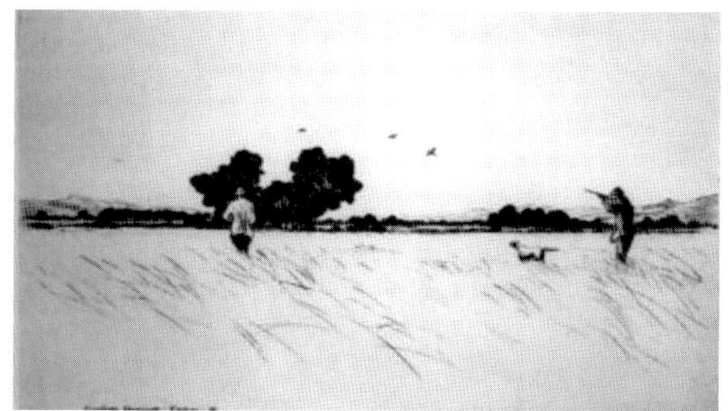

"Hunting Pheasants"
Medium: Etching
Image: 6.75 inches high by 11.75 inches wide

Hans Kleiber

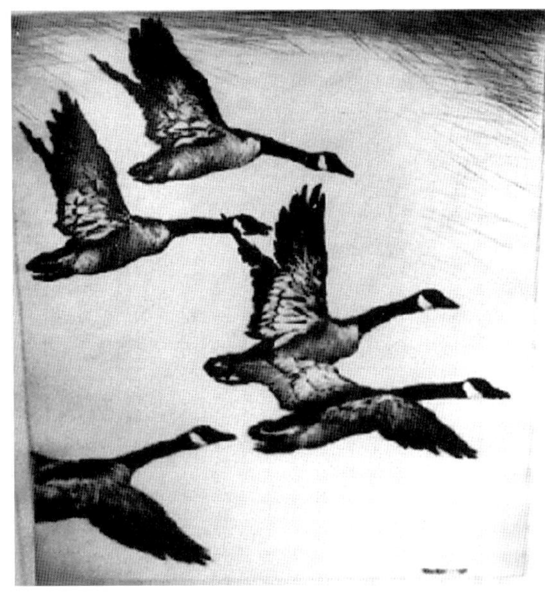

"In Full Flight"
Medium: Etching
Image: 12.75 inches high by 10.5 inches wide
Medium: Photogravure
Image: 6.875 inches high by 5.875 inches wide

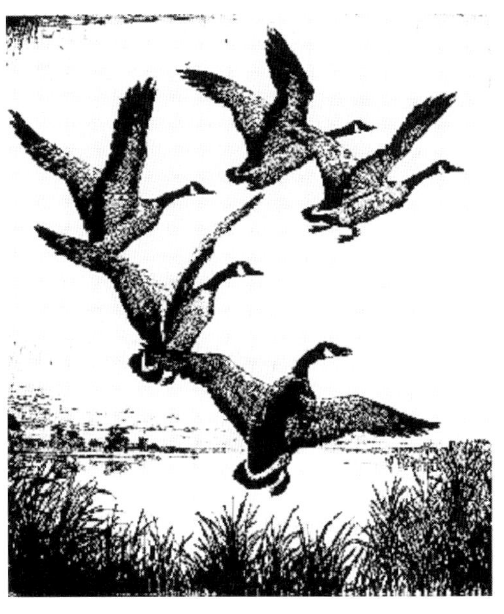

"In Full Flight"
Medium: Etching
Image: 13.75 inches high by 11.75 inches wide

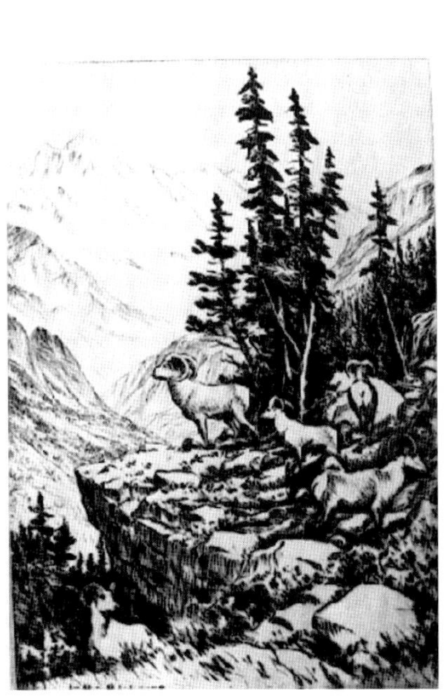

"In the Bighorns"
Medium: Etching
Image: 6.375 inches high by 4.25 inches wide

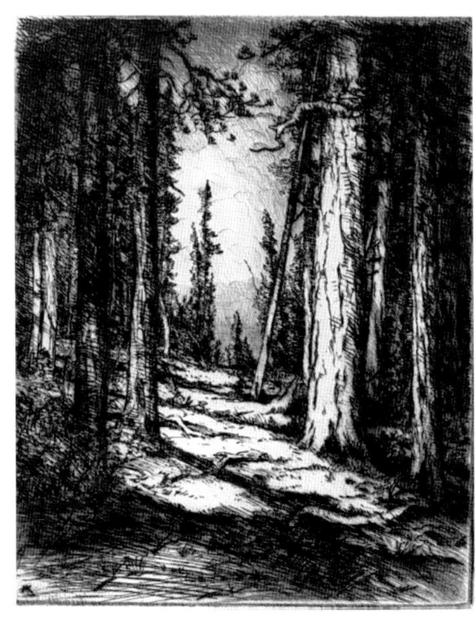

"In the Forest"
Medium: Etching
Image: 8.875 inches high by 6.875 inches wide

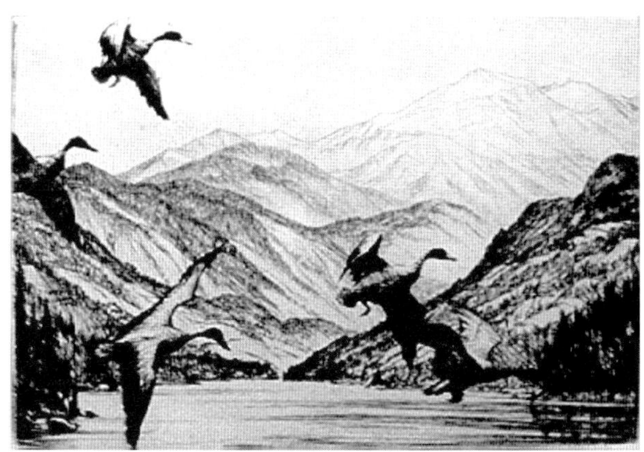

"In the Mountains"
Medium: Etching
Image: 3.4375 inches high by 4.875 inches wide

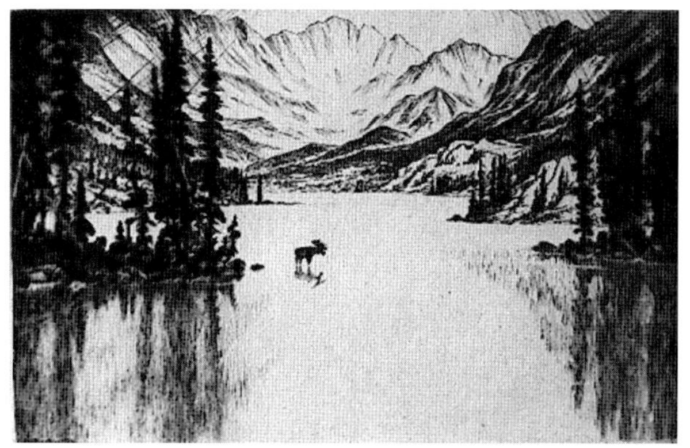

"In the Rockies"
Medium: Photogravure
Image: 3.625 inches high by 5.875 inches wide

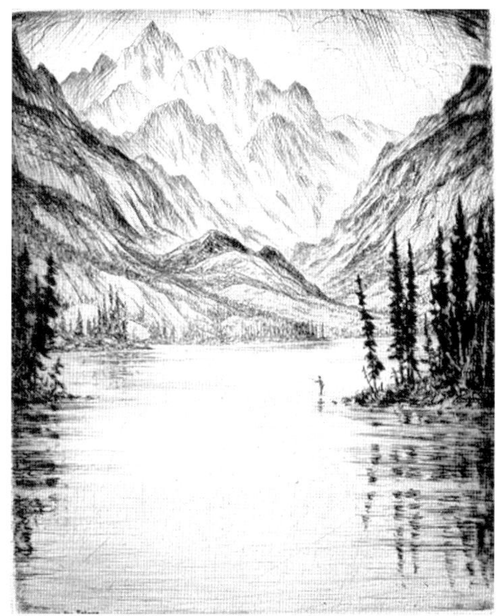

"In the Tetons"
Medium: Etching
Image: 4.75 inches high by 3.875 inches wide

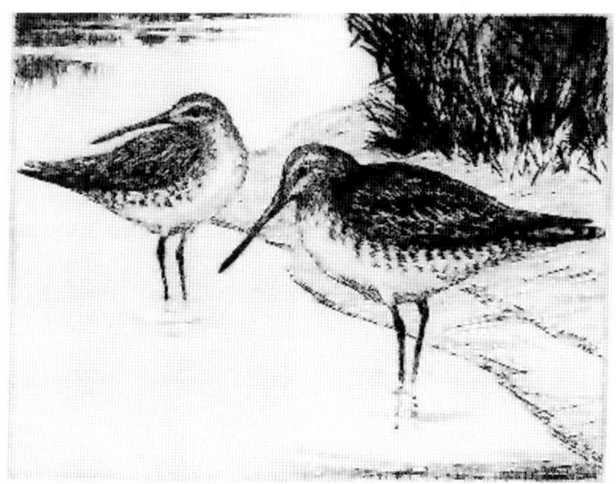

"Jack Snipes"
Medium: Etching
Image: 3.875 inches high by 4.875 inches wide

Hans Kleiber

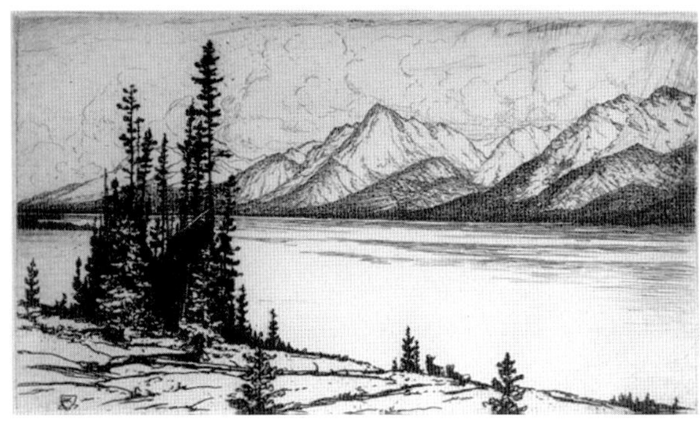

"Jackson Lake and the Tetons"
Medium: Etching, Photogravure
Image: 5.25 inches high by 8.75 inches wide

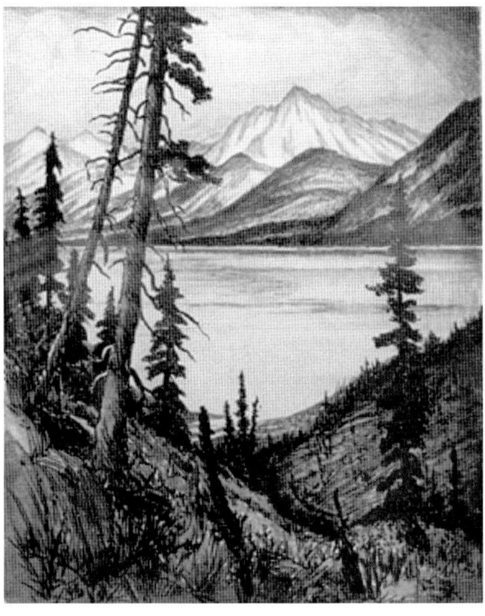

"Jackson Lake and Tetons I"
Medium: Etching
Image: 6.75 inches high by 5.25 inches wide

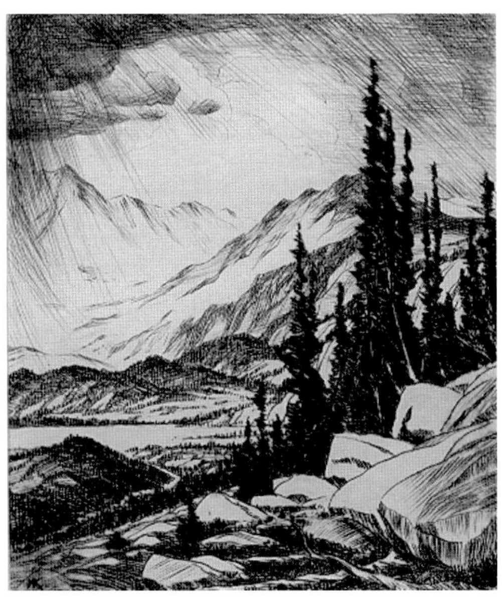

"Kearney Lake"
"Piney"
"Piney - Kearney Lake"
Medium: Etching
Image: 4.25 inches high by 3.5 inches wide

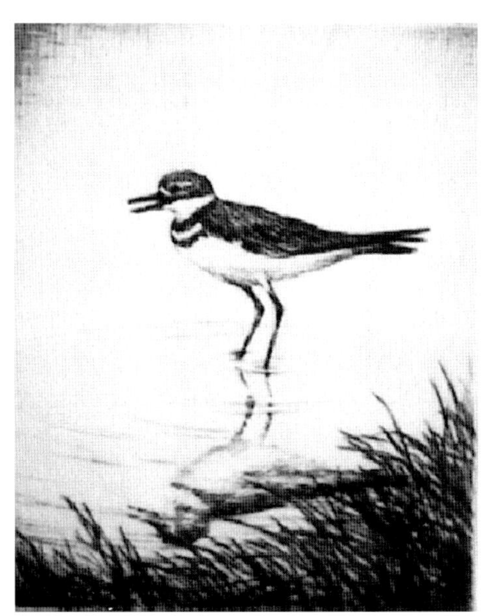

"Killdeer"
Medium: Etching
Image: 4.375 inches high by 3.375 inches wide

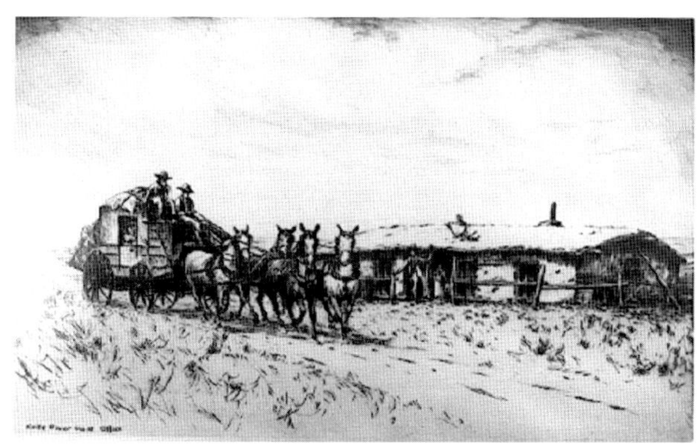

"Knife River Post Office"
Medium: Etching
Image: 6.75 inches high by 10.75 inches wide

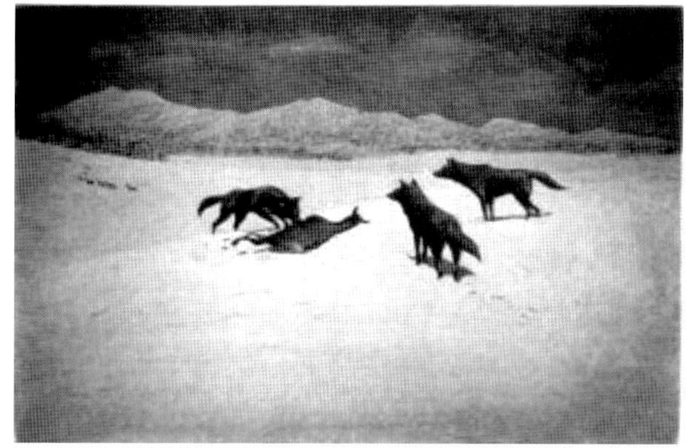

"Killers"
Medium: Photogravure
Image: 6.25 inches high by 9.375 inches wide

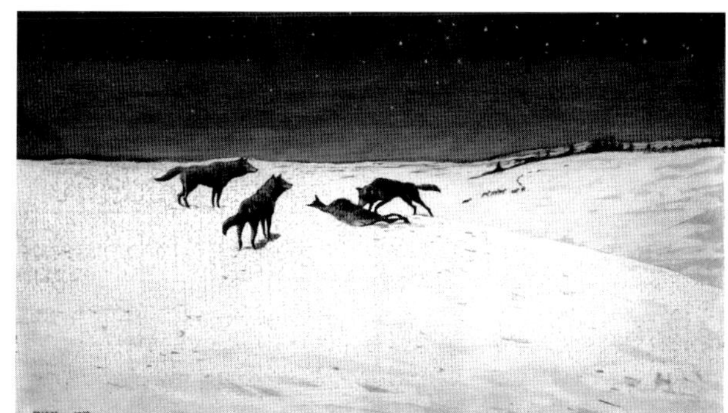

"Killers"
Medium: Hand Colored Etching
Image: 7.875 inches high by 13.25 inches wide

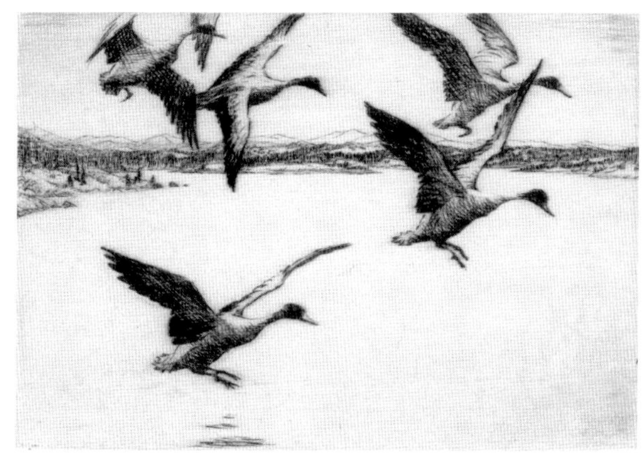

"Lake Adelaide"
"Lake Adelaide - Pintails"
Medium: Etching
Image: 3.375 inches high by 4.75 inches wide

Hans Kleiber

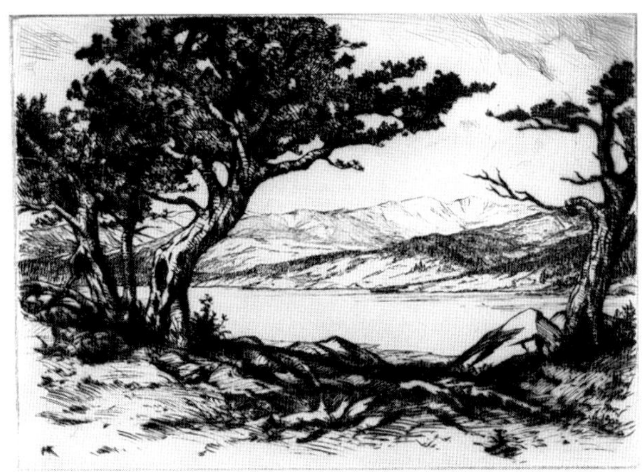

"Lake Adelaide, Wyoming"
First State
Medium: Etching
Image: 6.875 inches high by 9.375 inches wide

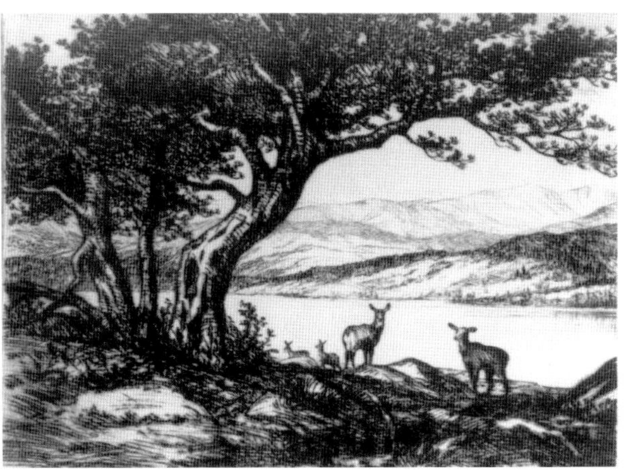

"Lake Adelaide"
"Lake Adelaide - Bighorns"
Second State of "Lake Adelaide, Wyoming"
Medium: Etching
Image: 5.375 inches high by 7.125 inches wide

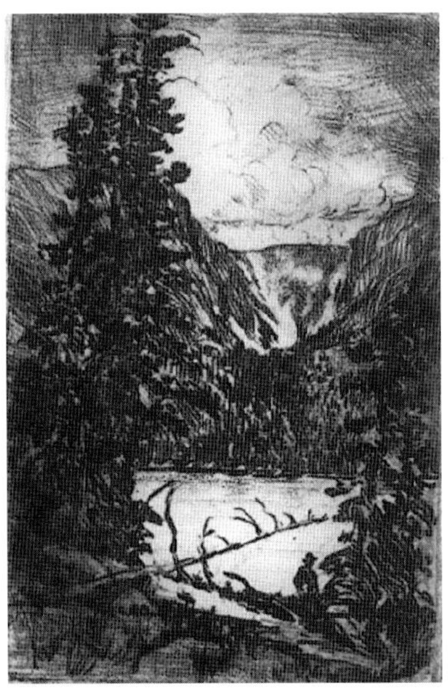

"Lake Geneva - Bighorns"
Medium: Etching
Image: 6.875 inches high by 4.375 inches wide

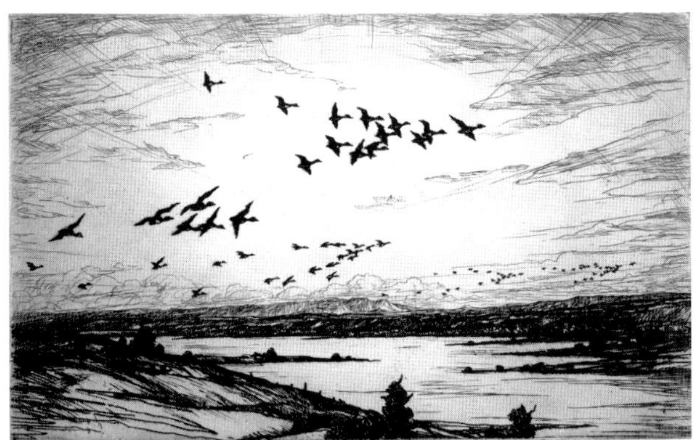

"Lake DeSmet"
Medium: Photogravure
Image: 6.375 inches high by 10 inches wide

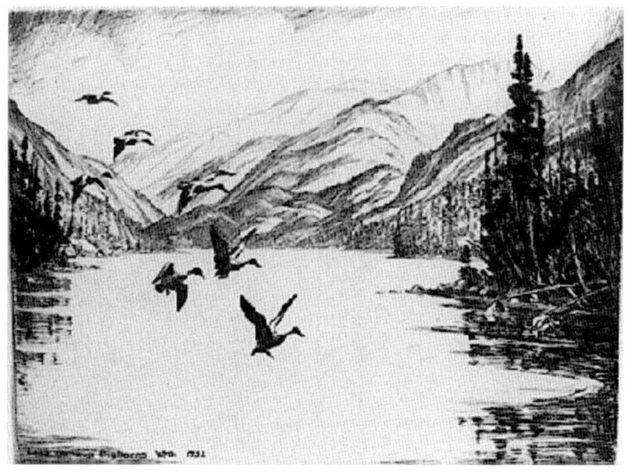

"Lake Geneva Bighorns, Wyo. 1932"
First State
Medium: Etching
Image: 4.875 inches high by 6.25 inches wide

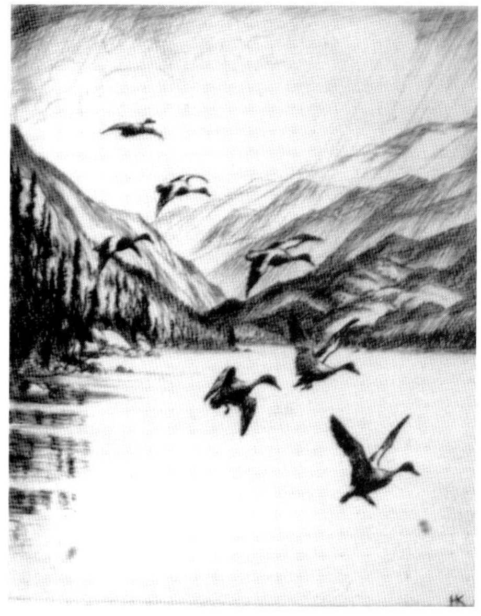

"Coming In"
Second State of
"Lake Geneva Bighorns, Wyo. 1932"
Medium: Etching
Image: 4.375 inches high by 3.4375 inches wide

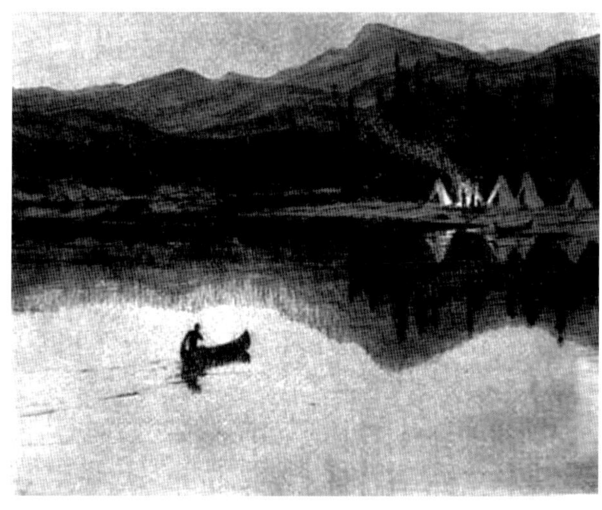

"Lake O' the Woods"
"Lake O' the Woods II"
"Union Pass, Wind River Mts."
First State
Medium: Etching
Image: 4.75 inches high by 6.375 inches wide

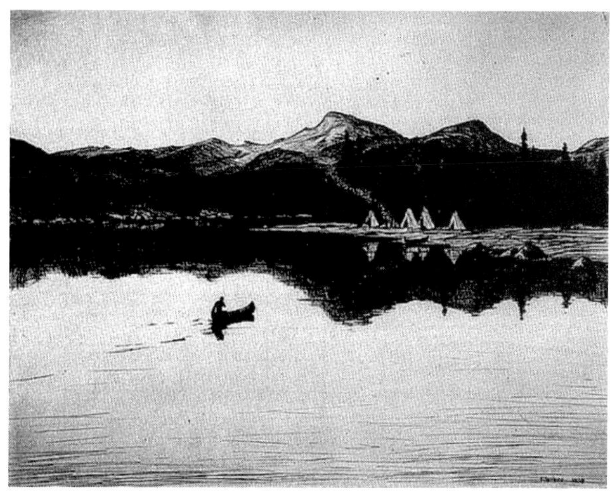

"Lake O' the Woods"
Second State of "Lake O' the Woods"
Medium: Photogravure
Image: 7.375 inches high by 10.25 inches wide

Hans Kleiber

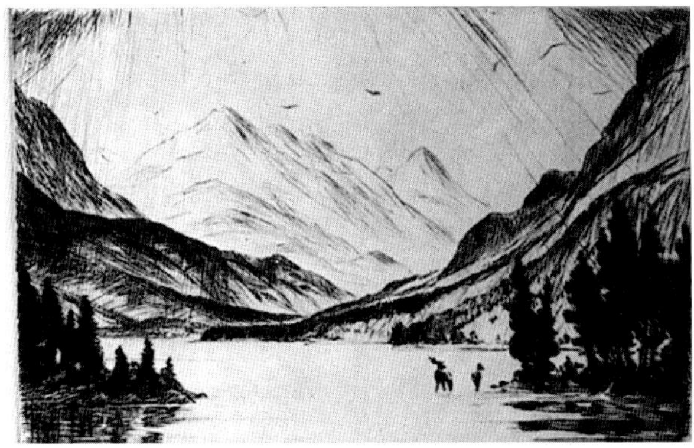

"Lake Solitude"
"Lake Solitude I"
"Solitude I"
Medium: Etching
Image: 3.8125 inches high by 5.8125 inches wide

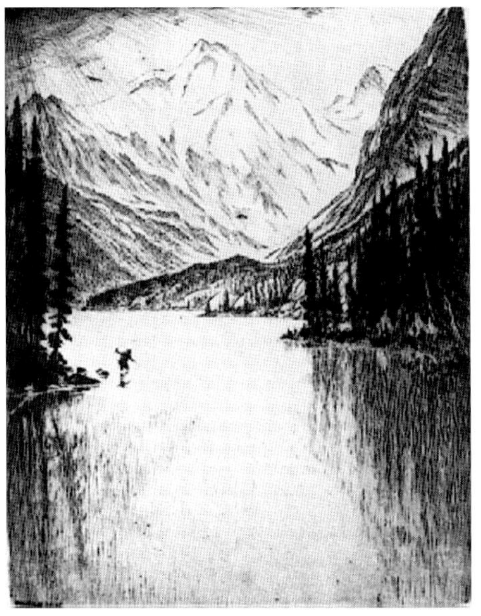

"Lake Solitude II"
"Maligne Lake"
Medium: Etching
Image: 5.75 inches high by 4.375 inches wide

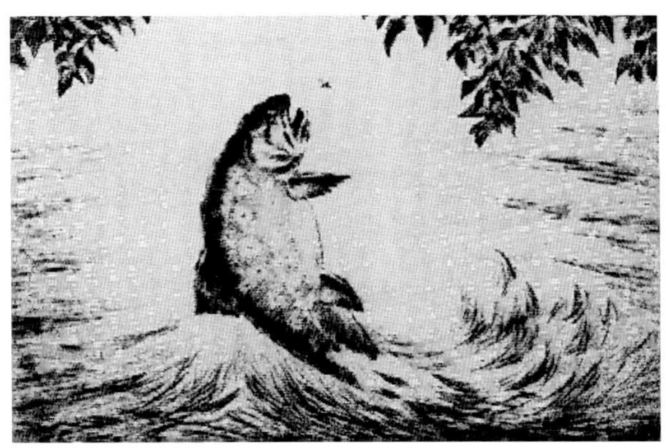

"Leaping Trout"
Medium: Etching
Image: 3.75 inches high by 5.5 inches wide

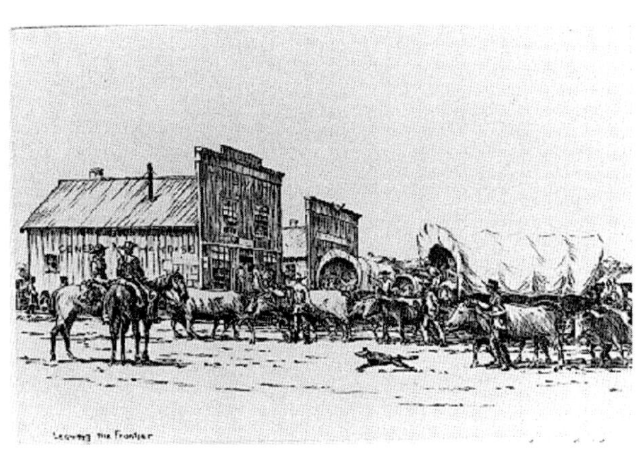

"Leaving the Frontier"
Medium: Etching
Image: 6.75 inches high by 9.75 inches wide

Medium: Photogravure
Image: 5.375 inches high by 7.625 inches wide

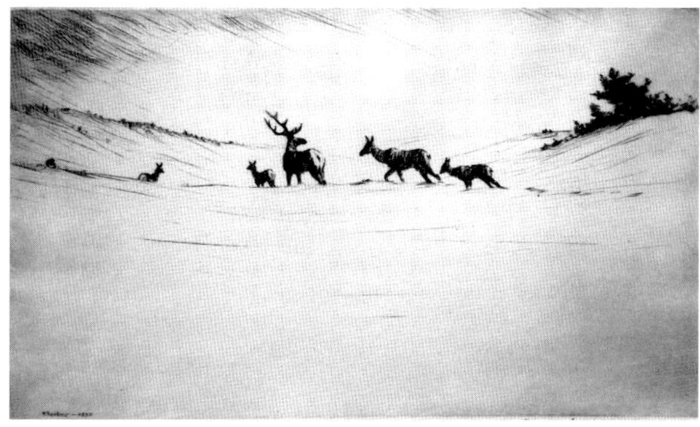

"Leaving the High Country"
Medium: Etching
Image: 7.75 inches high by 12.75 inches wide

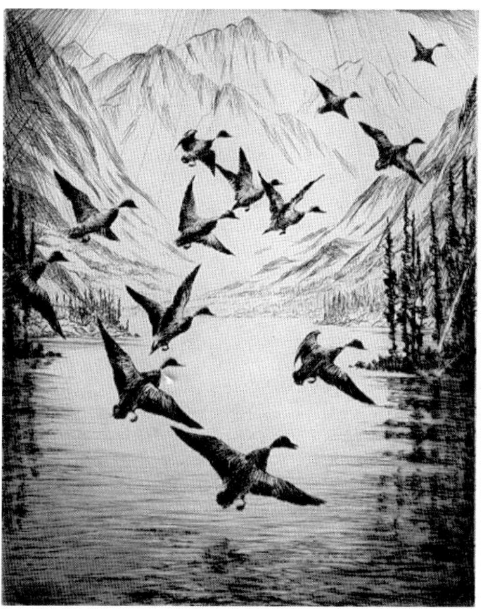

"Leigh Lake"
Medium: Etching
Image: 4.875 inches high by 3.875 inches wide

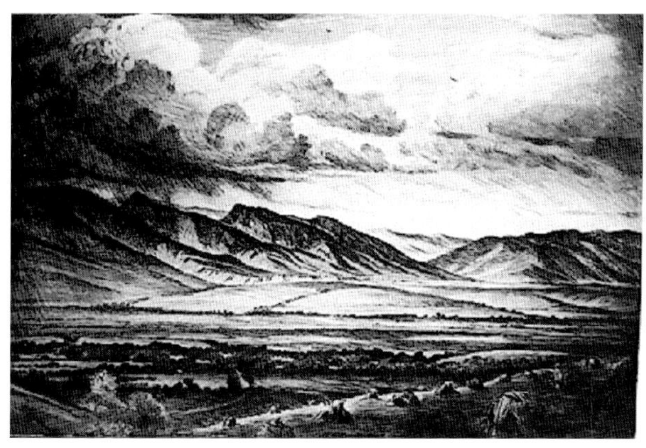

"Little Goose Valley"
"Little Goose Valley, Bighorns"
Medium: Etching
Image: 5.5 inches high by 8 inches wide

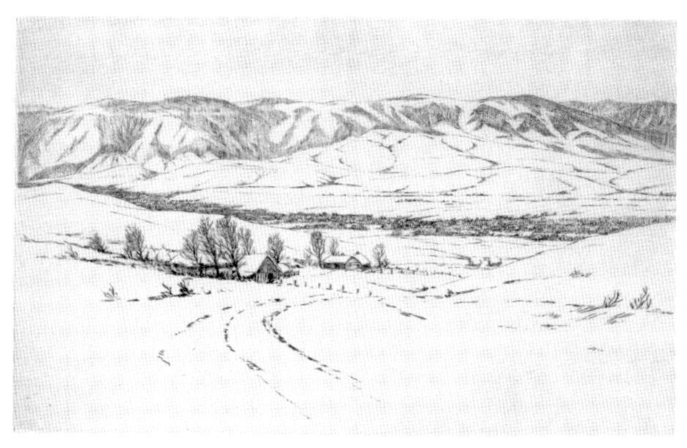

"Little Goose - Wyo."
First State
Medium: Etching
Image: 6.75 inches high by 10.75 inches wide

Hans Kleiber

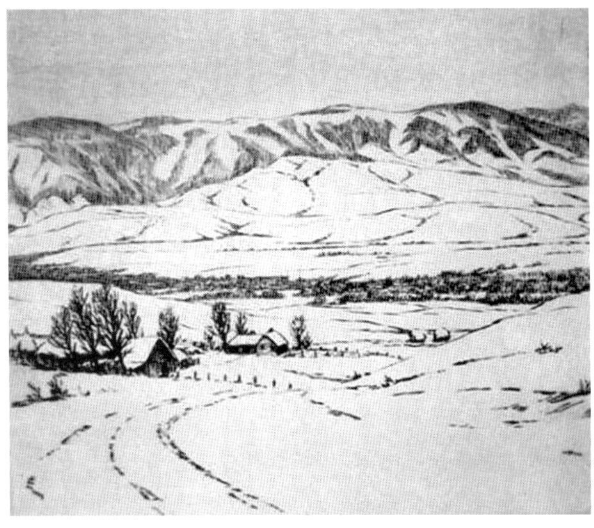

"Little Goose Valley"
"Little Goose, Wyoming"
"Little Goose, Wyo."
"Winter"
Second State of
"Little Goose - Wyo."
Medium: Etching
Image: 6.25 inches high by 7.875 inches wide

"Long's Peak"
Medium: Etching
Image: 6.875 inches high by 4.875 inches wide

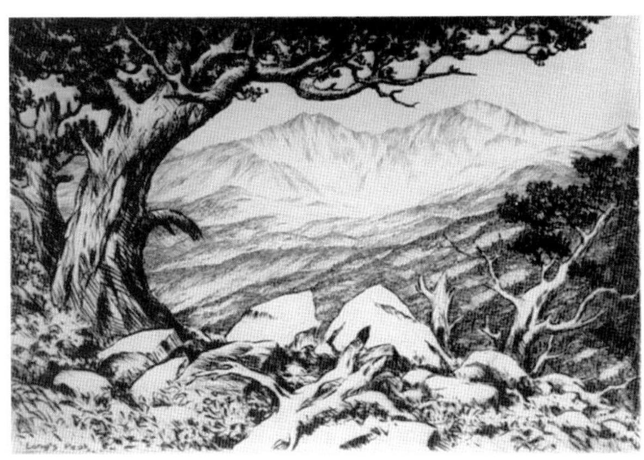

"Long's Peak, II"
Medium: Etching
Image: 4.8125 inches high by 6.875 inches wide

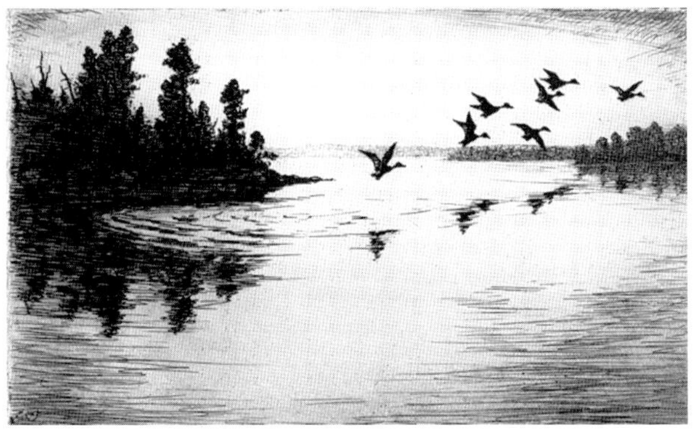

"Loon Lake, Minnesota"
Medium: Etching, Photogravure
Image: 6.3125 inches high by 10.0625 inches wide

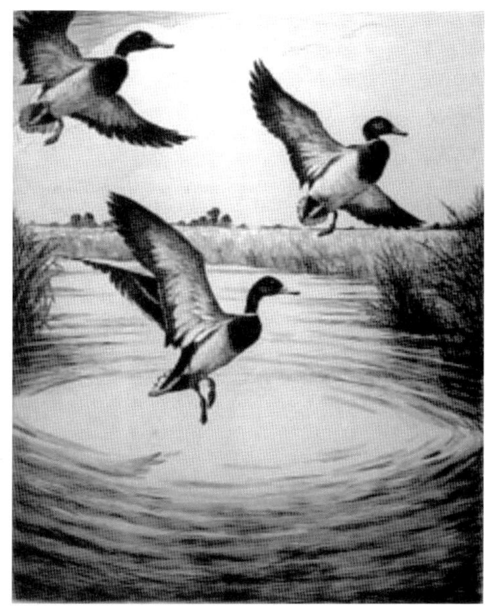

"Louisiana Honkers"
"Mallard Drakes"
Medium: Etching
Image: 9.8125 inches high by 7.75 inches wide

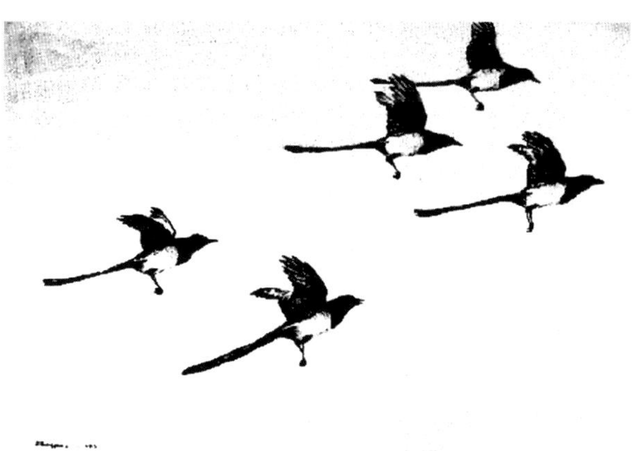

"Magpies"
First State
Medium: Etching
Image: 7.875 inches high by 10.875 inches wide

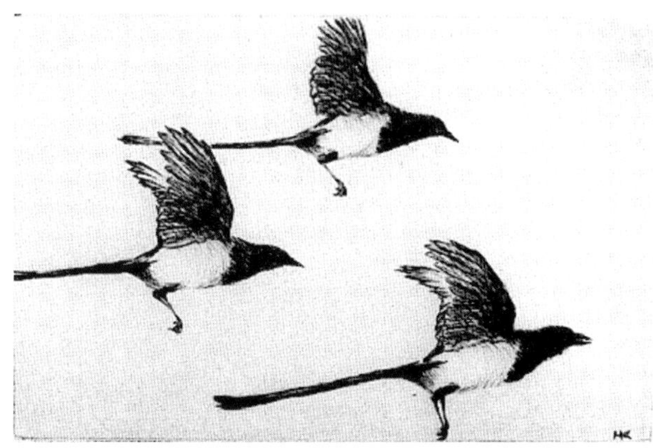

"Magpies"
"Magpies in Flight"
Second State of "Magpies"
Medium: Etching
Image: 3.625 inches high by 5.375 inches wide

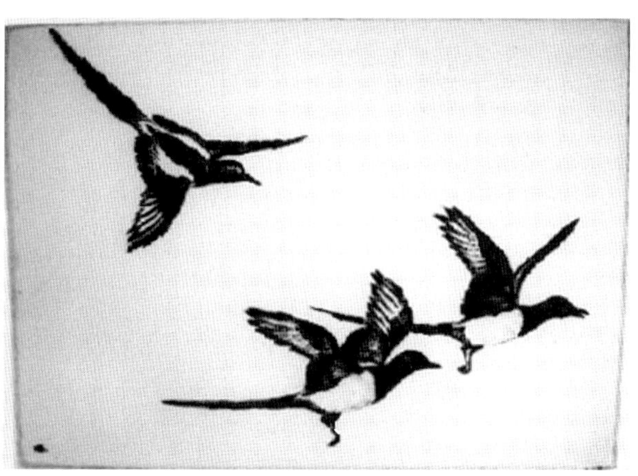

"Magpies"
Medium: Etching
Image: 5.8125 inches high by 7.875 inches wide

Hans Kleiber

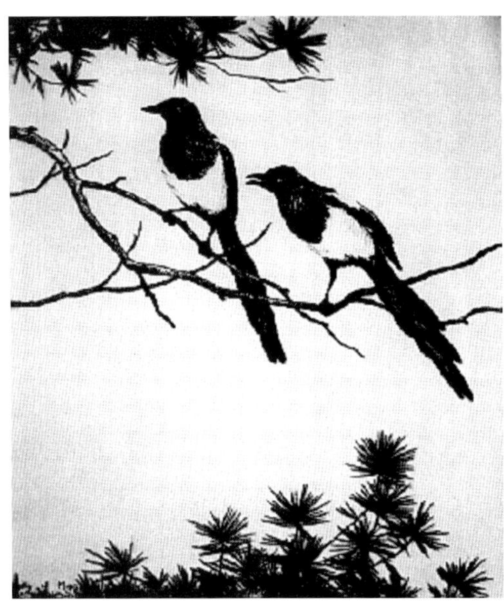

"Magpies"
"Study of Magpies"
Medium: Etching
Image: 8.375 inches high by 7.3125 inches wide

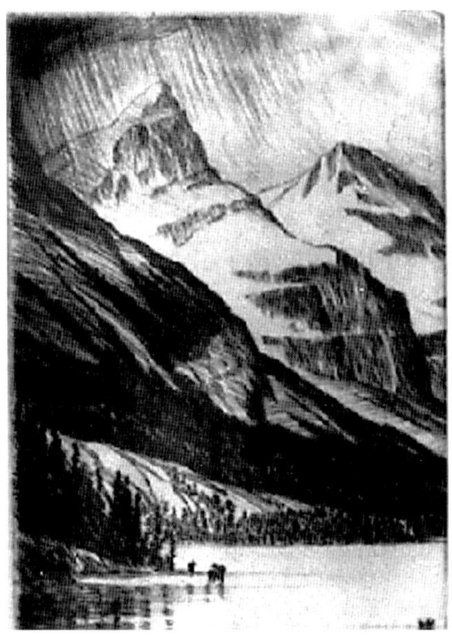

"Maligne Lake I"
Medium: Etching
Image: 3.8125 inches high by 2.625 inches wide

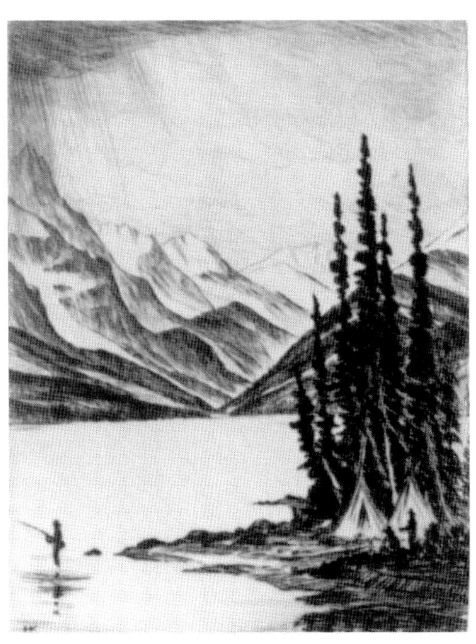

"Maligne Lake II"
Medium: Etching
Image: 4.875 inches high by 3.625 inches wide

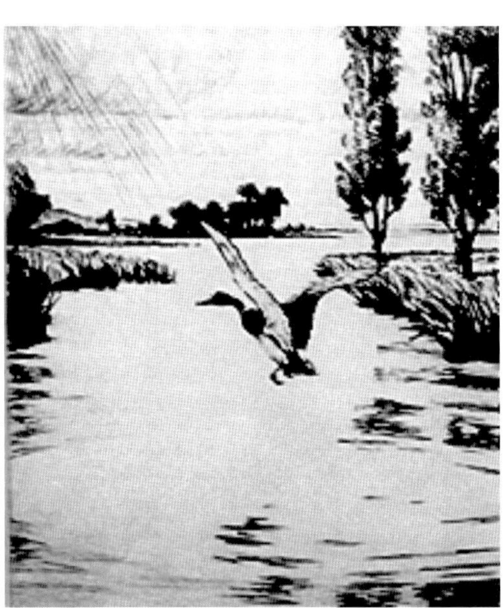

"Mallard Drake"
Second State of "Poplars II"
Medium: Etching
Image: 6.625 inches high by 5.875 inches wide

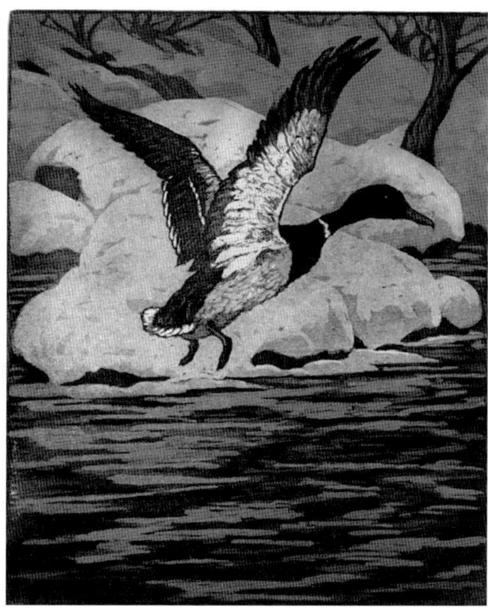

"Mallard Drake on Snow"
Medium: Etching
Image: 9.875 inches high by 7.875 inches wide

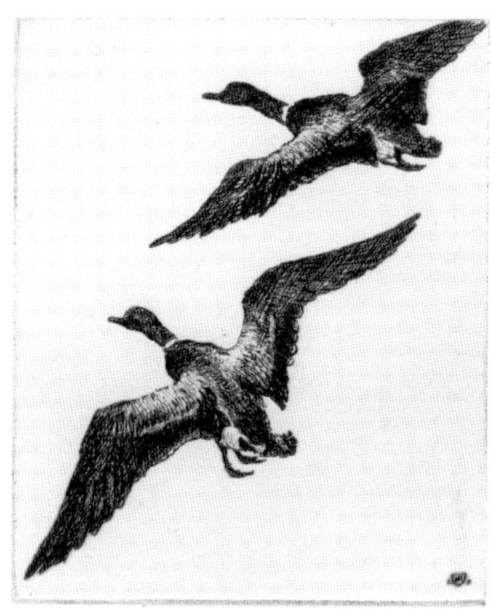

"Mallard Drakes"
"Pair of Mallard Drakes"
Medium: Etching
Image: 5 inches high by 4 inches wide

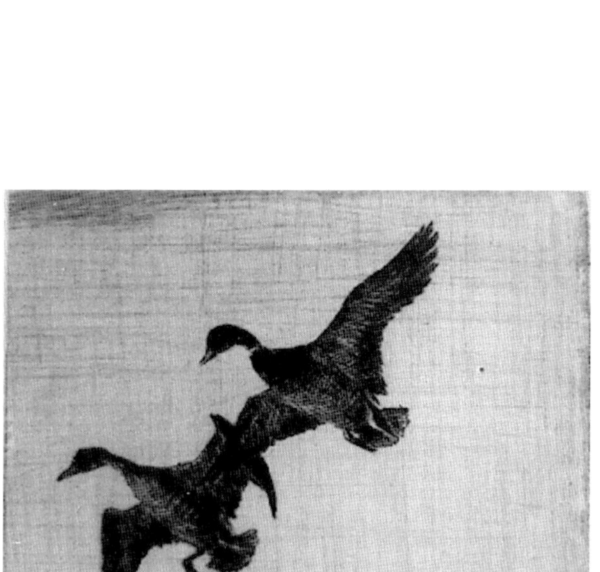

"Mallards"
Second State of Unknown First State
Medium: Etching
Image: 3.125 inches high by 4 inches wide

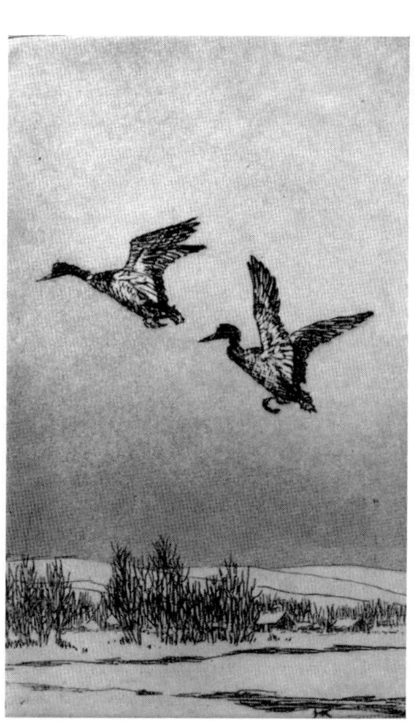

"Mallards"
"Mallards Rising"
Medium: Photogravure
Image: 4.375 inches high by 2.625 inches wide

Hans Kleiber

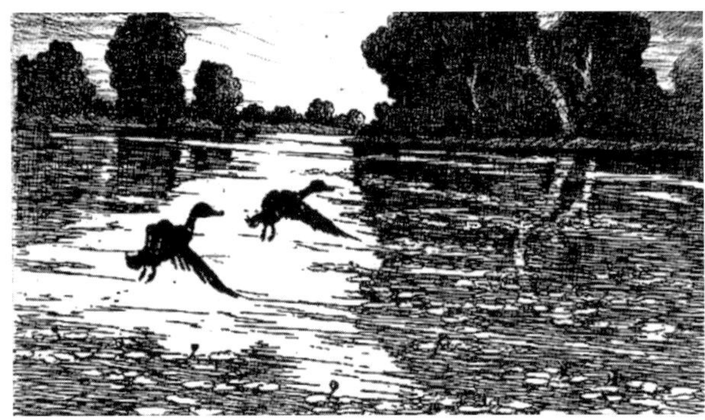

"Mallards at Dusk"
Medium: Etching, Photogravure
Image: 4.75 inches high by 8.75 inches wide

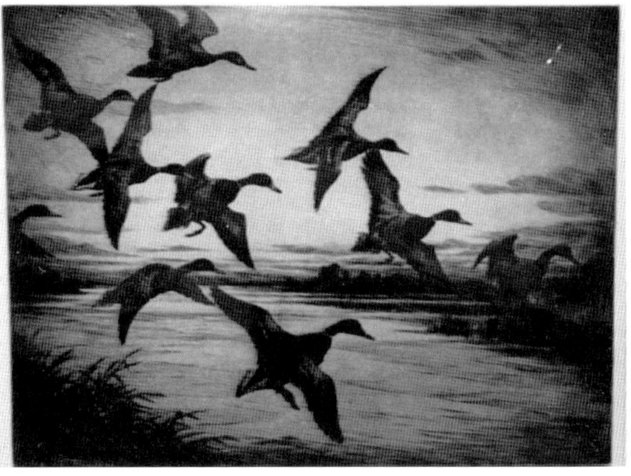

"Mallards Coming In"
First State
Medium: Etching
Image: 10.75 inches high by 13.75 inches wide

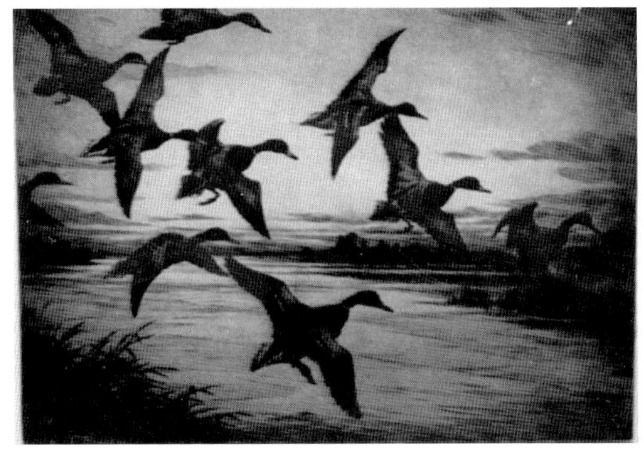

"Mallards Coming In"
Second State of "Mallards Coming In"
Medium: Etching
Image: 9.625 inches high by 13.75 inches wide

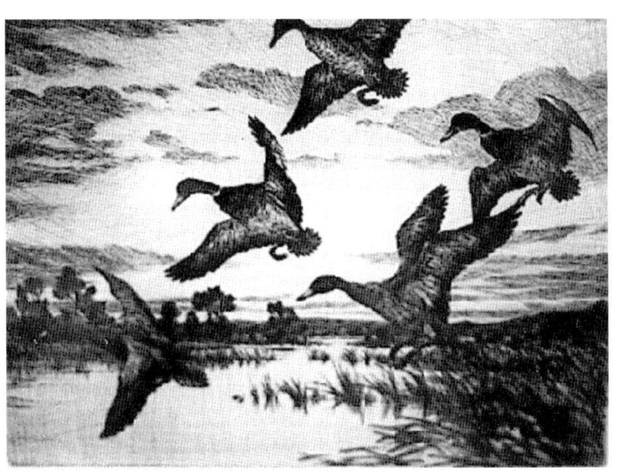

"Mallards - Evening"
"Mallards - Evening II"
Medium: Etching
Image: 5.75 inches high by 7.625 inches wide

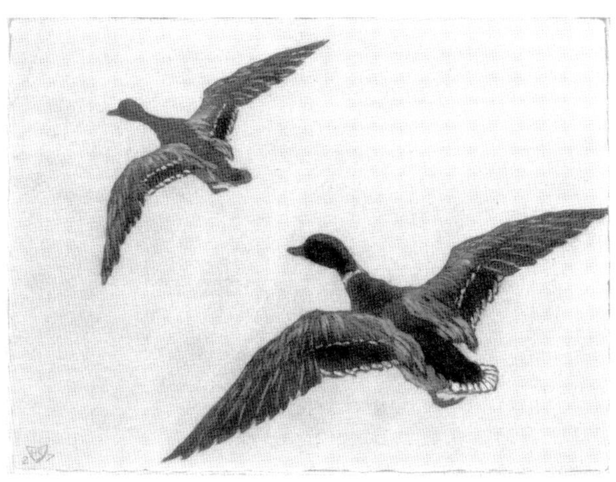

"Mallards Flying"
Medium: Etching
Image: 4.75 inches high by 6.25 inches wide

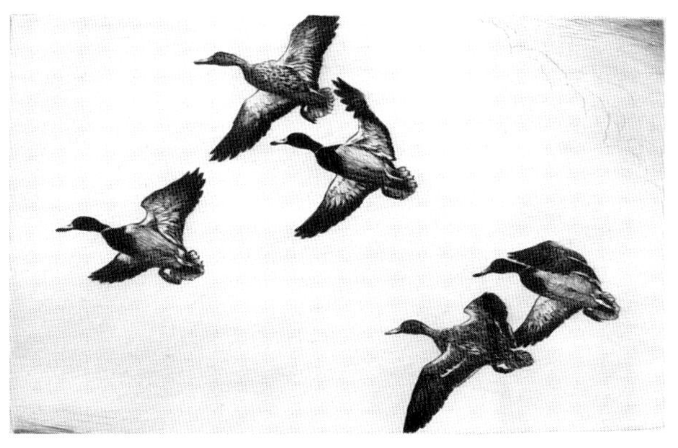

"Mallards in Flight"
Medium: Etching
Associated American Artists
Image: 7.75 inches high by 11.75 inches wide

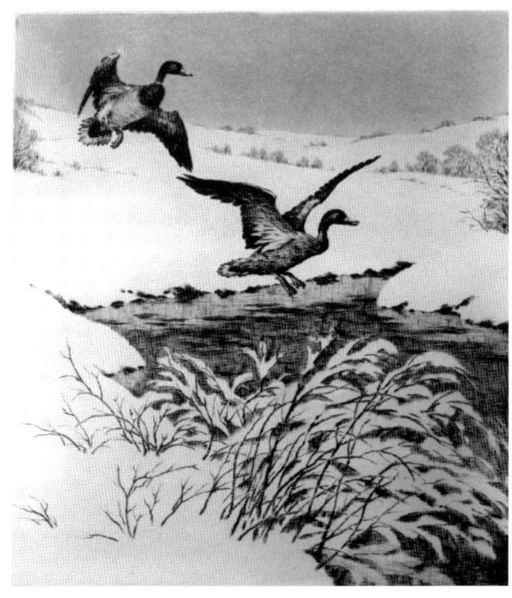

"Mallards in the Snow"
"Winter Guests"
"Winter Guests I"
Medium: Etching
Associated American Artists
Image: 10.75 inches high by 9.25 inches wide

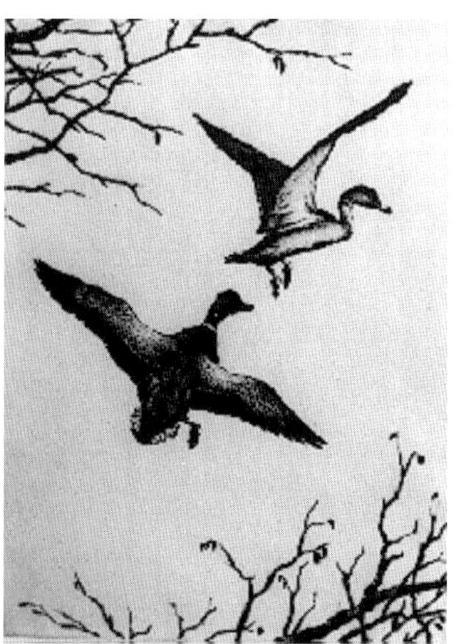

"Mallards - Mating Time"
"Mallards--Mating Time No. 1"
"Mating Time"
Medium: Etching
Image: 8.875 inches high by 6.375 inches wide

Hans Kleiber

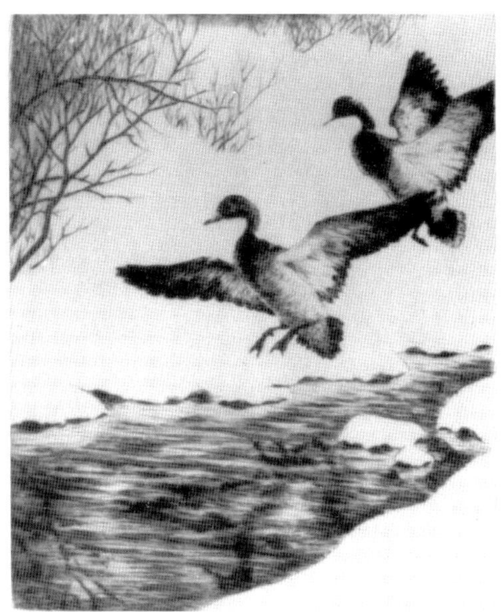

"Mallard Drakes"
"Mallards - Winter"
Medium: Etching
Image: 4.8125 inches high by 3.875 inches wide

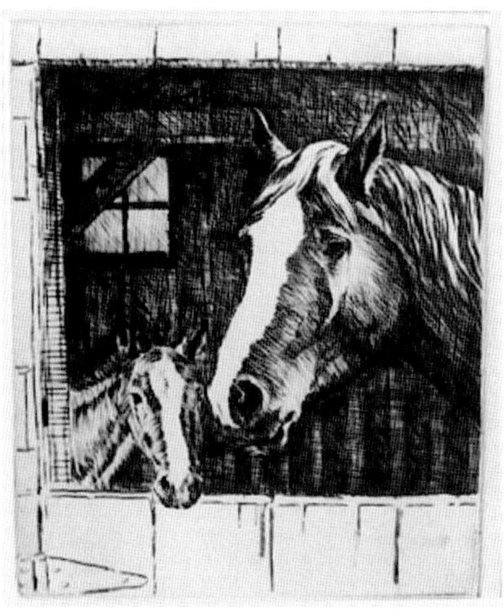

"Mare and Colt"
Medium: Etching
Image: 4.875 inches high by 3.875 inches wide

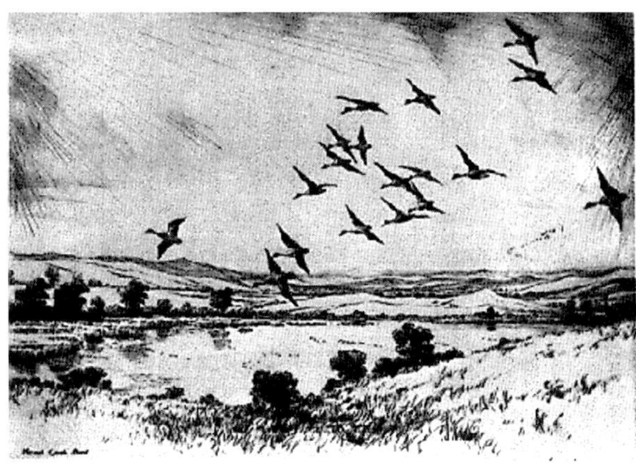

"A Pond in the Hills, Mead Creek"
"Mead Creek Pond"
Medium: Etching
Image: 7.625 inches high by 10.625 inches wide

Medium: Photogravure
Image: 5.25 inches high by 7.25 inches wide

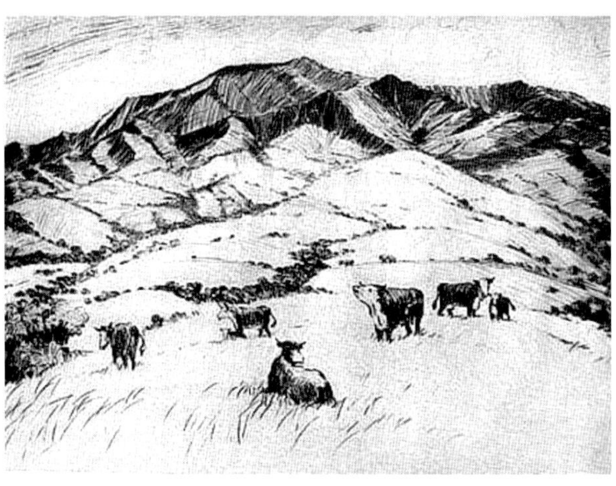

"Mead Creek Ranch"
"On Little Goose"
"On Little Goose - Bighorns"
Medium: Etching
Image: 7.3125 inches high by 10.8125 inches wide
Paper Size: 10.8125 inches high by 13.5 inches wide

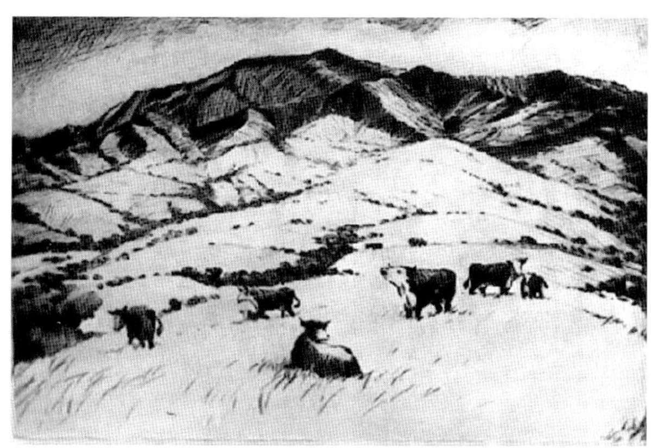

"Mead Creek Ranch"
"On Little Goose"
"On Little Goose - Bighorns"
Medium: Photogravure
Image: 4 inches high by 5.875 inches wide

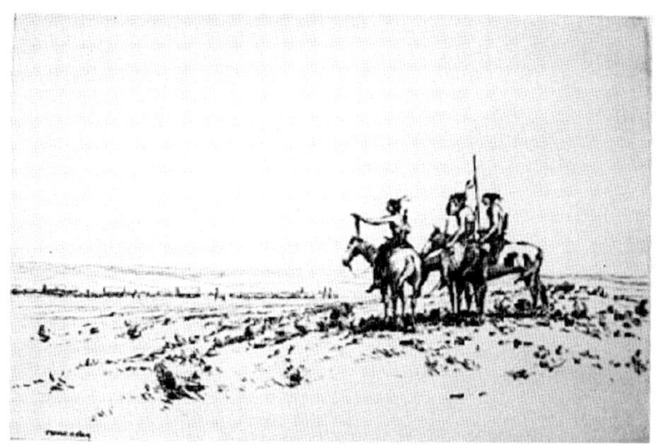

"Meneaska"
"Meneasky"
Medium: Etching
Image: 6.75 inches high by 9.75 inches wide

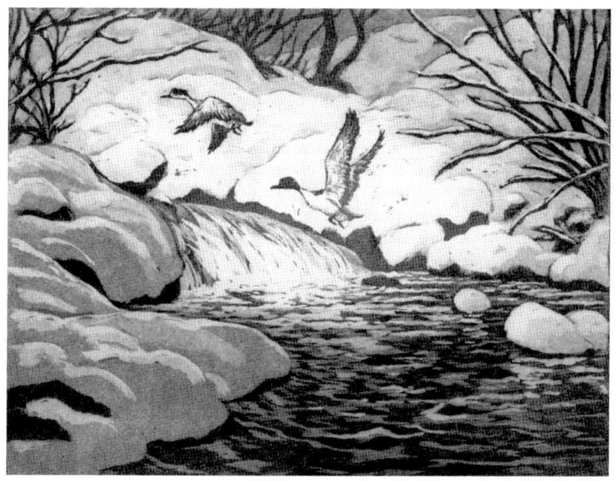

"Mergansers"
Medium: Etching
Image: 7.375 inches high by 9.375 inches wide

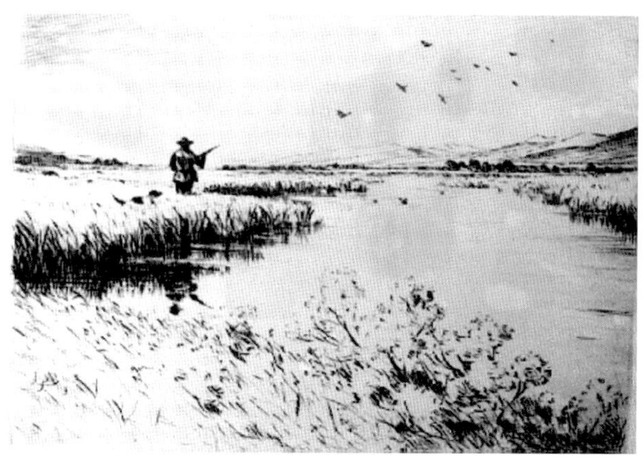

"Marsh Along Snake River"
"Marshes Along Snake River"
"Snake River Marshes"
Medium: Etching
Image: 4.625 inches high by 6.375 inches wide

Hans Kleiber

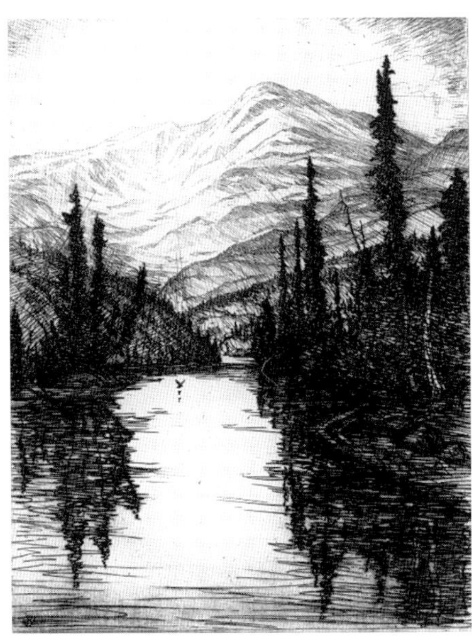

"Mather Peak, Wyo."
Medium: Photogravure
Image: 9.8125 inches high by 7.375 inches wide

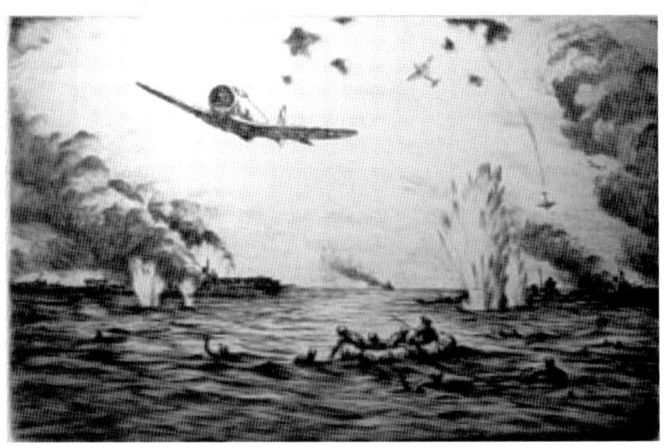

"Midway"
Medium: Etching
Image: 5.75 inches high by 8.75 inches wide

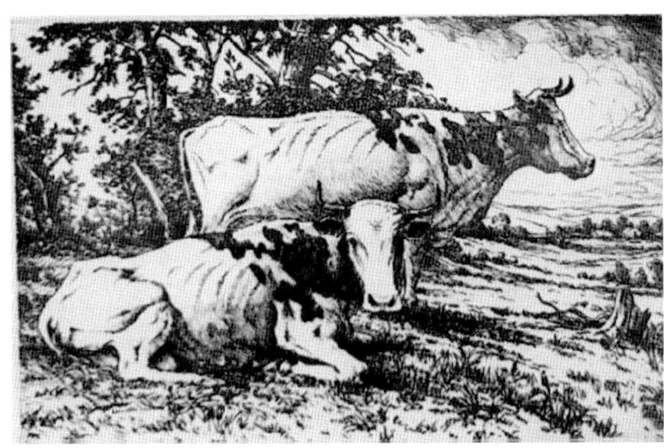

"Milk Cows"
Medium: Photogravure
Image: 3.75 inches high by 5.75 inches wide

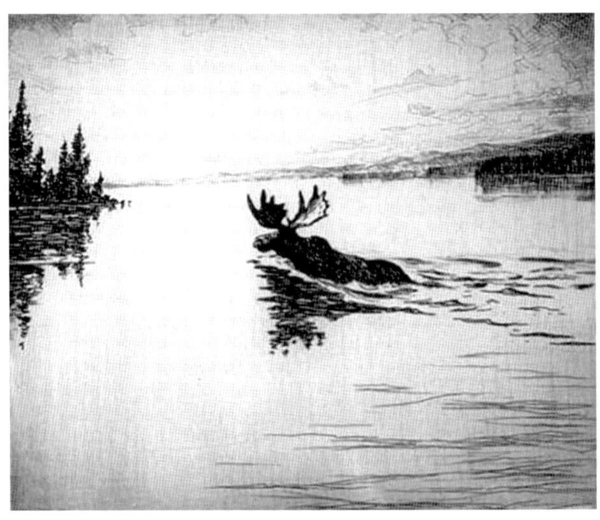

"Moose Swimming"
First State
Medium: Etching
Image: 6.25 inches high by 7.75 inches wide

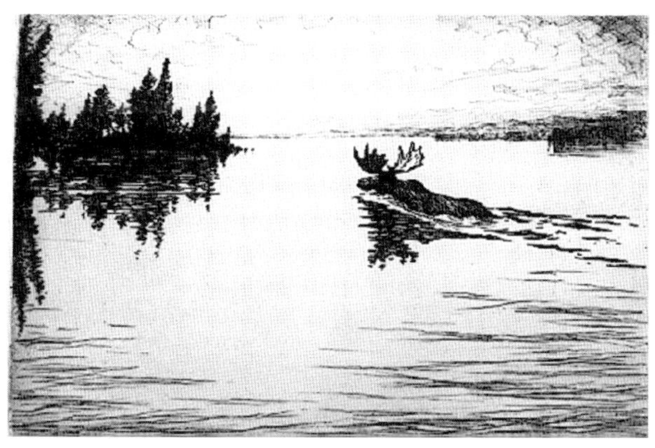

"Moose Swimming"
Second State of "Moose Swimming"
Medium: Photogravure
Image: 6.875 inches high by 9.875 inches wide

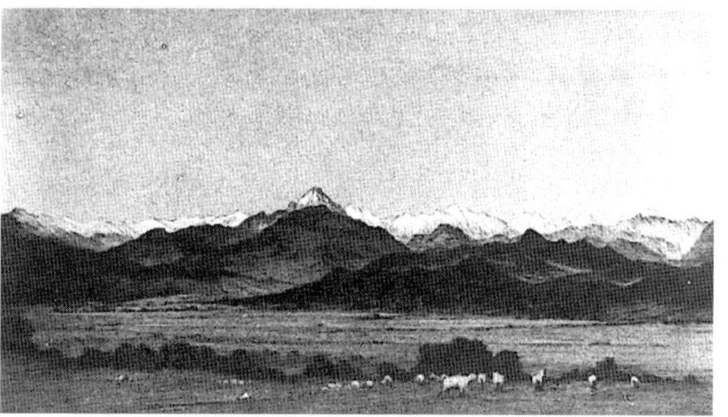

"Morning in the Rockies"
"Sangre De Christa Mountains, Colorado"
Medium: Etching
Image: 6.75 inches high by 11.75 inches wide

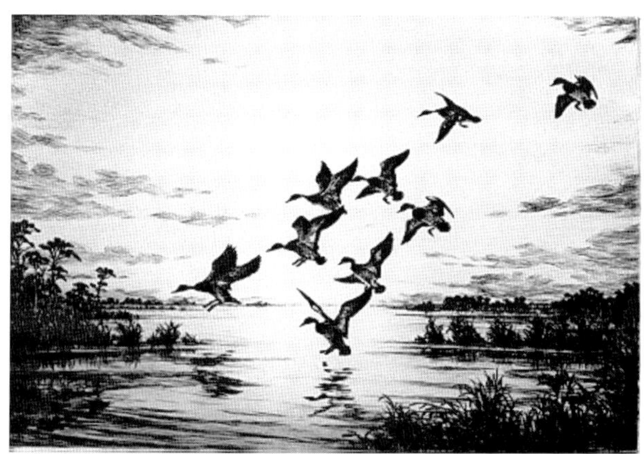

"Morning on the Marshes"
Medium: Etching
Associated American Artists
Image: 7.5 inches high by 10.875 inches wide

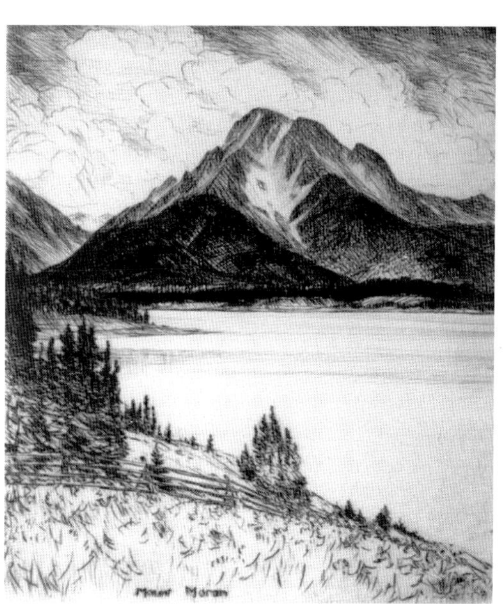

"Mount Moran"
Medium: Etching
Image: 5.875 inches high by 4.9375 inches wide

Hans Kleiber

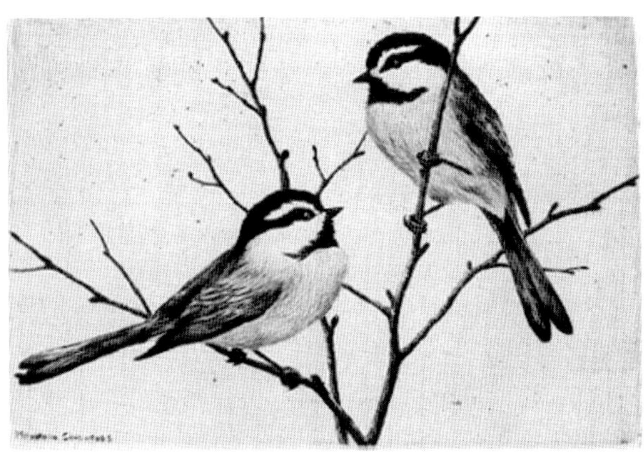

"Mountain Chicadees"
Medium: Etching
Image: 3.875 inches high by 5.5 inches wide

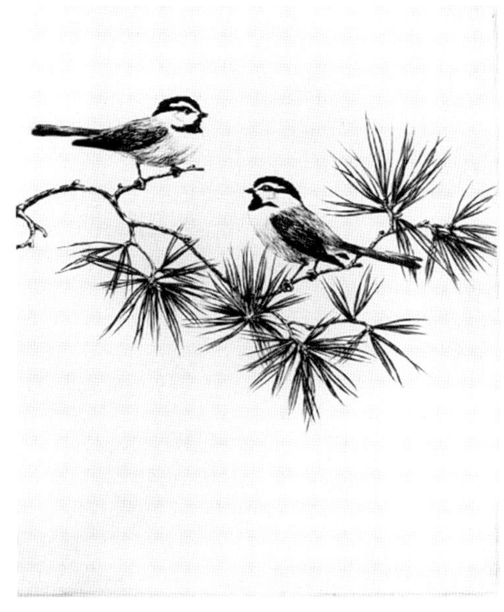

"Mountain Chicadees"
First State
Medium: Etching
Associated American Artists
Image: 9.75 inches high by 7.75 inches wide

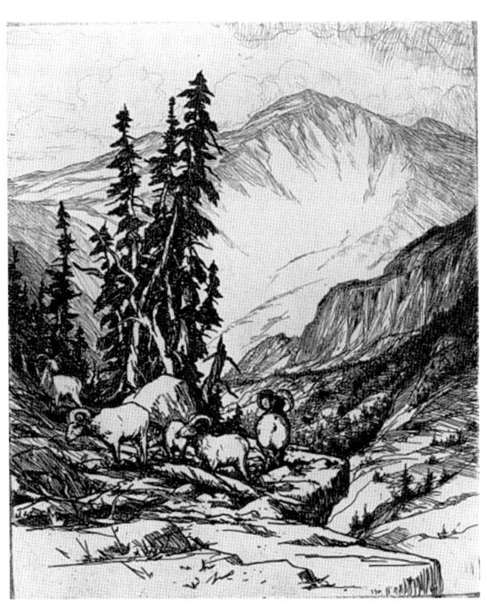

"Mountain Sheep"
"Mt. Sheep in Wind River Mts."
Medium: Etching, Photogravure
Image: 7.875 inches high by 6.3125 inches wide

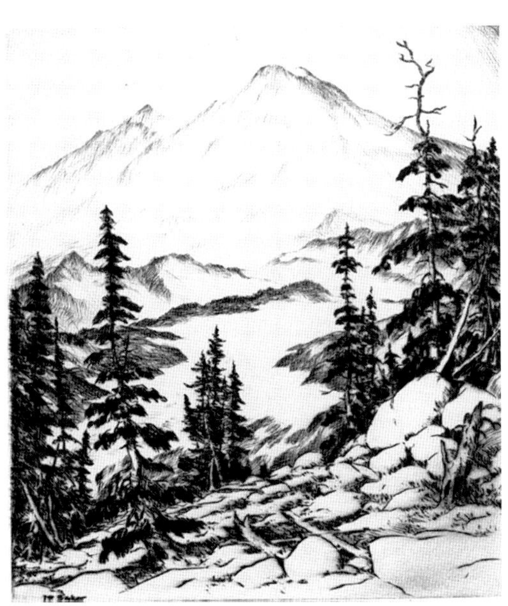

"Mt. Baker"
Medium: Etching
Image: 5.875 inches high by 4.875 inches wide

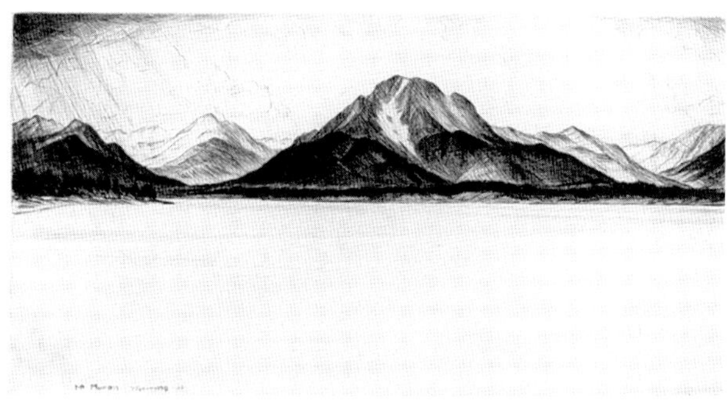

"Mt. Moran, Wyoming"
"Mt. Moran, Jackson Lake - Wyoming"
Medium: Etching
Image: 5.75 inches high by 10.75 inches wide

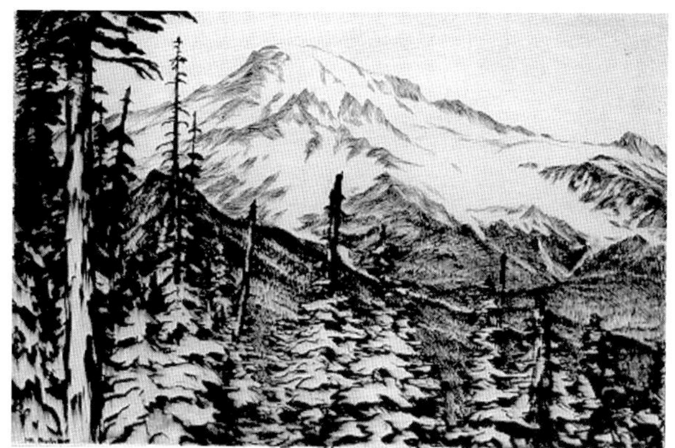

"Mt. Rainier"
Medium: Etching
Image: 4.375 inches high by 6.375 inches wide

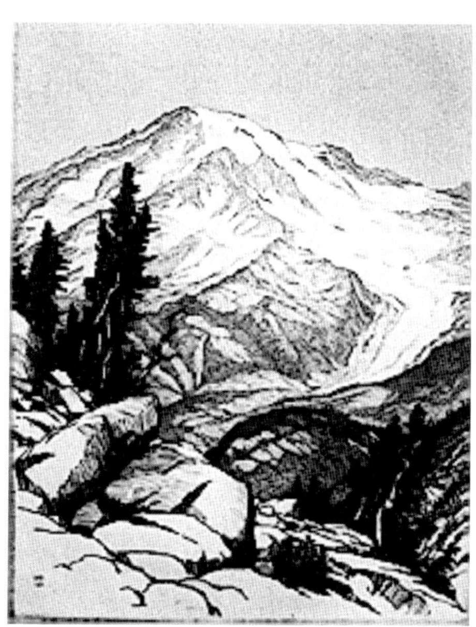

"Mt. Rainier"
Medium: Photogravure
Image: 9.25 inches high by 7 inches wide

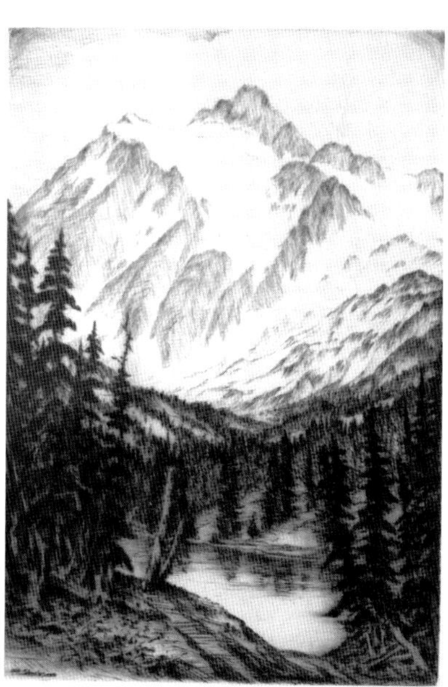

"Mt. Shuksan"
Medium: Etching
Image: 6.75 inches high by 4.75 inches wide

Hans Kleiber

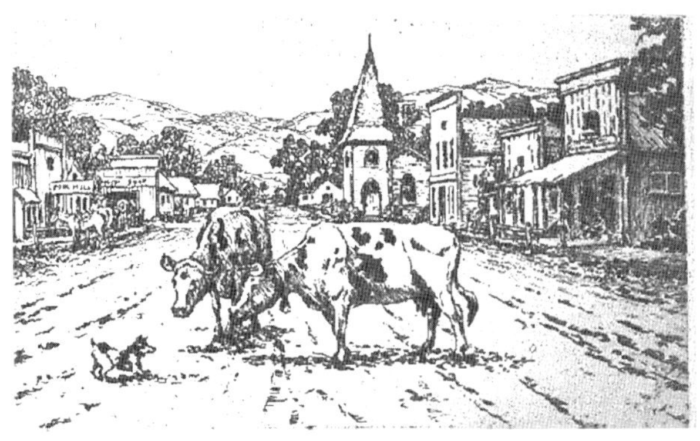

"My Home Town"
"My Home Town - Dayton, Wyoming"
"The Old Home Town - Dayton, Wyoming"
Medium: Etching, Photogravure
Image: 3.875 inches high by 6.25 inches wide

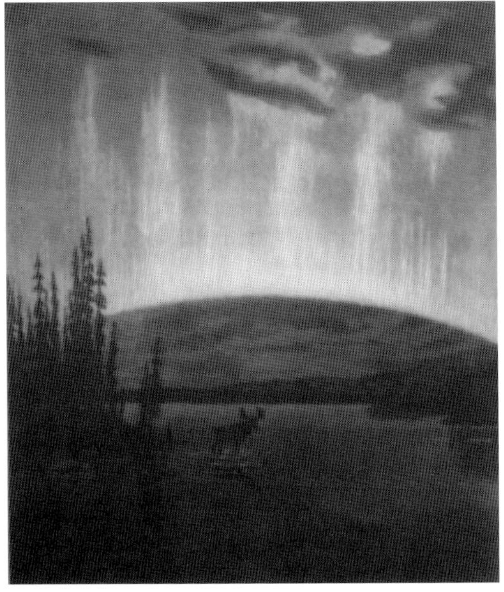

"Northern Lights"
Medium: Etching
Image: 11.75 inches high by 9.75 inches wide

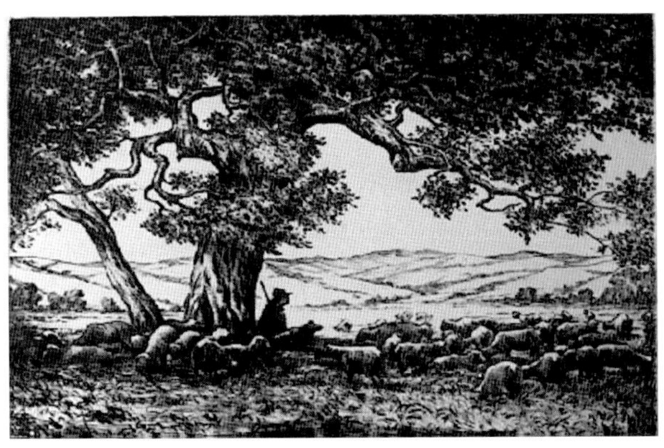

"Old Cottonwood Tree"
"The Old Cottonwood"
"The Old Cottonwood Tree"
Medium: Etching
Associated American Artists
Image: 7.125 inches high by 10.75 inches wide

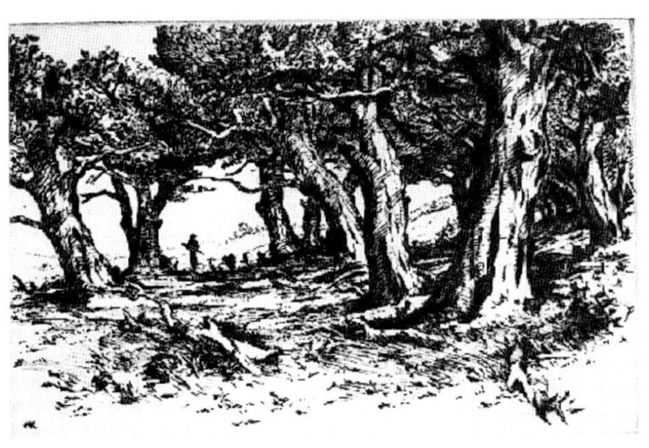

"Old Pines on Sheep Creek,Wyoming"
First State
Medium: Etching
Image: 6.25 inches high by 9.25 inches wide

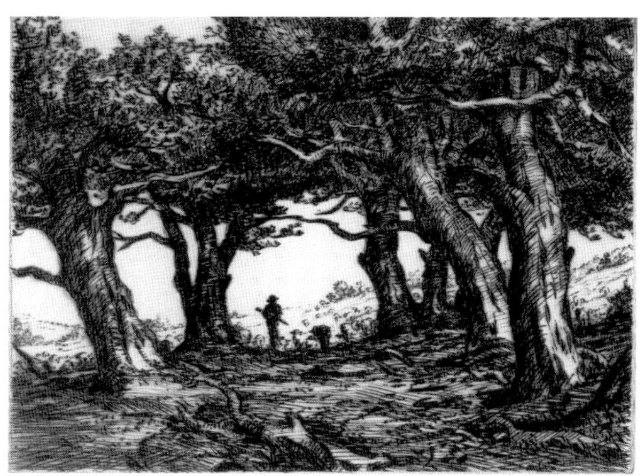

"Sheep Creek Ridge"
Second State of "Old Pines on Sheep Creek, Wyoming"
Medium: Etching
Image: 4.875 inches high by 6.5 inches wide

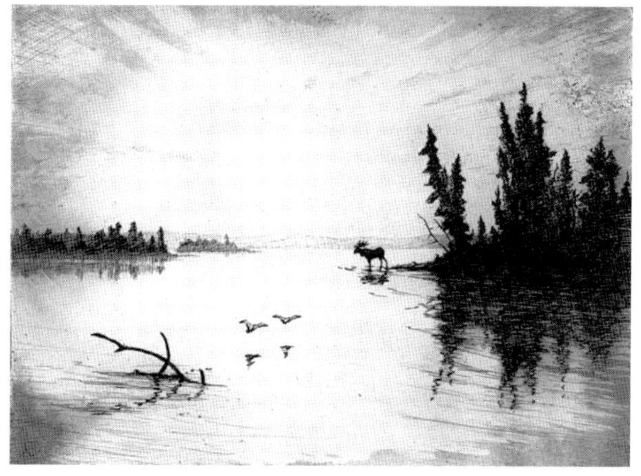

"Lake LaCroix - Minnesota"
First State
Medium: Etching
Image: 7.75 inches high by 10.25 inches wide

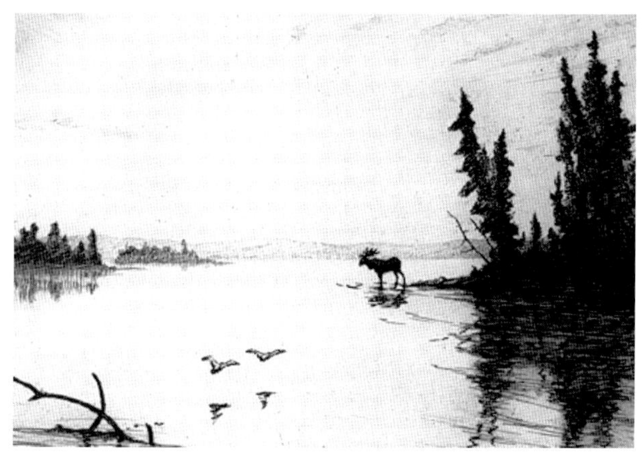

"In the Lake LaCroix"
"On Lake LaCroix"
Second State of "Lake LaCroix - Minnesota"
Medium: Etching
Image: 5.25 inches high by 7.25 inches wide

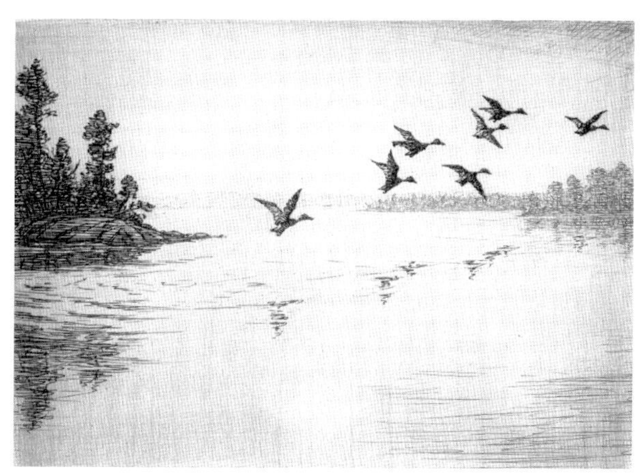

"On Lake LaCroix on a Rainy Day"
a.k.a. "Ducks on Loon Lake"
Medium: Etching
Image: 5.375 inches high by 7.375 inches wide

Hans Kleiber

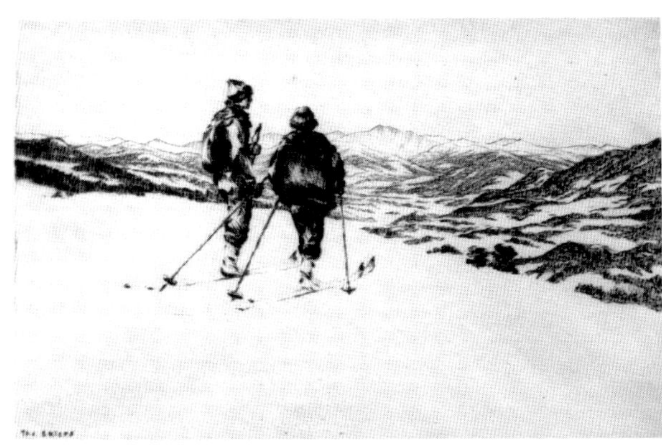

"On Tepee Creek - Little Goose - Bighorns"
"The Skiers"
Medium: Etching
Image: 3.8125 inches high by 5.75 inches wide

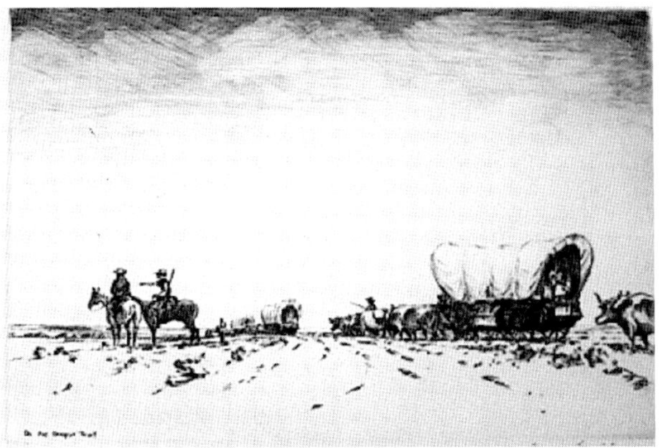

"On the Oregon Trail"
First State
Medium: Etching
Image: 6.75 inches high by 9.75 inches wide

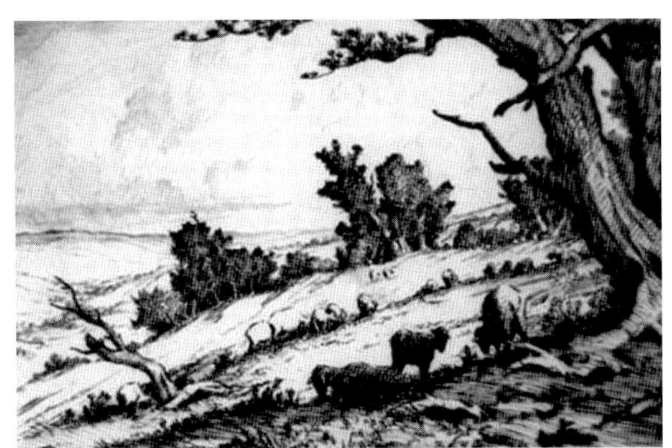

"On the Sheep Range"
First State
Medium: Etching
Image: 4.875 inches high by 8 inches wide

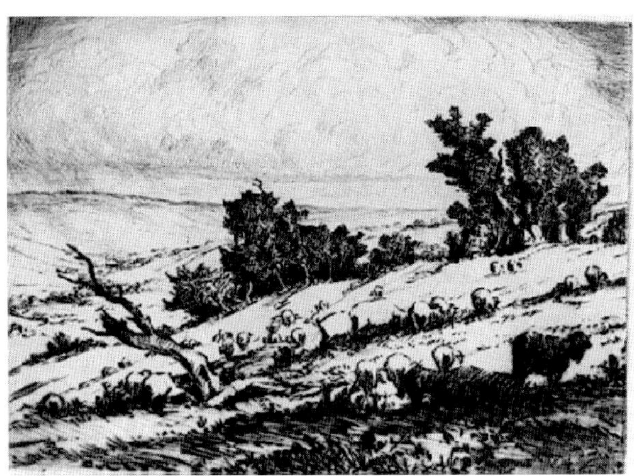

"On the Sheep Range"
Second State of "On the Sheep Range"
Medium: Etching
Image: 4.25 inches high by 5.625 inches wide

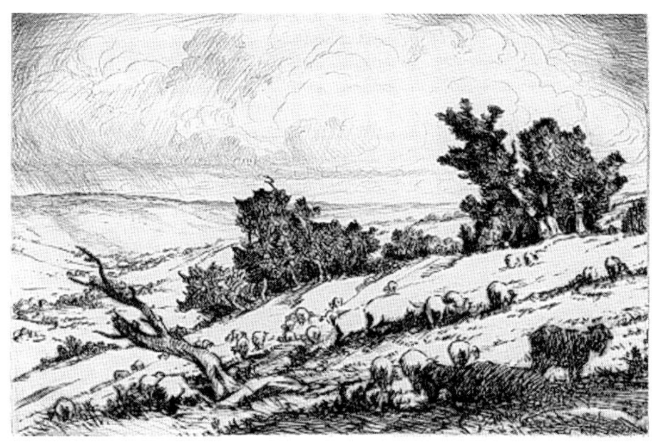

"On the Sheep Range"
"Sheep on the Range"
"Summer Range"
Third State of "On the Sheep Range"
Medium: Etching
Image: 3.875 inches high by 5.625 inches wide

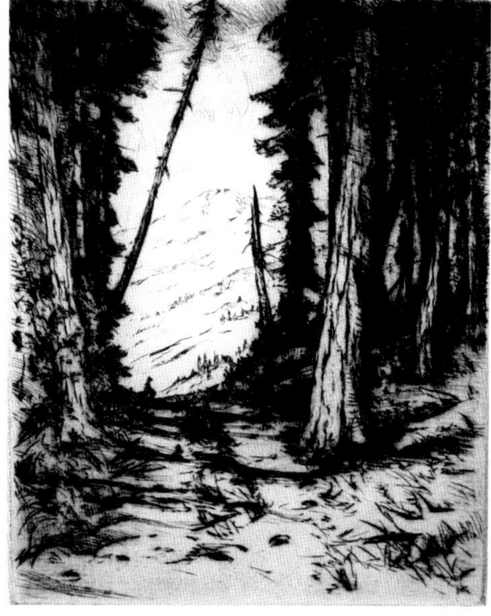

"On the Trail"
Medium: Etching
Image: 6.8125 inches high by 5.375 inches wide

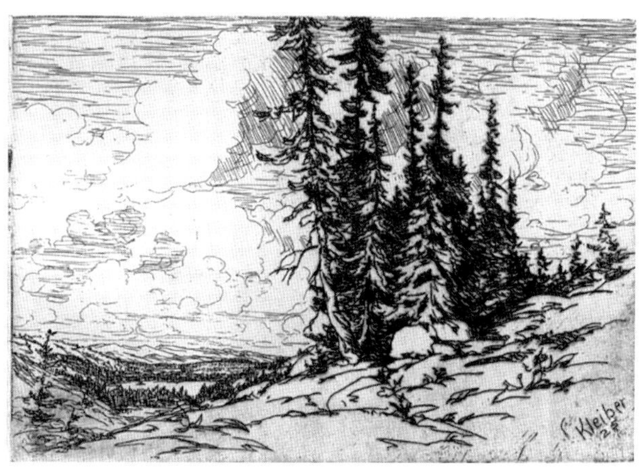

"On Top O' the Big Horns"
Medium: Etching, Photogravure
Image: 4.875 inches high by 6.875 inches wide

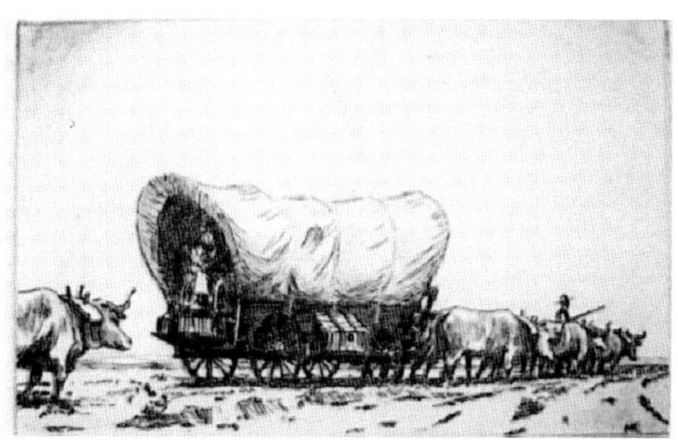

"Oregon Trail I"
"Pioneers I"
Second State of "On the Oregon Trail"
Medium: Photogravure
Image: 3.5 inches high by 5.25 inches wide

Hans Kleiber

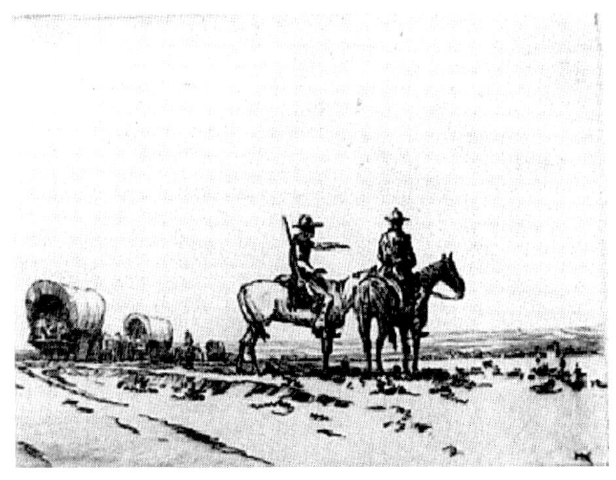

"Oregon Trail II"
"Pioneers II"
Third State of "On the Oregon Trail"
Medium: Photogravure
Image: 3.5 inches high by 4.5 inches wide

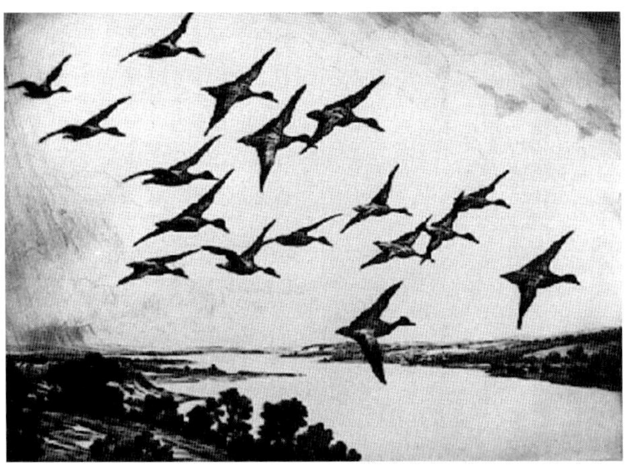

"Out of the Clouds"
"Out of the Sky"
Medium: Etching
Image: 5.875 inches high by 7.875 inches wide

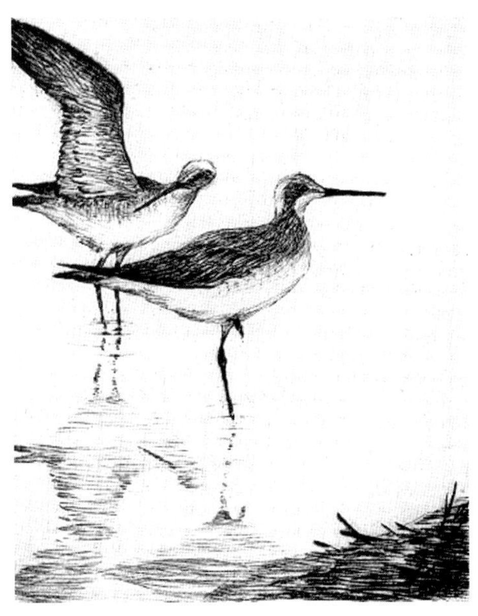

"Phalaropes"
Medium: Etching
Image: 4.375 inches high by 3.375 inches wide

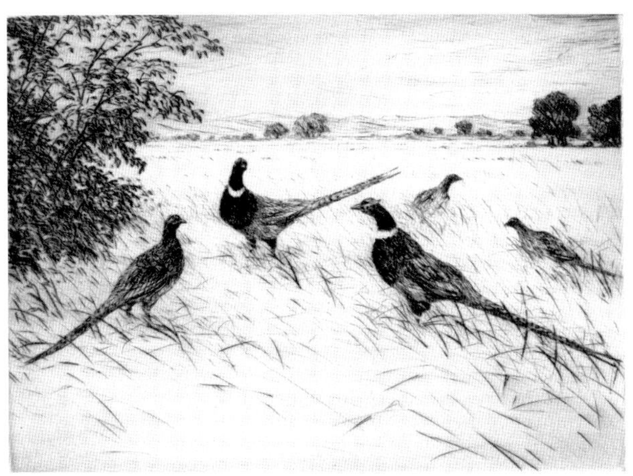

"Pheasants II"
Medium: Etching
Image: 6.3125 inches high by 8.3125 inches wide

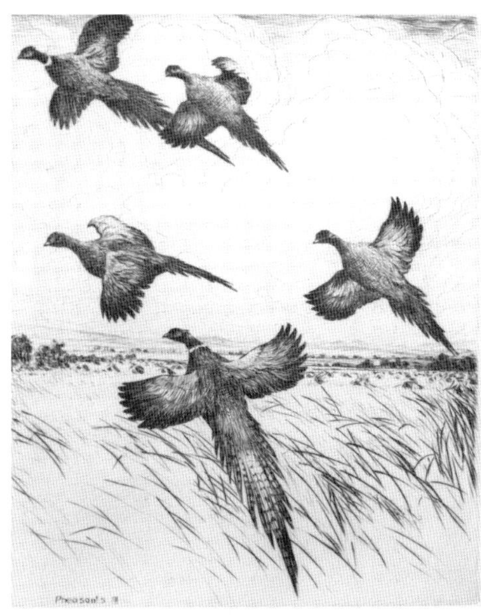

"Pheasants III"
Medium: Etching
Image: 9.75 inches high by 7.625 inches wide

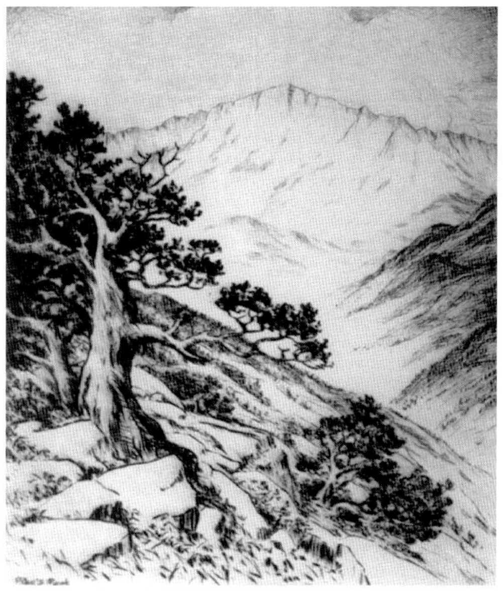

"Pike's Peak"
Medium: Etching, Photogravure
Image: 5.875 inches high by 5 inches wide

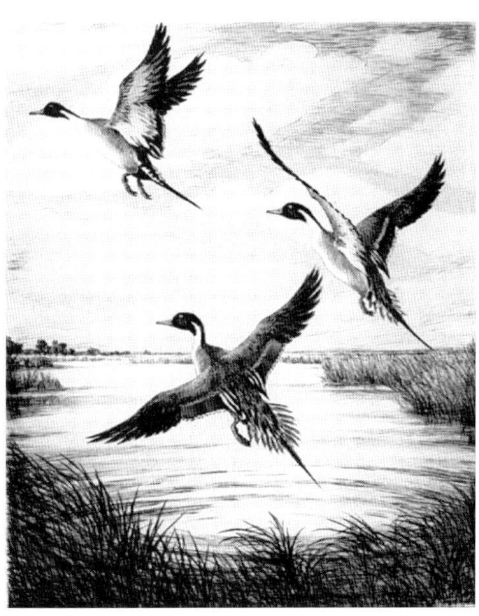

"Pintail Drakes"
Medium: Etching
Image: 9.5 inches high by 7.75 inches wide

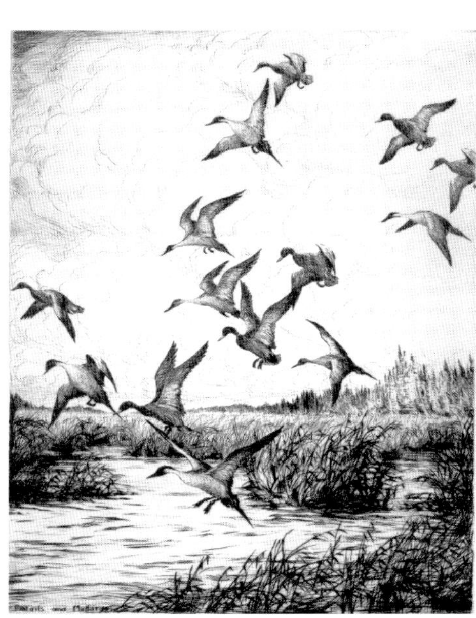

"Pintails and Mallards"
Medium: Etching
Associated American Artists
Image: 9.75 inches high by 7.875 inches wide

Hans Kleiber

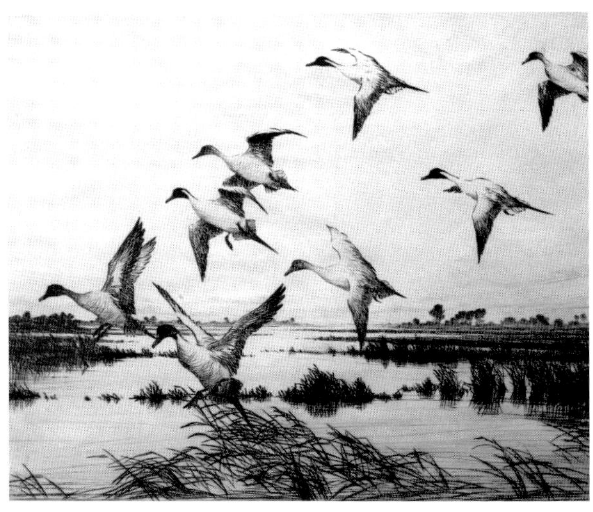

"Pintails Coming In"
Medium: Etching
Associated American Artist
Image: 10.75 inches high by 12.75 inches wide

Medium: Photogravure
Image: 5.625 inches high by 7 inches wide

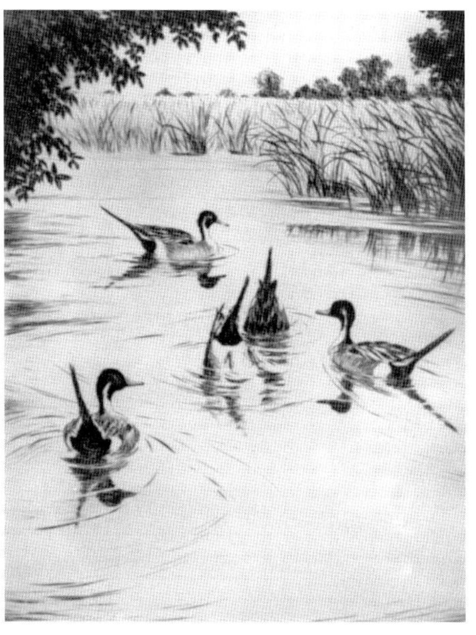

"Pintails Feeding"
Medium: Etching
Associated American Artists
Image: 8.5 inches high by 6.75 inches wide

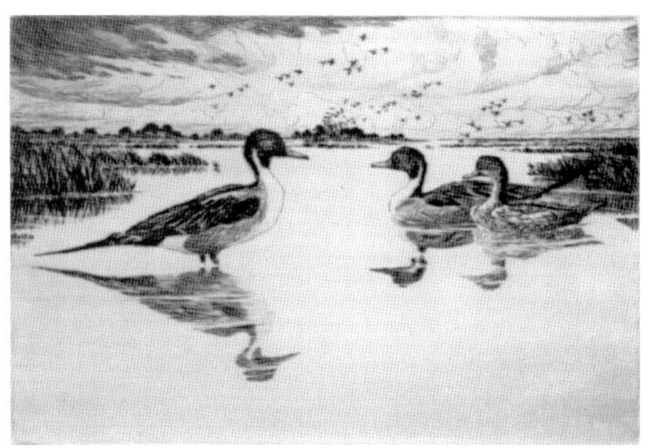

"Pintails Loafing"
Medium: Etching
Image: 4.75 inches high by 6.75 inches wide

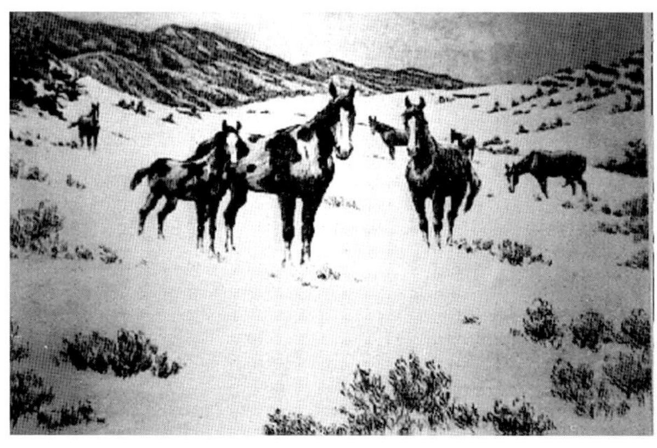

"Pinto Mare and Colt"
Medium: Etching
Image: 8.25 inches high by 11.75 inches wide

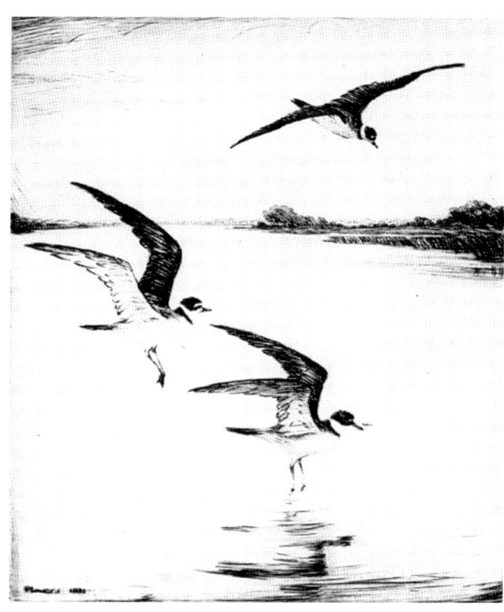

"Plovers"
First State
Medium: Etching
Image: 7.1875 inches high by 5.875 inches wide

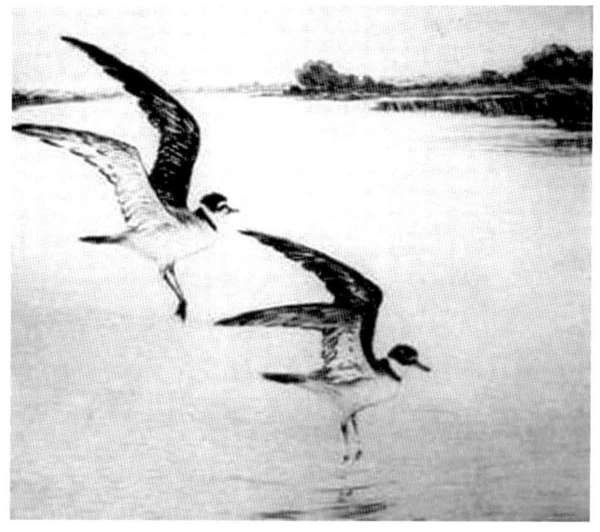

"Plover"
Second State of "Plovers"
Medium: Etching
Image: 4.5 inches high by 5.75 inches wide

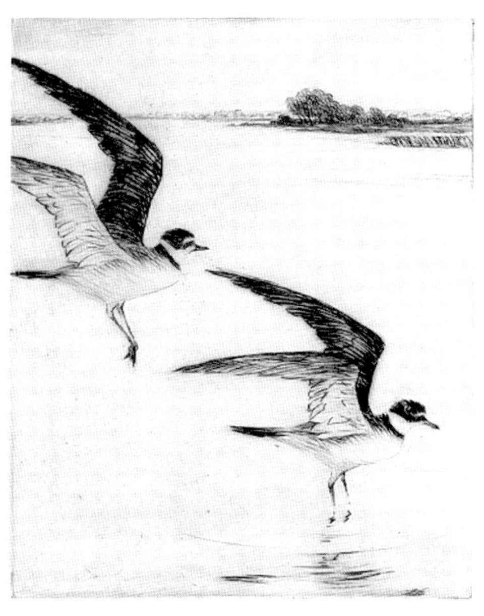

"Plover"
Third State of "Plovers"
Medium: Etching
Image: 4.625 inches high by 3.625 inches wide

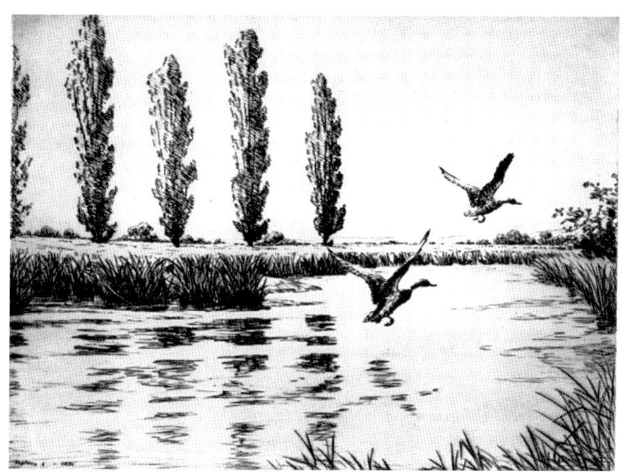

"Poplars I"
First State
Medium: Etching
Image: 8.3125 inches high by 10.75 inches wide

Hans Kleiber

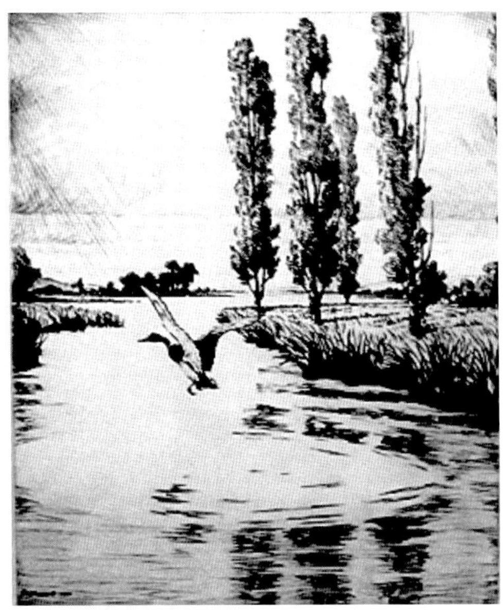

"Poplars II"
First State
Medium: Etching
Image: 10.75 inches high by 8.625 inches wide

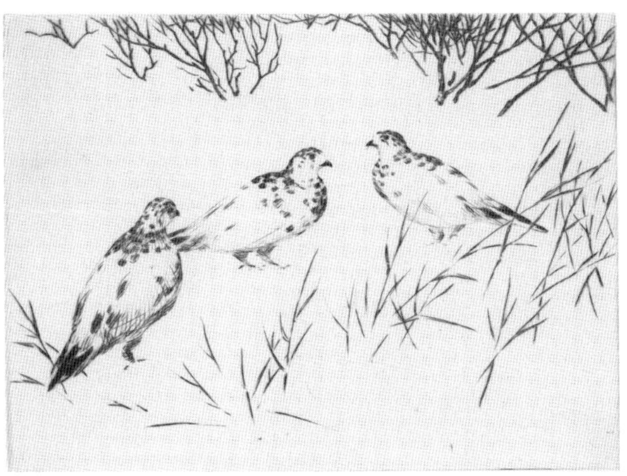

"Ptarmigan"
"Ptarmigan (Spring Plumage)"
Medium: Etching
Image: 4.875 inches high by 6.375 inches wide

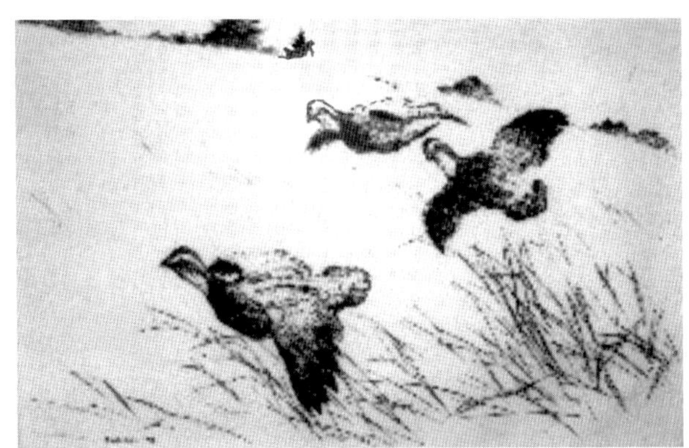

"Quail"
First State
Medium: Etching
Image: 5.25 inches high by 8.25 inches wide

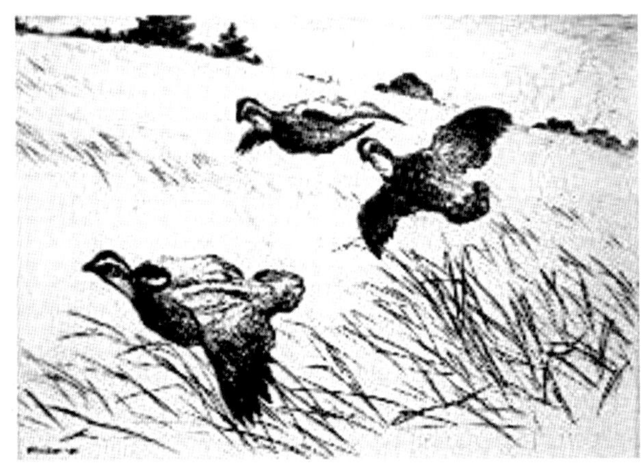

"Quail"
Second State of "Quail"
Medium: Etching
Image: 5.375 inches high by 7.25 inches wide

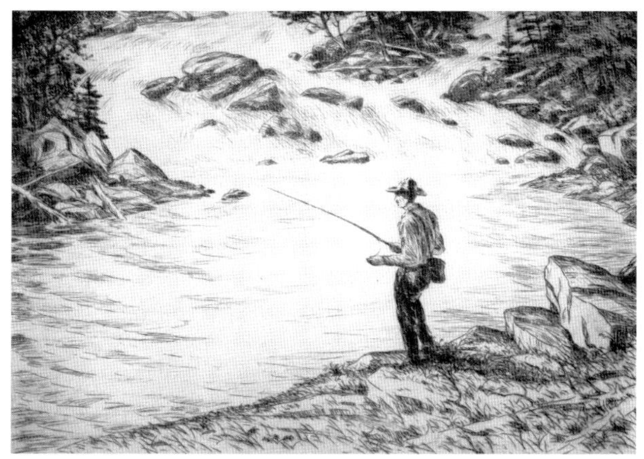

"Rainbow Water"
Medium: Etching
Image: 7.875 inches high by 10.75 inches wide

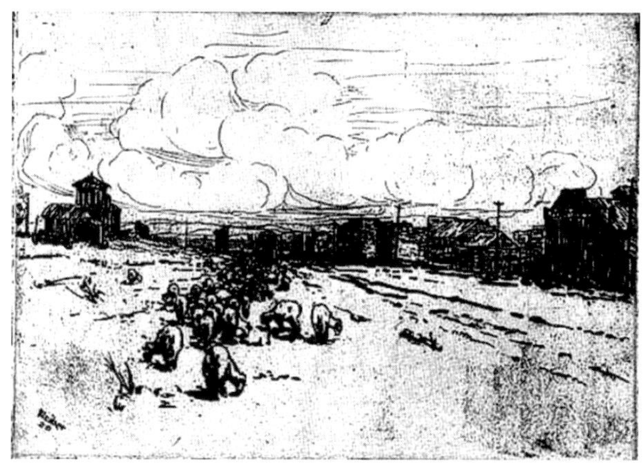

"Ranchester, Wyoming"
Medium: Etching, Photogravure
Image: 4.5 inches high by 6.875 inches wide

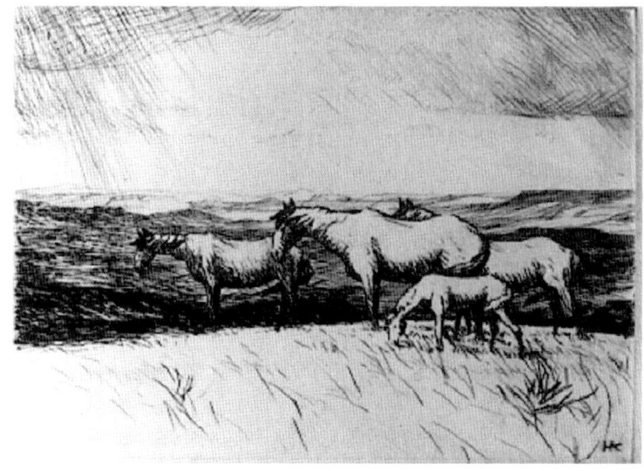

"Range Horses"
"Range Horses, Summer"
"Range Horses in Summer"
Medium: Photogravure
Image: 3.375 inches high by 4.5 inches wide

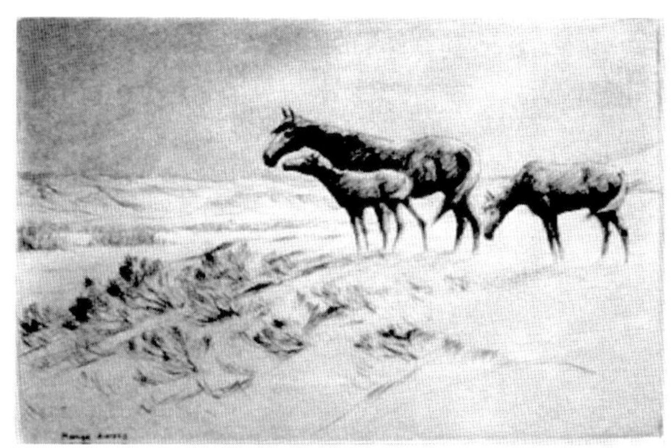

"Range Horses"
Medium: Etching
Image: 3.75 inches high by 5.75 inches wide

Hans Kleiber

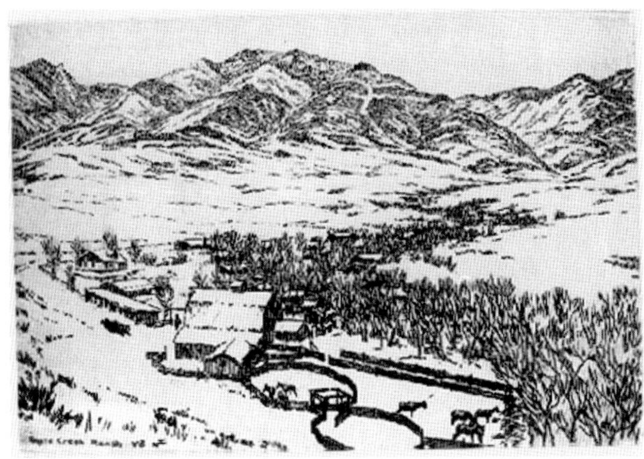

"Rapid Creek Ranch"
Medium: Photogravure
Image: 4.75 inches high by 6.75 inches wide

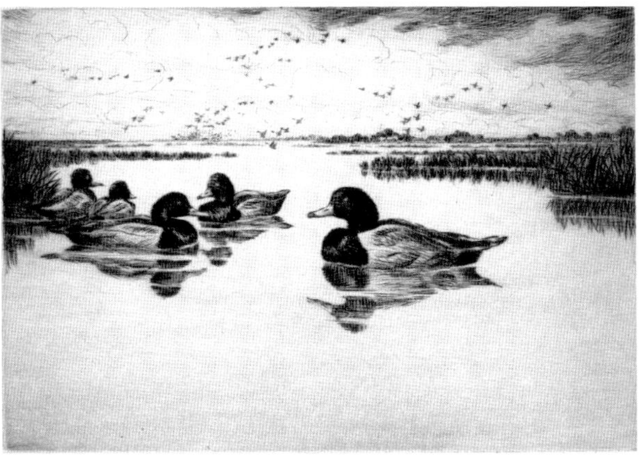

"Redheads--Loafing"
Medium: Etching
Image: 4.75 inches high by 6.75 inches wide

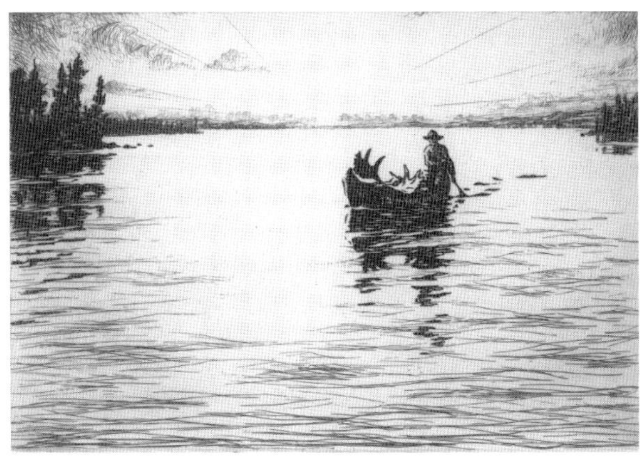

"Returning from the Hunt"
First State
Medium: Etching
Image: 7.8125 inches high by 11.3125 inches wide

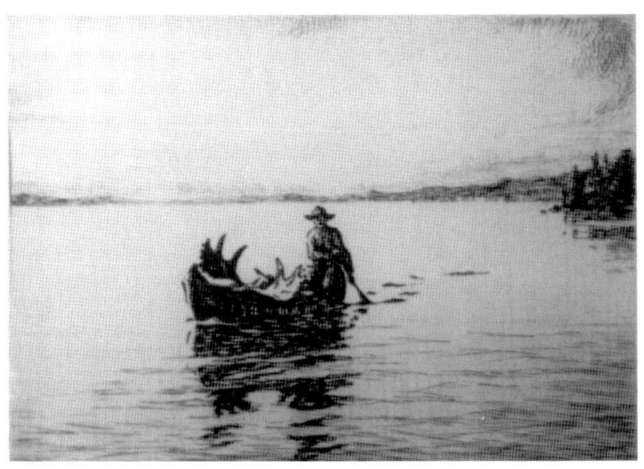

"Returning from the Hunt"
Second State of "Returning from the Hunt"
Medium: Photogravure
Image: 5.25 inches high by 7.375 inches wide

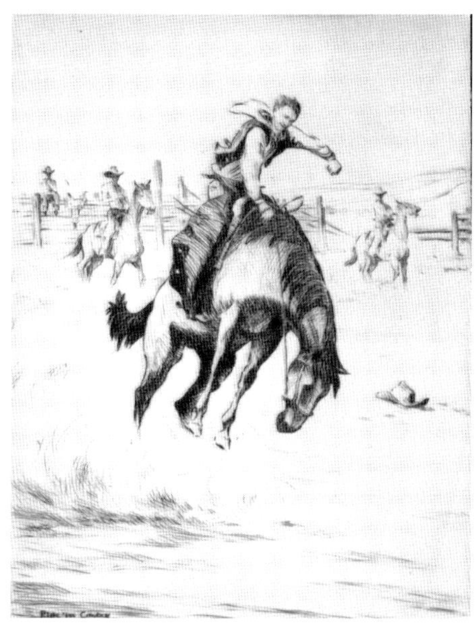

"Ride 'im Cowboy"
Medium: Etching
Image: 6.25 inches high by 4.75 inches wide

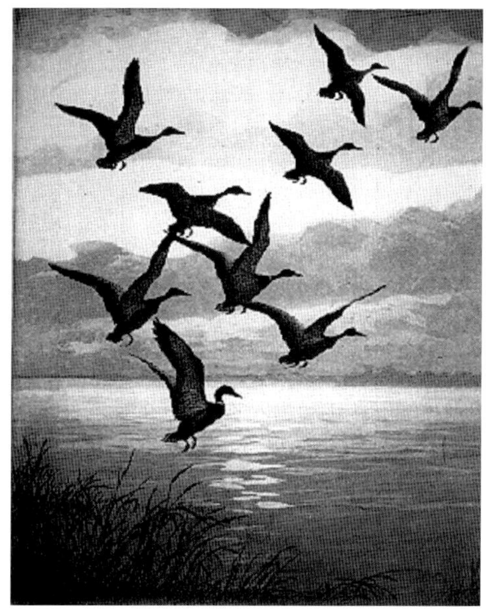

"Rising"
Medium: Etching
Image: 10.875 inches high by 8.75 inches wide

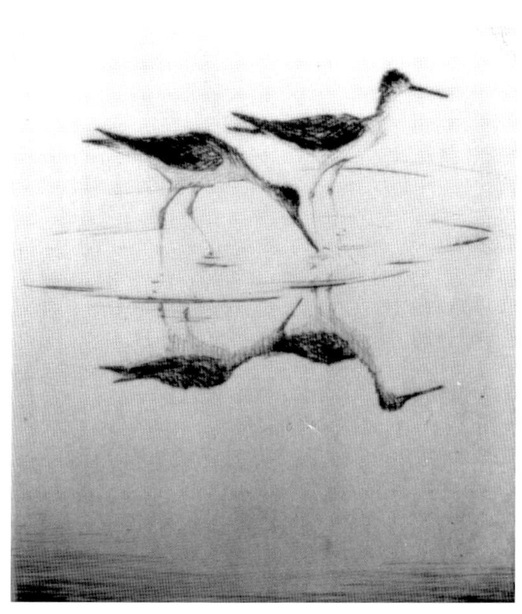

"Sandpipers"
"Yellowlegs, III"
Second State of "Yellow Legs"
Medium: Etching
Image: 3.875 inches high by 3.25 inches wide

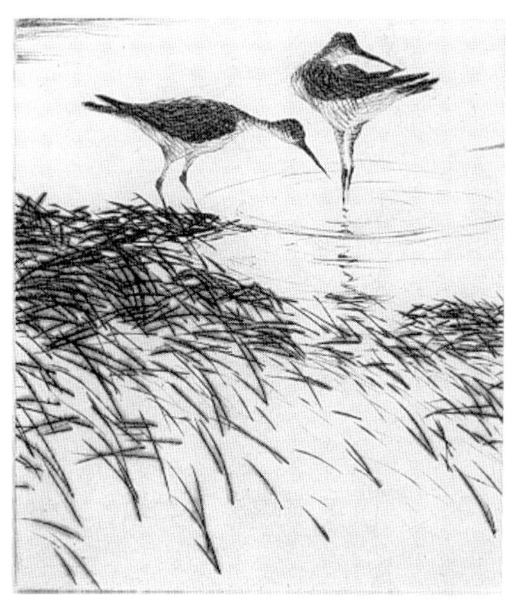

"Sand Pipers II"
"Sandpipers II"
Second State of
"Yellowlegs, No. II"
Medium: Etching
Image: 3.875 inches high by 3.25 inches wide

Hans Kleiber

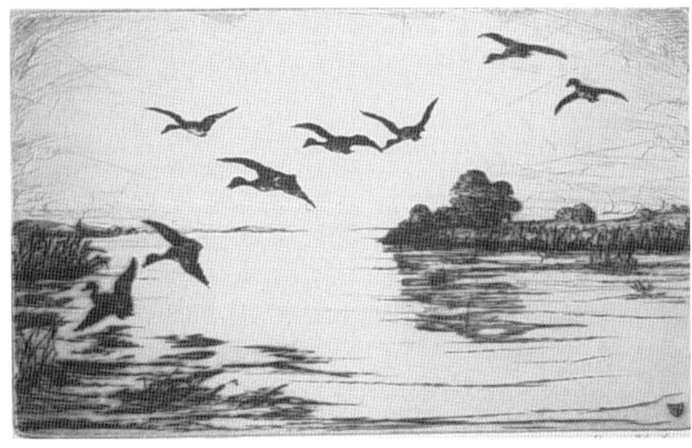

"Settling at Sundown"
Medium: Etching
Image: 5.375 inches high by 8.625 inches wide

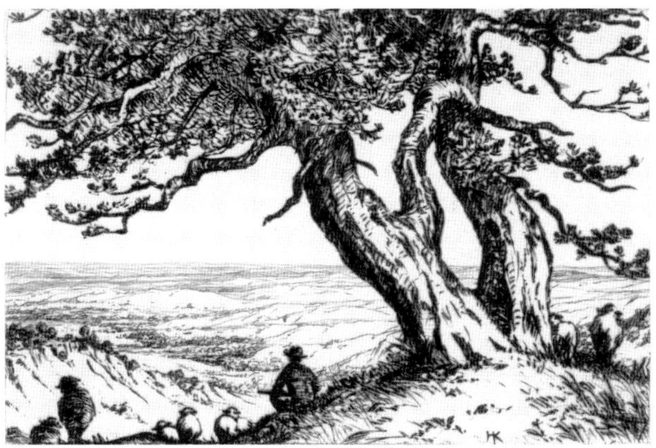

"Sheep Herder I"
"Sheepherder"
"Sheepherder II"
"The Sheep Herder I"
"The Sheepherder"
Medium: Etching
Image: 3.75 inches high by 5.5 inches wide

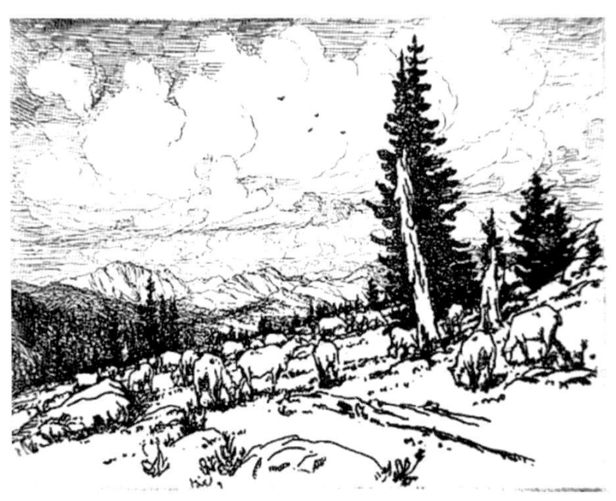

"Sheep on Paintrock - Wyoming"
Medium: Etching, Photogravure
Image: 4.875 inches high by 6.75 inches wide

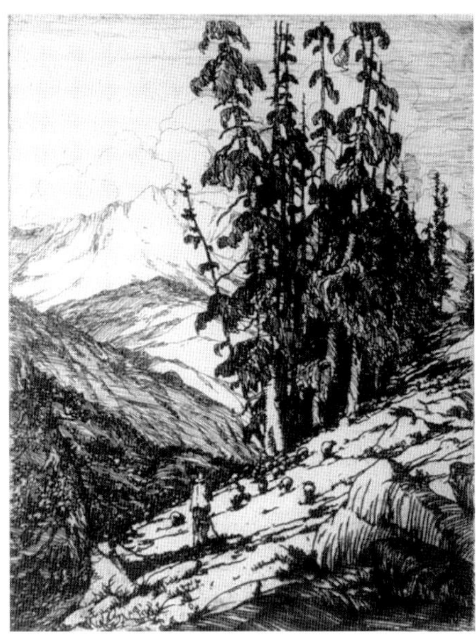

"Sheep in the Bighorns"
"Sheep on the Bighorns - Wyoming"
Medium: Etching, Photogravure
Image: 7.75 inches high by 5.75 inches wide

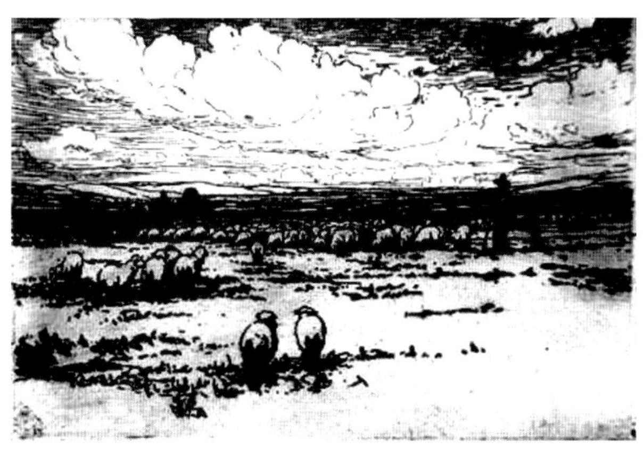

"Sheep on the Range"
"Sheep on the Spring Range"
Medium: Etching
Image: 4.75 inches high by 7.75 inches wide

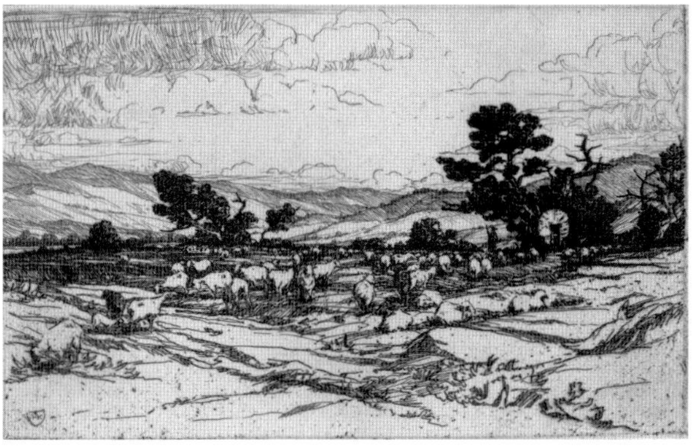

"Sheep Wagon I"
Medium: Etching
Image: 5.75 inches high by 9.25 inches wide

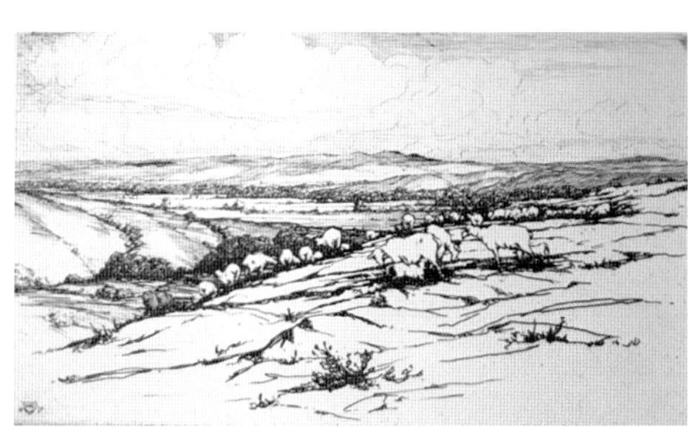

"Sheep on Tongue River - Wyoming"
Medium: Etching, Photogravure
Image: 5.5 inches high by 9.25 inches wide

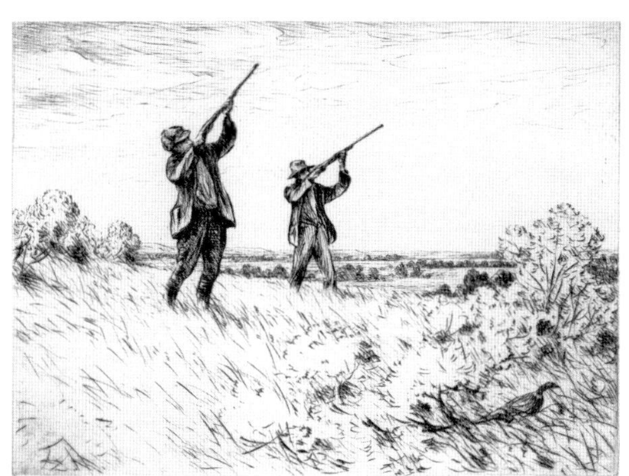

"Shooting Pheasants"
Medium: Etching
Image: 4.75 inches high by 6.375 inches wide

Hans Kleiber

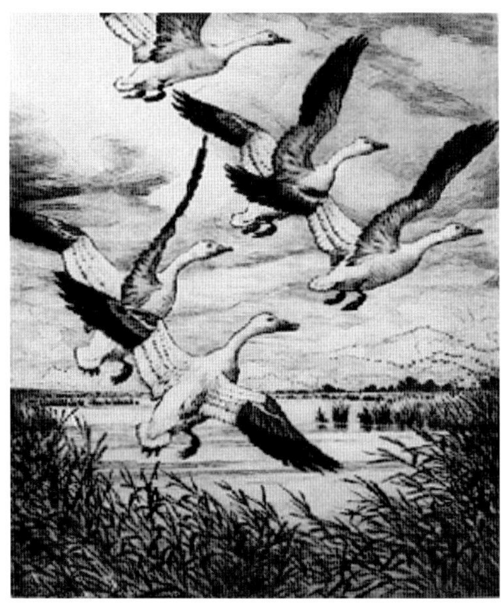

"Snow Geese"
Medium: Etching
Image: 8.25 inches high by 6.75 inches wide

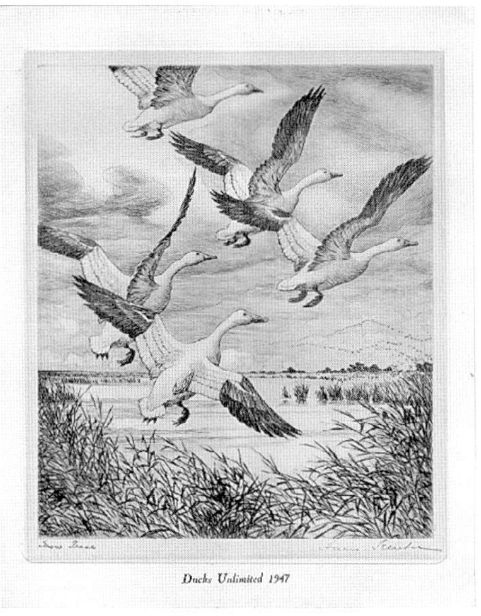

"Snow Geese"
Ducks Unlimited 1947
Medium: Photogravure
Image: 8.625 inches high by 7 inches wide

Ducks Unlimited, the national organization, was unable to find any record of this image but highly suspected that it was done on a regional or state level.

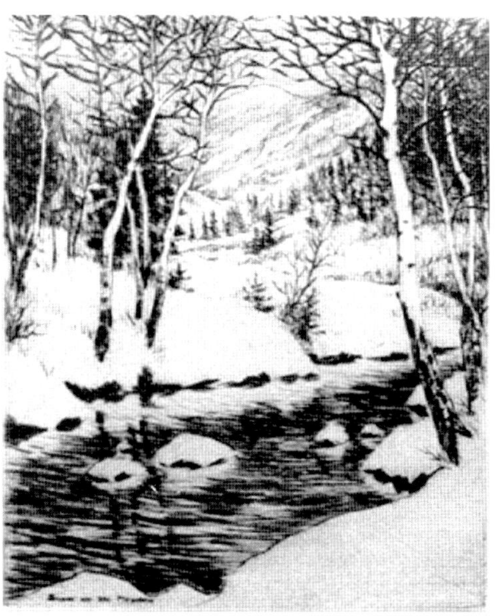

"Snow in the Meadow"
"Snow on the Meadow"
Medium: Etching
Image: 5 inches high by 3.875 inches wide

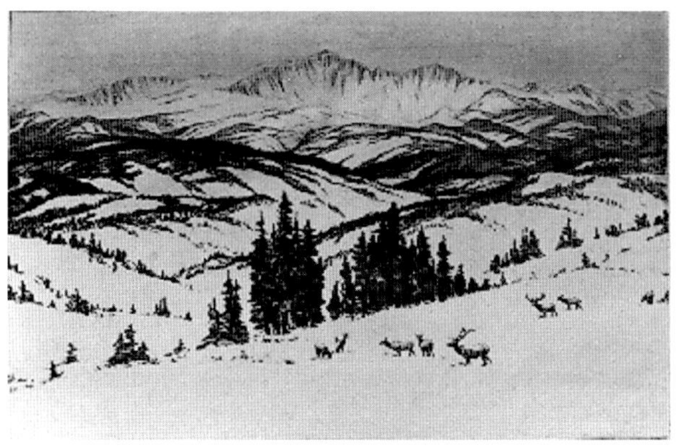

"Snow in the Rockies"
Medium: Etching
Image: 8.25 inches high by 11.75 inches wide

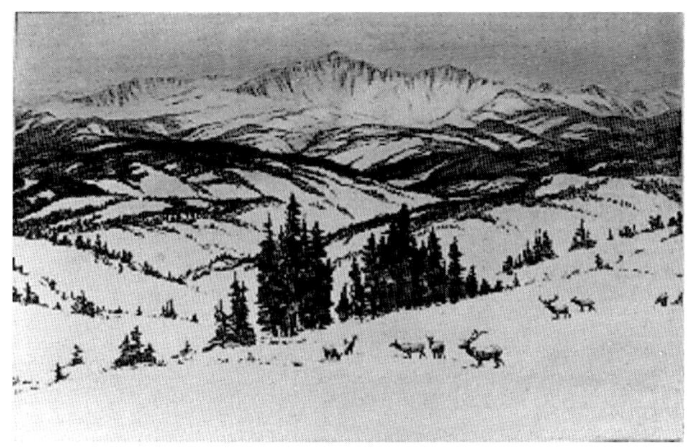

"Snow in the Rockies"
Medium: Photogravure
Image: 8.75 inches high by 11.75 inches wide

Medium: Photogravure
Image: 3.5 inches high by 4.4375 inches wide

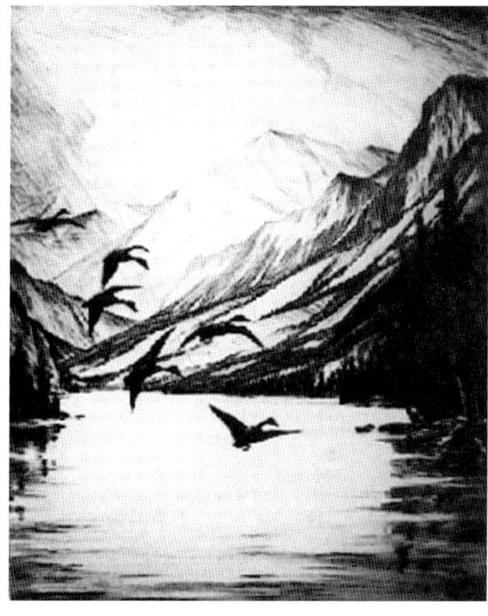

"Solitude II"
Medium: Etching
Image: 6.375 inches high by 4.75 inches wide

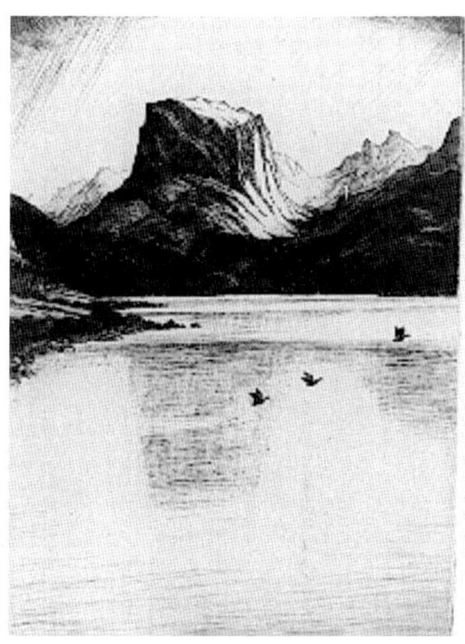

"Square Top - Green River"
"Table Mountain - Green River Lake"
Medium: Etching
Image: 10.375 inches high by 7.375 inches wide

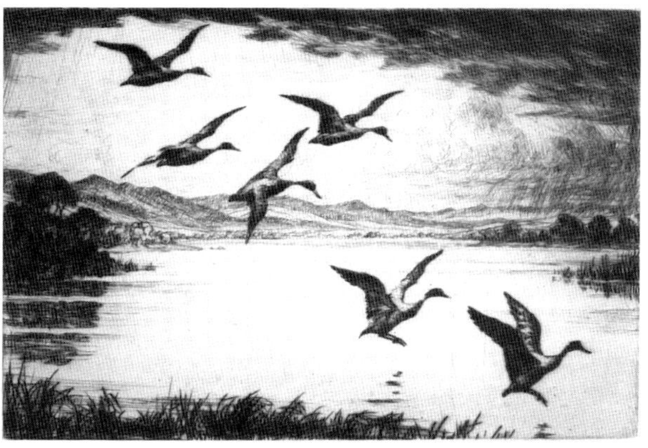

"Cloudy Afternoon"
"Stormy Afternoon"
Medium: Etching
Image: 3.625 inches high by 5.3125 inches wide

Hans Kleiber

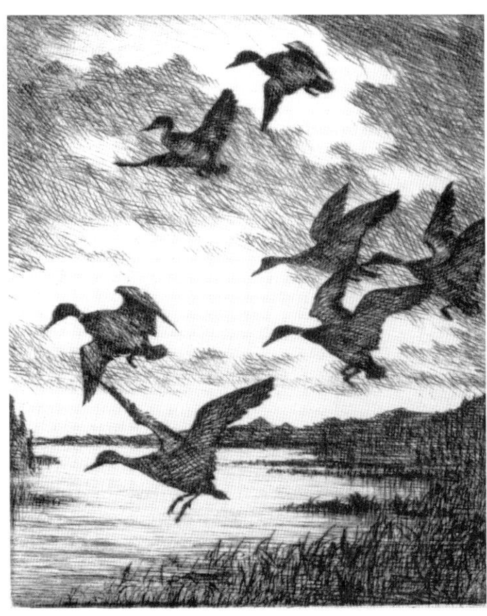

"Stormy Evening"
Medium: Etching
Image: 4.75 inches high by 3.75 inches wide

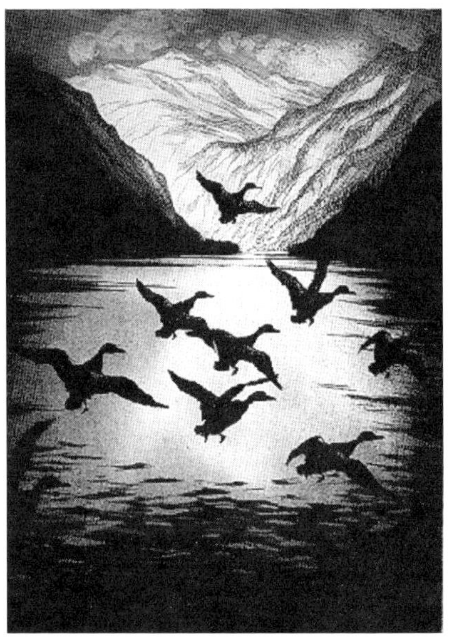

"Stormy Sunset"
Medium: Etching
Image: 11.75 inches high by 8.375 inches wide

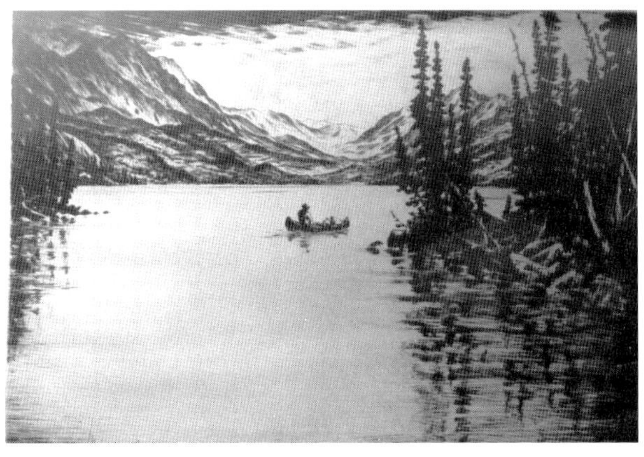

"Summer in the Rockies"
Medium: Etching
Associated American Artists
Image: 7.75 inches high by 10.75 inches wide

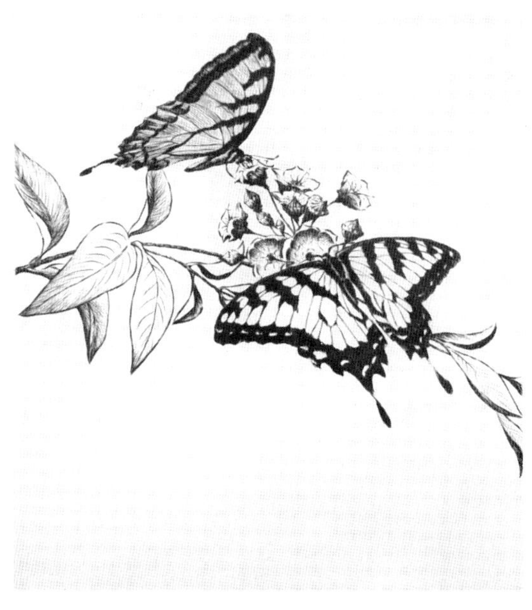

"Swallow Tails"
"Swallowtails"
Medium: Etching
Associated American Artists
Image: 10.75 inches high by 9.125 inches wide

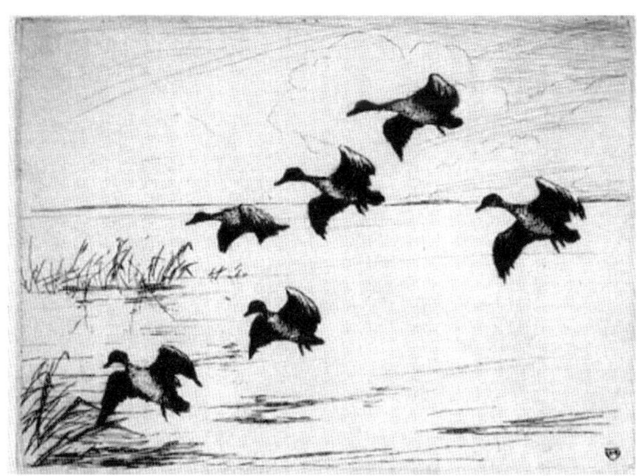

"Teal"
Medium: Etching
Image: 5.125 inches high by 6.75 inches wide

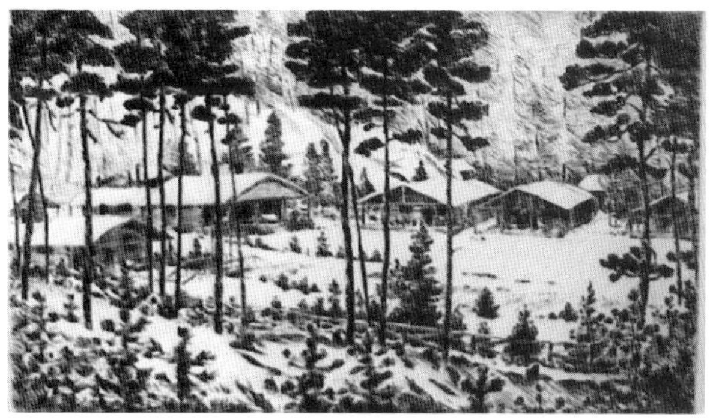

"Tepee Lodge"
Medium: Etching
Image: 4.75 inches high by 7.25 inches wide

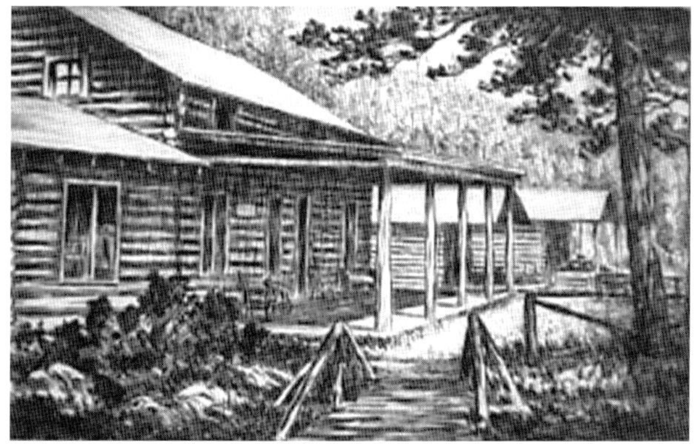

"Untitled - Tepee Lodge"
Medium: Etching
Image: 5 inches high by 7.25 inches wide

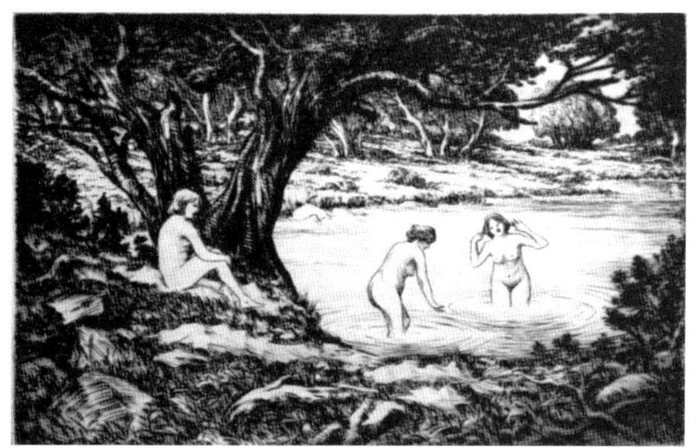

"The Bathers I"
Medium: Etching
Image: 4 inches high by 6.25 inches wide

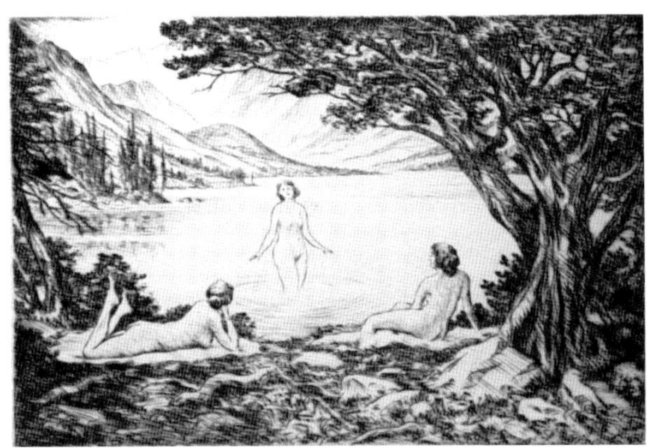

"The Bathers II"
Medium: Etching
Image: 4.25 inches high by 6.25 inches wide

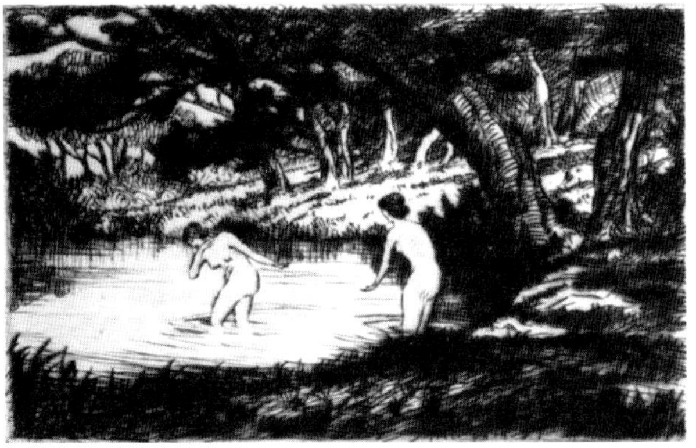

"The Bathers No. 1"
Medium: Etching
Image: 3.25 inches high by 5 inches wide

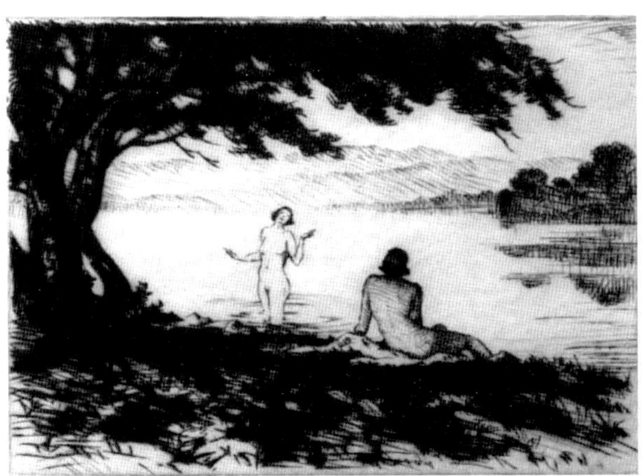

"The Bathers No. 2"
Medium: Etching
Image: 3.8125 inches high by 5.25 inches wide

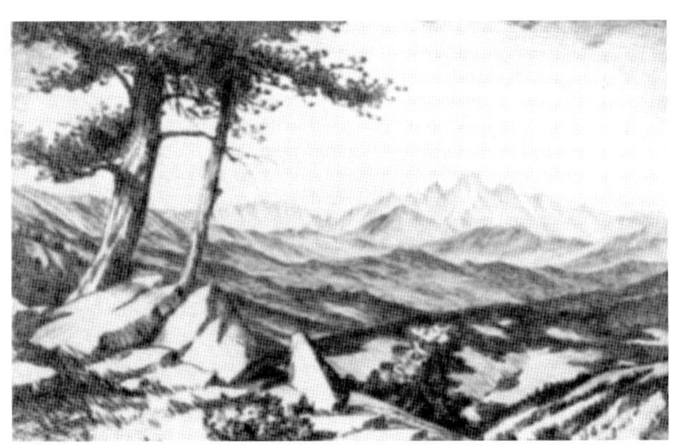

"Big Horn Peaks"
"The Bighorns"
"The Bighorns - Black Tooth"
Medium: Etching
Image: 3.625 inches high by 5.25 inches wide

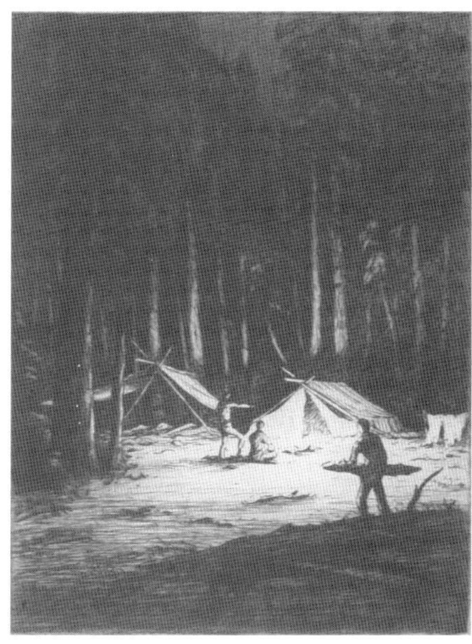

"The Campfire"
Medium: Etching
Image: 10.75 inches high by 7.75 inches wide

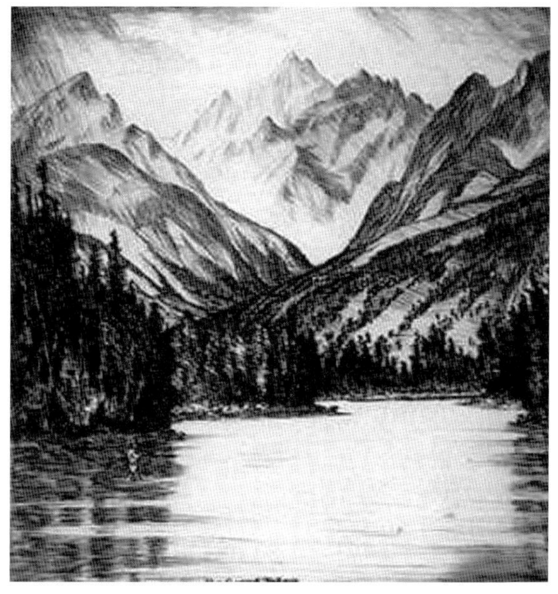

"The Grand Teton"
First State
Medium: Etching
Image: 5.75 inches high 4.75 inches wide

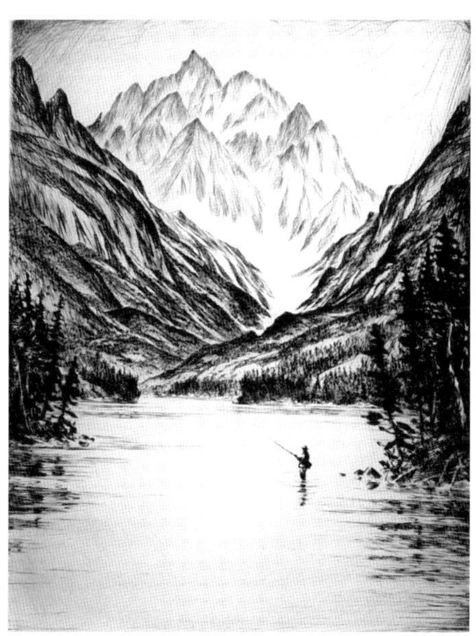

"The Grand Teton"
"The Teton"
"Grand Teton"
Medium: Etching
Associated American Artists
Image: 11.75 inches high by 8.75 inches wide

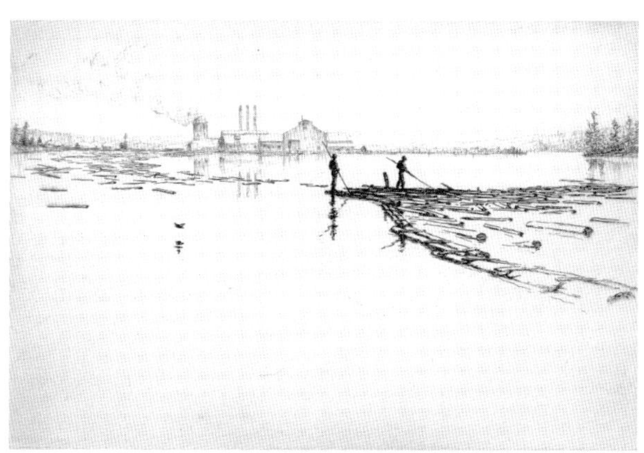

"The Log Boom"
Medium: Etching
Image: 7.25 inches high by 10.75 inches wide

Hans Kleiber

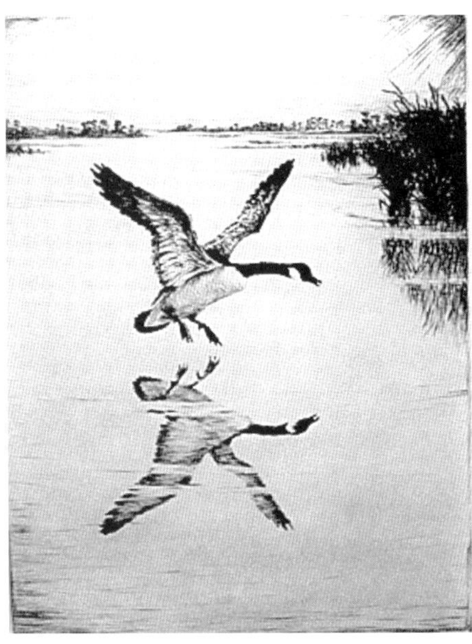

"The Lone Goose"
Medium: Etching
Image: 11.75 inches high by 8.5 inches wide

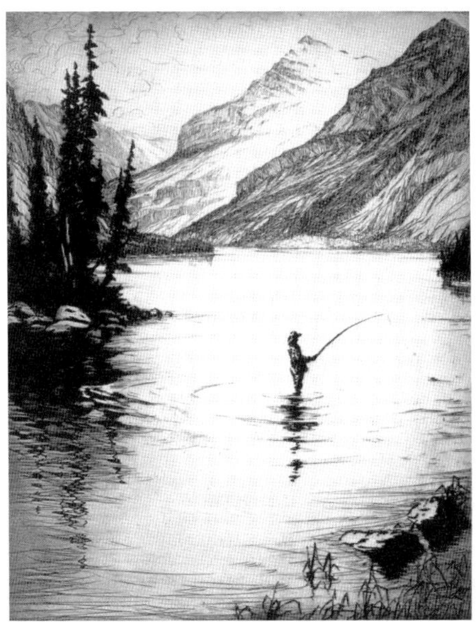

"The Lone Fisherman"
Medium: Etching
Image: 11.75 inches high by 8.75 inches wide
Medium: Photogravure
Image: 7.375 inches high by 5.375 inches wide

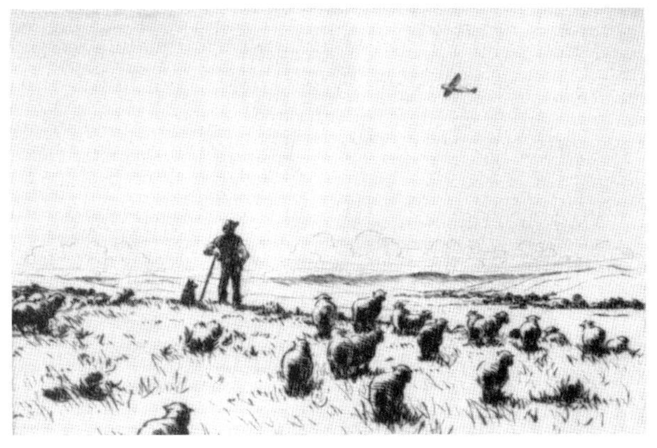

"The Old and the New"
First State
Medium: Etching
Image: 6.25 inches high by 9.25 inches wide

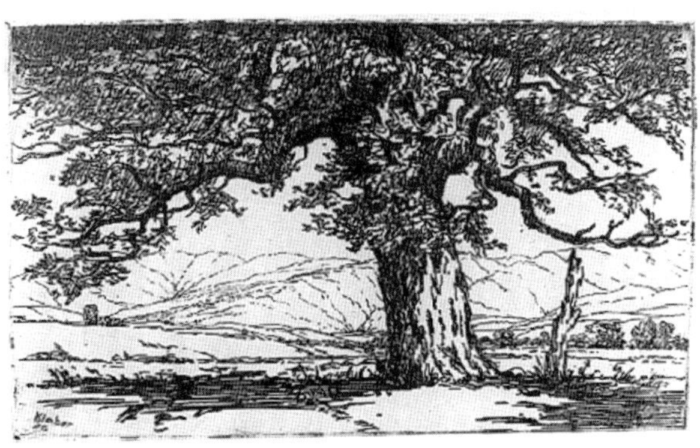

"The Old Cottonwood Tree"
Medium: Etching
Image: 4.875 inches high by 7.875 inches wide

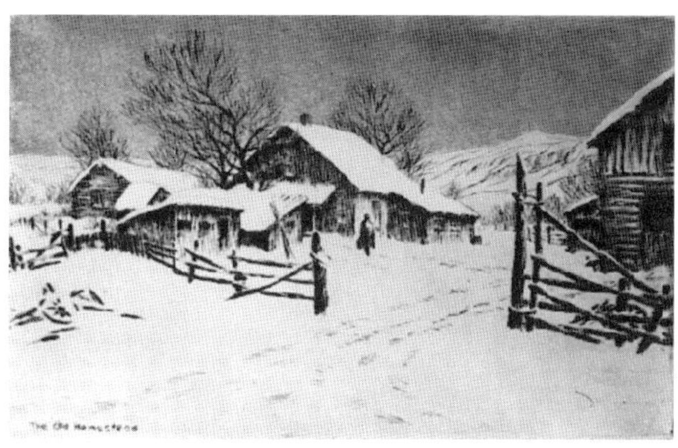

"The Old Homestead"
Medium: Photogravure
Image: 3.75 inches high by 5.875 inches wide

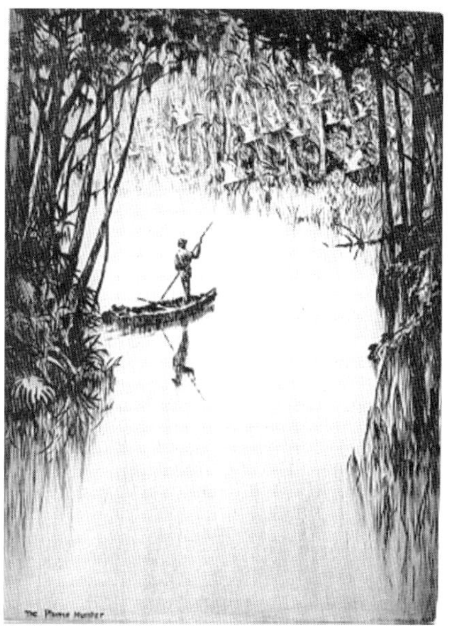

"The Plume Hunter"
Medium: Etching
Associated American Artists
Image: 11.75 inches high by 8.25 inches wide

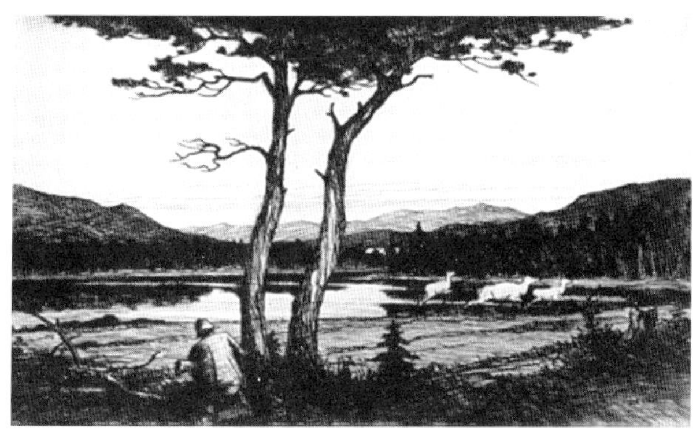

"The Poacher"
First State
Medium: Etching
Image: 5.25 inches high by 8.25 inches wide

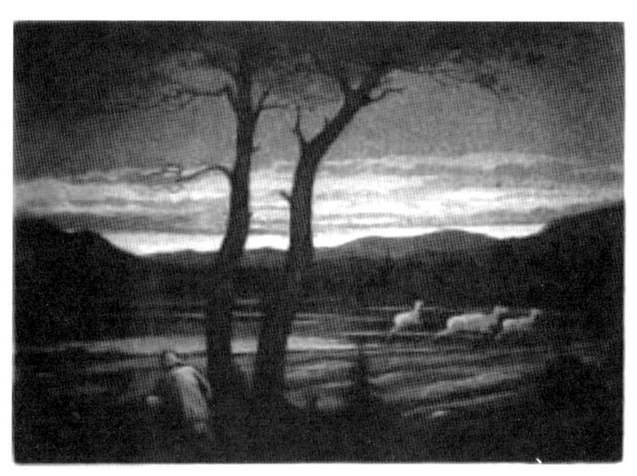

"The Poacher"
Second State
Medium: Etching
Image: 5.25 inches high by 7.25 inches wide

Hans Kleiber

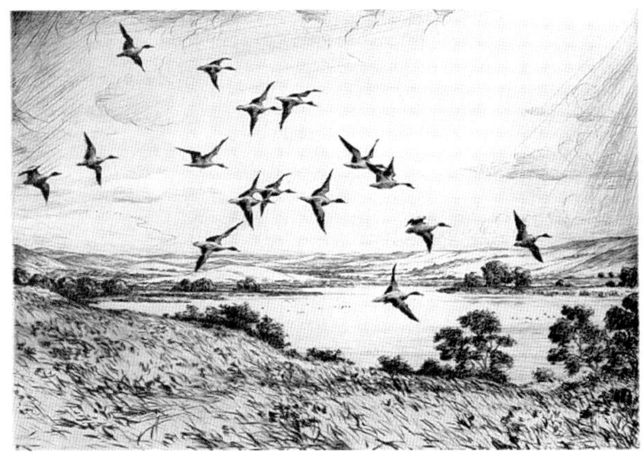

"The Pond in the Hills"
Medium: Etching
Associated American Artists
Image: 7.75 inches high by 11.75 inches wide

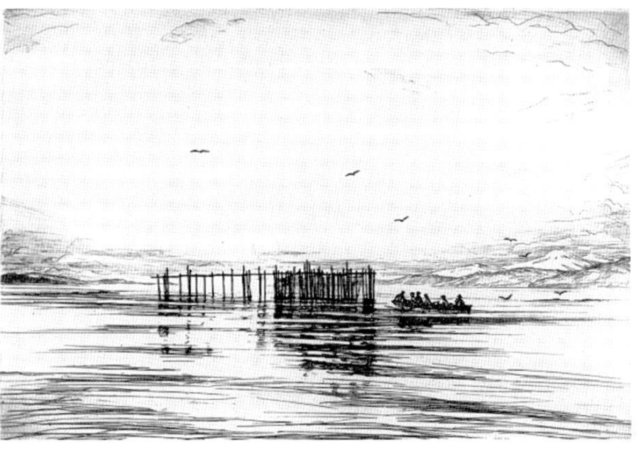

"The Salmon Trap"
Medium: Photogravure
Image: 8.375 inches high by 11.875 inches wide

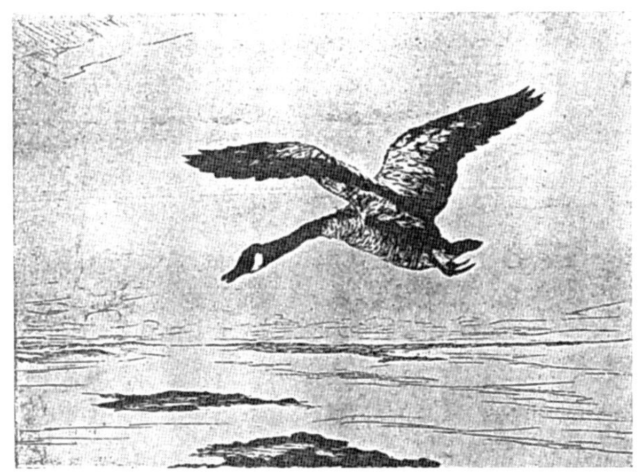

"The Scout"
Medium: Etching
Image: 6.25 inches high by 8.5 inches wide

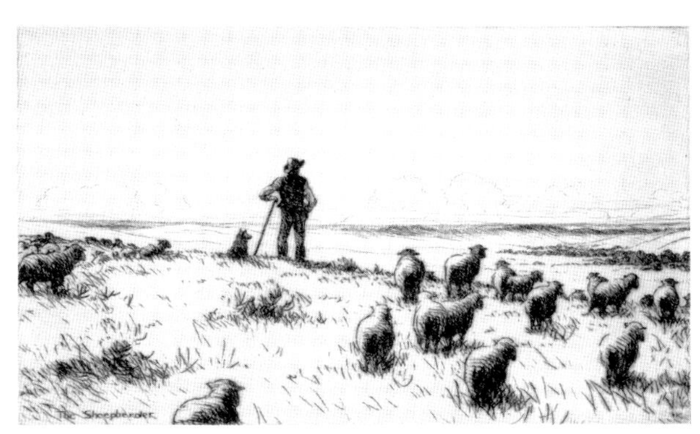

"The Sheepherder"
Second State of "The Old and the New"
Medium: Etching
Image: 4.8125 inches high by 7.75 inches wide

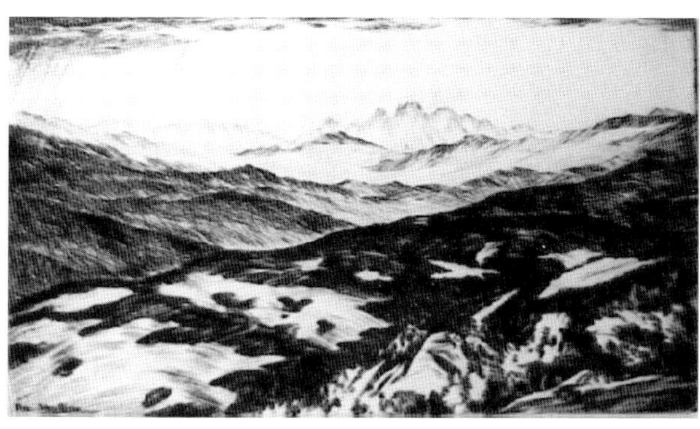

"The Skyline"
Medium: Etching
Image: 4.0625 inches high by 6.8125 inches wide

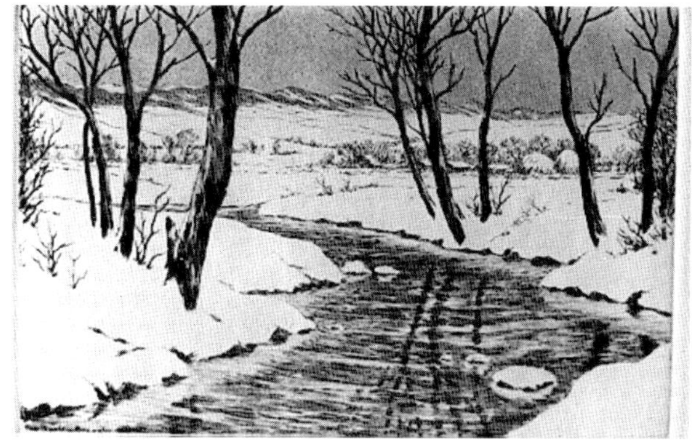

"The Spring Branch"
Medium: Photogravure
Image: 3.8125 inches high by 5.75 inches wide

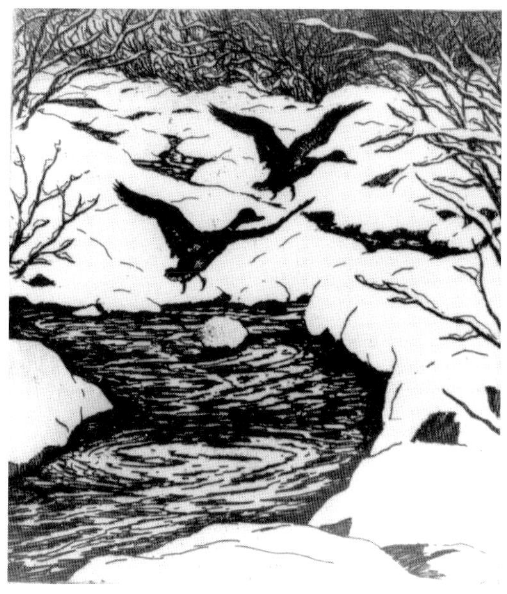

"The Spring Branch"
Medium: Etching
Image: 9.25 inches high by 7.75 inches wide

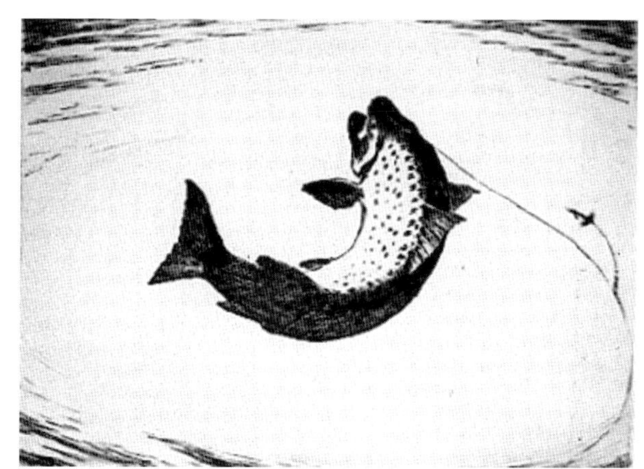

"The Strike"
Medium: Etching
Image: 5.75 inches high by 7.75 inches wide

Hans Kleiber

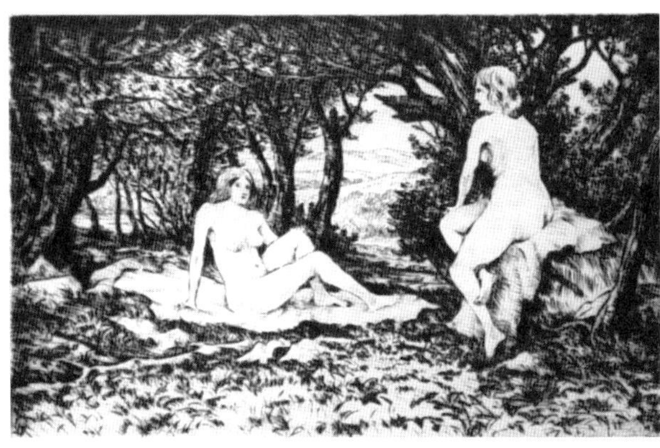

"The Sun Bath"
Medium: Etching
Image: 3.75 inches high by 5.75 inches wide

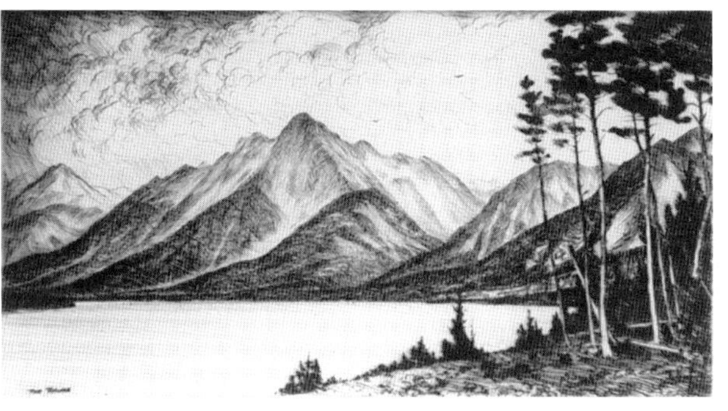

"The Tetons"
Medium: Etching
Image: 3.875 inches high by 6.875 inches wide

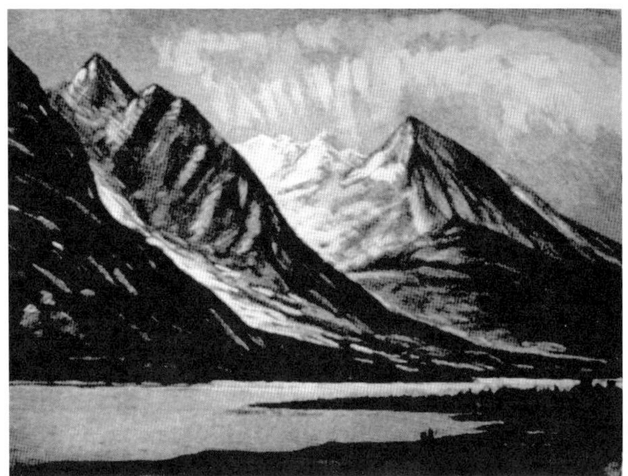

"The Tetons from the South"
"The Tetons, Wyoming"
Medium: Etching
Image: 6.0625 inches high by 7.75 inches wide

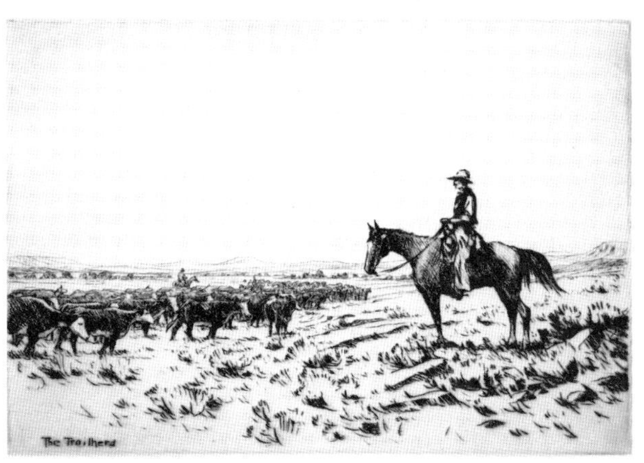

"The Trailherd"
Medium: Etching
Image: 4.75 inches high by 6.75 inches wide

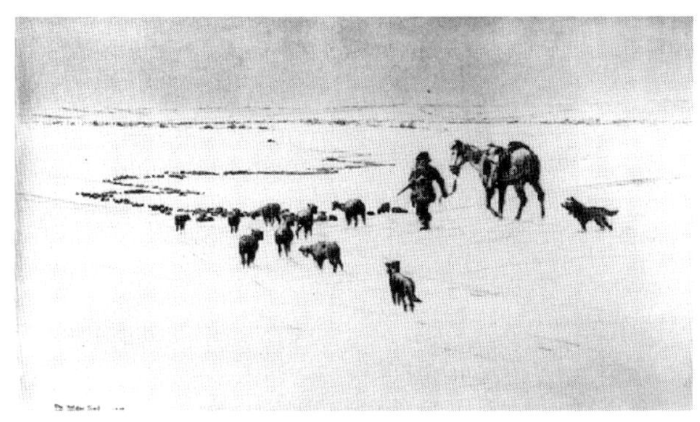

"The Winter Trail"
"Winter Trail"
Medium: Etching
Image: 7.625 inches high by 12.75 inches wide

Medium: Photogravure
Image: 5 inches high by 7.75 inches wide

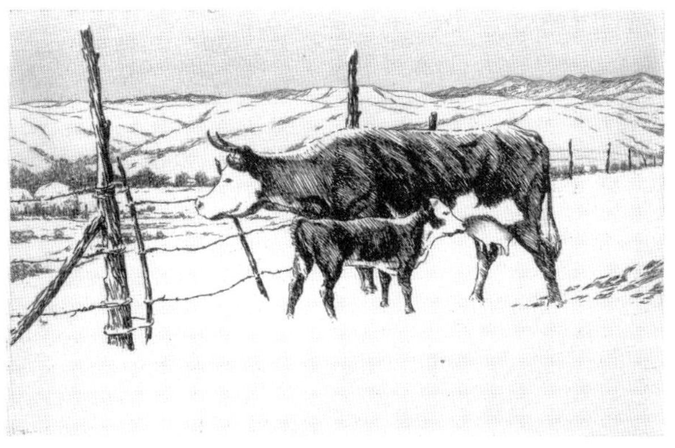

"The Wire Gate"
Medium: Photogravure
Image: 3.75 inches high by 5.875 inches wide

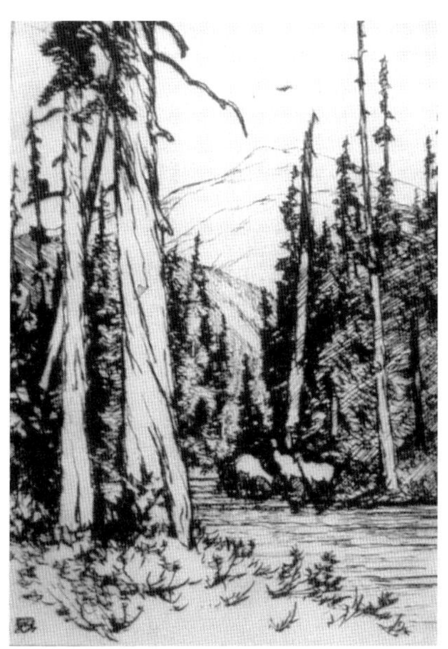

"Three Deer"
Medium: Etching
Image: 8.25 inches high by 5.75 inches wide

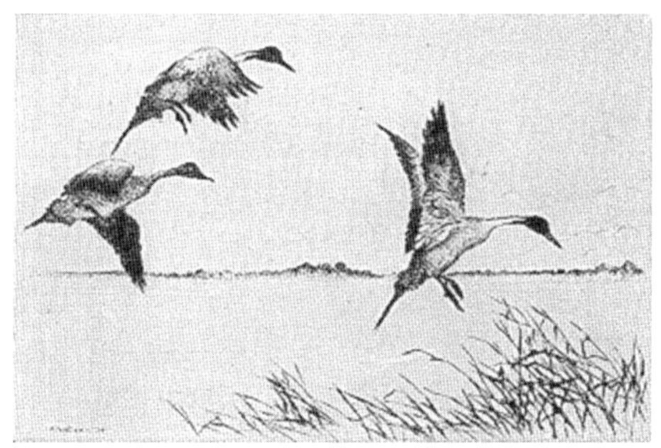

"Three Pintails"
Medium: Etching
Image: 6.0625 inches high by 8.75 inches wide

Hans Kleiber

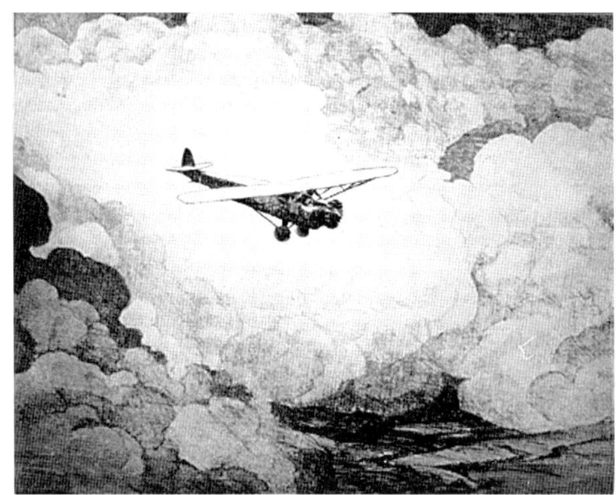

"Through the Clouds"
Medium: Etching
Image: 7.875 inches high by 9.75 inches wide

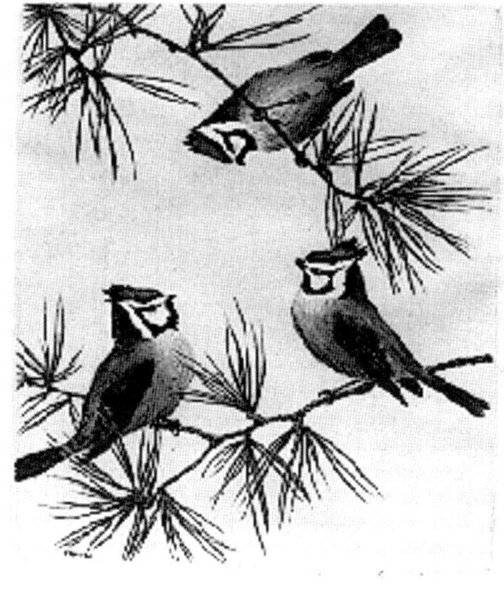

"Titmice"
Medium: Etching
Image: 5.8125 inches high by 4.8125 inches wide

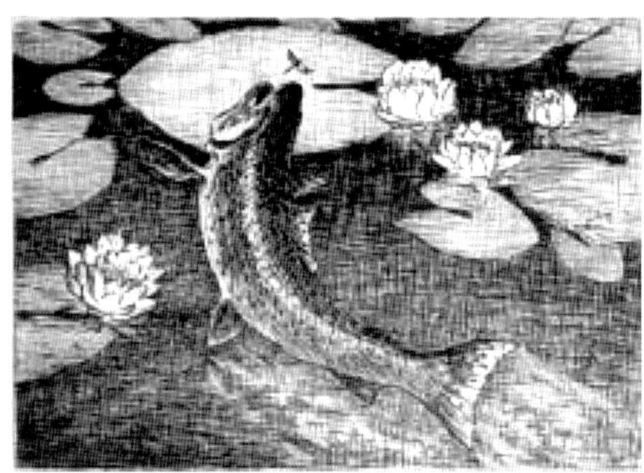

"Trout and Lilies"
Medium: Etching
Image; 3.75 inches high by 5.25 inches wide

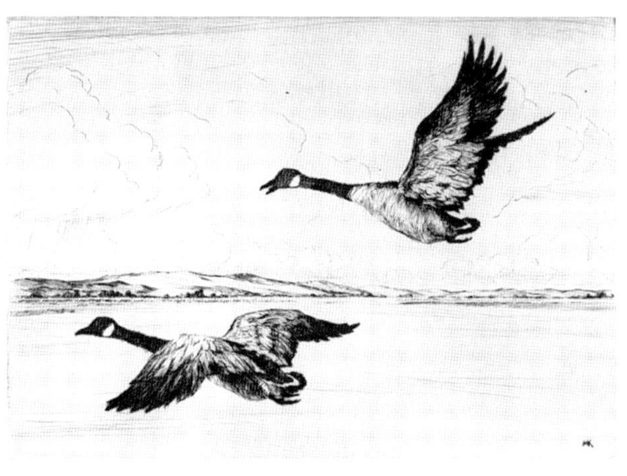

"Two Geese"
First State
Medium: Etching
Image: 7.25 inches high by 9.875 inches wide

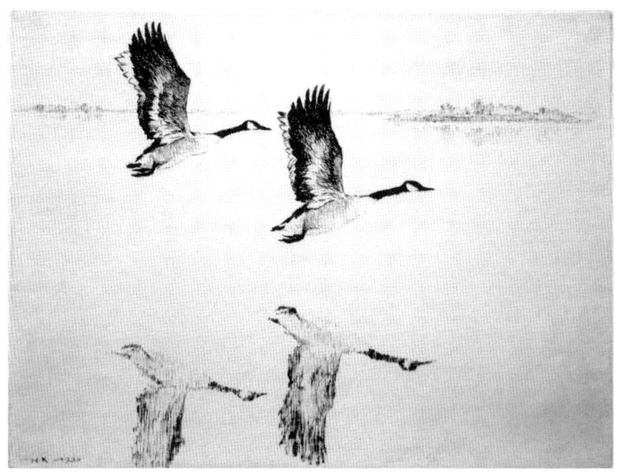

"Two Honkers"
Medium: Etching
Image: 6.75 inches high by 8.75 inches wide

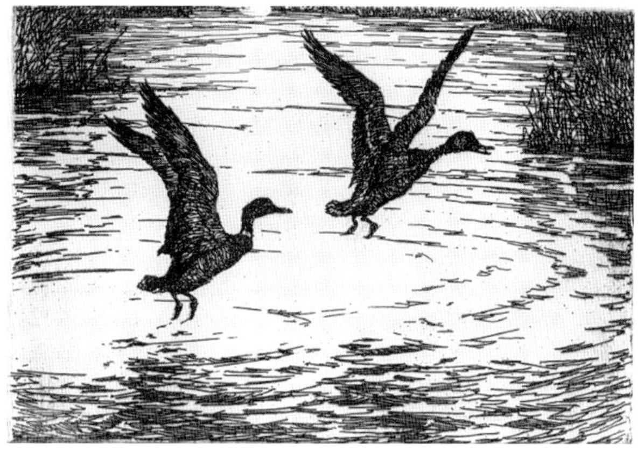

"Two Mallards"
Medium: Photogravure
Image; 4.875 inches high by 6.8125 inches wide

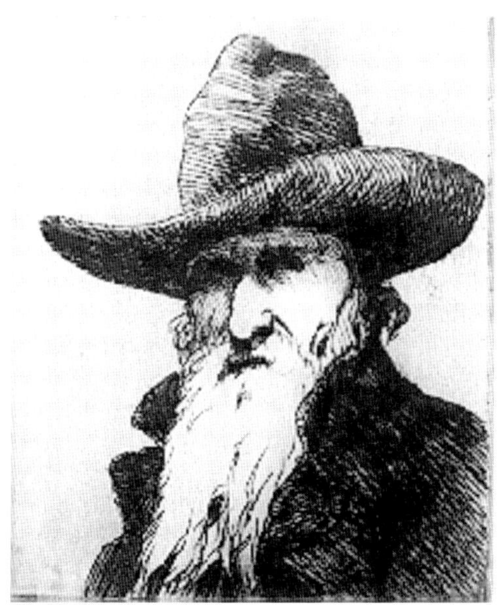

"Uncle Ben"
Medium: Etching
Image: 4.875 inches high by 4 inches wide

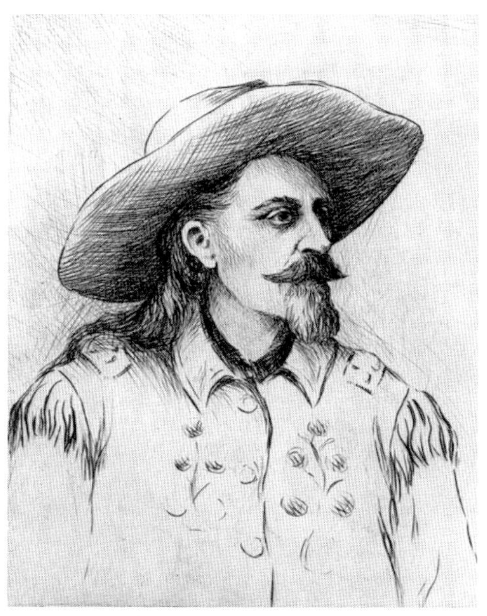

"Untitled - Buffalo Bill Cody"
Medium: Etching
Image: 5.625 inches high by 4.375 inches wide

Hans Kleiber

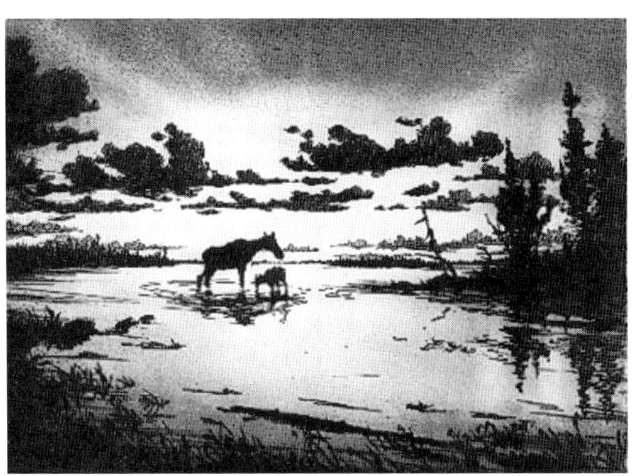

"Untitled - Cow Moose and Calf"
Medium: Etching
Image: 8.75 inches high by 11.625 inches wide

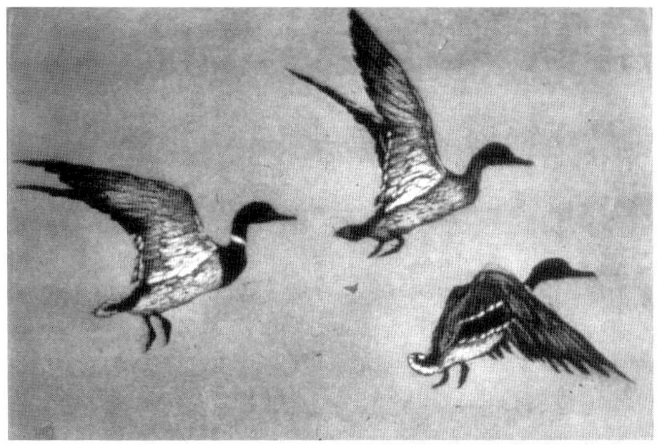

"Untitled - Three Mallards"
Medium: Etching
Image: 5.25 inches high by 7.5 inches wide

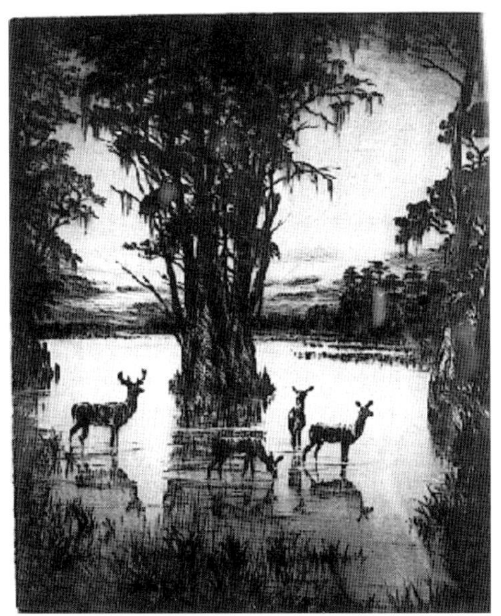

"Virginia Deer"
Medium: Etching
Image: 9.75 inches high by 7.75 inches wide

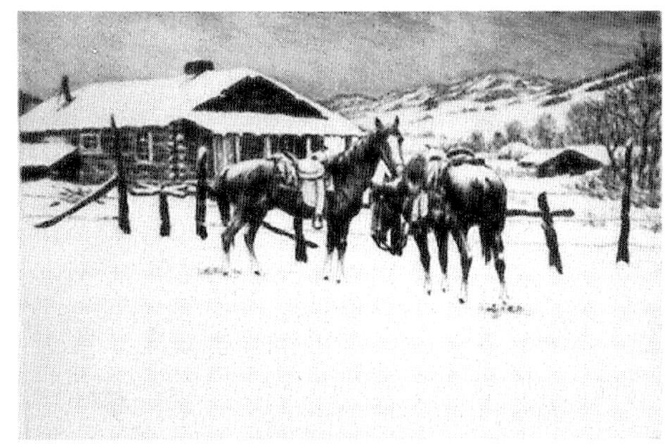

"Visitors"
Medium: Etching
Image: 7.5 inches high by 10.75 inches wide

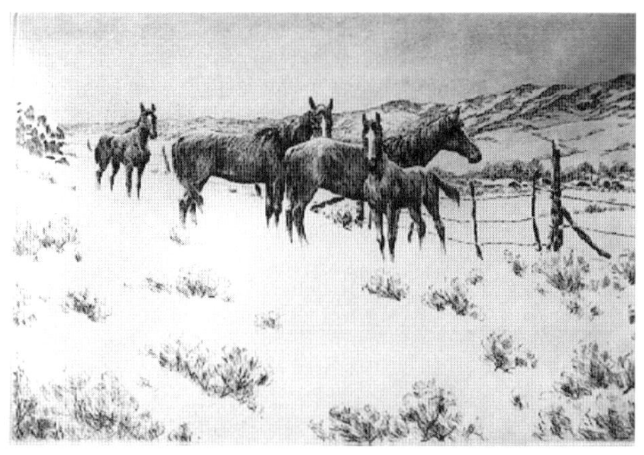

"Waiting at the Gate"
Medium: Etching
Image: 8.25 inches high by 11.75 inches wide

Medium: Photogravure
Image: 5.25 inches high by 8 inches wide

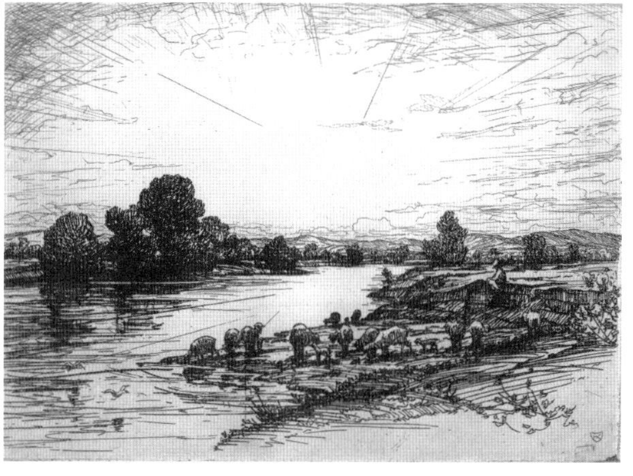

"Watering Sheep"
Medium: Etching, Photogravure
Image: 5.875 inches high by 7.875 inches wide

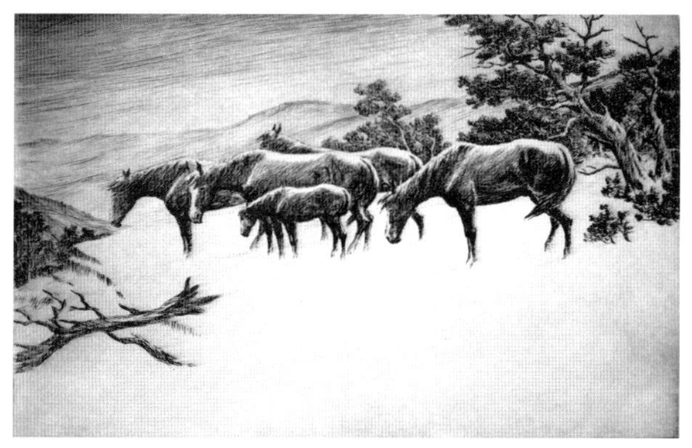

"Weathering a Storm"
Medium: Etching
Image: 7.875 inches high by 11.75 inches wide

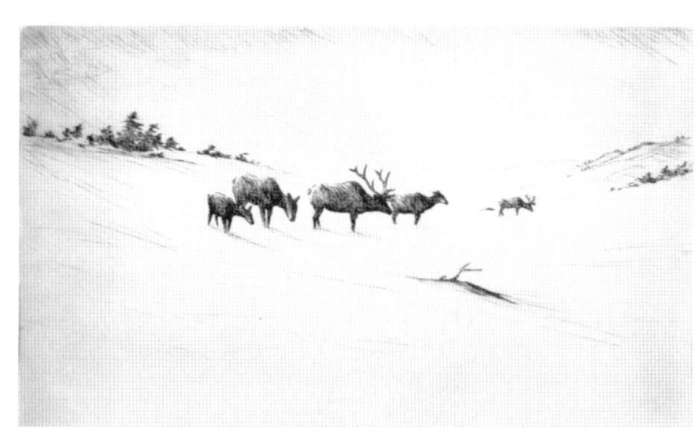

"Weathering the Storm"
"Weathering a Storm"
Medium: Etching
Image: 7.75 inches high by 11.75 inches wide

Hans Kleiber

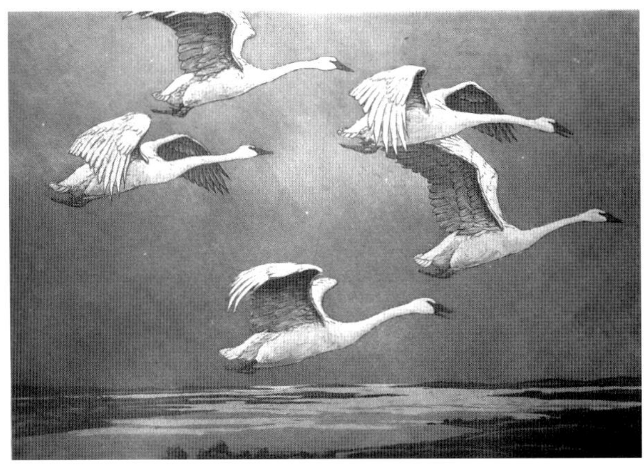

"Whistling Swans"
Medium: Etching
Image: 9.75 inches high by 13.625 inches wide

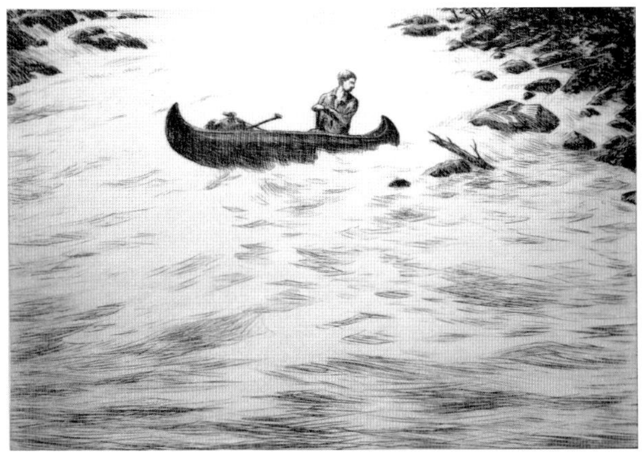

"White Water"
Medium: Etching
Image: 6.25 inches high by 7.875 inches wide

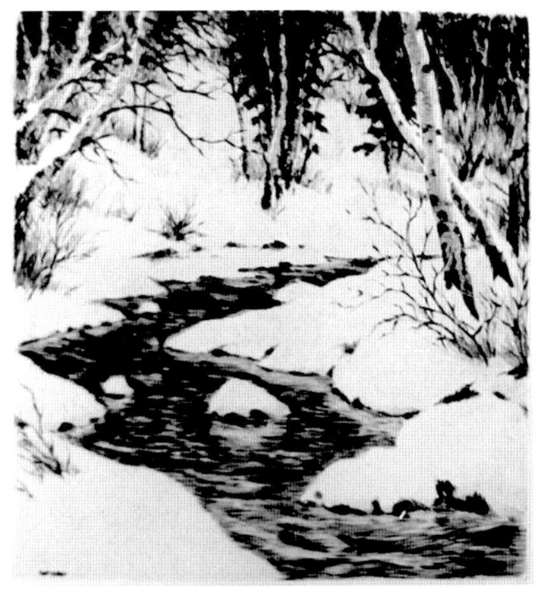

"Winter"
Medium: Etching
Image: 4.875 inches high by 4.375 inches wide

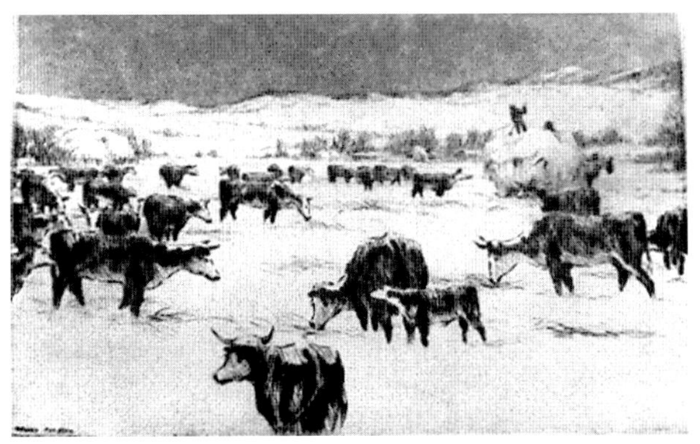

"Winter Feeding"
Medium: Photogravure
Image: 3.75 inches high by 5.75 inches wide

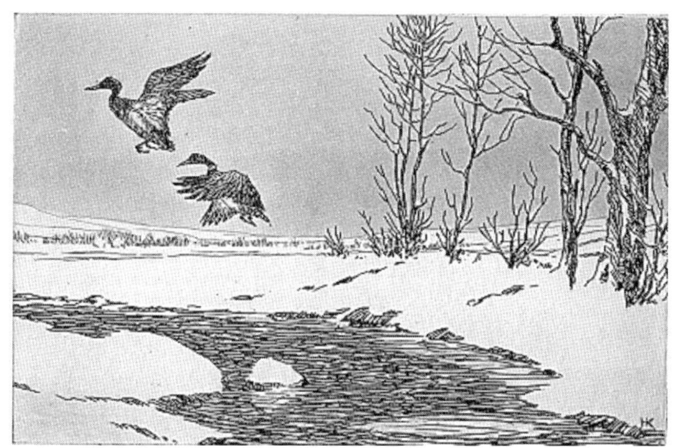

"Winter Guests"
Medium: Photogravure
Image: 3.625 inches high by 5.375 inches wide

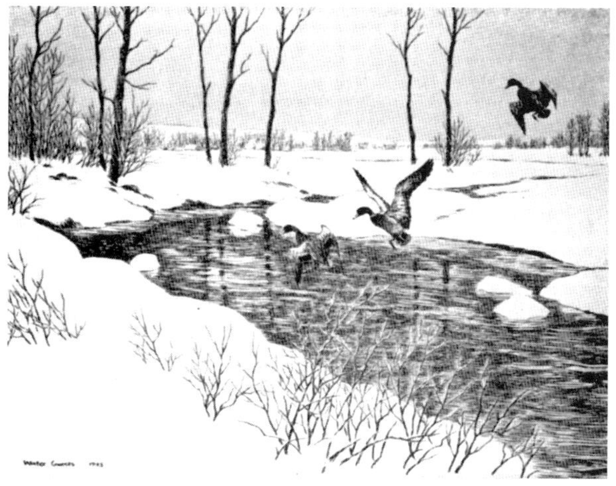

"Winter Guests"
First State
Medium: Etching
Image: 10.75 inches high by 13.75 inches wide

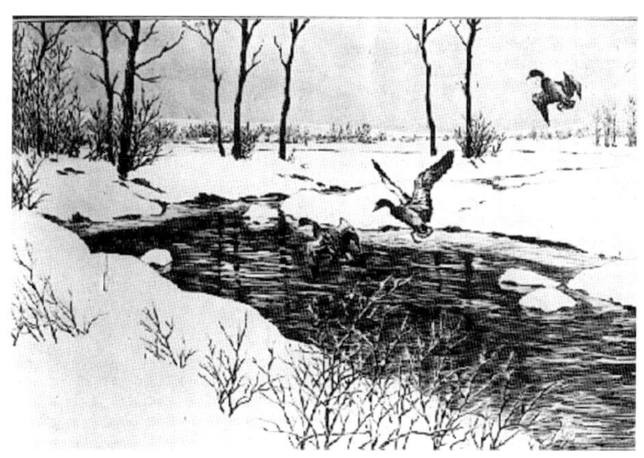

"Winter Guests"
"Winter Inlets"
a.k.a., "Winter Residents"
Second State of "Winter Guests"
Medium: Etching
Image: 9.75 inches high by 13.75 inches wide

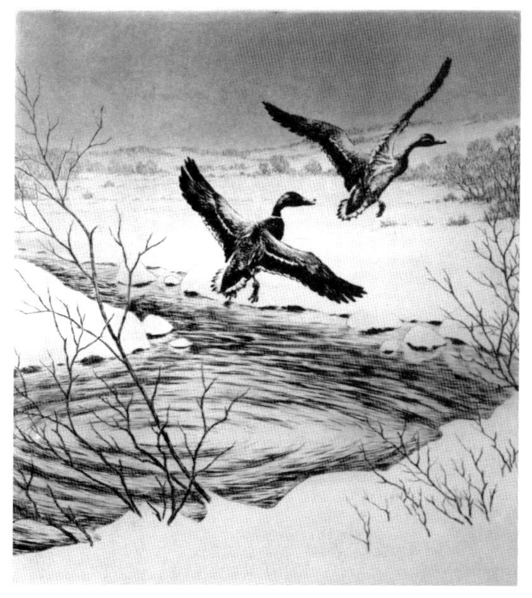

"Winter Guests II"
Medium: Etching
Associated American Artists
Image: 10.75 inches high by 9.25 inches wide

Hans Kleiber

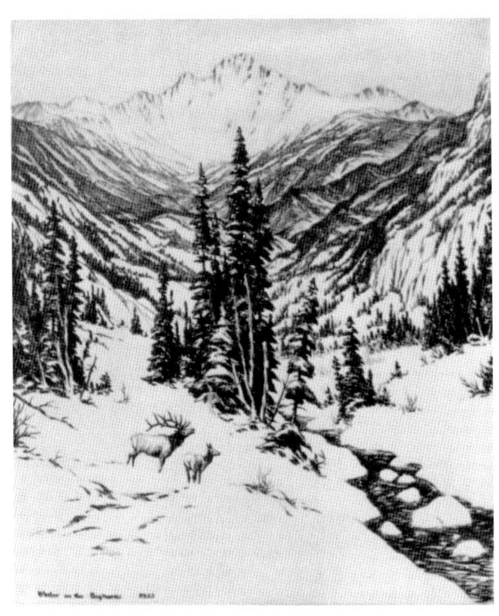

"Winter in the Bighorns"
Medium: Etching
Image: 12.625 inches high by 10.75 inches wide

Medium: Photogravure
Image: 6.875 inches high by 5.875 inches wide

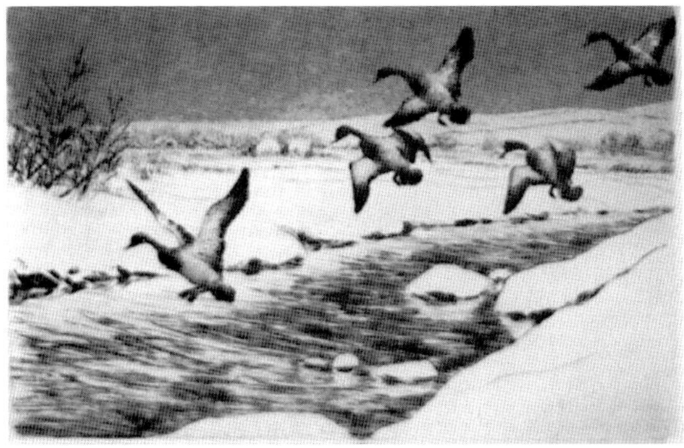

"Winter Guests II"
Medium: Etching, Photogravure
Image: 3.75 inches high by 5.75 inches wide

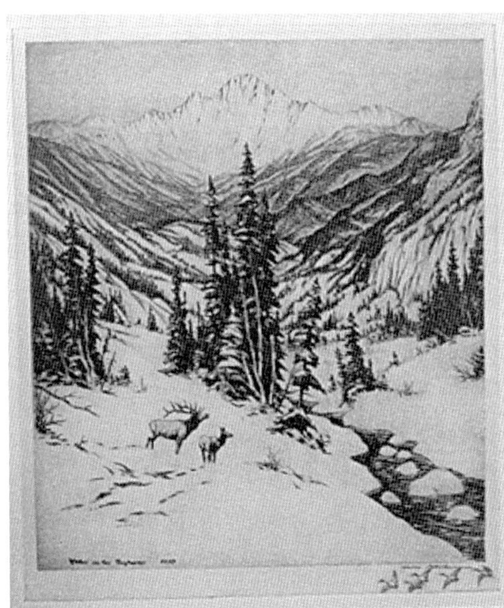

"Winter in the Bighorns"
Medium: Photogravure
Image: 5.5 inches high by 4.625 inches wide
Photogravure with remarque reproduced.

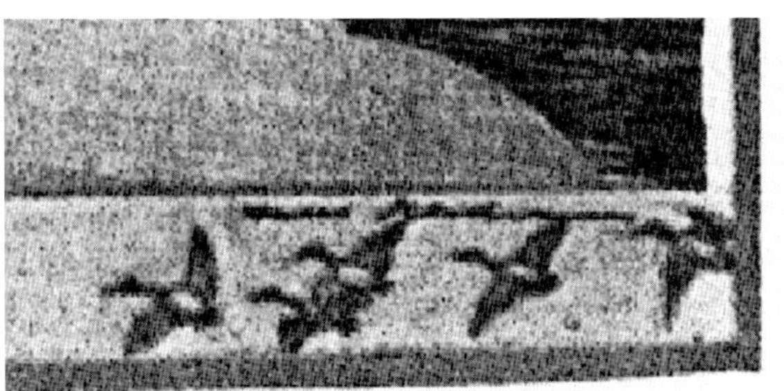

Detail view of reproduced remarque.

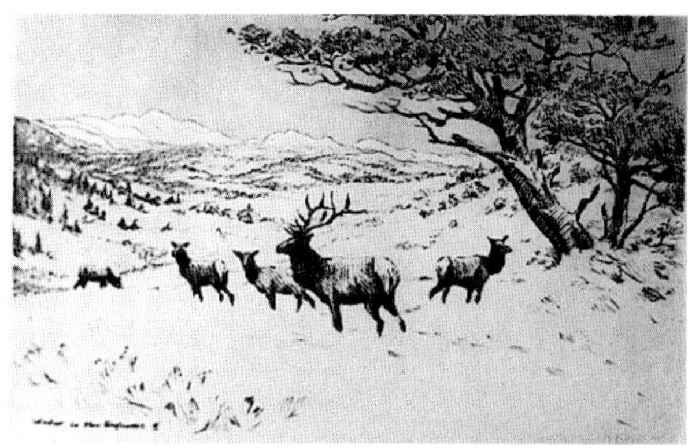

"Winter in the Bighorns II"
Medium: Photogravure
Image: 4 inches high by 6.25 inches wide

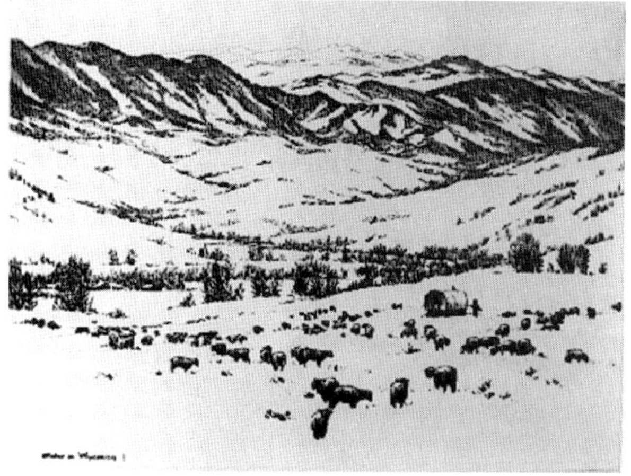

"Winter in Wyoming I"
Medium: Etching
Image: 6.75 inches high by 8.75 inches wide

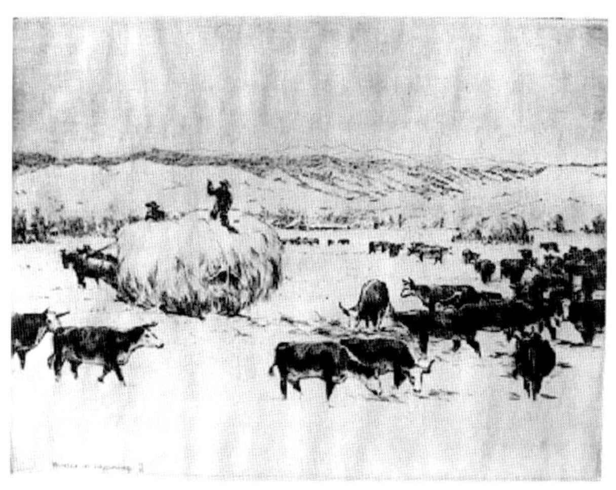

"Winter in Wyoming II"
Medium: Etching
Image: 6.875 inches high by 8.75 inches wide

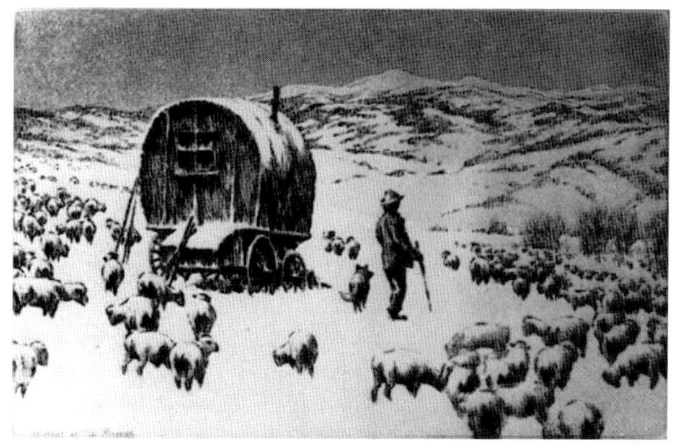

"Winter on the Range"
Medium: Etching
Image: 3.75 inches high by 5.875 inches wide

Hans Kleiber

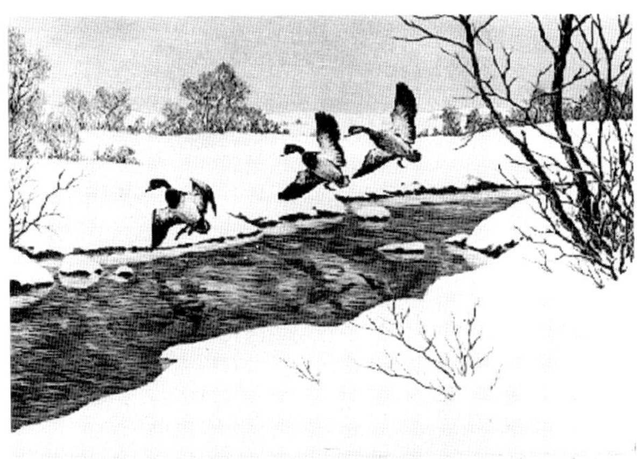

"Winter Guests"
"Winter Residents"
"Winter Residents - Mallards"
First State
Medium: Etching
Associated American Artists
Image: 7.75 inches high by 10.75 inches wide

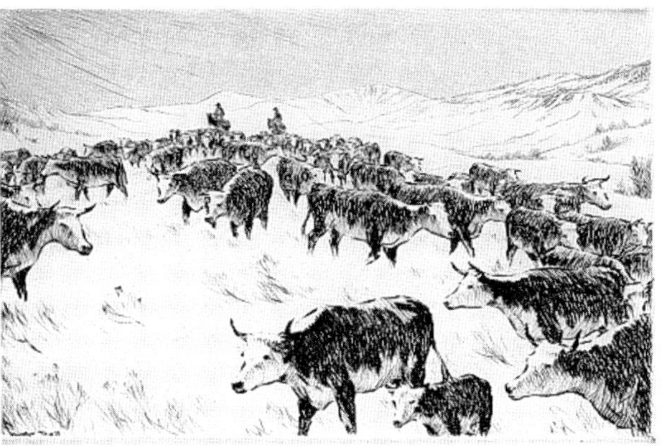

"Winter Trail"
Medium: Etching
Image: 3.875 inches high by 5.75 inches wide

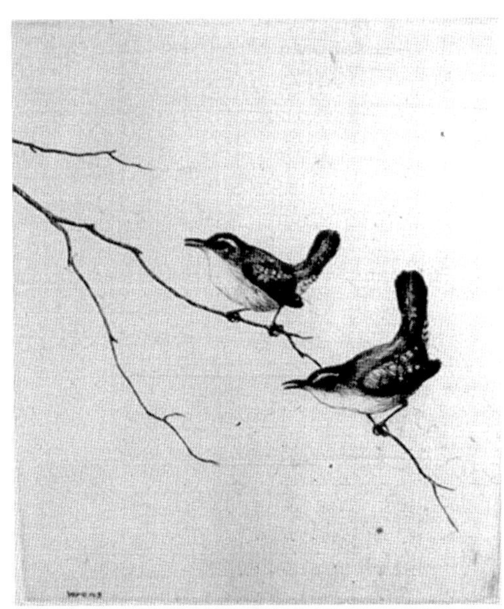

"Wrens"
Medium: Etching
Image: 5.75 inches high by 4.75 inches wide

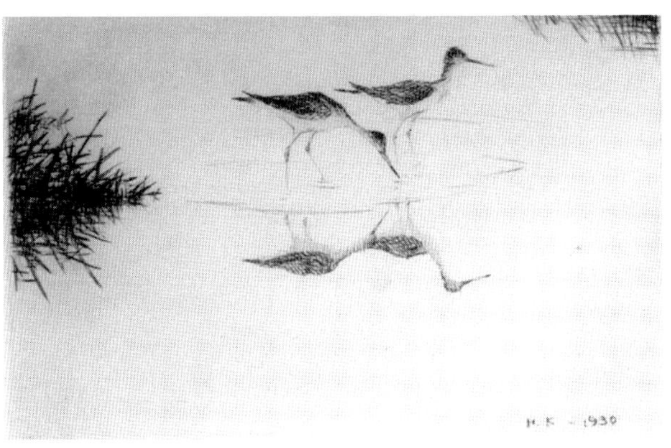

"Yellow Legs"
"Yellow Legs - 1930"
"Yellow Legs I"
"Yellow Legs II"
First State
Medium: Etching
Image: 3.875 inches high by 5.875 inches wide

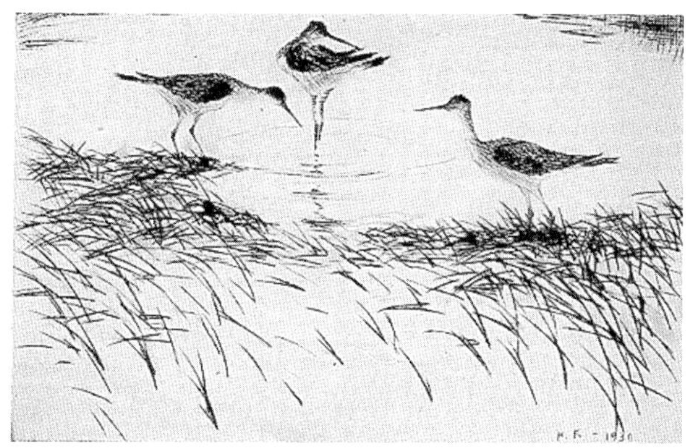

"Yellowlegs, No. II"
First State
Medium: Etching
Image: 3.875 inches high by 5.875 inches wide

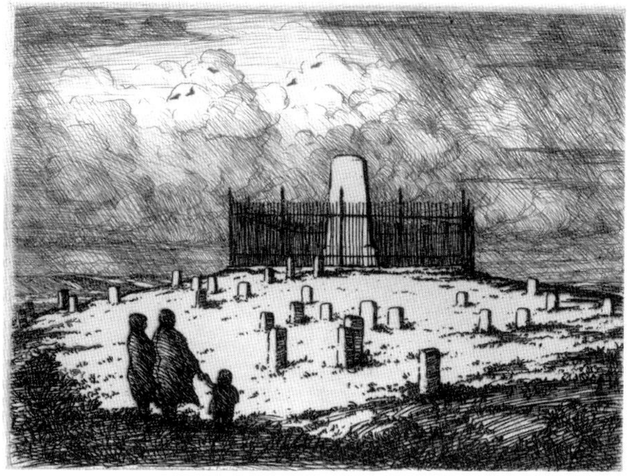

"Custer Battlefied Monument, Montana"
First State
Medium: Etching
Image: 4.75 inches high by 6.3125 inches wide

New Discovery at Press Time!!

Hans Kleiber

Chapter Eleven

Associated American Artists

James Watrous in his book, "American Printmaking, A Century of American Printmaking 1880-1980"[41] explained about the low prices for unlimited editions by various galleries in 1940. The years of the Depression found many dealers with inventory that reflected extremely low prices. The author, James Watrous, made the additional comment that "marketing by dealers offered artists scant income, in 1933 a Contemporary Print Group had been formed to sell works by mail order."[42]

Later in mid-1934, Reeves Lewenthal formed the Associated American Artists. Lewenthal was a former reporter for the Chicago Tribune. The

---

[41]"American Printmaking, A Century of American Printmaking 1880-1980 by James Watrous; The University of Wisconsin Press, 1984; page 107.

[42]Ibid., page 107-108.

Associated American Artists through the Federal Arts Project offered assistance to artists during the Great Depression. Artwork was marketed and sold to the general public. Artists were offered a flat fee of $200.00 for each edition with additional increments if more than ten impressions were sold.[43] The Associated American Artists marketed the work through intense mass mailings, women's clubs, and exhibitions. The primary purpose of the Associated American Artists was to promote printmaking and to bring in artists that had worked in other two dimensional areas. The editions were usually of 250 impressions.[44] The Associated American Artists would pay the flat fee to the artist and then have the editions pulled by master printers. The paper used by those master printers was of a very high quality. Current conservation efforts have been greatly enhanced due to those initial, consistent standards for printmaking.

"The Associated American Artists issued many lively etchings and lithographs, but its course was cautious. Prints by Americans who were inclined toward abstract art were omitted in favor of works steeped in narrative or pictorial subject matter."[45]

---

[43]Ibid.

[44] All of the edition sizes by the Associated American Artists were 250 except for two titles. "Deep In The Rockies" was an edition of 179 and "Grand Teton" was an edition of 211. This information was provided courtesy of Sylvan Cole, Jr..

[45]"American Printmaking, A Century of American Printmaking 1880-1980 by James Watrous; The University of Wisconsin Press, 1984; page 109.

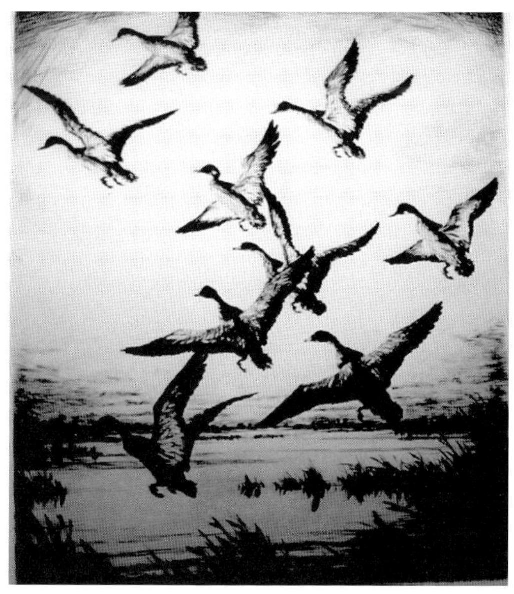

"Black Ducks"
Image: 11.75 inches high by 9.75 inches wide
Published in 1964.

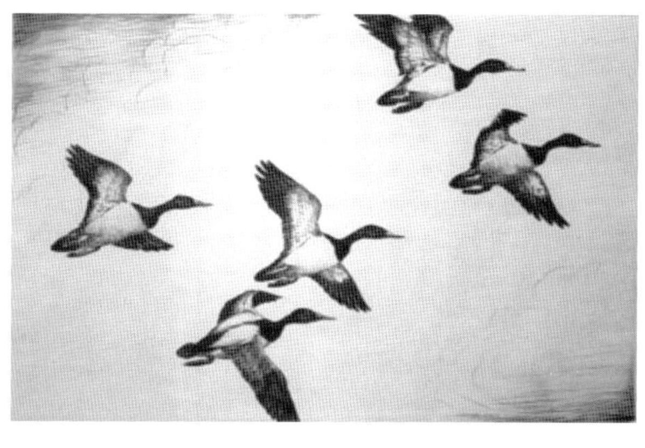

"Canvasbacks in Flight"
Image: 7.625 inches high by 11.75 inches wide
Published in 1952.

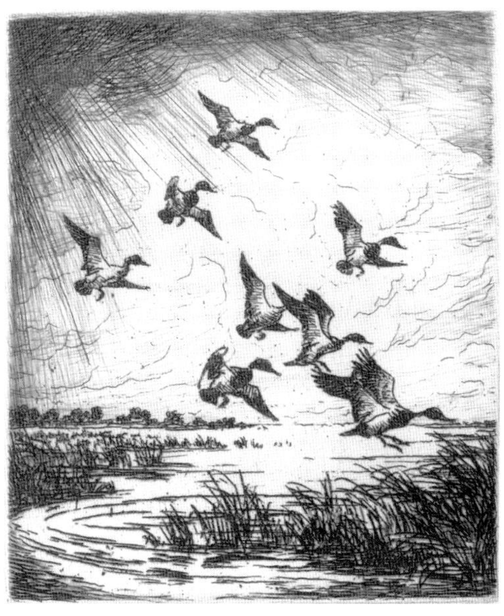

"Coming In"
Image: 3.25 inches high by 2.5625 inches wide
Published in 1948.

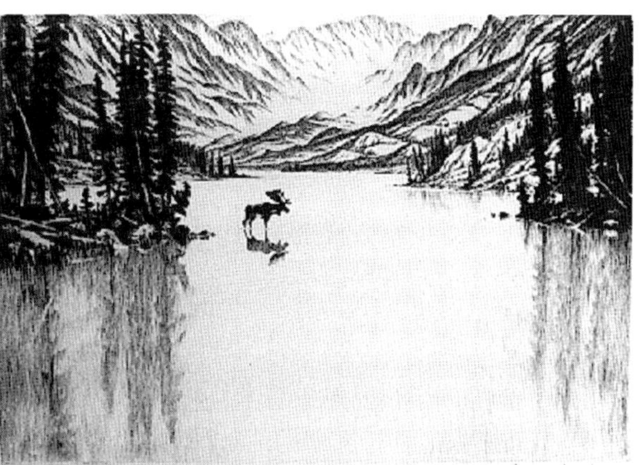

"Deep in the Rockies"
Image: 7.75 inches high by 10.75 inches wide
Edition size of 179.
Published in 1942.

Hans Kleiber

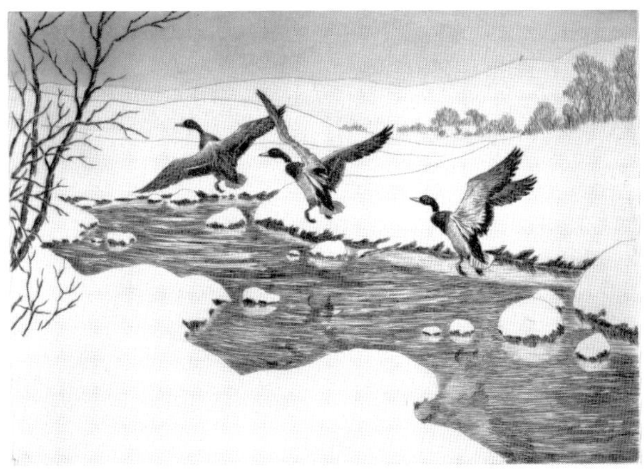

"Disturbed Mallards"
Image: 7.75 inches high by 10.75 inches wide
Published in 1951.

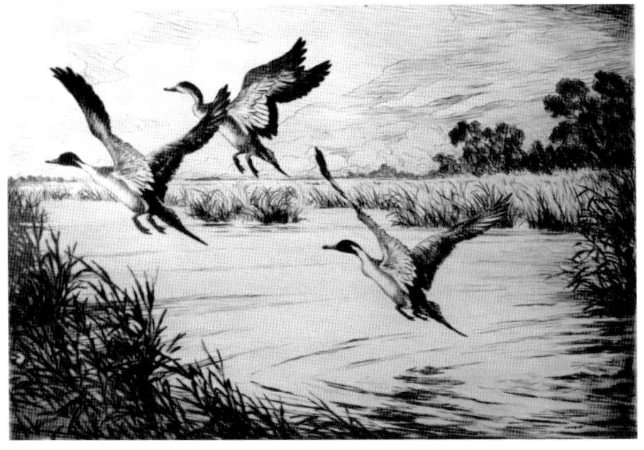

"Disturbed Pintails"
Image: 6.25 inches high by 8.75 inches wide
Published in 1948.

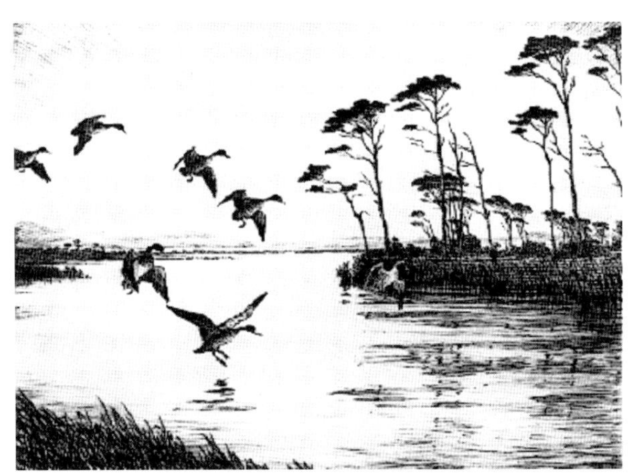

"Evening"
Image: 8.25 inches high by 10.75 inches wide
Published in 1963.

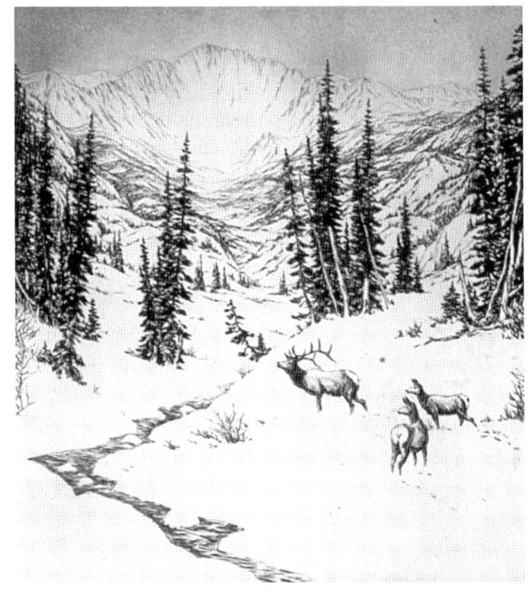

"Fall in the Rockies"
Image: 10.75 inches high by 9.25 inches wide
Published in 1942.

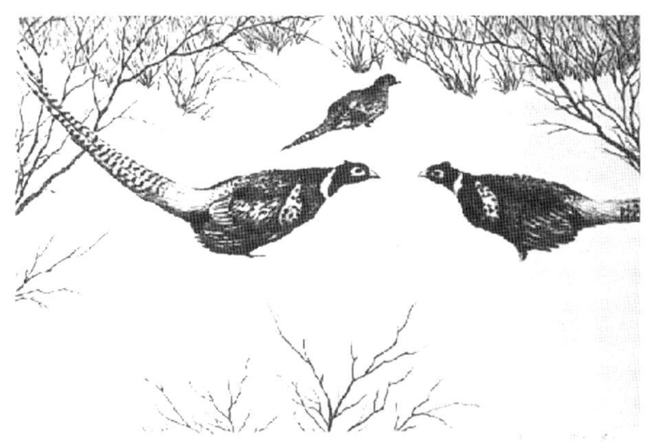

"Fighting Pheasants"
Image: 8.25 inches high by 11.75 inches wide
Published in 1950.

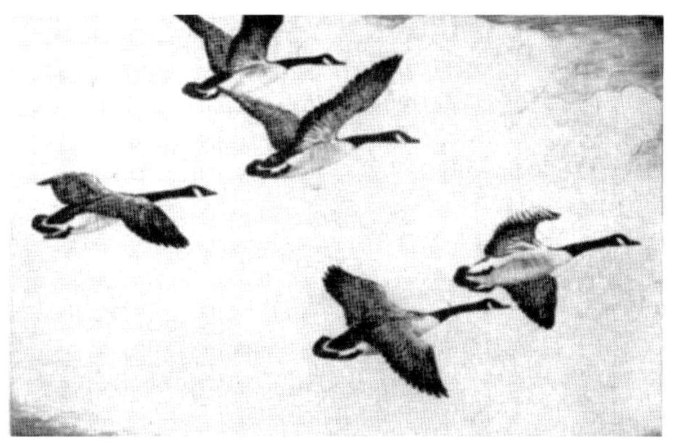

"Flying Honkers"
Image: 7.75 inches high by 11.75 inches wide
Published in 1950.

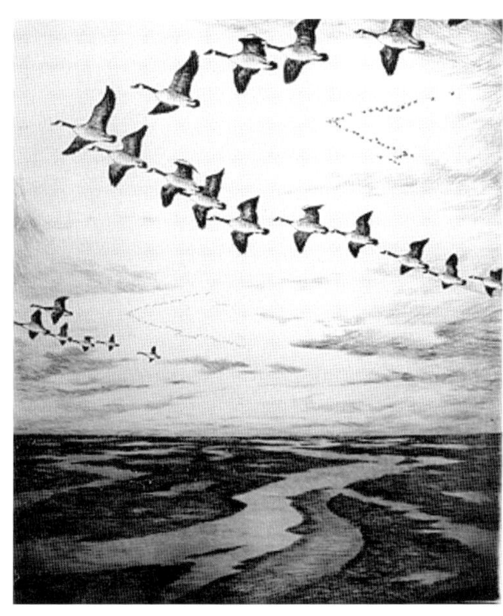

"Geese over the Marshes"
Image: 11.75 inches high by 9.5 inches wide
Published in 1949.

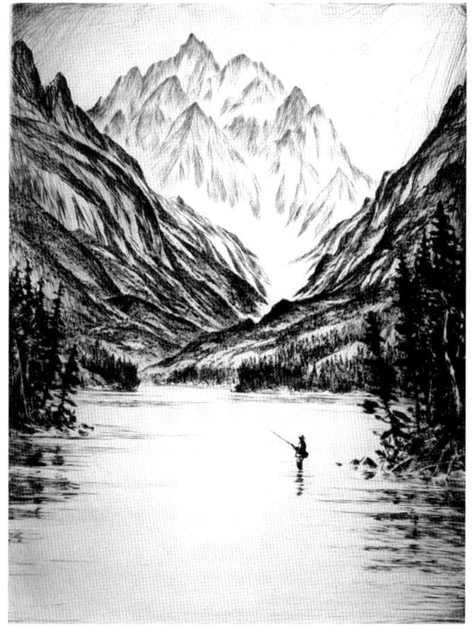

"Grand Teton"
Image: 11.75 inches high by 8.75 inches wide
Edition size of 211.
Published in 1941.

Hans Kleiber

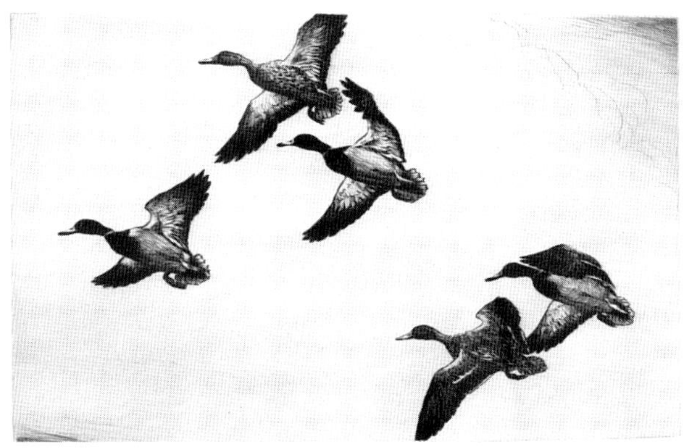

"Mallards in Flight"
Image: 7.75 inches high by 11.75 inches wide
Published in 1949.

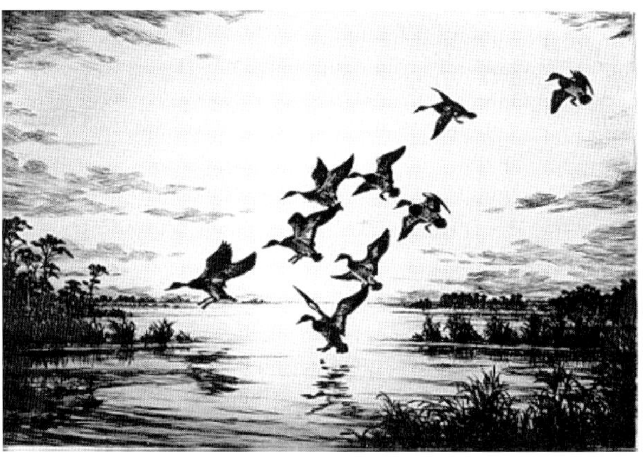

"Morning on the Marshes"
Image: 7.5 inches high by 10.875 inches wide
Published in 1950.

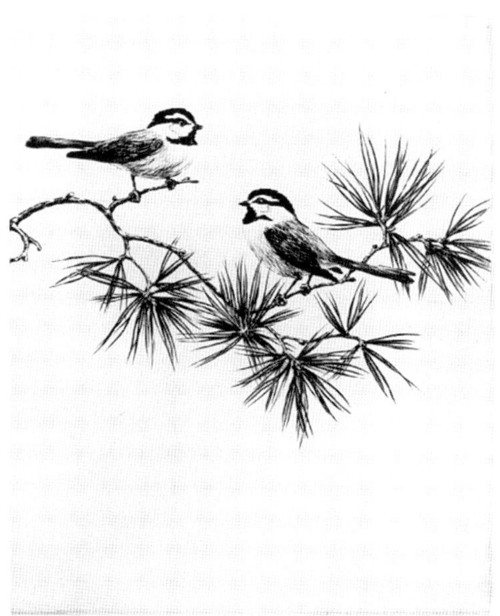

"Mountain Chicadees"
First state
Medium: Etching
Image: 9.75 inches high by 7.75 inches wide
Published in 1943.

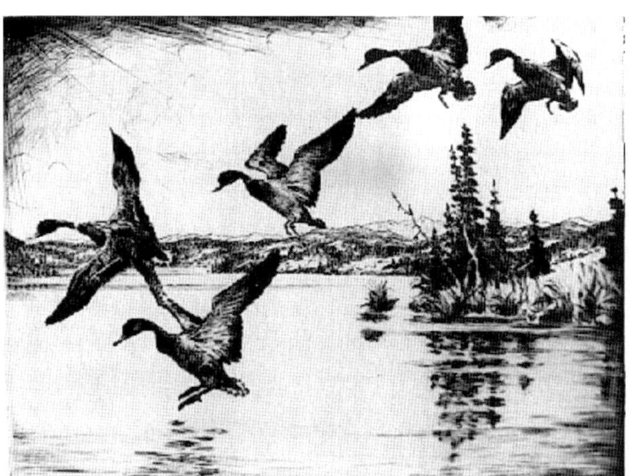

"On Yellowstone Lake"
Image: 5.875 inches high by 7.75 inches wide
Published in 1945.

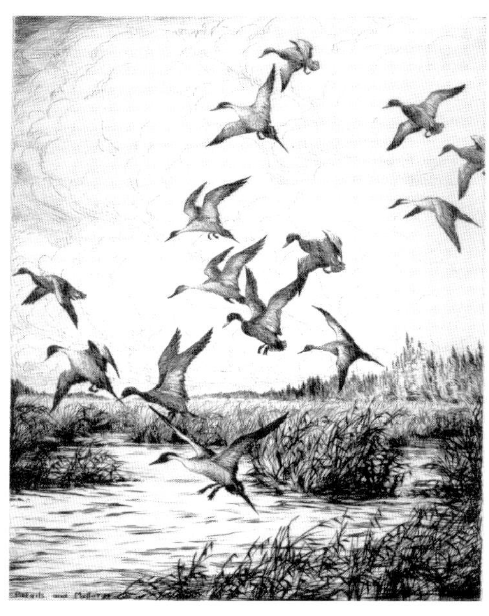

"Pintails and Mallards"
Image: 9.75 inches high by 7.875 inches wide
Published in 1966.

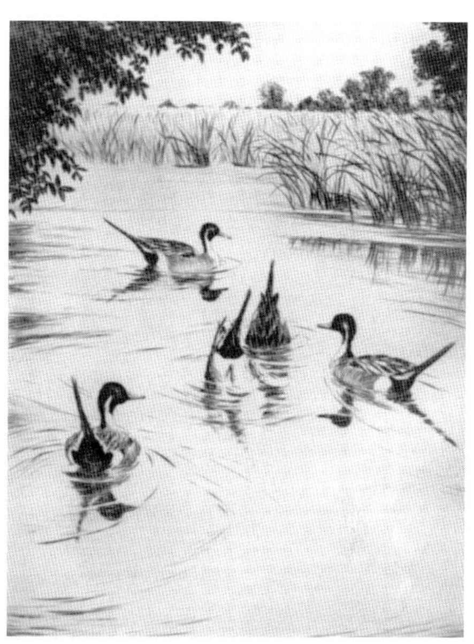

"Pintails Feeding"
Image: 8.5 inches high by 6.75 inches wide
Published in 1958.

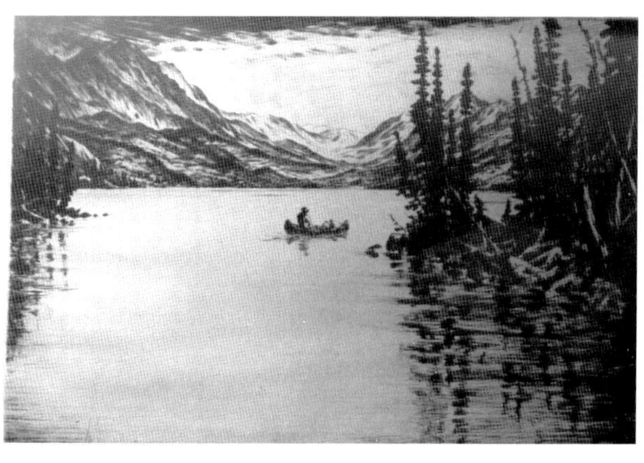

"Summer in the Rockies"
Image: 7.75 inches high by 10.75 inches wide
Published in 1944.

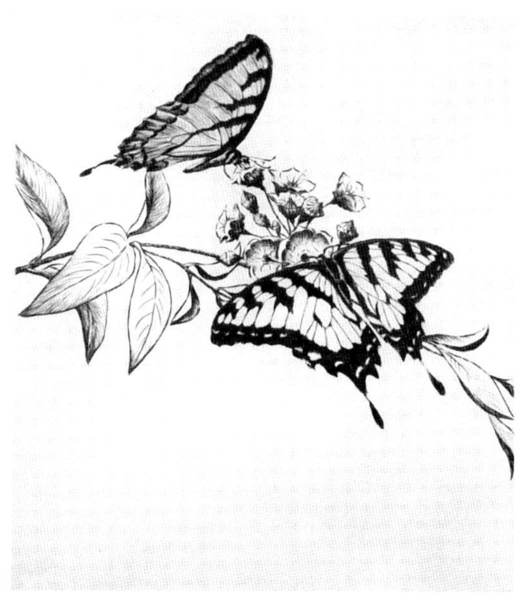

"Swallow Tails"
Image: 10.75 inches high by 9.125 inches wide
Published in 1945.

Hans Kleiber

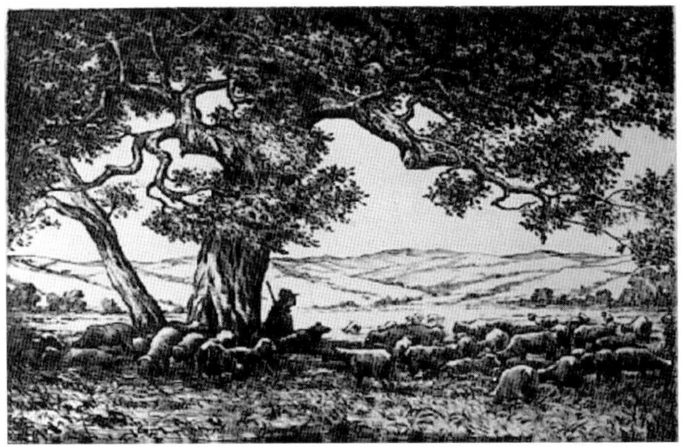

"The Old Cottonwood Tree"
Image: 7.125 inches high by 10.75 inches wide
Published in 1946.

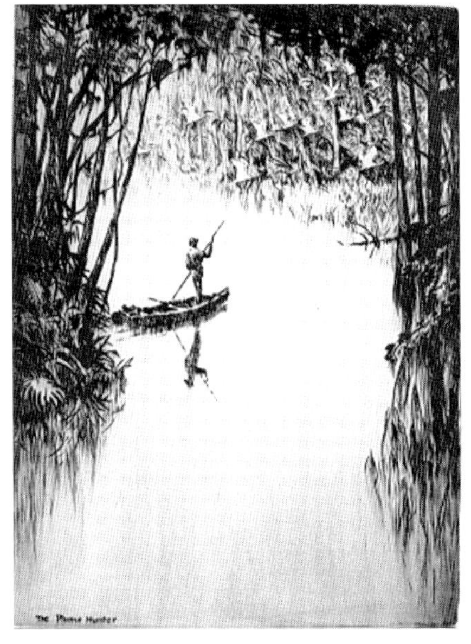

"The Plume Hunter"
Image: 11.75 inches high by 8.25 inches wide
Published in 1942.

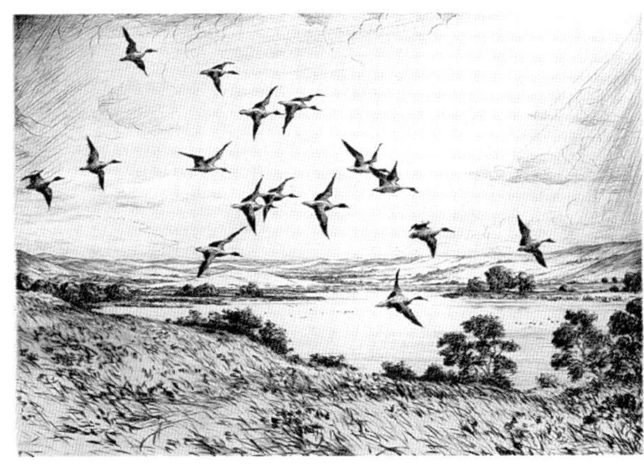

"The Pond in the Hills"
Image: 7.75 inches high by 11.75 inches wide
Published in 1944.

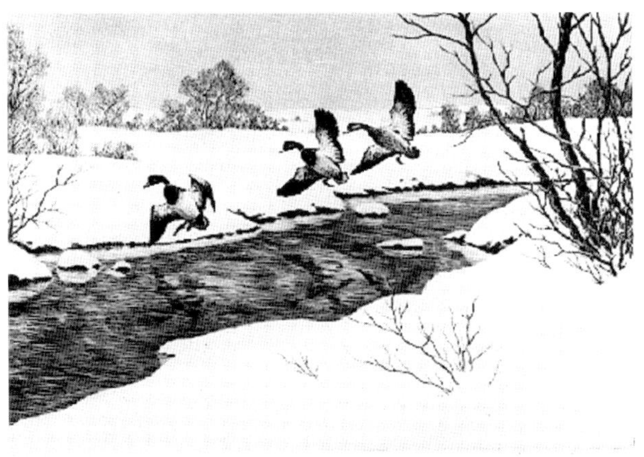

Published by Associated American Artists as "Winter Residents" a.k.a. "Winter Residents - Mallards"
Image: 7.75 inches high by 10.75 inches wide
Published in 1947.

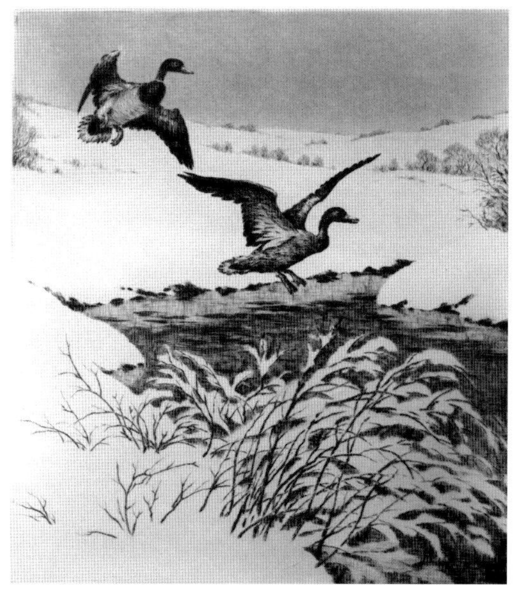

Published by Associated American Artists as "Mallards in the Snow" a.k.a. "Winter Guests" a.k.a. "Winter Guests I"
Image: 10.75 inches high by 9.25 inches wide
Published in 1945.

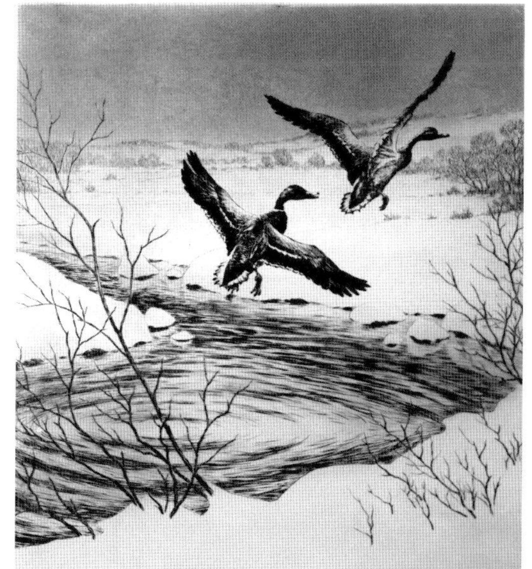

"Winter Guests"
Image: 10.75 inches high by 9.25 inches wide
Published in 1944.

Hans Kleiber

Examples of Associated American Artists brochures

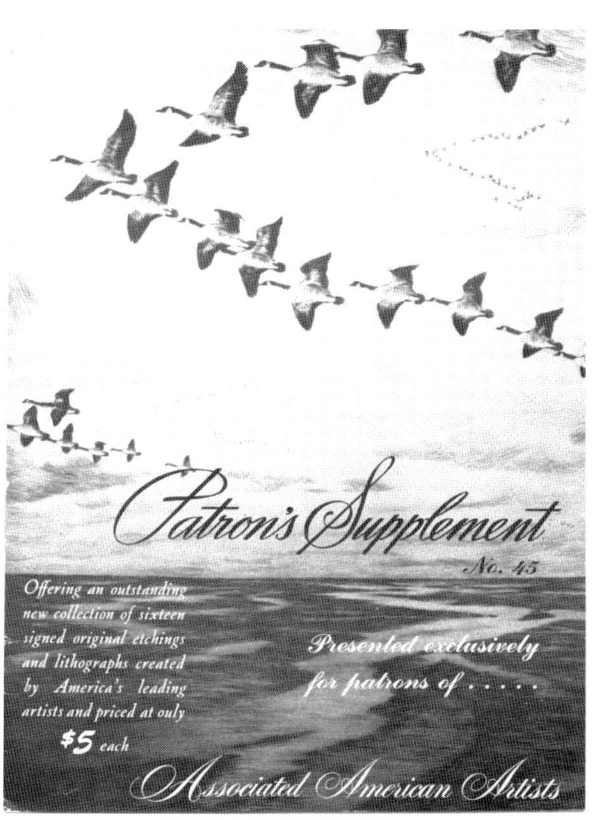

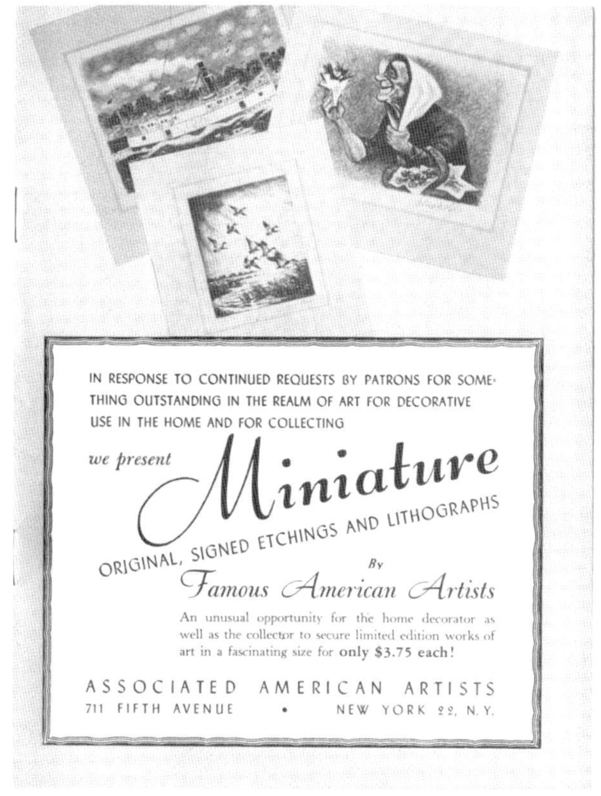

Hans Kleiber

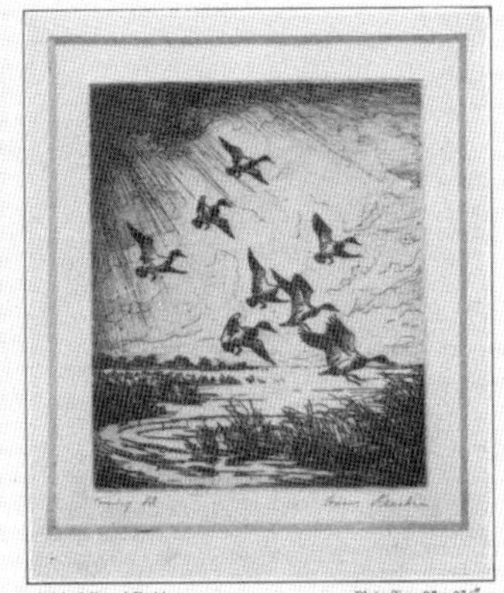

Original Signed Etching — Plate Size: 3" x 2⅞"

"Coming In" by Hans Kleiber

HANS KLEIBER

"Many of our waterfowl winter along the Gulf Coast. Coming In *is my impression of a flock of ducks doing just that, on the marshes near Grand Chenier, Louisiana."*

EARLY in the century, Kleiber found himself in the Big Horn country of Wyoming. The years that followed included a tour of duty with the U. S. Forestry Service throughout the Western states and gave Kleiber an unforgettable picture of the beauty and solemnity of the Western scene. It was in this atmosphere that he learned to draw. His self-developed talent has been accorded many of the leading art awards given by this country.

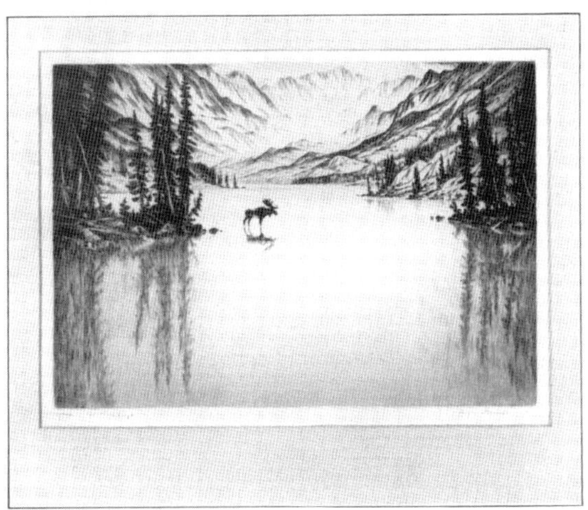

"DEEP IN THE ROCKIES" by Hans Kleiber

AN ORIGINAL SIGNED ETCHING

PLATE 10¾" x 7¾": MAT 18" x 14"

Hans Kleiber's self-developed talent has achieved its expression in the surroundings he has inhabited and loved since the peak popularity of the Buffalo Bill legends. Early in the century Kleiber, then a lad of eighteen, found himself drawn irresistibly to the Big Horn country of Wyoming. Once he saw its grandeur and breathed its invigorating air, he was content to stay, and it is that inspiring atmosphere that stimulated his imagination and gave him the urge to draw. Among the tourists coming by the thousands to the Big Horn country at that time was an artist who brought some copper plates and did some etching. Kleiber found he could draw on the copper plates as well as on a drawing pad, and began etching. Some of his creations, taken East by tourists, aroused the enthusiasm of a dealer who gave Kleiber an exhibition. It was very successful, and the following year he was persuaded to come to New York to appear in person at a second one-man show. "It was the most trying ordeal of my life," he says. "I was scared half to death and returned home exhausted, convinced that my place is right here."

"Disturbed Pintails"
by
Hans Kleiber

HANS KLEIBER, one of the West's leading sportsman-etchers, writes: "I remember quietly walking along a dike one afternoon. Suddenly three pintails took to the air in a glitter of black and white and in a moment they were only a blurr against the sun."

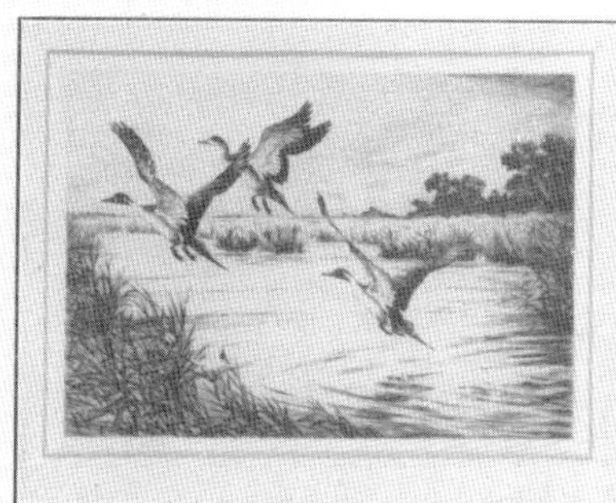

Plate Size: 8¼" x 6⅛" Mat Size: 18" x 14"
An Original Signed Etching

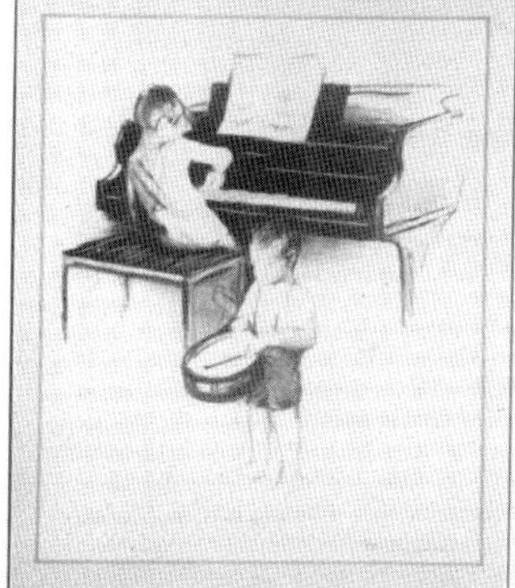

Plate Size: 7¼" x 8½" Mat Size: 14" x 18"
An Original Signed Lithograph

"Rainy Day Concert"
by
Margery Ryerson

MARGERY RYERSON's way with children, and her ability to catch their spirit and their moods, has brought her fame as a portrayer of them. She tells us: "How a child amuses himself during vacations is very important. We grown folks learn about him at these times — he learns about himself — tries out many things and discovers what he really likes. Day after day, when I was little, I painted paper dolls not too different from the children in this lithograph."

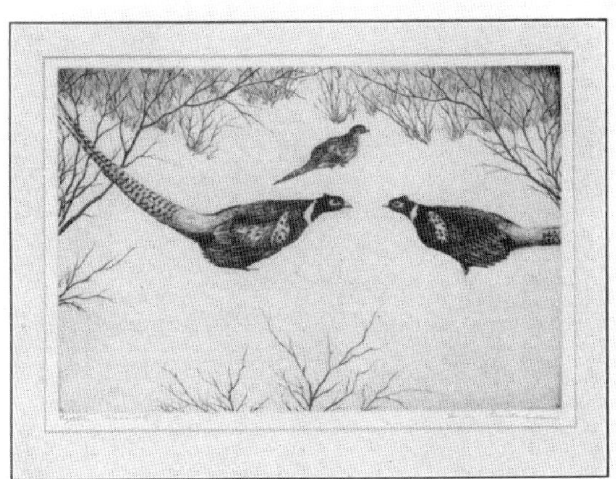

Plate Size: 11⅜" x 8¼" *An Original Signed Etching* Mat Size: 18" x 14"

"Fighting Pheasants" by Hans Kleiber

HANS KLEIBER's imagination, at the age of 18, was so caught by Buffalo Bill, by Wister's "*The Virginian*" and by Teddy Roosevelt's adventures in the Big Horn country, that he went West to work in a lumber camp. In years following, he was in the forestry service out in the Western states, and this gave Kleiber an unforgettable picture of the beauty and solemnity of the western scene. He had an insatiable desire to draw and through perseverance and courage, he used his talents at the etcher's plate. The years have seen him climb to the top ranks in the art world. Concerning his most recent rendering, he writes, "Cock pheasants are aggressive and quarrelsome birds, particularly in the spring. These two particular birds settled their differences just outside my studio window during a snow storm last April."

Hans Kleiber

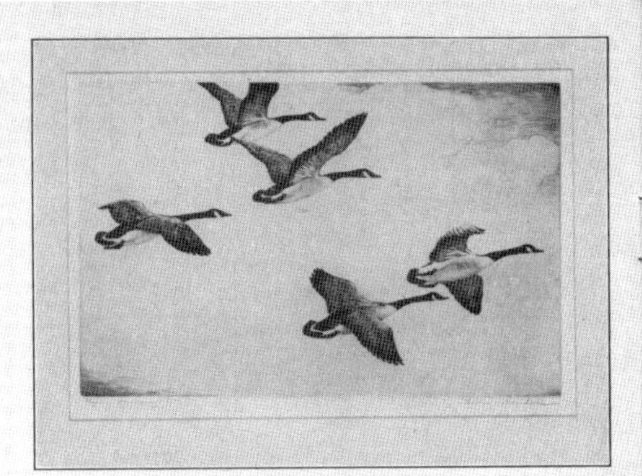

Plate Size: 11¾" x 7¾" *An Original Signed Drypoint* Mat Size: 18" x 14"

"Flying Honkers" by Hans Kleiber

EARLY IN THE CENTURY Hans Kleiber found himself in the Big Horn country of Wyoming working as a U. S. forester. To pass the time, he began drawing on the copper plate and his talent was recognized by a tourist who returned East with several of his renderings. An exhibition was arranged and Kleiber overnight went from an "unknown" to an artist of rank whose works are in constant demand by museums and private collectors throughout the world. He depicts here a sight familiar to all sports-loving Americans. He writes: "In the drypoint of *Flying Honkers*, I tried to show five Canadian Geese winging southward in their characteristic V-formations. They are by common consent the best known and most impressive waterfowl on our continent, and I know of no other birdcall which announces the coming of winter more poetically."

"Geese over the Marshes" by Hans Klieber

"DURING a recent mid-winter field trip over some of the Louisiana marshes," Klieber writes, "I saw many geese, including great flocks of the Blue and Snow geese. I chose the Canada geese for this drypoint because their markings and characteristic V-shaped formations lend themselves better to an expression in black and white than any of the others."

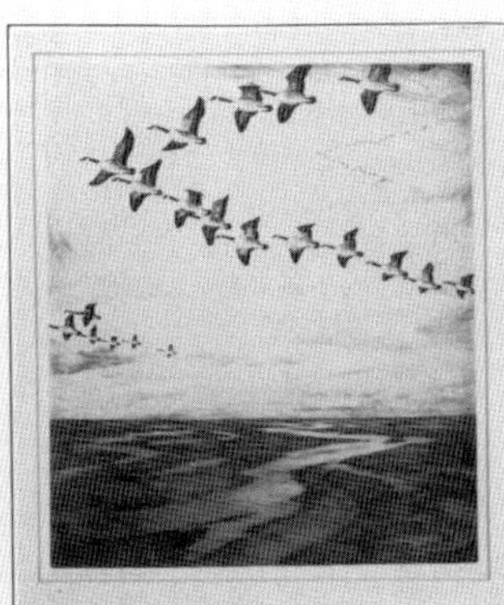

Plate Size: 9⅞" x 10¾"
Mat Size: 14" x 18"
An Original Signed Drypoint

"Mallards in Flight" by Hans Klieber

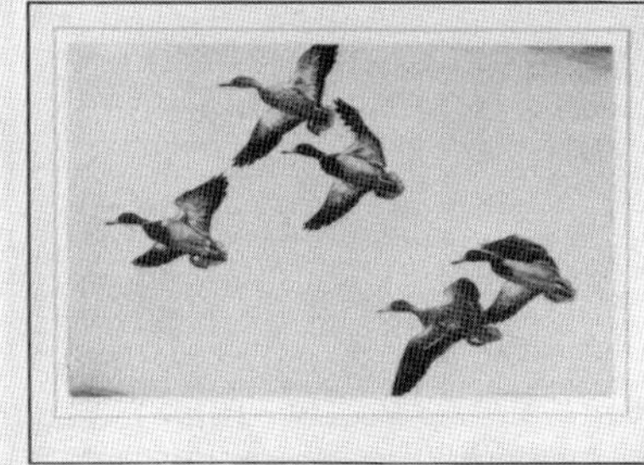

Plate Size: 11⅞" x 7¾" *An Original Signed Drypoint* Mat Size: 18" x 14"

"ALL I tried to show in this plate," writes the artist, "are the five mallards in strong, straight flight, just as a hunter or humble observer like myself would see them fly past against the sky. I purposely left out any indication of landscape to focus attention on the fast moving birds."

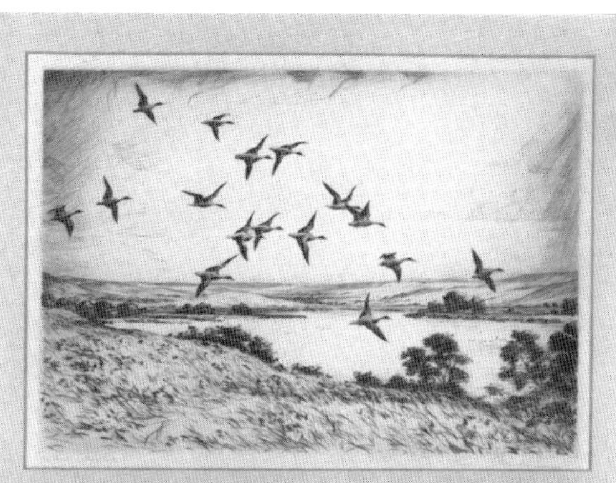

HANS KLEIBER
An Original Signed Etching

"THE POND IN THE HILLS"
Plate: 10¾" x 7⅞"; Mat: 18" x 14"

"The Bighorn Mountains in Wyoming are a prolific source of small streams that water the semi-arid range country around them, but there are few lakes or ponds. The pond in the hills is one of those few. It lies tucked away in the foothills, and few people, except neighboring ranchers, know it's there.

"Its reedy shores make it an ideal spot for all sorts of waterfowl. During the migrating seasons, especially on blistery days, it's a welcome stopping place where they rest and feed until they are ready to go on again. It was just such a day when I was last there. Great clouds were endlessly tearing across the heavens from the Northwest, bringing ducks and occasional flocks of geese with them. They would circle the pond trying to make sure that they would not be disturbed here. A few went on when they spotted me sitting on a grassy knoll just above the pond. I almost wished that I had some way of letting them know that I had not come to shoot, but just to see them in the throes of migration and to soak up the landscape under the spell of a coming storm." . . . HANS KLEIBER

9

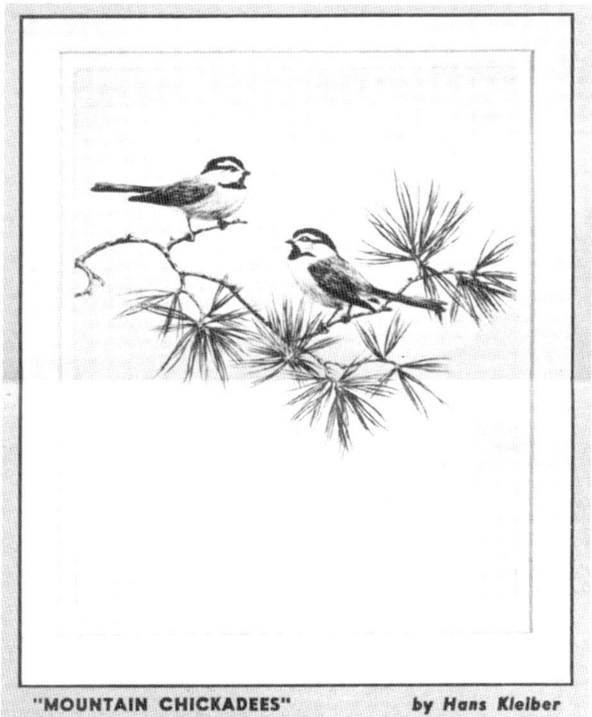

"MOUNTAIN CHICKADEES" ***by Hans Kleiber***

AN ORIGINAL SIGNED ETCHING
PLATE: 7¾" x 9⅝"; MAT: 14" x 18"

Hans Kleiber

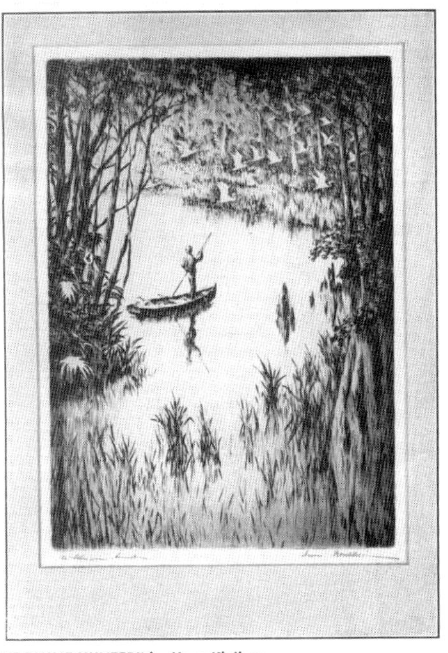

"THE PLUME HUNTER" by Hans Kleiber
AN ORIGINAL SIGNED ETCHING
PLATE 8⅜" x 11⅞": MAT 14" x 18"
From the Big Horn country of Wyoming where Hans Kleiber has lived since almost the turn of the century, and which he loves with immeasurable devotion, comes this lovely etching, his most recent. Kleiber's sporting subjects are eagerly sought and he is represented in many famous collections.

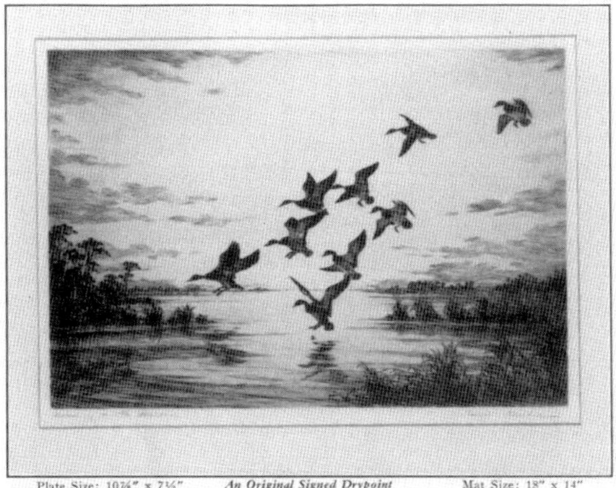

Plate Size: 10⅜" x 7½" *An Original Signed Drypoint* Mat Size: 18" x 14"

"Morning on the Marshes" by Hans Kleiber

EARLY IN THE CENTURY Kleiber found himself in the Big Horn country of Wyoming. The years that followed included United States Forestry Service throughout the Western states and in this atmosphere of scenic grandeur he started to draw. Among the tourists who visited this region was an artist who brought some copper plates and Kleiber soon found he could draw on the copper as well as a drawing pad. His early work, taken East by tourists, aroused the interest of art collectors and art critics alike and it was only a matter of a few years before leading museums throughout the country had acquired his work for their permanent collections. "In this drypoint," he writes, "I am reminiscing about an early morning on a Louisiana marsh when a flock of mallards suddenly appeared out of nowhere and settled in the cane breaks not far from me."

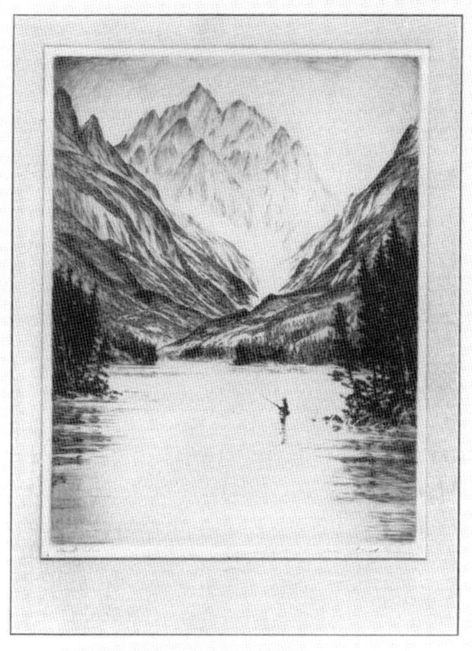

"GRAND TETON" by Hans Kleiber

AN ORIGINAL SIGNED ETCHING — PLATE 8⅞" x 12"; MAT 14" x 18"

Hans Kleiber's imagination, at the age of eighteen, was so caught by Buffalo Bill and Wister's "Virginian" that he went west to work in a lumber camp. Gradually he found himself drawn to a brush; later, he used his new-found talents at the etcher's plate. Perseverance and courage landed him in the top ranks. This first A.A.A. offering of Kleiber's work shows him at his finest.

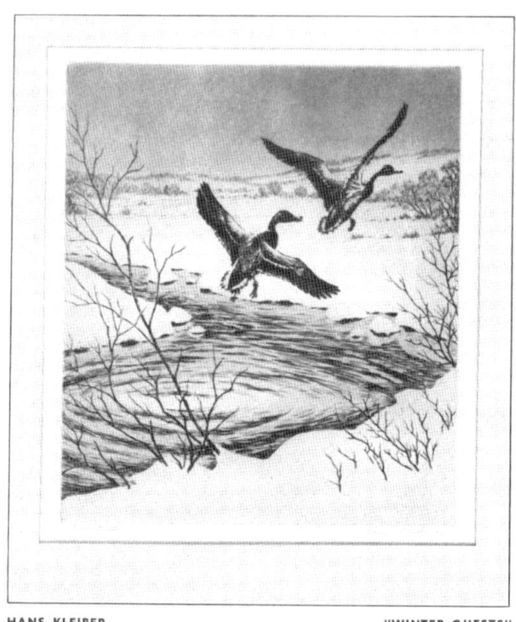

HANS KLEIBER — **"WINTER GUESTS"**

An Original Signed Etching — Plate: 9⅜" x 10⅞"; Mat: 18" x 14"

"The winters along the Bighorn Mountains are as a rule severe, and practically all of our water fowl move South to more congenial environments. However, some our locally raised Mallards undertake to spend the winter with us. They seem to divide their time between the harvested grain fields or feed lots in the day time, and what little open water they can find at night. This open water is usually a big spring where water will run some distance before freezing.

"I have one such spring on my place, scarcely 200 feet from the house, and there was hardly a winter day when I couldn't flush a pair or two from it." . . . HANS KLEIBER

12

HANS KLEIBER

HANS KLEIBER'S self-developed talent has achieved its expression in the surroundings he has inhabited since the peak popularity of the Buffalo Bill legends.

Early in the century Kleiber found himself drawn to the Big Horn country of Wyoming; the years that followed included U. S. Forestry Service throughout the western states and gave Kleiber an unforgettable picture of the beauty and solemnity of the western scene. It is that atmosphere which inspired him to draw.

Among the tourists at that time was an artist who brought some copper plates. Kleiber found he could draw on the copper as well as on a drawing pad, and began etching. Some of his creations, taken East by tourists, aroused the enthusiasm of a dealer who gave Kleiber an exhibition. The following year his second one-man show assured his success.

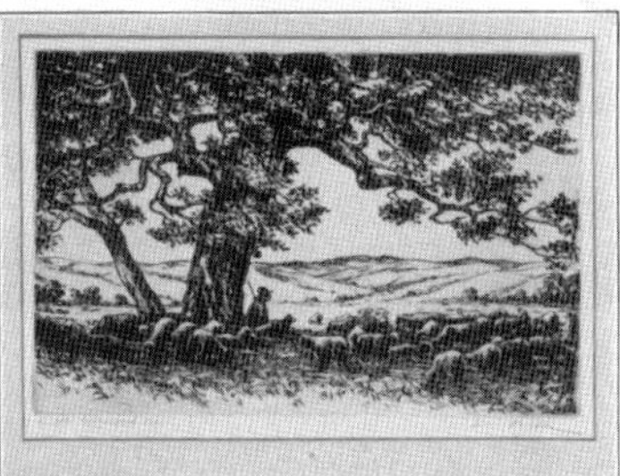

HANS KLEIBER "THE OLD COTTONWOOD TREE"
Original Signed Etching Plate: 10¾" x 7½" Mat: 18" x 14"

"Under the canopy of this ancient, solitary cottonwood tree that stood there long before the white man took possession of its surroundings, a herder with his dog and sheep have taken refuge from the sun and heat of midsummer."

Winner of many prizes, the artist's work is to be found in the permanent collections of several leading museums.

HOWARD BAER

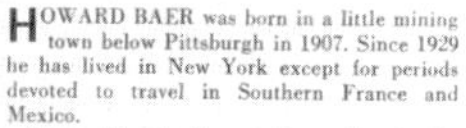

HOWARD BAER was born in a little mining town below Pittsburgh in 1907. Since 1929 he has lived in New York except for periods devoted to travel in Southern France and Mexico.

Baer achieved widespread attention for his drawings, illustrations and cartoons which appeared regularly in the *New Yorker*, *Esquire* and other magazines, but in 1941 he began to devote more time to easel painting. He is very much in the forefront of American art today.

During the past two years he has executed commissions for the recording of naval and military operations in the war theatres.

This lithograph is one of a series inspired by the artist's visit to his home town of Finleyville, Pa., after an absence of twenty-seven years. The population was still 700, and all of the houses were there exactly as Baer had remembered them, including the old Schoolhouse with its four rooms for the eight grades.

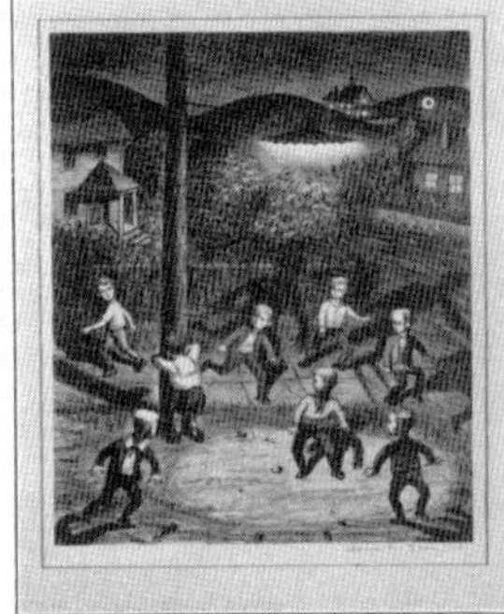

HOWARD BAER
"STILL POND, NO MORE MOVING"
Original Signed Lithograph Plate: 9⅝" x 11⅞" Mat: 14" x 18"

"One of my fondest memories . . . this childhood game played at night under the 'Main Street' light."

13

Chapter Twleve

Pen and Ink

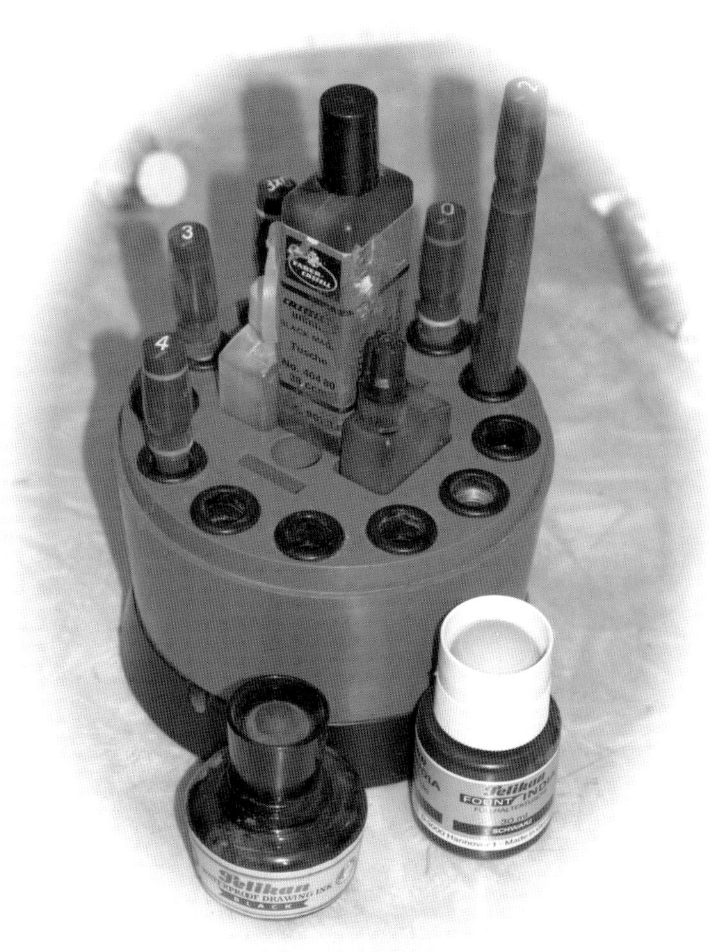

Hans Kleiber

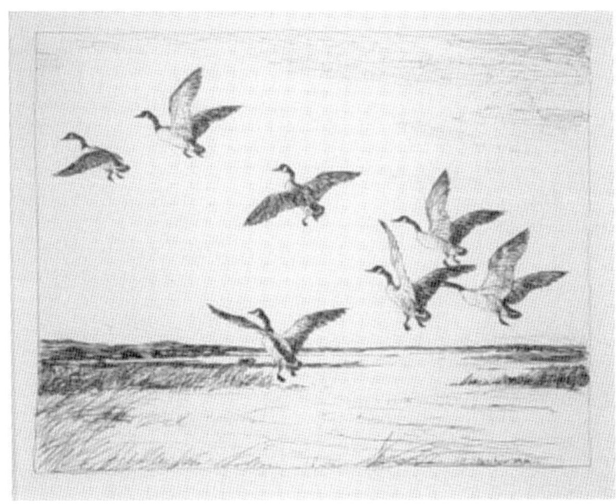

"A Flock of Honkers"
Image: 8.125 inches high by 10.125 inches wide

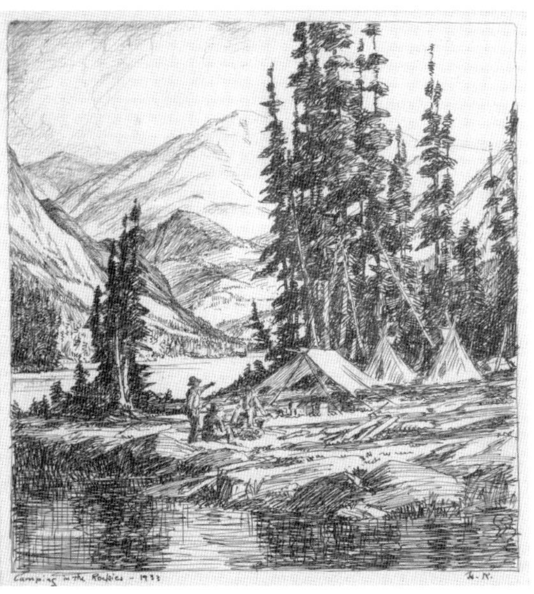

"Camping in the Rockies 1933"
Image: 8.875 inches high by 8 inches wide

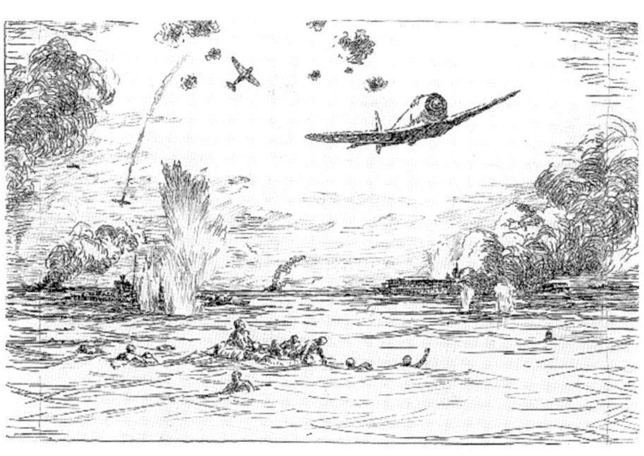

"Midway"
Image: 6 inches high by 9 inches wide

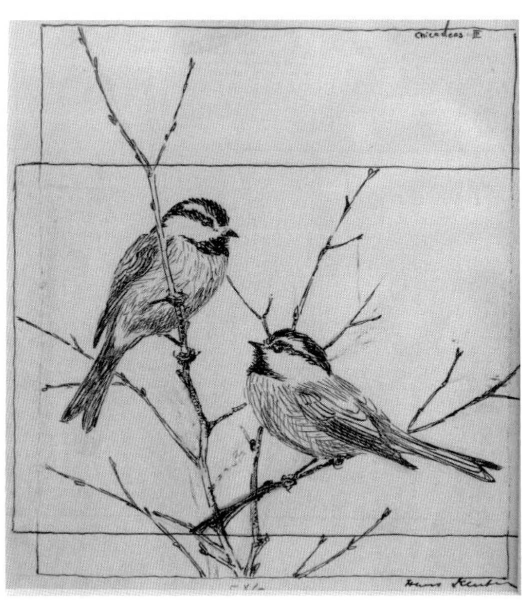

"Mountain Chicadees"
Image: 6 inches high by 5.5 inches wide

"Before" and "After"

As the story goes, Hans Kleiber was continually requested by many of the sportsman groups to provide artwork for some of their fund raising efforts. Hans was annoyed with one of the groups, thus "Before" and "After" were created for them. The two works vividly describe the pursuits of unethical hunters who do not respect the land or its wildlife.

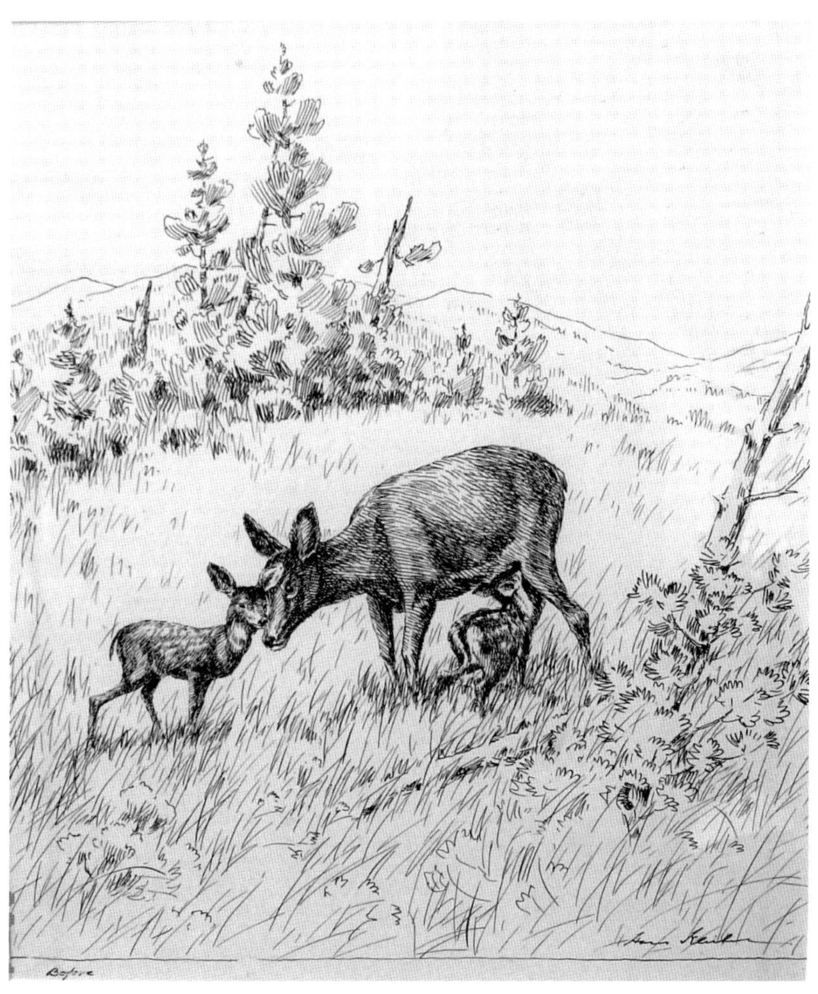

"Before"
Image: 16 inches high by 14 inches wide

Hans Kleiber

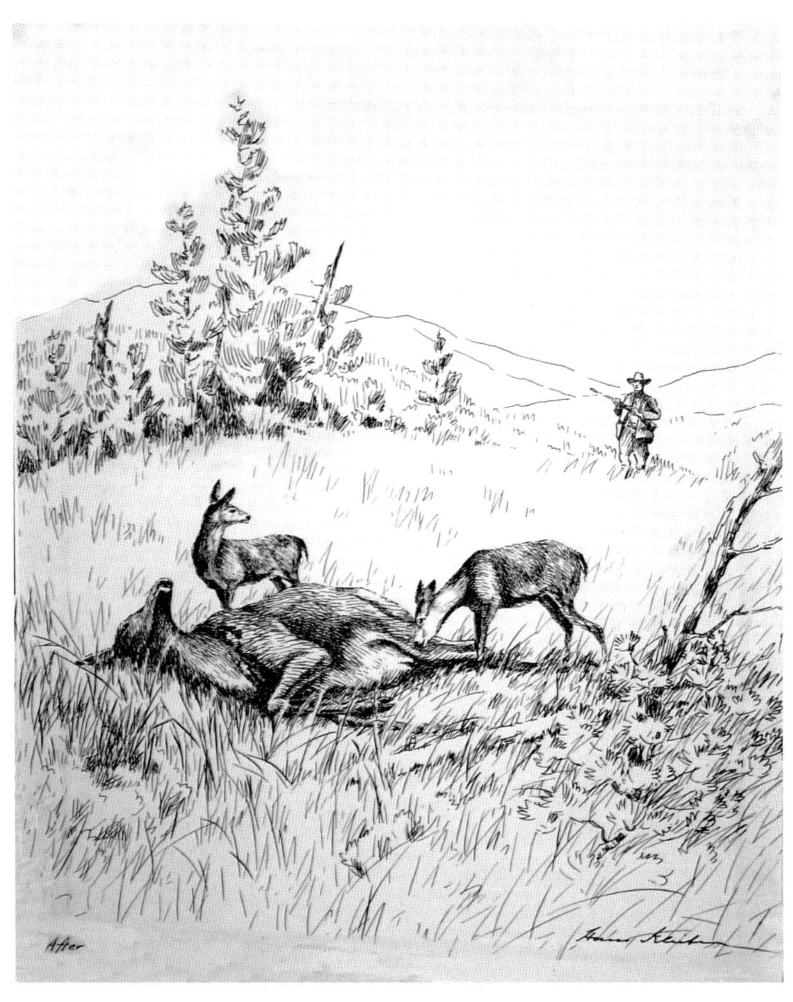

"After"
Image: 16 inches high by 14 inches wide

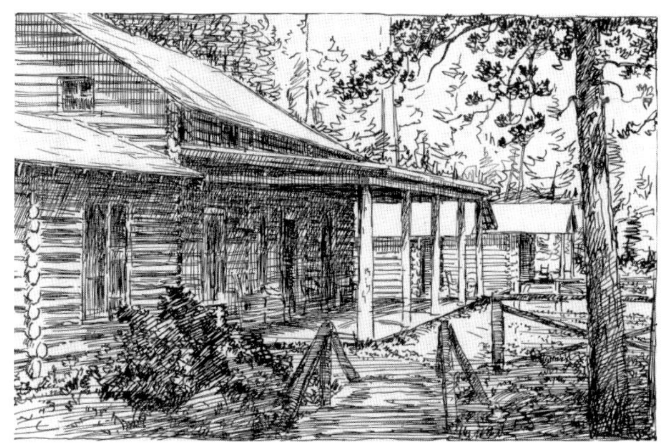

"Untitled--Tepee Main Lodge"
Image: 5 inches high by 7.5 inches wide

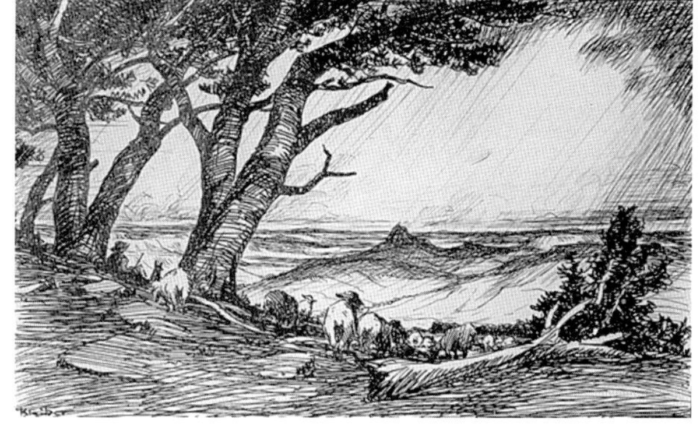

"Untitled--Sheepherder"
Image: 5.5 inches high by 8.75 inches wide

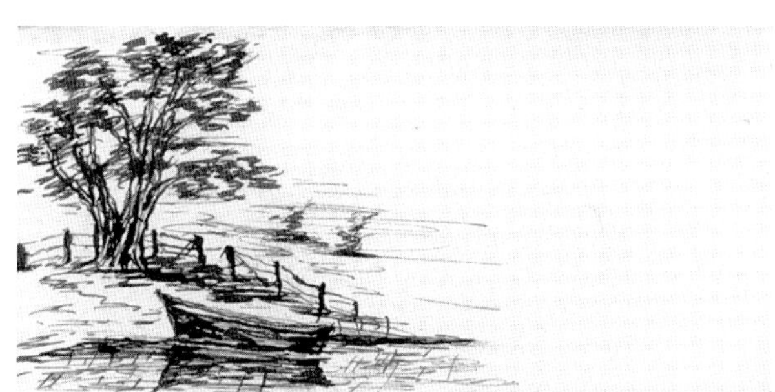

"Untitled--Landscape with Boat in Stream"
Unsigned
Image: 1.625 inches high by 2.125 inches wide

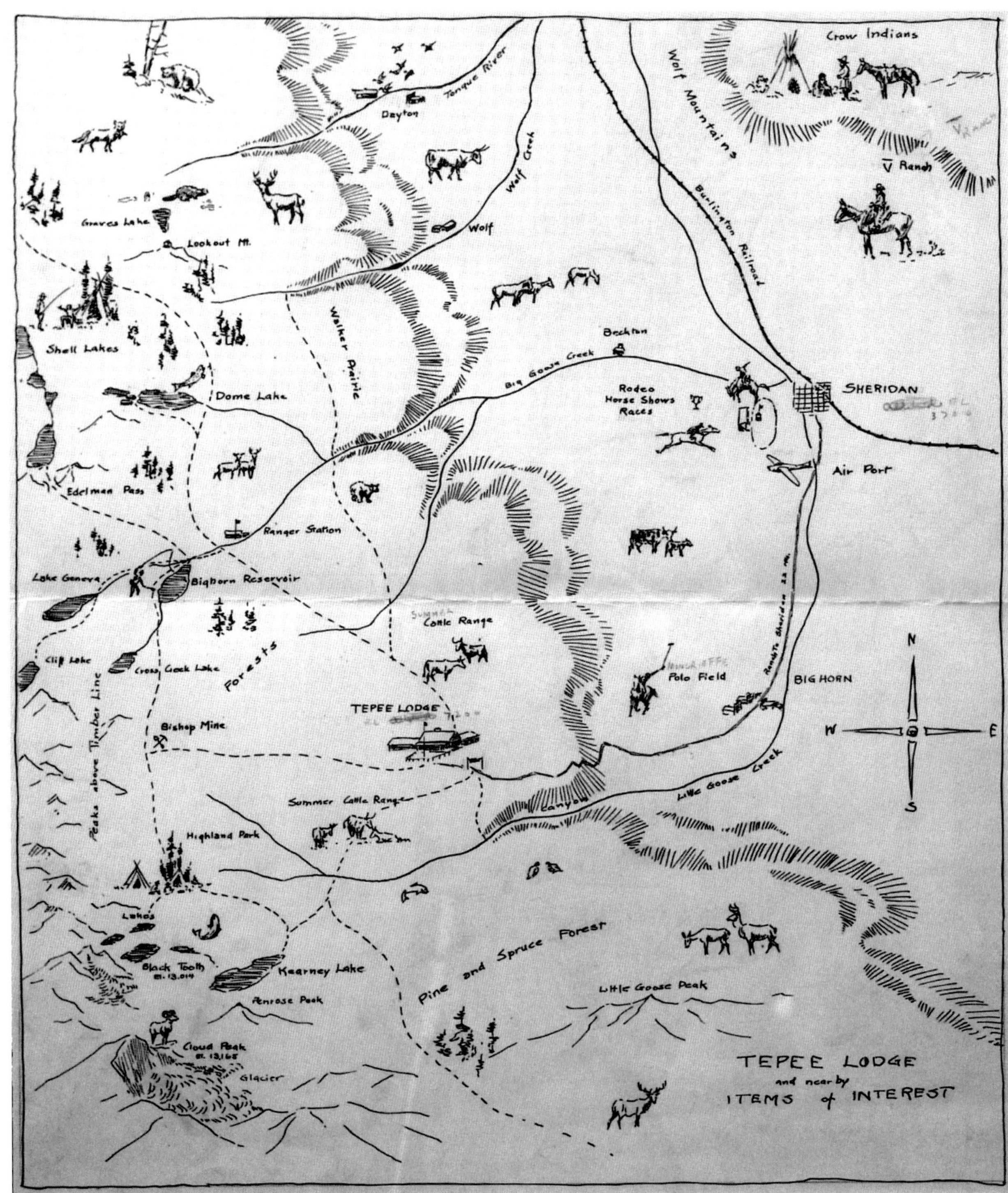

"Tepee Lodge and Nearby Items of Interest"
Image: 18 inches high by 15 inches wide

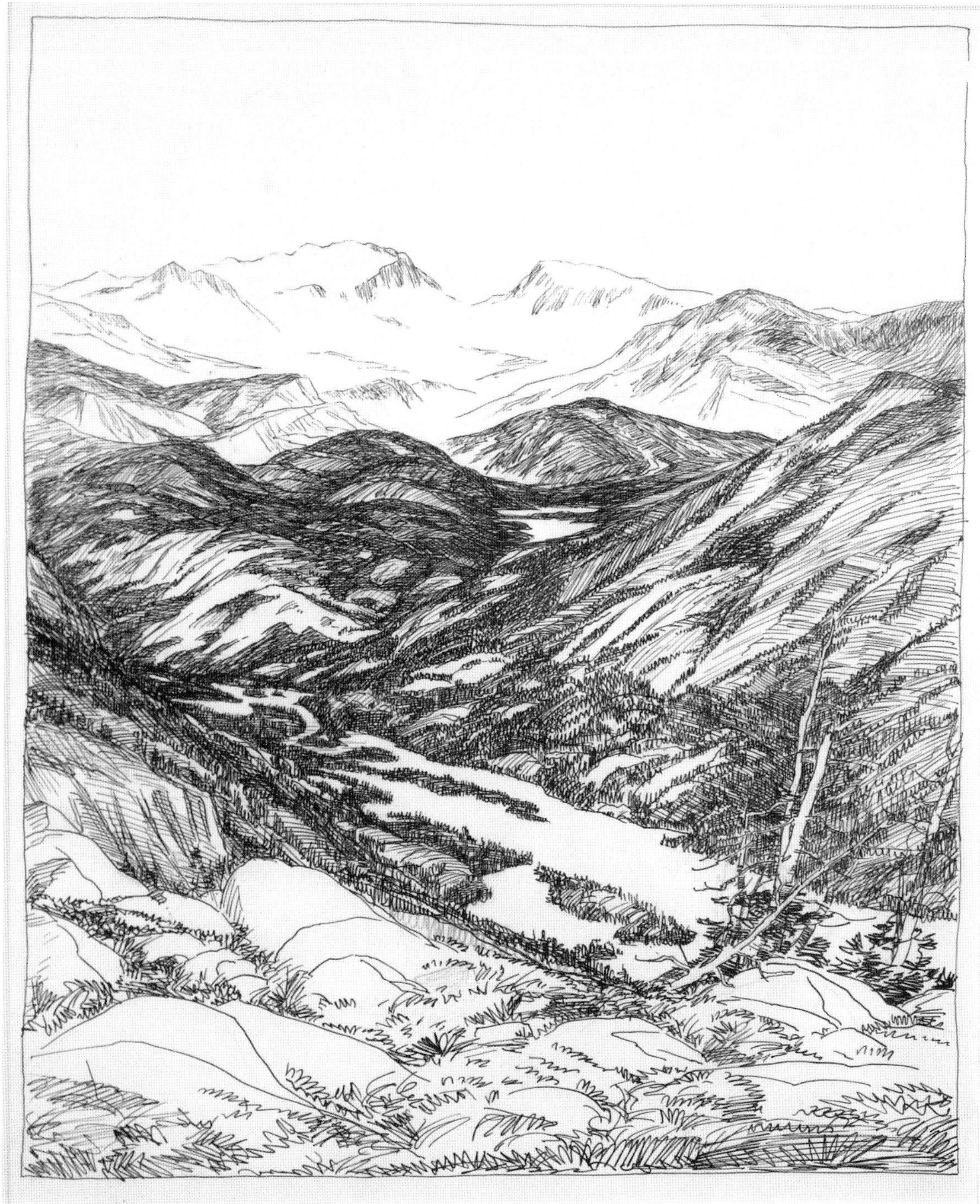

"Wind River Range"
Image: 10 inches high by 8 inches wide

Hans Kleiber

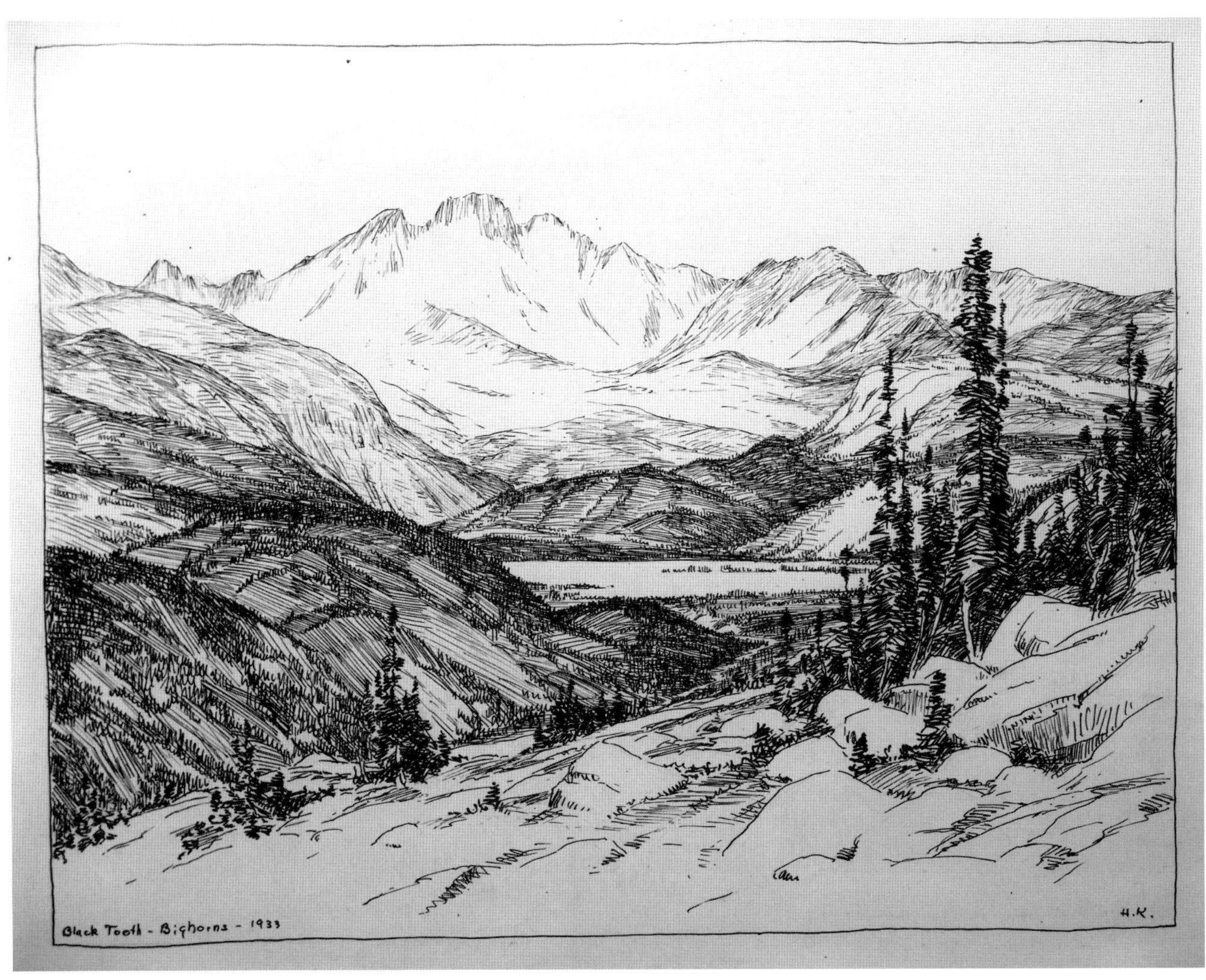

"Black Tooth Bighorns 1933"
Image: 8 inches high by 10 inches wide

Chapter Thirteen
Note Cards

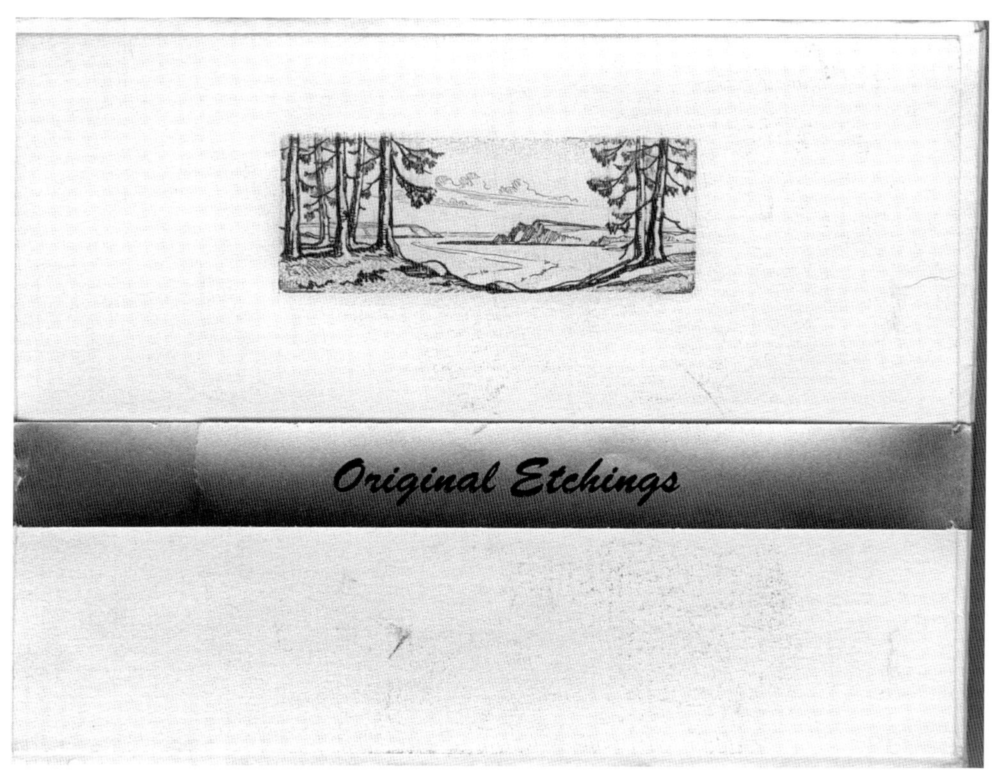

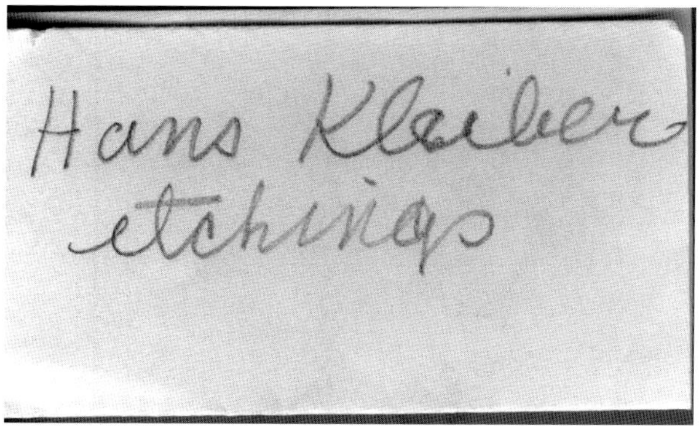

Hans Kleiber
etchings

Authors Note: The note cards were offered for sale through the Snook Art Company of Billings, Montana. The box label indicates that they were etchings. If it was not for Miss Snook's handwriting, no one could be sure that the cards were from Hans Kleiber as they are unsigned. Carole Tucker of the Golden Crown told us about some very small etchings that Kleiber had done. These note cards fit her description.

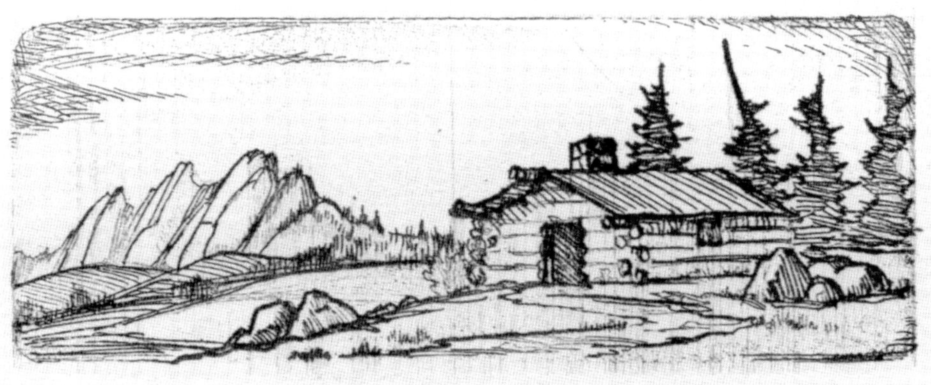

"Untitled--Log Cabin"
Medium: Etching
Image: 0.75 inches high by 2.00 inches wide
Unsigned

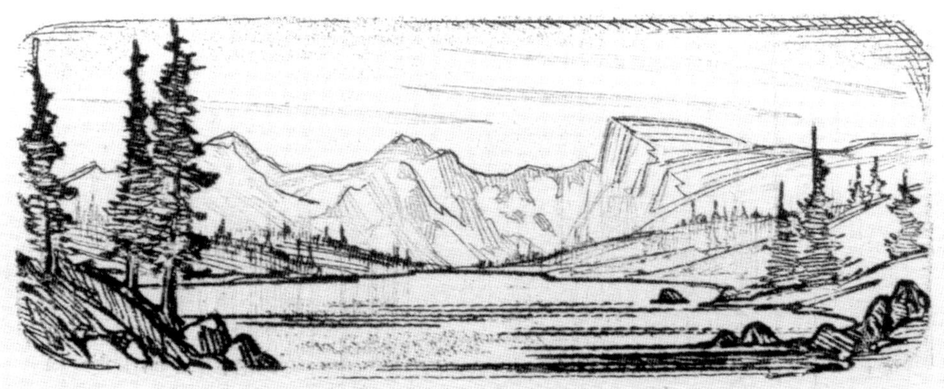

"Untitled--Mountain Lake"
Medium: Etching
Image: 0.75 inches high by 2.00 inches wide
Unsigned

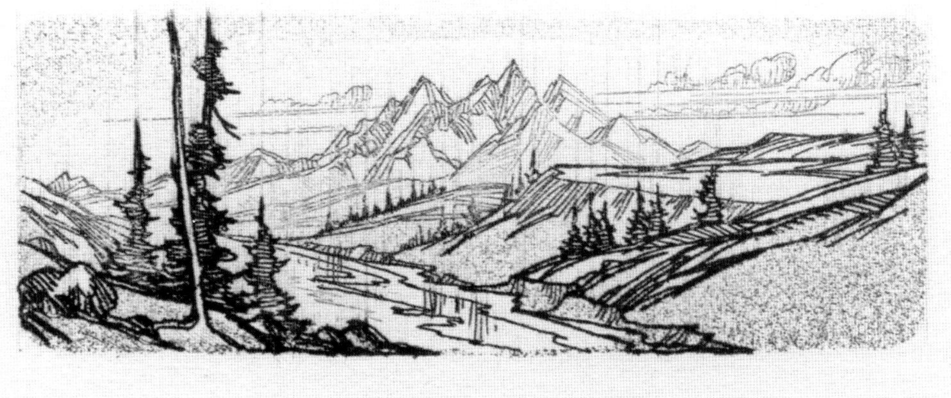

"Untitled--Mountain Scene with River"
Comment: This could very likely be the Tetons.
Medium: Etching
Image: 0.75 inches high by 2.00 inches wide
Unsigned

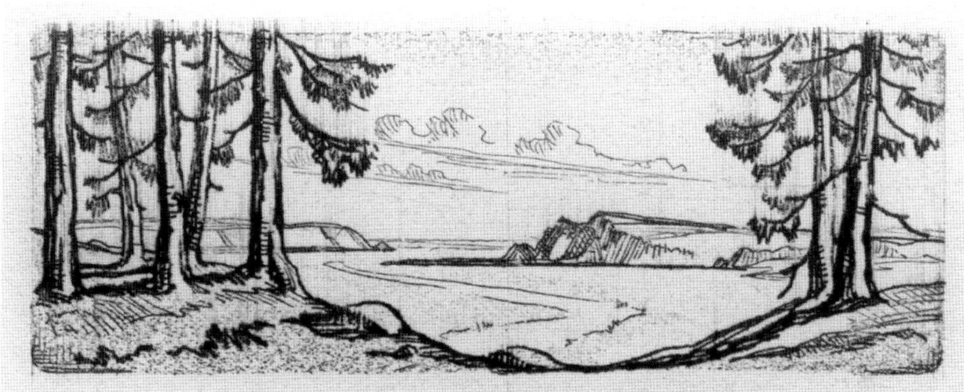

"Untitled--Landscape with River"
Medium: Etching
Image: 0.75 inches high by 2.00 inches wide
Unsigned

Hans Kleiber

Chapter Fourteen

Hand Colored Impressions

Authors Note: This section includes examples of not only hand watercolored impressions but also those that were done as a two ink process. This section contains examples for the readers reference, but does not constitute all of the impressions hand colored by the artist.

Hans Kleiber

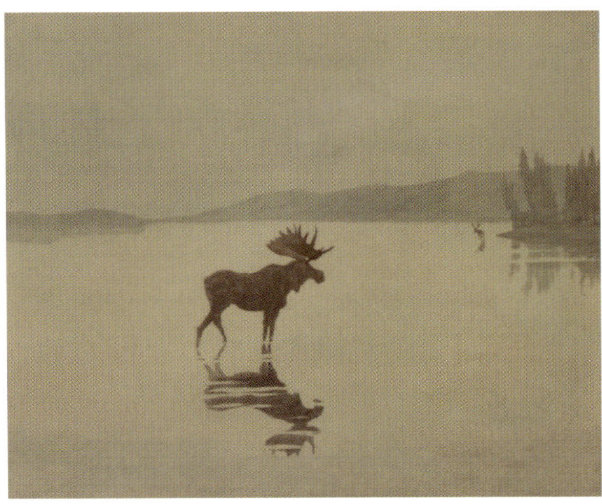

"A Moose"
"Moose--Night"
Two Ink Impression
Image: 9.75 inches high by 11.75 inches wide

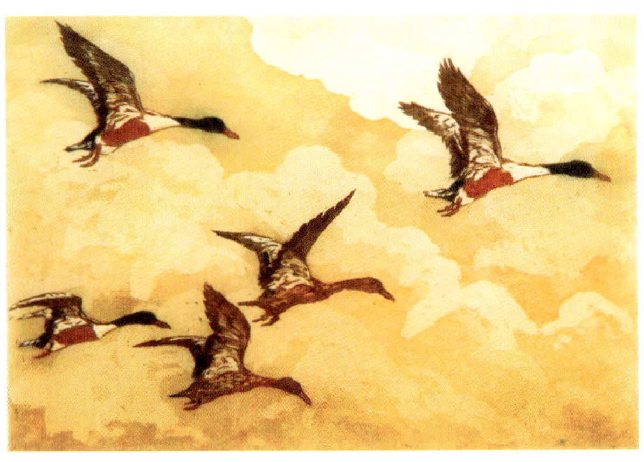

"A Flock of Shovellers"
"Spoonbills"
Two Ink Impression
Image: 7.25 inches high by 10.25 inches wide

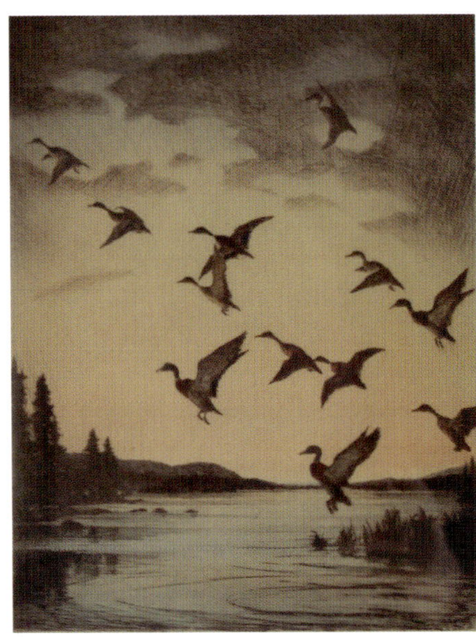

"A Rising Flock"
Image: 9.75 inches high by 7.25 inches wide

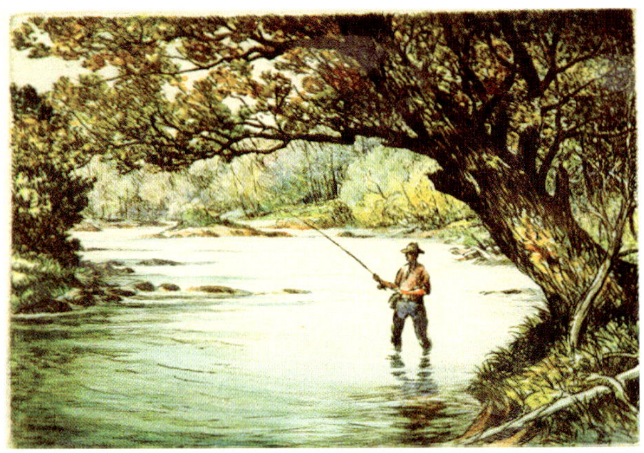

"A Quiet Stream"
Image: 3.8125 inches high by 5.3125 inches wide

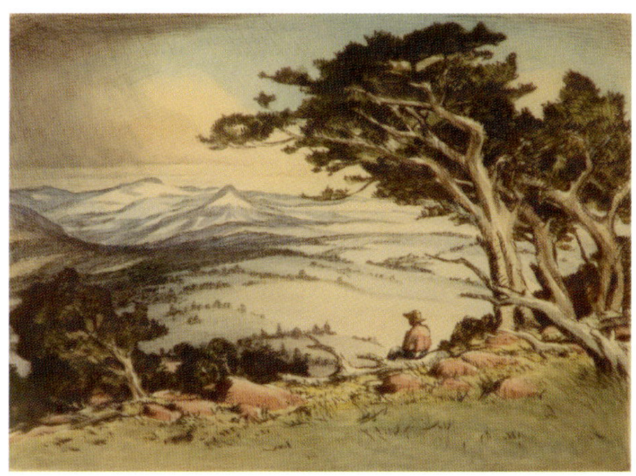

"Across the Hills"
"The Absoraka"
"The Absorakas"
Image: 4.375 inches high by 5.75 inches wide

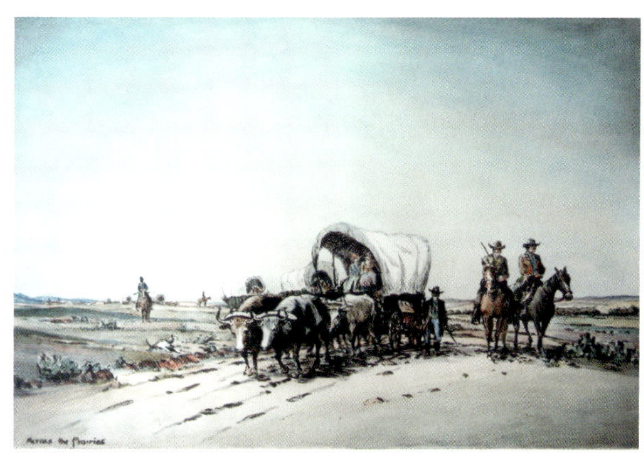

"Across the Prairies"
Medium: Hand Colored Photogravure
Image: 5.25 inches high by 7.5 inches wide

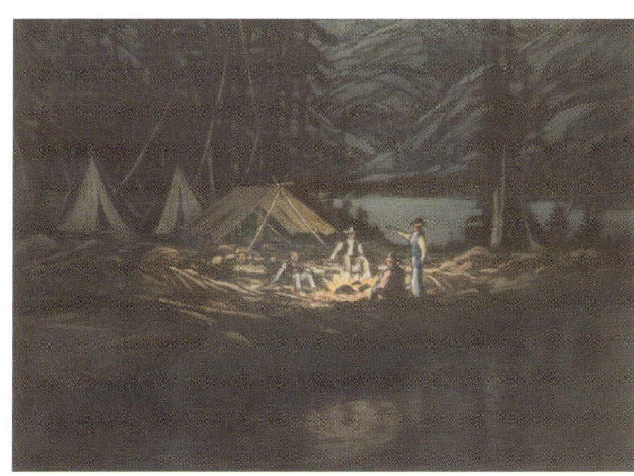

"Around the Campfire"
Second State of "Campfire" a.k.a. "Campfire II"
Image: 5.75 inches high by 7.75 inches wide

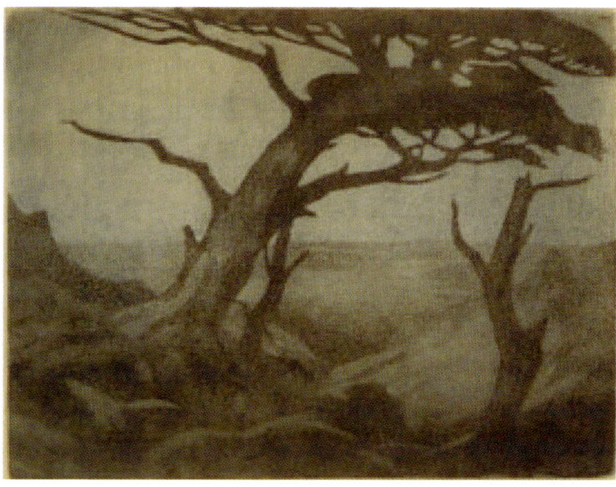

"At the Canyon Pine"
"On the Canyon Rim"
Second State
Medium: Two Ink Impression
Image: 6.125 inches high by 7.875 inches wide

Hans Kleiber

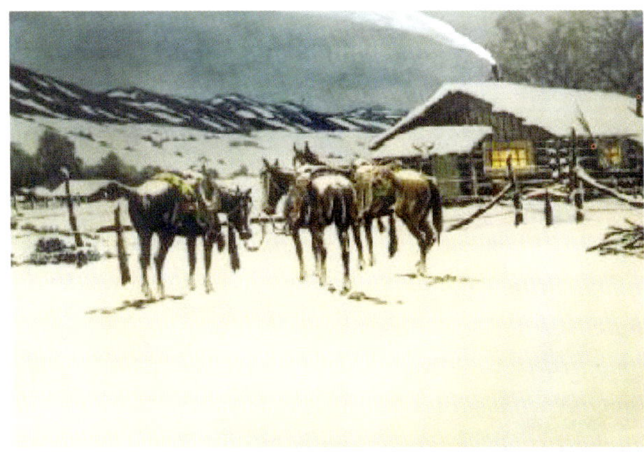

"At the Hitchrack"
Image: 9.5 inches high by 13.75 inches wide

The difference between the regular hand pulled impression and the hand colored is the smoke from the chimney of the cabin.

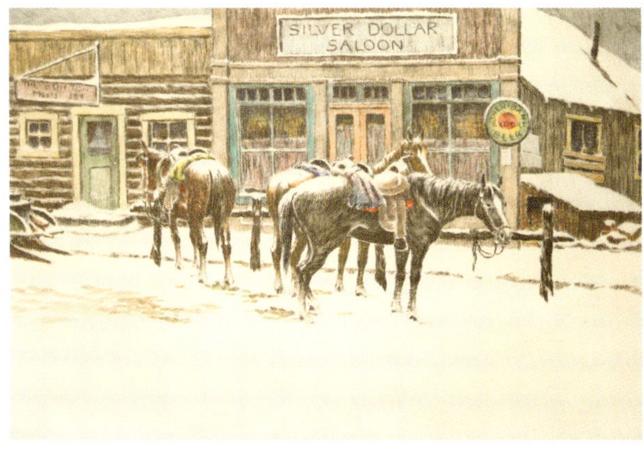

"At the Silver Dollar"
Image: 8.25 inches high by 11.75 inches wide

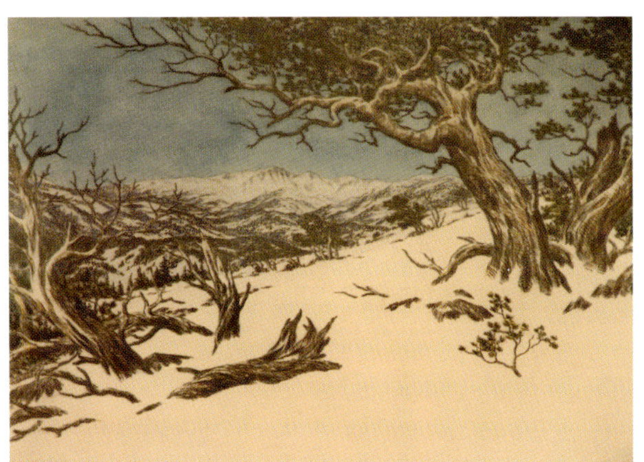

"At Timber Line"
"At Timberline"
Image: 7.75 inches high by 10.75 inches wide

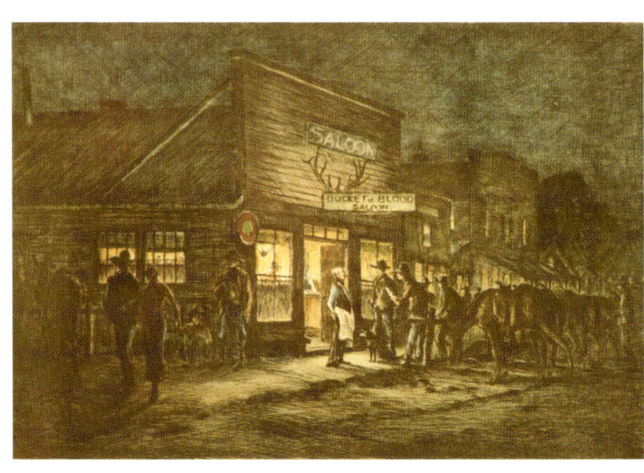

"Bucket of Blood Saloon"
"The Bucket of Blood Saloon"
Medium: Hand Colored Photogravure
Image: 5.25 inches high by 7.625 inches wide

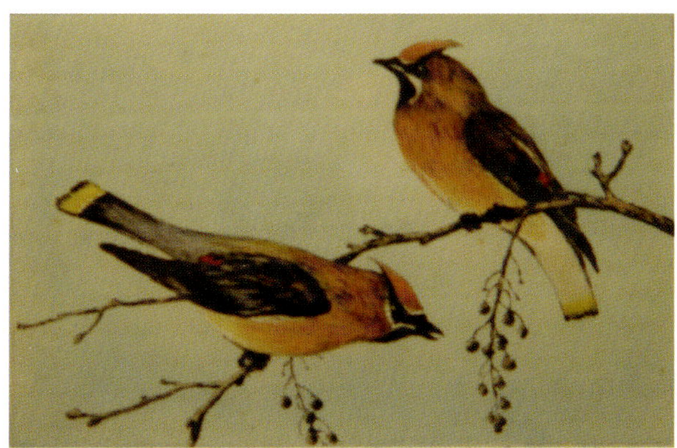

"Cedar Waxwings"
Image: 3.875 inches high by 5.875 inches wide

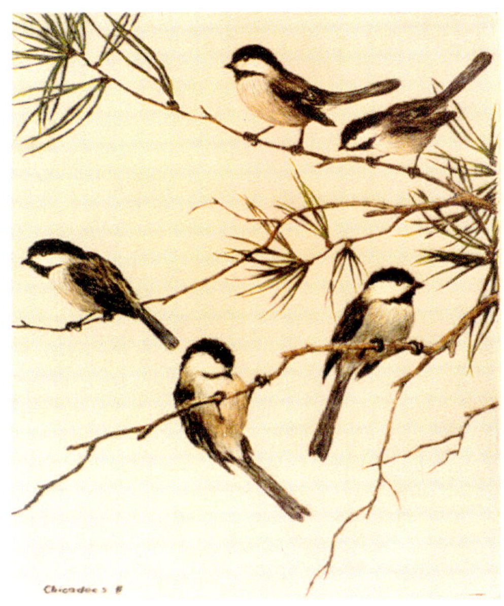

"Chicadees II"
Image: 5.75 inches high by 4.75 inches wide

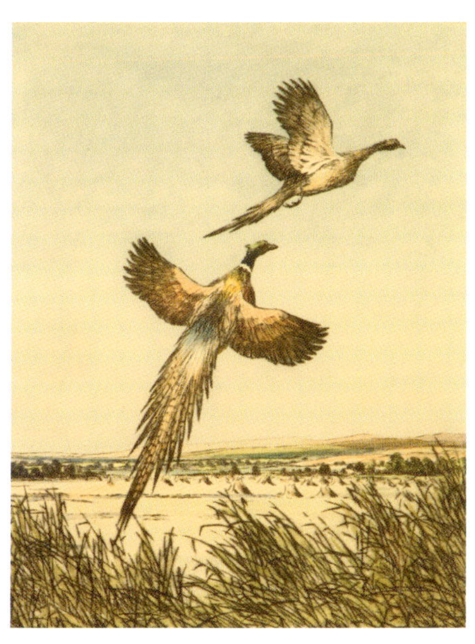

"Chinese Pheasants"
"Pheasants"
Image: 6.25 inches high by 4.875 inches wide

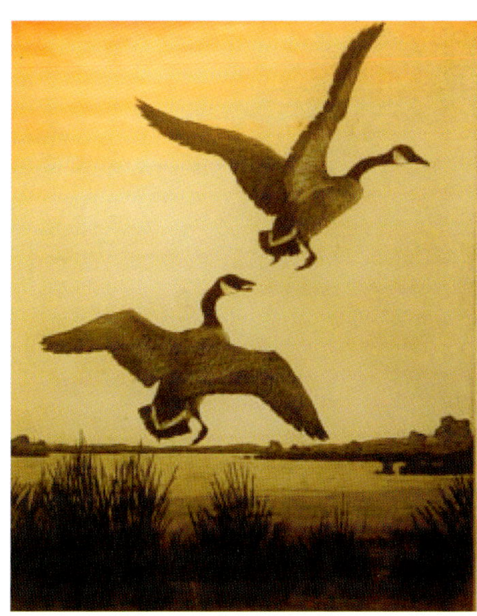

"Disturbed Geese"
"Disturbed Honkers"
Two Ink Impression
Image: 9.375 inches high by 7.375 inches wide

Hans Kleiber

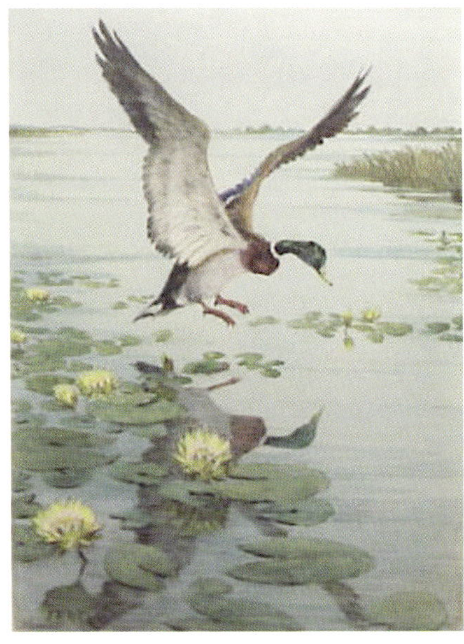

"Drake and Lilies"
"Drake and Lilies I"
Image: 8.75 inches high by 6.25 inches wide

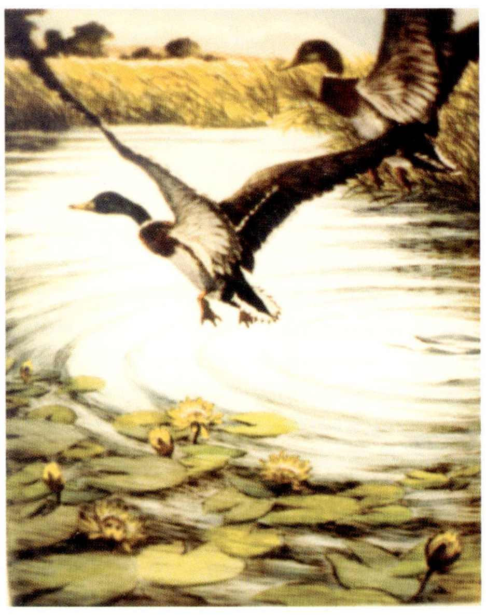

"Drakes and Lilies II"
"Drakes in Lilies II"
"Drakes in Summer"
Image: 8.75 inches high by 6.75 inches wide

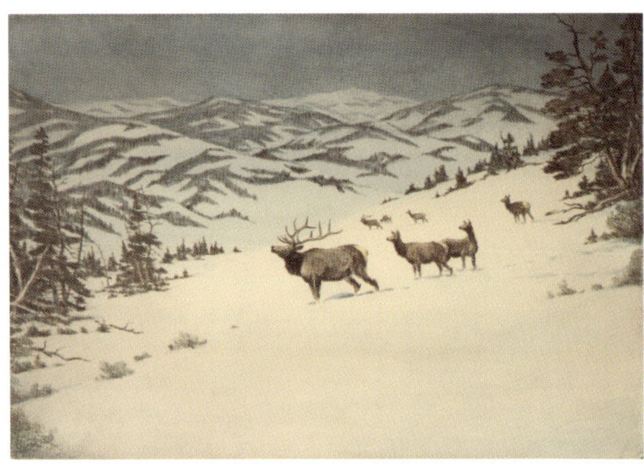

"Elk in the Bighorns"
"Elk in the Rockies"
Image: 9.75 inches high by 13.75 inches wide

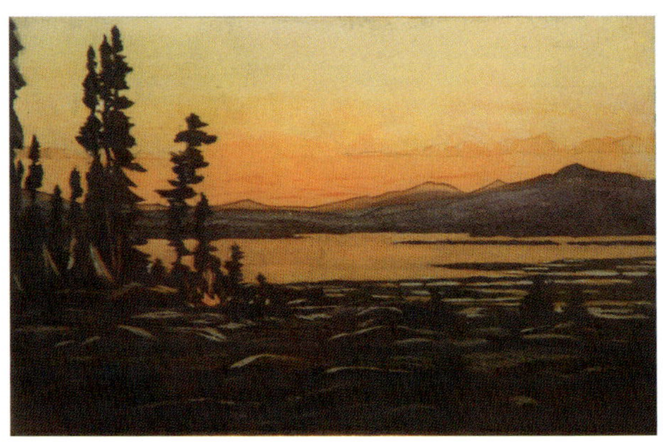

"Evening at Elk Lake--Wyoming"
Medium: Two Ink Impression
Image: 5.875 inches high by 8.875 inches wide

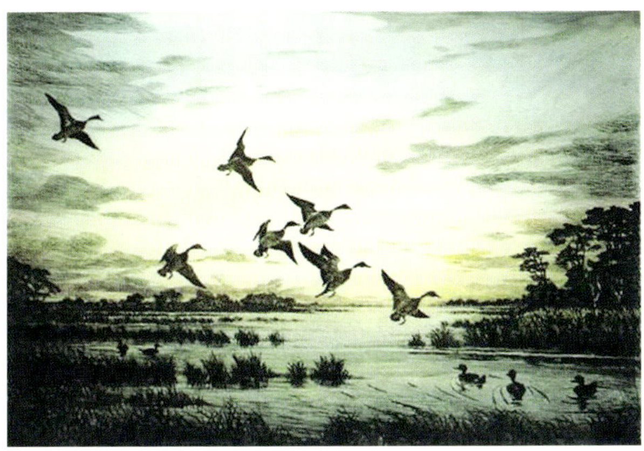

"Evening on the Marshes"
Image: 8.125 inches high by 11.75 inches wide

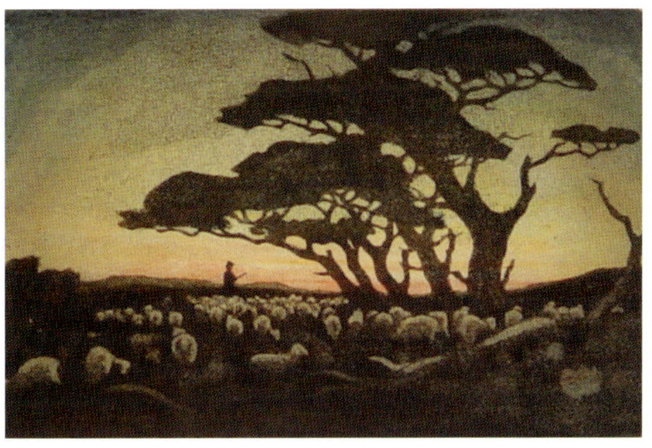

"Evening on the Range"
Two Ink Impression
Image: 6.375 inches high by 9.375 inches wide

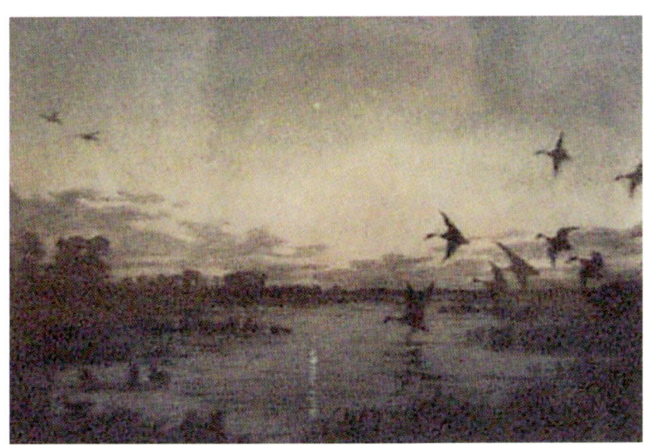

"Evening Star"
Hand Colored Photogravure
Image: 5.125 inches high by 7.125 inches wide

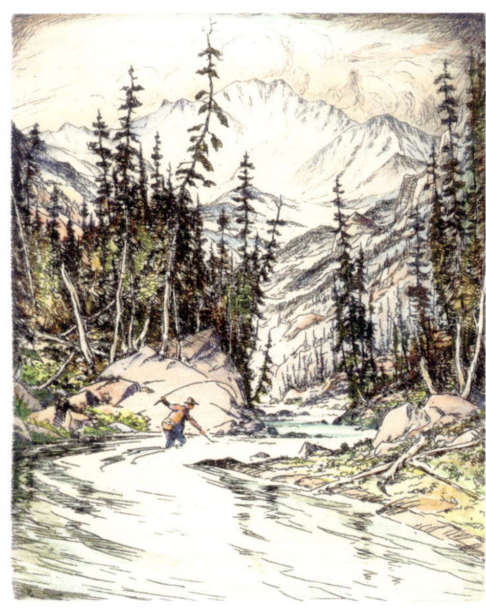

"Fishing on Paint Rock"
Image: 4.875 inches high by 3.75 inches wide

Hans Kleiber

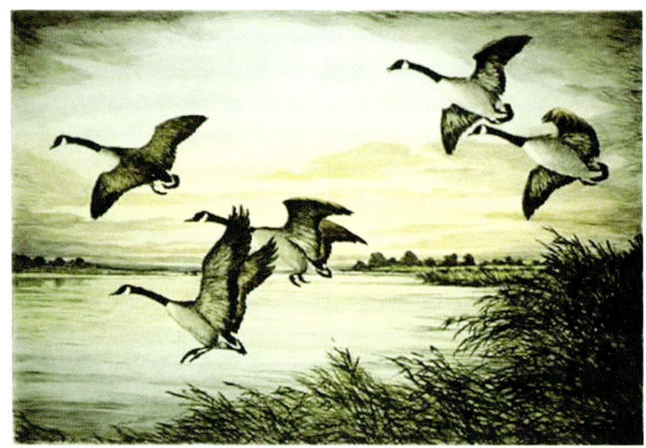

“Honkers Settling”
Image: 9.75 inches high by 13.75 inches wide

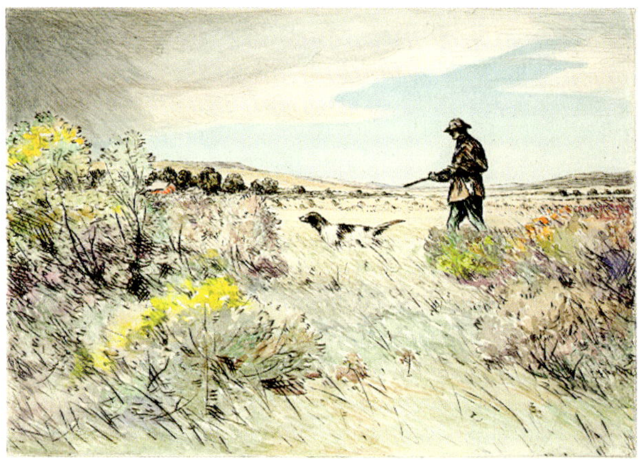

“Hunting Pheasants”
“Looking for Pheasants”
Image: 4.75 inches high by 6.5 inches wide

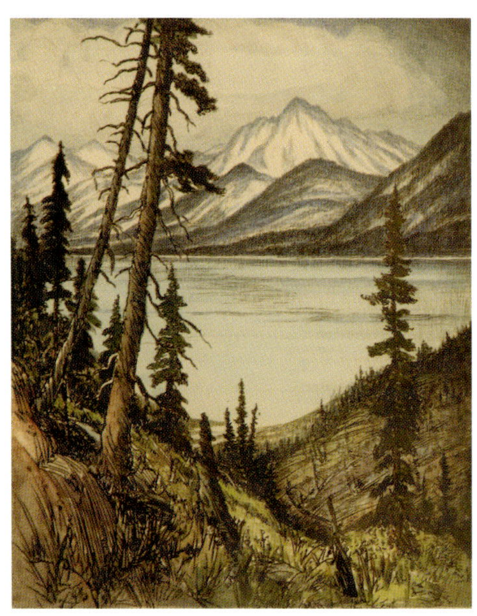

“Jackson Lake and Tetons I”
Image: 6.75 inches high by 5.25 inches wide

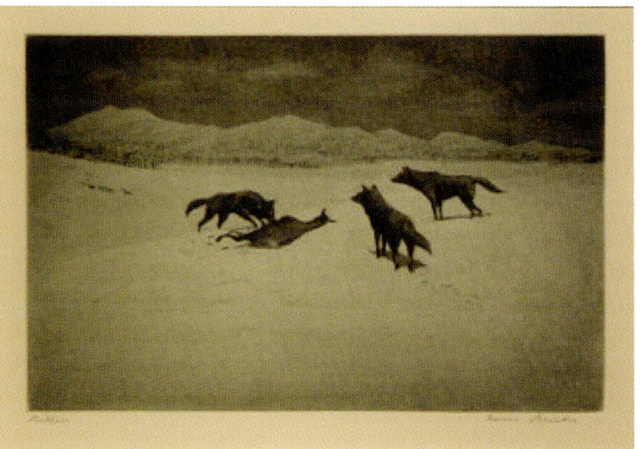

“Killers”
Medium: Hand Colored Etching
Image: 7.875 inches high by 13.25 inches wide

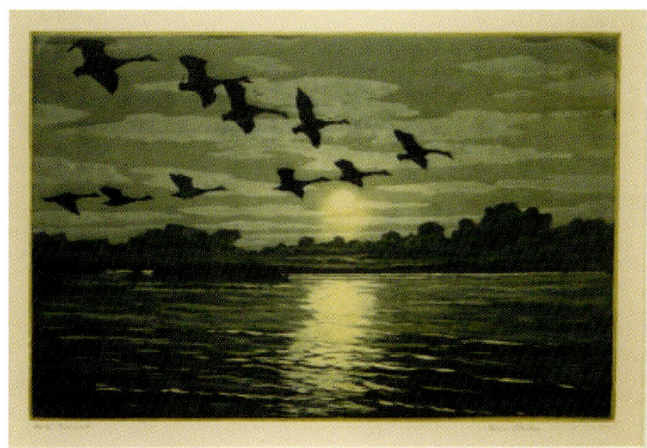

"Late Arrivals"
Two Ink Impression
Image: 8.25 inches high by 12.25 inches wide

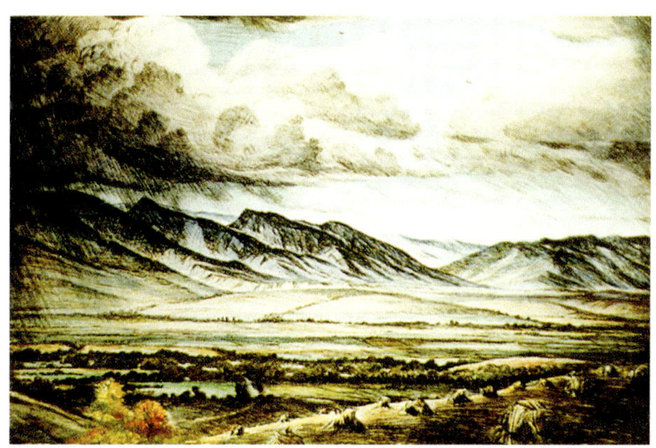

"Little Goose Valley"
"Little Goose Valley, Bighorns"
Image: 5.5 inches high by 8 inches wide

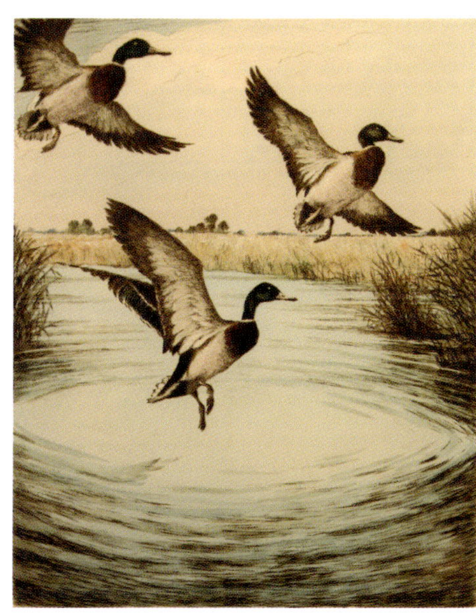

"Mallard Drakes"
"Louisiana Honkers"
Image: 9.8125 inches high by 7.75 inches wide

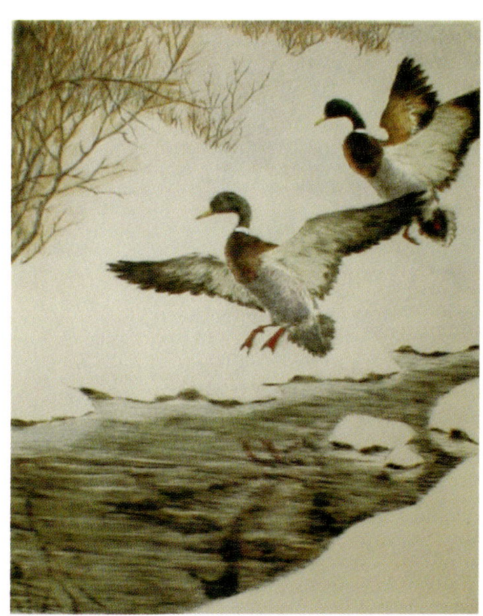

"Mallard Drakes"
"Mallards--Winter"
Image: 4.8125 inches high by 3.875 inches wide

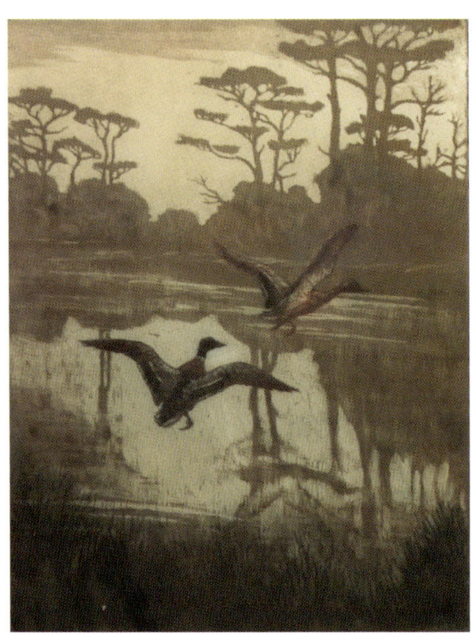

"Mallards Disturbed"
"Disturbed"
Medium: Two Ink Impression
Image: 11.875 inches high by 8.75 inches wide

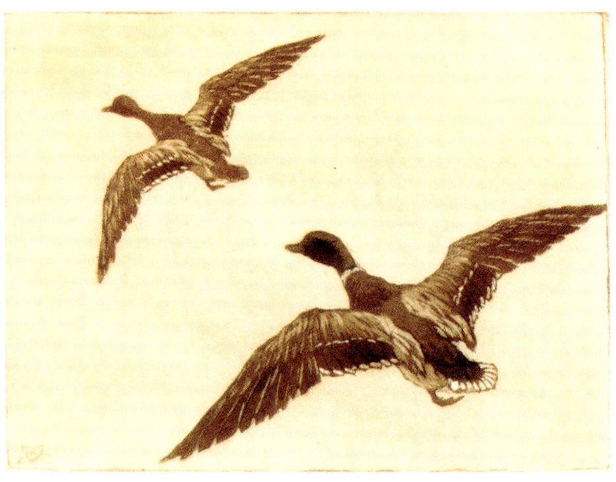

"Mallards Flying"
Medium: Two Ink Impression
Image: 4.75 inches high by 6.25 inches wide

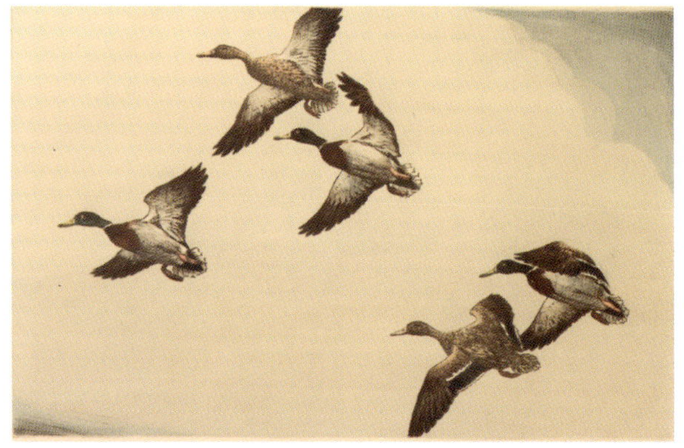

"Mallards in Flight"
Image: 7.75 inches high by 11.75 inches wide

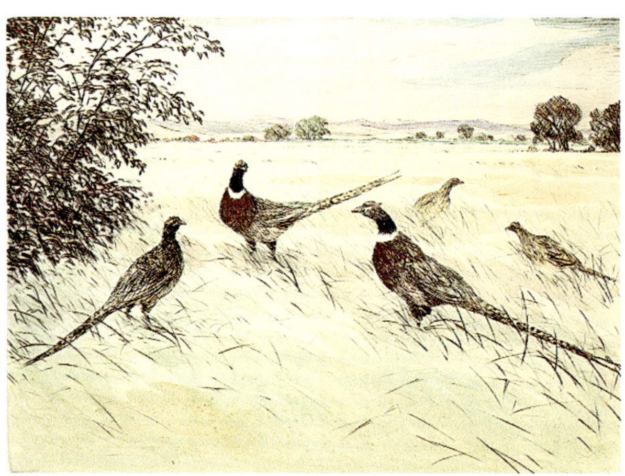

"Pheasants II"
Image: 6.3125 inches high by 8.3125 inches wide

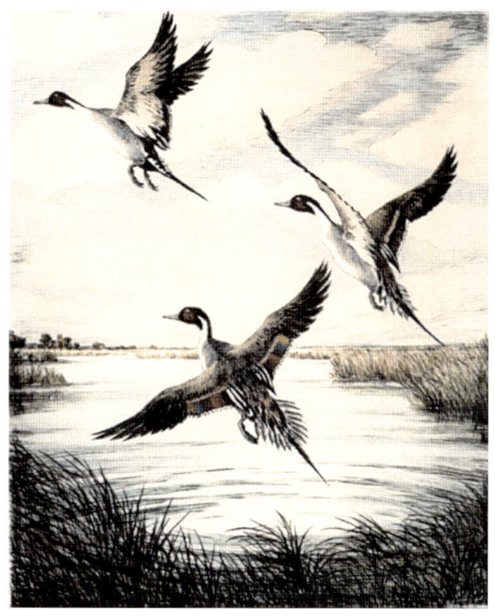

"Pintail Drakes"
Image: 9.5 inches high by 7.75 inches wide

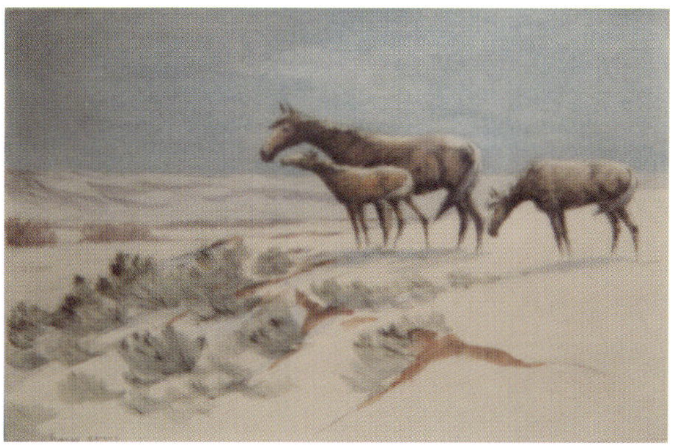

"Range Horses"
Image: 3.75 inches high by 5.75 inches wide

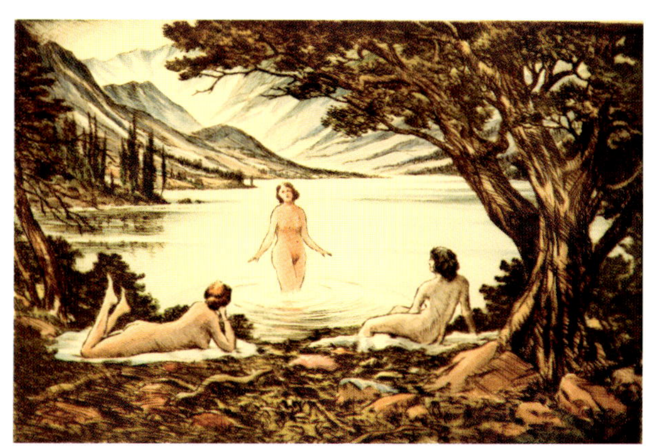

"The Bathers II"
Image: 4.25 inches high by 6.25 inches wide

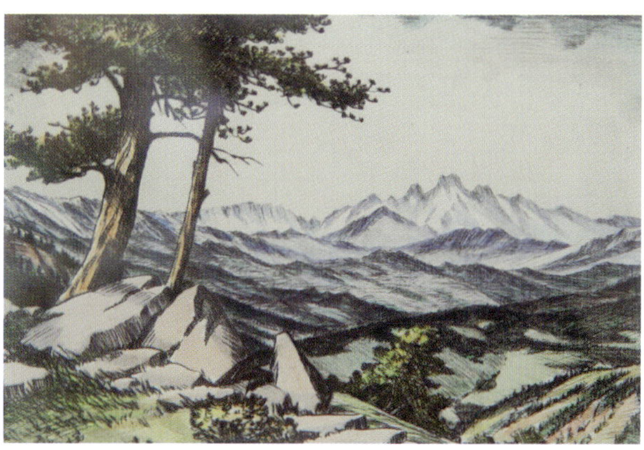

"The Bighorns"
"The Bighorns--Black Tooth"
"Big Horn Peaks"
Image: 3.625 inches high by 5.25 inches wide

Hans Kleiber

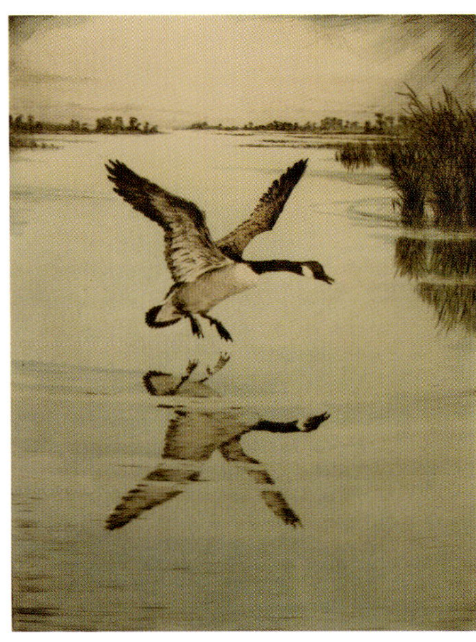

"The Lone Goose"
Image: 11.75 inches high by 8.5 inches wide

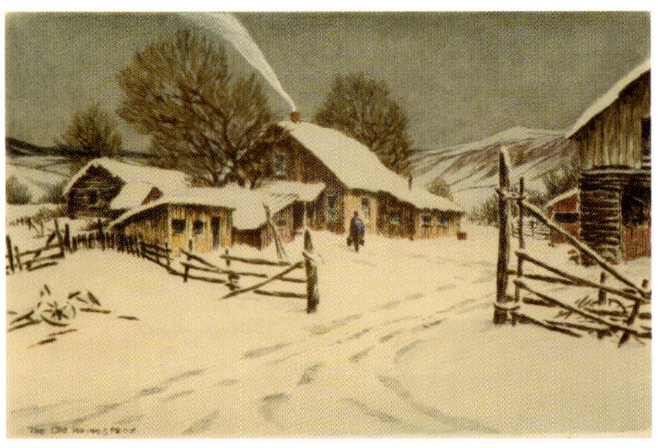

"The Old Homestead"
Image: 3.75 inches high by 5.875 inches wide

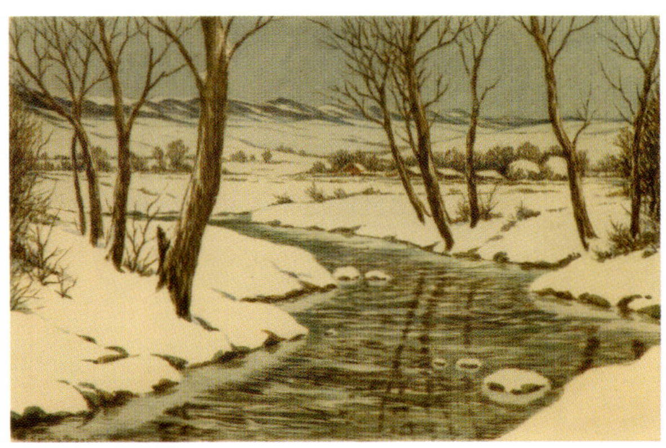

"The Spring Branch"
Image: 3.875 inches high by 5.875 inches wide

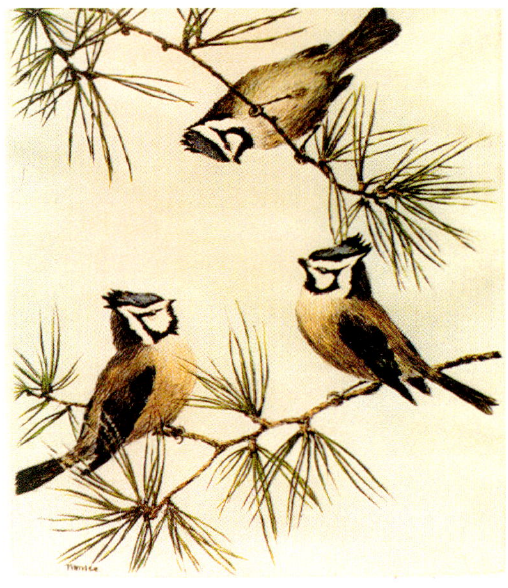

"Titmice"
Image: 5.8125 inches high by 4.8125 inches wide

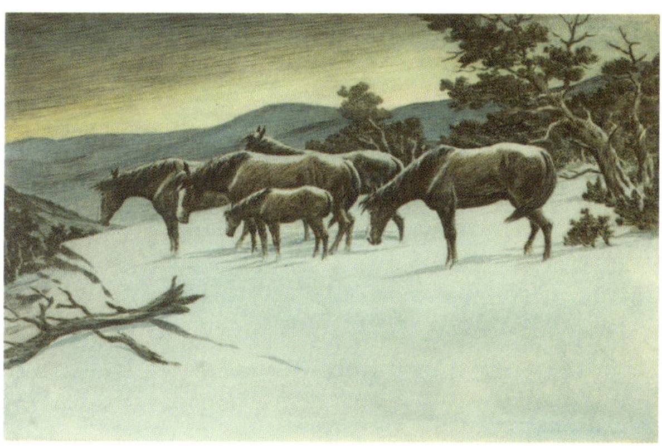

"Weathering a Storm"
Image: 7.875 inches high by 11.75 inches wide

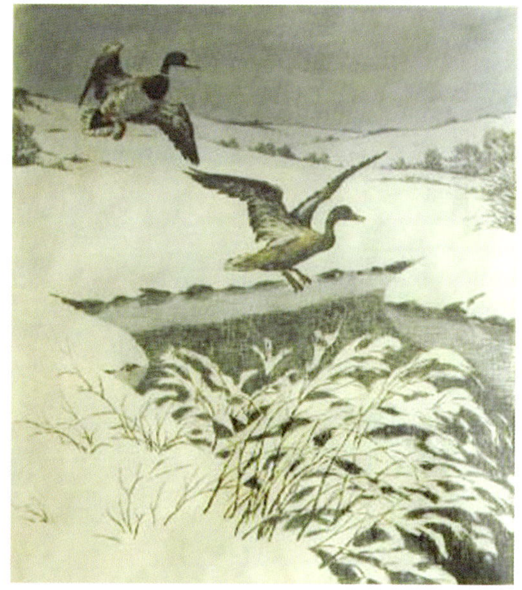

"Winter Guests"
"Winter Guests I"
"Mallards in the Snow"
Image: 10.75 inches high by 9.25 inches wide

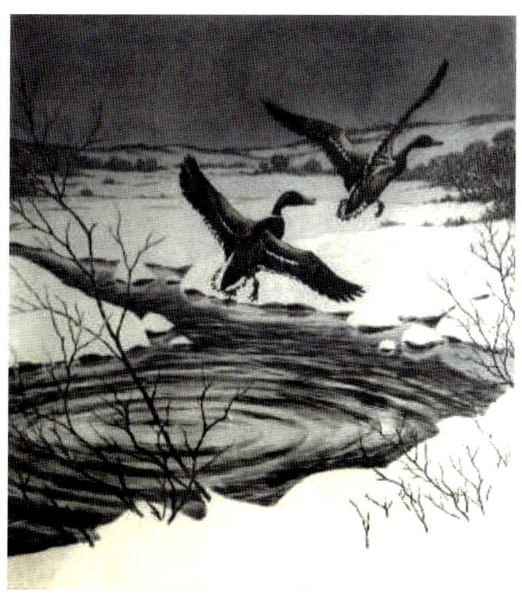

"Winter Guests II"
Image: 10.75 inches high by 9.25 inches wide

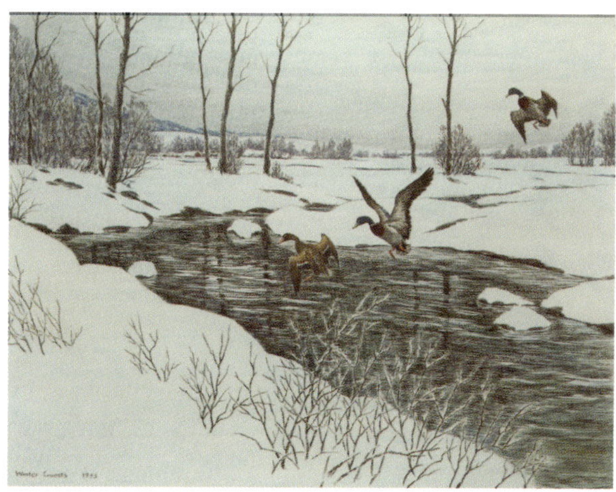

"Winter Guests"
Image: 10.75 inches high by 13.75 inches wide

Hans Kleiber

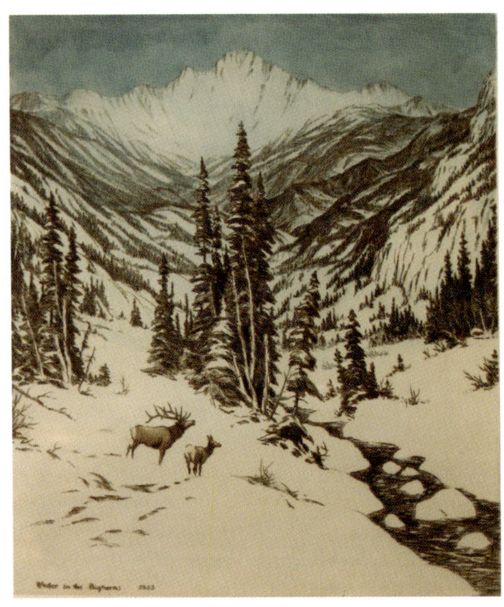

"Winter in the Bighorns"
Image: 12.625 inches high by 10.75 inches wide

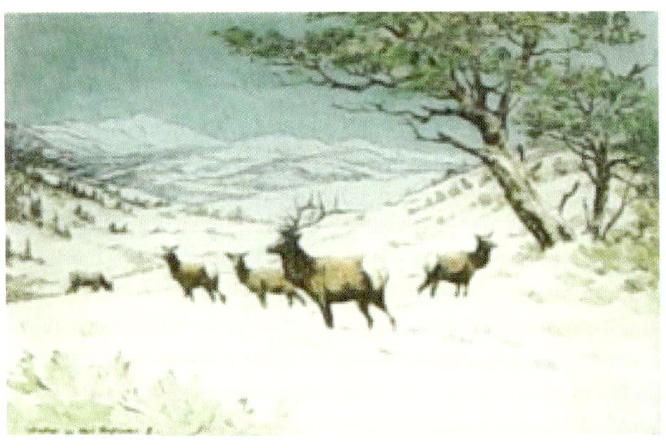

"Winter in the Bighorns II"
Image: 4 inches high by 6.25 inches wide

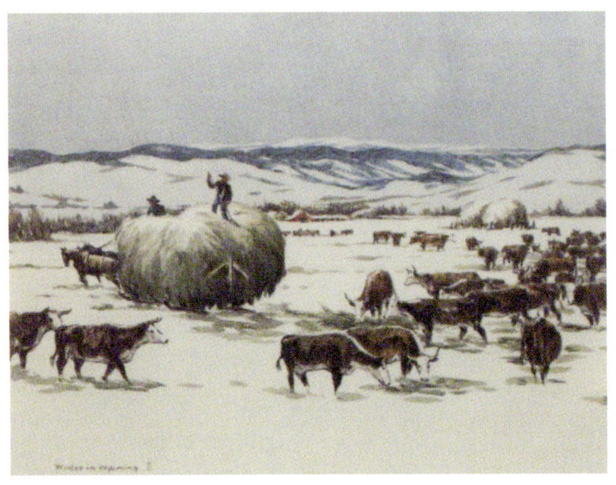

"Winter in Wyoming II"
Image: 6.875 inches high by 8.75 inches wide

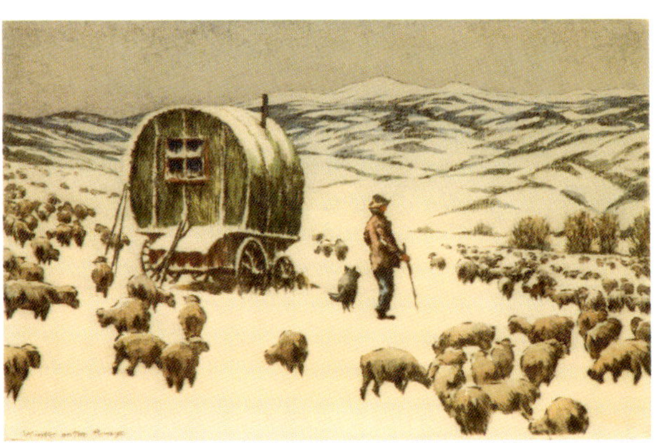

"Winter on the Range"
Image: 3.75 inches high by 5.875 inches wide

Chapter Fifteen

Watercolor Paintings

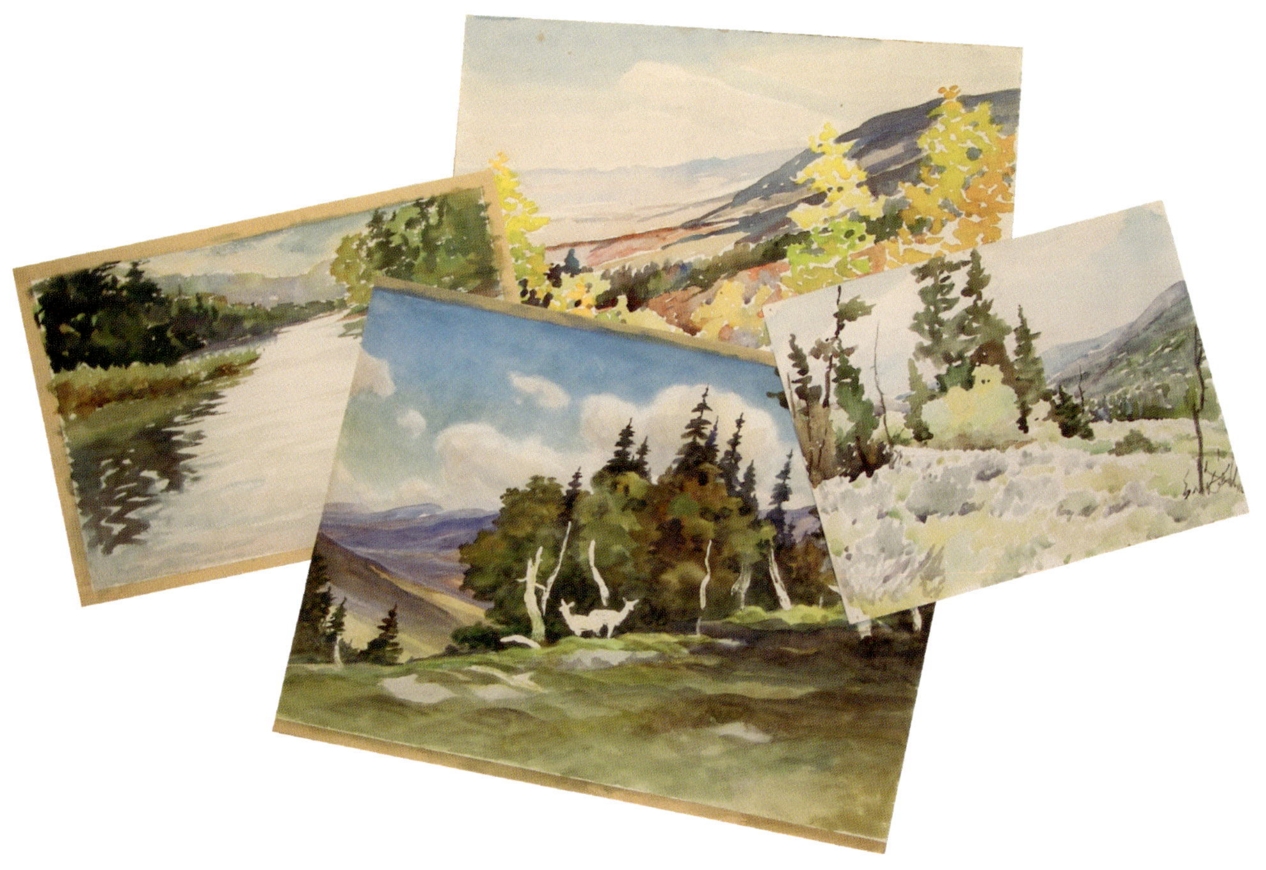

Unfinished watercolors by Hans Kleiber.

Hans Kleiber

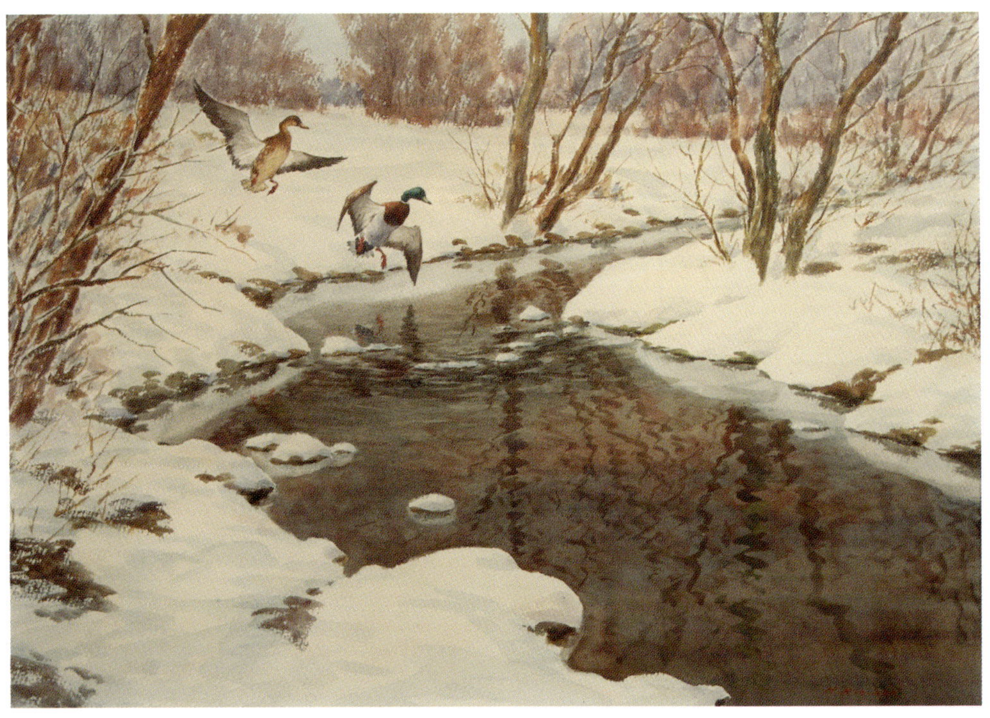

"A Pair of Mallards on a Winter Day"
Image: 13.5 inches high by 18.5 inches wide

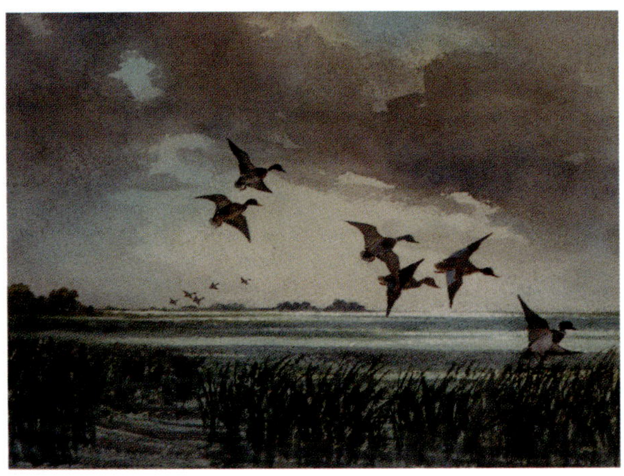

"A Stormy Interlude"
Image: 8.5 inches high by 11.25 inches wide

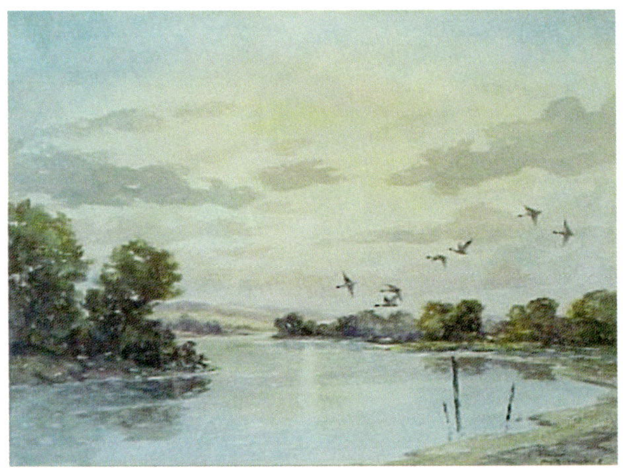

"Along the Yellowstone"
Image: 14 inches high by 18 inches wide

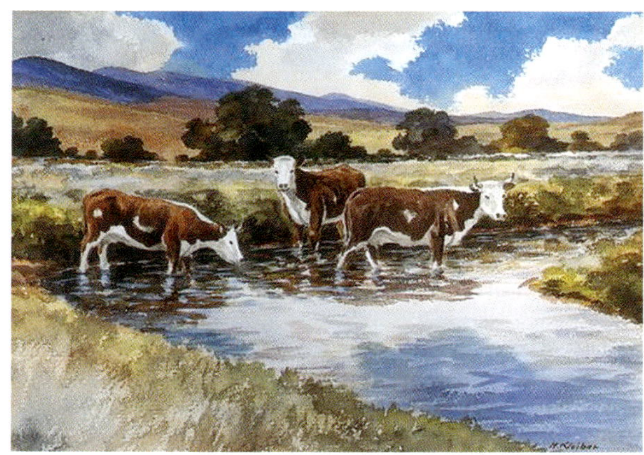

"At the Water Hole"
Image: 11.5 inches high by 15.75 inches wide

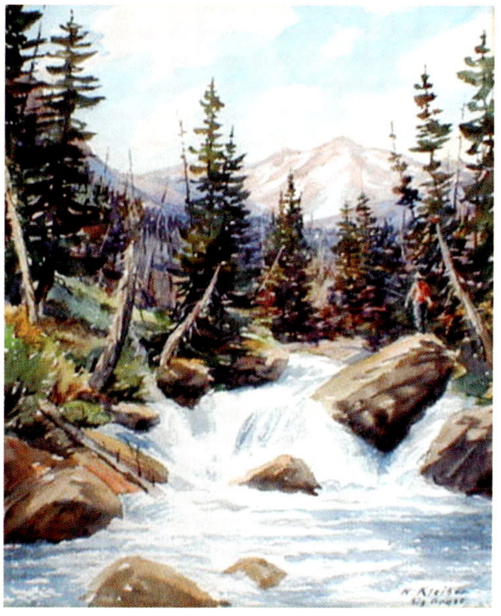

"Big Goose"
Image: 10.5 inches high by 8.5 inches wide

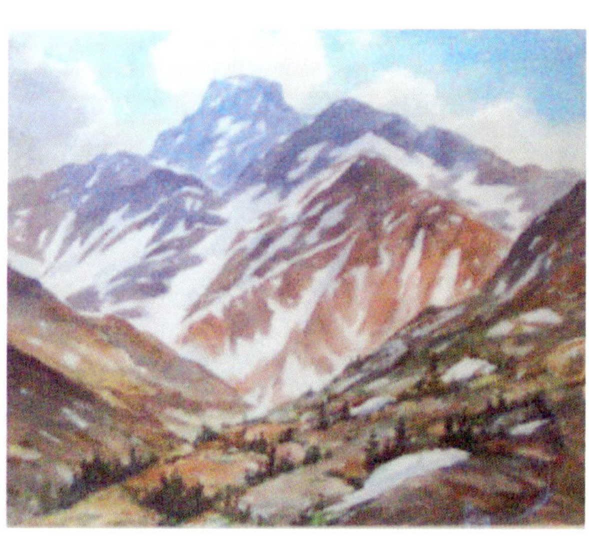

"Black Tooth--Bighorns"
Image: 13.75 inches high by 15.75 inches wide

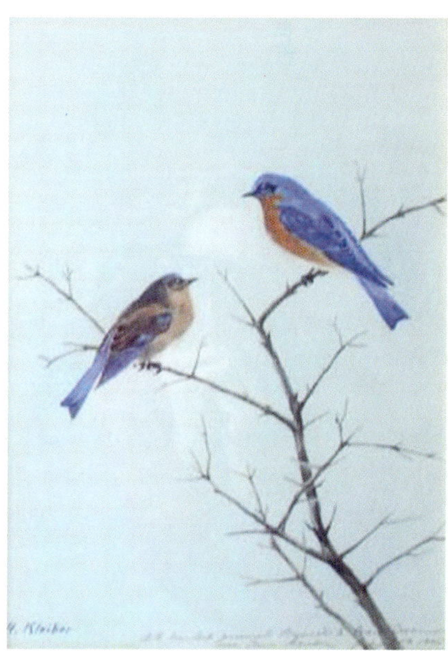

"Blue Birds"
Image: 14.5 inches high by 10.5 inches wide

Hans Kleiber

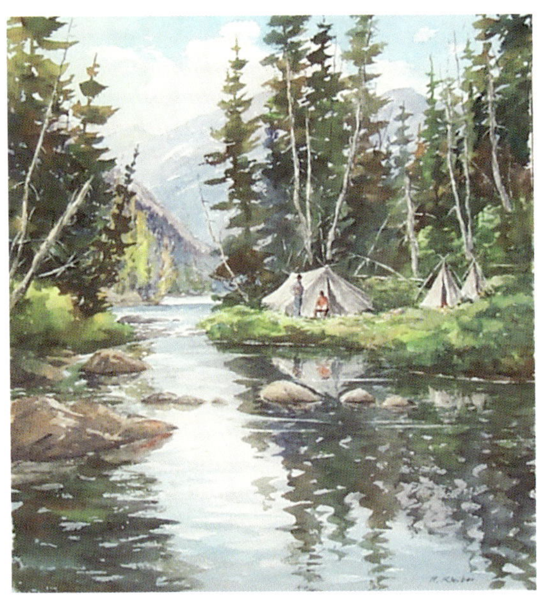

“Camp at Lake Geneva--Bighorns”
Image: 14 inches high by 13.5 inches wide

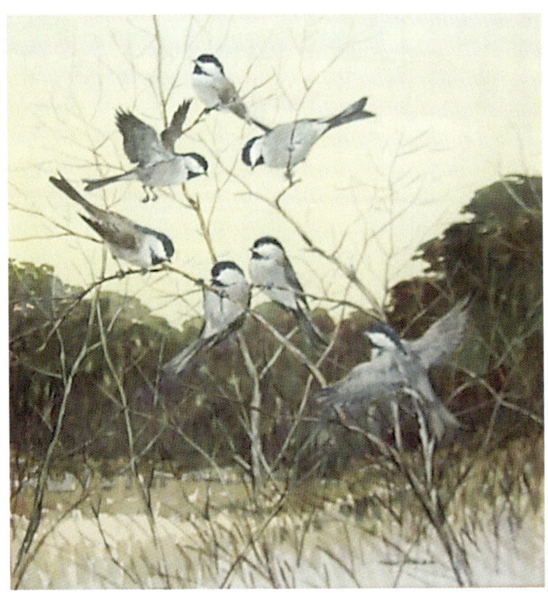

“Chicadees”
Image: 15.5 inches high by 14 inches wide

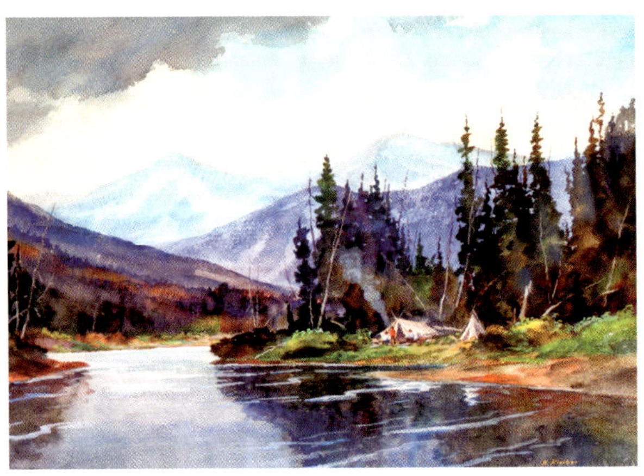

“Cloudy Day in Camp”
Image: 10.5 inches high by 14.5 inches wide

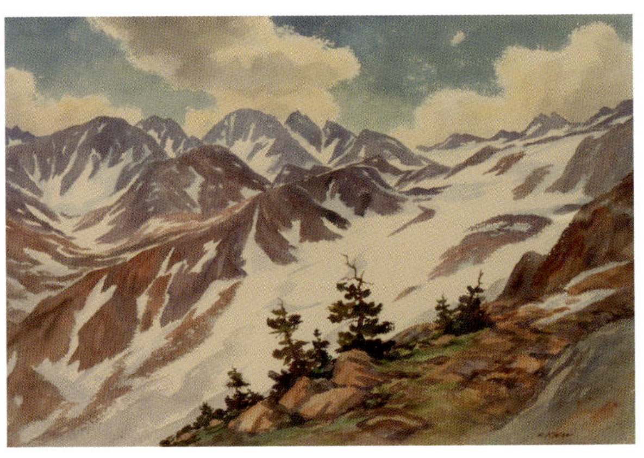

“Core of the Wind River Range, North of Fremont Park”
Image: 14.625 inches high by 21 inches wide

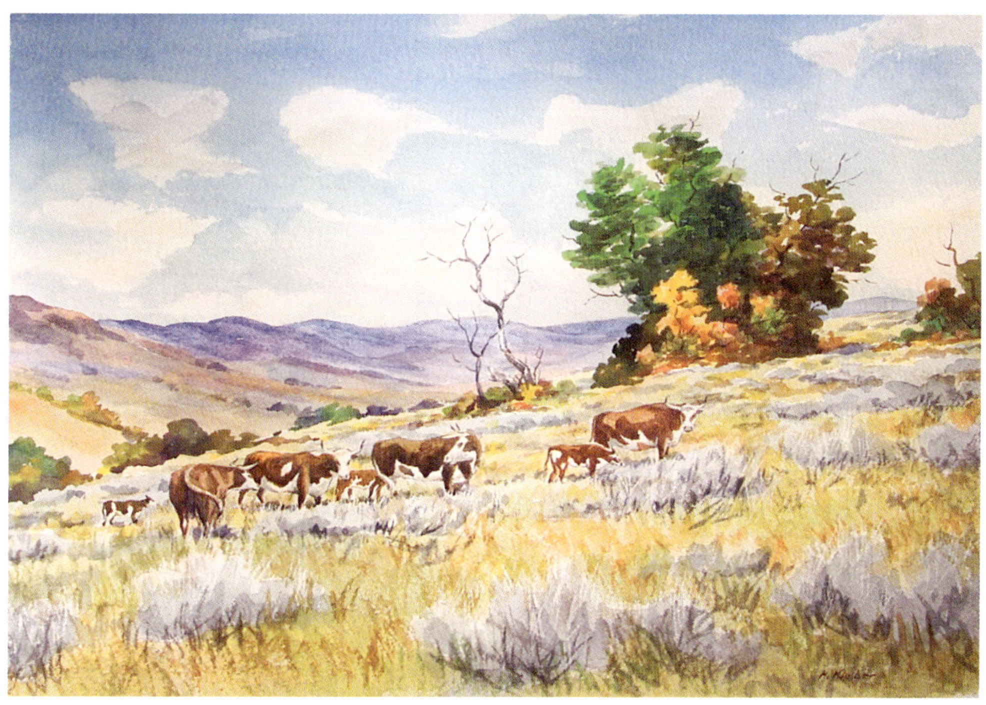

"Cows and Calves on the Reservation"
Image: 10.375 inches high by 14.5 inches wide

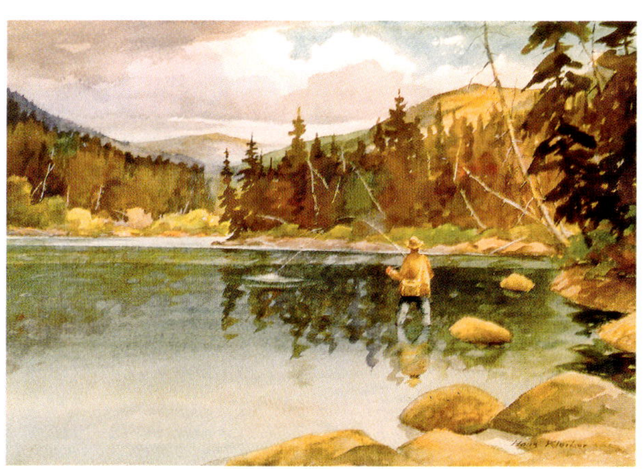

"Dome Lake"
Image: 9.25 inches high by 13.75 inches wide

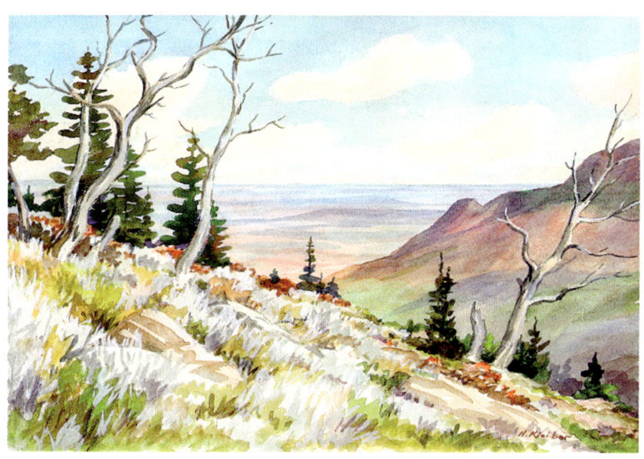

"Down Tongue River Canyon and the Valleys Beyond"
Image: 7.5 inches high by 10.625 inches wide

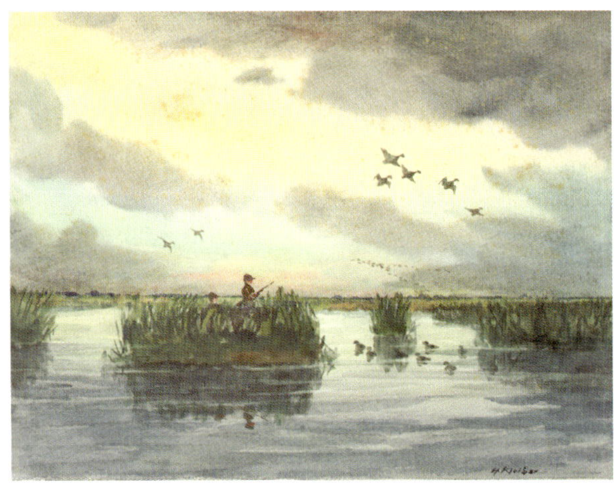

"Duck Blind Grand Chenier, La."
Image: 7.5 inches high by 9.625 inches wide

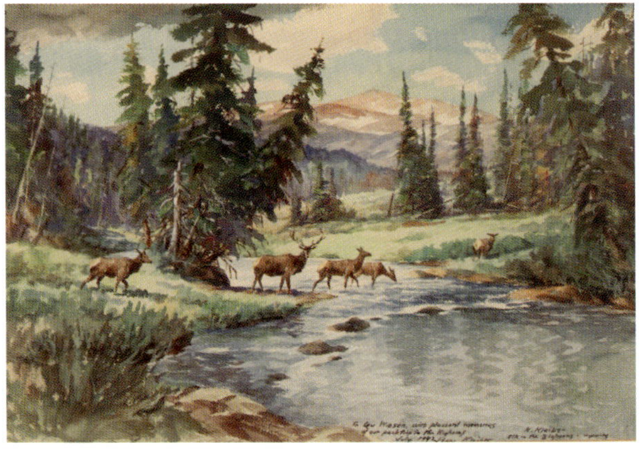

"Elk in the Bighorns--Wyoming"
Image: 10.5 inches high by 15 inches wide
Painting dated 1942.

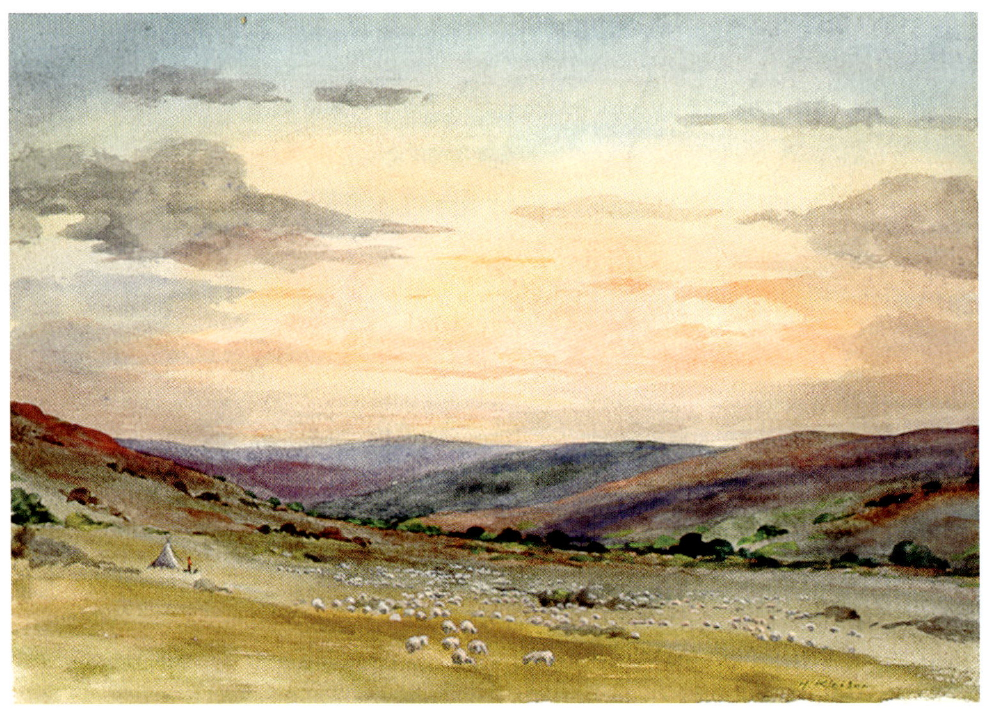

"Evening at a Sheep Camp"
Image: 7.125 inches high by 9.75 inches wide
Painting documented as 1956.

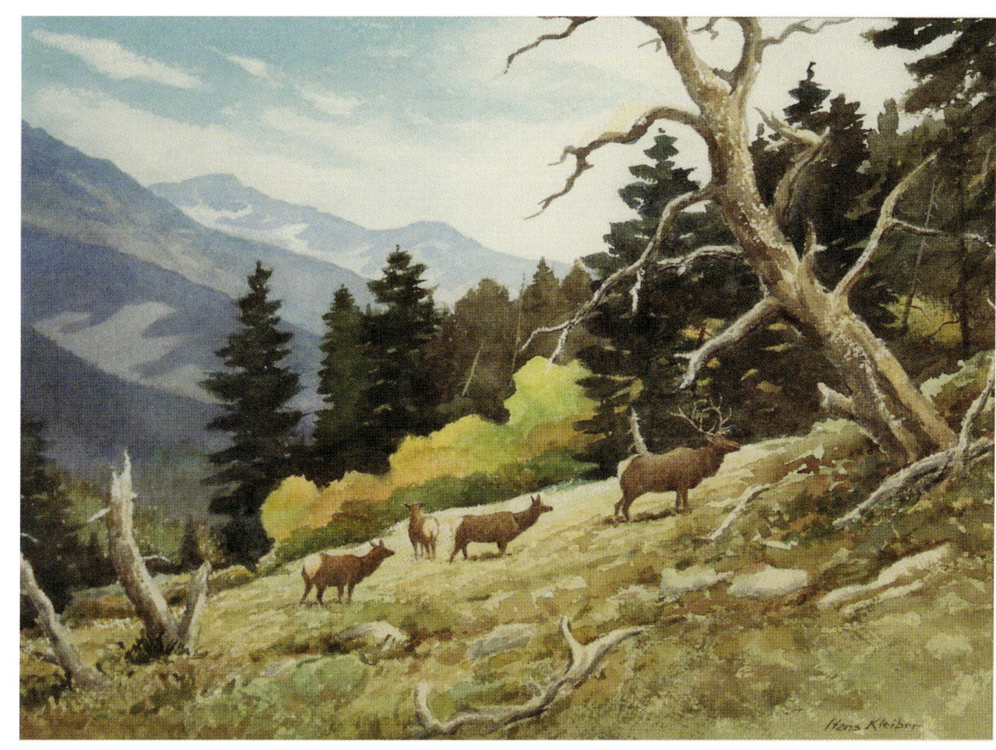

"Elk in the Bighorns"
Image: 9.25 inches high by 12.5 inches wide

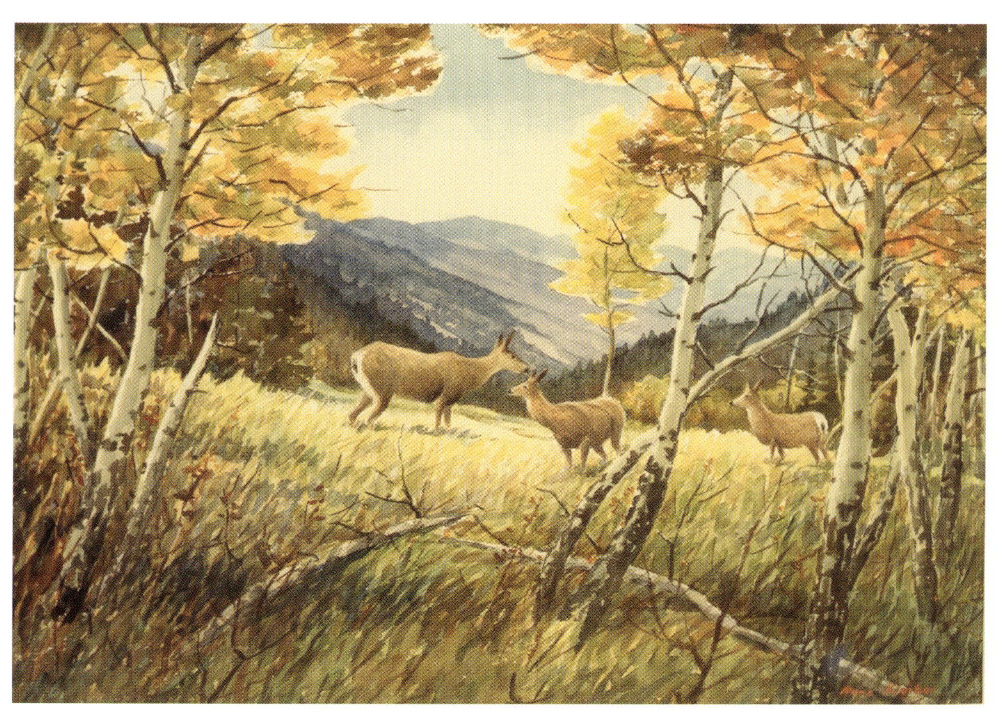

"Fall in the Bighorns"
Image: 10 inches high by 14 inches wide

Hans Kleiber

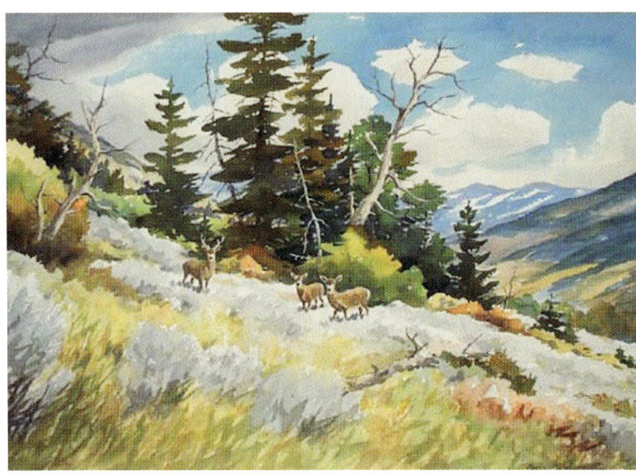

"Fall in the Bighorns"
Image: 15 inches high by 20.25 inches wide

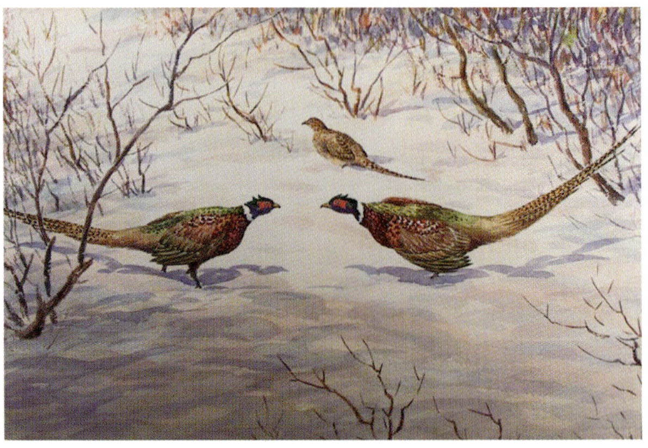

"Fighting Pheasants"
Image: 11 inches high by 16 inches wide

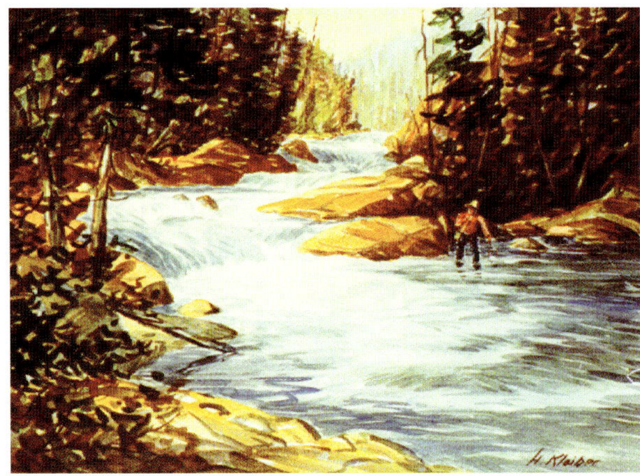

"Fishing on the Tongue River"
Image Size Unavailable

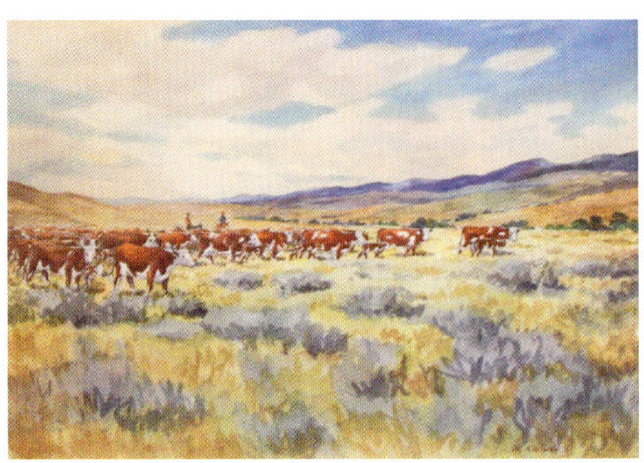

"Heading for the Summer Range"
Image: 10.5 inches high by 14.5 inches wide

“Golden Crowned Kinglets”
Image: 14.625 inches high by 10.625 inches wide

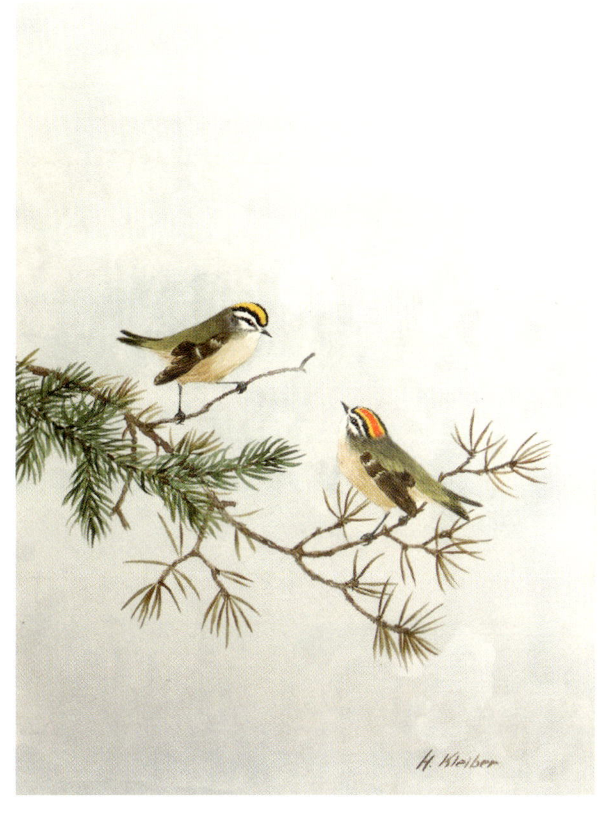

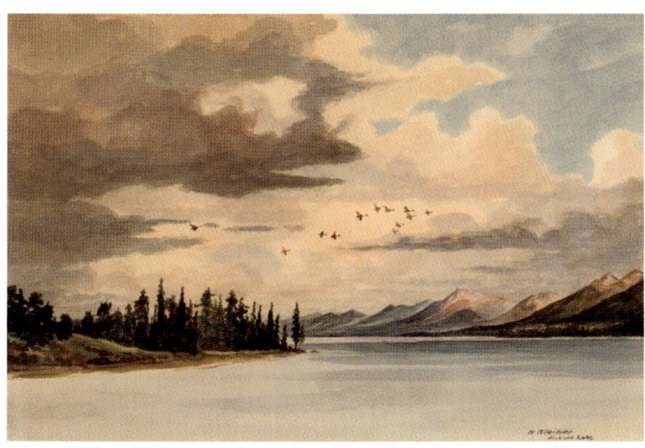

“Jackson Lake”
Image: 10.25 inches high by 14.5 inches wide

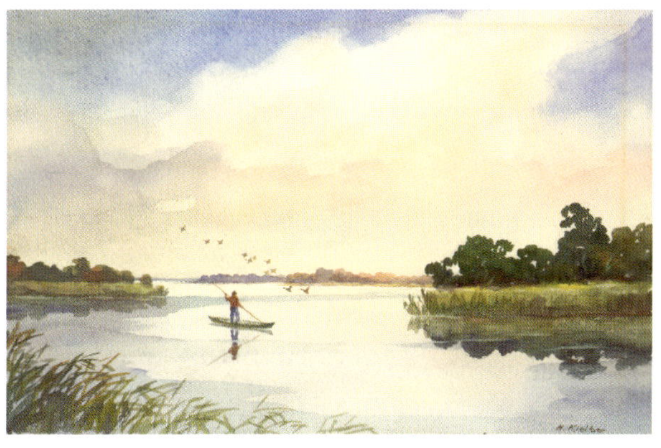

“Lake Salvadore”
Image: 6.875 inches high by 10.375 inches wide

Hans Kleiber

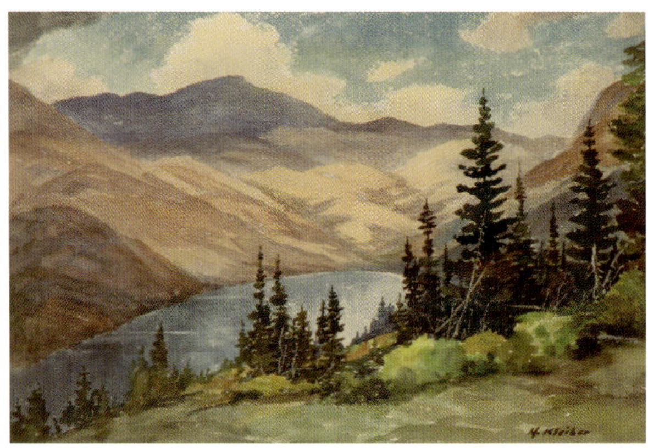

"Lake Solitude"
Image: 7 inches high by 10.25 inches wide

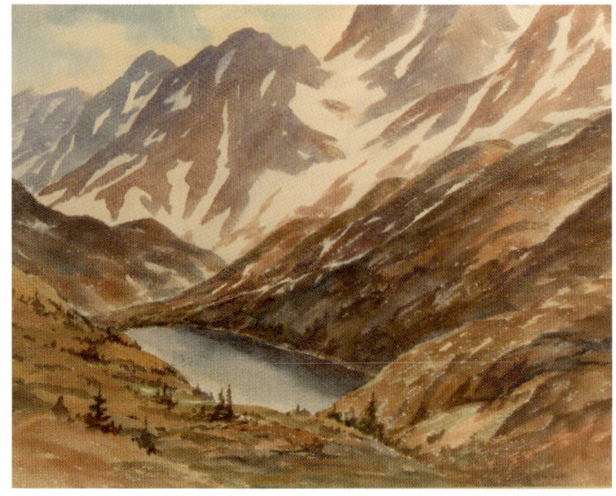

"Lake Solitude Above Timberline"
Image: 11.5 inches high by 14 inches wide

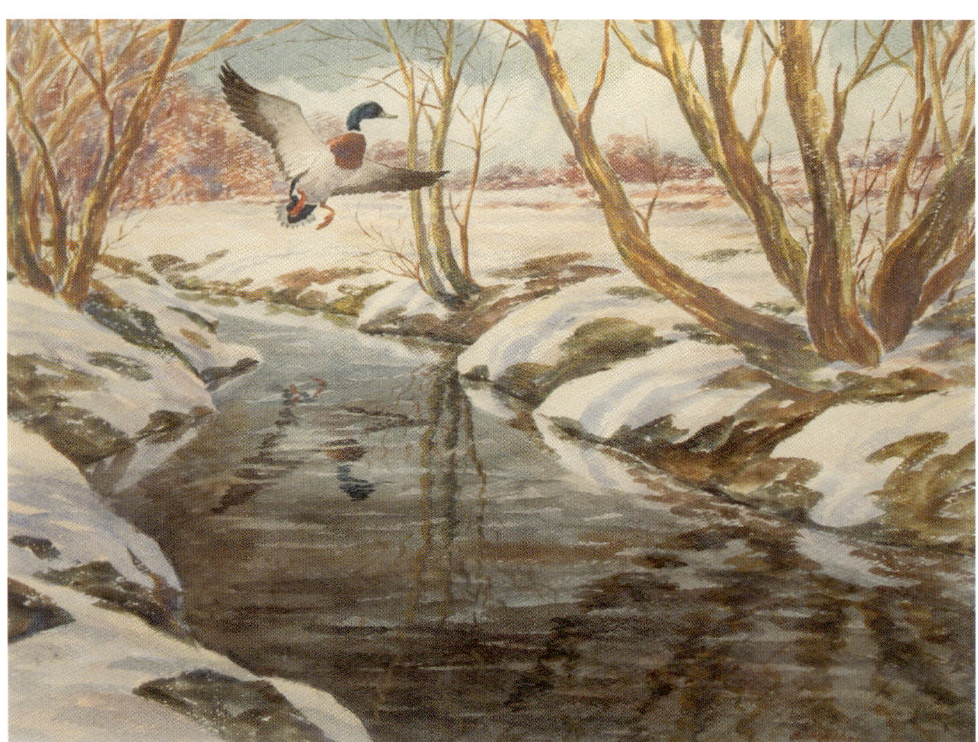

"Mallard On A Winter Day"
Image: 12.25 inches high by 16 inches wide

"Mallards Settling--
Evening"
Image: 21 inches
high by 28.75
inches wide
Painting
documented 1952.

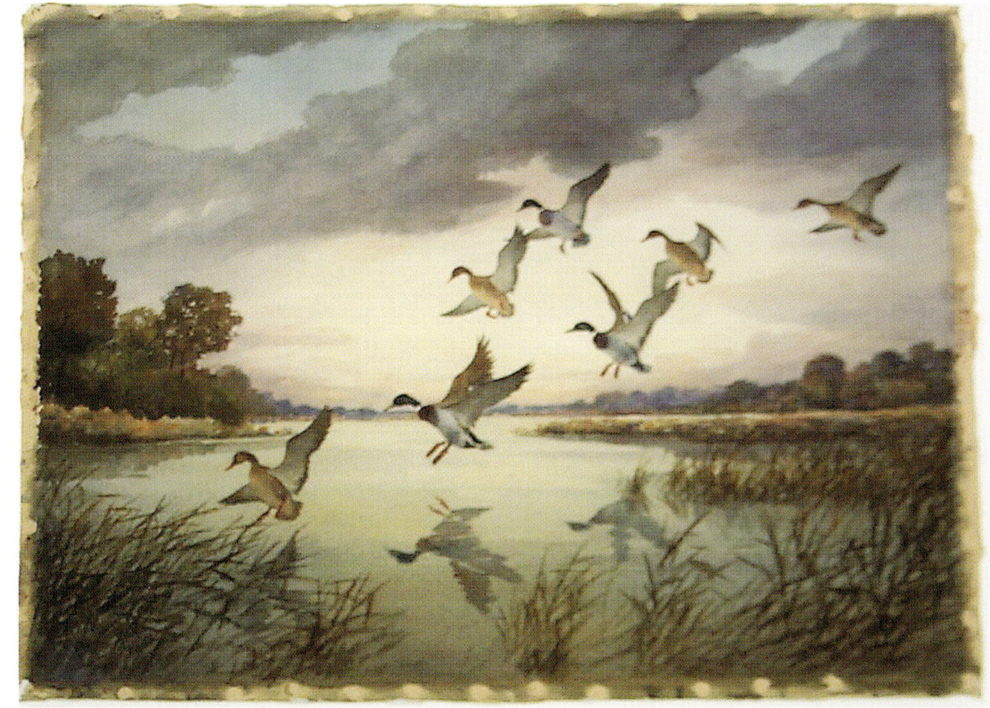

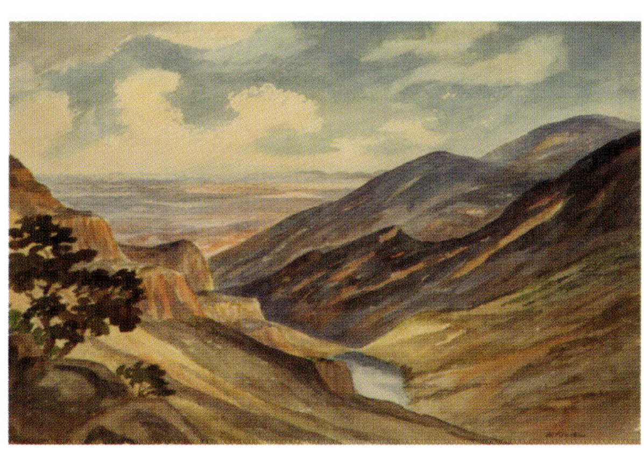

"Little Tongue River Canyon and the Valleys Beyond"
Image: 7.375 inches high by 10.75 inches wide

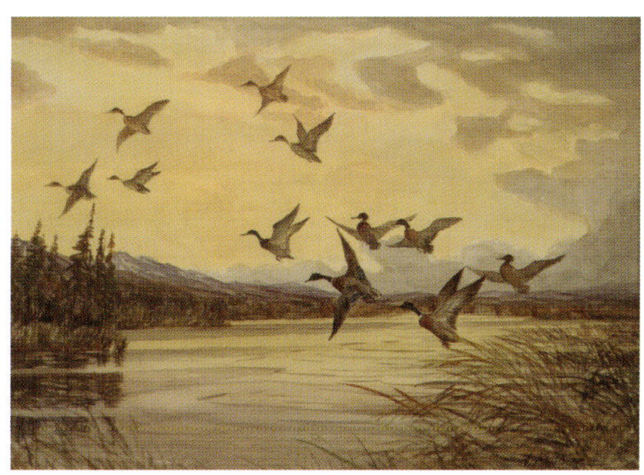

"Mallards at Sunrise"
Image: 10.375 inches high by 14.375 inches wide

Hans Kleiber

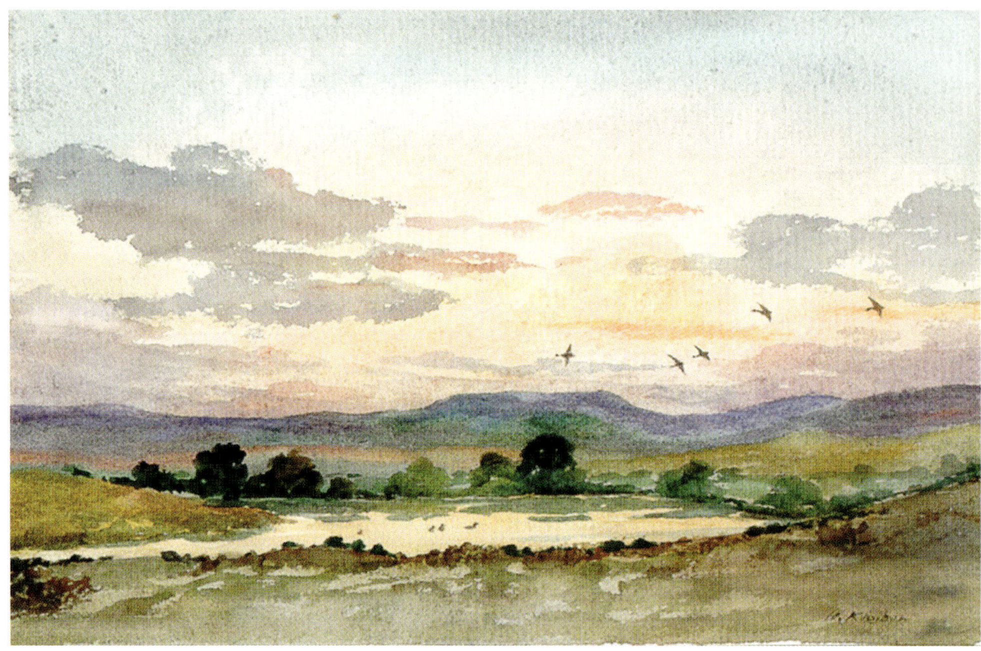

"Sheeley Pond"
Image: 7.25 inches high by 11 inches wide
Painting documented 1956.

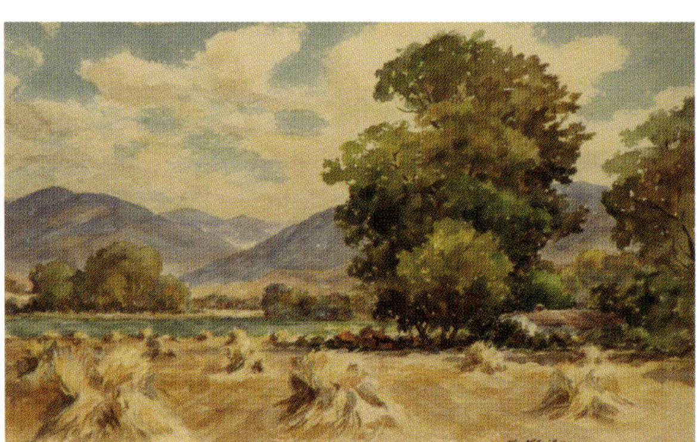

"IXL Ranch, Dayton, Wy."
Image: 6.75 inches high by 10.75 inches wide

The IXL Ranch or Ninth Lancers Ranch is on the Tongue River above Dayton, Wyoming. Captain Frank D. Grizzel was with the Ninth British Lancers and homesteaded the ranch in 1891.

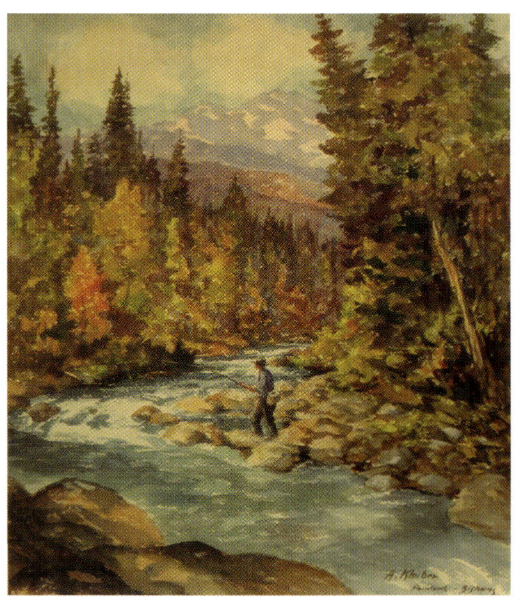

"Paintrock--Bighorns"
Image: 17 inches high by 14.5 inches wide

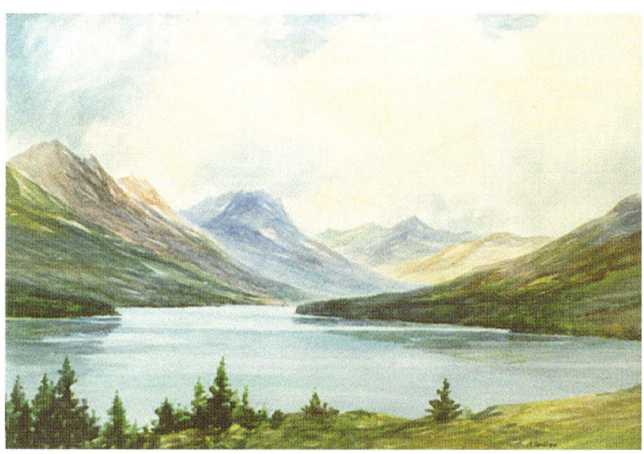

"St. Mary's Lake"
Image: 10.25 inches high by 14.25 inches wide

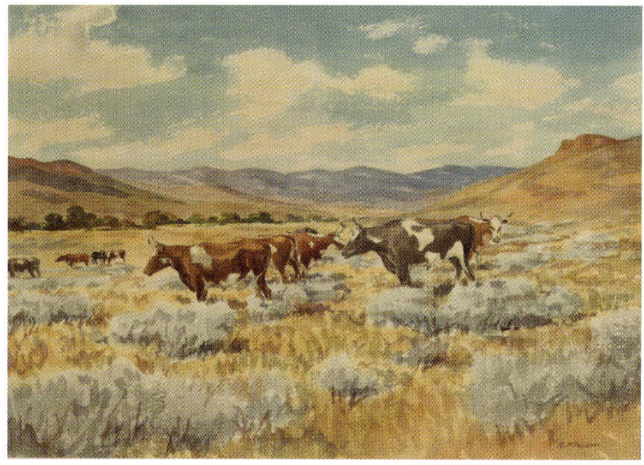

"Steers on the Reservation"
Image: 10.5 inches high by 14.5 inches wide

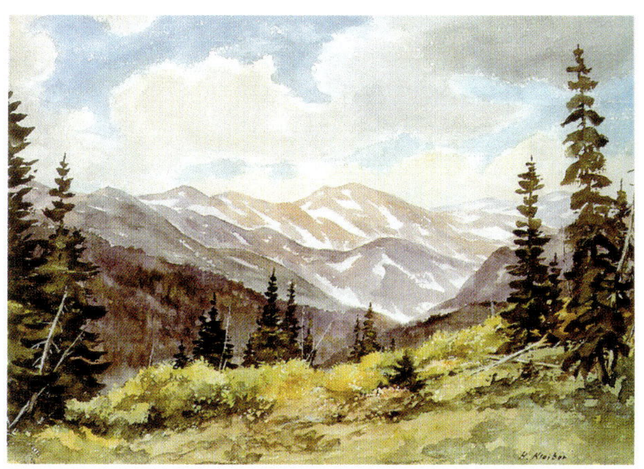

"Summer in the Rockies"
Image: 11 inches high by 14.75 inches wide
Painting documented 1944.

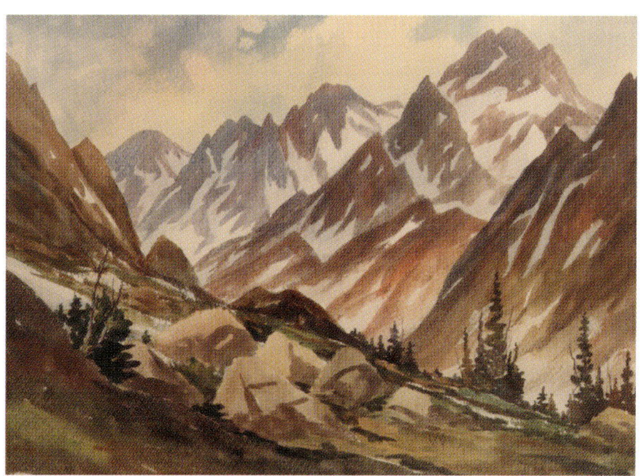

"Teton Peaks"
Image: 10.75 inches high by 14.75 inches wide

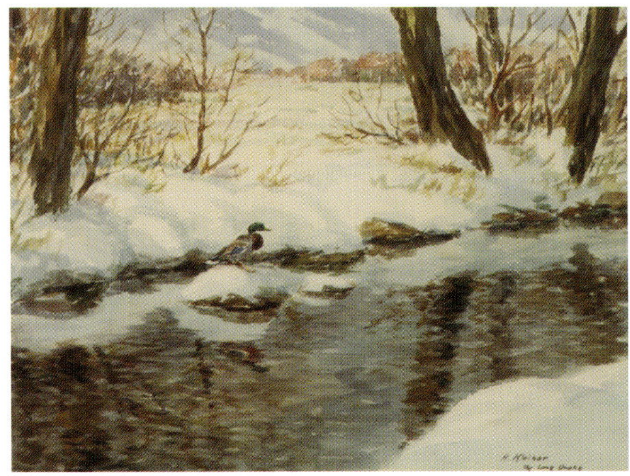

"The Lone Drake"
Image: 10.5 inches high by 13.875 inches wide

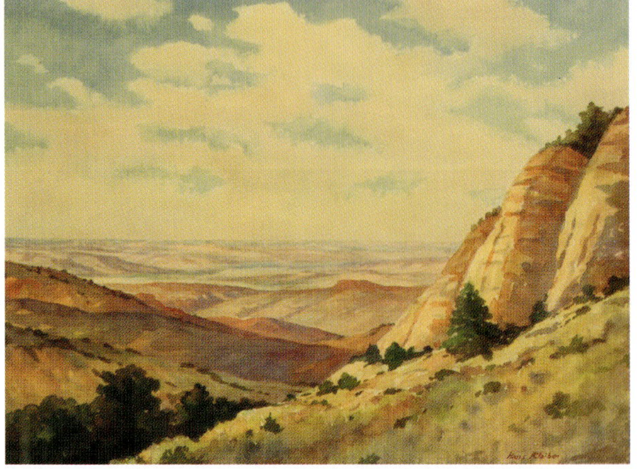

"The Valleys Below"
Image: 11 inches high by 14.5 inches wide

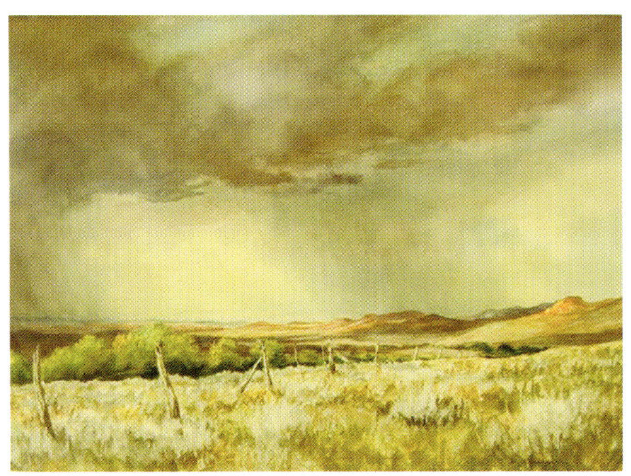

"Thunderstorm on the Crow Reservation"
Image: 9.5 inches high by 13 inches wide
Painting documented 1952.

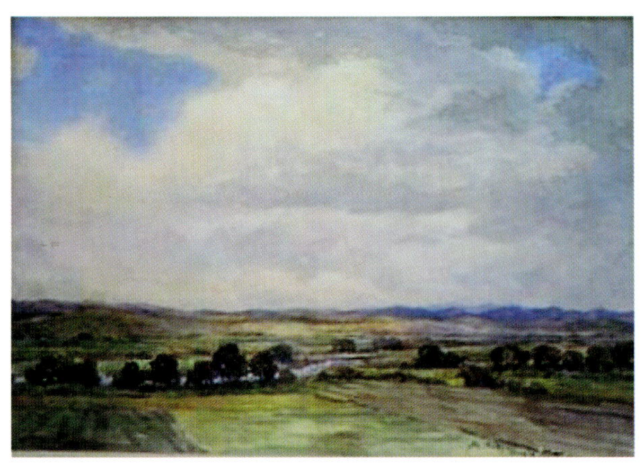

"Tongue River"
Image: 10 inches high by 14 inches wide

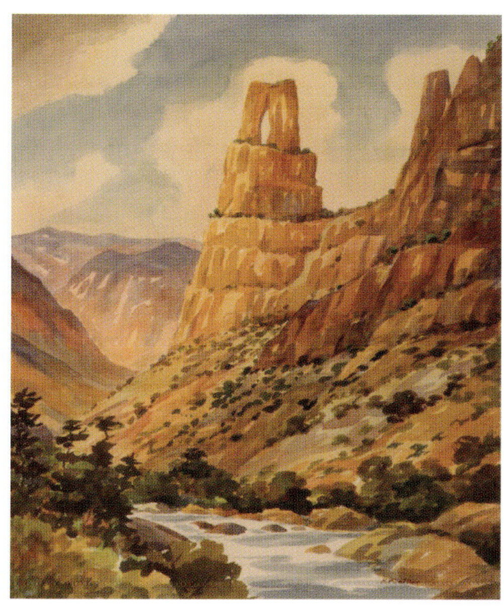

"Tongue River Canyon Big Horns, Wyoming"
(Eye of the Needle)
Image: 12.75 inches high by 10.5 inches wide

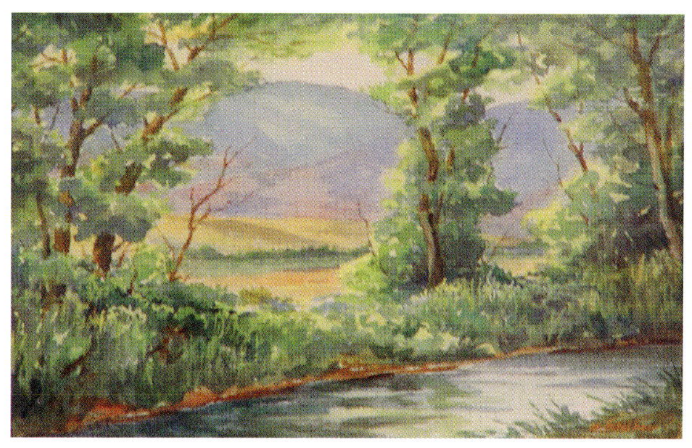

"Tongue River Ditch"
Image: 6 inches high by 9.25 inches wide

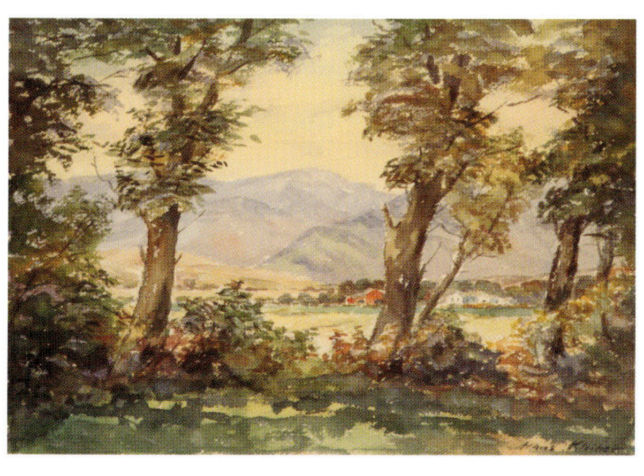

"Tongue River Valley above Dayton"
Image: 10.625 inches high by 15 inches wide

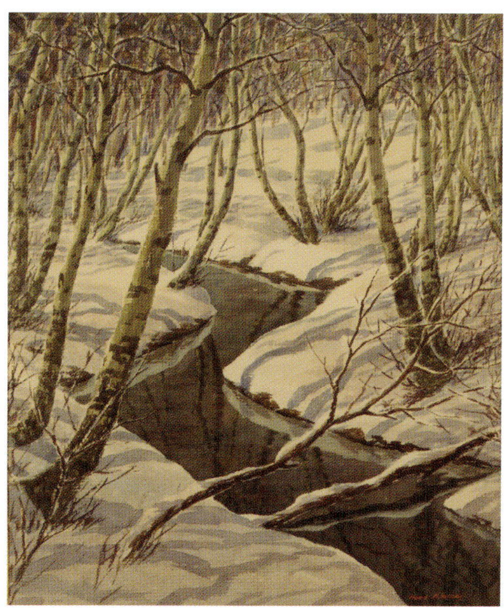

"Untitled--Creek Scene"
Image: 17 inches high by 14.125 inches wide

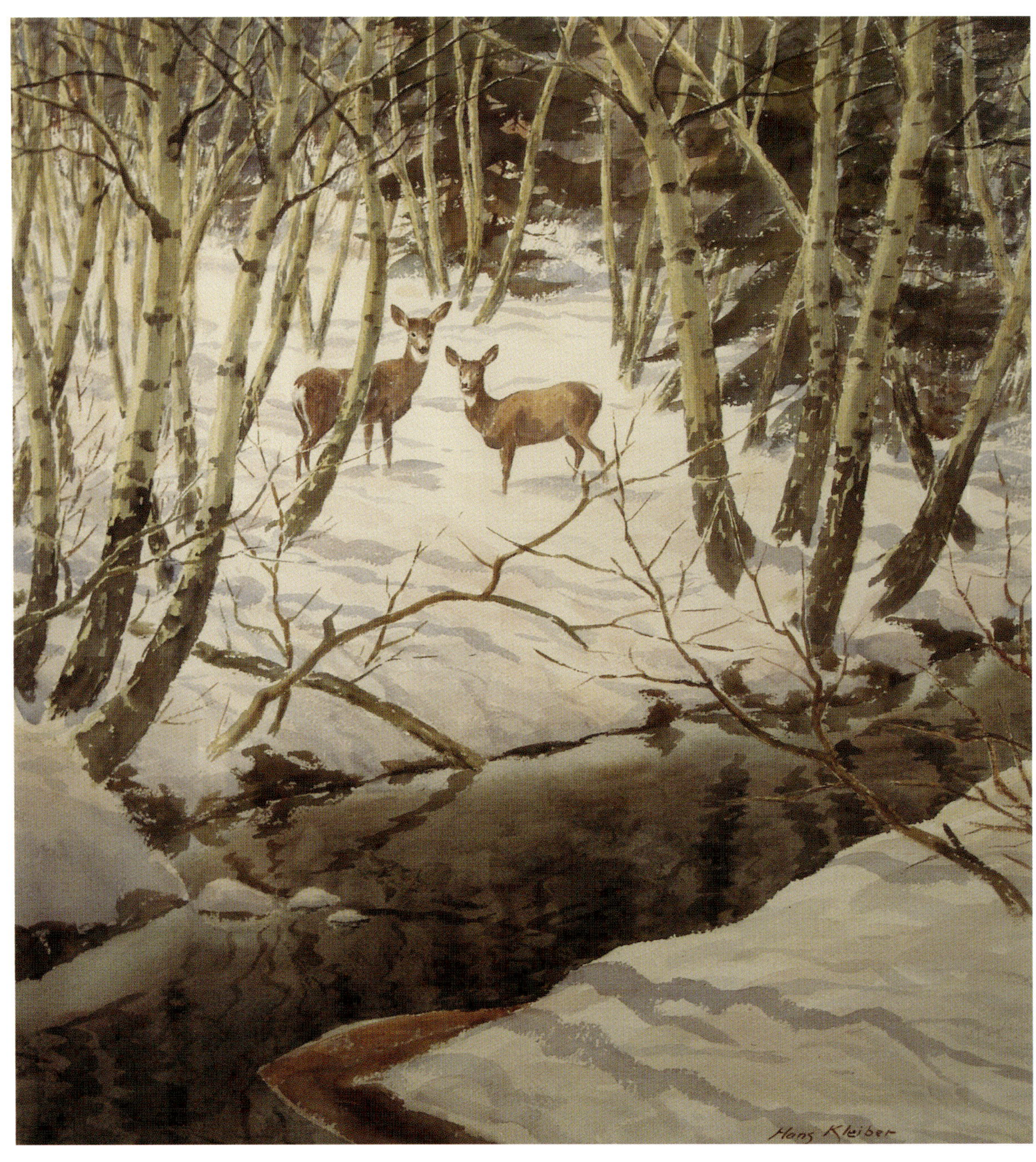

"Untitled--Deer in Aspen"
Image: 24 inches high by 21 inches wide

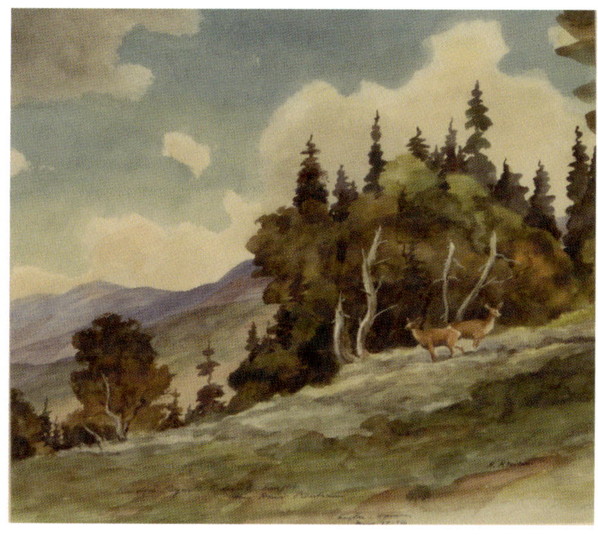

"Untitled--Deer"
Image: 10 inches high by 11.25 inches wide
Dated March 27, 1966.

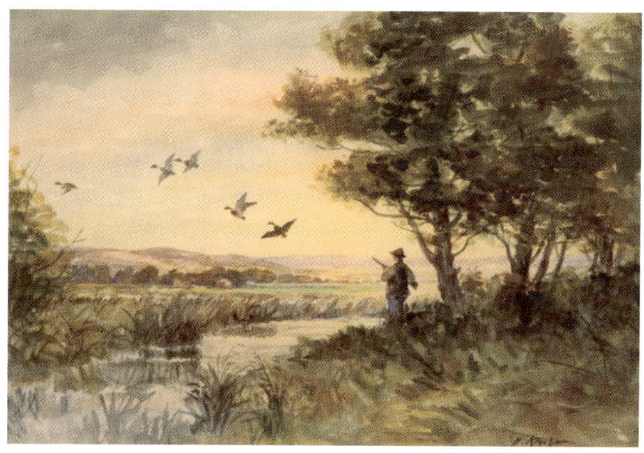

"Untitled--Duck Hunter"
Image: 10.375 inches high by 14.875 inches wide

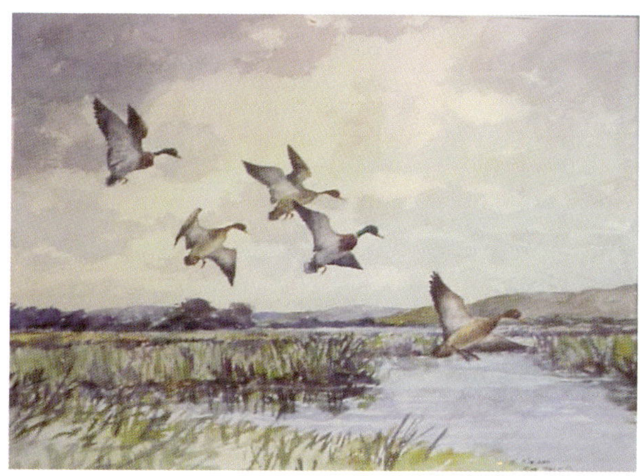

"Untitled--Five Mallards"
Image: 10.5 inches high by 14.5 inches wide

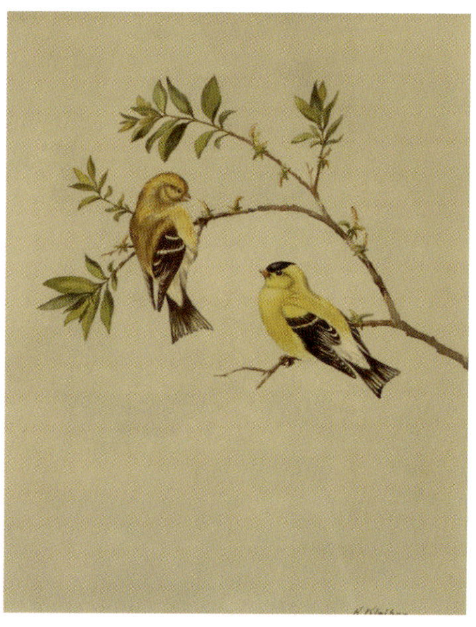

"Untitled--Gold Finches"
Image: 12.25 inches high by 9.5 inches wide

Hans Kleiber

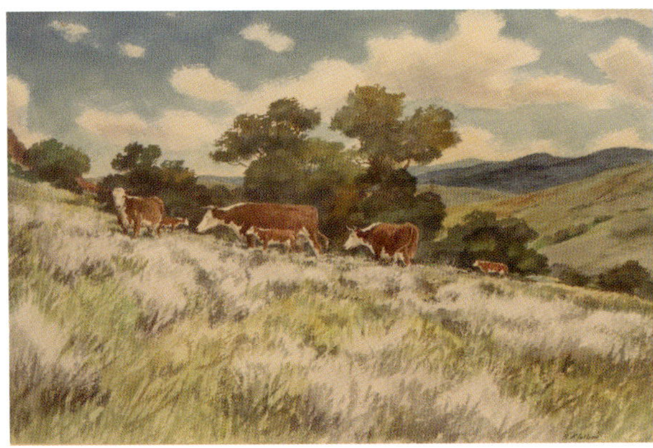

"Untitled--Herefords"
Image: 14.5 inches high by 21.375 inches wide

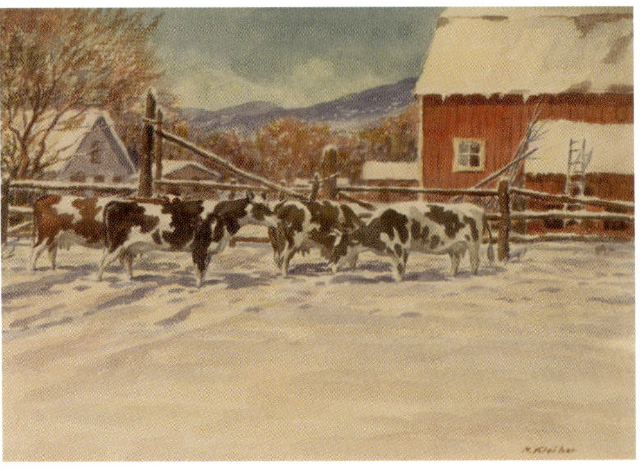

"Untitled--Holsteins in Snow"
Image: 10.75 inches high by 14.75 inches wide

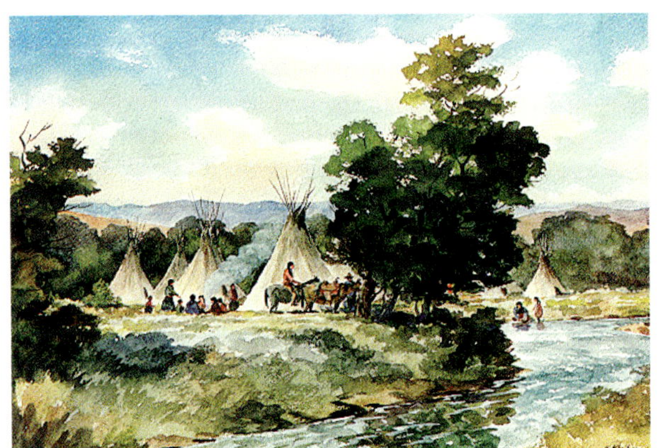

"Untitled--Indian Camp"
Image: 10.5 inches high by 14.75 inches wide

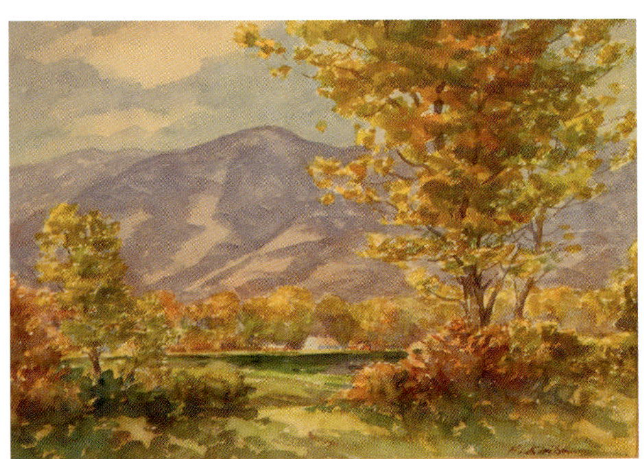

"Untitled--Landscape"
Image: 10.5 inches high by 14.5 inches wide

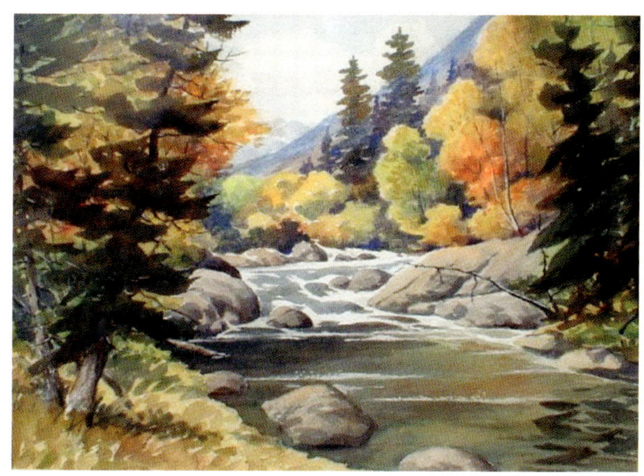

"Untitled --Landscape"
Image: 9 inches high by 12 inches wide

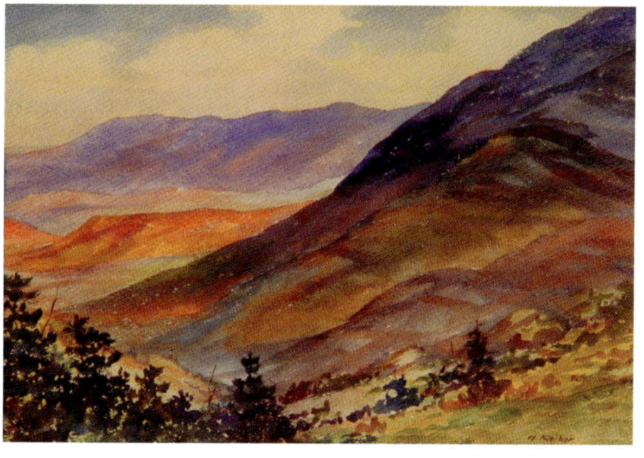

"North of Hell Creek"
Image: 11 inches high by 14 inches wide

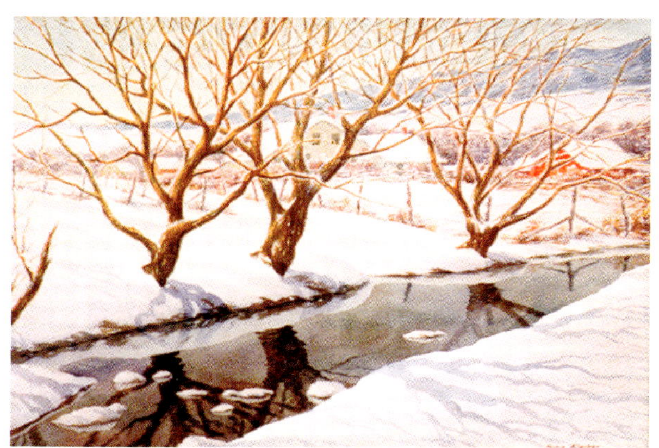

"Untitled --Landscape"
Image: 14.25 inches high by 20.5 inches wide

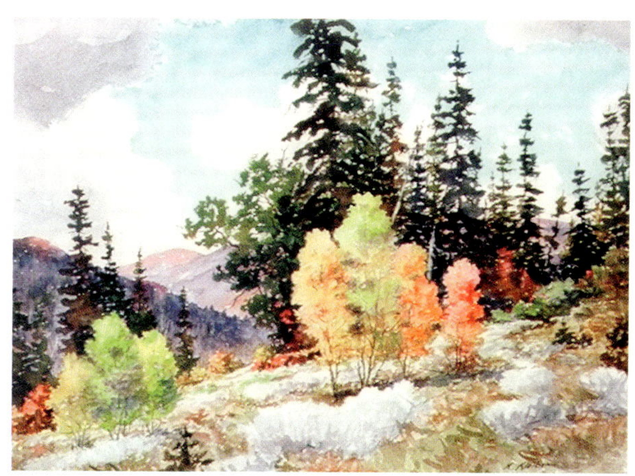

"Untitled--Landscape"
Image Size Unavailable

Hans Kleiber

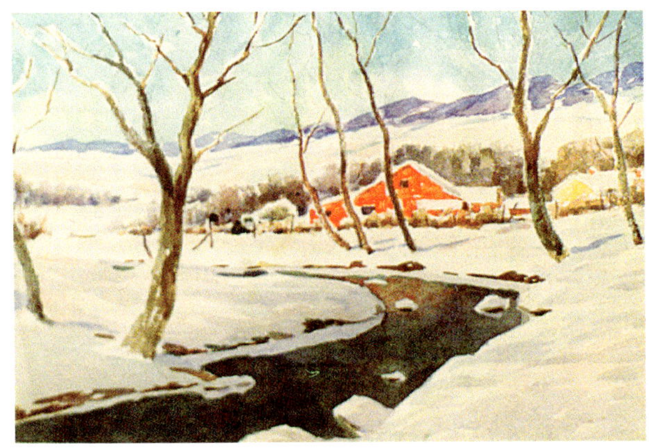

"Untitled--Landscape"
Unsigned
Image: 9.25 inches high by 13.25 inches wide

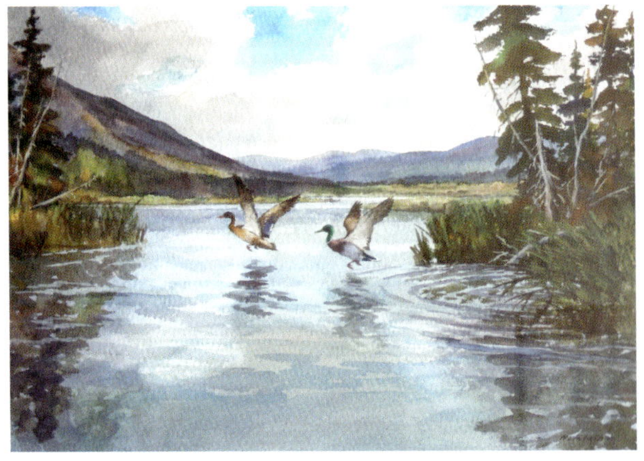

"Untitled--Mallards"
Image: 10.5 inches high by 14.5 inches wide

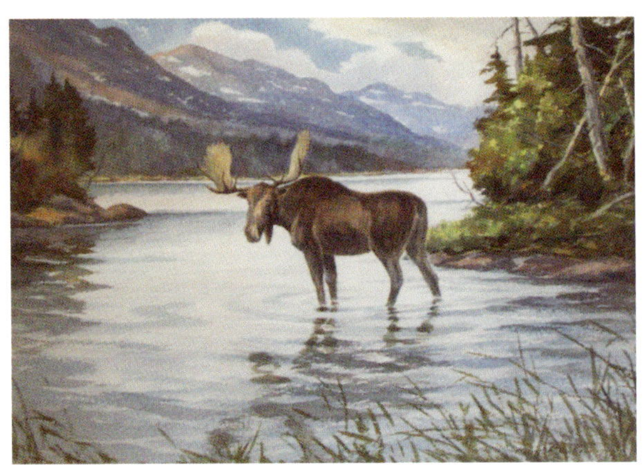

"Untitled--Moose"
Image: 10 inches high by 14.125 inches wide

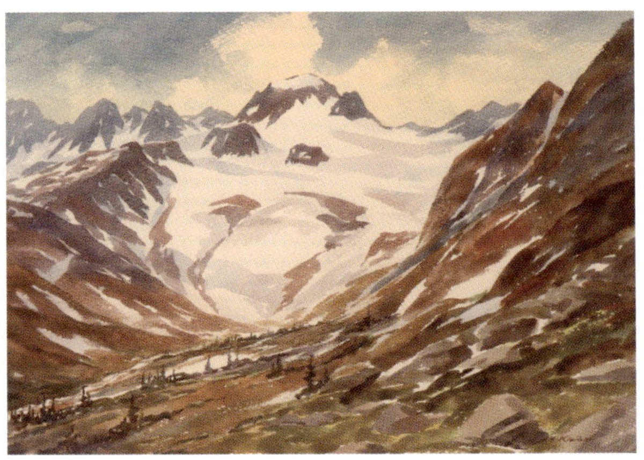

"Untitled--Mountain Scene"
Image: 10.25 inches high by 14.25 inches wide

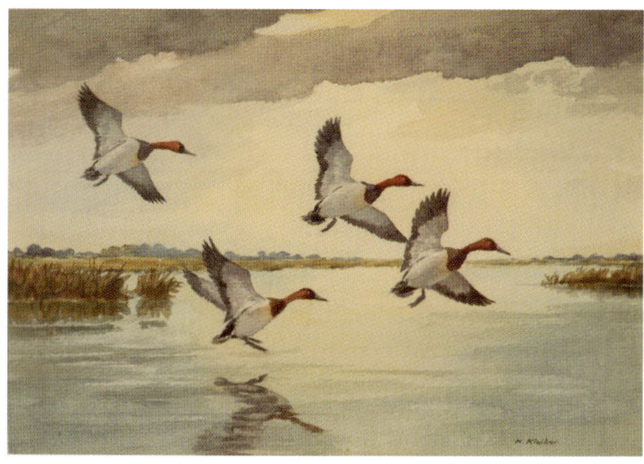

"Untitled--Redheads"
Image: 7.625 inches high by 10.5 inches wide

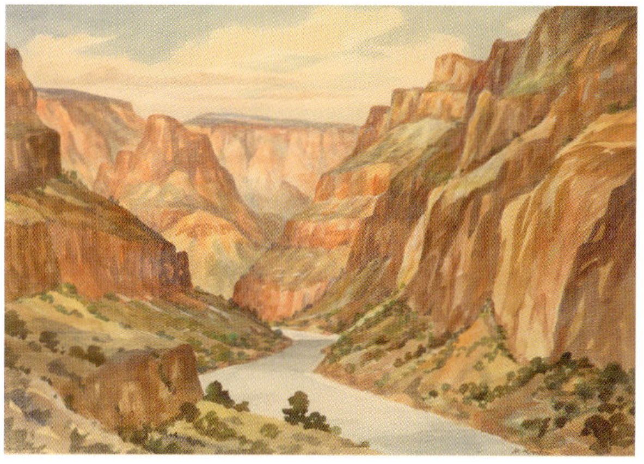

"Untitled--River Canyon Scene"
Image: 7.875 inches high by 10.875 inches wide

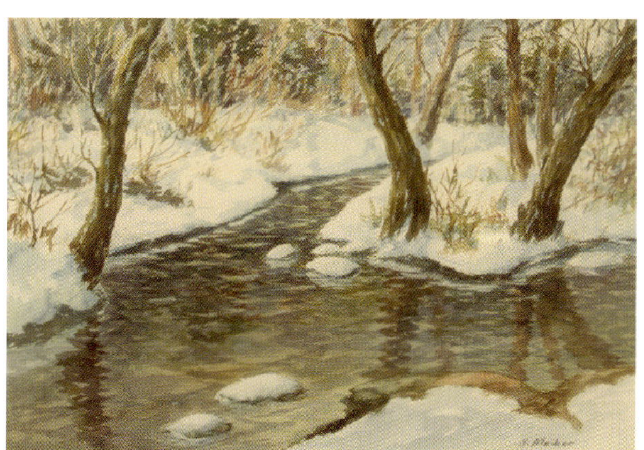

"Untitled--River Scene"
Image: 14.75 inches high by 20.75 inches wide

"Unfinished--Robins"
Image: 9 inches high by 14.5 inches wide

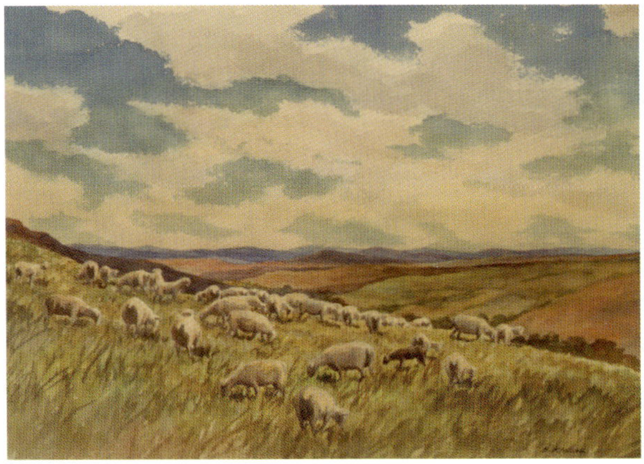

"Untitled--Sheep Grazing"
Image: 10.5 inches high by 14.5 inches wide

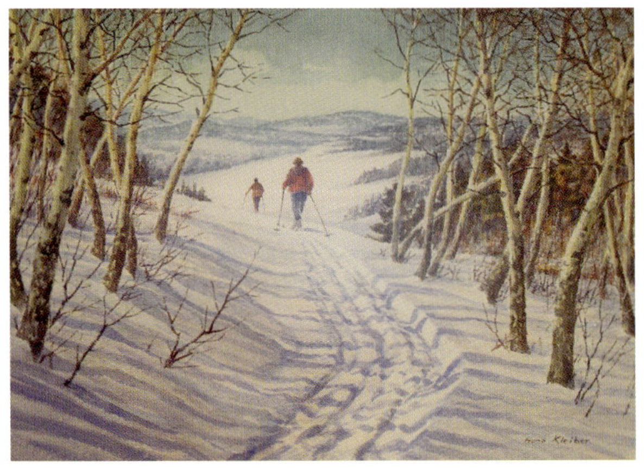

"Untitled--Skiing"
Image Size Unavailable

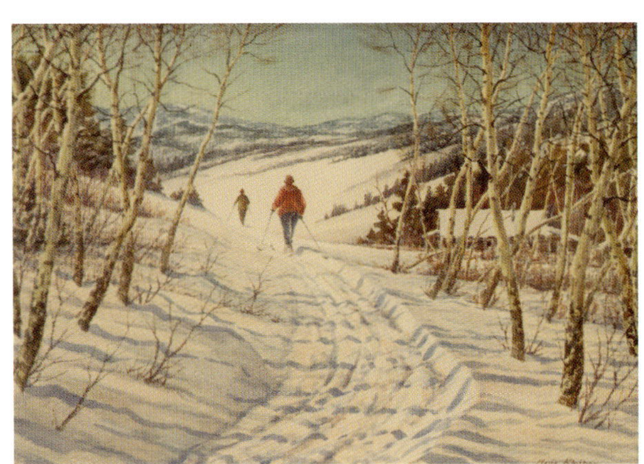

"Untitled--Skiing"
Image: 9.75 inches high by 13.75 inches wide

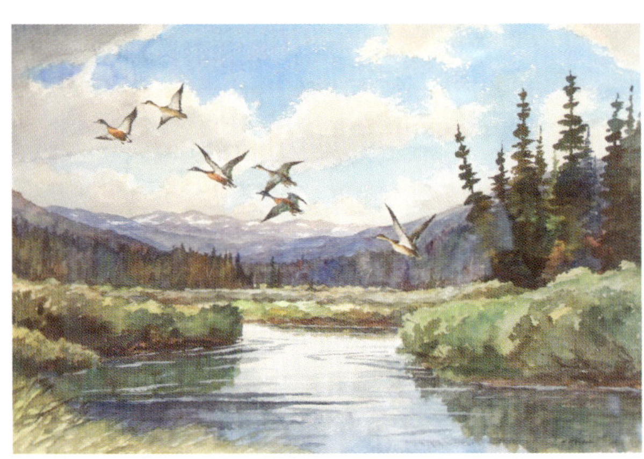

"Untitled--Teal"
Image: 15 inches high by 21.25 inches wide

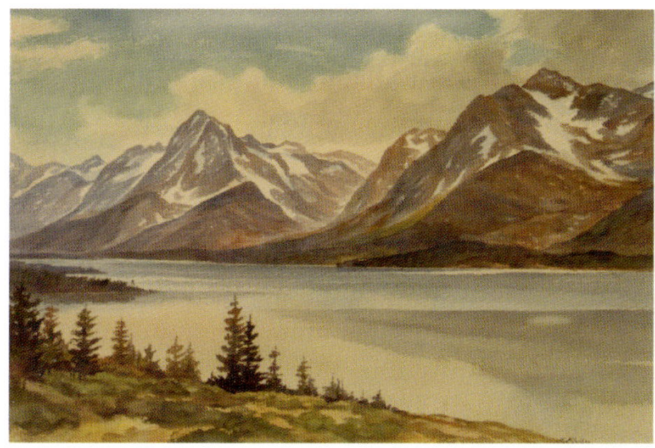

"Untitled--The Tetons"
Image: 14.5 inches high by 20.875 inches wide

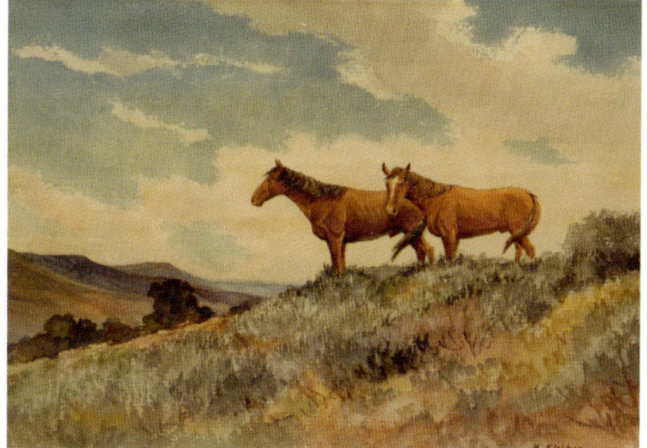

"Untitled--Two Horses"
Image: 10.625 inches high by 14.75 inches wide

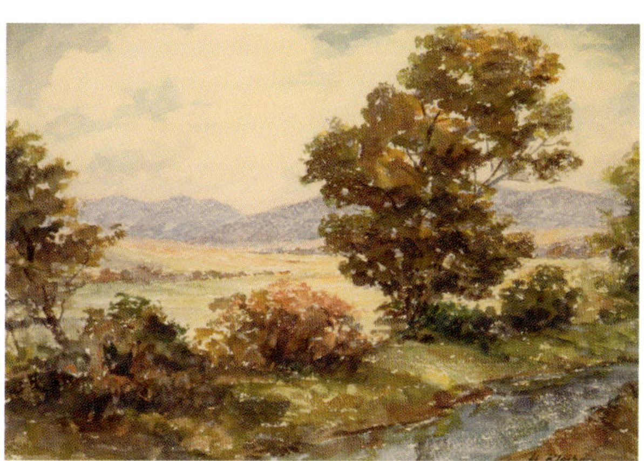

"Untitled--Valley Scene"
Image: 10.625 inches high by 15 inches wide

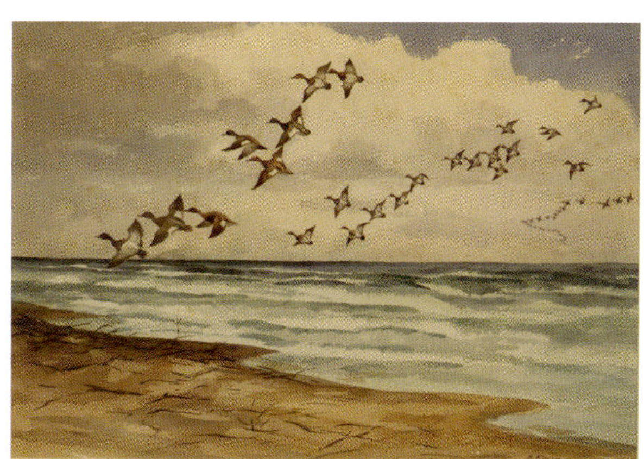

"Untitled--Waterfowl Southern Scene"
Image: 10.375 inches high by 14.75 inches wide

Hans Kleiber

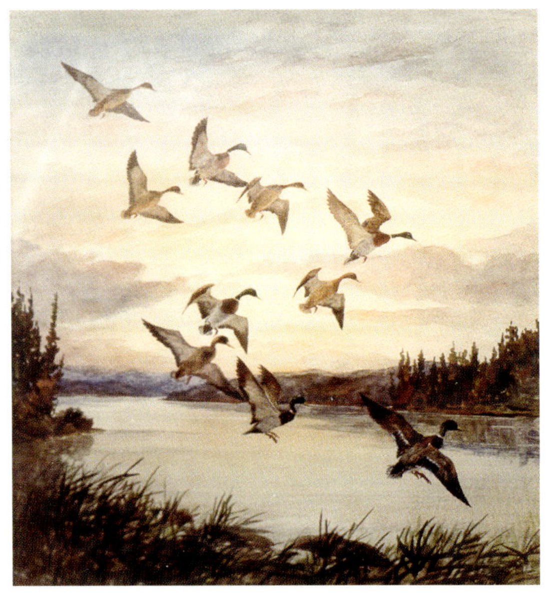

"Untitled--Waterfowl"
Image: 16.5 inches high by 15.5 inches wide

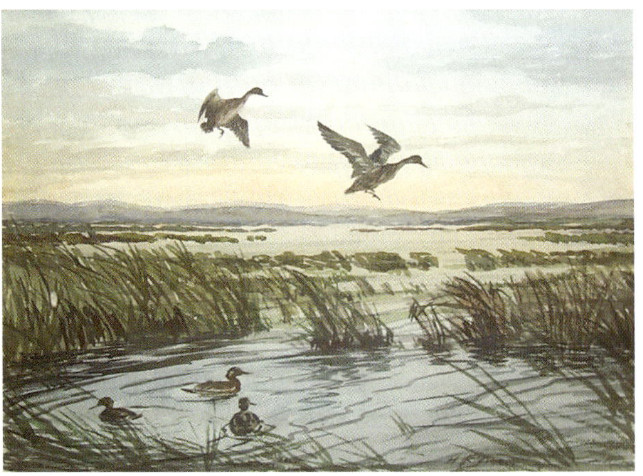

"Untitled--Waterfowl"
Image: 9.625 inches high by 13.125 inches wide

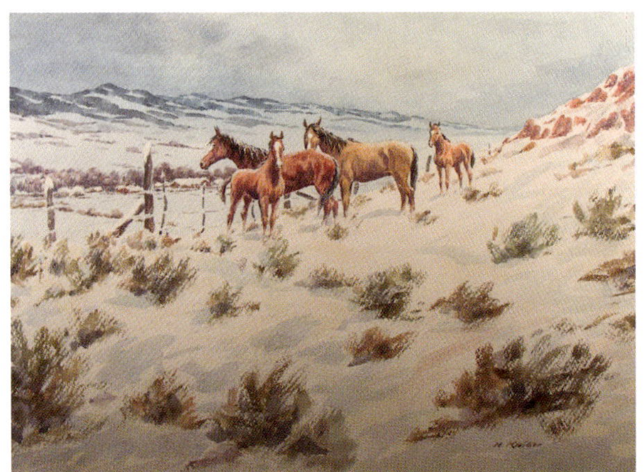

"Waiting at the Gate"
Image: 14 inches high by 18 inches wide

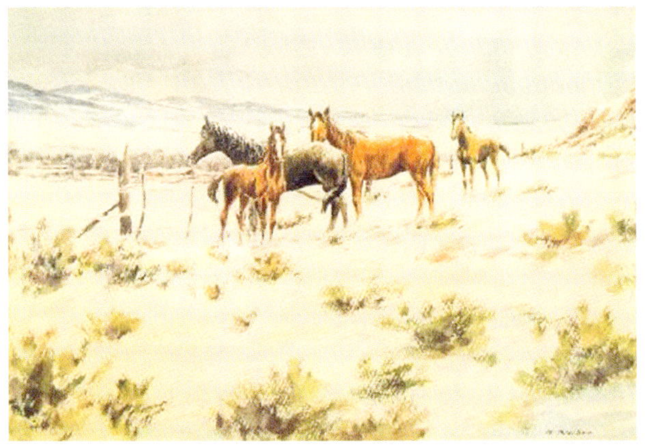

"Waiting at the Gate"
Image: 10 inches high by 16 inches wide

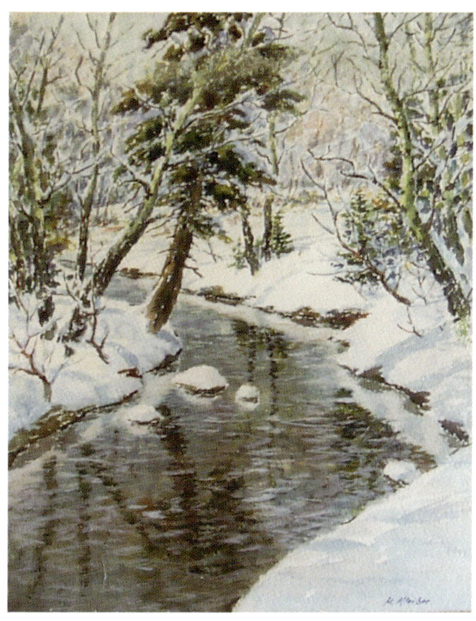

"Winter Afternoon"
Image: 17.75 inches high by 13.75 inches wide

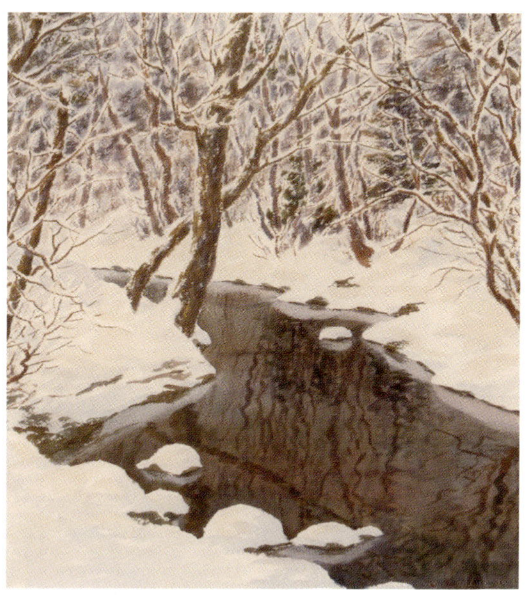

"Untitled--Winter Creek Scene"
Image: 16 inches high by 14.25 inches wide

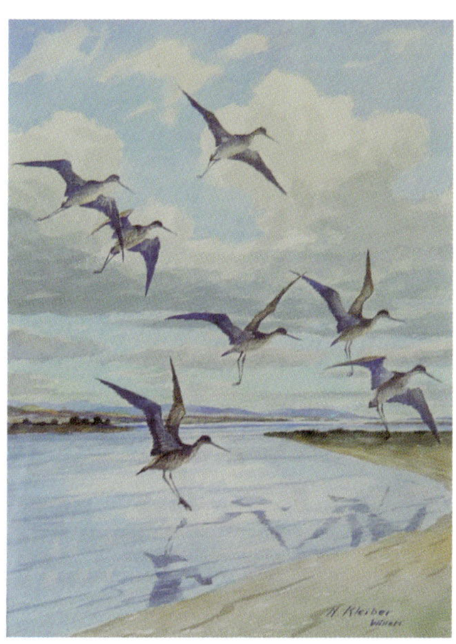

"Willets"
Image: 14.375 inches high by 10.25 inches wide

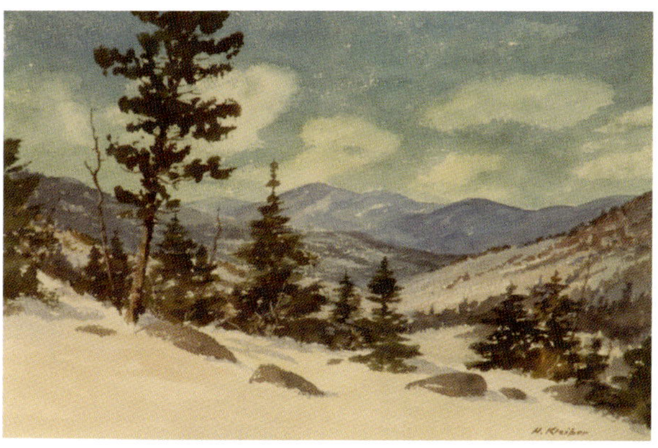

"Winter in the Big Horn Shell Creek"
Image: 7.25 inches high by 10.875 inches wide

Hans Kleiber

Chapter Sixteen

Oil
Paintings

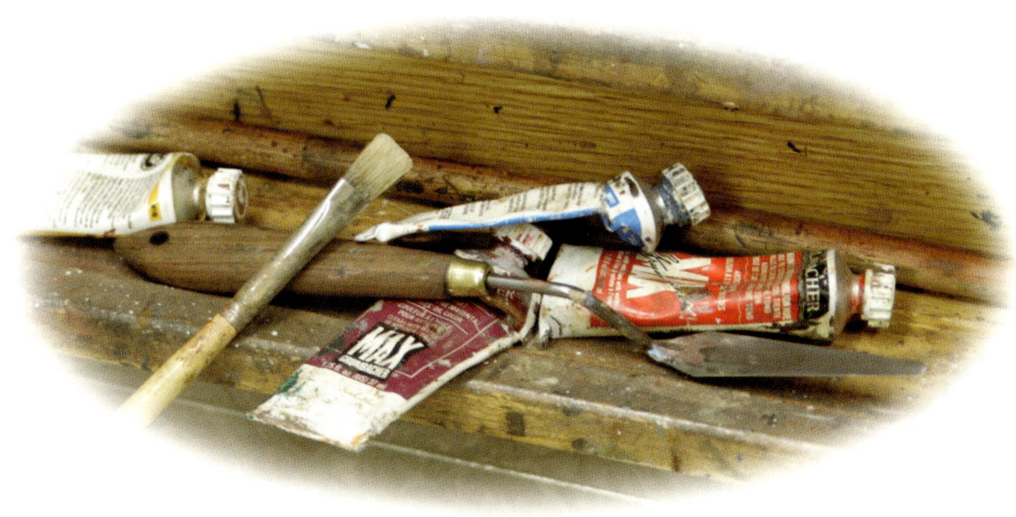

Hans Kleiber

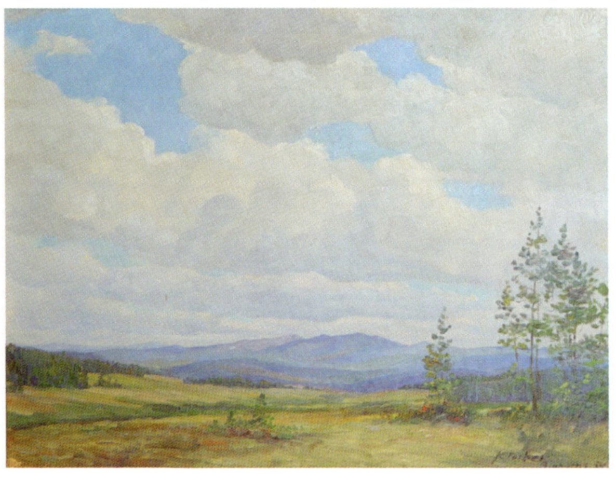

"Bighorns"
Image: 10 inches high by 12 inches wide
Dated 1934.

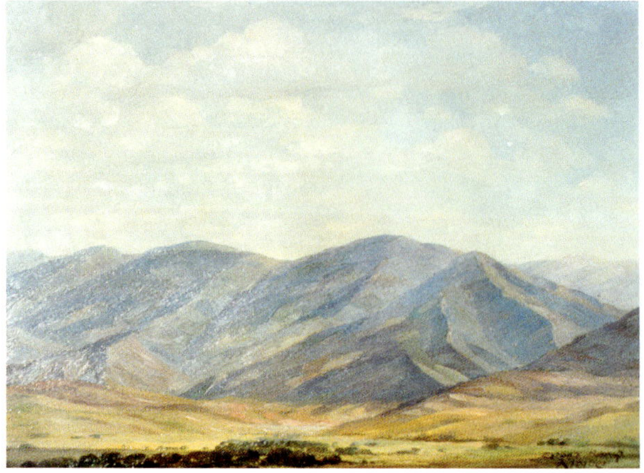

"Eaton's Ranch"
Image: 10 inches high by 13 inches wide

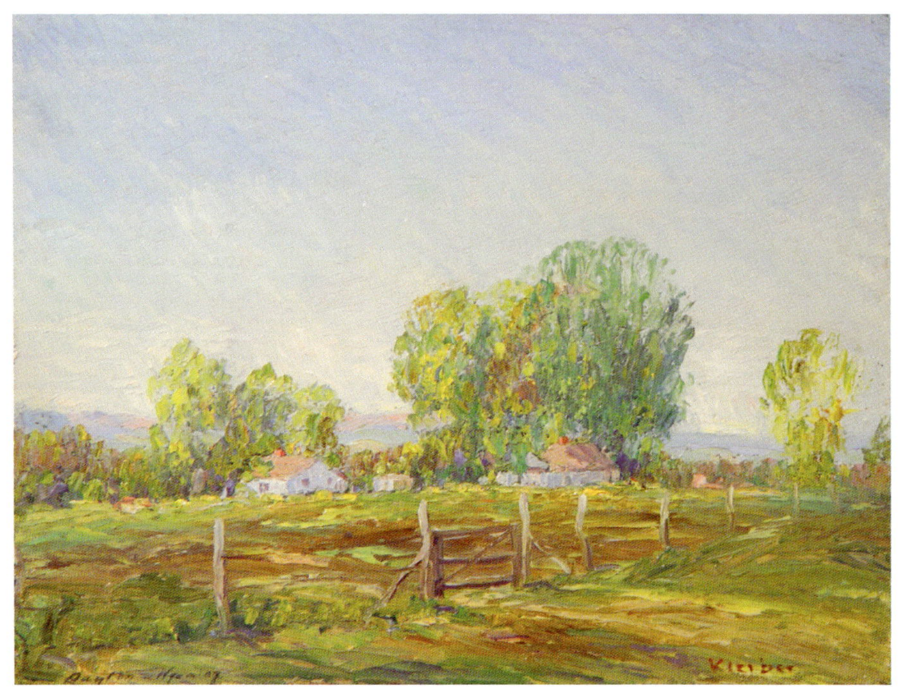

"Dayton, Wyoming"
Image: 7 inches high by
8.9375 inches wide

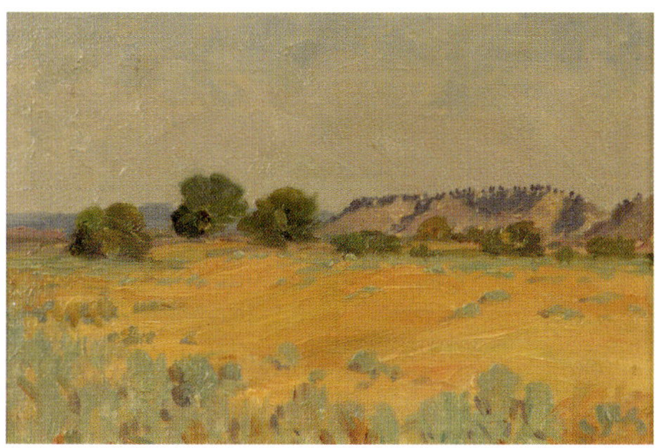

"Eaton's Horse Ranch"
Image: 7 inches high by 10 inches wide

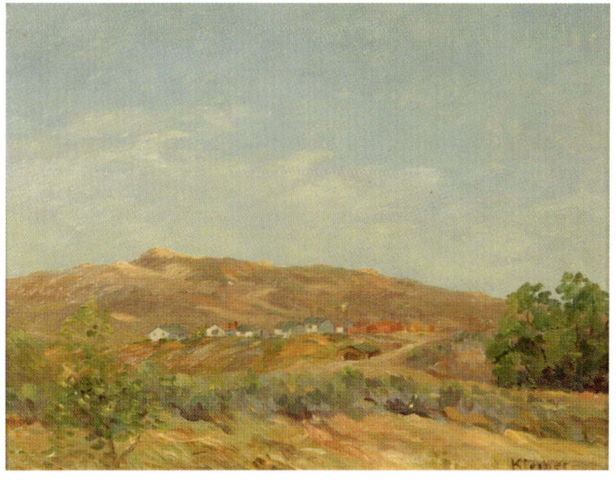

"Eaton's Horse Ranch"
Image: 12 inches high by 15 inches wide

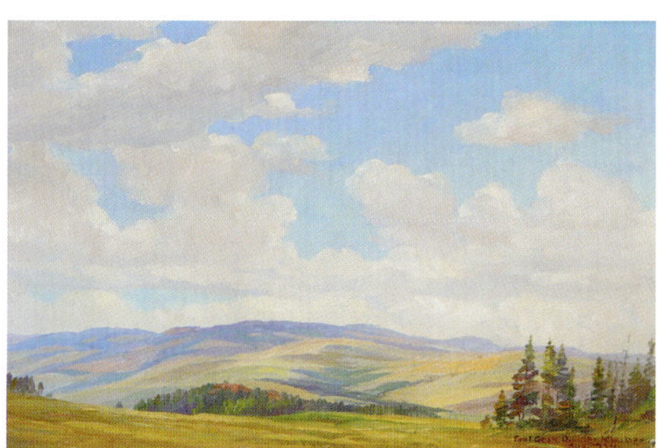

"Fool Creek Divide"
Image: 9.5 inches high by 14 inches wide
Dated 1934.

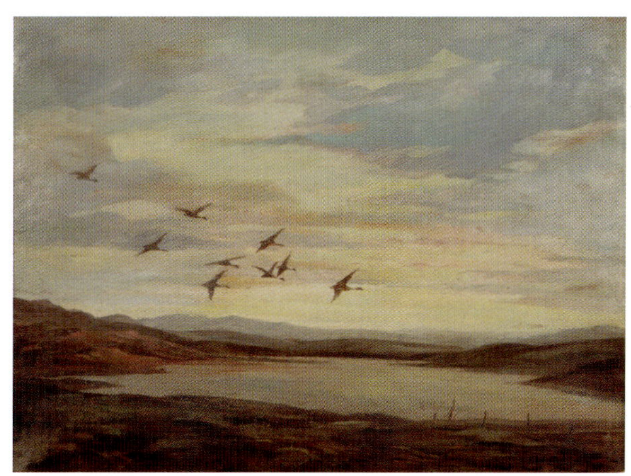

"Lake DeSmet, Wyoming"
Image: 12 inches high by 16 inches wide

Hans Kleiber

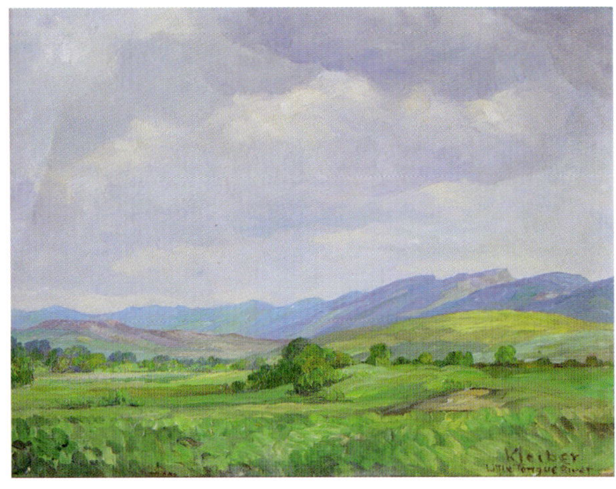

"Little Tongue River"
Image: 10 inches high by 12.875 inches wide

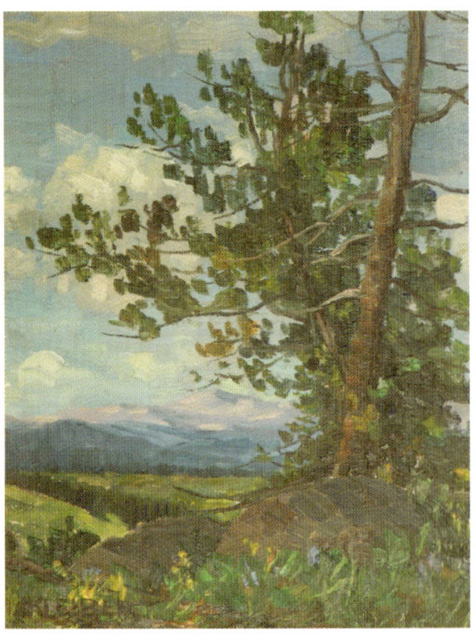

"Lone Tree in Tetons"
Image: 12 inches high by 9 inches wide

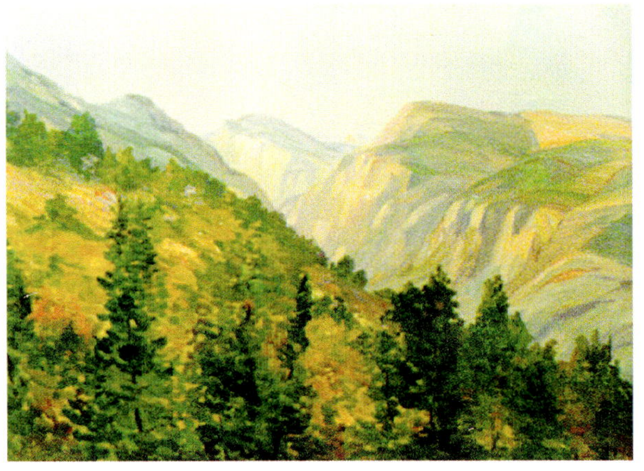

"Looking Toward Dayton-Kane"
Image: 9 inches high by 11.75 inches wide
Dated 1933

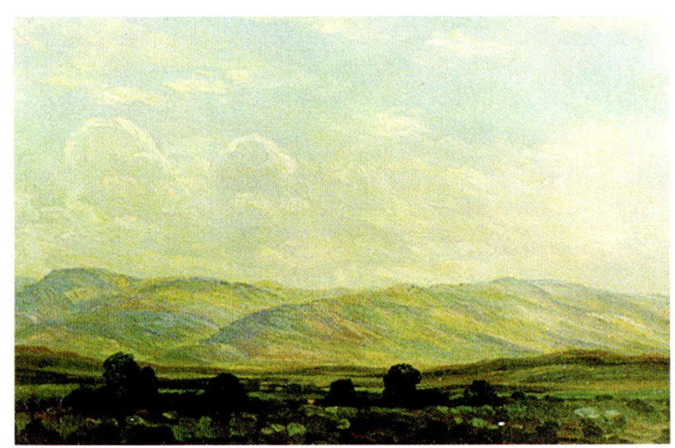

"Sage in Valley"
8.5 inches high by 12.5 inches wide
Unsigned

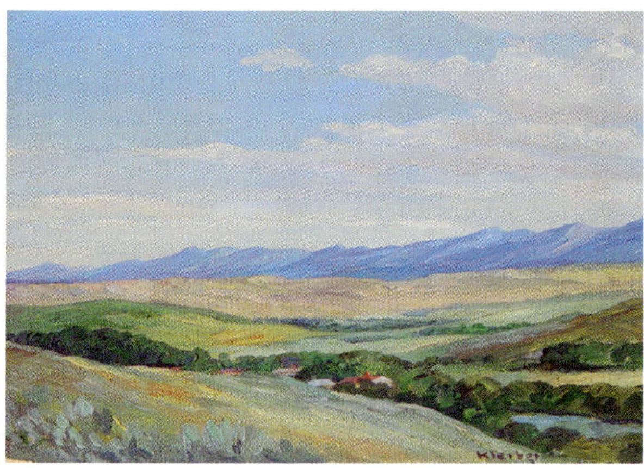

"The Big Horns From Dayton Wy"
Image: 8.75 inches high by 12 inches wide

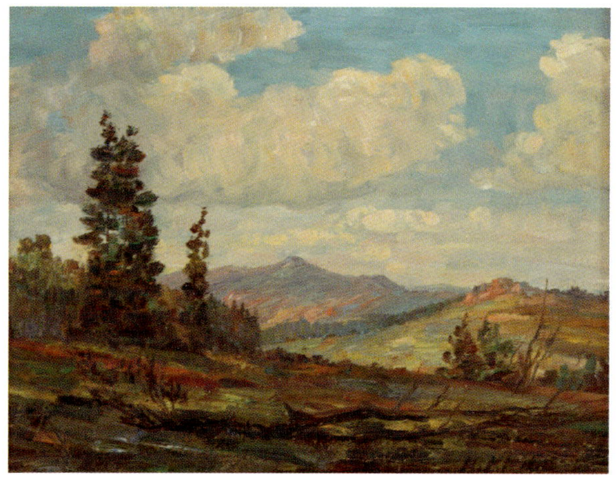

"The Tetons"
Image: 8 inches high by 10 inches wide

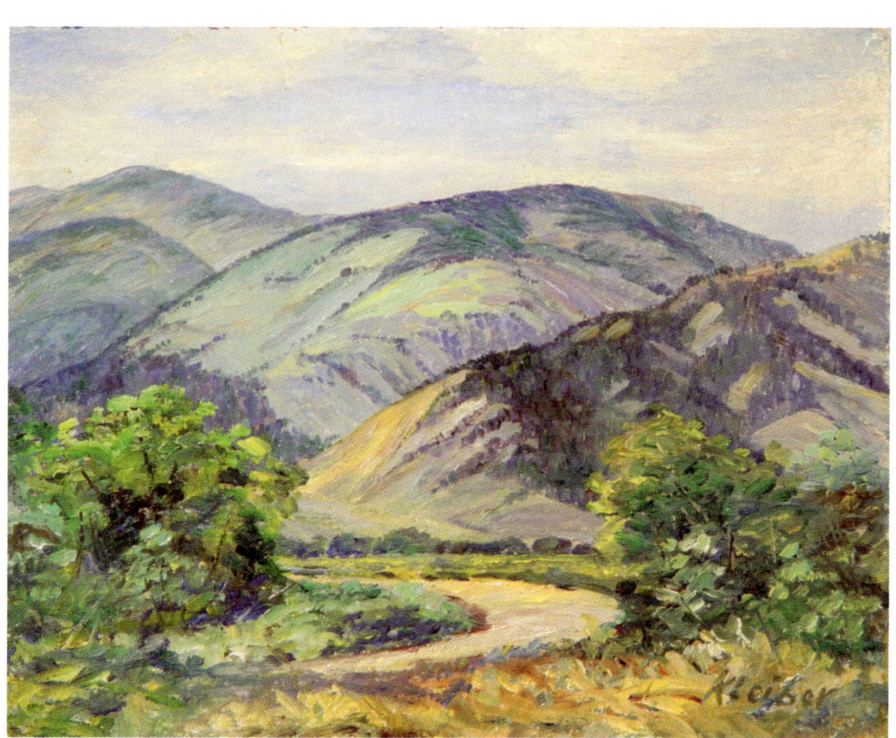

"Tongue River Valley"
Image: 8 inches high by 9.75 inches wide

Hans Kleiber

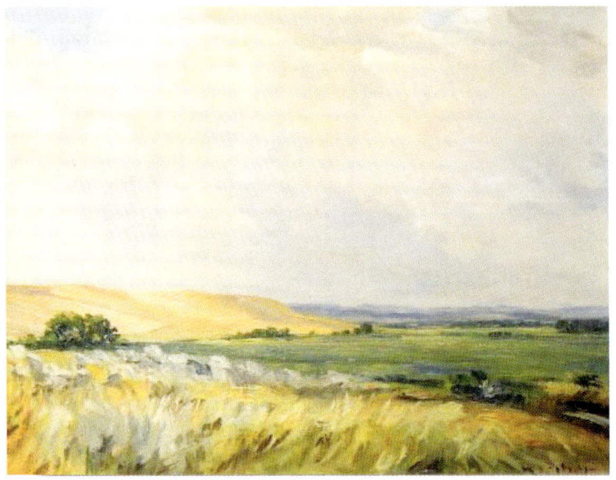

"Tongue River Valley"
Image: 9.5 inches high by 12 inches wide

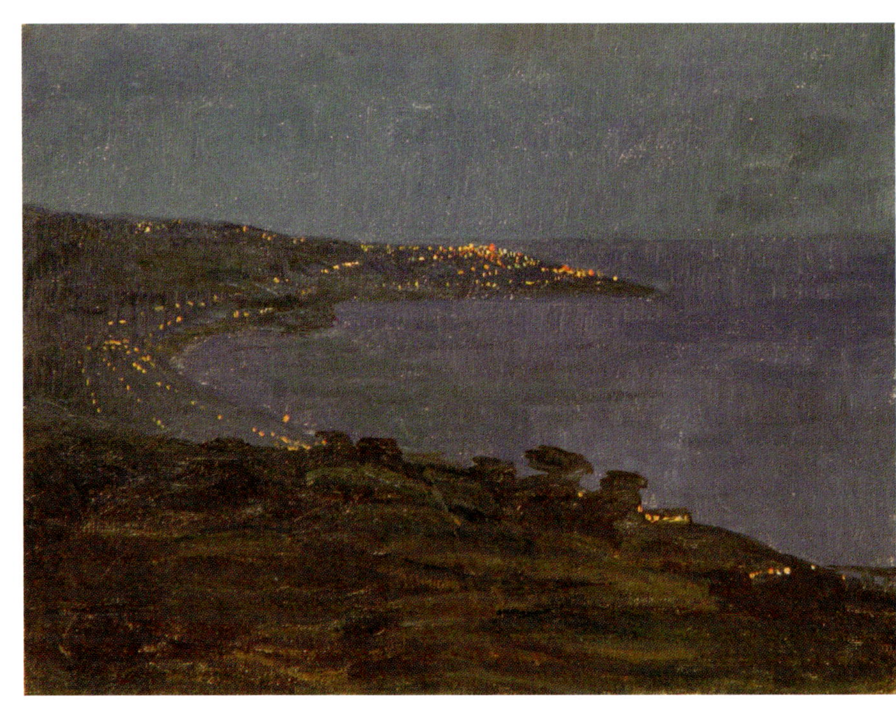

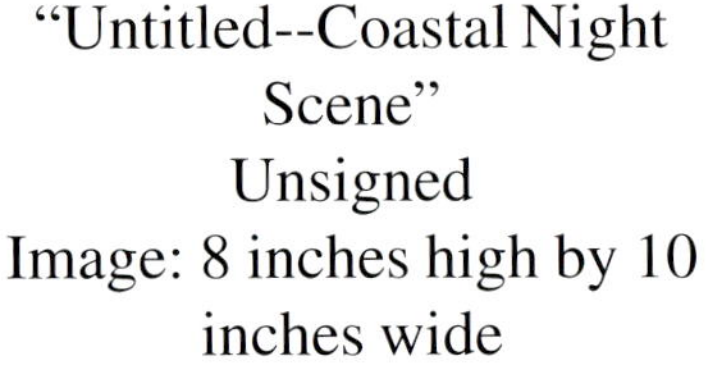

"Untitled--Coastal Night Scene"
Unsigned
Image: 8 inches high by 10 inches wide

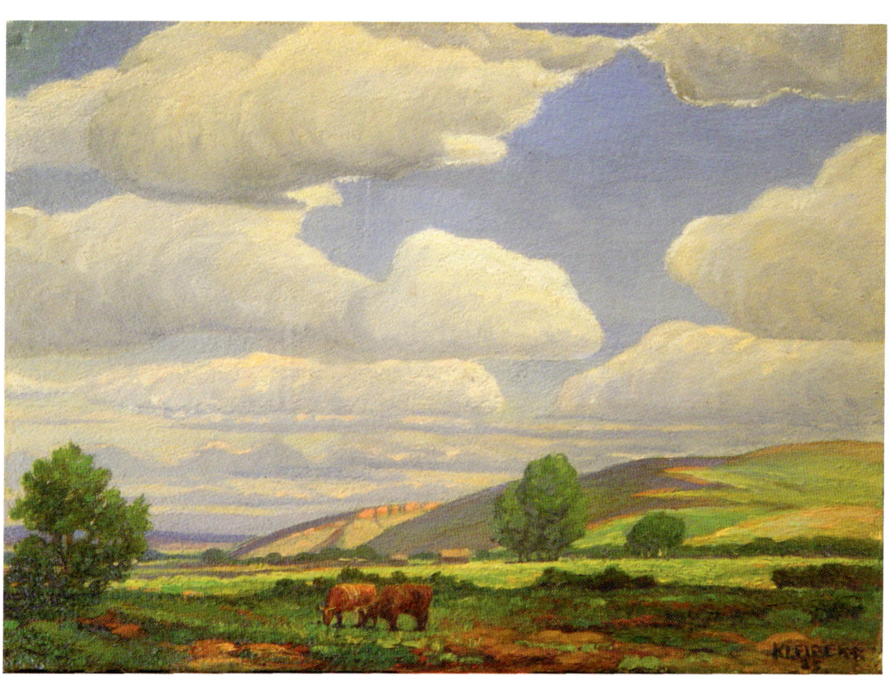

"Untitled--Cows in Pasture"
Image: 9.75 inches high by 13 inches wide
Dated 1923.

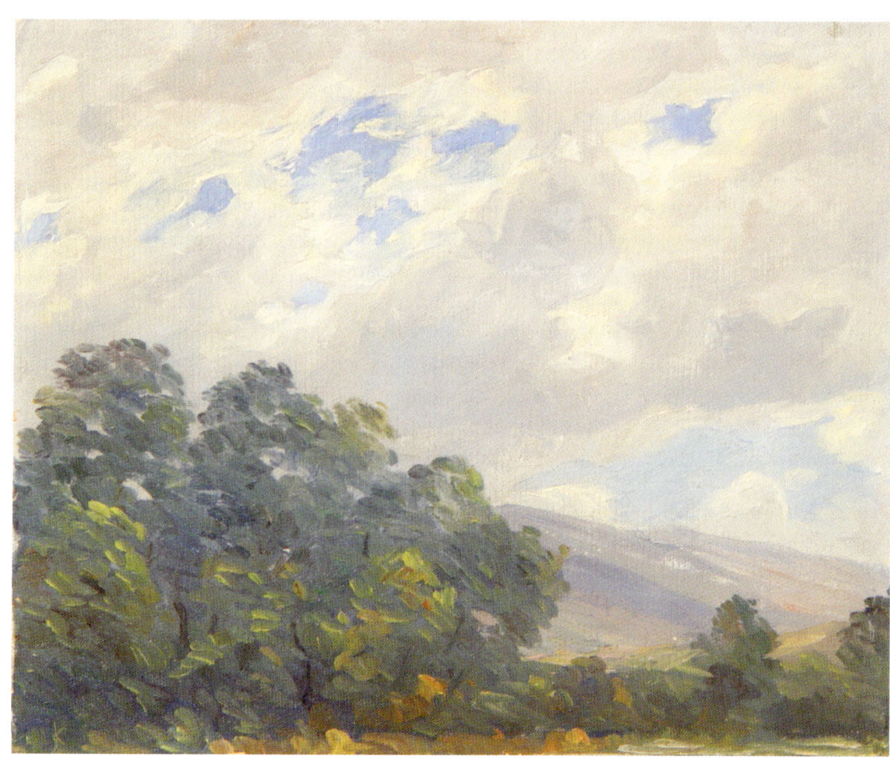

"Untitled--Dark Clouds and Trees"
Image: 9.25 inches high by 10.875 inches wide

Hans Kleiber

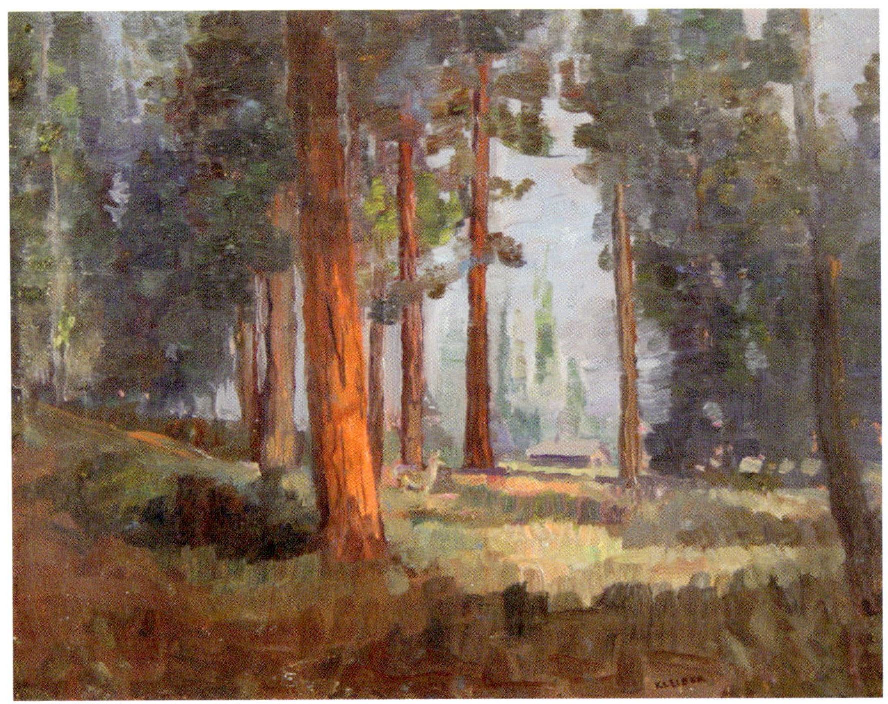

"Untitled--Deer and Cabin"
Image: 12 inches high by 14.75 inches wide

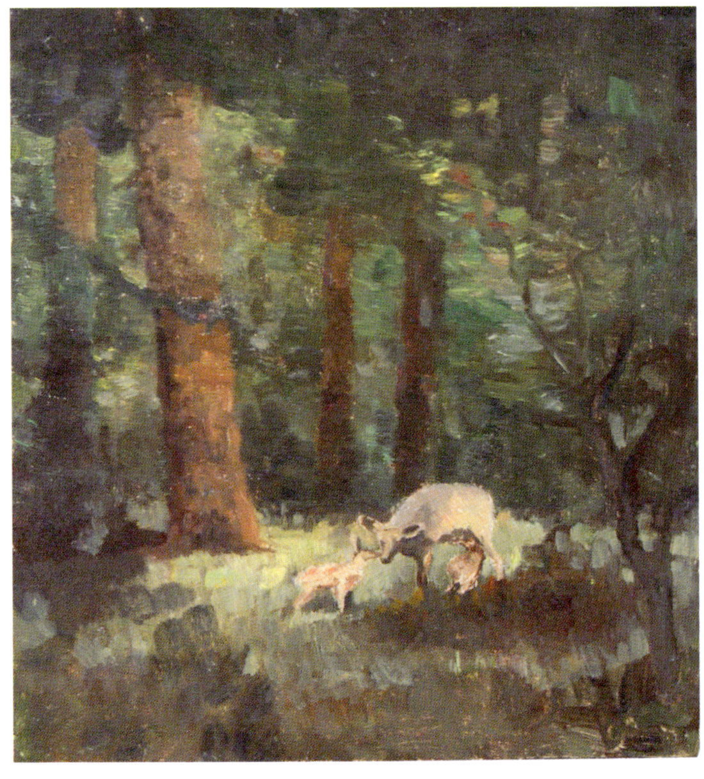

"Untitled--Doe and Two Fawns"
Unsigned
Image: 12.875 inches high by 11.4375 inches wide

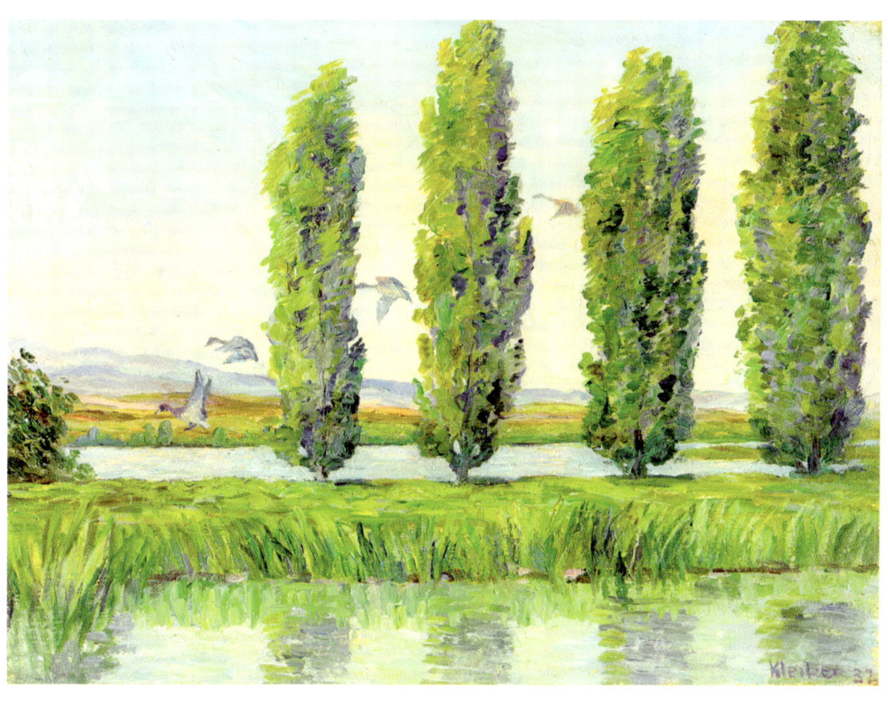

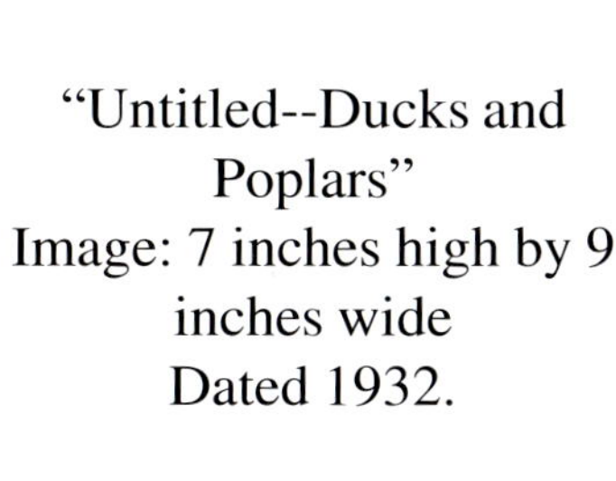

"Untitled--Ducks and Poplars"
Image: 7 inches high by 9 inches wide
Dated 1932.

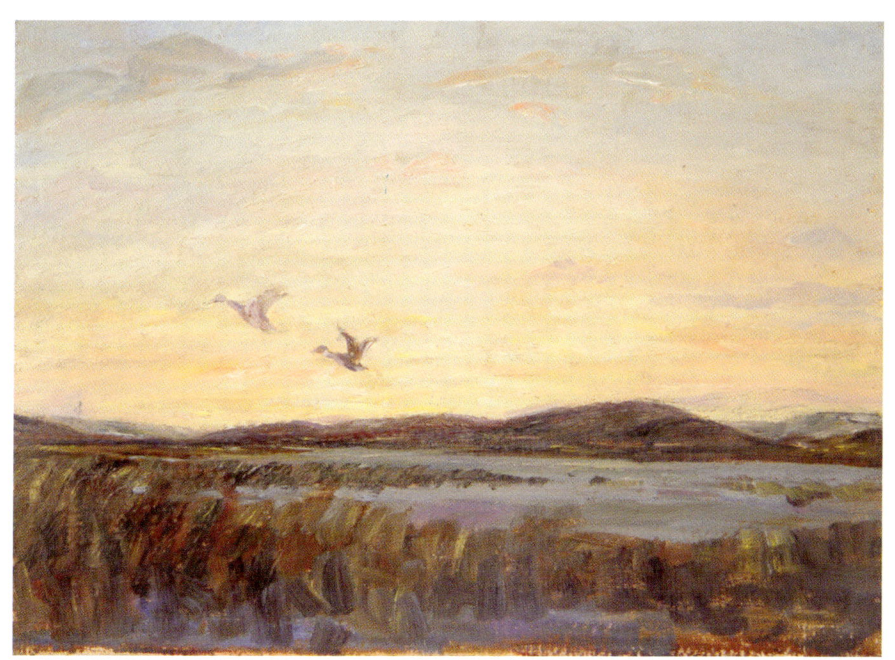

"Untitled--Ducks"
Image: 9 inches high by 12.125 inches wide
Unsigned

Hans Kleiber

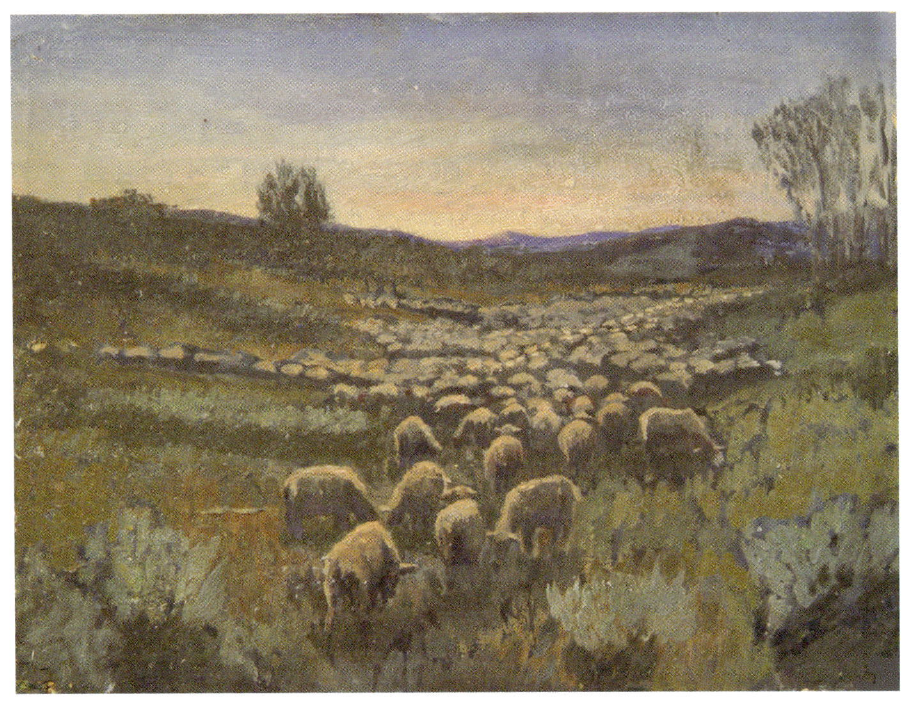

"Untitled--Evening Flock of Sheep"
Image: 9.25 inches high by 11.875 inches wide
Unsigned

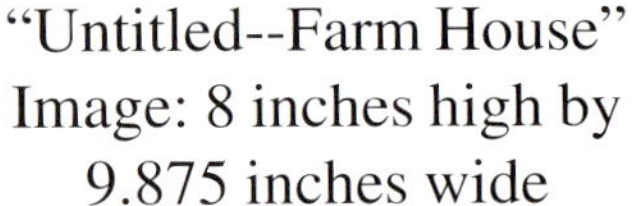

"Untitled--Farm House"
Image: 8 inches high by 9.875 inches wide

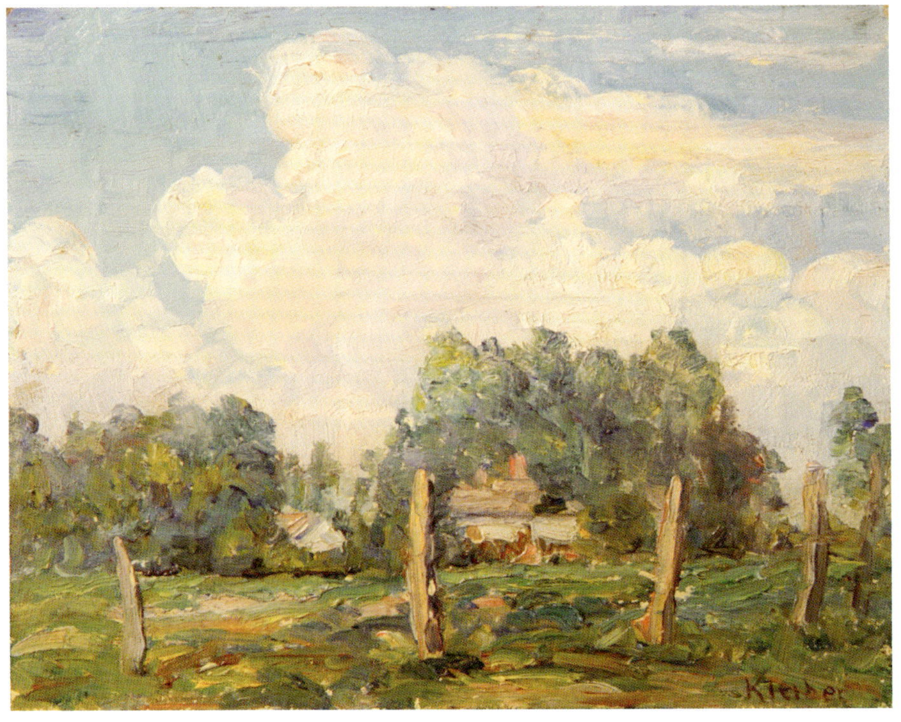

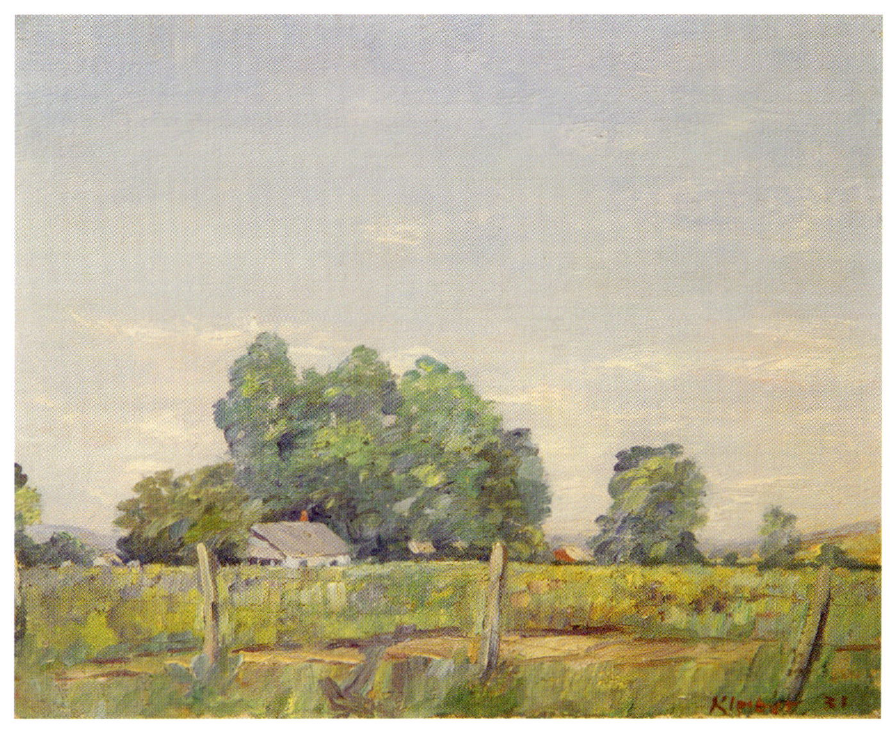

"Untitled--Farm House"
Image: 8 inches high by
9.75 inches wide
Dated 1931

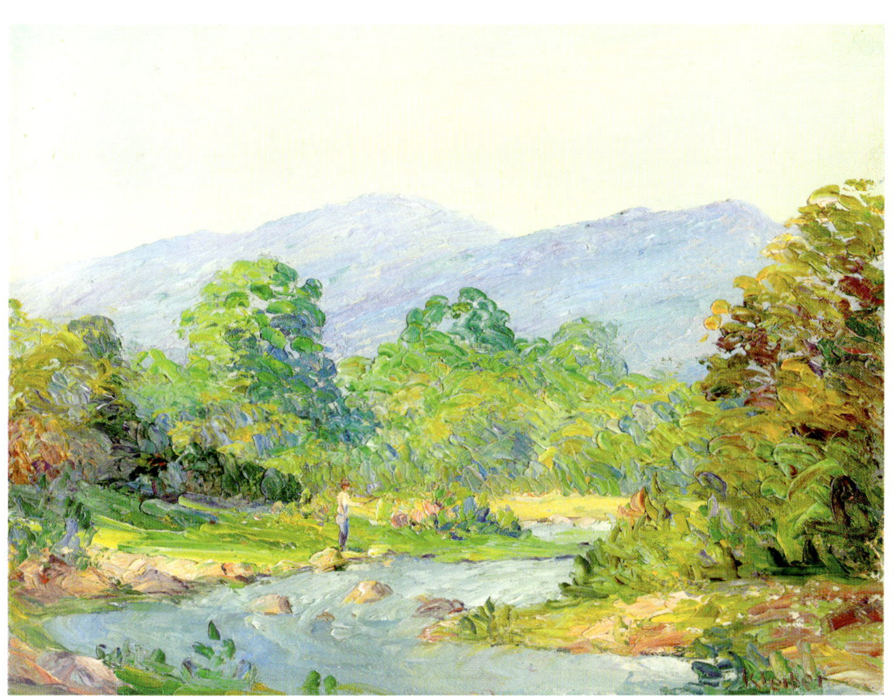

"Untitled--Fisherman"
Image: 9 inches high by 11
inches wide

Hans Kleiber

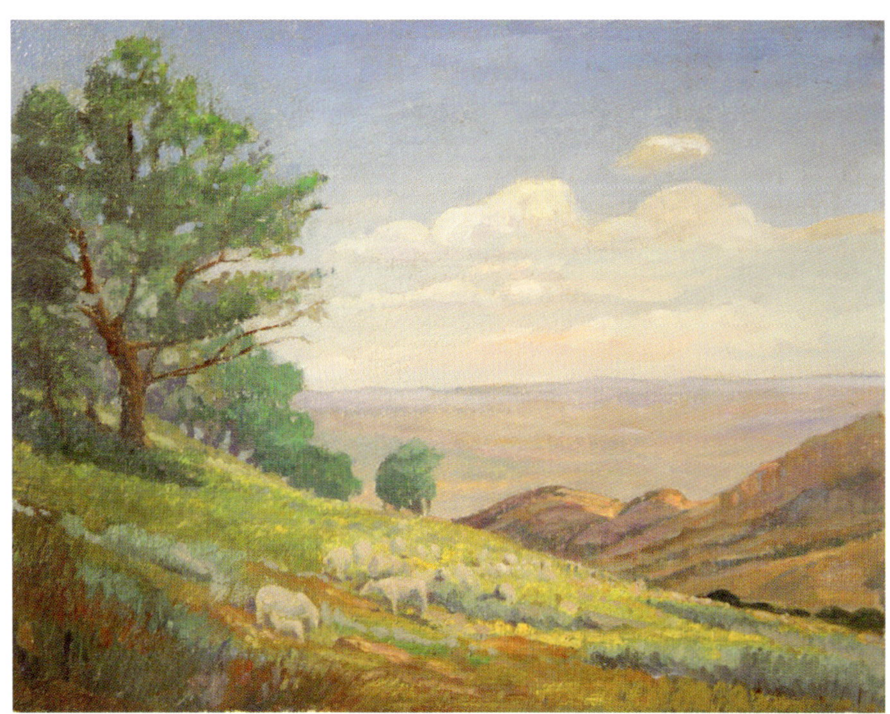

"Untitled--Flock of Sheep"
Image: 12 inches high by 15 inches wide
Unsigned

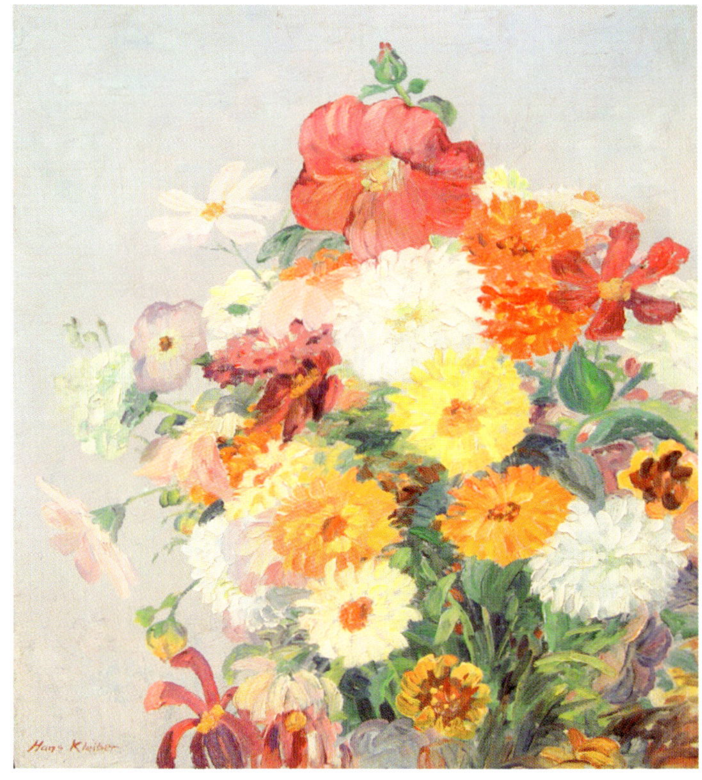

"Untitled--Flowers"
Image: 12.875 inches high by 11.5 inches wide

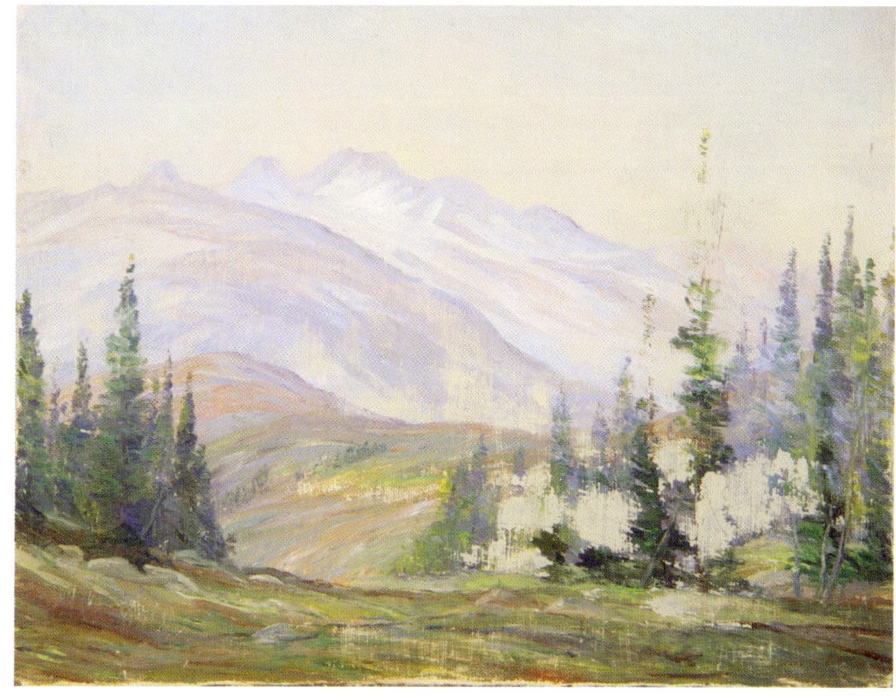

"Untitled--High Meadow"
Image: 8 inches high by 10 inches wide
Unsigned

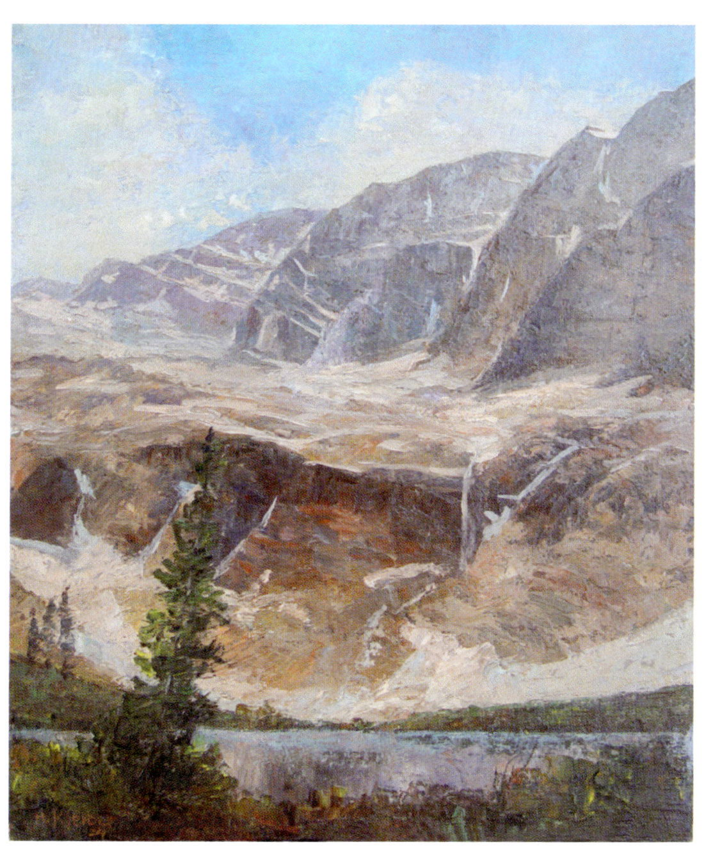

"Untitled--High Mountain Scene"
Image: 14.5625 inches high by 12.0625 inches wide
Dated 1924

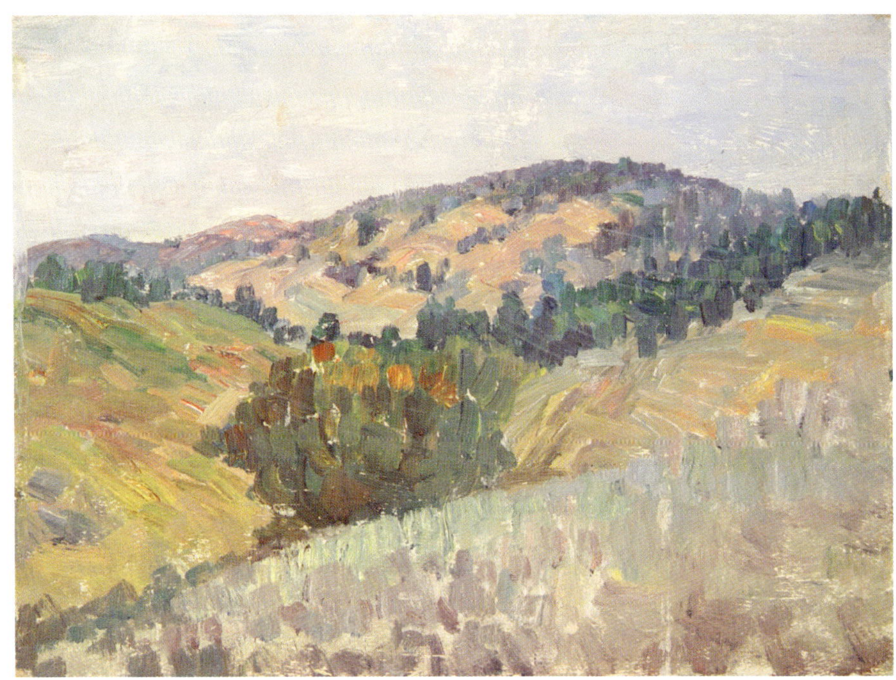

"Untitled--Hills"
Image: 10 inches high by
13 inches wide
Unsigned

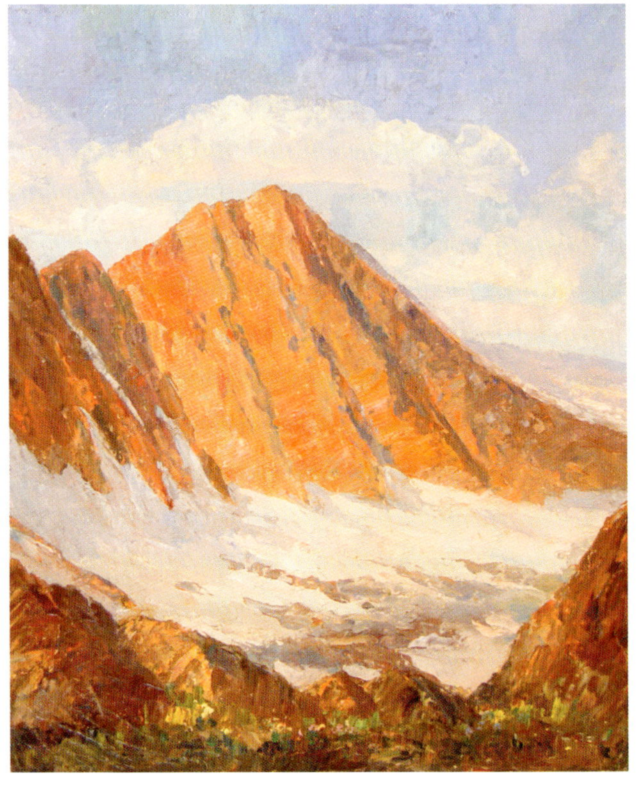

"Untitled--High Mountain Scene"
Image: 13.875 inches high by 11.125
inches wide

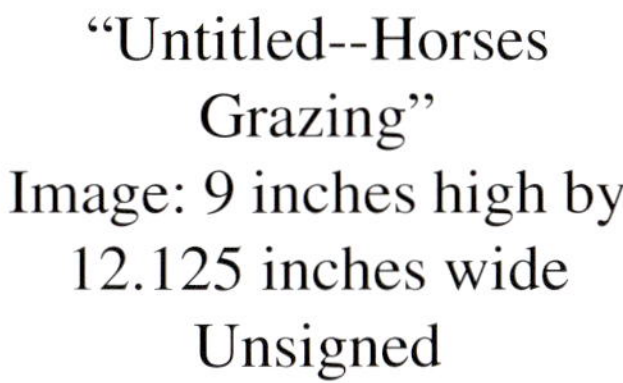

"Untitled--Horses Grazing"
Image: 9 inches high by 12.125 inches wide
Unsigned

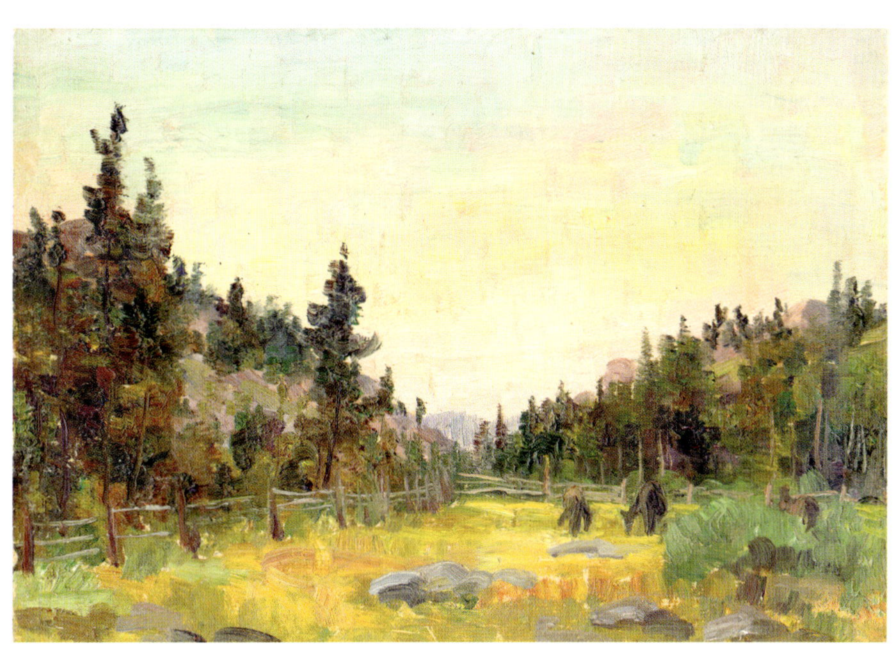

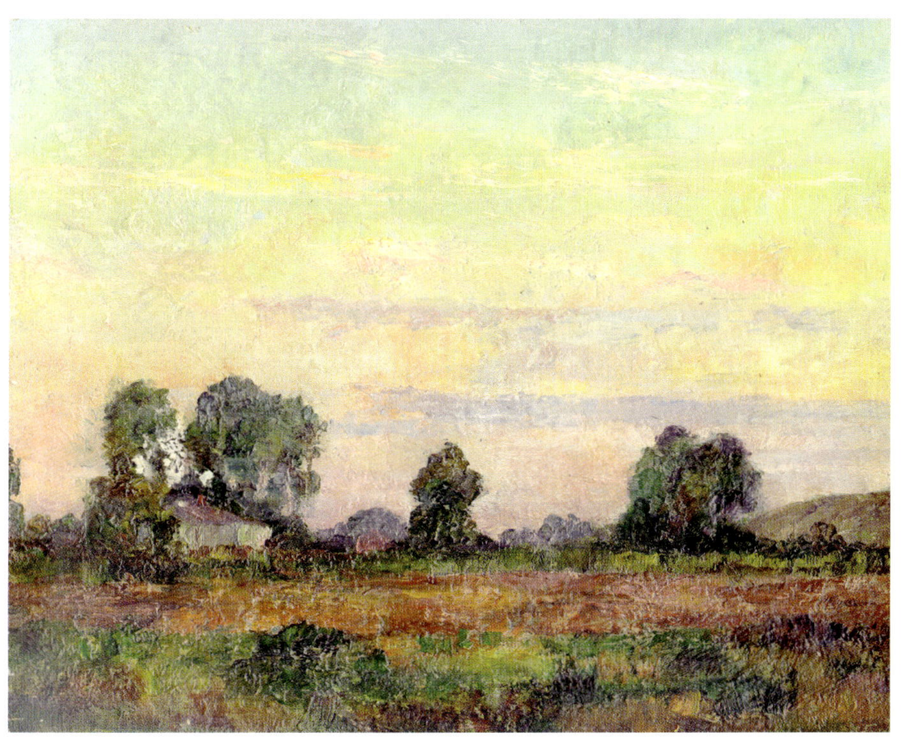

"Untitled--House at Sunset"
Image: 7.875 inches high by 9.625 inches wide
Unsigned

Hans Kleiber

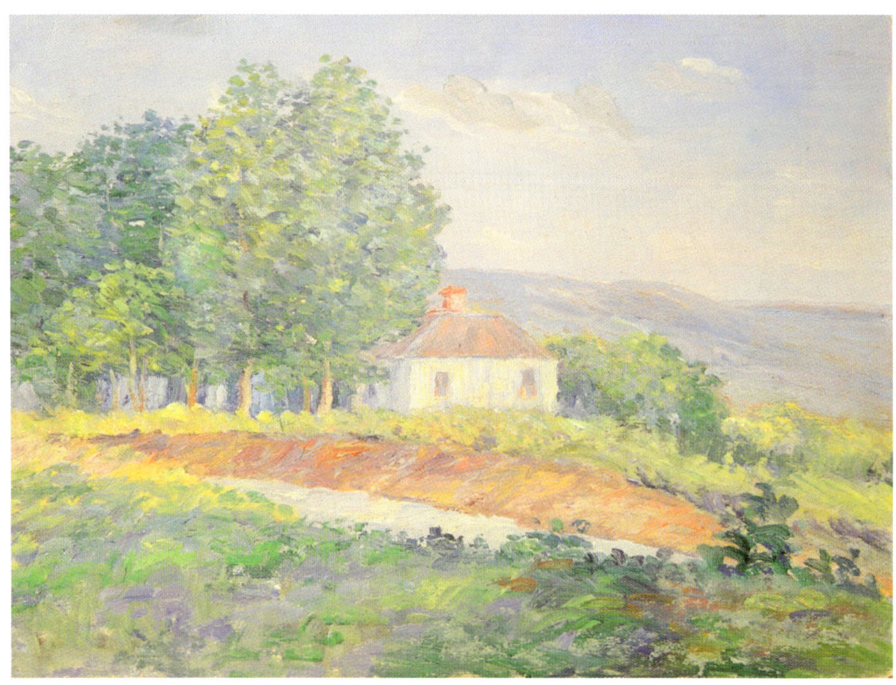

"Untitled--House by Stream"
Image: 10 inches high by 13 inches wide
Unsigned

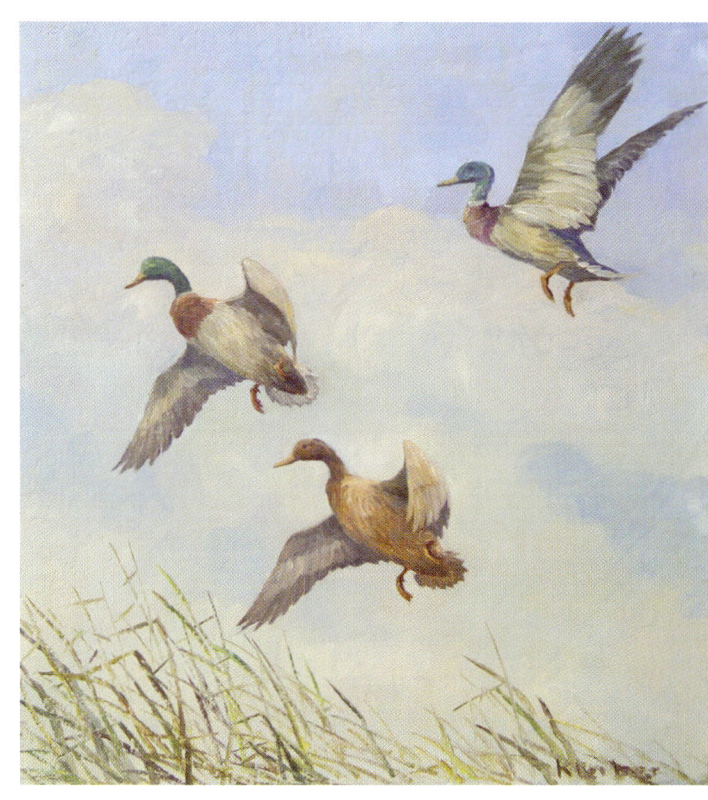

"Untitled--Mallards"
Image: 12.875 inches high by 11.4375 inches wide

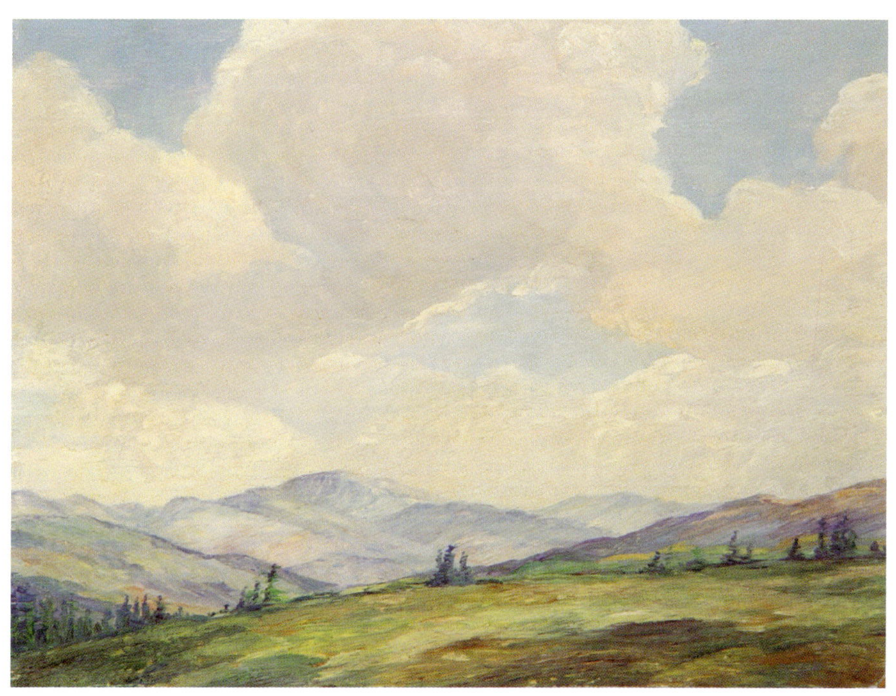

"Untitled--Landscape"
Image: 7 inches high by 9 inches wide

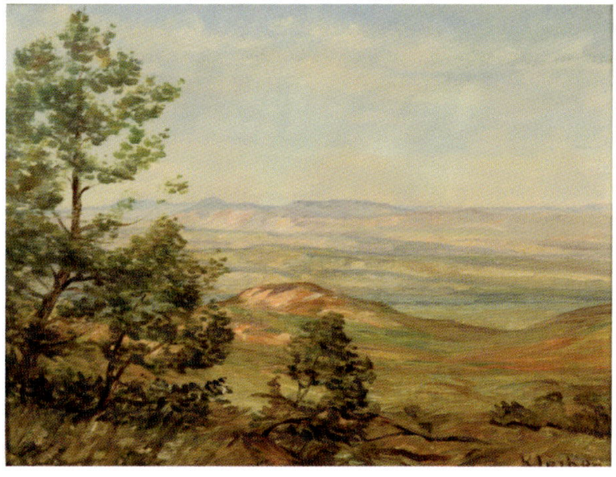

"Untitled--Landscape"
Image:9.5 inches high by 12.25 inches wide

Hans Kleiber

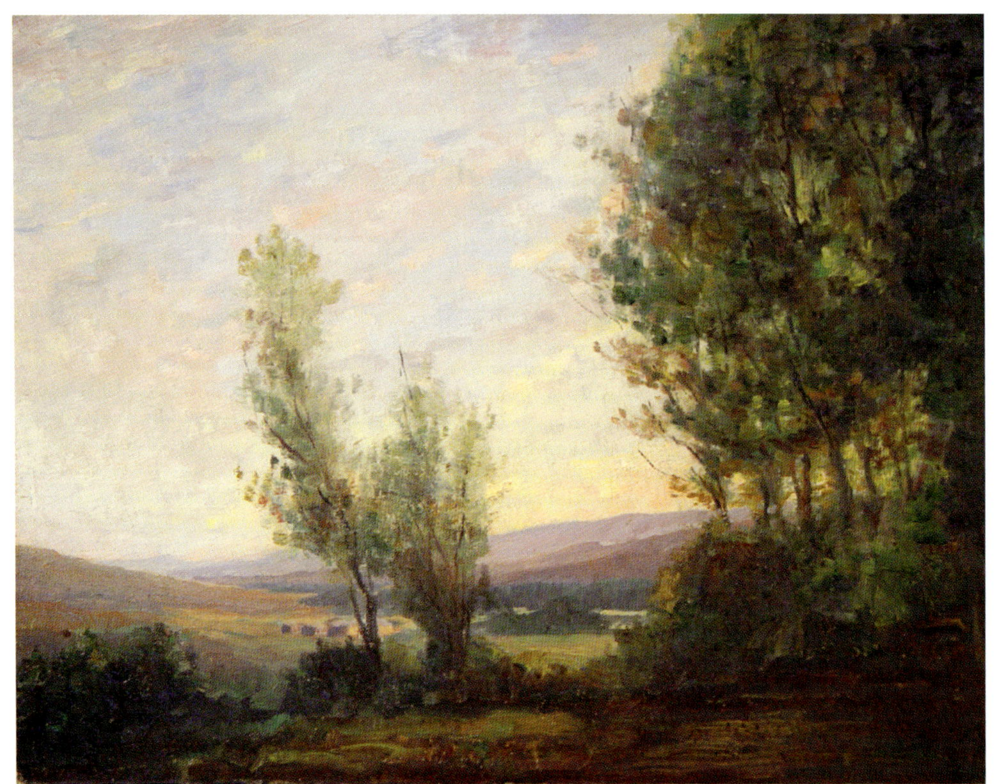

"Untitled--Meadow Scene"
Image: 12 inches high by 15 inches wide
Unsigned

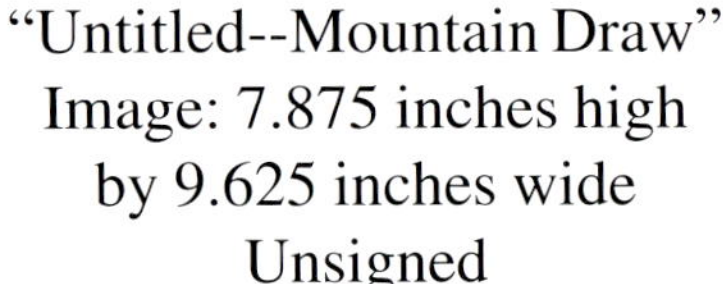

"Untitled--Mountain Draw"
Image: 7.875 inches high by 9.625 inches wide
Unsigned

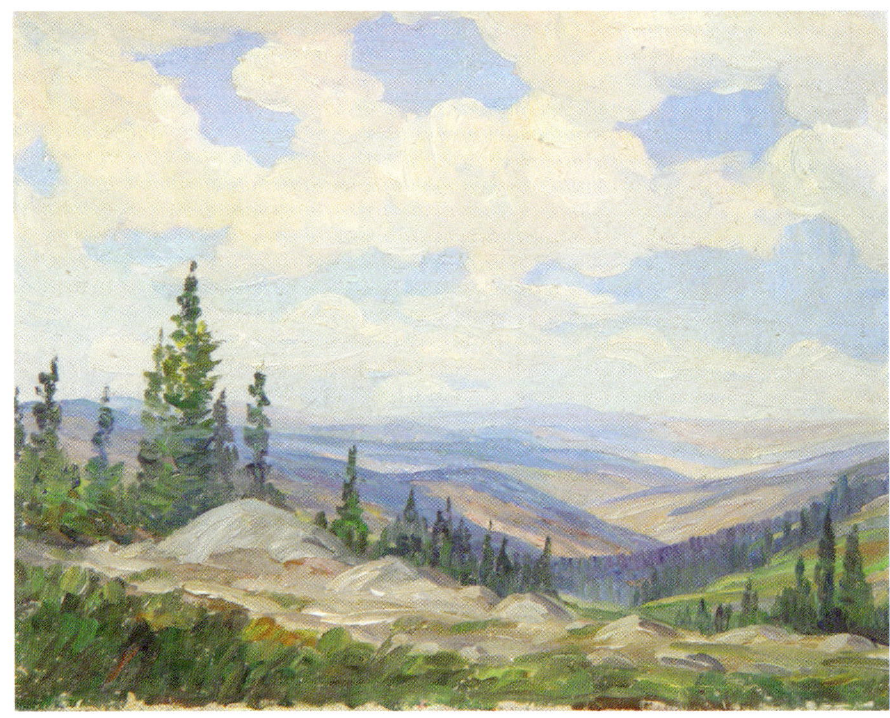

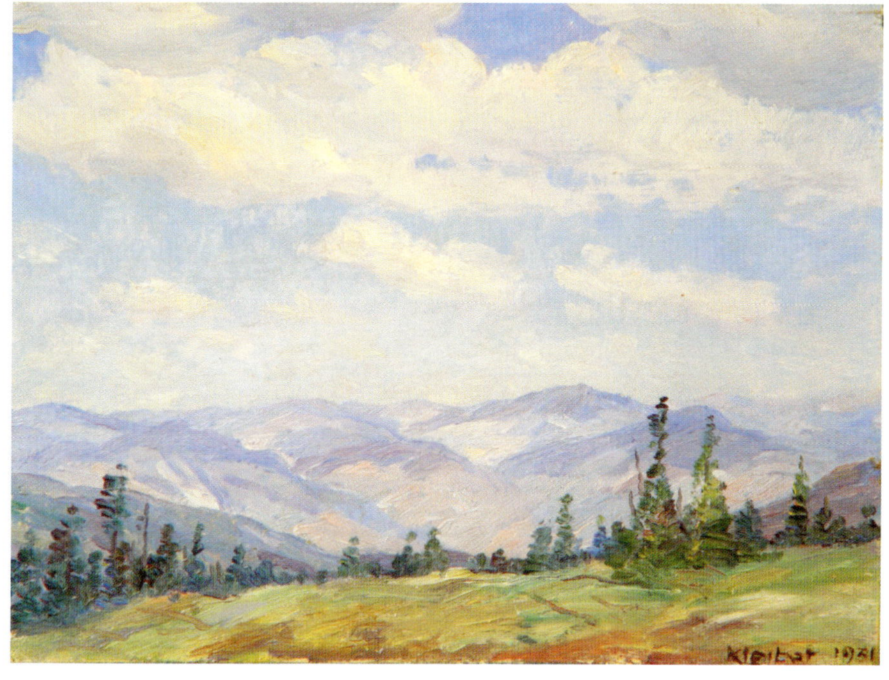

"Untitled--Mountain Landscape"
Image: 6.875 inches high by 9 inches wide
Dated 1931

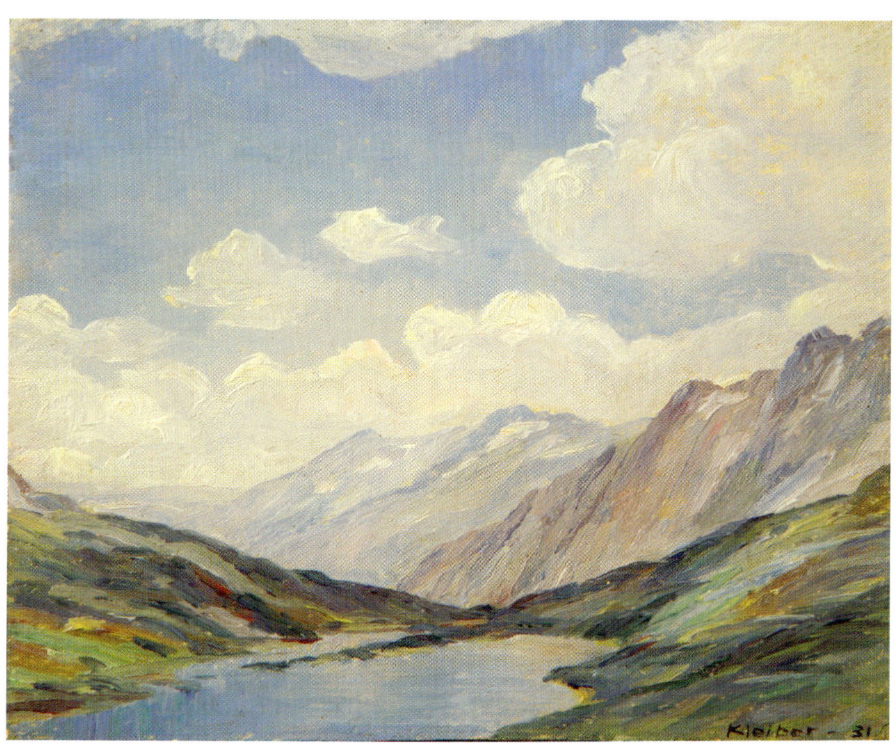

"Untitled--Mountain Lake"
Image: 8.0625 inches high by 9.75 inches wide
Dated 1931

Hans Kleiber

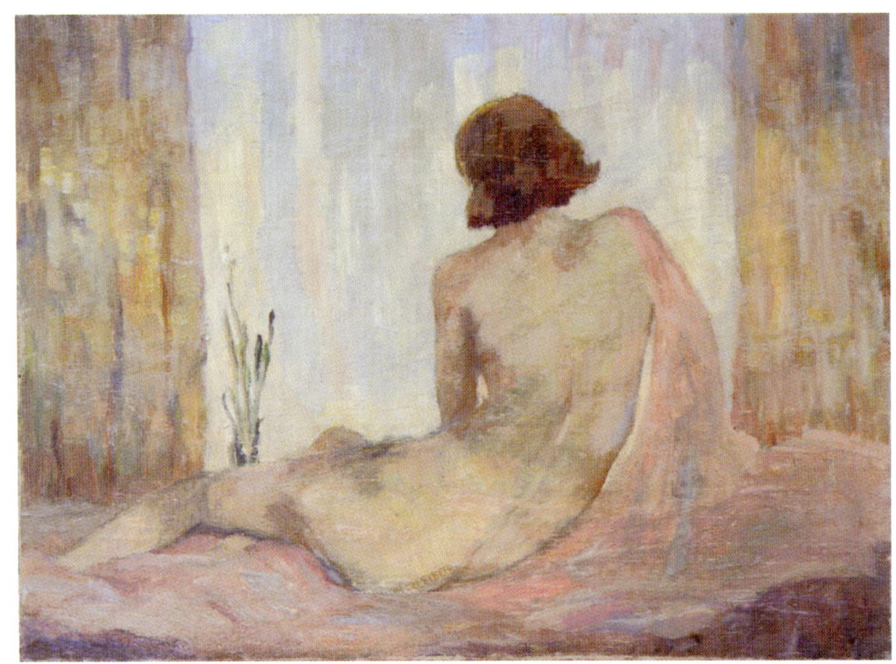

"Untitled--Nude"
Image: 9.75 inches high by 13 inches wide

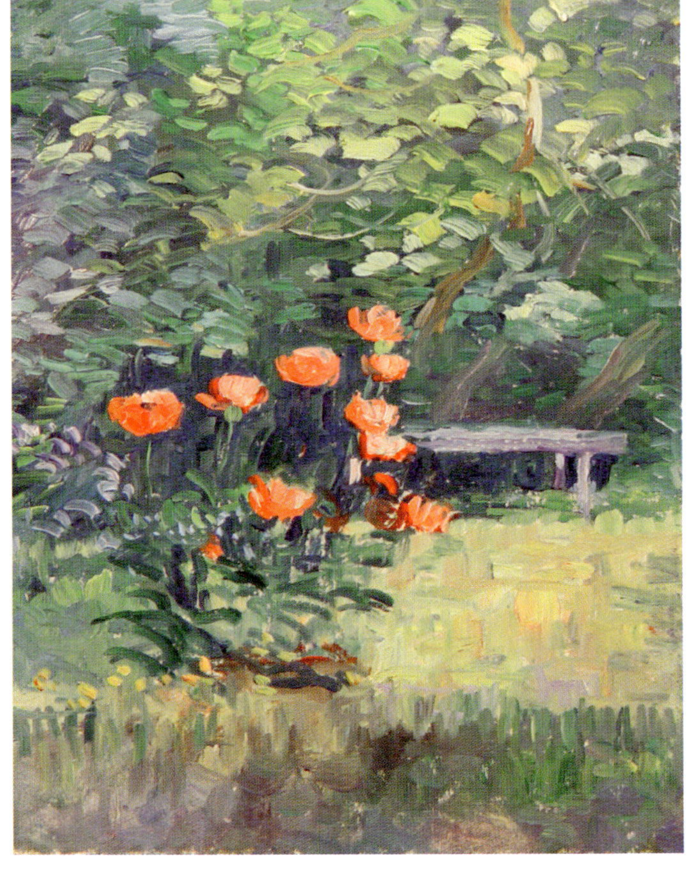

"Untitled--Oriental Poppies"
Image: 9 inches high by 7 inches wide
Unsigned

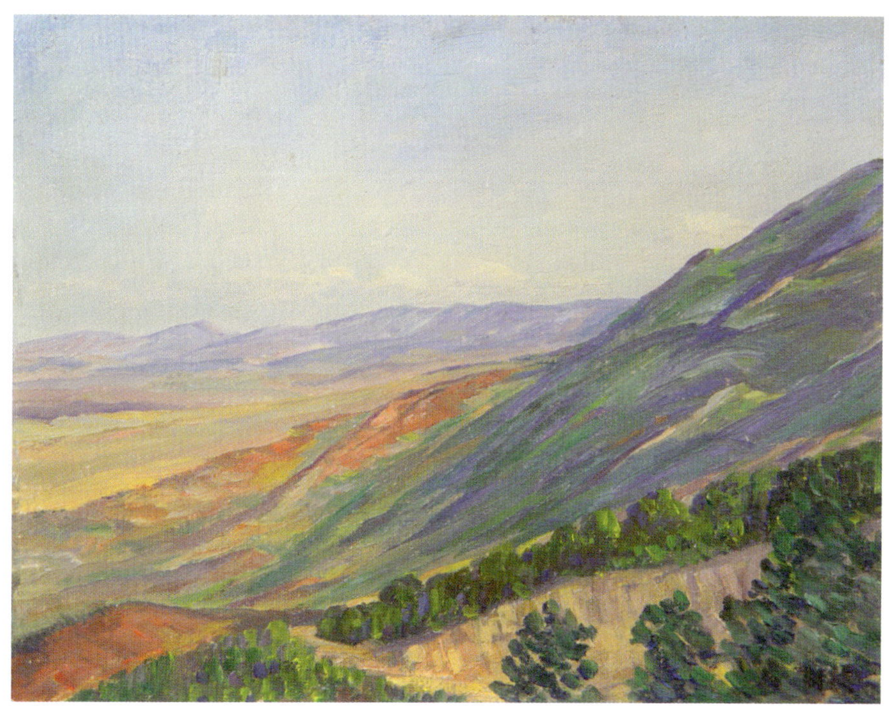

"Untitled--Red Grade"
Image: 8 inches high by
10 inches wide
Unsigned

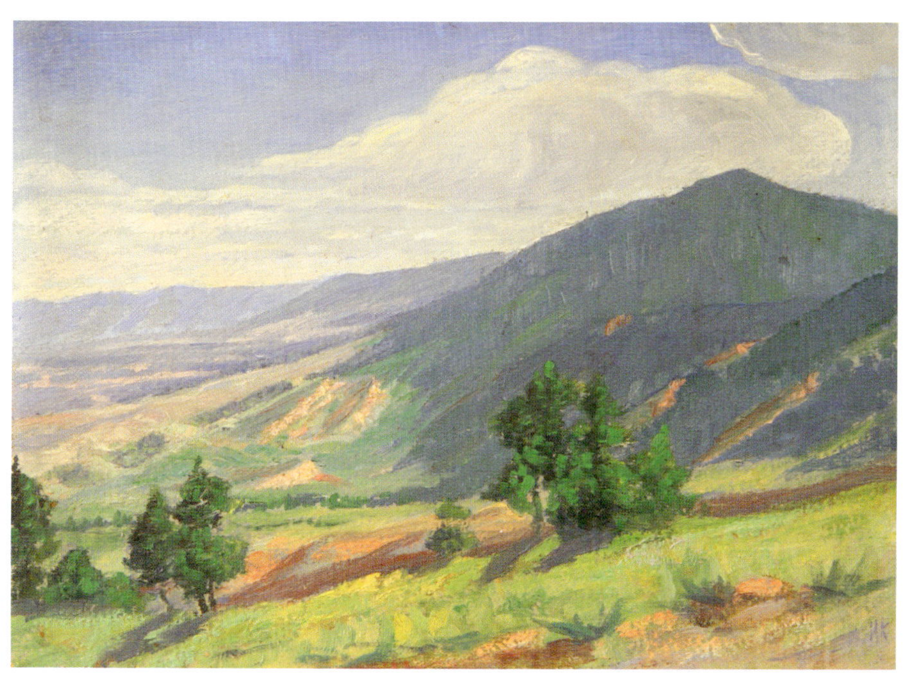

"Untitled--Red Grade"
Image: 9.75 inches high by
13 inches wide

Hans Kleiber

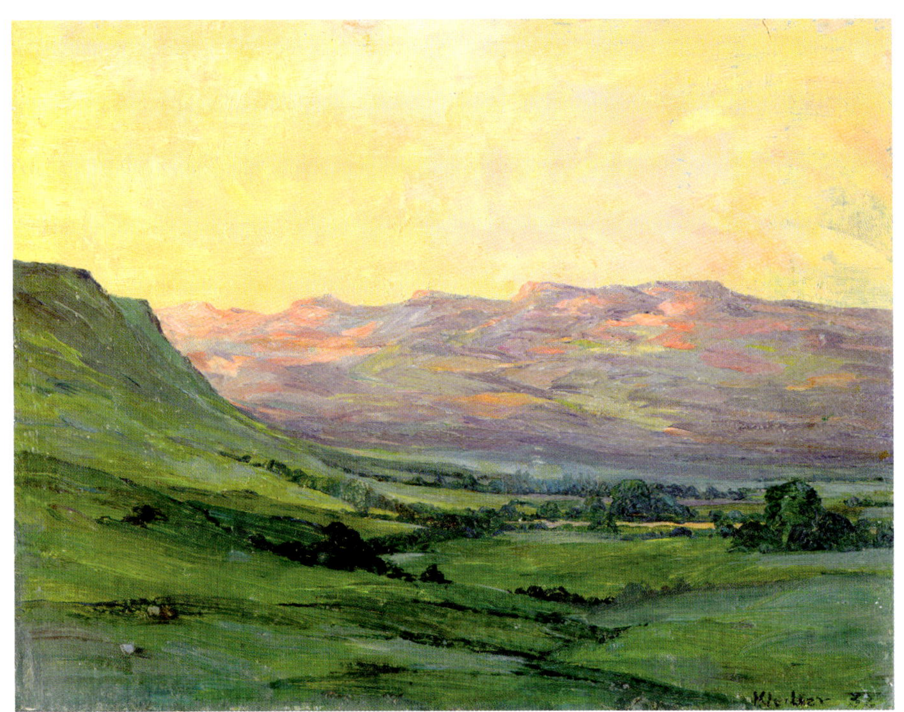

"Untitled--Rims and Valley"
Image: 7 inches high by 9 inches wide
Dated 1932

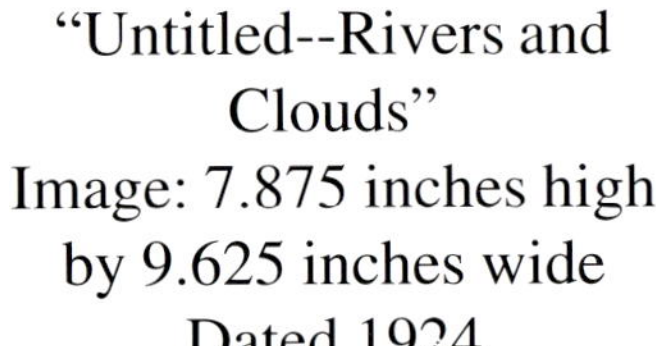

"Untitled--Rivers and Clouds"
Image: 7.875 inches high by 9.625 inches wide
Dated 1924

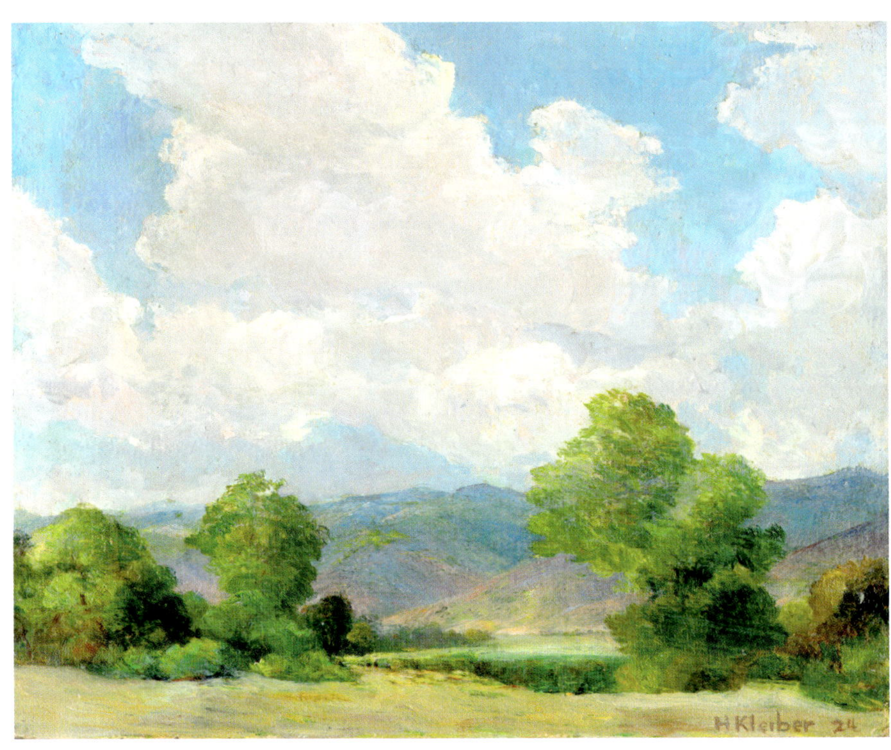

"Untitled--Sheep at Sunset"
Image: 9.9375 inches high by 13 inches wide

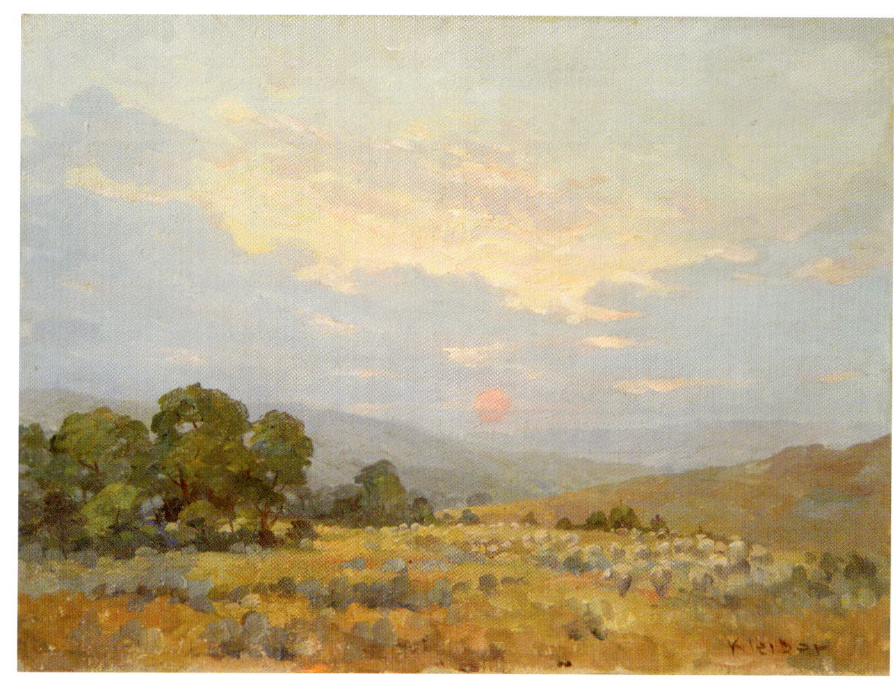

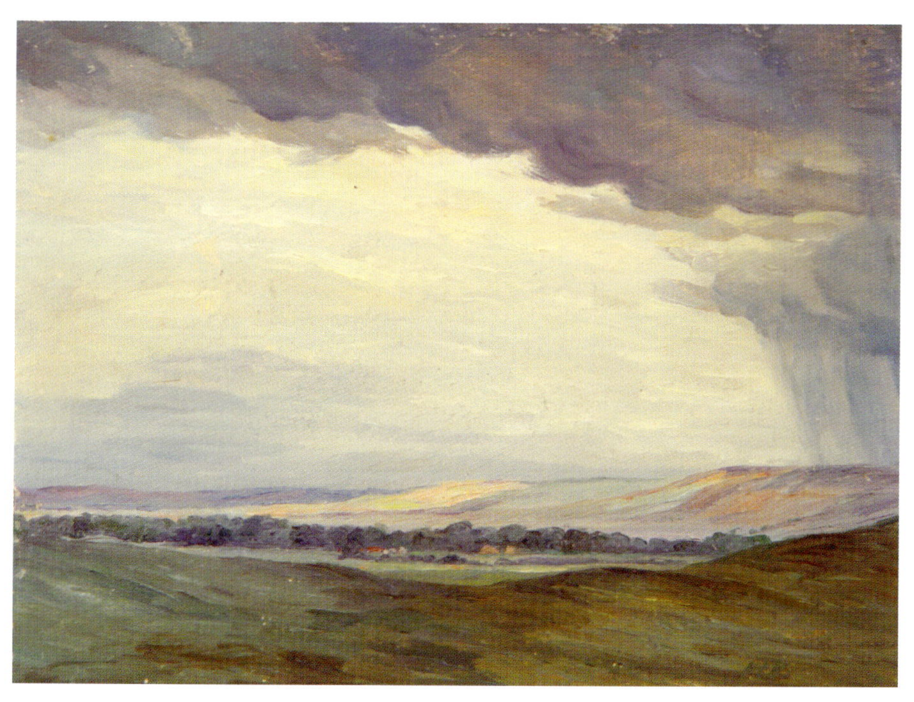

"Untitled--Storm"
Image: 7 inches high by 9.0625 inches wide

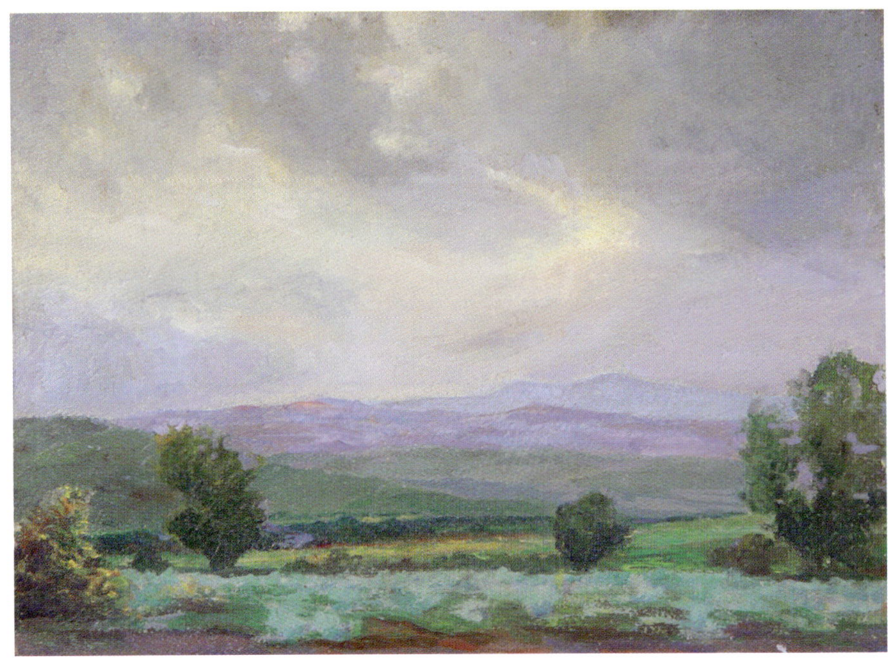

"Untitled--Stormy Clouds"
Image: 9.75 inches high by
13 inches wide
Unsigned

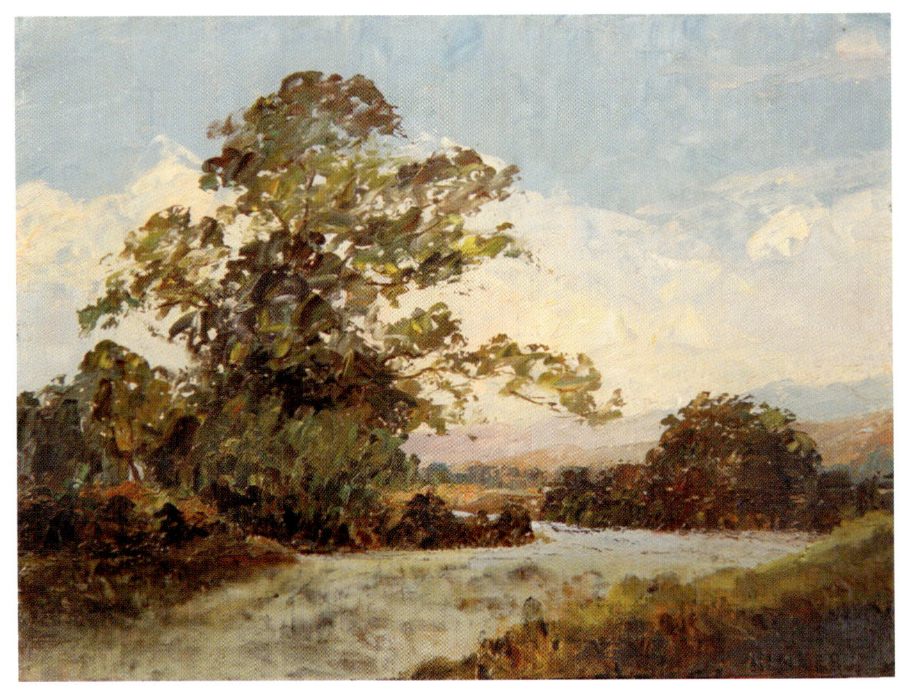

"Untitled--Stream Scene"
Image: 7 inches high by
9.0625 inches wide

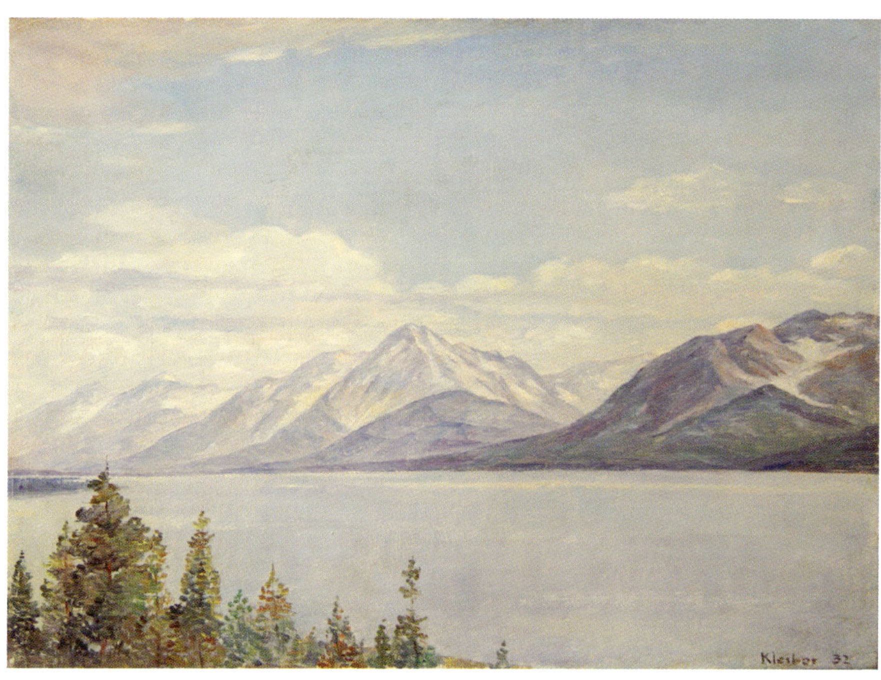

"Untitled--Tetons"
Image: 9.8125 inches high
by 12.9375 inches wide
Dated 1932

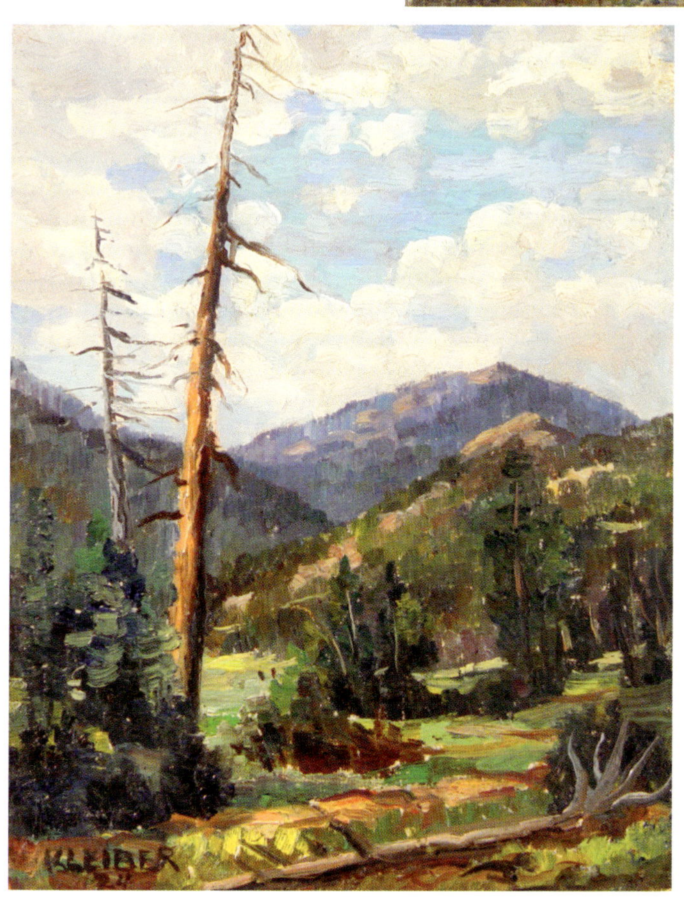

"Untitled--Timber Scene"
Image: 12.125 inches high by 9 inches wide
Dated 1924

Hans Kleiber

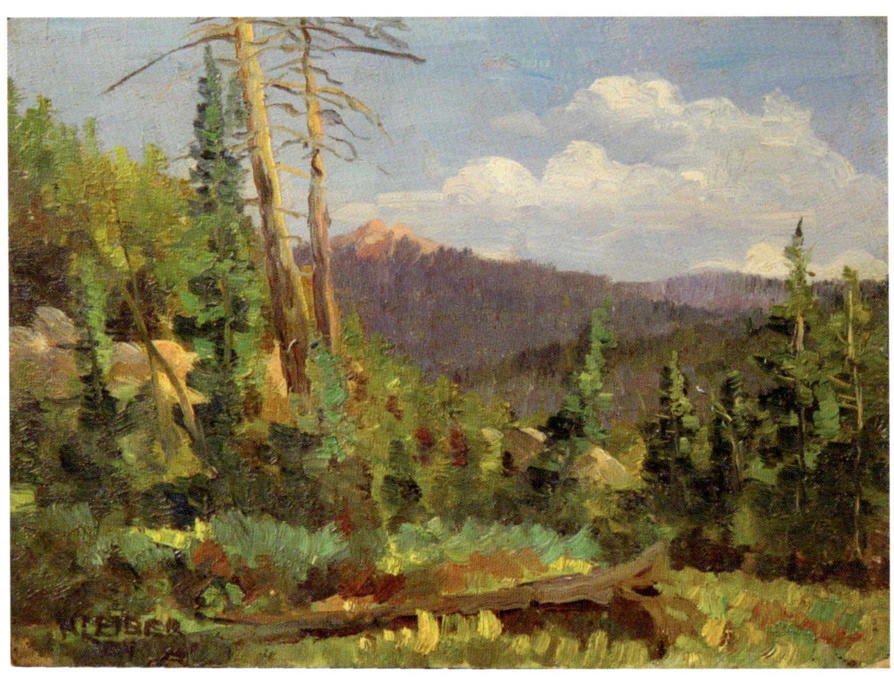

"Untitled--Timber Scene"
Image: 9 inches high by 12 inches wide
Dated 1924

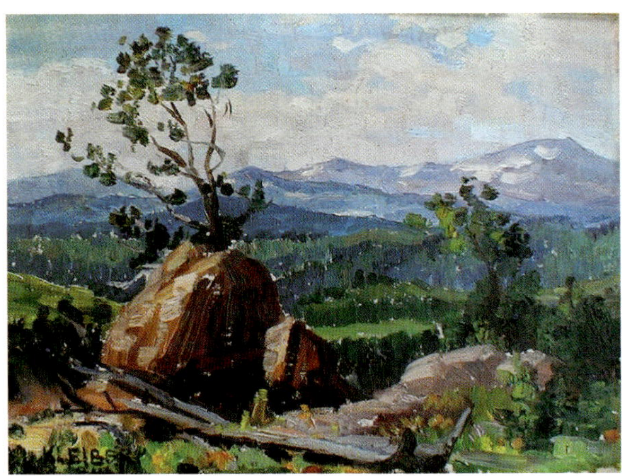

"Untitled--Landscape"
Image: 9 inches high by 12 inches wide
Dated 1924

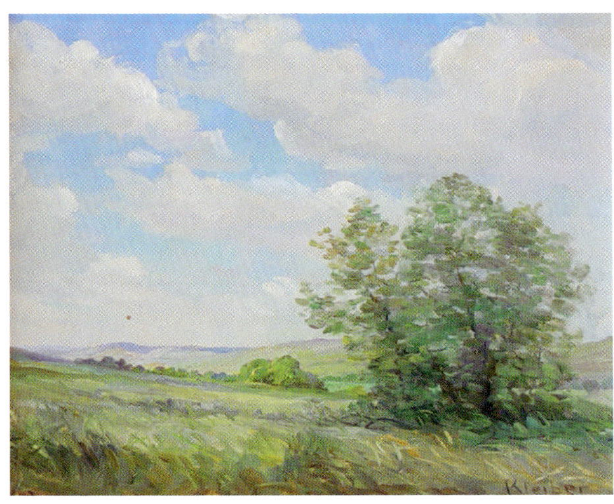

"Untitled--Trees and Clouds"
Image: 8 inches high by 10 inches wide

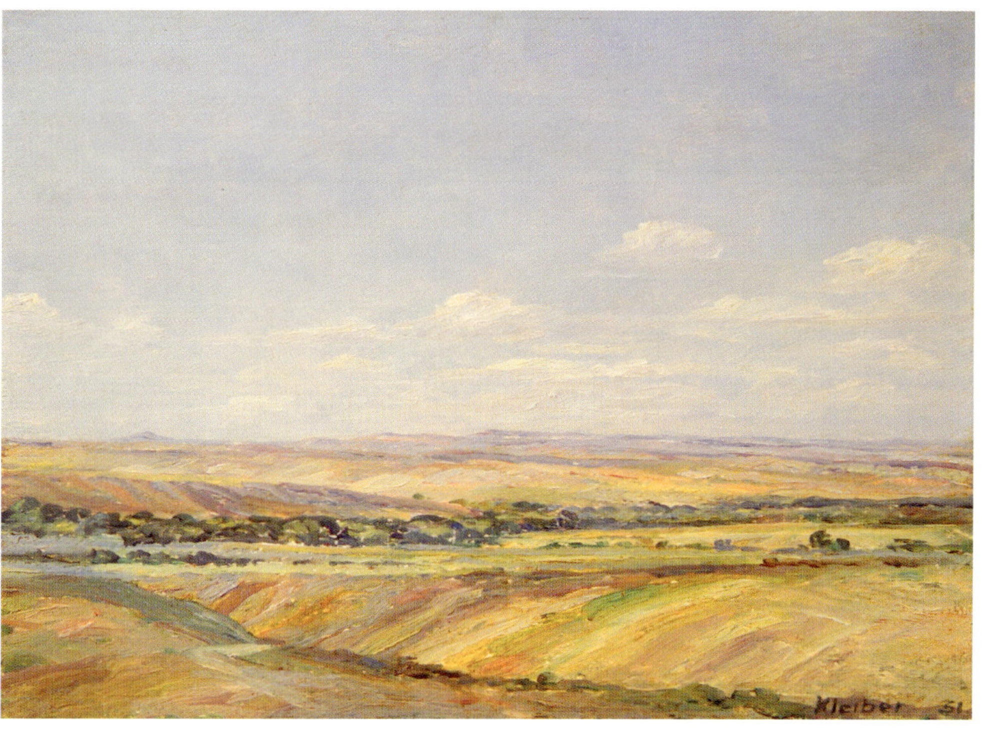

"Untitled--Valley Scene"
Image: 9.625 inches high by 13 inches wide
Dated 1931

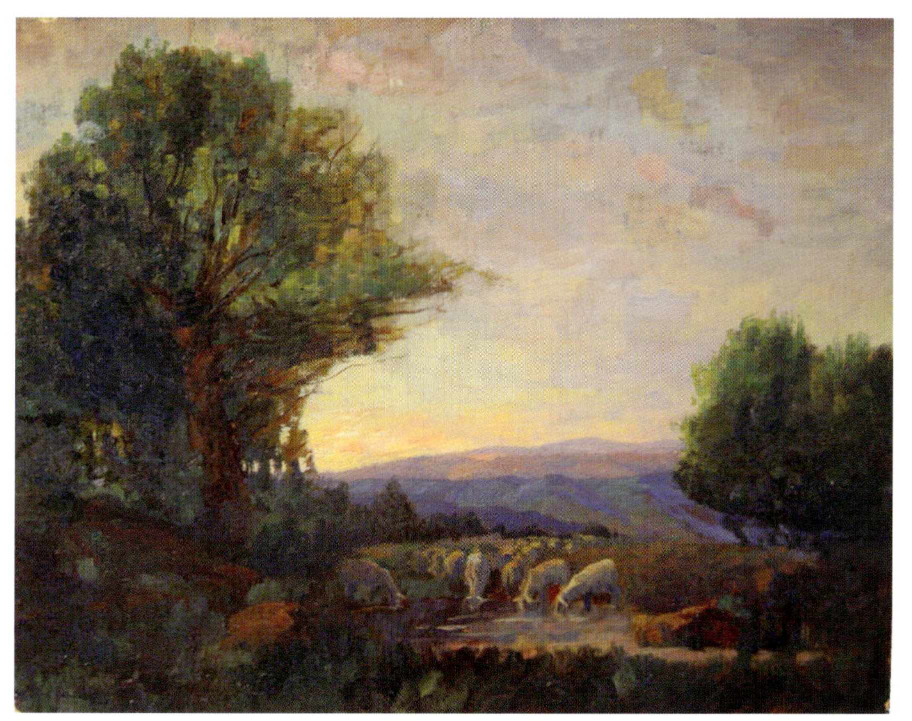

"Untitled--Watering Sheep"
Image: 12 inches high by 15 inches wide
Unsigned

Hans Kleiber

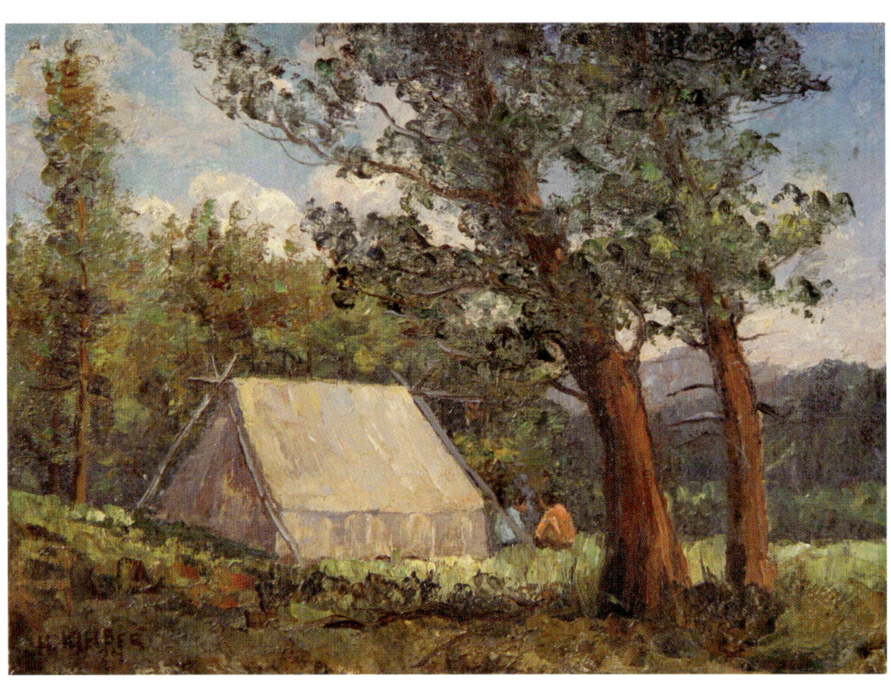

"Untitled--Wall Tent"
Image: 9 inches high by 12 inches wide
Dated 1924

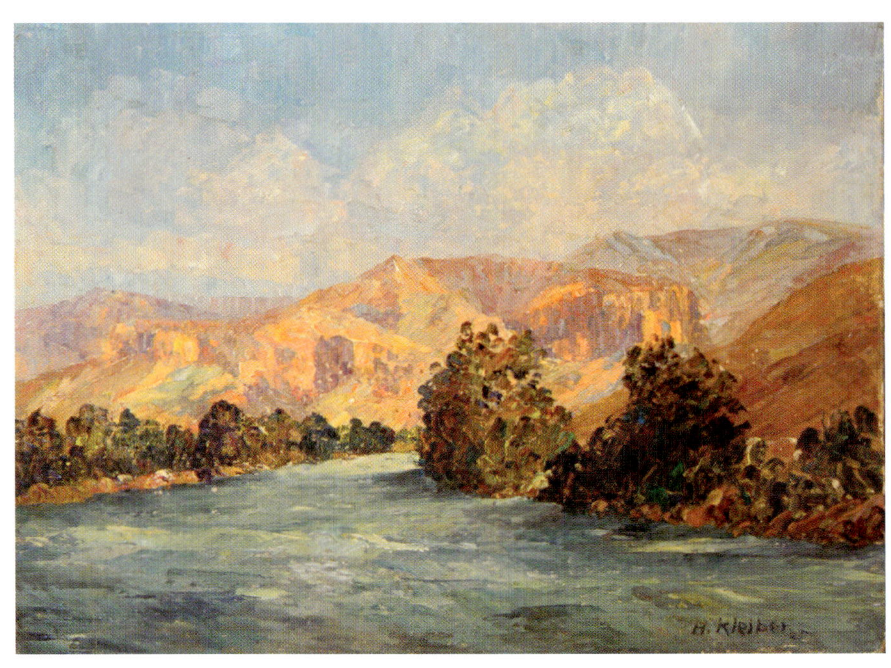

"Wind River Upper"
Image: 9.875 inches high by 13 inches wide
Dated 1927

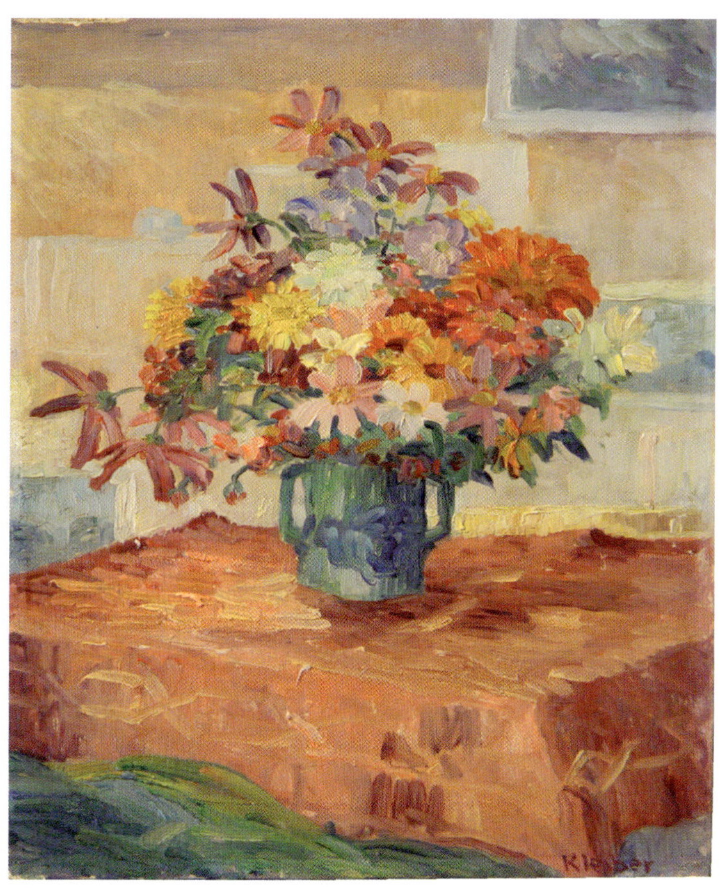

"Untitled--Vase of Flowers"
Image: 9.875 inches high by 8 inches wide

Hans Kleiber

Appendix One
Letter to Branson Stevenson

This is a transcript of a letter by Hans Kleiber to Branson Stevenson, dated January 18, 1926. (The letter was to a Mr. Stevenson, but according to Marion Ruth, it was to Branson Stevenson.)

My Dear Mr. Stevenson

Your letter and prints came a few days ago and I was glad to hear from you, as well as to use a couple of your prints. They were interesting to use and no bones about it.

Yes, I was pretty nearly crazy with the printing problems before Xmas, due to poor paper, the press going on the blink, but principally to several wretched ink that I got from Webers in Philadelphia. Everything turned out allright though finally after having gotten some good old ink from Winsor and Newton in New York. By the way, never get any etching materials from Weber's. They are the most expensive and poorest, including their highly advertised ground, that it was my misfortune to get hold of. The best luck with materials I had so far, was from the "American Steel and Copper Plate Co." 101 fairmount Ave. Jersey City, N. Jersey. They are reasonable and good. For sure when one is groping in the dark, like I was on this proposition, one flops around considerably, spends a lot of money and time on this and that, you doubly appreciate when solid ground is hit.

As I'm not much in frills in getting acquainted I'll get on —down to business in what letter I may be able to tell you from my experience with acid and needle. I have never bit "dry point" because I finish the bitten lines for all around purposes is the more vital of the two in the long run. Please understand though that my eyes are not closed to the ravishing effects that can be obtained by it, when handled properly and that never can be reached with the acid.

I use an English ground "Sands" from the outfit that I recommended. A double point needle with a cork grip is all I use. I have a lot of others both fine and coarse that I got when I started out, but they are all discarded now and I doubt if I will ever use them again. Visiting current etchers might fair(sp) was for now, but for what impression I wish to record, they use not needed. The main thing to my way of thinking is to understand the acid, steel jars the lines their proper life and color, which is the main thing I'm after.

To begin with I used all zinc plates. Zinc hasn't the quality and the vitality like copper, but its cheaper and thought over the notations. Often when our idea is not quite clear in my mind I do it on zinc first and perhaps later on copper. Nitric 10 to 1 can be depended on to do the biting. There is nothing to be feared in the biting of zinc to that ratio and if the ground is first properly it will behave like a gentle horse tied to a tree with an inch rope. Only don't use any acid that has previously had copper in it, for that will cause it to bite a dirty line.

For copper, nitric acid 50-50 is at once the touch etone of delight and despair. You never quite know what it's going to do, there seems to be so many factors that influence it, heat sustained experiments is the only way to get aquatinted with its moods, to my way of thinking. Time—pertains a lot to do with it, but is try far not the only thing. I would hear ditched long ago, only, the quality of the lines its bites for emotional expressions cannot be equalled by any other acid, and Themium bits its temptations. Nitrous acid and chloride of sro—rs will bit beautiful lines, absolutely to be dependent on, but they are cold and clear nothing more to be said. Especially chloride Trous, which is the vilest stuff in small and looks. This you use in a pure state, cheap at its sources but expensive by the time one gets it out here. My last experiments were with Chloride to start with and ending with Nitric, it worked allright, but somehow it left me cold and the plates went into the discard with a goodly company.

Lately I haven't been doing anything along these lines, as my experiments on the burn in the last session. I went through about 35 plates in 6 weeks, experimenting day and night almost continually with lines and soft ground work. I have not much to show for it exceptions for the feeling of having much more as hid ground under me. As soon as I can get hold of more junk for plates another session is to come off though.

In regards to printing. I started in with using most any kind of paper, this is a poor policy its <u>hard</u> on your plates and it doesn't do justice to it in printing it. So lately I've gotten in couple of batches of haye— matt Trojan paper, its expensive as hell, but its the only stuff to use. To begin with I don't only wet my paper, but I soak it for at least 2 days between boards. The longer the better, not so long as it doesn't rot. Her is some things about printing, keep your whole outfit warm, the warmer the better press, plates, paper and all. Instead of working the ink in with a dabber or your fingers I bought me a flexible roller and use it when printing a big batch.

The press I built myself. A strictly original idea, never had seen one in my life. You wouldn't think it works by looking at it, but it does in spells, like me. I am missing a blotter or two on top of the plate, but have come to the conclusion that a soft flour ell instead, pushes the paper into the luuls much better. The only thing is to get hold of the right king of flannel, that bothers me just now, on the other hand with a blotter the print sticks to it and doesn't cockle so easily, which is a good thing. Do you burn your own linseed oil for diluting ink, or do you buy it?—Please tell me about it.

I'm a damn poor scribe, but I'm glad you wrote and, hope you will do so again. Don't be backward about asking anything, if I can tell you anything it doesn't hurt me in the least to part with it. I'm sending you a few experimental proofs, they are not good ones you understand, and I do not care to have them around much, but you may get something out of them, if you are seriously considering the quesr. I ought to lr ul it right now only my eyes are still giving me hell, so I'm fooling with color, and fooling is about all too, but I can't leave it alone. What I really should do is to close up shop and go on a prolonged jamboree. That would help more than anything I know.

I don't use thermometers, hydrometers or anything with my acids. I keep the room good and warm, that is important and about the only thing you can do for often it gets erratic in spite of hell, and all one can do is to take the medicine. Thus all is a days work who the man that has really something to say. Art is long and life about an it gag, but a true one and a good one to remember when things slip away from you. You can use most any good paper for printing, no matter how hard it, if you work it long enough, least its not always suitable as the thing to sue. White paper is with everything else I floundered from one thing to another and used a lot that I shouldn't have. Hard —er papers are the only kind to us and according the plate, slightly tinted, away from or dead white, but you may know all this. If you ever get any stuff from the 'outfit' I receommended tell them I put you next, you can get discounts if you buy in quantities.

Another thing when you go in for line etching "Forget Pen and Ink". Also to a larger extent forget your needle, but always "keep in mind the acid." The more you can get it to work for you, the nearer one comes to being an ethcer. Remember me to Joe, if you see him.

Very sincerely yours
Hans Kleiber

Hans Kleiber

Appendix Two

Biographical Sketch for Business Womans Club

The following is from a paper entitled by the artist himself as a "Biographical Sketch For Business Womans Club, Sheridan (Wyoming), May 22, (19)36." This biography was also sent to the American Artists Group as it was in their records.

"I was nineteen years old when I got to Wyoming in the summer of 1906 in the quest of romance and, incidentally, to get into the United States Forestry Service if I could. Forestry work seemed to fit better into my ideal of outdoor work at that time than anything else. To begin with, though, I had to be satisfied with work around a logging camp at Woodrock at the head of Tongue River and it wasn't until the following year that I began to work for the Forest Service. And, on account of my age, it was several years before I got a permanent place with them.

One of the first things I did was to build a log cabin along the banks of the river so that I would be independent and able to read and study and do the things that were dearest to my heart. Strange to say I did very little drawing or painting in that time although I did occasionally do a sketch to amuse myself but never with any particular idea of going in for it seriously. There were too many other and more interesting things to do during those years. The Bighorns to me were a sort of terra incognito that had to be explored very personally, on horseback and on foot during the summer, for five or six years I seldom left the mountains. After that, my work took me to other forests in Wyoming, Montana, Idaho, Washington, and Minnesota but somehow I always loved the Bighorns the best and finally in 1915 decided to build a permanent home in Dayton at the foot of the mountains.

Along about 1920 I began to think seriously of trying to put down some of the things that I had seen and felt about the landscapes and wildlife of the mountains but it wasn't for several years, until the summer of 1923 that I really made the break and then not all at once. About the first thing I found out was that it is quite a different thing to see a thing with mind's eye or even to feel about it strongly and to put it down either as a drawing or in paint. The manual difficulties for one who had had no training along those lines proved infinitely greater than I had anticipated and I was forced to back off again and, again for a new start. It wasn't until 1927 that people began to show some interest in what I was trying to do. In 1928 Goodspeed's Book Shop in Boston gave me my first exhibition of etchings which proved a tremendous encouragement. In 1930 the(y) gave another one-man show of my work and asked me to be present. I was scared to death but I went and felt it was the greatest ordeal I had ever been through. I suppose it is one of the necessary evils in an artist's career.

It can't be said that things came easier after that for an artis(t's) struggles are much the same as those of any one else. They never cease and it is one thing to hammer out a certain amound of reputation and another thing to keep it. However, this recognition put me definitely in the rin(g) and it was up to me to stay in it. Since then my work has been shown in New York, Chicago, St. Louis, Los Angeles, Denver, Seattle, elsewhere I have been elected a member of the California Print Maker's Society and one of my prints won the Silver Medal at one of their international exhibitions. I exhibit in all the major print exhibitions such as the Brooklyn show, the Chicago annual show, etc., and my prints are in many museums and public and private collections.

My studio is at Dayton, Wyoming, on the same property that I bought in 1915, and I suppose it will always be there. The subjects that are nearest and dearest to me are mostly to be found in this northwestern country which can be reached so easily from here and I rather feel that an artist can say what he has to much more faithfully and convincingly when he lives on the same sod with them.

Hans Kleiber

Appendix Three

Restrikes of the "Frontier Series"

As we mentioned in "Hans Kleiber, A Reference Manual," Appendix Three, Volume I, page 69; the entire Frontier Series was done after Hans Kleiber's death with the photogravure process. There was quite a bit of concern that when collectors found out that Stuart Kleiber, his son, was having restrikes done of the Frontier series. One collector said that he visited with Stuart Kleiber about his concerns and Stuart agreed to cancel the plates. There had to be quite a bit of humor in that conversation as one party thought they were solving a problem and the other one knew that the request had no effect as to their actions. To produce the quote "restrikes" or actually photogravures, the original plate was not needed at all.

Also, in Appendix Three, Volume I, page 69, we did error in listing "Pioneers I" and "Pioneers II" as members of the Frontier Series. According to Carole Tucker of the Golden Crown in Sheridan, Wyoming, the Frontier Series had already been selected and established by Hans Kleiber before their, she and her husband, taking over the marketing of his work after Totman's. This is a contradiction to the theory that the Frontier Series was a marketing ploy of Vern Tucker. There was no basis, as well, to the fact that "At The Silver Dollar" was not part of the Frontier Series.

The Frontier Series or Pioneer Series, according to the Inventory Numbering System done by Carole Tucker and Missy Kleiber before Hans Kleiber died, states the designated impressions. Many times, we have heard from one source or another that they had a letter from so and so stating the members of the

Pioneer or Frontier Series. Now how more factual can it be than from the actual inventory listing done by the artist, his wife, and Carole A. Tucker.

Appendix Four

Estate Stamps

After the death of Hans Kleiber, it is our understanding that the attorney for the estate required that all works sold after the date of death bear certain information. There were two versions of the stamping. The first required that the heir, Stuart Kleiber, sign each stamping which became a fairly significant task. In addition the stamped date of death was not correct on both methods of stamping and was actually December 8, 1967. Later a rubber stamp was made that did not require any signatures. We have examined impressions where the stamping was done on the back of it and directly in the center of the impression. Eventually the ink from the rubber stamped information could "bleed" through the paper to the front of the impression.

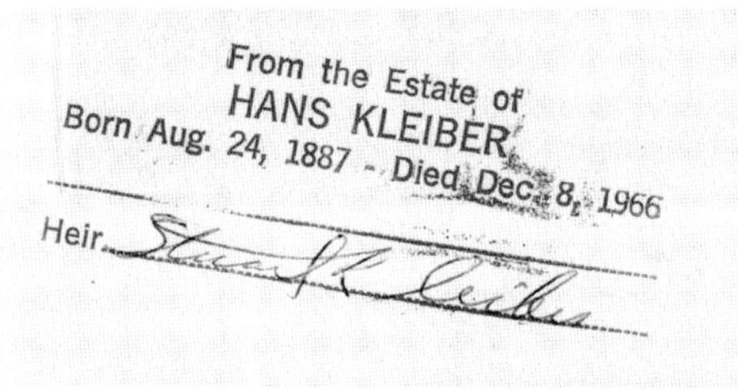

FROM THE ESTATE OF HANS KLEIBER
BORN: AUGUST 24, 1887
DIED: DECEMBER 8, 1966

Hans Kleiber

Appendix Five
Anderson-Lamb Photogravure Corporation

The Associated American Artists would have all of their published impression editions done through the Anderson-Lamb Photogravure Corporation.[46] George Miller and Sons did all of the lithographs. Anderson-Lamb Photogravure Corporation was in business from before 1934 and possibly into the late 1970's according to Sylvan Cole.[47] The Associated American Artists introduced Hans Kleiber to the firm of Anderson-Lamb Photogravure Corporation.

---

[46] Sylvan Cole, Jr. of Sylvan Cole Gallery in New York, New York.

[47] Ibid.

Hans Kleiber

Appendix Six

Will James (1892-1942)

Will James was introduced by E. W. "Bill" Gollings to the printmaking skills of Hans Kleiber. From this meeting, Hans Kleiber produced plates for the printing of several works by Will James. Very little information is really known about the impressions pulled by Hans Kleiber for and after the death of Will James. We have not ever inspected a signed impression by Will James. Some collectors have impressions with supposed initials of Will James, but after closer inspection nothing is conclusive.

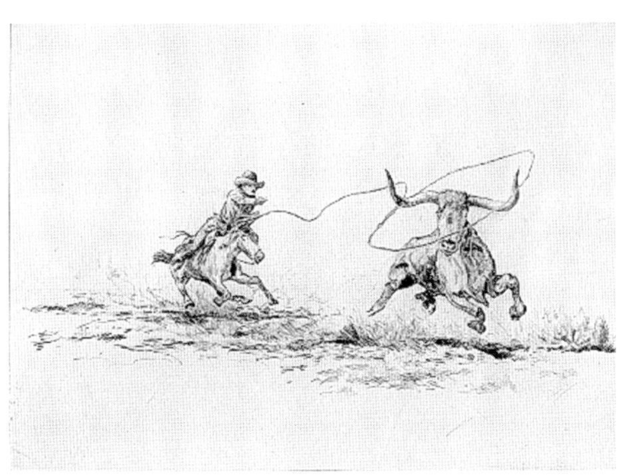

Impression pulled by Hans Kleiber for Will James.

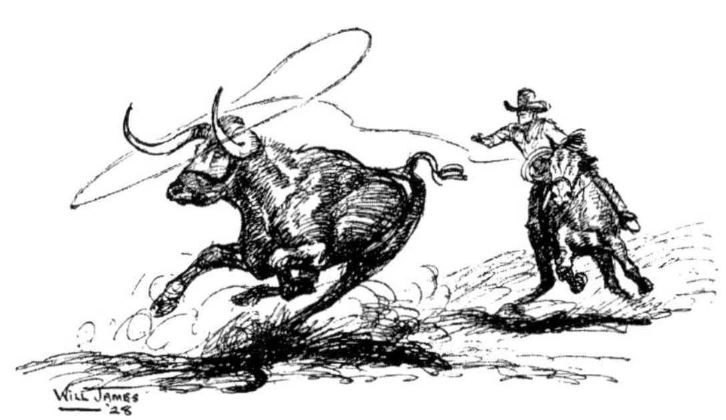

I've seen mighty fine ropers in the hills that wasn't so good in the arena.

This above illustration by Will James and the reproduction of this work is courtesy of the Will James Art Company of Billings, Montana.

Hans Kleiber

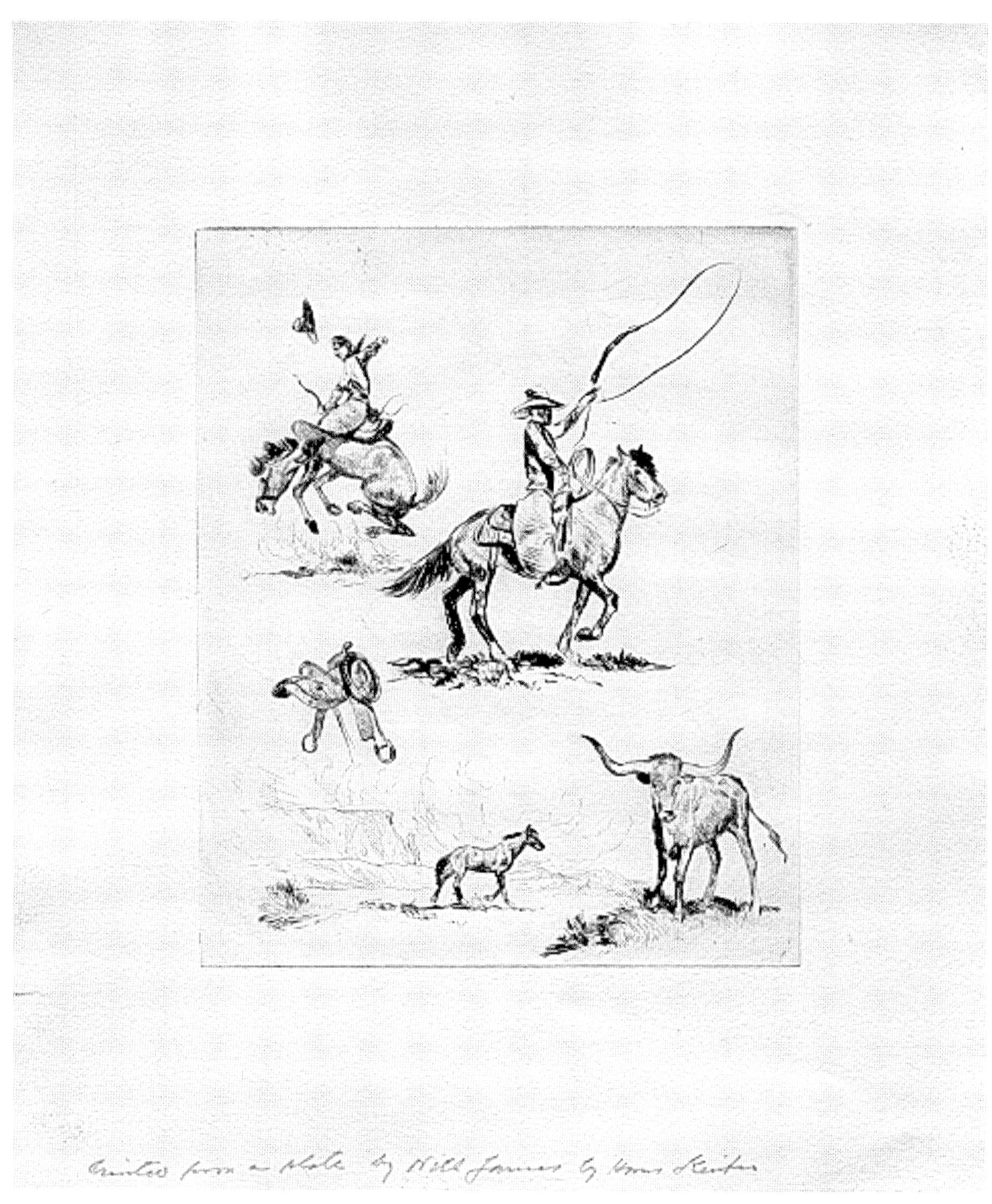

Glossary of Terms

Aquatint

"Aquatint is an etching process in which tonal areas are created instead of lines. This is achieved by dusting powdered resin on the plate which when heated will cause the resin to contract and thus allow the acid to bite the plate in the small crevices of the grain."[48•6]

"An etching process in which a mordant acid is made to bite both lines and tonal areas in the copper plate. An aquatint resembles a watercolor in its tonal effects."[49]

Drypoint

"Lines can also be scratched onto the plate with a thin steel tipped needle if no varnish is applied, and the result is called a drypoint. However, drypoint lines wear out much faster than etching lines. Etching and drypoint are sometimes used in combination."[50]

"In the dry-point the instrument used is a

---

[48] "The Etchings Of Edward Borein, A Catalogue of his work" by John Galvin, Compiled with the assistance of Warren R. Howell, In collaboration with Harold G. Davidson; page vi; John Howell—Books, 1971.

[49] "The Pocket Dictionary of Art Terms," Edited by Julia M. Ehresmann; New York Graphic Society, 1979, page 6.

[50] Ibid.

steel or diamond point. This method allows more freedom than the burin and the lines are therefore more spontaneous and elastic. The distinguishing feature of dry-point is the burrr thrown up by the needle, on both sides of the furrow if held perpendicularly, and on only one side if held at a slant. Dry-point is very often used in conjunction with etching, adding the finishing touches to a plate."[51]

Etching

"Etching is simply a process of printing an intaglio. That is, instead of a method for taking an impression on paper from a series of raised lines, etching is a form of engraving in which lines are eaten into a flat surface, these depressions being filled with ink and the ink then transferred to paper under pressure."[52]

The following is from "The Etchings of Edward Borein, A Catalogue Of His Work" by John Galvin:

"A plate of copper (or sometimes of zinc)is cleaned and polished, and a coating of varnish—the etching ground—is applied in preparation. The artist then draws his design through the ground with an etching needle, aware that in the print it will appear reversed. In a bath of diluted nitric acid, the

---

[51] "Making an Etching" by Levon West; New York: The Studio Publications, Inc., 1932; page 7.

[52] Ibid.

lines traced by the needle are bitten into the plate, the rest of the plate being protected from the acid by the varnish."[53]

"The etching proper differs from the engraving or dry-point in that the furrows or lines are not cut into the plate by main force, but are the result of chemical action. A copper penny dropped into a tray of nitric acid disappears in a few minutes–dissolved by the acid just as sugar is dissolved by water. But if the coin were coated in wax or resin before being placed in the acid, nothing would happen, since nitric acid does not eat into wax. It is on this principle that all etching is based. Specifically, a copper plate is covered with a protective substance, or "ground," into which the design is scratched with a sharp needle. The plate is then put into a bath of nitric acid. Since the acid can only act on the copper in places where it is unprotected, the design that has been scratched through the wax is etched, or the plate is left in the acid the deeper the lines will be. When the plate is removed from the acid and the wax washed off, the plate is ready to be inked and printed."[54]

---

[53] "The Etchings Of Edward Borein, A Catalogue of his work" by John Galvin, Compiled with the assistance of Warren R. Howell, In collaboration with Harold G. Davidson; page vi; John Howell—Books, 1971.

[54] "Making an Etching" by Levon West; New York: The Studio Publications, Inc., 1932; page 7-8.

> "To summarize, etching is a process whereby a polished metal plate is covered with an acid-resistant ground, into which a design is drawn with a needle that exposes, but does not penetrate, the metal. Acid is then introduced to bite the design into the plate. Finally, ink is forced into the bitten lines which, under pressure, will yield an impression on paper. The print so produced is known as an etching."[55]

Impression

> "The term used to describe the pressing of plates on paper, and all copies printed in a single edition."[56]

Intaglio

> "The metal plate processes, etching and line engraving, are classed as intaglio processes; the ink is applied to the plate and wiped off, the lines being left charged with ink, which is deposited on the paper by running plate and paper through a roller press in contact with each other."[57]

---

[55] Ibid., page 8.

[56] "Art Print and Graphics Glossary" by the Professional Picture Framers Association; 1985, page 21.

[57] "The Artist's Handbook of Materials and Techniques" by Ralph Mayer; The Viking Press, New York, 1970; page 573.

Photogravure

"Photographic images may be produced on plates to be printed by intaglio, relief, or both methods, just as they have been used for silk screen, litho, offset, and electronic-deposit printing."[58]

A plate that has been created photographically and then also had the ink applied mechanically, or the same amount each time, guarantees that each impression will be exactly the same as well. At this point the world of fine art has ceased, and the mechanical reproduction world has stepped in.

Print

A fine art print can be produced from a metal plate of copper or zinc, a woodblock, silkscreen, linoleum, or a stone. The image is created by hand by the artist. The medium is then filled with ink by hand by the artist and the print pulled. The application of the ink by hand each time supports the process of a fine art print as the impressions all vary when pulled. A mechanical process severely removes the artist from any further creativity or uniqueness to the printing process as each impression is exactly the same.

---

[58] Ibid.

Reductions

"Reductions" was an early term that we encountered having to do with the printmaking career of Hans Kleiber. For years, the public had viewed various image sizes of the same impression, and lacking the proper fine art terminology, they were labeled as reductions.

Restrike

"The term used to describe the reprinting of an edition (generally of etchings, engravings, etc.) from original or reworked plates, usually after the death of the artist."[59]

---

[59] "Art Print and Graphics Glossary" by the Professional Picture Framers Association, Richmond, Virginia; 1985, page 29.

Photographic Credits:

Bradford Brinton Memorial of Big Horn, Wyoming

Buffalo Bill Historical Center of Cody, Wyoming

Collection of University of Wyoming Art Museum of Laramie, Wyoming

Mary Hawkins of Billings, Montana

Montana Historical Society of Helena, Montana

Richard P. Bodine and Charlene L. Bodine of Sheridan, Wyoming

Sam Scott and Mona Scott of Dayton, Wyoming

Will James Art Company of Billings, Montana

Wyoming Division Of Cultural Resources of Cheyenne, Wyoming

Bibliography

"American Printmaking, A Century of American Printmaking 1880-1980" by James Watrous; The University of Wisconsin Press, 1984.

"Art Print and Graphics Glossary" by the Professional Picture Framers Association; 1985

"Daydreams and Fantasies, Stories of the Secret Forest" by Hans Kleiber, published by Kay Kleiber, 1989.

"Edward Borein, The Update" by Harold G. Davidson; Harold G. Davidson, Santa Barbara, California, 1991.

"Hans Kleiber, Artist of the Bighorn Mountains" by Emmie Mygatt and Roberta Cheney; The Caxton Printers, Ltd., Caldwell, Idaho; 1975.

"How Prints Look" by William M. Ivins, Jr.; Beacon Press, 1943.

"How to Identify Prints: A Complete Guide to Manual and Mechanical Processes from Woodcut to Ink-jet" by Bamber Gascoigne; Thames and Hudson, 1986.

"Making an Etching" by Levon West; New York: The Studio Publications, Inc.; 1932.

"New Ways of Gravure, Revised Edition" by Stanley William Hayter; Watson-Guptill Publications, New York, 1981.

Hans Kleiber

"Reminiscences of Hans Kleiber, Early Day Forest Ranger, Big Horn National Forest" by Hans Kleiber, 1942; Sheridan County Historical Society.

"Printmaking, History and Process" by Donald Saff and Deli Sacilotto; Holt, Rinehart, and Winston, 1978.

"The Artist's Handbook of Materials and Techniques" by Ralph Mayer; The Viking Press, New York, 1970

"The Etchings Of Edward Borein, A Catalogue of his work" by John Galvin, Compiled with the assistance of Warren R. Howell, In collaboration with Harold G. Davidson; John Howell—Books, 1971.

"The Pocket Dictionary of Art Terms," Edited by Julia M. Ehresmann; New York Graphic Society, 1979.

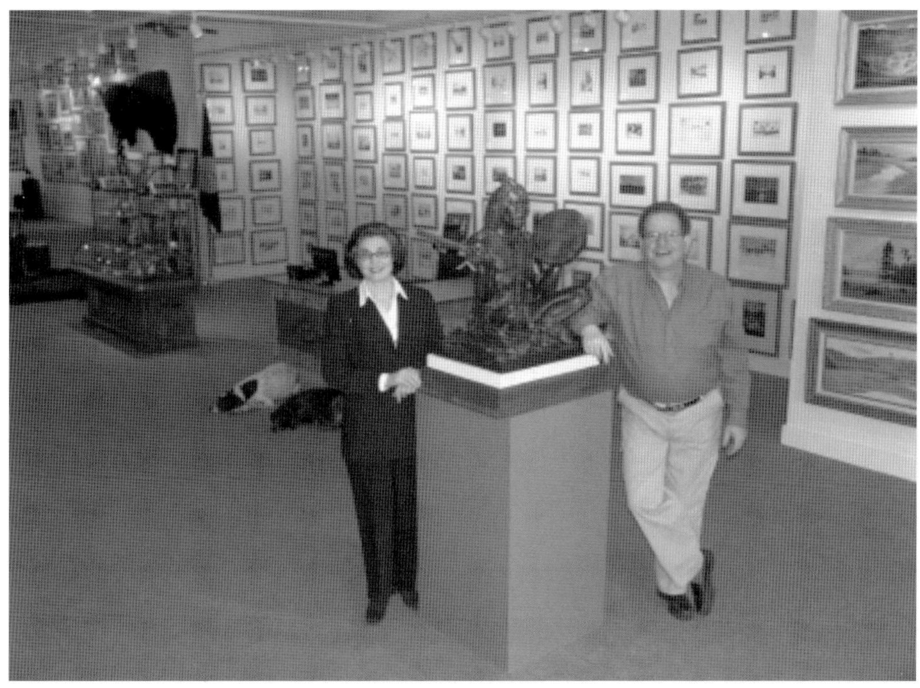

Marylee M. Moreland and Gary L. Temple

About the Authors

Marylee M. Moreland received her Bachelor of Art Degree from Montana State University in Bozeman, Montana, with extended study in Art from Arizona State University in Tempe, Arizona. She is a professional painter, sculptor, and Certified Picture Framer with the Professional Picture Framers Association. Gary L. Temple received his Bachelor of Art Degree in Speech Communication from Montana State University in Bozeman, Montana. Gary is a past President of the Northern Rockies Chapter of the Professional Picture Framers Association. He was prolific in welded metal sculpture for nine years and currently is active in the marketing of original fine art. With his wife, Marylee M. Moreland, they have created, framed, and sold artwork together since 1978. Together they wrote and published "Hans Kleiber: A Reference Manual," Volumes I and II. They have also produced and marketed the video tape, "Edward Borein, Cowboy Artist" by Harold G. Davidson. In 1995, they presented their seminar on Hans Kleiber at the C. M. Russell Art Show and Auction. Their research and expertise on Hans Kleiber is accepted by major museums that include the Montana Historical Society in Helena, Montana; the C. M. Russell Museum in Great Falls, Montana; the University of Wyoming Art Museum in Laramie, Wyoming; and the Whitney Gallery of Western Art, Buffalo Bill Historical Center in Cody, Wyoming. Fine art appraisals and art research claim work has been accepted by major insurance companies. Gary L. Temple and Marylee M. Moreland have owned and operated The Meadowlark Gallery, Inc., since 1987.

Hans Kleiber

Index

A

C

D

E

G

H

M

Hans Kleiber

N

O

R

S

T

Y

Hans Kleiber